Shared Decision-Making in Health Care
Achieving evidence-based patient choice

D1464411

Shared Decision-Making in Health Care
Achieving evidence-based patient choice

SECOND EDITION

Edited by

Adrian Edwards
School of Medicine
Cardiff University, UK

Glyn Elwyn
School of Medicine
Cardiff University, UK

OXFORD
UNIVERSITY PRESS

OXFORD

UNIVERSITY PRESS

Great Clarendon Street, Oxford ox2 6DP

Oxford University Press is a department of the University of Oxford.
It furthers the University's objective of excellence in research, scholarship,
and education by publishing worldwide in

Oxford New York

Auckland Cape Town Dar es Salaam Hong Kong Karachi
Kuala Lumpur Madrid Melbourne Mexico City Nairobi
New Delhi Shanghai Taipei Toronto

With offices in

Argentina Austria Brazil Chile Czech Republic France Greece
Guatemala Hungary Italy Japan Poland Portugal Singapore
South Korea Switzerland Thailand Turkey Ukraine Vietnam

Oxford is a registered trade mark of Oxford University Press
in the UK and in certain other countries

Published in the United States
by Oxford University Press Inc., New York

First edition published as Evidence-based patient choice: inevitable
or impossible by Oxford University Press, 2001

This edition published by Oxford University Press 2009

British Library Cataloguing in Publication Data

Data available

Library of Congress Cataloging in Publication Data

Data available

Typeset in Minion by Cepha Imaging Private Ltd., Bangalore, India
Printed in Great Britain
on acid-free paper by
Ashford Colour Press Ltd., Gosport, Hampshire, UK

ISBN 978–0–19–954627–5 (pbk)

10 9 8 7 6 5 4 3 2 1

Foreword

Practice variation, shared decision-making, and health care policy

The challenge to the research community is to provide the intellectual basis for a transition from a healthcare economy where healthcare utilization is based on physician's opinion to an economy where the demand is based on informed patient choice. The publication of the second edition of 'Shared Decision-Making in Health Care: Achieving Evidence-based Patient Choice' signals the emergence of an international community of social scientists, epidemiologists, and clinical science dedicated to advancing the field. It summarizes the current state of knowledge and lays out the research challenges yet to be met. Its editors and contributors are to be congratulated for consolidating in one volume the essential features of this emerging science of informed patient choice.

The policy imperative behind the transition to informed patient's choice is found in the practice variation phenomenon. Largely out of concern over costs, policy makers are increasingly concerned over the striking geographic variation in the incidence of elective surgery and other preference-sensitive treatments. The variation is judged to be unwarranted because it cannot be explained on the basis of illness, medical evidence, or patient preference. One important reason for unwarranted variation is the weakness in clinical science. In the absence of the constraints that sound clinical science place on clinical ideas, professional opinions on the value of the treatments they prescribe are necessarily subjective, with inferences made from personal experience and anecdote or on the basis on an untested clinical theory that might or might not prove true, were it subjected to clinical investigation.

Another important reason for unwarranted variation resides in flaws in the clinical decision-making—in the willingness to delegate decision-making to physicians under the assumption that they can accurately diagnose the treatment preferences of their patients. The evidence from practice variation research challenges this assumption. Even physicians who base their decision to operate on up to date "evidence-based" guidelines risk committing a serious medical error: they risk operating on the wrong patient—on a patient who if adequately informed would not want the procedure they provide.

Reducing unwarranted variation in preference–sensitive care and establishing the 'right rate' for discretionary surgery and other preference-sensitive interventions require fundamental changes in the doctor–patient relationship and the standards governing the determination of medical necessity: delegated decision-making should be replaced by shared decision-making; and the doctrine of informed patient consent superceded by informed patient choice.

The challenge to policy makers is to promote the transition from delegated decision-making to informed patient choice: to support improvements in clinical science to assure evidence-based patient choice; and encourage practicing physicians and their patients to adopt shared decision-making as a principle strategy for avoiding the risk of operating on the wrong patient and ensuring that the utilization of preference-sensitive care is based on the decisions of informed patient.

The implications seem clear. More effort is needed to develop models for implementing shared decision-making into everyday practice and measuring the quality of patient decision-making. Policy makers need to undertake experiments in reimbursement reform that support the necessary infrastructure and reward clinicians who successfully implement shared decision-making.

Legal scholars and legislators need to advance the case for establishing informed patient choice as the legal standard for determining the medical necessity for preference-sensitive care. If, over the next few years, progress in healthcare policy can catch up with the advances in science, the third edition of 'Shared Decision-Making in Health Care: Achieving Evidence-based Patient Choice' may tell the history of the transition to a healthcare economy where demand is based on informed patient choice.

Jack Wennberg
Peggy Y. Thompson Professor of the Evaluative Clinical Sciences
Dartmouth Institute for Health Policy and Clinical Practice
Dartmouth College
New Hampshire
USA

Contents

Section 3 **Conceptual developments**

Section 4 **Shared decision-making in health care practice**

Section 5 **The next and possible future developments**

Biographies

Adrian Edwards is Professor in General Practice at the Department of Primary Care and Public Health at Cardiff University. He is also a part-time general practitioner in Cwmbran, Gwent, South Wales, seeing about 80 patients per week and holds a visiting chair at the University of South Denmark in Odense. His two main research interests are in risk communication as part of shared decision-making, and in quality improvement in primary care. Among the former, research work has included the development and evaluation of training for doctors in risk communication approaches, and simple decision aids for use in consultations. More recently, this has focused on development of interactive decision aids that might be used outside consultations. Other more 'fundamental' work is looking at the notion and application of Health Literacy initiatives that may underpin patient's involvement in shared decision-making. He was a member of the lead faculty at the Summer Institute for Informed Patient Choice, Dartmouth College, New Hampshire (2007). He co-edited the first edition of this volume (*Evidence-based Patient Choice – inevitable or impossible?*) with Glyn Elwyn in 2001, and they co-hosted the first and second International Shared Decision-Making conferences in Oxford (2001) and Swansea (2003).

His methodological research interests centre on systematic reviews, and Professor Edwards has conducted over 25 different reviews using meta-analysis, meta-regression, and meta-synthesis methods. He is a co-editor in the Melbourne-based Consumers and Communication Review Group of the Cochrane Collaboration. His main Cochrane reviews in this topic area have addressed the effects of personalized risk communication in screening, interventions to enhance patients' participation in consultations, and culturally appropriate health education for people from ethnic minorities with diabetes. The Quality Improvement research centres on organizational development in primary care practices, using the 'Maturity Matrix' method (http://www.maturitymatrix.co.uk/). This includes both a dedicated version in Denmark and an international version across 12 European countries, currently being evaluated.

Glyn Elwyn is a primary care clinician who has research interests in shared decision-making, decision support technologies, risk communication and the integration of health informatics into clinical practice. He has published 150 peer-reviewed articles. He was appointed as one of the inter-school Link Chairs at Cardiff University in May 2005 and leads the Clinical Epidemiology Interdisciplinary Research Group at the School of Medicine (2007). In collaboration with Professor Adrian Edwards, he convenes a research group on decision-making and the development of web-based interactive decision support (see www.prosdex.com, www.amniodex.com, www.bresdex.com). He is involved in the supervision of ten PhD students.

He holds a visiting chair position at 'IQ', the Scientific Institute for Quality of Healthcare, Radboud University & Medical Centre, Nijmegen, The Netherlands. He co-leads the International Patient Decision Aids Standards Collaboration with Professor Annette O'Connor, Ottawa, and has been a member of the lead faculty at the Summer Institutes for Informed Patient Choice, Dartmouth College, New Hampshire (2007 and 2008). He is the Royal College of General Practitioners' UK delegate for the European Association of Quality Improvement (EQUIP). He is the author of '*Groups*' – a guide to teaching and working in small groups, published by Radcliffe Medical Press in 2001 and which won the European Association for Healthcare Management's Baxter Prize.

Acknowledgements

Adrian Edwards and Glyn Elwyn are indebted to the many contributors from several countries to this volume. They thank the authors for their commitment to submit chapters through 2008 and in many cases for their involvement in several chapters. They also want to thank several other people – colleagues, friends, and family – who have influenced the content of this book through discussions, correspondence, and conference presentations over the last 10 years or more in the exciting and expanding field of health care practice and research that is described in this volume.

Contributors

Joan Austoker
Director, Cancer Research UK
Primary Care Education Research Group,
Reader in Public Health and
Primary Health Care, Oxford, UK

Alexandra Barratt
Associate Professor of Epidemiology,
School of Public Health, University
of Sydney, Australia

Michael J. Barry
Massachusetts General Hospital & Harvard
Medical School, Boston, USA

Hilda Bastian
German Institute for Quality and
Efficiency in Health Care, Cologne,
Germany

Hilary Bekker
Institute of Health Sciences,
University of Leeds, UK

Jeff Belkora
University of California,
San Francisco, USA

Carol Bennett
University of Ottawa,
Ottawa Health Research Institute,
Ottawa Hospital, Ontario, Canada

Cathy Charles
McMaster University, Canada

Marla L. Clayman
Center for Communication and Medicine,
Division of General Internal Medicine,
Northwestern University Feinberg School
of Medicine, Chicago, Illinois USA

Nananda Col
Center for Outcomes Research
and Evaluation, Maine Medical Center,
Portland, USA

Angela Coulter
Picker Institute Europe,
King's Mead House, Oxford, UK

Myfanwy Davies
Department of Primary Care and
Public Health, School of Medicine,
Cardiff University, UK

Marie-Anne Durand
Department of Primary Care and
Public Health,
Centre for Health Sciences Research,
Cardiff University, UK

Karen Eden
Oregon Health and Science University, USA

Adrian Edwards
Professor in General Practice,
School of Medicine,
Cardiff University, UK

Michelle Edwards
Department of Primary Care and
Public Health, School of Medicine,
Cardiff University, UK

Benjamin Elwyn
Postgraduate student,
Philosophy Department, Kings College,
London, UK

Glyn Elwyn
Professor, Department of Primary Care and
Public Health, School of Medicine,
Cardiff University, Cardiff, UK

Vikki Entwistle
Universities of Dundee and
St. Andrews, UK

Rhodri Evans
Department of Primary Care and
Public Health, School of Medicine,
Cardiff University, UK

Deb Feldman-Stewart
Associate Professor, Department of Oncology,
Division of Cancer Care and Epidemiology,
Cancer Research Institute, Queen's
University, Kingston, Ontario, Canada

Dominick Frosch
Assistant Professor, Division of General
Internal Medicine and Health Services
Research, UCLA Department of Medicine,
Los Angeles, USA

Clara L. Gaff
Genetic Health Services Victoria,
Departments of Medicine and Paediatrics,
University of Melbourne, Melbourne,
Australia

Amiram Gafni
McMaster University, Canada

William Godolphin
University of British Columbia, Canada

Ian D. Graham
Associate Professor, School of Nursing,
University of Ottawa; Senior Social Scientist,
Ottawa Health Research Institute, Canada

Karine Gravel
France Legare, Department of Family
Medicine, Université Laval,
Centre Hospitalier Universitaire de Québec,
Hôpital St-François d'Assise10 Rue Espinay,
Québec, Canada

Dorte Gyrd-Hansen
Professor of Health Economics,
Institute of Public Health, Unit for Health
Economics, University of Southern Denmark,
Odense, Denmark

Martin Härter
Department of Psychiatry and Psychotherapy,
Section of Clinical Epidemiology and Health
Services Research, University of Freiburg,
Germany

Sophie Hill
Cochrane Consumers and Communication
Review Group, School of Public Health,
La Trobe University, Victoria, Australia

Søren Holm
Professor, Cardiff Law School,
Cardiff University, UK

Margaret Holmes-Rovner
Professor, Health Services Research,
Michigan State, University College of
Human Medicine, USA

Donald W. Kemper
Healthwise, Idaho, USA

Anne Kennedy
Manchester University, UK

Sara Khangura
University of Ottawa, Ottawa Health
Research Institute, Ottawa Hospital,
Ottawa, Ontario, Canada

J. Kievit
Department of Medical Decision Making,
Leiden University Medical Center, Leiden,
The Netherlands

Paul Kinnersley
Cardiff University, UK

Marco Knelangen
German Institute for Quality and
Efficiency in Health Care, Cologne,
Germany

Marije S. Koelewijn-van Loon
Department of General Practice and Centre
for Quality of Care Research, Maastricht
University, The Netherlands

Sascha Köpke
University of Hamburg, Germany

Ivar Sønbø Kristiansen
Professor, Institute of Public Health,
The Research Unit of General Practice,
University of Southern Denmark,
Odense, Denmark

Jennifer Kryworuchko
Faculty of Health Sciences, School
of Nursing, University of Ottawa,
Ottawa, Canada

Julie Leask
University of Sydney, Australia

France Légaré
Department of Family Medicine,
Université Laval, Centre Hospitalier
Universitaire de Québec, Hôpital St-François
d'Assise10 Rue Espinay, Québec, Canada

Matthias Lenz
University of Hamburg, Germany

Carmen Lewis
University of North Carolina Chapel Hill,
Department of Medicine, Sheps Center for
Health Services Research, USA

Hilary A. Llewellyn-Thomas
Center for the Evaluative Clinical Sciences,
Department of Community and Family
Medicine, Dartmouth Medical School, USA

Gregory Makoul
Center for Communication and Medicine,
Division of General Internal Medicine,
Northwestern University Feinberg School of
Medicine, Chicago, Illinois USA

Theresa M Marteau
King's College London, Psychology and
Genetics Research Group, Department of
Psychology (at Guy's), Institute of Psychiatry,
Guy's Campus, London, UK

Carl May
Health Technology and Human Relations,
Institute of Health and Society, Newcastle
University, UK

Dennis J. Mazur
Professor, Department of Veterans Affairs
Medical Center, Portland, Oregon, USA

Bettina Meiser
Psychosocial Research Group, Prince of Wales
Hospital and Prince of Wales Clinical School,
The University of New South Wales,
Sydney, Australia

Talya Miron-Shatz
Research scholar, Center for Health and
Wellbeing, Princeton University, USA

Alan Montgomery
BRTC Director and Senior Lecturer,
University of Bristol, UK

Albert G. Mulley
Massachusetts General Hospital,
Harvard Medical School, USA

Elizabeth Murray
University College London, UK

Ingrid Mühlhauser
University of Hamburg, Germany

Madeleine J Murtagh
Newcastle University, UK

Annette M. O'Connor
Professor and Tier 1 Canada Research Chair,
University of Ottawa and Ottawa Health
Research Institute, Clinical Epidemiology
Program, Ottawa, Ontario, Canada

Michael Pignone
University of North Carolina Chapel Hill,
Department of Medicine, Sheps Center for
Health Services Research, USA

Christopher Price
School of Postgraduate
Medical and Dental Education,
Cardiff University, UK

Joanne Protheroe
Manchester University, UK

Tim Rapley
Health Technology and Human Relations,
Institute of Health and Society,
Newcastle University, UK

Stéphane Ratté
Doctorale candidate in epidemiology,
Department of Family Medicine,
Université Laval, Centre Hospitalier
Universitaire de Québec,
Hôpital St-François d'Assise10
Rue Espinay, Québec, Canada

Anne Rogers
University of Manchester, UK

David Rovner
Professor Emeritus, Endocrinology,
Michigan State University,
College of Human Medicine,
East Lansing, USA

Anton Saarimaki
University of Ottawa,
Ottawa Health Research Institute, Canada

Lisa M. Schwartz
The Veterans Affairs Outcomes Group,
White River Junction, VT and the Center for
Medicine, the Media and the Public at the
Dartmouth Institute for Health Policy and
Clinical Practice, USA

Karen R. Sepucha
Massachusetts General Hospital, Harvard
Medical School, USA

Daniela Simon
Department of Psychiatry and Psychotherapy,
Section of Clinical Epidemiology and Health
Services Research, University of Freiburg,
Germany

Dawn Stacey
Population Health PhD Program and
Research Associate, Ottawa Health Research
Institute, Ottawa Hospital, Canada

Anne M. Stiggelbout
Department of Medical Decision Making,
Leiden University Medical Center, Leiden,
The Netherlands

Richard Thomson
School of Population and Health Sciences,
Medical School, Framlington Place,
Newcastle upon Tyne, UK

Hazel Thornton
Honorary Visiting Fellow, Department of
Health Sciences, University of Leicester, UK

Angela Towle
University of British Columbia, Canada

Lyndal Trevena
University of Sydney, Australia

Trudy van der Wiejden
Department of General Practice and Centre
for Quality of Care Research, Maastricht
University, The Netherlands

Ben van Steenkiste
Department of General Practice and Centre
for Quality of Care Research, Maastricht
University, The Netherlands

Bob Volk
Associate Professor, Vice Chair for Research,
Department of Family and Community
Medicine, Baylor College of Medicine,
Houston, Texas, USA

H. Gilbert Welch
The Veterans Affairs Outcomes Group,
White River Junction, VT and the Center for
Medicine, the Media and the Public at the
Dartmouth Institute for Health Policy and
Clinical Practice, Hanover, NH, USA

Celia E. Wills
Department of Psychiatry and Psychotherapy,
Section of Clinical Epidemiology and Health
Services Research, University of Freiburg,
Germany

Anna Winterbottom
Institute of Psychological Sciences,
University of Leeds, UK

Steven Woloshin
The Veterans Affairs Outcomes Group,
White River Junction, VT and the Center for
Medicine, the Media and the Public at the
Dartmouth Institute for Health Policy and
Clinical Practice, USA

Beate Zschorlich
German Institute for Quality and Efficiency
in Health Care, Cologne, Germany

Section 1

Shared decision-making and evidence-based patient choice

Chapter 1

Shared decision-making in health care: Achieving evidence-based patient choice

Adrian Edwards and Glyn Elwyn

Health care communication

The relationship between a patient and their health professional is viewed as one of the most complex interpersonal relationships. It involves the interaction between people in unequal positions, often non-voluntary, often addressing vitally important issues, emotionally laden, and requiring close co-operation (Ong *et al.*, 1995). It has also long been recognized as a vital influence on the course of illness: Hippocrates observed that 'some patients, though conscious that their condition is perilous, recover their health simply through their contentment with the goodness of the physician' (Heritage and Maynard, 2006). There is a long history of studying the doctor–patient relationship in social sciences with seminal work from several authors, identifying the importance of the 'sick role' for the patient (Parsons, 1951), but also how doctor-centred behaviours attenuate therapeutic possibilities (Byrne and Long, 1976), and how the extent to which patients adopt passive roles and accept medical expertise and authority vary with the character time scale and severity of their illness and its treatment or options for self-treatment (Szasz and Hollander, 1956).

More recently, Roter and Hall (1992) described four basic forms of the doctor–patient relationship: default, paternalistic, consumerist, and mutualistic. *Default* relationships are characterized by a lack of control on either side and are far from ideal. *Paternalism* is characterized by dominant doctors and passive patients, whereas *consumerism* is associated with the reverse and a focus on patients' rights and doctors' obligations. Consumerism in health care is an extension of the value of individual autonomy, independence, control, and rationality seen in western societies today (Bishop and Yardley, 2004). However, this is also problematic, and analysis suggests that this may be because it privileges the representation of patients as 'rational actors' in medical encounters, when a central feature of these encounters is their embodied and emotional nature (Bishop and Yardley, 2004). *Mutuality* is characterized by a sharing of decision-making and often advocated as the best type of relationship.

Shared decision-making

Emanuel E.J. and Emanuel L.L. (1992) suggest that a medical encounter can be judged by three main dimensions – the extent to which the agenda is set by the doctor, patient, or both in negotiation, the status of the patient's values (assumed by doctor, jointly explored, or unexamined), and the doctor's functional role as guardian, advisor, or consulting technician. The mutualistic relationship is characterized by a broad balance in power and symbolic resources for each participant; the agenda is negotiated; the patient's values are explored, and the doctor takes an advisory role regarding the patient's goals and decisions. There is a range of views about what constitutes patient involvement and participation in health care (Thompson, 2007) and a range of interpretations of what constitutes shared decision-making (Makoul and Clayman, 2005). However, the most commonly cited and generally accepted conceptualization of shared decision-making is that of Charles *et al.*, who identified the key features of shared decision-making as 'involvement of both the patient and the doctor, a sharing of information by both parties, both parties taking steps to build a consensus about the preferred treatment, and reaching an agreement about which treatment to implement' (Charles *et al.*, 1997).

Shared decision-making (or mutuality, 'active involvement', 'partnership') has gained a high level of policy support (Coulter, 2001; Coulter and Ellins, 2006). Paternalistic health care has fallen out of favour, replaced by the 'patient-centred model' (Stewart and Brown, 2001) which emphasizes patient autonomy, informed consent, and empowerment (supported also, for example, in General Medical Council descriptions of 'Good Medical Practice'(Council, 1998)). However, there is recognition that mutuality or shared decision-making may not suit all types of patients (Brundage *et al.*, 2005; Deber *et al.*, 2007; Edwards *et al.*, 2005). Furthermore, it is often difficult to achieve in practice (Berry, 2007; Towle *et al.*, 2006), and it appears something of an ideal that is far from reality in the everyday practice of doctors and experiences of patients.

Increased patient involvement and shared decision-making do produce beneficial results. Crawford *et al.*'s (2002) systematic review showed that higher levels of involvement resulted in better quality of care, increased satisfaction (for both patients and medical staff), and improved self-esteem for patients. Other systematic reviews also show the benefits of patient-centred care (Lewin *et al.*, 2003), and specific interventions such as those before consultations for helping patients address their information needs (Kinnersley *et al.*, 2007) and decision aids (interventions such as interactive websites, videos, leaflets to promote deliberative treatment decisions) (Murray *et al.*, 2005; O'Connor *et al.*, 2003). They report a range of cognitive, affective, behavioural, and health-status benefits.

Despite some caution on the extent of the benefits of shared decision-making on patient-based and health outcomes (Joosten *et al.*, 2008), it seems reasonable to continue to promote shared decision-making or other mutualistic approaches to health care, even though they are not widely adopted or achieved in practice (Carlsen and Aakvik, 2006). But to achieve change in practice, we need to examine the process afresh, in more depth, and gain greater understanding of the issues and influences at work. Some barriers to implementation in practice, such as professionals' attitudes, skills, and time available, have been studied widely (Gravel *et al.*, 2006). But experiences of decision-making are likely to be highly influenced by personal preferences, experiences, and relationships, and also structural constraints (class, education, ethnicity, and culture). They will also vary over time as people are more exposed or familiar with involvement in decision-making (Longo *et al.*, 2006) and to vary from one situation or context to another for an individual patient. There is also recognition that people exhibit potentially contradictory or ambivalent stands in relation to assuming responsibility for their health and health care at different times and in different situations.

Reflection and questions

People are becoming more autonomous and taking responsibility for their health and health care (Coulter, 2002). However, the relatively slow rate of progress towards the model of fully health literate consumers, exercising their own agency rather than requiring an agent (the clinician) to act for them, warrants reflection. We need a deeper understanding of how decision-making is occurring (whether shared or not). We need to examine what is happening in the shared decision process and in the unequal process. This examination can be both theoretical and empirical. If we can gain this deeper understanding, particularly perhaps when efforts are being made to adopt the shared or mutualistic approach, we will be in a stronger position to identify strategies to overcome the difficulties and promote shared decision-making.

However, the difficulties also generate more fundamental questions on which to reflect. Are we clear what we want as stakeholders in the field of shared decision-making practice and research – whether as patients, researchers, or clinicians? What is our understanding of shared decision-making and is it really what we want to achieve? It may have ethical justifications. It may or may not be efficient health care when examined from health economic perspectives. A range of health and health care benefits may be of different importance to different stakeholder groups including also policy-makers and payers for health care. We need to identify ways of implementing shared decision-making, but there is a more fundamental question to be answered first – *Do patients really want it*? The authors in this volume examine debate and explore a number of issues around these questions. Here we will outline the contributions to the volume, but first will make a few comments about terminology.

Shared decision-making or 'evidence-based patient choice'?

The first edition of this volume was entitled *Evidence-based patient choice – inevitable or impossible?* in 2001, reflecting work through the late 90s; this appeared to be a term gaining favour. There are also a number of related terms in the literature. As well as those noted in the Introduction, these include informed (shared) decision-making (Towle and Godolphin, 1999), patient-centred care (Stewart *et al.*, 1995), concordance (Marinker, 1997), participation and partnership (Coulter, 1997), informed consent (Gigerenzer, 2002), autonomy (Schneider, 1998), consumer involvement and consumerism (Entwistle *et al.*, 1996), expert patient (Kennedy and Rogers, 2001), and evidence-informed patient choice (Entwistle *et al.*, 1998). These have different meanings, nuances, and may be for different purposes.

We believe, however, that the term which has endured, and arguably has the highest profile, is shared decision-making (Charles *et al.*, 1997; Elwyn *et al.*, 2000). It has deficiencies, not least because it might be assumed to promote shared decision-making as the ideal model for all circumstances, when clearly this is not the case. We believe it can be viewed as a short-hand term, but which perhaps has the greatest impact and recognition, clearly signalling to wider constituencies what is proposed as a change in the way health care is practiced. Being short hand, it requires clarification. We suggest that what really represents is 'involving the patient in decision making, to the extent that they desire' (Edwards and Elwyn, 2006). Health care practitioners need to be able to gauge the patient's preferred level of involvement, and then employ skills and competencies to achieve that preferred level of involvement, whether a clinician-led, shared, or patient-led decision. A key contribution to this process comes from health information, effectively presented, and the scope of decision aids to enhance decision-making (O'Connor *et al.*, 2007).

The other area of terminological debate is around the labels and terms for the provider and the person using health care services. We clearly recognize that the terms 'doctor' and 'patient' are now somewhat outdated, and terms such as clinician or health care professional, and patient, client, user, citizen, or consumer (among others) may be more inclusive or appropriate depending on the context. These were discussed in the first volume (Elwyn and Edwards, 2001) and arguably this is an area where little updating is required eight years later, the range of terms remains varied, and is appropriate given the range of health care circumstances and contexts, and the purposes for which the terms are used in debate. However, where in the first volume we to some extent standardized terminology around 'clinicians' and 'consumers', in this volume authors have used various from among these terms, suitable to their field of analysis.

Overview of the second edition

The shared decision-making field has developed and broadened considerably in recent years. It is now 12 years since the seminal paper by Charles *et al.* (1997) and 8 years since the first International Shared Decision Making Conference in Oxford, UK, and the first edition of this volume (Edwards and Elwyn, 2001). The second edition retains the same five sections as the first examining the nature of health care, theoretical perspectives, conceptual development, evidence of shared decision-making in practice, and debating potential future developments. However, as the field has broadened, so have the number of issues and aspects worth including and debating. More particularly, the number of authors able to contribute expertize and experience has also increased, and the range of countries from which they come. Thus, we have invited over a hundred authors from 10 countries to contribute to this volume.

Section 1: Shared decision-making and evidence-based patient choice

Some of the headline issues have been introduced above and these are explored in more depth in the first section. Holmes-Rovner relates how the field has developed and evolved, particularly focusing on the progress with the international conferences and their showcasing of research and development (Chapter 2). The body of the section is devoted to the developments both in the concept of patient involvement (Entwistle, Chapter 3), but also in terms of how shared decision-making can fit in with the way health care is increasingly provided by teams of professionals (Legare, Chapter 4) and how this affects the roles of those professionals and of patients (Stacey and Thornton, Chapters 5 and 6, respectively).

Section 2: Theoretical perspectives

Several disciplines can shed light on the nature and purposes of shared decision-making. Chapters in this section contribute a range of theoretical analyses and discussions, from psychological (Bekker, Chapter 7), sociological (Rapley, Chapter 8; Murtagh, Chapter 12), ethics (Holm, Chapter 9), and economics perspectives (Kristiansen and Gafni, Chapters 10 and 11). These chapters show how the analysis of shared decision-making has progressed in recent years, in particular how a stronger theoretical base is now seen as vital for interventions. However, we also see the introduction of a more sceptical note – it is not assumed that shared decision-making is automatically 'where we want to go' (Gafni, Chapter 12).

Section 3: Conceptual developments

We start this section with the discussion of exciting developments that are arguably more usually not associated automatically with the shared decision-making field. These concern informed choice (Marteau, Chapter 13) and initiatives around the Expert Patient (Rogers, Chapter 14) and Health Literacy (Edwards, Chapter 15). Clayman and Makoul review how the concept of shared decision- making itself has developed (Chapter 16) and subsequent chapters examine how shared decision-making competencies (Elwyn, Chapter 17), values clarification (Llewellyn-Thomas, Chapter 18), and risk communication (Edwards, Chapter 19) are seen as part of that.

Again though, more questions arise, including fundamental ones about 'what is a good decision'? Perhaps the differing views of this, expounded by Elwyn (Chapter 20) and Sepucha (Chapter 21), and noted also by Marteau (Chapter 13), show how difficult the theoretical and conceptual issues are in shared decision-making. With these difficulties – the lack of a clear understanding of what shared decision-making is, what its purpose is, and how to achieve it and measure it – it is unsurprising that the shared decision-making field has encountered implementation barriers (Edwards, Chapter 19).

Section 4: Shared decision-making in health care practice

Despite these theoretical and conceptual concerns, a huge volume of evidence has accrued now about shared decision-making in practice – the pragmatic end of the spectrum is thriving! Coulter describes the experience and extent of shared decision-making in different international health care systems (Chapter 22), and Mazur describes the medico-legal perspectives (Chapter 23). Kinnersley summarizes a Cochrane review on how consumers can be helped in quite simple ways with their information needs in consultations – question prompt sheets may be a simple and modestly effective way of enhancing consumer involvement (Chapter 24). Schwartz shows how drug information, summarizing the benefits and harms of treatments, could be made available to consumers (Chapter 25). The vested interests of pharmaceutical companies militate against this currently in the United States, but Bastian describes how information resources have been made available in Germany under its universal insurance-based health care system (Chapter 26).

The main theme of this section, however, is around decision aids. Chapters 27–34 provide an overview (O'Connor, Chapter 27), summarize their effectiveness with data from the well-cited Cochrane review (O'Connor et al., 2003; Stacey, Chapter 28), and examine the role of psychological theory – often lacking – in their development (Durand, Chapter 29) and the use of 'narratives' or patient stories (Winterbottom, Chapter 30). Llewellyn-Thomas also examines further research needs concerning decision support and decision aids, in the context of the Dartmouth–Hitchcock 'Decision Lab' (Chapter 34). Perhaps related technologies concern internet-delivered interventions (Murray, Chapter 31) and decision analysis (Thomson, Chapter 32). However, an important issue around the proliferation of decision aids in recent years (see also http://decisionaid.ohri.ca/AZinvent.php) concerns quality assurance. The International Patient Decision Aids Standards Collaboration was formed in 2003 and had developed quality criteria for their development and assessment (Elwyn et al., 2006) (Chapter 33).

The rest of this section is given to illustrating decision support and decision aids in 15 health care topics. This is far from an exhaustive list of the important clinical topics where shared decision could be or is important – indeed it is likely to be important in any topic and any decision. We apologize to stakeholders in topics that have not been included. Rather a selection is included to illustrate the nature of decisions, the range of decision aids available, the experience available to date, and the lessons and prospects for the future that we may able to learn from these exemplars. They cover a variety of medical, surgical, and screening or prevention topics.

Section 5: The next and possible future developments

This section starts by returning to the sceptical refrain. Even the academics and policy proponents have been reflecting some doubts about the nature or purpose of shared decision-making, just beneath the surface in a number of chapters in this volume. An experienced clinician (Price, Chapter 50) examines whether patients really want it? Shared decision-making is increasingly advocated in health care but is not widely adopted in practice. There are a number of potential reasons for this, including professional resistance, lack of skills, lack of time, and other structural barriers (Gravel et al., 2006). These are summarized by Legare (Chapter 51) and analysed from a theoretical perspective using the Normalization Process Model, examining how shared decision-making and decision aids need to fit in with the usual *work* of the consultation (May, Chapter 52). However, shared decision-making (as currently proposed) pre-supposes that the patient is willing and able to participate. Earlier chapters have visited the issue in terms of patient autonomy, power asymmetry (Murtagh, Chapter 12), and also the 'agency relationship' in health care (Gafni, Chapter 11). But it remains pertinent to ask the 'emperor's new clothes question' about shared decision-making, decision aids, and so on: *do patients really want it?* Assuming for the moment that patients are willing and able to participate in health care encounters, and decision-making in particular, the implementation issues are important, as are issues around training and education of professionals, discussed by Towle (Chapter 53). There are exciting possibilities ahead in terms of how 'decision support technologies' and 'information therapy' can make invaluable contributions to shared decision-making, enabling consumers to be actively engaged in their health and health care. Elwyn describes the potential future development of decision support technologies (Chapter 54), and Kemper describes the development of information therapy in the context of commercial providers of health care, as evident in the United States (Chapter 55). All such developments require further evaluation and analysis of how they affect the patient's contribution to decision-making. If we can understand better what happens when shared decision-making occurs, and what the differences are when it does not, we will be better placed to know when it should be promoted, how to do this, and what this will achieve – and when it should not.

References

Berry, D. (2007). Communication between patients and professionals. New York: McGraw-Hill, Open University Press.

Bishop, F. and Yardley, L. (2004). Constructing agency in treatment decisions: Negotiating responsibility in cancer. *health: an Interdisciplinary Journal for the Social Study of Health, Illness and Medicine*, **8**, 465–482.

Brundage, M., Feldman-Stewart, D., Leis, A., *et al.* (2005). Communicating quality of life information to cancer patients: A study of six presentation formats. *Journal of Clinical Oncology*, **23**, 6949–6956.

Byrne, P. and Long, B. (1976). *Doctors talking to Patients*. London: HMSO.

Carlsen, B. and Aakvik, A. (2006). Patient involvement in clinical decision making: The effect of GP attitude on patient satisfaction. *Health Expectations*, **9**, 148–157.

Charles, C., Gafni, A., and Whelan, T. (1997). Shared decision-making in the medical encounter: What does it mean? (Or it takes at least two to tango). *Social Science & Medicine*, **44**, 681–692.

Coulter, A. (1997). Partnerships with patients: The pros and cons of shared clinical decision making. *Journal of Health Services Research and Policy*, **2**, 112–121.

Coulter, A. (2001). Empowering patients – The policy agenda. *Shared Decision Making in Health Care*: *1st International Conference, Oxford*.

Coulter, A. (2002). *The Autonomous Patient*. Oxford: Radcliffe Medical Press.

Coulter, A. and Ellins, J. (2006). Patient-focused interventions – A review of the evidence. *Quest for Quality and Improved Performance Programme*. London: The Health Foundation.

Council., G.M. (1998). *Maintaining Good Medical Practice* (1st Edition), London: General Medical Council.

Crawford, M., Rutter, D., Manley, C., *et al.* (2002). Systematic review of involving patients in the planning and development of health care. *British Medical Journal*, **325**, 1263–1266.

Deber, R., Kraetschmer, N., Urowitz, S., *et al.* (2007). Do people want to be autonomous patients? Preferred roles in treatment decision-making in several patient populations. *Health Expectations*, **10**, 248–258.

Edwards, A. and Elwyn, G. (2001). *Evidence-based Patient Choice – Inevitable or Impossible?* (1st Edition), Oxford: Oxford University Press.

Edwards, A. and Elwyn, G. (2006). Inside the black box of shared decision making – Distinguishing between the process of involvement and who makes the decision. *Health Expectations*, **9**, 307–320.

Edwards, A., Elwyn, G., Atwell, C., *et al.* (2005). Shared decision making and risk communication in practice: Qualitative study of general practitioners' experiences. *British Journal of General Practice*, **55**, 6–13.

Elwyn, G. and Edwards, A. (2001). Evidence-based patient choice? In Edwards, A. and Elwyn, G. (eds) *Evidence-based Patient Choice – Inevitable or Impossible?* (1st Edition), Oxford: Oxford University Press.

Elwyn, G., Edwards, A., Kinnersley, P., *et al.* (2000). Shared decision-making and the concept of equipoise: Defining the 'competences' of involving patients in health care choices. *British Journal of General Practice*, **50**, 892–899.

Elwyn, G., O'Connor, A., Stacey, D., *et al.* (2006). Developing quality indicators for patient decision aids: An online international Delphi consensus process. *British Medical Journal*, **333**, 417–419.

Emanuel, E.J. and Emanuel, L.L. (1992). Four models of the physician-patient relationship. *Journal of the American Medical Association*, **267**, 2221–2224.

Entwistle, V., Sheldon, T., Sowden, A., *et al.* (1998). Evidence-informed patient choice. Practical issues of involving patients in decisions about health care technologies. *Int. J. Technol Assess Health Care*, **14**, 212–225.

Entwistle, V., Sheldon, T., Sowden, A.J., *et al.* (1996). Supporting consumer involvement in decision making: What constitutes quality in consumer health information? *Journal for Quality in Health Care*, **8**, 425–437.

Gigerenzer, G. (2002). (Un)informed consent. *Reckoning with Risk – Learning to Live with Uncertainty*. (1st Edition), London: Penguin Press.

Gravel, K., Legare, F., and Graham, I. (2006). Barriers and facilitators to implementing shared decision-making in clinical practice: A systematic review of health professionals' perceptions. *Implementation Science*, **1**, 16.

Heritage, J. and Maynard, D. (2006). Problems and prospects in the study of physician-patient interaction: 30 years of research. *Annual Review of Sociology*, **32**, 351–374.

Joosten, E., DeFuentes-Merillasa, L., de Weertc, G., *et al.* (2008). Systematic review of the effects of shared decision-making on patient satisfaction, treatment adherence and health status. *Psychotherapeutics Psychosomatics*, **77**, 219–226.

Kennedy, A. and Rogers, A. (2001). Improving self-management skills: A whole systems approach. *British Journal of Nursing*, **10**, 734–737

Kinnersley, P., Edwards, A., Hood, K., *et al.* (2007). Interventions before consultations for helping patients address their information needs [review]. *Cochrane Database of Systematic Reviews*, 3, CD004565.

Lewin, S., Skea, Z., Entwistle, V., *et al.* (2003). Effects of interventions to promote a patient centred approach in clinical consultations: *Cochrane review*, 2.

Longo, M., Cohen, D., Hood, K., *et al.* (2006). Involving patients in primary care consultations: Assessing preferences using discrete choice experiments. *British Journal of General Practice*, **56**, 35–42.

Makoul, G. and Clayman, M. (2005). An integrative model of shared decision making in medical encounters. *Patient Education & Counseling*, **60**, 301–312.

Marinker, M. (1997). From compliance to concordance – Achieving shared goals in medicine taking. Working Party of the Royal Pharmaceutical Society of Great Britain, London.

Murray, E., Burns, J., See, T., *et al.* (2005). Interactive Health Communication Applications for people with chronic disease, *Cochrane Library*, 4.

O'Connor, A., Stacey, D., Entwistle, V., *et al.* (2003). Decision aids for people facing health treatment or screening decisions [Cochrane review]. *Update Software: Cochrane Library*, 2.

O'Connor, A., Wennberg, J., Legare, F., *et al.* (2007). Toward the 'tipping point': Decision aids and informed patient choice. *Health Affairs*, **26**, 716–725.

Ong, L., Dehaes, J., Hoos, A., *et al.* (1995). Doctor-patient communication – A review of the literature. *Social Science & Medicine*, **40**, 903–918.

Parsons, T. (1951). *The Social System*. Glencoe: Free Press.

Roter, D. and Hall, J. (1992). *Doctors talking with Patients/Patients talking with Doctors*. Westport: Connecticut Auburn House.

Schneider, C.E. (1998). *The Practice of Autonomy: Patients, Doctors and Medical Decisions*. New York: Oxford University Press.

Stewart, M. and Brown, J. (2001). Patient-centredness in medicine. In Edwards, A. and Elwyn, G. (eds) *Evidence-based Patient Choice*. London: Oxford University Press.

Stewart, M., Brown, J.B., Weston, W., *et al.* (1995). *Patient-centred Medicine. Transforming the Clinical Method*. Thousand Oaks, CA: Sage Publications.

Szasz, P. and Hollander, M. (1956). A contribution to the philosophy of medicine: The basic model of the doctor-patient relationship. *Archives of Internal Medicine*, **97**, 585–592.

Thompson, A. (2007). The meaning of patient involvement and participation in health care: A taxonomy. In Collins, S., Britten, N., Ruusuvuori, J. and Thompson, A. (eds) *Patient Participation in Health Care Consultations* (1st Edition), Maidenhead, UK: Open University Press.

Towle, A. and Godolphin, W. (1999). Framework for teaching and learning informed shared decision making. *British Medical Journal*, **319**, 766–771.

Towle, A., Godolphin, W., Grams, G., *et al.* (2006). Putting informed and shared decision making into practice. *Health Expectations*, **9**, 321–332.

Chapter 2

International collaboration in promoting shared decision-making: A history and prospects

Margaret Holmes-Rovner and David Rovner

Introduction and history

Evidence-based patient choice is closely allied with shared decision-making, both conceptually and as a social movement. In this chapter, we trace the development of an international network, The International Shared Decision Making Meeting (ISDM) and 'listserv', and reflect on how the focus of research has evolved over 8 years.

ISDM has held four biennial meetings, beginning in 2001. Attendance has grown steadily, from 140 in 2001 to more than 230 in 2007. Its organization grew out of its history, and perhaps out of its lack of a bureaucracy to support it. As participants, we can recount the early history, leading to the first meeting at St. Catherine's College, Oxford, in 2001. It reflects the spontaneity and spirit of collaboration that has continued. Both intellectual and personal associations provide background for its development. The intellectual threads include ethical standards for informed consent, technology assessment (e.g. decision aids), and patient-centered care. Direct impetus for deliberation about trade-offs among alternative health care interventions came from both decision analytic and regional variation studies. In this context, shared decision-making is part of the evidence-based medicine movement of the 1980s and 1990s, but focused on providing evidence about medical alternatives to patients and providers in order to improve their decisions.

The meetings of the Society for Medical Decision Making (SMDM) and the International Society for Technology Assessment in Health Care (ISTAHC) provided venues for discussions. In 1999, at the ISTAHC meeting in Edinburgh, a North American–UK collaboration began through a collective sabbatical among Annette O'Connor, Margaret Holmes-Rovner, Hilary Llewellyn-Thomas, Cornelia Ruland, and David Rovner to work at the Picker Institute (Europe) and the Institute for Health Sciences (IHS) in Oxford. Angela Coulter established the 'Shared Decision Making Forum 2000' to host this collaboration in Oxford for the first 6 months of 2000. Details of the seminars, personal interactions, and accomplishments can be found in a longer account published in Patient Education and Counseling (Holmes-Rovner, 2008). A critical decision was to begin a biennial meeting, the International Shared Decision Making conference. The first meeting of ISDM was held in collaboration with The European Association for Communication in Health Care (EACH) in Oxford, England. Subsequent meetings were held in Swansea, Wales, in 2003, Ottawa, Canada in 2005, and Freiburg, Germany, in 2007. By the time this book is published, the 2009 meeting will have taken place in Boston, USA.

ISDM meetings and accomplishments

Each of the meetings has entertained lively debate about the purpose and progress of shared decision-making. People have presented research, new decision support tools, and debated the proper focus and approach to evidence-based patient choice and decision-sharing between patients and their clinicians. A major collaborative enterprise was begun at the Swansea meeting, called the International Patient Decision Aid Standards (IPDAS) collaborative (Elwyn et al., 2006). This is described more fully in Chapter 33, but briefly, its purpose was to improve the quality of decision tools by establishing a set of quality rating criteria based on the best science. Following the Swansea meeting, a steering committee of 16 members commissioned 12 state-of-the-art papers on key topics, involving 56 authors. The key topics were as follows: providing information about treatment and screening options, presenting probabilities, clarifying and expressing values, using personal stories, guidance and coaching in deliberation and communication, health literacy and plain language, delivering decision aids on the internet, and basing information tools on scientific evidence. A final paper grappled with the problem of how to evaluate the effectiveness of information tools. A number of related papers were subsequently published: Information Provision (Feldman-Stewart et al., 2007), Decision Quality (Sepucha et al., 2004), Risk Communication (Barratt et al., 2004; Trevena et al., 2006), Values Clarification (O'Connor et al., 2005). All appear on the IPDAS website (Elwyn et al., 2008).

IPDAS used a consensus process involving stakeholder groups of patients, providers, researchers, and policy makers from 14 countries to establish best practices for design and content of patient decision aids, to be compiled into a simple quality rating system (Elwyn et al., 2006). The resulting criteria, described elsewhere, have yielded a checklist to guide decision aid development (Elwyn et al., 2006). A quality measure is being developed by the IPDASi Measurement Group. The presentation of the results generated debate and discussion stimulating development in the field.

ISDM functional style: Networking as a 'Worknet'

To date, ISDM has been an informal association of volunteers, largely of researchers and developers; few consumers or advocates have attended meetings. Annette O'Connor and Glyn Elwyn have led IPDAS, supporting the Delphi process and hosting the IPDAS website. Local groups have taken the entire responsibility for each meeting. David Rovner manages the monitored listserv (shared-l). ISDM has also been supported by its close ties to two related organizations. The European Association for Communication in Healthcare (EACH) has published two special issues of *Patient Education and Counseling* from ISDM meetings. The Society for Medical Decision Making has a shared decision-making interest group, hosted a symposium in 2006, and published a special issue of *Medical Decision Making* in 2007 on decision aids.

Is ISDM an organization or a network? Networks, as described by Christopher Meyer, are part of an emerging group of concepts, circulating mostly by internet, that have captivated the business world (Meyer, 2007). These include social webs, open innovation, and customer-created content. Meyer observes that to get a return on investment, the focus has to be on the *work* that, in the case of ISDM, is expanding and improving shared decision-making. Some ISDM participants have commercial interests in tools for patients (and health professionals) to use. Some have interests in how the tools affect the communication process between patients and providers. Some have interests in how health systems can be restructured to accommodate and support patients' voices being heard. These are interlocking aspects of an applied project: getting shared decision-making to work in health care.

How does ISDM rate on Meyer's basic tasks that network can serve? In an essay on break through ideas for 2007, in the Harvard Business Review, he lists five worknet tasks. They can *scan* the horizon for events and patterns with implications for strategies. The special issue of the German Journal for Evidence and Quality in Health Care (Haerter and Loh, 2007) did this for several countries.

A network can *solve* problems. ISDM has done this through the IPDAS process, which posed the problem of identifying attributes of a high-quality decision aid. The implementation of the IPDASi rating scale is proceeding through training at meetings and organizations. It is conceivable that the problems of using and improving the IPDASi rating scale might involve the ISDM listserv in a brainstorming and networking process.

A network can *innovate* for its own benefit. This function has been a primary function of the ISDM meetings where researchers and developers can seek new ideas for improving decision support tools, patient-professional health care encounters, and health system implementation of shared decision-making.

A network can exert *influence*. However, like many professional organizations, ISDM has not been particularly influential. Networks can also efficiently *allocate* resources. But ISDM has no financial resources to allocate, beyond the intellectual capital of the listserv.

As Meyer notes, since networks perform diverse functions, they require diverse forms. By identifying the most important work that a group wants a network to perform, it can design (or improve on the design) of the 'worknet' yielding benefits that are not just economic, but informational and emotional. The balance may vary for members participating for different reasons or having different roles, but all need to be satisfied.

The spirit of collaboration exhibited in ISDM appears to enhance the emotional and informational exchanges. The International meetings are collegial and energizing and much sharing of products and opportunities occur. At the Freiburg meeting, attendees represented 17 countries and the ability to see what goes on in other countries is highly simulating. ISDM is a vehicle for innovation and problem solving. However, the projects that have grown from the problem-solving activity have the potential to extend their influence if the power of the ISDM network is directly harnessed. Below are two feasible projects that exemplify the opportunity.

ISDM future potential

Extending IPDAS as a standard

IPDAS (the collaboration's criteria) and IPDASi (the instrument) are moving through the development and validation process under the leadership of Elwyn and O'Connor and the IPDAS Steering Committee. The IPDAS checklist and approach to rating decision support tools have been presented as a workshop at ISDM and SMDM in 2007. This checklist is being used to describe the quality of patient decision aids on the Ottawa Inventory of available patient decision aids (O'Connor 2008). The criteria for judging effectiveness of patient decision aids have been used in updating the Cochrane systematic review of patient decision aids (O'Connor *et al.*, 2007a). The IPDASi group is performing reliability and scaling studies to improve its performance. O'Connor and Stacey's work to present IPDAS to the producers of decision support tools provides on-the-ground demonstration of how IPDAS standards can guide the development of new tools in the voluntary health sector, the commercial sector, and the government sector across countries. Mention of the IPDAS standards in the informed choice legislation of the Washington State is also promising (O'Connor *et al.*, 2007b). In 2008, the American Agency for Health Care Research and Quality (AHRQ) issued a request for proposals for a large contract to produce decision aids including explicitly requirements to show how such decision aids met IPDAS standards. With this level of uptake of the standards, IPDAS can help to assure that decision support tools are balanced, display the evidence for all clinically viable options, and engage patient preferences. The dissemination effort could recruit members of the ISDM network to work in a co-ordinated fashion across countries and across sectors. The purpose would be to *allocate human resources* efficiently, maintain training standards, and to *influence* the field. The IPDAS standards will have to be updated periodically.

Integration of 'evidence review' into health care communication

Shared decision-making requires that patients and health professionals review evidence together in the clinical encounter. At the 2007 ISDM meeting, there was increased discussion of the importance of patient and clinician communication. However, the presentation of communication skills with a specific focus on evidence review remains under-developed. Early work in this area shows descriptive evidence that shared decision-making rarely happens in clinical encounters (Braddock *et al.*, 1997; Elwyn *et al.*, 1999; Haerter and Loh, 2007; Loh *et al.*, 2006; Loh *et al.*, 2007). The opportunity exists to expand existing training programs for physicians and other health professionals to teach procedures for eliciting the patient's knowledge base and reviewing evidence tools, in addition to the current focus on enhancing general communication skills.

The fact that neither patients nor clinicians expect to 'do evidence review' in a routine visit is problematic. Clinicians are in the best position to sort out fact from fiction, relevant from irrelevant. They are also in the position to make sure that all individuals have sufficient basic information about their diseases and treatment to care for themselves on a day-to-day basis. Patients may be very well informed about what they think is their condition and do a lot of searching for information and learn everything they can about their diagnosed or undiagnosed condition or symptoms. On the other hand, many patients do not seek out information, feeling this is the doctor's job. Both techniques may yield unintended adverse consequences. This basic bilateral information review is not something physicians are frequently trained to do with patients. They often have neither the time nor the confidence to take on this task, particularly when it involves explaining statistical inference and risk. Communication skills teaching, as it is currently practiced, allows clinicians to hold a bias against well-informed patients because of a fear that reviewing information will slow down the work flow. Ignoring the need for patients to be informed poses important risks. Misunderstanding about disease and treatment lead to errors in self-care. Patients do not easily disclose their concerns about the therapies being considered. If clinicians discourage questions about research that patients have done, they are likely to continue to seek and act upon information, without the guidance of a health professional. To address this gap in the basic framework to support shared decision-making, we have now begun teaching communication skills *to patients*.

How might the work of these two projects engage the ISDM network? Meyer notes that well-designed networks proceed deliberately to (1) define the work, (2) identify the talent, (3) engineer the exchanges among the participants, (4) design the experience, and (5) assemble the technology. Capitalizing on the power of the network could move shared decision-making into a more vibrant reform vehicle. Moving shared decision-making ahead requires careful attention to all the technologies involved, be they decision support tools, the IPDAS checklist, an evidence review protocol, specific SDM training programs for health care providers, or the choice of the specific resources for networking.

Conflict of interest statement

(Presented in part at the meeting of the 4th International Shared Decision Making Conference, Freiburg, Germany, 30th May–1st June 2007.)

References

Barratt, A., Trevena, L., Davey, H. M., *et al.* (2004). Use of decision aids to support informed choices about screening. *British Medical Journal*, **329**, 507–510.

Braddock, C. H., III, Fihn, S. D., Levinson, W., *et al.* (1997). How doctors and patients discuss routine clinical decisions. Informed decision making in the outpatient setting. *J Gen. Intern. Med*, **12**, 339–345.

Elwyn, G., Edwards, A., and Kinnersley, P. (1999). Shared decision-making in primary care: the neglected second half of the consultation. *Br. J. Gen. Pract.*, **49**, 477–482.

Elwyn, G., *et al.* (2008). International Patient Decision Aid Standards Collaboration. Available at http://ipdas.ohri.ca. Acessed on 19, June 2008.

Elwyn, G., O'Connor, A., Stacey, D., *et al.* (2006). Developing a quality criteria framework for patient decision aids: Online international Delphi consensus process. *British Medical Journal*, **333**, 417.

Feldman-Stewart, D., Brennenstuhl, S., McIssac, K., *et al.* (2007). A systematic review of information in decision aids. *Health Expect.*, **10**, 46–61.

Haerter, M. and Loh, A. (2007). Shared decision-making in diverse health care systems. *German Journal for Evidence and Quality in Health Care*, **101**, 4.

Holmes-Rovner, M. (2008). International collaboration in shared decision-making: The International Shared Decision Making (ISDM) conference history and prospects. *Patient Educ. Couns. Apr. 1 epub.* **73**, 402–406.

Loh, A., Simon, D., Hennig, K., *et al.* (2006). The assessment of depressive patients' involvement in decision making in audio-taped primary care consultations. *Patient. Educ. Couns.*, **63**, 314–318.

Loh, A., Simon, D., Wills, C. E., *et al.* (2007). The effects of a shared decision-making intervention in primary care of depression: A cluster-randomized controlled trial. *Patient. Educ. Couns.*, **67**, 324–332.

Meyer, C. (2007). The Best Networks are Really Worknets", *Harvard Business Review*, vol. 1–33.

O'Connor, A. M. (2008). The Ottowa Health Research Institute. Available at http://decisionaid.ohri.ca/AZinvent.php.

O'Connor, A. M., Bennett, C., Stacey, D., *et al.* (2007a). Patient decision aids for people facing health screening or treatment decisions: A systematic review and meta-analysis. *Med Decis Making*, **27**, 554–574.

O'Connor, A. M., Graham, I. D., and Visser, A. (2005). Implementing shared decision making in diverse health care systems: The role of patient decision aids. *Patient Educ. Couns.*, **57**, 247–249.

O'Connor, A. M., Wennberg, J. E., Legare, F., *et al.* (2007b). Toward the 'tipping point': Decision aids and informed patient choice. *Health Aff.(Millwood.)*, **26**, 716–725.

Sepucha, K. R., Fowler, F. J., Jr., & Mulley, A. G., Jr (2004). Policy support for patient-centered care: The need for measurable improvements in decision quality. *Health Aff (Millwood)*, vol. Suppl Web Exclusive, p. VAR54–VAR62.

Trevena, L. J., Davey, H. M., Barratt, A., *et al.* (2006). A systematic review on communicating with patients about evidence. *J. Eval. Clin. Pract.*, **12**, 13–23.

Chapter 3

Patient involvement in decision-making: The importance of a broad conceptualization

Vikki Entwistle

Introduction

The idea that patients should be enabled to be involved in decision-making about their own health care is now widely accepted – at least in general terms. But behind the broad consensus that patient involvement is 'a good thing', there are differences of opinion about why it is important, what it might look like, and how it should be promoted in practice.

Arguments for patient involvement are variously based on claims that it matters to patients, is indicative of (health professionals' respect for) patients' personal autonomy, and is beneficial for health and wellbeing. The currently dominant conceptualization of patient involvement in decision-making focuses on the following: (1) an exchange of information between health professional(s) and patient about a menu of health care options and the patient's understanding of these options and (2) the influence the patient has over the selection made from the option menu. This conceptualization underpins several variant models of patient involvement, including those referred to as 'shared decision-making' and 'informed choice'. It is also evident in most efforts to promote and assess patient involvement in practice. However, it has recently been criticized for being too narrow in two respects: it fails to cover key aspects of decision-making surrounding the selection of one option from a menu and it neglects health professionals' and patients' attitudes towards each other and their feelings about their interactions and engagement in decision-making activities. In this chapter, I will refer to the second of these areas as the 'relational and subjective-affective aspects' of involvement.

This chapter describes the origins and key features of the dominant conceptualization of patient involvement in decision-making. It summarizes recent critiques of this conceptualization and suggests that a broader conceptualization might better accommodate what matters to patients, be more consistent with recent ideas about patient autonomy, and facilitate consideration of the relationship between patient involvement and health and wellbeing.

Patient involvement: The dominant conceptualization

Contemporary interest in involving patients in decisions about their own health care has been shaped by a complex array of factors, including the following:

- Expansion of the range of possible health care interventions and growing awareness that for many health problems, there are several management options; choosing between these options often involves making trade-offs between different benefits, harms, and uncertainties; and individuals vary in terms of the trade-offs they will make.

◆ Moral reaction against situations in which people were given health care interventions that they would not have accepted if they had been informed and given a choice.

◆ The strong emphasis within the field of bioethics, and in legal and policy developments relating to informed consent, on respect for patients' personal autonomy; also an understanding of respect for autonomy as a matter of ensuring that competent patients make intentional choices about their health care with sufficient understanding of the salient options and free from controlling influences (Beauchamp and Childress, 2001).

◆ The development of 'evidence-based medicine' and the increase in the availability and perceived importance of information about the likely outcomes of different health care options.

Patient involvement is often regarded as a means of ensuring that health care decisions combine health professionals' knowledge of health care options and outcomes with individual patients' knowledge of their life plans and preferences relating to the implications of different health care options (Charles et al., 1997). Although various models of patient involvement such as 'shared decision-making' and 'informed choice' have been proposed, and various definitions offered (Makoul and Clayman, 2006), a dominant basic conceptualization can be identified. This focuses on

1 health professionals' disclosure and/or patients' understanding of information about a menu of health care options and their likely outcomes; and

2 the questions of who makes the decision and/or whether the option chosen is congruent with the individual patient's values and preferences.

This conceptualization is evident in efforts to ensure that health professionals have the required competences to facilitate patient involvement in decision-making (Towle and Godolphin, 1999; Elwyn et al., 2000) and to develop supportive resources such as patient decision aids (O'Connor et al., 2003). It is also clearly reflected in the tools developed to 'measure' patient involvement – usually for professional assessment and research purposes. Measures based on observations of professional behaviour in consultations look particularly for an explicit acknowledgement that a decision needs to be made and that the patient can be involved; presentation of information about options; checking of patients' understanding; and attendance to patients' preferences and concerns (Braddock et al., 1999; Elwyn et al., 2005). Attempts to elicit patients' perspectives on whether and how well they were involved have often focused on the question of 'who made the decision?', asking respondents to pick one from a menu of descriptions such as 'The doctor made the decision', 'The doctor and I made the decision together', and 'I made the decision' (Ford et al., 2006; Hack et al., 2006). Alternatively, they have used a structured series of questions and invited people to indicate, for example, their agreement with statements such as 'The doctor informed and explained to me about my health problems and its possible treatment' and 'The doctor gave me the chance to express my opinions about the different treatments available' (Wensing et al., 2007).

Concerns about the dominant conceptualization

Several critiques of the dominant conceptualization of patient involvement have emerged in recent years. These claim that it focuses too narrowly on particular aspects of decision-making and patient–professional interaction, neglecting both (1) patients' roles in relation to the activities surrounding the selection from a menu of health care options and (2) the relational and subjective-affective aspects of involvement.

The tendency to consider patients' influence primarily in terms of their contribution to the selection of one option from a given menu set has been criticized for obscuring the potential importance of patients' engagement in discussions about the nature of their problems (Bugge *et al.*, 2006), the question of who defines the option set (Wirtz *et al.*, 2006), and the facilitation of patients' contributions to the delivery of, and monitoring response to, the health care interventions selected (Entwistle and Watt, 2006). Studies of the psychology of decision-making have also suggested that an emphasis on the provision of more sophisticated information about health care options and outcomes, and on encouraging people to make the best decisions they can, may not always be beneficial (Schwartz, 2004; Douglas and Jones, 2007).

The tendency to neglect key relational and subjective-affective aspects of patient involvement has been identified via consideration of both usual understandings of the word 'involvement' and investigations of patients' perspectives on their involvement.

In everyday talk, people can be said to be involved *in* activities and *with* others. Judgements about involvement are based not only on manifest behaviours but also on their thoughts and feelings about their role in activities and their interactions and relationships with others (Entwistle and Watt, 2006).

Patients' own assessments of their involvement do not always correlate well with assessments based on researchers' observations of consultations (Martin *et al.*, 2003; Ford *et al.*, 2006; Saba *et al.*, 2006), and some patients talk of having been involved in decision-making when they have not been given information about a menu of treatment options and have not significantly influenced the selection of a course of action (Beaver *et al.*, 2005; Entwistle *et al.*, 2006).

Patients often find questions about who made particular treatment decisions difficult to answer (Entwistle *et al.*, 2001; Edwards and Elwyn, 2006), and their answers are not consistently related to their descriptions of how those decisions were reached (Entwistle *et al.*, 2001; Entwistle *et al.*, 2004). Their perceptions of who made decisions may be less important to them than the processes by which decisions were discussed, although being given too much decisional responsibility can be significantly problematic (Edwards and Elwyn, 2006).

All this suggests that reports from surveys indicating that many patients would prefer health professionals to take the lead in 'making' treatment decisions (Say *et al.*, 2006; Deber *et al.*, 2007) should not necessarily be interpreted as evidence that patients do not want to be or to feel involved in decisions about their care. It may reflect differences between patients' understandings and the dominant conceptualization of patient involvement in decision-making.

Recent studies suggest that when patients consider their involvement in decision-making, they reflect on more than the information they receive and the influence they have over the selection of a treatment option. A study in Scotland found that people with diabetes associated involvement in treatment decisions with features of the 'ethos and feel of health care encounters' (practitioners being friendly and welcoming, interested and respectful of patients and their perspectives, facilitative of patients' contributions to discussions and to their care, and not unduly judgemental) and communication about health problems as well as communication about treatments (Entwistle *et al.*, 2008). A Swedish study found that not being listened to, not being respected as an individual, and feeling insecure in health care interactions were all associated with perceptions of non-participation in secondary care, alongside not being given appropriate information (Eldh *et al.*, 2008).

A broader conceptualization and its potential advantages

The notions of information exchange about health care options and patient influence over the selection of one option are not irrelevant and may be key aspects of involvement in some situations. However, the above concerns suggest that the conceptualization of involvement should be extended to cover (1) a broader range of decision-making activities or health-related behaviours and (2) the relational and subjective-affective aspects of involvement.

The potential benefits of examining and understanding patients' engagement in the activities that precede and follow the selection of a health care option include extending the applicability of the concept of patient involvement to a broader range of health care contexts (Murray *et al.*, 2006); enhancing recognition and support for patients' contributions to several key aspects of their health care; and facilitating recognition of the potential 'knock forward' benefits or implications of involvement (Entwistle and Watt, 2006).

Attention to the relational and subjective-affective aspects of involvement could also have advantages. A conceptualization that attended to a fuller notion of 'partnership' (Towle and Godolphin, 1999; Montori *et al.*, 2006) and to communication as 'being in relation' as well as communication as a skill or means of information transfer (Zoppi and Epstein, 2002) would better accommodate what matters to patients about involvement. It would also better reflect the fact that patients value positive relationships with health professionals not only (or not mainly) because of the benefits of task-related information exchange and choice but also because it matters to them that they feel cared for as individuals and respected as part of the care team (Burkitt-Wright *et al.*, 2004). It would also be consistent with the 'relational' accounts of autonomy that are responding to concerns about understandings of personal autonomy that focus simply on informed and independent individual choice. In contrast, these relational accounts emphasise 'the inter-subjective and social dimensions of selfhood and identity' and the implications of the ways individuals are viewed and treated by others for their own beliefs, preferences, and actions (Mackenzie and Stoljar, 2000:p4). Attention to these dimensions of involvement might also benefit investigations of links between involvement and health care outcomes (Entwistle and Watt, 2006) because relationships between health professionals and patients can plausibly affect the emotional states and health of both parties (Adler, 2002).

Conclusion

Relatively narrow conceptualizations of involvement that focus on the observable skills and behaviours of information transfer, and offering of choice or influence to patients can more readily be used to specify measurable learning objectives for trainee clinicians and to assess professional facilitation of patient involvement for clinical audit or quantitative research purposes (Saba *et al.*, 2006, Makoul and Clayman, 2006). However, there is a danger that the requirement of measurability drives conceptualization and that what is important about involvement is neglected because it is difficult to measure (Weiss and Peters, 2008). If policy makers, clinicians, and researchers aspire to attend to what matters to patients, respect patient autonomy in a meaningful way, and conduct more nuanced investigations of the relationships between involvement and health care outcomes, they need to think in terms of broader conceptualizations of patient involvement that attend to how patients and health professionals think and feel about their relationships and interactions as well as what they communicate about health care options.

References

Adler, H.M. (2002). The sociophysiology of caring in the doctor–patient relationship. *Journal of General Internal Medicine*, **17**, 883–890.

Beauchamp, T.L. and Childress, J.F. (2001). *Principles of Biomedical Ethics* (5th edition), Oxford: Oxford University Press.

Beaver, K., Jones, D., Susnerwala, S., *et al.* (2005). Exploring the decision-making preferences of people with colorectal cancer. *Health Expectations*, **8**, 103–113.

Braddock, C.H., Edwards, K.A., Hasenbert, N.M., *et al.* (1999). Informed decision-making in outpatient practice – Time to get back to basics. *JAMA,* **282**, 2313–2320.

Bugge, C., Entwistle, V.A., and Watt, I.S. (2006). Information that is not exchanged during consultations: Significance for decision-making. *Social Science & Medicine,* **63**, 2065–2078.

Burkitt-Wright, E., Holcombe, C., and Salmon, P. (2004). Doctors' communication of trust, care, and respect in breast cancer: Qualitative study. *British Medical Journal,* **328**, 864–866.

Charles, C., Gafni, A., and Whelan, T. (1997). Shared decision-making in the medical encounter: What does it mean? (Or it takes at least two to tango). *Social Science & Medicine,* **44**, 681–692.

Deber, R., *et al.* (2007). Do people want to be autonomous patients? Preferred roles in treatment decision-making in several patient populations. *Health Expectations,* **10**, 248–258.

Douglas, K. and Jones, D. (2007). Top 10 ways to make better decisions. *New Scientist,* **2602**, 35–43.

Edwards, A. and Elwyn, G. (2006). Inside the black box of shared decision-making: Distinguishing between the process of involvement and who makes the decision. *Health Expectations,* **9**, 307–320.

Eldh, A.C., Ekman, I., and Ehnfors M. (2008). Considering non-participation in health care. *Health Expectations,* **11**, 263–271.

Elwyn, G., Edwards, A., Kinnersley, P., *et al.* (2000). Shared decision-making and the concept of equipoise: The competences of involving patients in healthcare choices. *British Journal of General Practice,* **50**, 892–897.

Elwyn, G., Hutching, H., Edwards, A., *et al.* (2005). The OPTION scale: Measuring the extent that clinicians involve patients in decision-making tasks. *Health Expectations,* **8**, 34–42.

Entwistle, V., Skea, Z., and O'Donnell, M. (2001). Assessing the roles that people play in decisions about their health care: A study of women's interpretations of two measures of control. *Social Science and Medicine,* **53**, 721–732.

Entwistle, V.A., Watt, I.S., Gilhooly, K., *et al.* (2004). Assessing patients' participation and quality of decision-making: Insights from a study of routine practice in diverse settings. *Patient Education and Counselling,* **55**, 105–113.

Entwistle, V.A., Williams, B., Skea, Z., *et al.* (2006). Which surgical decisions should patients participate in? Reflections on women's recollections of discussions about different types of hysterectomy. *Social Science and Medicine,* **62**, 499–509.

Entwistle, V.A. and Watt, I.S. (2006). Patient involvement in treatment decision-making: The case for a broader conceptual framework. *Patient Education and Counselling,* **63**(3), 268–278.

Entwistle, V.A., Prior, M., Skea, Z.C., *et al.* (2008). Involvement in decision-making: A qualitative investigation of its meaning for people with diabetes. *Social Science and Medicine,* **66**, 362–375.

Ford, S., Schofield, T., and Hope, T. (2006). Observing decision-making in the general practice consultation: Who makes which decisions? *Health Expectations,* **9**, 130–137.

Hack, T.F., Degner, L.F., Watson, P., *et al.* (2006). Do patients benefit from participating in medical decision-making? Longitudinal follow-up of women with breast cancer. *Pscyho-oncology,* **15**, 9–19.

Mackenzie, C. and Stoljar, N. (eds). (2000). *Relational Autonomy: Feminist Perspectives on Autonomy, Agency and the Social Self.* New York: Oxford University Press.

Makoul, G. and Clayman, M. L. (2006). An integrative model of shared decision-making in medical encounters. *Patient Education and Counseling,* **60**, 301–312.

Martin, L.R., Jahng, K.H., Golin, C.E., *et al.* (2003). Physician facilitation of patient involvement in care: Correspondence between patient and observer reports. *Behavioral. Medicine,* **28**, 159–164.

Montori, V., Gafni, A., and Charles, C. (2006). A shared treatment decision-making approach between patients with chronic conditions and their clinicians: The case of diabetes. *Health Expectations,* **9**, 25–36.

Murray, E., Charles, C., and Gafni, A. (2006). Shared decision-making in primary care: Tailoring the Charles *et al.* model to fit the context of general practice. *Patient Education and Counseling,* **62**, 205–211.

O'Connor, A.M., Stacey, D., Entwistle, V., *et al.* (2003). Decision aids for people facing health treatment or screening decisions [Cochrane review: Substantive update]. Update Software: *Cochrane Library,* **2**.

Saba, G., Wong, S., Schillinger, D., *et al.* (2006). Shared decision-making and the experience of partnership in primary care. *Annals of Family Medicine,* **54**, 54–62.

Say, R. and Thomson, R. (2003). The importance of patient preferences in treatment decisions—challenges for doctors. *British Medical Journal,* **327**, 542–545.

Schwartz, B. (2004). *The Paradox of Choice: Why More is Less.* New York: Harper Collins.

Towle, A. and Godolphin, W. (1999). Framework for teaching and learning informed shared decision-making. *British Medical Journal,* **319**, 766–771.

Weiss, M.C., and Peters, T.J. (2008). Measuring shared decision-making in the consultation: A comparison of the OPTION and informed decision-making instruments. *Patient Education and Counseling,* **70**, 79–86.

Wensing, M., Wetzels, R., Hermsen, J., *et al.* (2007). Do elderly patients feel more enabled if they had been actively involved in primary care consultations? *Patient Education and Counseling,* **68**, 265–269.

Wirtz, V., Cribb, A., and Barber, N. (2006). Patient–doctor decision-making about treatment within the consultation: A critical analysis of models. *Social Science & Medicine,* **62**, 116–124.

Zoppi, K., and Epstein, R.M. (2002). Is communication a skill? Communication behaviours and being in relation. *Family Medicine,* **34**, 319–324.

Chapter 4

Shared decision-making: The implications for health care teams and practice

France Légaré and Dawn Stacey

Introduction

With the increased emphasis on engagement of patients as partners in their care, there is a need to determine effective ways to involve them in the process by which health care decisions are made. As clinical options multiply and health-related decisions become more challenging, it is expected that patients will require more guidance to make informed decisions. At the same time, in response to the growing needs of their population and the shortage in the health care labour force, in many industrialized countries, there is also an expectation that interprofessional health care team approaches will be encouraged and developed. Consequently, the process by which patients are engaged to share their preferences and become involved in decisions with their practitioners will have to change to accommodate this new interprofessional health care environment (Coulter, 1999).

Shared decision-making is defined as a decision-making process jointly shared by patients and their health care provider. It aims at helping patients play an active role in decisions concerning their health, which is the ultimate goal of patient-centered care. Nonetheless, shared decision-making has not yet been widely adopted. We argue that interprofessionality should be used to strengthen these new decision-making processes within a broader perspective of the health care team. Indeed, barriers to shared decision-making may be minimized with an interprofessional approach. This chapter reviews the state of knowledge regarding the interprofessional health care team's approaches and how they relate to shared decision-making. It also summarizes the lessons learned from current initiatives and provides suggestions for future research and development in this area.

Interprofessional health care teams

An interprofessional health care team approach is a process by which two or more professionals collaborate to provide integrated and cohesive patient care to address the needs of their population (D'Amours et al., 2005). Professionals include any health care workers involved in patient care across the spectrum from prevention to treatment and/or rehabilitation. Interprofessionality involves continuous interaction, open communication and knowledge sharing, understanding of professional roles, and common health goals (Xyrichis et al., 2008b). Interprofessionality also involves exploring a variety of education and care issues, all while seeking to optimize the patient's participation.

Interprofessional collaborations build on the strengths of each profession's approach to care delivery such that professionals practice within their full scope of practice and without intentional duplication of services. A Cochrane systematic review revealed that interprofessional collaborative practice produced positive outcomes on (a) emergency department culture and patient satisfaction; (b) collaborative team behaviour and reduction of clinical error rates for emergency department teams; (c) management of care delivered to domestic violence victims; and (d) mental health practitioner competencies related to the delivery of patient care (Reeves *et al.*, 2008). Of six included studies, two had positive outcomes, two observed mixed outcomes (positive and neutral), and two reported that interprofessional collaborative practice had no impact on either professional practice or patient care. It is notable that no included studies assessed the impact of interprofessional collaborative practice on patient's participation in decision-making. Due to the small number of studies, the heterogeneity of interventions, and the methodological limitations of the included studies, the authors stated that it was not possible to draw generalizable inferences about the key elements of interprofessional collaborative practice.

Notwithstanding some of the positive outcomes of interprofessional collaborative practices on processes of care and patient outcomes, barriers to its effective implementation in health care environments remain. Key elements influencing successful implementation are at the practitioner level (e.g., partnerships, effective communication, power), organizational level (e.g., leadership, training and development, processes, division of labour), and socio-political level (e.g., leadership, funding, pre-licensure uni-professional educational environments) (Reeves *et al.*, 2007).

Interprofessional education and learning

Interprofessional education and learning environments need to be considered at the same time as interprofessional collaborative practice, as well as linkages between these worlds. Individuals from diverse groups of professionals need to learn how to reconcile their differences and synergistically influence patient care through continuous interaction, sharing of their knowledge, and optimizing patients' participation. The World Health Organization (1988) defines interprofessional education as 'the process by which a group of students or workers from the health-related occupations with different backgrounds learn together during certain periods of their education, with interaction as the important goal, to collaborate in providing promotive, preventive, curative, rehabilitative, and other health-related services'.

Interestingly, post-licensure interprofessional collaborative practice interventions appear to have positive effects on care delivery. However, there is a lack of evidence on pre-licensure interprofessional education (Zwarenstein *et al.*, 2005). This is important because it could partly explain why interprofessional approaches to patient care by diverse health professions remain limited. Furthermore, legislation in most industrialized countries is based on distinct professions with their own educational requirements, practice standards, and regulatory colleges. More recently, policy makers have called for patient-centered care provided by an interprofessional team and have provided funding to enhance educational initiatives at all levels of licensure (Health Canada, 2006). For example, from 2000 to 2006, the Government of Canada demonstrated its commitment towards supporting the necessary changes to primary health care by establishing an $800M Primary Health care Transition Fund for provinces and territories to reform their primary health care systems. Across Canada, teams of researchers, educators, and decision makers applied for funding to elaborate and test interprofessional approaches to health care. This large national initiative has given birth to a Canadian consortium dedicated to interprofessional health care initiatives (Canadian Interprofessional Health Collaborative, 2008). This consortium serves as a national hub, the aim of which is to strengthen interprofessional education for collaborative, patient-centred practice and the knowledge base for interprofessional education. The model adopted by this consortium clearly depicts that both the professional system and the educational system are interdependent (Figure 4.1). However, outcomes of many of these large research and educational initiatives have yet to be evaluated and published.

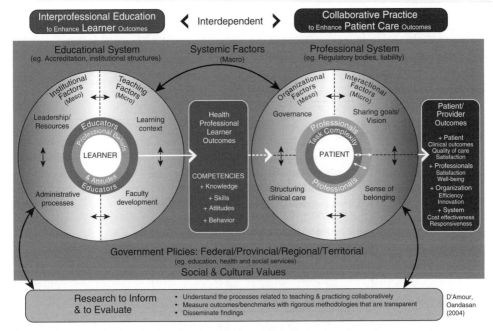

Figure 4.1 Interprofessional education for collaborative patient-centred practice: an evolving framework (D'Amours et Oandasan, 2004).

Interprofessional health care team approach to shared decision-making

The majority of current conceptual models of shared decision-making are essentially focused on the process by which decisions are made between one health care provider and one patient and more specifically, between one physician and one patient. An interprofessional approach to shared decision-making is the process by which patients are supported to become involved in decision-making, have their decisional needs met, and reach health care choices that are agreed upon by them and their interprofessional health care team (Légaré et al., 2008). An interprofessional approach to shared decision-making has the potential to improve the quality of decision support provided within the health care system. Although there are conceptual models of interprofessional practice and other models of shared decision-making, there is only limited view of how these important approaches to quality patient care should be integrated. Table 4.1 shows elements that an interprofessional health care team approach to shared decision-making should include.

Table 4.1 Elements of an interprofessional approach to shared decision-making

1. Sharing the common goal of quality health decisions (e.g. informed and based on patients' values).

2. Having a sense of trust among professionals participating in the shared decision-making process.

3. Being governed by leaders who value shared decision-making.

4. Having organizational structures to facilitate implementation of shared decision-making within the processes of care.

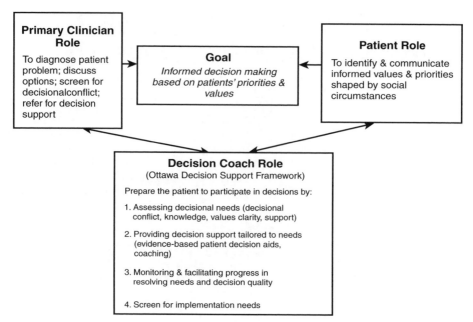

Figure 4.2 Decision support coaching framework (Stacey *et al.*, 2008).

Models that could help foster an interprofessional health care team approach to shared decision-making are only starting to emerge in the literature. For example, the Decision Coaching to Support Shared Decision-Making Framework proposes two roles for health professionals (Figure 4.2) (Stacey *et al.*, 2008). The role of one health professional would be to diagnose the problem requiring a shared decision-making process, provide options, and assess the degree of decisional conflict. The role of a second health professional would be to focus on decision coaching. This would involve (a) assessing factors influencing patients' decisional conflict, (b) providing support to address decisional needs, (c) monitoring progress in decision-making, and (d) screening for factors influencing implementation.

Patient decision aids also can play an important role in fostering an interprofessional approach to shared decision-making. For example, Lalonde and her colleagues (2004) have developed and piloted a patient decision aid regarding cardiovascular disease prevention with the goal of improving an interprofessional approach to active participation of patients in decisions. This patient decision aid is perceived as playing an important role for an integrated and cohesive patient care pathway.

In the last year, an international research team was initiated to develop and validate with key stakeholders a conceptual model and set of measurement tools for enhancing an interprofessional approach to shared decision-making in primary health care practices, education, and applied health services research (Légaré *et al.*, 2008). This research project involves four main steps. First, it includes a theoretical analysis of the existing conceptual models and theories in shared decision-making to ascertain their characteristics, strengths, and limitations, including their acknowledgement of interprofessional roles in the process of shared decision-making. This will also explore the extent to which they have been tested in applied health services research and educational activities in primary health care. Second, it will assess the validity and reliability of identified measurement tools that would be relevant to an interprofessional approach to shared decision-making. Third, a consensus will be sought among the research team for a new conceptual model and a set of measurement tools for an interprofessional approach to shared decision-making in primary health care practices, education, and applied health services research. Lastly, the research team will identify the perceived barriers and facilitators to the implementation of the proposed conceptual model and set of measurement tools for an interprofessional approach to shared decision-making with representatives from clinical practice, research, education, and policy environments. The results of this research initiative were also to be used to lay the ground for discussion and international linkages at the 2008 Summer Institute for Informed Patient Choice; the main theme of which was 'Interprofessional Education in Decision Support' (Center for Informed Choice at The Dartmouth Institute for Health Policy & Clinical Practice, 2008).

Conclusion

Overall, in many industrialized countries, their current health care context reinforces the need for interprofessional teams that will address the new challenges in health care. These challenges include (a) explosion of health information, (b) expanding roles and participation of patients in clinical decision-making, (c) increasing burden of chronic diseases and multi-morbidity in patients, and (d) shortage and constraints in the health care labour force. However, the literature points to a lack of guidance in how the existing conceptual models and measurement tools in shared decision-making and interprofessionalism relate to enhancing current practice, applied health services research, and training activities to support an interprofessional approach to shared decision-making.

The literature does not provide sound evidence on how to implement interprofessional approaches effectively in health care nor shared decision-making itself. For both, a number of factors have been speculated but not tested. For example, factors potentially influencing the implementation of teamworking include (a) team premises, (b) team size and composition, (c) organizational support, (d) team meetings, (d) clear goals and objectives, and (e) audit (Xyrichis et al., 2008a). Factors potentially influencing the implementation of shared decision-making in health care professional practices include among others (a) time constraints, (b) lack of applicability due to patient characteristics and the clinical situation, (c) provider motivation, and (d) perceived impact on the clinical process and patient outcomes (Gravel et al., 2006). Drawing attention on the larger body of the literature pertaining to the implementation of innovative clinical practices (Grol et al., 2003), one might hypothesize that a combination of strategies at the individual level (e.g. training of individuals), organizational level (e.g. team processes such as regular meetings), and policy level (e.g. regulations by the state) could be effective.

Therefore, future research initiatives need to propose and test appropriate conceptual models and measures that will foster an interprofessional health care team approach to shared decision-making. This will provide a foundation for conducting future studies and educating health professionals to improve how the health care system understands and responds to public expectations in a more coordinated fashion. Effective implementation strategies for an interprofessional health care team approach to shared decision-making also need to be tested. Importantly, this may also be instrumental in realigning patients' unrealistic expectations of health care treatment outcomes and how the system manages to ensure safe delivery of high-quality services to patients who most value them – two important priority themes in health services and policy research.

References

Canadian Interprofessional Health Collaborative (CIHC). (2008). Retrieved May 3, 2008, from http://www.cihc.ca/

Center for Informed Choice at The Dartmouth Institute for Health Policy and Clinical Practice. (2008). 2008 Summer Institute on Informed Patient Choice: Interprofessional Education in Decision Support. Retrieved May 3, 2008, from http://www.dartmouth.edu/~cecs/cic/2008/index.html

Coulter, A. (1999). Paternalism or partnership? Patients have grown up and there's no going back [editorial comment] [see comments]. *British Medical Journal*, **319**, 719–720.

D'Amours, D., Ferrada-Videla, M., San Martin Rodriguez., *et al.* (2005). The conceptual basis for interprofessional collaboration: Core concepts and theoretical frameworks. *J. Interprofessional Care*, **19** (1), 116–131.

Gravel, K., Légaré, F., and Graham, I. D. (2006). Barriers and facilitators to implementing shared decision-making in clinical practice: A systematic review of health professionals' perceptions. *Implement Science*, **1**, 16.

Grol, R. and Grimshaw, J. (2003). From best evidence to best practice: Effective implementation of change in patients' care. *Lancet*, **362**, 1225–1230.

Health Canada. (2006). Primary Health Care Transition Fund. Retrieved September 11, 2006, from http://www.hc-sc.gc.ca/hcs-sss/prim/phctf-fassp/index_e.html

Lalonde, L., O'Connor, A. M., Drake, E., *et al.* (2004). Development and preliminary testing of a patient decision aid to assist pharmaceutical care in the prevention of cardiovascular disease. *Pharmacotherapy*, **24**, 909–922.

World Health Organization. (1988). *Learning together to work together for health. Report of a WHO study group on multiprofessional education of health personnel: The team approach.* (No. 769). Geneva: World Health Organization.

Légaré, F., Stacey, D., Graham, I. D., *et al.* (2008). Advancing theories, models and measurement for an interprofessional approach to shared decision making in primary care: A study protocol. *BMC Health Serv. Res.,* **8**, 2.

Reeves, S., Goldman, J., and Oandasan, I. (2007). Key factors in planning and implementing interprofessional education in health care settings. *J. Allied Health*, **36**, 231–235.

Reeves, S., Zwarenstein, M., Goldman, J., *et al.* (2008). Interprofessional education: Effects on professional practice and health care outcomes. *Cochrane Database Systematic Review* (1), CD002213.

Stacey, D., Murray, M. A., Légaré, F., *et al.* (2008). Decision coaching to support shared decision making: A framework, evidence, and implications for nursing practice, education, and policy. *Worldviews Evidence Based Nurs.,* **5**, 25–35.

Xyrichis, A. and Lowton, K. (2008a). What fosters or prevents interprofessional teamworking in primary and community care? A literature review. *Int J Nursing Studies*, **45**, 140–153.

Xyrichis, A. and Ream, E. (2008b). Teamwork: A concept analysis. *J. Advanced Nursing*, **61**, 232–241.

Zwarenstein, M., Reeves, S., and Perrier, L. (2005). Effectiveness of pre-licensure interprofessional education and post-licensure collaborative interventions. *J. Interprofessional Care*, **19** (1), 148–165.

Chapter 5

Evidence-based health care decision-making: Roles for health professionals

Dawn Stacey, France Légaré, and
Jennifer Kryworuchko

Introduction

A goal of evidence-based health care is to optimize decision-making by integrating clinical expertise and patients' values with the best available evidence (Sackett *et al.*, 2000). This is consistent with shared decision-making, defined as a decision-making process jointly shared by patients and their health care provider. It aims to help patients play an active role in decisions concerning their health, which is the ultimate goal of patient-centered care.

More recently, there has been a shift to preferring an interprofessional approach to shared decision-making (see Chapter 4). Interprofessional shared decision-making is defined as the process by which patients are supported to become involved in decision-making, have their decisional needs met, and reach health care choices that are agreed upon by them and their inter-professional health care team (Legare *et al.*, 2008). Consequently, key players in interprofessional evidence-based health care decision-making are the patient and his/her significant others, as well as two or more health care professionals. We contend that an interprofessional approach to shared decision-making can be reinforced by the presence of a member of the health care team functioning in a *decision coaching* type role (O'Connor *et al.*, 2008).

The purpose of this chapter is to (a) discuss the roles of those involved in interprofessional evidence-based health care decision-making including the role of a decision coach, (b) distinguish the role of a decision coach from the role of the other health care professionals in facilitating the process of shared decision-making, (c) review the evidence on the decision coaching role, and (d) explore strategies to implement decision coaching roles.

Patient role

The patient is the individual confronted with the clinical situation requiring a choice, often supported by family members or significant others involved in the decision-making. An important patient role in shared decision-making is to communicate their personal values and preferences that are shaped by their knowledge of the options and social circumstances (Coulter, 2002; Stacey *et al.*, 2008; Towle and Godolphin, 1999; Kristjansson E. *et al.*, 2007). Elements of patients' involvement in decision-making include establishing partnership with health care professionals; communicating their health problem, values, and priorities; seeking and using information; and implementing the decision (Table 5.1). Chapter 6 further discusses the patient's role in evidence-based health care.

Given the majority of patients experience uncertainty about the best course of action and require support to achieve an active role in decision-making, health care professionals should

Table 5.1 Patients' role responsibilities in shared decision-making

Patient competencies (Towle and Godolphin, 1999)	Effective consumer attributes and skills (Kristjansson E. *et al.*, 2007)
◆ Define preferred doctor – patient relationship	◆ Seek evidence-based information
◆ Establish partnership with a physician	◆ Make decisions
◆ Articulate health problems, feelings, beliefs, and expectations in an objective and systematic manner	• adapt information to self
	• set goals
	• determine values
◆ Communicate with the physician to understand and share relevant information	• set priorities
	◆ Implement decisions
◆ Access information	◆ Negotiate role
◆ Evaluate information	◆ Negotiate the system
◆ Negotiate decisions, give feedback, resolve conflict, agree on an action plan	◆ Interact within social environment
	◆ Acknowledge individual differences

screen for uncertainty and provide decision support (O'Connor *et al.*, 2008). Furthermore, providing decision support proactively may also lead to higher quality health care decisions. International consensus defines higher quality decisions as informed with the best available evidence and based on patients' informed values (Elwyn *et al.*, 2006).

Clinician role

Another key player in shared decision-making is the clinician primarily accountable for the specific health care situation. This clinician works together with patients and/or fosters a team-based approach to the way in which decisions are made and implemented. Clinicians in this context include physicians, nurse practitioners, midwives, dieticians, physiotherapists, or occupational therapists. The clinician role involves diagnosing the problem, discussing the options, and reaching agreement with the patient on the best option to implement in their situation (Elwyn *et al.*, 2000; Stacey *et al.*, 2008a; Towle and Godolphin, 1999; Makoul and Clayman, 2005). Chapter 17 discusses the competencies necessary for clinicians. Unfortunately, emerging evidence suggests that decision quality resulting from standard counselling in clinicians' practice is less than optimal (Guimond *et al.*, 2003; Elwyn *et al.*, 2005; Loh *et al.*, 2006; Stevenson *et al.*, 2004).

In studies that evaluated standard counselling, physicians largely focused on information giving without explicitly considering patients' expectations or values associated with outcomes of options. As well, many barriers interfere with implementing shared decision-making in clinical practice (Gravel *et al.*, 2006). As a result, patients exposed to current practice do not necessarily reach health care decisions that are based on patients' evidence-informed values associated with the outcomes of the possible options. Although there are advantages to train clinicians, potential disadvantages include clinician bias, increased time required for consultations, and the need for further skill development (Table 5.2). To overcome some of these barriers and better support patients in their role, there are initiatives to explore a decision coach role for other health care professionals within the team.

Decision coach role

A decision coach is a skilled health professional who supports the patient's involvement in health care decision-making but does not make the decision for the patient (O'Connor *et al.*, 2008). The decision coach has also been described as a facilitator and a knowledge broker (Myers, 2005; Woolf *et al.*, 2005). Many coaches are nurses that have evolved the patient educator role to be

Table 5.2 Comparison of factors influencing the use of decision coaches and trained clinicians in shared decision-making (Woolf *et al.*, 2005)

	Trained clinicians	Decision coaches
Advantages	◆ Within patient–clinician relationship ◆ Integrated in care ◆ Potential for reimbursement ◆ Less need to coordinate roles	◆ More neutral ◆ Less demanding on clinician ◆ Consistent with interprofessional collaboration ◆ Higher quality counselling
Disadvantages	◆ Provider bias ◆ Clinician time for counselling ◆ Need for training and skill development	◆ Lack of clinical expertise ◆ Inefficient if not coordinated with clinicians' role ◆ Reimbursement issues

knowledgeable and skilled as decision coaches; but decision coaches are also other health care professionals such as social workers, psychologists, pharmacists, and palliative care consultant physicians. Overall, the decision coach is an *adjunct* to the clinical consultation and assists patients to be active participants in shared decision-making.

Key elements involved in decision coaching (as viewed by three different authors) are summarized in Table 5.3 (Myers, 2005; Stacey *et al.*, 2008a; Woolf *et al.*, 2005). The decision coach facilitates the process of shared decision-making by assessing decision-making needs and intervening as appropriate. Coaches can help patients understand the best evidence about the options, clarify their values, communicate with others involved in the decision, and negotiate the barriers to implementation. Decision coaches need to assess the patient's self-confidence with their preferred role in decision-making and encourage them to discuss their preferences with the clinician. Although decision coaches may lack clinical expertise and use of this role may be inefficient if not coordinated with the clinician's role, advantages include being more neutral in the decision, provide higher quality counselling, sharing workload across the team, and having an interprofessional team that allows members to function to their full potential (see Table 5.2).

Table 5.3 Decision coach role competencies

	Myers 2005	Stacey 2008	Woolf 2005
Assess factors influencing patient decision-making	√	√	
Assess patient understanding of options and evidence	√	√	√
Clarify patients' preferred option	√	√	√
Discuss patients' decision support needs and resources		√	
Determine patients preferred role			√
Provide educational resources, including patient decision aids		√	√
Encourage patient selection of preferred option	√	√	
Coach patients to discuss preferences with clinician(s)			√
Screen/plan for barriers to implementation	√	√	
Monitor and facilitate progress in decision-making		√	

Five studies have evaluated the effect of the decision coach role (Kennedy *et al.*, 2002; Myers, 2005; National Steering Group for Decision Support Aids in Urology, 2005). Myers reported on a decision counselling intervention that was used in three prospective cohort studies: the decision to undergo prostate cancer screening, the decision to participate in a trial of prostate cancer chemoprevention, and the decision to undergo genetic and environmental screening for colorectal cancer. Decision counselling was reported to be effective in helping participants identify factors that influence their decision, clarify personal preference regarding the options, and select the option that best matched their preferences.

Two other studies evaluated the effect of decision coaching combined with patient decision aids (Kennedy *et al.*, 2002; National Steering Group for Decision Support Aids in Urology, 2005). Patient decision aids are interventions designed also as adjuncts to clinician counselling that at a minimum provide evidence-based information on the options and the associated benefits and harms of each option (O'Connor *et al.*, 1999). In a large randomized controlled trial, women considering hysterectomy for heavy uterine bleeding, exposed to a patient decision aid followed by nurse coaching to clarify their preferences, were more satisfied and the intervention was more cost-effective compared to decision aid alone or usual care (Kennedy *et al.*, 2002). Women who received decision coaching less frequently chose hysterectomy and incurred lower costs. A cohort study of men considering treatment for benign prostate hypertrophy or prostate cancer found that after exposure to the decision aid and decision coaching, men made higher quality decisions and were more satisfied (National Steering Group for Decision Support Aids in Urology, 2005).

Models for integrating the various roles

There are three approaches for integrating the patient, clinician, and decision coach roles in the process of evidence-based health care decision-making. In a *serial model*, the patient receives decision support for salient decisions as they pass from one clinician to another. For example, patients may (a) be provided with treatment options by an oncologist at a cancer facility; (b) subsequently telephone a call centre to receive decision coaching by health care professionals; and (c) return to their oncologist to make the decision. A *group model* occurs when health care professionals have a team conference with the patient and/or family to discuss the options and reach a shared decision based on the patient's informed preferences. A third approach is the *specialist role* where the decision coach is a consultant to the team and located within the clinical setting. Regardless of factors in the clinical setting that influence how the role is integrated, the key elements involved in decision coaching remain consistent across models.

Strategies to develop and implement decision coach role

The challenge lies in developing and implementing the decision coach role, given the limited decision coaching skills of health care professionals and constraints of clinical environments. Effective interventions to improve decision coaching knowledge and skills are (a) the Ottawa Decision Support Tutorial (publicly available at www.ohri.ca/decisionaid); (b) skills building workshop using examples of higher quality decision coaching and role play; (c) protocols or decision aids to guide the coaching process; and (d) feedback using the Decision Support Analysis Tool (Stacey *et al.*, 2009b). Studies in Australia and Canada of call centre health care professionals (e.g. nurses, psychologists, health promotion professionals) that were exposed to these interventions had significant improvement in their knowledge of decision coaching and skills in supporting standardized patients (Stacey *et al.*, 2006b; Stacey *et al.*, in press a). At baseline, all participants were likely to provide information about the decision but after exposure to the interventions

Table 5.4 Process to develop decision coach competencies

Exposure	◆ Aware of decision support roles
	◆ Aware of decisional conflict and related factors
	◆ Recognize personal attitudes about patient involvement in decision-making
Immersion	◆ Participate in educational activities
	◆ Provide decision coaching with standardized patients
	◆ Obtain commitment to try decision coaching in clinical practice
Competence	◆ Provide higher quality decision coaching
	◆ Facilitate implementation of coaching within interprofessional teams
	◆ Role model/mentor novice coaches

they were more likely to assess information needs before providing the required information, discuss values associated with outcomes of the options, and discuss support issues influencing the decision (e.g. pressure from others, advice required, resources needed). Unfortunately, barriers in the environment continued to influence sustainable practice changes.

Key barriers to sustainability of a decision coaching role for health care professionals are poor access to electronic protocols and tools to guide decision coaching, managers who do not value the contributions of decision coaches, lack of patient awareness of these services, and lack of reimbursement for these types of services (Stacey *et al.*, 2006a; Woolf *et al.*, 2005). Despite known barriers, decision coach roles are being integrated into the processes of care. The process is as outlined in Table 5.4, and some centers show how this can be achieved. For example, patients who call into the Cancer Council Queensland Helpline for information related to a specific cancer treatment or screening decision receive information and decision coaching by health care professionals working at the Call Centre (Hutchison *et al.*, 2006). At Dartmouth-Hitchcock Medical Centre in NH, USA, patients are either referred to or drop into the Centre for Shared Decision-Making where the decision coach provides access to patient decision aids and, if necessary, coaches patients through the process of decision-making (Dartmouth-Hitchcock Medical Center, 2008). Most of this center's activity is invested in helping teams embed decision support in the care processes of clinics and inpatient units. The centre can also provide decision quality reports back to the referring clinician. Another project is building upon the results from a demonstration project to implement patient decision aids and decision coaching by nurses in urology practices across the United Kingdom (National Steering Group for Decision Support Aids in Urology, 2005).

Conclusions

Overall, the literature indicates that within an interprofessional health care team making shared decisions, patients, clinicians, and decision coaches collaborate to achieve the common goal of a higher quality health decision. Decision coaches are able to facilitate patient understanding of the evidence and prepare patients to discuss their preferences with clinicians and important others in the decision-making process. Studies indicate that patients exposed to decision coaches achieve higher quality decisions and are satisfied with the process of decision-making.

However, given that decision coaches are relatively new to the health care team, there is still a need to articulate the role and determine optimal ways to incorporate this role within the team. Emerging evidence should be strengthened by future research initiatives that propose effective strategies for implementing decision coach roles within health care teams in diverse care settings.

References

Coulter, A. (2002). *The Autonomous Patient. Ending Paternalism in Medical Care*. London: The Nuffield Trust.

Dartmouth-Hitchcock Medical Center (2008). Center for Shared Decision Making. Available at http://www.dhmc.org/shared_decision_making.cfm [On-line]. Accessed on June 8, 2008.

Elwyn, G., Edwards, A., Kinnersley, P., *et al.* (2000). Shared decision making and the concept of equipoise: The competencies of involving patients in healthcare choices. *British Journal General Practice,* **50,** 892–899.

Elwyn, G., Hutchings, H., Edwards, A., *et al.* (2005). The OPTION scale: Measuring the extent that clinicians involve patients in decision-making tasks. *Health Expectations,* **8,** 34–42.

Elwyn, G., O'Connor, A., Stacey, D., *et al.* (2006). Developing a quality criteria framework for patient decision aids: Online international Delphi consensus process. *British Medical Journal,* **333,** 417–422.

Gravel, K., Legare, F., and Graham, I.D. (2006). Barriers and facilitators to implementing shared decision-making in clinical practice: A systematic review of health professionals' perceptions. *BMC Implementation Science,* **1,** 1–15.

Guimond, P., Bunn, H., O'Connor, A.M., *et al.* (2003). Validation of a tool to assess health practitioners' decision support and communication skills. *Patient Education & Counseling,* **50,** 235–245.

Hutchison, S., Steginga, S.K., and Dunn, J. (2006). The tiered model of psychosocial intervention in cancer: A community based approach. *Psycho-Oncology,* **15,** 541–546.

Kennedy, A., Sculpher, M.J., Coulter, A., *et al.* (2002). Effects of decision aids for menorrhagia on treatment choices, health outcomes, and costs. A randomized controlled trial. *Journal of the American Medical Association,* **288,** 2701–2708.

Kristjansson, E., Tugwell, P.S., Wilson, A.J., *et al.* (2007). Development of the effective musculoskeletal consumer scale. *Journal of Rheumatol.,* **34,** 1392–1400.

Legare, F., Stacey, D., Graham, I., *et al.* (2008). Advancing theories, models and measurement for an interprofessional approach to shared decision making in primary care: A study protocol. *BMC Health Services Research,* **8,** 1–8.

Loh, A., Simon, D., Hennig, K., *et al.* (2006). The assessment of depressive patients' involvement in decision making in audio-taped primary care consultations. *Patient Education & Counseling,* **63,** 314–318.

Makoul, G. and Clayman, M.L. (2006). An integrative model of shared decision making in medical encounters. *Patient Education & Counseling.* **60,** 301–312.

Myers, R. E. (2005). Decision counseling in cancer prevention and control. *Health Psychol.,* **24,** S71–S77.

National Steering Group for Decision Support Aids in Urology (2005). Implementing patient decision aids in urology – *Final Report.* Available at http://www.pickereurope.org/Filestore/Research/Urology_steering_group_report.pdf [On-line]. Accessed on June 8, 2008.

O'Connor, A.M., Rostom, A., Fiset, V., *et al.* (1999). Decision aids for patients facing health treatment or screening decisions: A Cochrane systematic review. *BMJ,* **319,** 731–734.

O'Connor, A.M., Stacey, D., and Legare, F. (2008). Coaching to support patients in making decisions. *British Medical Journal,* **336,** 228–229.

Sackett, D.L., Straus, S.E., Richardson, W.S., *et al.* (2000). *Evidence-Based Medicine. How to Practice and Teach EBM*. Edinburgh: Churchill Livingstone.

Stacey, D., Pomey, M.P., O'Connor, A.M., *et al.* (2006a). Adoption and sustainability of decision support for patients facing health decisions: An implementation case study in nursing. *Implementation Science,* **1,** 1–10.

Stacey, D., O'Connor, A.M., Graham, I.D., *et al.* (2006b). Randomized controlled trial of the effectiveness of an intervention to implement evidence-based patient decision support in a nursing call centre. *Journal of Telemedicine and Telecare,* **12,** 410–415.

Stacey, D., Murray, M.A., Legare, F., *et al.* (2008). Decision coaching to support shared decision making: A framework, evidence, and implications for nursing practice, education, and policy. *Worldviews on Evidence-Based Nursing, 5,* 25–35.

Stacey, D., Steginga, S.K., Jacobsen, M.J., *et al.* (2009). Overcoming barriers to cancer helpline professionals providing decision support for callers: An implementation study. *Oncology Nursing Forum.*

Stacey, D., Taljaard, M., Drake, E.R., *et al.* (2009). Audit and feedback using the brief Decision Support Analysis Tool (DSAT-10) to evaluate nurse-standardized patient encounters. *Patient Education and Counseling.*

Stevenson, F.A., Cox, K., Britten, N., *et al.* (2004). A systematic review of the research on communication between patients and health care professionals about medicines: The consequences for concordance. *Health Expectations, 7,* 235–245.

Towle, A. and Godolphin, W. (1999). Framework for teaching and learning informed shared decision making. *British Medical Journal, 319,* 766–771.

Woolf, S.H., Chan, E.C.Y., Harris, R., *et al.* (2005). Promoting informed choice: Transforming health care to dispense knowledge for decision making. *Annals of Internal Medicine, 143,* 293–300.

Chapter 6

Evidence-based health care: What roles for patients?

Hazel Thornton

Introduction

The optimistic foreword by Richard Grol to the first edition of this book, published in 2001, ended with the words 'And, it manages to show us the way to a potential future: health care provision where patients and professionals operate as real partners with shared goals, playing an equal music in deciding on the best management of the health problems' (Grol, R. 2001). Forging and maintaining real partnerships of any kind requires a settled environment in which to develop them, continued desire and determination of both parties to make them work, a shared set of values, good communication, and constant hard work. I will examine the changing nature of health care consultations in this chapter, starting first with a broader view of health care developments and of research in particular, as I believe these are important contexts and influences on the everyday business of patients seeing clinicians in consultations.

Background

To examine what roles there might be for patients in evidence-based health care, particularly with respect to decisions taken in consultations between patients and health care professionals, perhaps we should step back to review the varied cultural, political, sociological, and structural changes that have occurred within and around health services since that foreword was written. 'Empowerment' (in developed countries) is generally encouraged and promoted (Department of Communities and Local Government, 2008); medical professionalism is evolving (Royal College of Physicians, 2005; Department of Health, 2008); government policies change and their promotions are usually neither evidence-based nor piloted (Fotaki M, *et al.*, 2005); 'achieving targets' is their measure of 'success'; health services are subjected to constant re-organization and changes of boundary. In consequence, patients and clinicians become bewildered and uncertain and less confident about being able to contribute. The context is continually changing; participating voices compete to be heard. When the composition of any group of stakeholders changes, the power dynamics are altered. At the same time, as the authority of the medical profession is being eroded by government, the patient's role, including research in particular, is gaining ground (Thornton, 2008).

What roles for patients in research? The evidence base

Undertaking reviews of the effect of patient involvement in research is essential, if we are to know what is occurring within these partnerships and to learn from collective experiences. Oliver and colleagues (Oliver SR, *et al.*, 2008) undertook a systematic review of research literature, policy documents, and reflective reports about public involvement in research agenda setting.

They developed a multidimensional framework of the implications for policy and practice that can facilitate learning across diverse experiences. They also identified gaps in the evidence base about public involvement, particularly with respect to its promotion and the effectiveness of different approaches.

The UK Clinical Research Collaboration has set up an Activities Log (UK Clinical Research Collaboration, 2008). This is a database to capture and share information about research, evaluations, or reflections on the impact of patient and public involvement in research. Its purpose is to create an openly accessible up-to-date resource that facilitates knowledge sharing and better co-ordination of activities in this field. The Activities Log aims to complement the work of 'invoNET'.

InvoNET is a network of people working to build evidence, knowledge and learning about public involvement in the NHS, public health and social care research, and to encourage collaborations (http://www.invo.org.uk/invoNET.asp). It has a broad range of members, including researchers, service users, carers, research funders, academics, and health and social care practitioners. In summary, there are many instances of important patient involvement in research, significantly influencing both direction and process of the research. There are valuable resources collating these experiences, and these efforts are likely to increasingly permeate through to health care practice.

Evidence-based patient choice

The difficulties of advocating and practicing evidence-based health care or enabling evidence-based patient choice in over-regulated 'western' health settings are many and varied. But the emancipation of patients is evident in many countries. Involvement of patients and the public in research and in the delivery and organization of health care is being accommodated. The balance of power has changed, with risks, responsibilities, and duties more likely to be shared. Political endorsement is explicit; health service encouragement for involvement is unequivocal.

The relationship between doctor and patient in the consultation has also been affected with rapid but uneven change in the flight from the culture of dependence to more self-reliant, involved, respectful, and responsible liaisons. With that change, exchanges and interactions, individual and group, have necessarily challenged and modified the language and conventions of the old order. Whilst mostly retaining respect for the healing profession, dialogues increasingly require directness and robustness to enable exchanges to lead to learning, action, and ultimately to improved health care and health. This paves the way for more satisfactory decision-making within consultations.

Who are these patients?

When asking, 'what roles for patients?' it is necessary to consider who these patients might be and which patients will be affected by or attracted to these new approaches to involvement and shared decision-making. Today's ease of communication brings both beneficial and perverse consequences. Both within inter-continental co-operation of health professionals and within patient groups, there are opportunities for exchanges, insights, collaboration, and rapid transference of findings. But also for anyone to speak on behalf of 'patients' demands', not just with knowledge of available evidence, but a constant awareness of the huge variety of expectation and aspirations, ranging from those within highly organized Western patient groups, who purport to speak for their patient constituency, to individuals struggling to acclimatise and survive as newcomers in a strange and different environment. It might seem that the former group have the advantage, but the membership of large organized groups is inevitably varied, leading to doubts about the accuracy of representation by spokespersons. Internet communication facilitates rapid dissemination amongst and between groups, but can sweep along those who perhaps do not fully understand and are not necessarily ready to accept new approaches. Maintaining individuals' desires to take personal responsibility, according their own culture, values, and preferences can be difficult; and for well-meaning others to recognize or fully respect. The boundaries of different attitudes, cultures, customs, and beliefs when it comes to the doctor–patient relationship should be carefully respected and not trodden down in the rush to emancipate 'the patient'. Today, a national boundary can encompass an even broader range of cultures and accepted traditional modes of behaviour than in earlier times, and at a time when access to health care is now more widely available. Integrating such diversity into national health care systems and practices is challenging.

Shared decision-making

Shared decision-making has been defined as 'the process of involving patients in clinical decisions'. The ethos is one where professionals (should) work to define problems with sufficient clarity and openness so that patients can comprehend the uncertainties that surround most decisions in medicine and therefore appreciate that choices have to be made between competing options (Edwards *et al.*, 2004). The clinician's expertise lies in diagnosing and identifying treatment options according to clinical priorities; the patient's role is to identify and communicate their informed values and personal priorities, as shaped by their social circumstances (Stacey *et al.*, 2008).

In June 2008, the UK General Medical Council replaced its 1998 booklet 'Seeking patients' consent: the ethical considerations', giving new guidance 'on the importance of the doctor–patient partnership'. It is entitled 'Consent: patients and doctors making decisions together' (General Medical Council, 2008). It sets out the key principles of good decision-making for all health care, from simple treatments under minor conditions to major surgery. It takes account of changes in the law and reflects the shift in professional and public attitudes towards more patient-centred care. It 'expands on the guidance in Good Medical Practice' (General Medical Council 2006), which requires doctors to be satisfied that they have consent from a patient, or other valid authority, before undertaking any examination or investigation, providing treatment, or involving patients in teaching and research.

This shift in emphasis by the GMC from doctors 'seeking consent' to doctors 'making decisions together' with patients is a clear indication of the considerable changes in attitude and practice that have taken place in the last 10 years. Formerly, it was the doctor's responsibility to seek consent; now, ensuring that proper consent is obtained is portrayed as a shared responsibility. The new guidance also signals that seeking consent in research should be no different from seeking consent in routine clinical practice. Hitherto, the GMC guidance for seeking consent for patients being invited to participate in research was much more onerous. It is to be hoped that former 'double standards', particularly with respect to information provision (Chalmers and Lindley, 2001), will have been smoothed away, particularly as the GMC state that 'the principles apply more widely, including decisions on taking part in research' (General Medical Council, 2008, p. 4.). They promise more details in their forthcoming separate guidance on research.

The consultation

Individual expectation of an ideal consultation will differ widely from one individual to another, depending on whether they wish to adopt a dependent, leading, or participating role in the decision-making. So, how much should we try to influence people's expectations for an improved consultation by suggesting that greater involvement in the decision-making process is a desirable goal? Do patients want and expect it? Do they value it when they experience it? What evidence do we have?

We can draw encouragement from Harry Cayton's Foreword to the official report of the *Health in Partnership* Programme research:

> *science confirms anecdote and objective scrutiny confirms subjective opinion. At last the evidence is here and I hope we can use it to extend and deepen patient and public involvement in the health service. Patient and public involvement is now, I am pleased to say, not only right but evidence based.*
>
> (UK Department of Health, 2004)

He went on to say:

> [The report] *reviews and summarizes twelve pieces of research about patient and public involvement. The outcomes for patients, for staff, for communities, and for health delivery are almost universally positive. The report shows that patient involvement improves patient satisfaction and is rewarding for professionals. Public involvement influences planning and services, and increases confidence and understanding.*

Changing patient expectations

A discrete choice experiment (Longo MF *et al.*, 2006) concluded that shared treatment decisions were valued less than some other attributes of a consultation. The consultation attribute that patients valued most was that the doctor listens, followed by 'information easy to understand', 'who chooses', 'amount of information', and length of consultation. Most patients preferred a consultation in which they contributed but did not have sole responsibility for the decision taken. Least preferred were consultations where the doctor alone makes the decisions (paternalistic) (Thornton *et al.*, 2003). Significantly, however, patient utilities for involvement appeared responsive to changes in experiences (i.e. of shared decision-making) of consultations. This suggests that shared decision-making may gain a greater value among patients once they have experienced it. We must remain aware though that patients feel involved in their care only when they are treated as equal partners, that privacy and time for discussion are required to achieve this, and that patients have different expectations of the responsibility they want to accept (Edwards *et al.*, 2004).

The benefits

There are benefits for both patients and health professionals. Professionals not only value the personal rewards of patient involvement but also see the process as a means of managing consultations more effectively. Patient satisfaction with consultations increases when health professionals involve them in decision-making. Other benefits that patients perceive are greater confidence; reduction in anxiety; greater understanding of personal needs, improved trust, better relationships with professionals, and positive health effects.

Provision of good quality, understandable information not only leads to better understanding of their condition, but also leads to a greater ability to discuss issues with their doctor in a more positive relationship (Thornton *et al.*, 2003). People also seek information to reinforce their existing knowledge.

The future

The goal of 'playing an equal music' (Grol, 2001) is now more achievable: evidence to sharpen our aim is rapidly accumulating; new guidance (General Medical Council, 2008) has set out the key principles of good decision-making emphasizing partnership; people have come to value it.

The 'brave new partnership between clinical trialists and patients' that the ethicist Raanon Gillon proposed in 1994 (Gillon, 1994) is becoming reality and this will increasingly permeate through to health care practice.

References

Chalmers, I. and Lindley, R. (2001). Double standards on informed consent to treatment. In L. Doyal and J.S. Tobias (eds) *Informed Consent in Medical Research. London: BMJ*, pp. 266–275.

Department of Communities and Local Government. (2008). The Community Power Pack April 2008. ISBN: 978-1-8511-2920-1. Available at http://www.communities.gov.uk/publications/communities/powerpack

Department of Health. (2008). Medical revalidation – Principles and next steps. The Report of the Chief Medical Officer for England's Working Group, 23rd July 2008.

Edwards, A., Elwyn, G., Atwell, C., *et al.* (2004). Shared decision making and risk communication in general practice – A study incorporating systematic literature reviews, psychometric evaluation of outcome measure, and quantitative, qualitative and health economic analyses of a cluster randomised trial of professional skill development. Report to the 'Health in Partnership' programme, UK Department of Health. Available at http://www.dh.gov.uk/en/Publicationsandstatistics/Publications/PublicationsPolicyAndGuidance/DH_4082332 (No. 11.)

Fotaki, M., Boyd, A., Smith, L., *et al.* (2005). Report of a *Scoping Review on Patient Choice and the Organisation and Delivery of Health Services* for the National Co-ordinating Centre for NHS Service Delivery and Organisation R&D (NCCSDO), December 2005.

General Medical Council. (2008). Consent: Patients and doctors making decisions together, June 2008.

General Medical Council. (2006). Good Medical Practice.

Gillon, R. (1994). Recruitment for clinical trials: The need for public-professional co-operation. *J Med Ethics*, **20**, 3–4.

Grol, R. (2001). Foreword. In A. Edwards and G. Elwyn (eds) Evidence-Based Patient Choice: Inevitable or Impossible? New York: Oxford University Press. p. xvii.

Longo, M.F., Cohen, D.R., Hood, K., *et al.* (2006). Involving patients in primary care consultations: Assessing preferences using discrete choice experiments. *British Journal of General Practice*, **56**(8), 35–42.

Oliver, S.R., Rees, R.W., Clarke-Jones, L., *et al.* (2008). A multidimensional conceptual framework for analysing public involvement in health *services research. Health Expectations*, **11**(1), 72–84.

Royal College of Physicians. (2005). Doctors in society – Medical professionalism in a changing world. Report of a Working Party of the Royal College of Physicians of London. London: RCP.

Stacey, D., Hawker, G., Dervin, G., *et al.* (2008). Making a difference. Management of chronic pain. Improving shared decision making in osteoarthritis. *British Medical Journal*, **336**, 954–955.

Thornton H. (2008). Patient and public involvement in clinical trials – Is established worldwide, but encouragement is needed to promote institutional collaboration and to avoid duplication of effort. *British Medical Journal*, 336, 903–904. Available at http://www.bmj.com/cgi/content/full/336/7650/903 toll free link: http://www.bmj.com/cgi/content/full/336/7650/903?ijkey=dcyiroiHlyb4Nc6&keytype=ref

Thornton, H., Edwards, A., and Elwyn, G. (2003). Evolving the multiple roles of 'patients' in health-care research: Reflections after involvement in a trial of shared-decision making. *Health Expectations*, **6**, 189–197. Available at http://www.blackwell-synergy.com/links/doi/10.1046/j.1369-6513.2003.00231.x/abs/

UK Clinical Research Collaboration activities log. Available at http://www.ukcrc.org/patientsandpublic/currentppiprojects/activitieslog.aspx

UK Department of Health. (2004). Patient and public involvement in health: The evidence for policy implementation. A summary of the results of the Health in Partnership research programme, compiled by Christine Farrell, April 2004. Available at http://www.dh.gov.uk/en/Publicationsandstatistics/Publications/PublicationsPolicyAndGuidance/DH_4082332

Section 2

Theoretical perspectives

Chapter 7

Using decision-making theory to inform clinical practice

Hilary L. Bekker

Introduction

This chapter provides an overview of the types of decision-making theories that can inform clinical practice. Theories enable us to understand, predict, and change phenomena or processes by providing a framework within which to develop and test hypotheses, and interpret data. Decision-making theories identify the generic components or processes that *all* individuals employ to reach a decision. As I cannot describe the strengths and weaknesses of each decision-making theory in a single chapter, exemplars from three categories of decision-making theory are used. These broad classifications are top-down, axiomatic theories outlining the ideal of how individuals think (normative); bottom-up, data-derived theories describing how people think in the real-world (descriptive); and yardstick theories suggesting how people should think in order to make the best decision (prescriptive) (Baron, 1994; Beach and Lipshitz, 1993; Chapman and Sonnenberg, 2000). Patient decision aids – interventions to help patients make deliberative choices between two or more options (Bekker *et al.*, 1999; O'Connor *et al.*, 2004) – are used to illustrate how theories can guide the content, and measurement, of interventions to facilitate decision-making about treatment options involving risk or uncertainty.

Normative theories of decision-making

Normative theories provide frameworks for reaching the optimal choice (see Baron, 1994). Expected utility theory (EUT) is the most widely recognized normative model, often referred to as formal decision theory, classical decision theory, or economic [man] theory. The theory provides a model of rational behaviour based on mathematical axioms and rules of logic that is internally consistent (see Beach and Lipshitz, 2003; Baron, 1994; Over, 2004). Its philosophy is that under ideal conditions, individuals should choose the *option* with the maximum expected utility. The *expected utility* is a trade-off between the *probability* of a consequence occurring and the *utility* placed on that consequence. Often, the terms value and utility are used interchangeably to refer to an individual's strength of preference for a consequence; however, the value is used for options with certain, and utility for options with uncertain, consequences (Keeney and Raiffa, 1976). EUT has a range of assumptions, including all the necessary information about the decision options being available, individuals being motivated to evaluate all the decision information without bias, and that individuals can combine the utility and risk figures to identify the option with the greatest expected utility. EUT endures because it is seemingly (a) simple, choose the option that does the most good; (b) intuitive, your choice is consistent with how much you judge something to be good and likely it to happen; and (c) measurable – values and risk (perceptions) can be elicited (Baron, 1994; Ubel and Loewenstein, 1997; Stiggelbout, 2000; Ryan *et al.*, 2001).

Decision analysis is the decision aid intervention based on EUT. The purpose of decision analysis is to help people be rational when making hard decisions (von Winterfeldt and Edwards, 1986). A rational decision is one that accords with the theory, i.e the choice with the maximum expected utility. The structure provided by decision analysis enables decision makers to represent a decision according to EUT. Modelling a medical decision by decision analytic techniques requires clarification of the decision problem, construction of a decision tree (a representation of the decision using *nodes* and *branches* to depict the decision, options, and consequences), elicitation of utilities, assessment of probabilities, and analysis (see von Winterfeldt and Edwards, 1986; Baron, 1994; Roberts and Sonnenberg, 2000). A range of methods to measure utilities in health contexts have been developed, some involving patients to rate outcomes on a simple visual analogue or Likert scale, others requiring more complex choice-based techniques forcing the patient to trade-off options or attributes (see Baron, 1994; Stiggelbout, 2000; Ryan *et al.*, 2001). The final stage of decision analysis requires a method of information integration to run the model and calculate the option with the maximum expected utility, usually by a third party (i.e. computer-based or by another person). For more details see Chapter 32 by Thomson.

The application of decision analysis to patients making decisions about treatment options in the real-world is limited (Bekker *et al.*, 2004; Dowding *et al.*, 2004; Montgomery *et al.*, 2007; Protheroe *et al.*, 2007). For a pragmatic reason, few of these applications have operationalized fully the decision analytic framework. Further, although some measures of decision quality change as a result of this intervention type, patient decisions are no more rational or theoretically consistent (Bekker *et al.*, 2004; Montgomery *et al.*, 2007). These findings suggest that expected utility theory or rational decision-making is not a useful theory to inform interventions to help patients make treatment decisions (Beach and Lipshitz, 1993; Baron, 1996).

Descriptive theories of decision-making

Descriptive theories of decision-making are those explaining how individuals make judgements and decisions (see Lipshitz, 1993; Baron, 1997; Gigerenzer, 2004; Chaiken, 1980). The dominant paradigm is that of information processing which represents the individual as an active problem solver, purposively reasoning about decisions in a complex world (see Carrol and Johnson, 1990; Payne and Bettman, 2004). As the cognitive processes involved in judgment and decision-making are unobservable, psychologists have developed a range of indirect techniques to investigate thinking. These include verbal think-aloud techniques, self-report verbal and questionnaire measures, and information tracing or communications monitoring (see Carroll and Johnson, 1990; Baron,1997; Payne and Bettman, 2004). The data from these methods are used to derive theories and models to explain how individuals make different types of decisions (e.g. ones with certain and uncertain outcomes) in different contexts (e.g. business, medicine, army, etc.) by people with different skills and experiences (e.g. novices versus experts) (Lipshitz, 1993; Payne and Bettman, 2004). Two key areas that are explained further are (a) the cognitive limitations of human processing and (b) the strategies explaining how individuals process information.

Heuristic and systematic processing of information

We all make decisions whilst being bombarded with information from environmental and internal sources. It is accepted that individuals have finite cognitive resources that affect the information they select from this maelstrom, and the way it is attended to, processed, stored, and retrieved (see Hogarth, 1988; Simon, 1988; Baron, 1994; Payne and Bettman, 2004). The ability to consciously attend to the decision-relevant information, and associated decision-making activities, is believed to be the scarce resource. It is also accepted that individuals employ two types of strategy to process information: heuristic processing (intuitive, 'rules-of-thumb', unconscious, and system 1) and systematic processing (analytic, conscious, and system 2) (see Chaiken, 1980; Eagly and Chaiken, 1993; Payne and Bettman, 2004; Hammond, 2007; Acker, 2008). The latter requires the decision maker to exert a considerable amount of conscious effort in evaluating completely the details of the decision information; the former is a simpler strategy, requiring less cognitive effort, as the decision maker evaluates a part of the decision information that initiates a general, often subconscious, rule to guide the choice. Although heuristic processing tends to lead to satisfactory decisions being made most of the time, it is more likely to result in the wrong choice being made if a systematic strategy is employed (Chaiken, 1980; Baron, 1994; Payne and Bettman, 2004).

Many investigate how decisions are made by patients and professionals (Gigerenzer, 2002; Reyna, 2005; Chapman and Elstein, 2000); behavioural scientists want to test their theories in different contexts and health researchers want to understand or enhance patient and professional decision-making. Although it is beyond the scope of this chapter to summarize systematically these findings, some implications for patient decision-making are considered. First, individuals, and therefore patients, are rarely aware of the way they make decisions or the factors that influence their judgements, preferences, and choices. Second, as individuals have a preference for using heuristic processing strategies, particularly in personal situations and those that involve trade-offs (Hogarth, 1988; Carrol and Johnson, 1990; Baron, 1994; Sjöberg, 2003), patients will tend to make treatment decisions using mostly heuristic processes. Third, heuristic processing means that patients are unlikely to search for the best treatment option but rather choose the first option that appears satisfactory. Fourth, patients will be selective about what information they attend to, screening out treatment options initially judged to be non-relevant (Zey, 1992), either excluding information about a no testing option because it is perceived not to be part of the decision frame (Bekker, 2003), or attending to contextual information to make their choice such as making a judgement about the person providing the information rather than the information content (Chaiken, 1980; Tversky and Kahneman, 1981). Fifth, the decisions patients make will be based on their interpretation of the decision information, rather than the objective reality; these evaluations are prone to bias, particularly in the context of risk (Tversky and Kahneman, 1981). For example, how patients interpret a risk figure will depend on how it is presented (Gigerenzer and Edwards, 2003; Covey, 2007; Cuite, 2008) and what information contextualizes the figure – a woman receives a screening test result of 1 in 150 for having a child with Down's syndrome, her perception of this figure as high or low is influenced by prior experience such as being told that 1 in 50 babies are born with an abnormality, or her age-related risk is 1 in 75, or 1 in 250 is a screen positive (high risk) result.

Prescriptive theories of decision-making

Prescriptive theories of decision-making are those that identify criteria for 'good thinking' and methods to encourage individuals to make decisions well (see Carrol and Johnson, 1990; Frisch and Jones, 1993; Baron, 1994; Frisch and Clemen, 1994; Janis and Mann, 1977; Zey, 1992). Essential to this approach is a belief that individuals can be helped to employ a decision process that is better for those difficult decisions with serious consequences than the one they use for everyday situations. It is acknowledged that this vigilant processing (Janis and Mann, 1977), active open-mindedness (Baron, 1994), and reasoned choice (Zey, 1992) strategy are unusual and effortful, demanding conscious engagement with the decision information and decision-making process. The premise is that by making decisions well, individuals reduce the gap between the preferences evaluated during decision-making with the experience of the decision consequences

(Frisch and Jones, 1993; Bekker *et al.*, 2003). To make a decision well requires the individual to make a choice after evaluating the possible consequences of all the options, appraising the likelihood and desirability of these consequences as accurately as possible, and making trade-offs between these evaluations (Frisch and Clemen, 1994). Good decisions, then, should not be judged by the consistency or coherence of the final choice with evaluations made during decision-making, rather by evidence of the process, i.e. the decision information was evaluated by an individual illustrating that s/he was aware of the realistic implications of the consequences before the choice was made. These criteria have been used to define informed (patient) decision-making (Bekker, 1999, 2003). Other chapters in this volume also address 'informed choice' (Chapter 13; Marteau), 'good decisions' (Chapter 20; Elwyn), and 'decision quality' (Chapter 21; Sepucha).

Proponents of the prescriptive approach to decision-making identify techniques aimed at de-biasing decision-making and encouraging better thinking (Janis and Mann, 1977; Baron, 1994; Larrick, 2004). Broadly interventions need to include techniques to (a) raise conscious awareness of the decision-making process and the need for assistance to make a decision well (e.g. state the decision or use a decision tree), (b) reduce the environmental cues that lead to biases in evaluations and the selective attention of the decision information (e.g. full information immediately available and effective risk presentation), (c) 'free-up' some cognitive capacities (e.g. using memory prompts like leaflets), (d) enable individuals to make explicit their evaluations about all the decision-relevant options and consequences (e.g. utility elicitation techniques), (e) help individuals confront their 'outworn' decisions or cognitions (e.g. use of belief statements from patient experience research), and (f) provide individuals with a way to integrate the different aspects of the decision information in order to facilitate trade-offs between evaluations (e.g. option by attribute tables and balance sheets). Although some techniques are incorporated in current patient decision aid interventions, many require further research to evaluate their effectiveness to facilitate informed decision-making either on their own or as part of a package (Bekker *et al.*, 1999; O'Connor *et al.*, 2004; see also Chapter 29, Durand).

Other models

Some other models are applied erroneously to understand and facilitate patient decision aid interventions. First, and briefly, social cognition and self-regulation theories are used to understand and change health and illness behaviours (see Petrie and Weinman, 1997; Conner and Norman, 2005). Decisions and behaviour are related but are different phenomena with different theoretical underpinnings and different measures of efficacy. An intervention, then, to facilitate decision-making about having a screening test should not be the same as one to increase screening test uptake; the latter aims to encourage a behaviour (to have a test), the former to enhance the decision-making process (to choose between having or not having a test). However, the findings from these types of studies may be useful in identifying the (full) information of patient decision aids and measures to assess (realistic) evaluations of the decision information. Second, there are models concerned with improving the style of communication between patient and professions – patient-centred care (Stewart and Brown, 2001; Epstein *et al.*, 2005), shared decision-making (Charles *et al.*, 2005; Edwards and Elwyn, 2006; Makoul and Clayman, 2006; Legare *et al.*, 2008), and collaborative health care (Legare *et al.*, 2008). The theoretical underpinning for such models is unclear but seems to combine the perspectives of social scientists exploring interactions between dyads, and medical and patient educationalists developing communication skills (Wirtz *et al.*, 2006; van den Borne, 1998; Epstein *et al.*, 2005; Street, 2007). These models are valuable in describing and changing clinical practice but do not address factors associated with making decisions well. Interventions to facilitate patient and/or professional decision-making may impact on the professional–patient encounter but this effect is not an explicit aim of decision aid interventions.

Conclusion

In summary, there are three categories of decision-making theory to inform interventions to improve patient decision-making. Decision aid interventions informed by a normative theory will have the same framework, techniques, and aim because they are operationalizing a theory of idealized decision-making rather than responding to individuals' decision-making needs. The main advantage of this top-down approach is having criteria guiding, for example, the development of a decision aid for any decision (O'Connor *et al.*, 2004). The main disadvantage is that the theory, and therefore the decision aid, may not be fit for purpose (Nelson *et al.*, 2007). Proponents of descriptive theories of decision-making question whether or not patient decision aid interventions should be developed or applied. It is argued that the best way to make a decision is for individuals to rely on the (subconscious) processes individuals use most often rather than to intervene and change them (Wilson *et al.*, 1993; Dijksterhuis *et al.*, 2006). However, the evidence that subconscious processes lead to 'good' decisions being made is weak (Acker, 2008). Decision aid interventions informed by the prescriptive approach identify a range of techniques to encourage individuals' *better thinking* about a decision (Bekker *et al.*, 1999). The advantage of bottom-up approaches is that interventions will be responsive to the differing needs of the decision context making them effective and efficient interventions. The disadvantage is that there are many techniques to support decision-making, and research is required to identify the active ingredients facilitating good decision-making in different contexts (Bekker, 1999; Medical Research Council, 2000).

References

Acker, F. (2008). New findings on unconscious versus conscious thought in decision making: Additional empirical data and met-analysis. *Judgment and Decision Making*, **3**, 292–303.

Baron, J. (1997). *Thinking and Deciding (2nd Edition)*. Cambridge: Cambridge University Press.

Baron, J. (1996). Why expected utility theory is normative, but not prescriptive. *Medical Decision Making*, **16**, 7–9.

Beach, L.R. and Lipshitz, R. (1993). Why classical decision theory is an inappropriate standard for evaluating and aiding most human decision making. In G.A. Klein, J. Orasanu, R. Calderwood, and E. Zsambok (eds) *Decision Making in Action: Models and Methods*. New Jersey: Ablex Publishing Corporation.

Bekker, H.L. (2003). Genetic screening: Facilitating informed choices. In D.N. Cooper and N. Thomas (eds) *Nature Encyclopaedia of the Human Genome*. New York: Nature Publishing Group, Macmillan Publishers Ltd. pp. 926–930.

Bekker, H.L., Hewison, J., and Thornton, J.G. (2003). Understanding why decision aids work: Linking process and outcome. *Patient Education and Counselling*, **50**, 323–329.

Bekker, H., Thornton, J.G., Airey, C.M., *et al.* (1999). *Informed decision making: An annotated bibliography and systematic review*. UK: Health Technology Assessment Number 3. NHS R&D.

Bekker, H.L., Thornton, J.G., and Hewison, J. (2004). Applying decision analysis to facilitate informed decision making about prenatal diagnosis for Down's syndrome: A randomised controlled trial. *Prenatal Diagnosis*, **24**, 265–275.

Carroll, J.S. and Johnson, E.J. (1990). *Decision Research: A Field Guide*. Newbury Park, CA: Sage.

Chaiken, S. (1980). Heuristic versus systematic information processing and the use of source versus message cues in persuasion. *Journal of Personality and Social Psychology*, **39**, 752–766.

Chapman, G.B. and Elstein, A.S. (2000). Cognitive processes and biases in medical decision making. In G.B. Chapman and F.A. Sonnenberg (eds) *Decision Making in Health Care: Theory, Psychology and Applications*. Cambridge: Cambridge University Press.

Chapman, G.B. and Sonnenberg, F.A. (eds) (2000). Introduction. In *Decision Making in Health Care: Theory, Psychology and Applications*. Cambridge: Cambridge University Press.

Charles, C., Gafni, A., Whelan, T., *et al.* (2005). Treatment decision aids: Conceptual issues and future directions. *Health Expectations*, **8**, 114–125.

Conner, M. and Norman, P. (eds.) (2005). *Predicting Health Behaviour (2nd edition)*. Berkshire: Open University Press.

Covey, J. (2007). A Meta-analysis of the effects of presenting treatment benefits in different formats. *Medical Decision Making*, **27**, 638–654.

Cuite, C.L., Weinstein, N.D., Emmons, K., *et al.* (2008). A test of numeric formats for communicating risk probabilities. *Medical Decision Making*, **28**, 377–384.

Dowding, D., Swanson, V., Bland, R., *et al.* (2004). The development and preliminary evaluation of a decision aid based on decision analysis for two treatment conditions: Benign prostatic hyperplasia and hypertension. *Patient Education and Counselling*, **52**, 209–215.

Dijksterhuis, A., Bos, M.W., Nordgren, L.F., *et al.* (2006). On making the right choice: The deliberation-without-attention effect. Science, **311**, 1005–1007.

Eagly, A.H. and Chaiken, S. (1993). *The Psychology of Attitudes*. Orlando: Harcourt brace and company.

Edwards, A. and Elwyn, G. (2006). Inside the black box of shared decision making – Distinguishing between the process of involvement and who makes the decision. *Health Expectations*, **9**, 307–320.

Epstein, R.M., Franks, P., Fiscella, K., *et al.* (2005). Measuring patient-centred communication in patient-physician consultations: Theoretical and practical issues. *Social Science and Medicine,* **61**, 1516–1528.

Frisch, D. and Clemen, R.T. (1994). Beyond expected utility: Rethinking behavioural decision research. *Psychological Bulletin*, **116**, 46–54.

Frisch, D. and Jones, S.K. (1993). Assessing the accuracy of decisions. *Theory and Psychology*, **3**, 115–135.

Gigerenzer, G. (2002). *Reckoning with Risk: Learning to Live with Uncertainty*. London: Penguin Books.

Gigerenzer, G. (2004). Fast and frugal heuristics: The tools of bounded rationality. In D.J. Koehler and N. Harvey (eds) *Blackwell Handbook of Judgment and Decision Making*. Malden, MA: Blackwell.

Gigerenzer, G. and Edwards A. (2003). Simple tools for understanding risks: From innumeracy to insight. *British Medical Journal*, **327**, 741–744.

Hammond, K.R. (2007). *Beyond Rationality: The Search for Wisdom in A Troubled Time*. New York: Oxford University Press.

Hogarth, R.M. (1988). *Judgment and Choice (2nd edition)*. UK: Wiley.

Janis, I.L. and Mann, L. (1977). *Decision Making: A Psychological Analysis of Conflict, Choice and Commitment*. New York: The Free Press.

Keeney, R.L. and Raiffa, H. (1976). *Decisions with Multiple Objectives: Preferences and Value Tradeoffs*. New York: Wiley.

Larrick, R.P. (2004). Debiasing. In D.J. Koehler and N. Harvey (eds) *Blackwell Handbook of Judgment and Decision Making*. Malden, MA, Blackwell.

Legare, F., Elwyn, G., Fishebin, M., *et al.* (2008). Translating shared decision-making into health care clinical practices: Proof of concepts. *Implementation Sci.*, **3**, *2 doi:10.1186/1748-5908-3-2.*

Lipshitz, R. (1993). Converging themes in the study of decision making in realistic settings. In G.A. Klein, J. Orasanu, R. Calderwood, and E. Zsambok (eds) *Decision Making in Action: Models and Methods*. New Jersey: Ablex Publishing Corporation.

Makoul, G. and Clayman, M.L. (2006). An Integrative model of shared decision making in medical encounters. *Patient Education and Counseling*, **60**, 301–312.

Medical Research Council. (2000). *A Framework for Development and Evaluation of RCTs for Complex Interventions to Improve Health*. London: Medical Research Council Publications.

Montgomery, A.A., Emmett, C.L., Fahey, T., *et al.* (2007). Two decision aids for mode of delivery among women with previous caesarean section: Randomised controlled trial. *British Medical Journal. Doi.10.1136/bmj.39217.671019.55.*

Nelson, W.L., Han, P.K.J., Fagerlin, A., *et al.* (2007). Rethinking the objectives of decision aids: A call for conceptual clarity. *Medical Decision Making, 27,* 609–618.

O'Connor, A.M., Stacey, D., Entwistle, V., *et al.* (2004). Decision aids for people facing health treatment or screening decisions. *The Cochrane Database of Systematic Reviews 2003, 1. CD001431. doi:10.1002/14651858.*

Over, D. (2004). Rationality and the normative/descriptive distinction. In D.J. Koehler and N. Harvey (eds) *Blackwell Handbook of Judgment and Decision Making.* Malden, MA: Blackwell.

Payne, J.W. and Bettman, J.R. (2004). Walking with the scarecrow: The Information-processing approach to decision research. In D.J. Koehler and N. Harvey (eds) *Blackwell Handbook of Judgment and Decision Making.* Malden, MA: Blackwell.

Petrie, K.J. and Weinman, J.A. (1997). *Perceptions of Health and Illness.* The Netherlands; harwood Academic Publishers.

Protheroe, J., Bower, P., Chew-Graham, C., *et al.* (2007). Effectiveness of a computerised decision aid in primary care on decision making and quality of life in menorrhagia: Results of the MENTIP randomised controlled trial. Effectiveness of computerised decision aid in primary care. *Medical Decision Making, 27,* 575–584.

Reyna, V.F. (2005). Fuzzy-trace theory, judgment, and decision-making: A dual processes approach. In C. Izawa and N. Ohta (eds) *Human Learning and Memory: Advances in Theory and Application.* New Jersey: Lawrence Erlbaum Associates and Publishers.

Roberts, M.S. and Sonnenberg, F.A. (2000). Decision modeling techniques. In G.B. Chapman and F.A. Sonnenberg (eds) *Decision Making in Health Care: Theory, Psychology and Applications.* Cambridge: Cambridge University Press.

Ryan, M., Scott, D.A., Reeves, C., *et al.* (2001). Eliciting public preferences for healthcare: A systematic review of techniques. *NHS R&D Health Technology Assessment Programme. 5,* 5.

Simon, H.A. (1988). Rationality as process and as product of thought. In D.E. Bell, H. Raiffa, and A. Tversky (eds) *Decision Making: Descriptive, Normative and Prescriptive Interactions.* Cambridge: Cambridge University Press.

Sjöberg, L. (2003). Intuitive vs. analytical decision making: Which is preferred? *Scand. J. Manage., 19,* 17–29.

Street, J. (2007). Aiding medical decision making: A communication perspective. *Med. Decis. Making, 27,* 550–553. Editorial.

Stewart, M. and Brown, J.B. (2001). Patient-centredness in medicine. In A. Edwards and G. Elwyn (eds) *Evidence-Based Patient Choice: Inevitable or Impossible.* Oxford: Oxford University Press.

Stiggelbout, A.M. (2000). Assessing patients' preferences. In G.B. Chapman and F.A. Sonnenberg (eds) *Decision Making in Health Care: Theory, Psychology and Applications.* Cambridge: Cambridge University Press.

Tversky, A. and Kahneman, D. (1981). The framing of decisions and the psychology of choice. *Science, 211,* 453–458.

Ubel, P.A. and Loewenstein, G. (1997). The role of decision analysis in informed consent: Choosing between intuition and systematicity. *Social Science and Medicine, 44,* 647–656.

Von Winterfeldt, D. and Edwards, W. (1986). *Decision Analysis and Behavioural Research.* Cambridge: Cambridge University Press.

Wilson, T.D., Lisle, D.J., Schooler, J.W., *et al.* (1993). Introspecting about reasons can reduce post0choice satisfaction. *Personality and Social Psychology Bulletin, 19,* 331–339.

Wirtz, V., Cribb, A., and Barber, N. (2006). Patient-doctor decision-making about treatment within the consultation – A critical analysis of models. *Social Science and Medicine, 62,* 116–124.

Zey, M. (ed) (1992). Criticisms of rational choice models. In *Decision Making: Alternatives to Rational Choice Models.* Newbury park, CA: Sage.

Chapter 8

Evidence and risk: The sociology of health care grappling with knowledge and uncertainty

Tim Rapley and Carl May

Introduction

This chapter argues that decisions are not only to be understood as cognitive acts and interactional exchanges that are confined to the consultation, but that they are extended and distributed beyond its boundaries. We are, therefore, concerned with how patients and practitioners work with and manage the diverse sources of knowledge, uncertainty, and risk and mobilise these in the consultation. In this chapter, we offer a conceptual framework to understand the *distributed* nature of decisions (Rapley, 2008).

Decisions

Initially, we could ask, *what is a decision?* Is it just something that goes on in peoples' minds? Everyday talk about decisions often assumes that decisions are merely cognitive acts, somehow adrift from the world of actions. Brown (2005), following the ordinary language philosopher Ryle (1949), reminds us that decisions are the central way we *manage and co-ordinate our actions* and that they are deeply social affairs. Research on shared decision-making (SDM) in consultations understands this. Essentially, the ideals of SDM are an attempt to

♦ manage and co-ordinate a specific set of actions – talk – in a consultation between a patient and health professional,

♦ to enable a specific act – a patient to produce an utterance like "I've decided on surgery", and

♦ to then manage and co-ordinate a future course of actions, rights, and responsibilities – a specific trajectory of treatment (or agree no further action is needed).

In this way, SDM research has routinely conceptualized decision-making as occurring in one-off dyadic encounters within the space of consultation rooms (Charles *et al.*, 1999; Elwyn, 2005). But, 'being ill' or 'receiving treatment' does not only occur at specific points in time and space. Instead, they have trajectories and a life beyond the consultation room. So rather than focus on decisions and decision-making as 'solo' individualized cognitive acts that are decoupled from their contexts, we need to see that they are governed under a set of conditions:

♦ *Patients' decisions can be ongoing and revisited over time.* Each new visit to a health professional offers *another-decision-in-a-series,* where the past decisions are reviewed in the light of the patients' 'new' history, examination, and test results (Rapley, 2008). This is especially clear when the patient has a chronic condition (Montori et al., 2006).

♦ *Multiple health professionals – in different clinical spaces – can be involved in a patients' decision-making.* This can occur over encounters with different members of a single clinical team (Lutfey, 2005) or over different specialisms as patients navigate their own care pathway (Calnan *et al.*, 2006).

♦ *Significant others – a patients' social network, family members, and friends – can be deeply involved in decision-making.* This could be to encourage the patient to discuss the decision, collaborate in the decision with the patient, persuade the patient to make a decision, or actually make the decision for the patient (Ohlen *et al.*, 2006). Here, helping someone to make a decision does not necessarily deny that person's autonomy, but rather such help can be a resource through which they can practically achieve their autonomy (Struhkamp, 2005).

Decision-making does not occur in one-off events, but rather is distributed over people, places, and time. Decisions emerge, transform, and solidify through multiple interactions, over a period of time, over multiple places. They are, thus, distributed socially, temporally, and spatially.

Knowledge and uncertainty

Uncertainty is normal in medicine. Since 1950s, observational studies of medical students in training have emphasized how managing personal and collective uncertainty is a central component of interactional work in medicine (Atkinson, 1984; Fox, 1957; Light, 1979; Timmermans and Angell, 2001). As they come face-to-face with real clinical situations, students are forced to learn how to manage the limitations inherent to the medical work. As Fox (2000) has outlined, training for uncertainty involves

♦ realizing the impossibility of personally grasping all aspects of medical knowledge, skills, and technology;

♦ learning how to manage the gaps inherent in medical understanding and knowledge; and

♦ becoming capable of judging whether uncertainty is due to personal ignorance of the field or gaps in medicines knowledge.

In practice, clinicians learn to manage and control the clinical uncertainties they face. However, patients – especially those in search of an initial diagnosis – expect a degree of authoritative knowledge about their problems and the best responses to them. The clinician often has to co-ordinate conflicting concerns; they have to engender *trust* and *confidence,* while simultaneously managing any personal uncertainty (May *et al.*, 2004). How patients orientate to the explicit discussion of uncertainty is intimately embedded in the broader relational issues of trust, faith, and confidence in the specific practitioner or clinical team (Brown, 2008), alongside the potential clinical implications of any choices they face. Any announcement and discussion of uncertainty in the space of the consultation often represents just one moment in patients' sense making trajectories. Patients routinely seek additional sources of evidence and collective experientially based health care knowledge – from formal and informal 'lay consultations' with significant others and other sufferers (e.g. Crossley M.L. and Crossley N., 2001; Ohlen *et al.*, 2006), medical texts, the radio, television, internet, and print-media (e.g. Moreira, 2006; Nettleton *et al.*, 2005) – to manage their knowledge and uncertainty.

Such laic forms of knowledge management echo the ways health professionals work. Gabbay and Le May (2004) have shown how family doctors work in 'communities of practice', where decisions are informed by formal and informal discussions with colleagues, drug company representatives and patients; experiences from treating other patients, teaching, and training; views of opinion leaders; reading, updates, and policy directives. Despite the growth in evidence-based resources, the practitioners they studied rarely directly accessed or used explicit evidence from research or other sources. Their practice was mediated by collective expertise. However, this expertise was locally developed practice-based evidence, not institutionally sanctioned evidence-based practice.

Knowledge and risk

Population-based risk information emerging from trials, systematic reviews, and meta-analysis does not seem to 'fit' easily with the practices of health professionals – it is mathematical rather than experiential – and it seems to fit poorly with the individualized heterogeneous accounts and moral responsibilities that emerge in consultations. When the trial-based knowledge is directly consulted, studies of research-conscious general practitioners in the United Kingdom (Lipman et al., 2004) and secondary practitioners (Tanenbaum, 1994) and residents in the United States (Timmermans and Angell, 2001) show how health professionals engage in something like 'evidence-based clinical judgement' (ibid: 354). Practitioners creatively work with epidemiological, population-based, deductive findings and merge them with clinical, inductive forms of knowledge. The meaning of research findings are reconstructed within the immediate clinical, ethical, interactional, practical, and organizational contexts. In this way, health professionals actively interpret evidence and (re)create the local validity and usefulness of research.

The rise of preventative health care – whether focusing on managing potential genetic-futures, ameliorating the progression of chronic disease, or modifying lifestyles of excess – emerges in a neo-liberal context in which we are all positioned as free individuals, free consumers, capable (and able) to make choices (Rose, 1996). The focus is on identifying and motivating 'at risk' and 'risky' patients to change behaviours and habits, or undertake a specific course of treatment, prior to the (further) onset of organic or psychosocial pathology.

It is no longer our 'duty to get well', but rather 'our duty to stay well' (Crawford, 1980; Greco, 1993). Given adequate knowledge, often in the form of risk information, we should then be able to make a rational, informed choice. However, as many have noted, how you express or frame risk has consequences as to how patients and practitioners make sense of it (e.g. Misselbrook and Armstrong, 2002), and patients make sense of risk-information in what can appear to be quite quirky or 'irrational' ways (e.g. Davidson et al., 1991, Walters et al., 2004). Moreover, talk about risk does not just emerge, but rather is produced in specific contexts. Linell et al. (2002), in their comparison of five different studies of clinic encounters, noted that explicit talk about risk is more probable when

> (a) patients can, in and through their own conduct, influence future risks; (b) the individual patient is known to be at high risk; (c) the patient is in the process of being informed rather than being already under medical treatment; (d) the topic of risks is an agenda point rather than something that is more incidentally brought up; (e) the professional has the legitimized right to issue medical (predictive or diagnostic) information; and (f) there is plenty of time available. Implicitness or avoidance is chosen as professional strategies in cases where the opposite conditions are at hand. (214)

So any explicit discussion of risks routinely occurs in auspicious environments, moments where, due to features of the encounter, talking about risk is less 'risky' for the smoothness of the ongoing interaction.

Involvement

The impulses towards interactions where the patient is involved are manifold, including the rise of patient support groups, feminist critiques of medical practice, new models of consumerism, alongside professional models, and theories around the dynamics of consultations. More recently, various tools, devices, and technologies have been developed in order to promote further involvement, to offer structured and sometimes tailored, advice, information, and risk-based knowledge. As discussed more fully elsewhere in this volume, this can take the form of relatively passive information sheets, screen shots, audio, or video-tapes, to interactive computer programmes, web-sites, or group discussions. However, such political and practical devices and designs rely on the idea that involvement is possible and inherently desirable.

Most of the empirical studies that attempt to find evidence of SDM in consultations find little evidence of its enactment. For example, Stevenson *et al.* (2000) analysed the interaction in general practice consultations and focused on the discussion of drugs and their side-effects and found that it was rare for both patients and doctors to be involved and rare for both parties to share information. They also found no evidence of them working to build a consensus or an agreement on treatment. They concluded that there was little evidence for the practices of SDM, let alone involvement *per se*. However, Collins *et al.* (2005), studying diabetes consultations in primary care and ENT cancer in oncology, did find evidence for a spectrum of approaches to decision-making about treatment:

> In 'bilateral' approaches, the practitioner talks in a way which actively pursues patient contributions, providing places for the patient to join in, and building on any contributions the patient makes: e.g. sign-posting options in advance of naming them; eliciting displays of understanding and statements of preference from the patient. In 'unilateral' approaches the practitioner talks in formats less conducive to [the] patient's participation: e.g. the scene for the decision is already set; the decision is presented as 'made'; the practitioner concludes the decision-making independently of the patient's contribution. (2625)

They note that, irrespective of what point along the spectrum that practitioners work, *within* consultations 'patient participation in decision-making is limited' (ibid: 2625). Given the inherent asymmetry in knowledge in consultations, especially with newly diagnosed patients, alongside the practical and professional status of practitioners as legitimate authorities in contributing biomedical expertise, it is perhaps unsurprising.

Conclusion

In this chapter, we have argued that (i) asymmetries of knowledge and practice mean that patient participation in *formal* decisions is often limited, but (ii) decisions and decision-making are distributed socially, temporally, and spatially – *within*, *between*, and *beyond* individual clinical encounters. (iii) That patients' orientation to any explicit discussion of professional uncertainty is intimately related to issues of interactional *trust, faith,* and *confidence,* and (iv) that decisions in practice are mediated by a *distributed collaboration* of collective professional and collective laic forms of knowledge, judgement, and expertise. This means that debates about the nature and structure of shared decision-making need to take into account the different terrain on which clinicians and patients are *working* when they enter into decisive interactions.

References

Atkinson, P. (1984). Training for certainty. *Social Science and Medicine*, **19**, 949–956.

Brown, B. (2005). Choice and mobility: Decision making on the move. Paper presented at *Society for the Advancement of Socio-Economics, 17th Annual Meeting on Socio-Economics*, Budapest, June 30 – July 2, 2005.

Brown, P. (2008). Trusting in the New NHS: Instrumental versus communicative action. *Sociology of Health & Illness*, **30**, 349–363.

Calnan, M., Wainwright, D., O'Neill, C., *et al.* (2006). Making sense of aches and pains. *Family Practice*, **23**, 91–105.

Charles, C., Gafni, A., and Whelan, T. (1999). Decision-making in the physician–patient encounter: Revisiting the shared treatment decision-making model. *Social Science and Medicine*, **49**, 651–661.

Collins, S., Drew, P., Watt, I., *et al.* (2005). 'Unilateral' and 'bilateral' practitioner approaches in decision-making about treatment. *Social Science and Medicine*, **61**, 2611–2627.

Crawford, R. (1980). Healthism and the medicalization of everyday life. *International Journal of Health Services*, **10**, 365–388.

Crossley, M.L. and Crossley, N. (2001). Patients' voices, social movements, and the habitus: How psychiatric survivors 'speak out'. *Social Science & Medicine.*, **52**, 1477–1489.

Elwyn, G. (2005). Arriving at the postmodern medical consultation. *Prim. Care*, **5**, 287–291. Available at www.primary-care.ch/pdf/2005/2005-12/2005-12-423.PDF

Fox, R. (1957). Training for uncertainty. In R. K. Merton, G. Reader, and P. L. Kendall (eds) *The Student Physician*. Cambridge, MA: Harvard University Press.

Fox, R. (2000). Medical uncertainty revisited. In G. L. Albrecht, R. Fitzpatrick, and S.C. Scrimshaw (eds.) *The Handbook of Social Studies in Health and Medicine*. London: SAGE Publications.

Gabbay, J. and le May, A. (2004). Evidence based guidelines or collectively constructed "mindlines?" Ethnographic study of knowledge management in primary care. *British Medical Journal*, **329**, 1013–1016.

Greco, M. (1993). Psychosomatic subjects and the "Duty to Be Well": Personal Agency within Medical Rationality. *Economy Society*, **22**, 357–372.

Light, D. (1979). Uncertainty and control in professional training. *Journal of Health & Social Behavior*, **20**, 310–322.

Linell, P., Adelswärd, V., Sachs, L., *et al.* (2002). Expert talk in medical contexts: Explicit and implicit orientation to risks. *Research on Language and Social Interaction*, **35**, 195–218.

Lipman, T., Murtagh, M. J., and Thomson, R. (2004). How research-conscious GPs make decisions about anticoagulation in patients with atrial fibrillation: A qualitative study. *Family Practice*, **21**, 290–298.

Lutfey, K. (2005). On practices of 'good doctoring': Reconsidering the relationship between provider roles and patient adherence. *Sociology of Health & Illness*, **27**, 421–447.

May, C., Allison, G., Chapple, A., *et al.* (2004). Framing the doctor–patient relationship in chronic illness: A comparative study of general practitioners' accounts. *Sociology of Health & Illness.*, **26**, 135–158.

Misselbrook, D. and Armstrong, D. (2002). Thinking about risk. Can doctors and patients talk the same language? *Family Practice*, **19**, 1–2.

Montori, V.M., Gafni, A., and Charles, C. (2006). A shared decision-making approach between patients with chronic conditions and their clinicians: The case of diabetes. *Health Expectations*, **9**, 25–36.

Moreira. T. (2006). Sleep, health and the dynamics of biomedicine. *Social Science and Medicine*, **83**, 54–63.

Nettleton, S., Burrows, R., and O'Malley, L. (2005). The Mundane realities of the everyday lay use of the internet for health and their consequences for media convergence. *Sociology of Health and Illness*, **27**, 972–992.

Ohlen, J., Balneaves, L., Bottorff, J., *et al.* (2006). The influence of significant others in complementary and alternative medicine decisions by cancer patients. *Social Science and Medicine*, **63**, 1625–1636.

Rapley, T. (2008). Distributed decision making: The anatomy of decisions-in-action. *Sociology of Health and Illnes*, **30**, 429–444.

Rose, N. (1996). *Inventing Our Selves: Psychology, Power and Personhood*. Cambridge: Cambridge University Press.

Ryle, G. (1949). *The Concept of Mind*. Chicago: The University of Chicago Press.

Stevenson, F.A., Barry, C.A., Britten, N., *et al.* (2000). Doctor–patient communication about drugs: The evidence for shared decision making. *Social Science and Medicine*, **50**, 829–840.

Struhkamp, R.M. (2005). Patient autonomy: A view from the kitchen. *Medicine, Health Care and Philosophy*, **8**, 105–114.

Tanenbaum, S.J. (1994). Knowing and acting in medical practice: The epistemological politics of outcomes research. *Journal of Health Politics, Policy and Law*, **19**, 27–44.

Timmermans, S. and Angell, A. (2001). Evidence-based medicine: Clinical uncertainty and learning to doctor. *Journal of Health & Social Behavior*, **42**, 342–359.

Walters, F., Emery, J., Braithwaite, D., *et al.* (2004). Lay understanding of familial risk of common chronic diseases: A systematic review and synthesis of qualitative research. *Annals of Family Medicine* **2**, 583–594.

Chapter 9

Ethical issues around evidence-based patient choice and shared decision-making

Søren Holm and Myfanwy Davies

Introduction

Evidence-based patient choice brings together the movements to promote evidence-based medicine and patient-centred medicine. While proponents of evidence-based medicine contend that interventions need to be based on evidence of effectiveness, patient-centred medicine is concerned with emphasizing the central role of patients in decisions about their care (Parker, 2001). Evidence-based patient choice may help to address the power imbalance inherent in many medical consultations and may serve to promote more effective patient care (Hope, 1997).

Shared decision-making has been advocated as an ideal model of treatment decision-making (Emanuel E. and Emanuel L., 1992). It is characterized by a broad balance in power and symbolic resources for each participant: the agenda is negotiated; the patient's values are explored; and the doctor takes an advisory role regarding the patient's goals and decisions. An important context for shared decision-making is the existence of 'equipoise' – where the clinician does not have a clear preference as to which treatment option should be chosen (Elwyn, 2000). However, many of the ethical issues occur when clinicians or society have clear treatment preferences and where a choice contemplated by the patient may therefore come to be conceptualized as 'wrong'.

Calls to promote evidence-based patient choice may appear to be justifiable and unproblematic. Nonetheless, promoting increased patient participation in decision-making through the use of evidence-based information poses its own ethical problems and illuminates others that would otherwise be addressed by clinicians alone. This chapter examines ethical issues in evidence-based patient choice at three levels: in defining goals for decision-making, in choosing methods, and in accepting responsibility for the outcomes (see Box 9.1). Given space constraints, we will rely on, rather than argue for, a set of core ethical values including respect for patient self-determination and a robust conception of social justice including a preference for providing benefit to those who are 'least well off' (Gillon, 1986; Rawls, 1999).

Some of the issues that are raised here are probably unresolvable in the sense that whereas it may be possible to justify a particular decision in a specific context, it is impossible to present a compelling general solution. There is, for instance, no compelling general solution to the epistemic question of the weight to give evidence at the group level in individual decision-making or to the moral question of the balancing of self-determination and the common good. This does not entail that we should not take these issues seriously when they occur. Every intervention to support shared decision-making embodies a view of how the balance should be struck.

Box 9.1: Ethical checklist for developers and implementers of evidence-based choice interventions

Goals

Is the goal to achieve the 'right' decision, or a well-informed decision?

Is the issue in itself ethically controversial, and if so has the ethical controversy been recognized and handled appropriately?

Populations

Have issues of social justice been considered in choice of target population?

Is there an acceptable balance between overall benefit and benefit to the least well off?

Methods

Are framing effects used deliberately to promote 'the right choice'?

Responsibility

Is the decision support tool well validated? Is it validated for the patient group that is likely to use it?

Is there potential for inappropriate use and has this been adequately handled?

Defining goals

Models of the 'competencies' needed to support shared decision-making tend to stress the need to define patients' expectations of the problem and the possible outcomes (Elwyn, 2000). However, a number of further dimensions shape the goals that patient choice may be intended to achieve, and these may vary between different health care systems. Commenting on the insurance-based US-health care system, Eddy (1990; 1991) and Morreim (1995) have suggested that patients should make their own decisions on health care in order to take direct personal responsibility for the costs incurred. Within the UK NHS, doctors have tended to strive to protect the interests of the patient from the wider imperative to control demand for less cost-effective treatments (Hunter, 2006). Evidence-based patient choice may, thus, increase a tension between the needs of the individual patient (traditionally defended by the general practitioner through paternalistic decision-making) and the projected collective needs of the population (defended by management, government, and policy initiatives; Hunter, 2006). In these cases, the ethical imperative to promote the greater good would be difficult for patients to sustain and would potentially be more difficult for doctors to sustain when faced with clear patient preferences. This indicates that there may be a tension between effectiveness in achieving a particular desired outcome and truly shared decision-making.

Care and treatments that are medically or technically preferable may not be best for the patient as a person. Researching attitudes to risky health behaviours, Popay (2003), for example, found that people in relative poverty understood the health risks entailed by behaviours such as smoking, excessive drinking, and poor diet but made judgements that these behaviours were necessary to counteract the emotional stress of their lives. Optimal health or longevity is not the principal life goals for everyone, and there is a possible tension between welfare, quality of life, and health. This tension is often glossed over methodologically as most of the current so-called quality-of-life scales actually only measure *health-related* quality-of-life.

Some choices also involve ethically contentious judgements, for instance in the area of reproduction. Here, there can often be no evidence in a strict sense concerning which option is best because the medically or technically preferable is ethically unacceptable to some patients. A choice process that ignored the ethical aspects would be deficient.

End-of-life care is a context in which a simple opposition between quality-of-life and clinically effective (and expensive) care has been identified (Drought, 2002). In the United States and United Kingdom, guidelines informing end-of-life care require the individual to make choices as an active and informed participant (Drought, 2002). In doing so, they assume that the individual can rationally confront their death and the physical conditions that precede it. Nonetheless, the permissibility of rejecting life-saving care through 'do not resuscitate' (DNR) orders, hospice eligibility criteria, or constraints on options available in insurance-based models may render 'choice' largely illusory. In these cases, the processes and tools intended to support patient choice are not value-neutral.

Choosing methods

Central to models of shared decision-making is the recognition that the patient must be respected as the decision maker (Charles *et al.*, 1997; Elwyn, 2000). These statements rest on commitments to the full disclosure of information and truth telling by clinicians. Nonetheless, where a clinically preferable option exists, full disclosure and truth telling may come into a direct conflict with commitments to providing the safest patient care and protecting public health. In these cases, clinicians may seek to frame the information provided in order to obtain the 'right' choice. Raffle (2001) for example suggests that information about screening is often biased towards achieving high uptake. She raises questions about the implications for patient choice but also outlines potential safety issues where the benefits of screening are over-emphasized and patients disregard relevant symptoms. At a more general level, it is important to remember that it is sometimes possible to deceive people, while telling them the truth if the truth is framed in a misleading way. Even though misleading is not lying, it is a distinct ethical wrong.

Interventions supporting patient choice must be available to and usable by everyone in relevant groups. A criticism of decision support technologies has focused on the highly individualistic model that is used. Where the effects of decisions on family and wider communities are not examined, models of patient decision-making will not reflect the social experience of many patients. These potentially exclusionary effects may be most pronounced among patients from non-Western cultures where social and family decision-making structures are more powerful (Davies, 2008). This conflicts with ideas of social justice. At a more practical level, the development of decision support technologies of all kinds has used the major national language(s) in the country of origin. Accordingly, these tools will not be equally available to most linguistic minorities. Where evidence-based patient choice is conceived as an ethical standard, decision support will also need to be tailored to people with disabilities including those with learning disabilities.

Within limited resources, problems may arise in reconciling arguments in favour of equity as opposed to best outcomes for the intervention. Participation in shared decision-making has been shown to be more valued by younger women, among those with higher educational attainment and among patients under non-acute conditions (Edwards, 2001). Decision support interventions targeting these groups are likely to have better outcomes than those targeting groups among which patient choice is less valued. Nonetheless, where patient choice is an ethical principle, the margin between optimal resource allocation and discrimination may prove to be narrow.

Shouldering responsibility

Responsibility for a shared decision is not a zero sum game. That one party becomes more responsible does not necessarily make the other party less responsible.

Nonetheless, the promotion of shared decision-making may lead indirectly to placing a greater decisional responsibility on patients. By introducing the information to support a decision and by requiring patients to make a decision on involvement, clinicians may create a context where rejecting the option to participate is difficult. A skilful practitioner will provide support where needed; however, contexts where support is needed may not be easily identifiable leading to a perception of 'abandonment' among patients facing choices that they feel unable to address (Schneider, 1998; Quill, 1995). Where decision support technologies replace personal contact with clinicians, the risk of failing to support vulnerable patients in making decisions may be amplified.

A final question of responsibility relates to the veracity and reliability of the information provided and its use in assessing individual risks and benefits. Decisions undertaken by patients and clinicians in consultations rely on the professional expertise and knowledge of the clinician. However, where information provided by decision support technologies is outdated or erroneous or the advice provided is inappropriate, patients have no legal protection. An important step forward in this regard is offered by the IPDAS quality control framework for decision support technologies that is becoming more widely used (Elwyn *et al.*, 2006), and we refer readers to Chapter 33 for more detail on this. Nonetheless, in the interim, patients may need to make judgements on clinical evidence for which they will be ill-prepared.

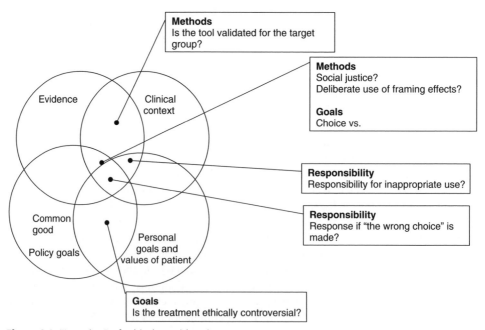

Figure 9.1 "Location" of ethical considerations.

These problems are especially acute where decision support is provided on open internet sites. The provider cannot rely on patients having a sophisticated understanding of the differences in disease prevalence, incidence, and treatment options between different countries and must share some responsibility for inappropriate use. Even if the support is quality-controlled and evidence-based in the country of origin, it may be misleading if relied upon by users in other countries, say someone from Pakistan using a US site to guide decision-making.

Conclusion

Evidence-based patient choice has a strong ethical basis drawing on the principal of respect for autonomy that is central to Western bioethics. This short review has outlined some areas of difficulty in identifying goals, where commitments to the common good, optimal health benefits, and individual needs and preferences may conflict. Similar issues may arise in the design of technologies to support patient choice. While promoting patient choice does not necessarily entail placing greater decisional responsibility on patients, it appears difficult to envisage how it will not lead to some vulnerable patients feeling abandoned by clinicians when faced with choices for which they are ill-equipped. Finally, in the absence of legal responsibilities for the standard of decisional support technologies, patients may face making further complicated judgments about what material to use.

In Figure 9.1, we have tried to illustrate where some of the ethical considerations should be located between evidence, clinical context, policy goals and patient values.

Models of evidence-based patient choice make far reaching assumptions about individual patient autonomy. If this important movement in health care is to improve the experience of all patients, the conception of autonomy on which it is based needs to accommodate principles such as the common good and social equity alongside recognition of individual differences and potential vulnerability.

References

Charles, C., Gafni, A., and Whelan, T. (1997). Shared decision-making in the medical encounter: What does it mean? (Or it takes at least two to tango). *Social Science & Medicine*, **44**, 681–692.

Davies, M. and Elwyn, G. (2008). Advocating mandatory patient 'autonomy' in health care: Adverse reactions and side effects. *Health Care Analysis*, **16**, 315–328.

Drought, T. and Koening, B. (2002). 'Choice' in end-of-life decision making: Researching fact or fiction? *Gerontologist*, **42**(Special Issue III), 114–128.

Eddy, D. (1990). Clinical decision making: From theory to practice. Connecting value and costs. Whom do we ask, and what do we ask them? *Journal of the American Medical Association*, **264**, 1737–1739.

Eddy, D. (1991). Clinical decision making: From theory to practice. The individual vs society. Resolving the conflict. *Journal of the American Medical Association*, **265**, 2399–2401.

Edwards, A., Elwyn, G., Atwell, C., *et al.* (2001). Consumers' views of quality: Identifying the consultation outcomes of importance to consumers, and their relevance to 'shared decision-making' approaches. *Health Expectations*, **4**, 151–161.

Elwyn, G., *et al.* (2000). Shared decision making and the concept of equipoise: The competences of involving patients in healthcare choices. *British Journal of General Practice*, **50**, 892–899.

Elwyn, G., O'Connor, A., Stacey, D., *et al.* (2006). Developing a quality criteria framework for patient decision aids: Online international Delphi consensus process. *British Medical Journal*, **333**, 417.

Emanuel, E. and Emanuel, L. (1992). Four models of the physician–patient relationship. *Journal of the American Medical Association*, **267**, 2221–2224.

Gillon, R. (1986). Philosophical Medical Ethics. Chichester: Wiley.

Hope, T. (1997). Evidence-Based Patient Choice. London: The King's Fund.

Hunter, D. (2006). From tribalism to corporatism: The continuing managerial challenge to medical dominance. In D. Kelleher, J. Gabe, and G. Williams (eds). *Challenging Medicine*. London: Routledge. pp.1–23.

Morreim, E. (1995). *Balancing Act: The New Medical Ethics of Medicine's New Economics*. Washington, DC: Georgetown University Press.

Parker, M. (2001). The ethics of evidence based patient choice. *Health Expectations*, **4**, 87–91.

Popay, J., Bennett, S., Thomas, C., *et al.* (2003). Beyond 'beer, fags, egg and chips'? Exploring lay understandings of social inequalities in health. *Sociology of Health & Illness*, **25**, 1–23.

Raffle, A. (2001). Information about screening – Is it to achieve high uptake or to ensure informed choice? *Health Expectations*, **4**, 92–98.

Rawls, J. A. (1999). Theory of Justice (revised edn). Cambridge, MA: The Belknap Press.

Schneider, C. (1998). *The Practice of Autonomy: Patients, Doctors, and Medical Decisions*. Oxford, UK: Oxford University Press.

Quill, T. and Cassel, C. (1995). Nonabandonment: A central obligation for physicians. *Annals of Internal Medicine*, **122**, 368–374.

Chapter 10

The economics of shared decision-making

Ivar Sønbø Kristiansen and Dorte Gyrd-Hansen

Introduction

What is economics?

The Nobel Prize laureate Paul Samuelson stated that 'economics is the study of how people and society choose to employ scarce resources that could have alternative uses in order to produce various commodities and to distribute them for consumption, now or in the future, among various persons and groups in society' (Samuelson and Nordhaus, 1985). The basic principle in economics is that society should be organized in a way such that overall welfare is maximized and that this is ensured if and only if we consume and produce those goods that provide us with the highest levels of utility. It can be proved that the production of goods and services is most efficient if it is left to a market with so-called perfect competition. The assumptions of perfect competition, however, are very strict and partly unrealistic, and the competitive market does not result in an optimal distribution of goods and services. Economics is about maximization and distribution of welfare where societal welfare is the sum of (possibly weighted) individuals' utilities. To the extent that distribution of utility across individuals is important, the utility gains of some individuals may be weighted higher or lower than others.

Due to a range of market failures (i.e. deviations from the assumptions about perfect competition), health care services are in most countries not sold on a competitive market, but offered free of charge (or at little cost) at the time of consumption to individuals who are insured through either a private or a publicly financed insurance system. Moreover, the patient does not demand health care services, but is represented by an agent (the clinician) who demands health care services on behalf of the patient. This principal–agent relationship can be seen to operate in the context of the relationship of figures 10.1 and 10.2:

The doctor has knowledge of the association between health care services and health (Figure 10.1), whereas the patient has knowledge of the association between different levels of health and aspects of health – and the utility she derives from the various health states (Figure 10.2). In the utility, function may also lay the (dis)utility associated with the process of consuming health care in order to obtain improved health. The ratio of benefit to harm is clearly dependent on patient values. If the aim is to ensure maximum utility for the individual patient, the challenge of shared decision-making is to ensure that the information and knowledge inherent in the two figures are assembled in order to maximize the individuals' utility given the health care options that are available. Clinicians and patients may play different roles in medical decision-making. A paternalistic physician will claim to have the final decisional authority, and he may focus primarily on the production function in Figure 10.1, with the aim of maximizing health. At the other end of the spectrum, we find clinicians who adhere to the informed choice model, in which they inform patients about the possible outcomes relating to different treatment options and leave the

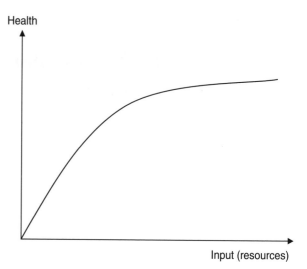

Figure 10.1 Health as a function of health care services/resources.

decisional authority to the patient. Shared decision-making seeks to offer middle ground between these extremes, involving patients in different degrees according to the patients' preferences for involvement (Elwyn *et al.*, 2000; Eriksson *et al.*, 2007).

Opportunity cost

When services are provided by a private or public health insurance program where out-of-pocket expenditures are zero or represent only a smaller proportion of the actual cost of a health care service, the patient's or consumer's consideration of whether the price of the health service does or does not exceed the utility associated with the good no longer ensures optimal resource alloca- tion from a societal perspective. Given that resources are taken from communal funds, an individual's consumption of health care services will always be associated with negative exter- nalities in the sense that one patient's use of services implies that these services are not available to other patients. Any use of resources will be associated with an *opportunity cost* in the form of lost opportunities for health care for others and, consequently, loss of health or utility elsewhere.

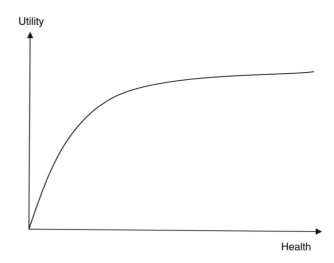

Figure 10.2 Utility as a function of health.

The challenge for society is to ensure that the resources are allocated fairly and efficiently across individuals in need, such that overall utility is maximized given the resources available. This challenge raises two important issues.

Firstly, the clinician naturally plays a central role in ensuring efficient allocation of services across all his patients. While a doctor according to traditional medical ethics 'owes his patient's complete loyalty and all the resources of his science' (Andersen *et al.*, 1987), the economics argument is that the doctor shall consider opportunity costs and whether resources spent on one patient may result in more health than for another. In some countries, such as Norway, this is explicitly stated that the patient has the right to treatment only if the benefits of the treatment are reasonable in relation to the costs (Patient's Right Act, 2008). In this way, the clinician is at the same time agent for the individual patient and for society at large (i.e. all future and present patients). Hence, decisions based on patient preferences may result in suboptimal decisions from a societal perspective, but only *if* there are externalities. In this context, externalities mainly mean taking resources that could be used by other patients (opportunity cost), but externalities could also be positive. Positive externalities are typically found in the area of immunization and forced mental health services (mental care against the patient's will). Here, the patient may prefer not to have immunization or mental treatment, to the disadvantage of others. The doctor should act as a perfect agent for his patients if choices involve no externalities, but is expected to act as a double agent if there are significant externalities. The existence of externalities, such as is the case in private and public insurance-based systems, raises the question of whether the principle of shared decision-making may be in conflict with society's objective of allocative efficiency (greatest benefit to the greatest number of patients). Shared decision-making requires that the patients are confident that the doctor is focused on which treatment will generate the greatest benefit for them (Sculpher *et al.*, 2002). It should be noted, however, that the clinician's challenge in choosing between the individual patient's interests and those of society at large is not necessarily less for doctors who practice paternalistic than for those doctors who practice informed choice medicine.

Secondly, it is necessary to define the concept of utility more precisely: What exactly is the objective of health care? Is it to maximize utility, where utility is defined by the public's or patients' preferences? Or is it to maximize objective measures of health such as life years or 'quality-adjusted life years' (QALYs)? The former accords well with the welfare economic framework (welfarist economics). The latter is aligned with the biomedical utility, where utility is associated with improved quality and duration of life (and Figure 10.2 is ignored) – 'extra-welfarist economics'. Even within the bounds of health economics, it has been argued that informational asymmetries in the market for health care jeopardize the status of the standard neo-classical demand curve as a normative construct (Evans, 1984; Culyer, 1989; Rice, 1992). Consequently, the health sector has proven fertile ground for extra-welfarist approaches that emphasize non-utility, and in particular health information, when guiding resource allocations (Hurley, 2008). Extra-welfarist methods (cost-effectiveness analyses and cost-utility analyses) have for many years largely supplanted welfare economic approaches (cost-benefit analysis) to the economic evaluation of individual health care services and procedures.

Welfarist and extra-welfarist economics

In cost-effectiveness and cost-utility analyses, measures of health are used as outcome measures. 'Gained life-years' is an often applied measure in cost-effectiveness analysis, and QALYs are classically used in cost-utility analysis (note that utility in 'cost-utility analysis' does not refer to the concept of utility referred to elsewhere in this chapter). In contrast, the outcome measure in a cost-benefit analysis is the patients' mean maximum willingness-to-pay (WTP) for a health care service.

Although one may criticize the concept of measuring utility by way of WTP, the essence of this approach is that there may be (dis-)utility bearing elements of a health care service beyond health improvements. A cost-benefit analysis will in principle include elements such as process (dis-) utility and information utility. These types of evaluation represent different viewpoints on what constitutes a good clinical decision for the patient: Is it a decision in which QALYs are maximized, or is it a decision in which utility is maximized?

These contrasting views are clearly aligned with different perceptions of whether the individual patient should be involved in deliberations about appropriate forms of clinical management (see Table 10.1). Greater patient involvement may potentially undermine the aim of QALY maximization, but does not necessarily threaten utility maximization. For example, if a patient needs to decide whether or not to participate in a colorectal cancer screening programme, SDM involves providing the patient with full information on the reduced risk of dying from colorectal cancer, but also on the nature and frequency of the screening test and the risk of a false positive diagnosis and subsequent unnecessary diagnostic testing. The patient may decide that the disadvantages outweigh the benefits and choose not to participate. From an extra-welfarist perspective this is a bad decision if participation incurs QALY gains at a low cost. From a welfarist perspective, the decision is optimal because society avoids spending resources on an intervention which is of a low value to the informed individual. Taking the welfarist approach of introducing shared decision-making as an alternative to the paternalistic approach to decision-making has a potential for welfare improvement because health care services are tailored to individual preferences. There is, however, a downside. While we may avoid using resources on services which individuals do not appreciate, shared decision-making may channel resources towards health care services which are much appreciated by the individual, but costly to society in the sense that the health improvement is small compared to the cost.

Whether the net impact of shared decision-making is beneficial to society depends on how the clinician manages his role as a double agent. Here, it is important to distinguish between 'decisional priority' (deciding which options are considered) and 'decisional authority' (who makes the decision) (Eriksson *et al.*, 2007). If the clinician upholds his decisional priority and defines the clinical question such that the options presented to the individual all represent cost-effective options, giving the decisional authority to the (rational!) individual will improve societal welfare from the welfarist perspective, while still ensuring some degree of QALY maximization.

Will shared decision-making result in more efficient health care?

We define efficient health care as health care that achieves the maximum of the objective of the care system within the existing resource limitations. It should be obvious from the previous section that there is no simple answer to the question of whether shared decision-making improves efficiency. First, it is not obvious what the objectives of health care systems are. Second, there are various models that the doctor can apply when executing shared decision-making (e.g. different perceptions of where decisional priority and authority lies), and the question of efficiency improvement may depend on which model it is applied (Eriksson *et al.*, 2008). Third, efficiency has two aspects: optimal technical production of health services (technical efficiency – 'doing the things right') and optimal choice of services (allocative efficiency – 'doing the right things').

If a change in the production of health services results in more of the same health services from the same amount of resources, or the same amount of services from fewer resources, this would be a change towards greater technical efficiency. As far as we understand, the concept and practice of shared decision-making entails no incentives or mechanisms that would improve

Table 10.1 Key characteristics of shared decision-making in the context of health economics

Welfarist approach		Extra-welfarist approach
Maximize utility	Societal level aim	Maximize life years or quality-adjusted life years (QALY),
Cost-benefit analyses	Methods for the economic evaluation of health programmes	Cost-effectiveness and cost-utility analyses*
Maximize utility, determined by preferences, values, and may include information utility	Objective for a 'good decision'	Maximize quality-adjusted life years
All options made available to patient	Constraints on shared decision making	Only cost-effective options made available to patient
Avoids allocating resources to services that patients do not want. Potential gain in welfare, but may be at high cost to society for small gain in health	Effects of greater patient involvement and shared decision making at an individual level	May limit QALYs gained, or increase cost-per-QALY gained

*Unfortunately, the term cost-utility is widely used for analyses that measure outcome in terms of QALYs even though the term may create confusion.

technical efficiency. In fact, the argument may go the opposite way. The practice of shared decision-making may imply that doctors spend more time on eliciting patient's preferences and discussing alternative diagnostic and therapeutic options. Cohen and co-workers found that the cost per consultation was £2.89 higher for those who practised shared decision-making (Cohen et al., 2004).

The question is then whether shared decision-making, in contrast to paternalistic or patient-led decision-making, improves allocative efficiency. It is impossible to answer this question, however, without knowing what the objectives of the health care system are, and the relative weighting of these. To our knowledge, few health care systems – whether private or public – state explicitly what their objectives are. By observing policy making in public systems such as those of the United Kingdom or the Nordic countries, it seems as if there are many and conflicting objectives: maximizing health (life years and quality), maximizing patients', and/or voters' utility or satisfaction, creating employment in remote areas, creating equity, etc.

If the health care system has utility maximization as its objective, economists would adopt a welfarist approach and use cost-benefit analysis as a tool for the evaluation of health services such as diagnostic tools, surgical procedures, medicines, etc. The value of specific health services will then be measured as (potential) patients' mean WTP for the service in question. If the cost-benefit analysis concludes that the aggregate benefit (measured in monetary terms) is greater than the aggregate cost, it would be efficient to adopt the service, shared decision-making implies no efficiency problem, and the recommendation would be that the service is among the services offered to patients. If the individual patient according to his or her values decides against the service, it may be optimal to respect the individual's decision, but only if such a decision does not involve externalities (other factors) that would in fact exceed the utility that the individual gains by this decision. Paternalistic decision-making, however, may be welfare reducing if the doctor for some reason (e.g. little health benefit) decides against the use of the service for an individual. If the cost-benefit analysis concludes that the benefits exceed the costs despite the little health benefit, it implies that the service is valued by the average patient (or society) for other reasons than health, and refusing to offer the service will result in loss of utility to the individual. To conclude, from a welfarist perspective, increasing patient participation in decision-making and thereby respecting patient values, may improve efficiency, but only if the decision does not involve significant externalities to others.

If the objective of the health care system is to maximize health as expressed in terms of (quality-adjusted) life years, the economic evaluation takes an extra-welfarist approach. If the cost per (quality-adjusted) life year for a specific health service is below some threshold (e.g. £20,000–30,000 in the United Kingdom; Devlin, 2004), the service in question will be considered cost-effective. Presumably, patients will then be offered the service, if they so prefer, in shared and informed decision-making, and even in paternalistic decision-making depending on the doctor's judgment. If the patient rejects the offer on the basis of his or her own values, this will undermine the objective of health maximization. Moreover, such a decision may also incur costs to society in the form of externalities, e.g. increased cost of treatment. According to the extra-welfarist approach, respecting patients' rejection of a cost-effective intervention will always be interpreted as undermining the efficiency of the service provision. Hence, shared decision-making which strengthens the patient's decisional authority will be seen as a threat to efficiency. This may also be the case if the doctor informs the patient about an intervention that is not cost-effective, and the patient opts for this intervention.

We have searched Medline for the literature on shared decision-making and efficiency (July 2008). We used the terms 'shared decision-making' and 'efficiency' or 'cost-benefit' or 'cost-effectiveness' or 'cost-utility' and received 30 hits. Only one of these hits referred to publications that explored the issue of shared decision-making and efficiency empirically (Wolters et al., 2006). The paper described a cluster-randomized trial of 187 older male patients with lower urinary tract symptoms in general practices. The intervention comprised distant teaching of general practitioners, evidence-based information, assessment of learning needs, and patient education materials. The control group received written guidelines. After 3 months, the mean cost of care per patient was lower in the intervention group, but the occurrence of symptoms was the same. The intervention was complex, and the trial does not allow for inference about the cost-effectiveness of shared decision-making in isolation.

Conclusions

Two important and relevant phenomena have occurred during the last 50–100 years. While medical decision-making typically has been paternalistic, ethicists, doctors, and others have argued that patients should have the right to be involved in decision-making on the grounds of patient autonomy. The emergence of shared decision-making can be seen in this context, and economists would typically applaud it because it is in line with basic economic theory about individuals' preferences. Another phenomenon, however, makes the case for shared decision-making more equivocal. The emergence of private and public insurance systems has undermined the traditional medical ethics that commanded doctors to offer all possible services to the patient in front of him, irrespective of the cost and lost opportunities for other patients (opportunity cost). It should be noted that hippocrates practised medicine at a time when insurance systems presumably were unknown, and externalities and opportunity cost were not issues. Increasingly, societies expect that doctors consider opportunity cost and, consequently, deny services on the grounds of lacking cost-effectiveness. Doctors, therefore, have to consider patients' legitimate wish to maximize preferences and society's need to allocate scarce resources to patients who benefit most. This conflict is not unique for shared decision-making, however.

Presumably, all insurance-based health care systems are based on the principles of autonomy as well as the principle of greatest benefit to the greatest number. The question of how doctors should resolve the conflict between the two principles needs to be discussed by patients and doctors, but ultimately, it is a political question. Meanwhile, conclusions about the economics of shared decision-making should be drawn cautiously.

References

Andersen, D., Mabeck, C.E., and Riis, P. (1987). Medical Ethics (in Danish: Medicinsk Etik). Copenhagen: FADL's Forlag.

Cohen, D., Longo, M.F., Hood, K., *et al.* (2004). Resource effects of training general practitioners in risk communication skills and shared decision making competences. *J. Eval. Clin. Pract.*, **10**, 439–445.

Culyer, A.J. (1989). The normative economics of health care finance and provision. *Oxford Reviewof Economic Policy*, **5**, 34–58.

Devlin, N. and Parkin, D. (2004). Does NICE have a cost-effectiveness threshold. . . . ? *Health Economics*, **13**, 437–452.

Elwyn, G., Edwards, A., Kinnersley, P., *et al.* (2000). Shared decision making and the concept of equipoise: The competences of involving patients in healthcare choices. *British Journal of General Practice*, **50**, 892–899.

Eriksson, T., Nilstun, T., and Edwards, A. (2007). The ethics of risk communication in life-style interventions: Consequences of patient centredness. *Health Risk* Soc., **9**, 19–36.

Evans, B. (1984). *Strained Mercy: The Economics of Canadian Health Care*. Toronto: Butterworth.

Hurley, J. (2008). An overview of the normative economics of the health care sector. In A.J. Culyer and J.P. Newhouse (eds) *Handbook of Health Economics*. Amsterdam: Elsevier Science.

Patient's Right Act. (2008). (in Norwegian: Lov om pasientrettigheter).

Rice, T. (1992). An alternative framework for evaluating welfare losses in the health care market. *J. Health. Econ.*, **11**, 86–92.

Samuelson, P.A. and Nordhaus, W.D. (1985). *Economics*. New York: McGraw-Hill.

Sculpher, M., Gafni, A., and Watt, I. (2002). Shared treatment decision making in a collectively funded health care system: Possible conflicts and some potential solutions. *Soc. Sci. Med.*, **54**, 1369–1377.

Wolters, R., Grol, R., Schermer, T., *et al.* (2006). Improving initial management of lower urinary tract symptoms in primary care: Costs and patient outcomes. *Scand. J. Urol. Nephrol.*, **40**, 300–306.

Chapter 11

The physician–patient encounter: An agency relationship?

Amiram Gafni and Cathy Charles

Introduction

The nature of the relationship between the physician and her patient has long fascinated social scientists and others. One feature, commonly agreed upon, that characterizes this relationship is the asymmetry of information between the patient and the doctor. Typically, a doctor is required to determine the patient's diagnosis on the basis of which a choice of treatment will be made. The doctor is also expected to know about available treatments, appropriate for the patient's specific case. As a result, the doctor–patient relationship has frequently been viewed, particularly in health economics, as an agency relationship where the physician is seen as an agent of the patient (Culyer, 1989; Evans, 1984; Feldstein, 1974; Phelps, 1992; Williams, 1988).

In the past decade, we have seen a growing interest in the physician–patient encounter and in the process of treatment decision-making. In particular, shared treatment decision-making, or shared decision-making (SDM), is a concept that has gained widespread appeal to both physicians and patients (Moumjid et al., 2007). Several definitions of SDM exist, which share some components but are not identical (for fuller discussion of the conceptual variation that exists, see Chapter 16 by Clayman and Makoul). Here, we use the Charles et al. (1997; 1999a) definition, which is most commonly cited (Moumjid et al., 2007).

In this chapter, we explore whether viewing the relationship between the physician and her patient as an agency relationship is consistent with attempts to promote SDM in the medical encounter. We first describe the main features of the agency paradigm in general and in health care. We than review the SDM process suggested by Charles et al. (1997; 1999a). Finally, we contrast the two approaches, exploring whether the physician is an agent or a partner of the patient. We conclude with a discussion.

The agency relationship

(a) In general

The agency paradigm addresses the question of how to optimize the behaviour of an organization of self-interested parties with conflicting goals in a world of incomplete information (Bamberg and Spremann, 1989; Levinthal, 1988; Rees, 1985a; Rees, 1985b). An agency relationship is said to exist between two (or more) parties when one, designated as an agent, acts on behalf of another, designated the principal. Consider, for example, this notion of agency in the context of the relationship between stockholders and the company's management. The stockholders act as principals, delegating the daily company operations to the management. What makes this (and other agency) relationship complex is the principal's uncertainty as to the agent's actions and goals.

Stockholders cannot closely monitor the managers' actions, nor are they as knowledgeable about appropriate actions to take in order to achieve their own goals. Stockholders also do not know what the goals of the managers are and whether they are in line with those of the stockholders. Thus, an agency problem is characterized by a situation where desired outcomes are clear but there is an incomplete knowledge (at least from the principal's perspective) of the cause/effect relationships (i.e. asymmetry of information) that will lead to the desired outcome. The agency paradigm incorporates two typical organizational features: uncertainty and goal conflict among members of the organization.

Agency theory (in economics) tries to address these features by introducing a contract – designed by the principal (e.g. stockholder) – which typically includes incentives for the agent (e.g. compensation schemes for management) to act in ways that achieve the principal goals (e.g. maximization of profits to stockholders). The various factors involved and the need to deal with uncertain payoffs and costs make the problem of designing a contract difficult to formulate and solve. Ideally, the contract should relate directly to the agent's behaviour; however, obtaining knowledge of the agent's actions and their impact on the goals to achieve is costly and not always possible.

(b) In health care

Agency relationships are claimed to be common in health care, such as in the raising of finance and the transfer of funds to hospitals (Smith *et al.*, 1997). Here we concentrate on the case of the physician–patient encounter in which a principal (a patient) delegates authority to an agent (the doctor) to take action (e.g. make medical decisions) for the principal, who defines the contract. This 'agency relationship' is justified as a direct consequence of the asymmetry of information between the patient and the doctor (explained earlier). The 'ideal' relationship is seen as a physician being a 'perfect agent' for the patient, i.e. using her extensive knowledge to make treatment decision for the patient taking the latter's viewpoint.

Because the agency model incorporates two basic features uncertainty and goal conflict among members of the organization, there are potential conflicts between the physician (i.e. agent) goals and the patient (i.e. principal) goals. Indeed physicians are increasingly requested to consider the economic consequences of their decisions with a view to optimizing the use of scarce health care resources allocated to the population. Hence, a conflict is likely to arise between the individual and the collective interest because doing all that can be done at the individual level implies fewer resources for other patients (Sculpher et al., 2002). Thus, physicians are placed today at the heart of this trade-off, as agents of two principals: the patient but also representatives of the collective interest, be it the state or a third party payer (Blomqvist, 1991; Rochaix, 1998). Finally, physicians are also human beings and it has been argued that things like maintaining a certain level of personal income can also affect their behaviour (Evans, 1984; Phelps, 1992). The latter is important because it will affect the ability to design a compensation scheme that will influence them to behave more in line with patients' interests.

The shared decision-making model

Traditionally, the dominant approach to making decisions in the medical encounter has been one of paternalism. More recently, doctors, patients, medical ethicists, and others have challenged this model. Their call for doctor–patient partnerships opened up options beyond paternalism for the task of making decisions about treatment, but also raised new complexities (Charles *et al.*, 1999b). Charles *et al.* (1997; 1999a), describe different types of treatment decision-making models, which can help us describe the kinds of partnerships (or sharing) that can be developed between a doctor and a patient in the context of making treatment decisions. In this conceptual framework, treatment decision-making is divided into different analytical stages (though in reality they may occur together or in an iterative process): information exchange (i.e. the flow, direction, type, and amount exchanged), deliberation or discussion of treatment preferences, and deciding on the treatment to implement. The framework identifies three 'pure models': paternalistic, informed, and shared but recognizes that in reality there are intermediate approaches. In other words, doctors and patients in a clinical encounter may not use a 'pure model', but rather a hybrid of elements of more than one model.

The essential characteristic of the *shared model* is its interactional nature in that the doctor and patient share all stages of the decision-making process simultaneously. In its purest form, the information exchange is two ways. At a minimum, the physician will inform the patient about all available treatment options and the potential benefits and risks of each. The patient needs to provide information to the physician on her values, preferences, life style, beliefs, and knowledge about her illness and its treatment. This ensures that (i) all relevant treatment options are considered and (ii) that both parties evaluate these options within the context of the patient's specific situation and needs, rather than a standard menu of options whose impact and outcomes are assumed to be similar for clinically similar patients.

The deliberation and decision-making stages reflect the fact that *both the patient and the doctor have a legitimate investment* in the treatment decision: the patient because her health is at stake and the physician out of concern for the patient's welfare. The deliberation stage is interactive which ensures patient's input into the process but can be cumbersome and time consuming. Negotiations as equal partners, however, are not easy for the patient because of the information and power imbalances in the relationship (Guadagnoli and Ward, 1998).

In the shared model, it is legitimate for the physician to give a treatment recommendation to the patient and try to persuade the latter to accept the recommendation. However, physicians should also be prepared to create a safe environment for the patient so that she feels comfortable in exploring information, expressing her views. The physician also needs to listen to and try to understand why the patient might favour a different treatment option. If the physician and the patient cannot agree on the treatment (or course of action) to implement, a shared treatment decision will not be reached, and the patient will have to go elsewhere if she hopes to have her preferred treatment implemented (unless her preferred option was to do nothing).

The physician: An agent or a partner?

In this section, we examine whether viewing the role of the physician as being the patient's agent (i) is consistent with the shared decision-making approach and (ii) can lead us to where we want to be (i.e. promotion of SDM between clinicians and patients – assuming that this is our goal).

When the agency paradigm is used in health care, the ideal physician is seen as a 'perfect agent' of her patient, one who 'would take on entirely the patient's point of view and act as if she were the patient' (Evans, 1984) or one 'ideally choosing in the way the individual would, had he or she been possessed of the same informational advantage of the profession' (Culyer, 1989). Health economists have long recognized that perfect agency relationships do not exist, but many see this as a benchmark from which one can study the departure from that ideal in a useful way. If making treatment decisions that reflect patient preferences and physician knowledge is truly the role that patients expect from their physicians, then using the paradigm of agency relationship might be appropriate.

Gafni et al. (1998) have argued that the goal of arriving at a treatment decision which is based on the physician's knowledge and the patient preferences is reflected in both the physician as a perfect agent for the patient and the *informed* treatment decision-making approaches. In the former, the patient delegates authority to her doctor to make medical decisions and the challenge is to encourage the physician to find out the patient's preferences. In the latter, the patient retains the authority to make medical decisions and the challenge is to induce physicians to transfer all relevant information in a clear and unbiased way to the patient. The choice of which approach to implement depends partly on the ease of implementation. They argue that the approach of transferring technical knowledge to patients is easier (but not easy) and hence more feasible than transferring each patient's preference to the physician in each medical encounter. They also argue that it is likely easier and more feasible to design 'contracts' to motivate physicians to transfer information to patients.

In contrast, the SDM approach describes a situation of partnership (ideally, equal partnership), which is built on trust and a positive patient–doctor relationship. As noted earlier, it is based on the premise that both patient and doctor have a legitimate investment in the treatment decision. This decision-making process is highly *interactive* as both parties describe their treatment preferences while trying to build a consensus on the appropriate treatment to implement.

The underlying features of the SDM approach differ from those of the agency relationship paradigm. The latter reflects a situation of conflicting goals between the physician and patient. The consequent lack of trust results in a need for a 'contract' with incentives for the agent (i.e. physician) to act in a way that is consistent with the principal's (i.e. patient's) goals. It assumes that what matters in the end is what the principal (i.e. patient) wants (or the principal's goals). In the SDM approach, the goals of the physician (i.e. in terms of improving the patient's welfare) are as important as those of the patient which explains why the final decision about the course of action to take should be arrived at by consensus. Furthermore, in the SDM approach the interactional nature of the process if properly done should create a trusting environment, which differs from the one underlying the agency relationship.

The fact that the underlying features of the agency paradigm and the SDM approach are different does not necessarily mean that one is right and the other is wrong. First, they reflect different goals to achieve: arriving at a decision that reflects the patient preferences and the physician knowledge (physician as agent paradigm) versus arriving at a decision that reflects both patient's and physician's knowledge and preferences (SDM approach). Second, they reflect different realities regarding the relationship between the physician and her patient: SDM assumes some form of partnership where the physician is seen as a benevolent person whose only goal is to improve her patient's health (even though she might define health differently than the patient). The agency relationship assumes conflicting goals, some lack of trust, and the need for a contract to motivate physicians to behave in a certain way. Because of these differences, it seems that the two treatment decision-making approaches are not compatible, i.e. they cannot be used to describe physicians' behaviour *at the same time* (but can be used to describe a physician's behaviour at different times). This raises the question of which model (or none) best describes reality (i.e. what happens in practice)? We do not address this empirical question here, but we will explore how this question can inform further policy developments in health care.

Where do we go from here?

"'Would you tell me please which way I ought to go from here?' Asked Alice. 'That depends a good deal on where you want to go' said the Cat. 'I don't much care where' said Alice. 'Then it does not matter which way you go' said the Cat"

(From Alice in Wonderland by Lewis Caroll)

The answer to the above question depends on where we want to go. Is the goal the advocacy of SDM as a way of *practicing* medicine? Should it be the only way to practice medicine? Or is the goal to arrive at a treatment decision that reflects only the patient's preferences, using physician knowledge about the risks and benefits of available treatment options as input? It is not clear that either of these approaches is or should be the only treatment decision-making approaches to promote. As already argued (Charles *et al.*, 1999a) there is no reason to believe that 'one size fits all'. For example, there is nothing wrong with a case where *both* patient and doctor, after discussing alternative decision-making approaches, agree that they prefer a paternalistic treatment decision-making approach. To the best of our knowledge, there is no empirical evidence demonstrating that all patients (and doctors) prefer one type of decision-making model. Also, we are not aware of any compelling normative argument why we should impose one type of decision-making process on everyone. In other words, the clarity of what we want to achieve is a prerequisite to determining how to get there. What this goal(s) should be is beyond the scope of this chapter.

It is also important to recognize that some of the underlying assumptions of both approaches are unrealistic. For example, as noted above physicians are increasingly urged to act as double agents – for both patients and third parties (Blomqvist, 1991; Rochaix, 1998; Sculpher *et al.*, 2002). It is also unrealistic to assume that all (or even most) doctors are willing to behave (or are behaving) as 'equal partners' with their patients. This does not mean that doctors are bad people, but rather that they work in a complex environment and under many constraints.

One lesson from this chapter is that adopting the agency paradigm is not the way to promote SDM; these approaches are incompatible. A second lesson is the realization that even physicians who are highly motivated to improve the patient's welfare (Mooney and Ryan, 1993) face practice constraints likely to limit their ability to dedicate as much time as needed to enable a SDM process to occur. Identifying potential conflicts between what is required in order to practice SDM and other goals and constraints that physicians face is the first step to finding strategies to deal with them (Sculpher *et al.*, 2002). The next step is to see whether physicians are willing to adopt these strategies. The broader policy issue which this situation raises is the extent to which the goal of promoting SDM for each patient should be advocated in the face of competing (and even conflicting) responsibilities to all patients which need to be undertaken within set time and financial constraints, and how to determine which goal trumps the others. The third lesson is the need for an acceptable definition of SDM and for conceptual clarity of this construct that will promote consensus on its meaning (Moumjid *et al.*, 2007). This task is key, if we want to enable SDM to exist as a viable form of treatment decision-making, encourage discussion of this construct in medical school curricula, and educate patients and potential patients to consider and ask for SDM in the medical encounter.

> "Oh, you're sure to get [some where]' said the Cat 'If you only walk long enough'"
> (From Alice in Wonderland, by Lewis Carroll)

Introducing SDM into the medical encounter is a complex issue. Following HL Menken, we too believe that every complex issue has a simple solution – which is wrong. For example, despite the recent popularity of treatment decision aids, we feel that SDM is unlikely to be achieved through the use of decision aids alone (*Charles et al.*, 2005; Nelson *et al.*, 2007). Nelson *et al.* (2007) also warn of the 'need to reexamine the assumptions and objectives that have thus far guided decision aid development'. We feel that the same comment applies to the advocacy of SDM as the best way of practicing medicine. Such advocacy is a value promotion task and lacks a rigorous scientific foundation. It seems that we missed the Cat's warning to Alice. Having walked long enough (i.e. advocating SDM as the best way of making decisions), we try to justify where we think we are rather than critically assessing whether this is where we want to be.

References

Bamberg, G. and Spremann, K. (eds). (1989). Agency theory: Information and incentives. Berlin: Springer-Verlag.

Blomqvist, A. (1991). The doctor as double agent: Information asymmetry, health insurance and medical care, *Journal of Health Economics*, **10**, 411–432.

Charles, C., Gafni, A., and Whelan, T. (1997). Shared decision-making in the medical encounter: What does it mean? (Or it takes at least two to tango). *Social Science and Medicine*, **44**, 681–692.

Charles, C., Gafni, A., and Whelan, T. (1999a). Decision-making in the medical encounter: Revisiting the shared treatment decision-making model. *Social Science and Medicine*, **49**, 651–661.

Charles, C., Whelan, T., and Gafni, A. (1999b). What do we mean by partnership in making decisions about treatment? *British Medical Journal*, **319**, 780–782.

Charles, C., Gafni, A., Whelan, T., *et al.* (2005). Treatment decision aids: Conceptual issues and future directions. *Health Expect*, **8**, 114–125.

Culyer, T. (1989). The normative economics of health care financing and provision. *Oxford Review of Economic Policy*, **5**, 34–58.

Evans, R.G. (1984). Strained Mercy: The Economics of Canadian Health Care. Toronto: Butterworths.

Feldstein, M.S. (1974). Econometric studies of health economics. In D.A. Kendrick and M.D. Intriligator (eds) *Frontiers of Quantitative Economics*. Amsterdam: North-Holland, **2**, 377–434.

Gafni, A., Charles, C., and Whelan, T. (1998). The physician–patient encounter: The physician as a perfect agent for the patient versus the informed treatment decision-making model. *Social Science and Medicine*, **47**, 347–354.

Guadagnoli, E. and Ward, P. (1988). Patient participation in decision-making. *Social Science and Medicine.*, **47**, 329–339.

Levinthal, D. (1988). A survey of agency models of organizations. *Journal of Economic Behavior and Organization* **9**, 153–185.

Mooney, G. and Ryan, M. (1993). Agency in health care: Getting beyond first principles. *Journal of Health Economics*, **12**, 125–135.

Moumjid, N., Gafni, A., Bremond, A., *et al.* (2007). Shared decision-making in the medical encounter: Are we all talking about the same thing? *Medical Decision Making*, **27**, 539–546.

Nelson, W.L., Han, P.K.J., Fagerlin, A., *et al.* (2007). Rethinking the objectives of decision aids: A call for conceptual clarity. *Medical Decision Making*, **27**, 609–618.

Phelps, C.E. (1992). *Health Economics*. New York: Harper Collins.

Rees, R. (1985a). The theory of principal and agent: Part 1. *Bulletin of Economic Research* **37**, 13–26.

Rees, R. (1985b). The theory of principal and agent: Part 2. *Bulletin of Economic Research*, **37**, 75–95.

Rochaix, L. (1998). The physician as perfect agent: A comment. *Social Science and Medicine*, **47**, 355–356.

Sculpher, M., Gafni, A., and Watt, I. (2002). Shared treatment decision-making in a collectively funded health care system: Possible conflicts and some potential solutions. *Social Science and Medicine*, **54**, 1369–1377.

Smith, P.C., Stepan, A., Valdmanis, V., *et al.* (1997). Principal-agent problems in health care systems: An international perspective. *Health Policy*, **41**, 37–60.

Williams, A. (1988). Priority setting in public and private health care: A guide through the methodological jungle. *Journal of Health Economics*, **7**, 173–183.

Chapter 12

Decision-making, power, and the doctor–patient relationship

Madeleine J. Murtagh

Introduction

There are many stories that could be told about how power in the doctor–patient relationship has been conceptualized. Perspectives on what has come to be seen as a crucial relationship in health care have emerged over the past half century or so from diverse disciplines (not least medical, sociological, psychological, anthropological) and epistemologies (positivist, realist, Marxist, feminist, post-structuralist, amongst others), though the importance of this relationship in shaping and defining medical practice is evident from the late 19th century. Moreover, within these perspectives, there have been shifts and schisms (albeit not linear and not total) over time. Marxist feminists of 1970s and 1980s and post-structural feminists of 1990s and 2000s, for example, produced very different accounts of the doctor–patient relationship. Indeed, even the term 'doctor–patient relationship' has transmogrified to include 'client–professional', 'consumer–clinician', and 'patient–professional' 'relationships', 'encounters', and 'interactions' with each permutation aligning to particular theoretical perspectives or to the context in which patients and doctors communicate and make decisions. However, I will use doctor–patient relationship as the common term throughout this chapter.

From broadly modernist to broadly post-modern epistemologies, quite different views of power have been proposed, explaining what has been an evolving doctor–patient relationship. Modernist sociologists, for example, largely produced descriptions of a malign medicine with doctor–patient relationships characterized by an unequal distribution of power in which the doctor was all powerful. In contrast, sociologists and others from post-modern and ethno-methodological perspectives have produced descriptions of negotiated power within the doctor–patient relationship. Shifting conceptualizations of the doctor–patient relationship also reflect developments in the social and organizational contexts of health care in which there are now increased expectations of patient involvement in decisions about their health care. The relationship itself has changed but so too has the social world in which this relationship occurs. The context of post-enlightenment views of the subject as rational, autonomous (mostly Western, male, and middle class) with the rise of the 'consumer society' and the 'information age' has produced *choice* as a defining value in Western society and thereby an imperative for patient involvement in health care decisions. It is the intersecting shifts in the doctor–patient relationship and increasing expectations of patient involvement in decision-making that are arguably of most interest to readers of this volume and are thus the focus of this chapter.

It is not possible here to detail each move and counter move around the conceptualization of power in the doctor–patient relationship, nor of its relationship to health care decision-making. Rather I unravel threads at the edge of a cloth, the textures of which are in ongoing processes of formation and reformation.

Decision-making, power, and the doctor–patient relationship

From social movements in the 1960s around gender and race evolved the dictum 'nothing about us without us'. This has been used by diverse communities of interest (disability and ageing amongst others) since that time to demand engagement in decision-making especially, but not exclusively, in relation to health care. In particular, the women's health movement spurred in the popular imagination a move away from a traditional paternalistic doctor–patient relationship in which the doctor *told* and the patient *did as they were told* (Ehrenreich and English, 2005). Resistance to 'medical power' was explicitly supported, for example, by the Boston Women's Health Collective's promotion of a new way for women to engage with health care practitioners (Collective, 1973; Ruzek, 2007). Though undoubtedly there were exceptions, the predominant doctor–patient relationship was understood as one in which the patient was passive and the doctor held power. Likewise, this was a view held by much contemporaneous sociologists of medicine[1].

Modernist sociological description of the doctor–patient relationship predominantly produced macro (or grand) theories of the operations of power in that relationship. Working from an understanding of power in terms of 'sovereign' power, power was conceived of as being 'held over' one agent by another more powerful agent. A totalizing view of medicine and its practitioners prevailed in sociological accounts. From Ehrenreich and English's (1973) accounts of the witch hunts of the 17th century as an outcome of the professionalization of medicine, Illich's (1976) proposition that 'medicine has become major threat to health', to Zola's (1972) view of medicine as a form of social control charging medicine with turning 'normal' life and life events into 'medical problems', the doctor–patient relationship was characterized in almost exclusively negative terms as a relationship which was uniformly disempowering of the patient.

Sociological accounts of the doctor–patient relationship provided the theoretical foundations for several radical accounts through a unidirectional view of sovereign power: Parsons' (1991) functionalist view of the normative roles in the doctor–patient relationship in the 'sick role', Friedson's (1970) accounts of professional dominance, and Waitzkin's (1984) view of the doctor–patient relationship as one in which the social and structural causes of ill-health are obscured and the potential for action muted, each positioned the patient as powerless. Medicine and medical professionals were conflated, and the possibility that doctors themselves might be caught up in relations of power was not admitted. Moreover, the commitment in these accounts to positioning patients as intrinsically passive constructed as logically impossible a doctor–patient relationship in which the patient could be empowered. They thereby precluded the very aim of these critiques of medicine. Scholarship examining the doctor–patient relationship in action (often micro analyses of practice) proffer a more differentiated account of power in the doctor–patient relationship describing elaborate preparation and subtle negotiation (Stimson and Webb, 1975), ritualized interactions (Strong, 1979), and the social organization of the verbal interaction (Heath, 1984) in which both parties in the relationship accomplish the reproduction of social relations of power.

The arrival and influence of 'patient-centredness'

At around the same time as political and academic calls for a changed power relationship between patients and doctors, reconfigurations were being attempted within medicine. The work of Balint

---

[1] For a fuller account of the sociology of the doctor–patient relationship than is possible in the sketch below see Nettleton, S. (2006), *The sociology of health and illness* (2nd Edition), Cambridge, MA: Polity Press.

and others (Balint, 2000; Balint et al., 1970) on the therapeutic potential of the doctor–patient relationship in general practice saw the emergence of the concept of 'patient-centredness' and the development of new practices, training, and research by small groups of general practitioners on the emotional content of the doctor–patient relationship – 'Balint groups'. It is important, however, to understand Balint's work as embedded in shifts in the social organization of medicine and certain power relationships within medicine that had been in contest since the late 19th century. Jewson (1974) described the shift from Bedside Medicine, in which the doctor was at the beck and call of wealthy patrons, to Hospital Medicine, where medical knowledge via the technologies of the laboratory remained the province of medicine[2].

With the rise of hospital medicine and the introduction of the National Health Service, the role for general practice medicine was diminished: left with the 'trivial complaints' of patients, general practice floundered (Armstrong, 1979; Gothill and Armstrong, 1999). Development of the concept of 'patient-centredness', which provided a mark of distinction from Hospital Medicine, was perhaps as much a part of defining a separate professional identity for general practice as it was a development in ethical practice that was the ideological underpinning of Balint groups. The more recent shift to engaging the patient in decision-making in the consultation (one elaboration of patient centredness) also serves a fundamental and instrumental function. The rise of biographical medicine, the interest in the psychological and social narratives patients bring to the clinic, rather than a shift in power relations was *oriented* to enhancing the efficacy of the clinical encounter (Armstrong, 1979; Burges Watson et al., 2008). That is not to say this was achieved: Chew-Graham and others have demonstrated that how the primacy of the doctor–patient relationship has produced a counter-intuitive result in which general practitioners felt unable to achieve clinically acceptable outcomes for their patients but rather colluded in the maintenance of illness producing behaviours (Chew-Graham et al., 2004; May et al., 2004). Whatever its origin and however incomplete (Burges Watson et al., 2008), it is apparent that a shift in orientation towards patients in the doctor–patient relationship has occurred.

Recent legislative and policy provisions in the United Kingdom that see the strengthening of patient and public engagement in health care decision-making as a key strategy for achieving population-wide health improvements reflect an increasing emphasis internationally on patient and public engagement. This is evident also in the move in clinical practice from paternalistic to shared decisions (Darzi, 2008; Florin and Dixon, 2004; Litva et al., 2002). The patient and public engagement agenda is based on understandings of individual autonomy, understood as the right to and capacity for freedom, crucially including freedom of choice and of consent. At the face value, the patient and public engagement agenda appears to meet the emancipatory project of the political movements in which involvement in decision-making about health care has been the marker of power relations: 'Nothing about us without us!'. However, choice is contextual and may not necessarily deliver the freedom imagined by its proponents.

Re-formulating power in the consultation

Drawing attention to the emergence of a differentiated understanding of power, following Foucault, a number of sociologists posit an alternative explanation (Dean, 2007; Dent, 2006; Lemke, 2001; Rose, 1999). This concept of power describes not the individual exertion of a sovereign

---

[2] See also Bell's account of the importance of the rise of the laboratory in reconstructing one particular life event, menopause, as a medical problem: **Bell, S.E.** (1987), 'Changing ideas: the medicalization of menopause', *Soc. Sci. Med.*, **24**(6), 535–542.

power by one individual (the doctor) over another (the patient), but the ways (via discourse) in which the social values and expectations in which the individuals (doctor or patient) are immersed, shape (or discipline) an individual's actions. Concepts of power, ethics, and freedom drawn from the work of Foucault and Rose enable us to read in practices of participation, decision-making, and choice forms of freedom that themselves limit freedom (Foucault et al., 1988; Greco, 1993; Rose, 1999). Specifically, the construction of a choosing subject *obliges* engagement, an 'ethic of autonomy' (Greco, 1993; Murtagh and Hepworth, 2003), and thereby serves to intensify power relations. The menopausal woman given the choice to take HRT or not to take HRT is not allowed the choice not to engage in this decision; the construction of menopause as a medical concern positions her as having no choice but to choose. On this reading 'decision-making' not the doctor–patient relationship becomes the disciplinary technology[3]. The exercise of agency in the doctor–patient relationship must, conceptually, include not choosing. But can you act as an agent and not choose? Resistance to 'decision-making' *per se* was indeed evident in research presented during the 2007 International Shared Decision-Making conference in Freiburg (see also Chapter 2, Holmes-Rovner). Emerging accounts demonstrate that some patients in some circumstances resist involvement in decision-making about their health. This refusal of decision-making should not be confused with meta-preferences that are associated with age, gender, and education (Say et al., 2006). Differentiation on the basis of these population level characteristics provide insufficient explanation of whether or not, in any given circumstance, an individual patient wants to be actively involved in decision-making.

Conclusion

The shift evident within the doctor–patient relationship towards patient-centredness and patient engagement in decision-making is not necessarily the emancipation demanded by the social movements of the last century. Arguably, it never could have been. Nonetheless, power relations continue (and will continue) to shape the experience and outcomes of health care decision-making. How these shifts will manifest themselves requires not only an elaboration of our understanding of power and the doctor–patient relationship but also of decision-making itself. Charles and colleagues argued that decision-making is a process that takes place over time, can involve many individuals, and certainly is not restricted to the doctor–patient relationship (Charles et al., 1999). Rapley (see also Chapter 8) demonstrated with empirical examples the distributedness of decisions over time, place, person, and technology (Rapley, 2008). But decisions are also contextual, both materially and symbolically. The socioeconomic and cultural environment, the experience of health and health care *matter* in decision-making; the meanings attached to health and illness *matter*. Moreover, decisions are always relational and we do not understand enough yet about the relational. If we are to engage with issues of power in decision-making we need at a minimum to engage in a more fully formed concept of decision-making than available to us via descriptions of the rational autonomous subject. A schema that at least includes decision-making as relational, contextual, and distributed is essential.

---

[3] Elsewhere I outline the problems with this reading. **Murtagh, M.J.** (2008), 'A funny thing happened on the way to the journal: A commentary on Foucault's ethics and Stuart Murray's 'Care of the self', *Philosophy, Ethics and Humanities in Medicine*, 2008, **3**, 2.

References

Armstrong, D. (1979). The emancipation of biographical medicine. *Social Science and Medicine*, **13**, 1–8.

Balint, M. (2000). *The Doctor, His Patient and the Illness*, Churchill Livingstone.

Balint, M., Hunt, J., Joyce, D. *et al.* (1970). *Treatment or Diagnosis: A Study of Repeat Prescriptions in General Practice*. London: Tavistock Publications.

Bell, S.E. (1987). Changing ideas: The medicalization of menopause. *Social Science and Medicine*, **24**, 535–542.

Burges Watson, D., Thomson, R.G. and Murtagh, M.J. (2008). Professional centred shared decision making: Patient decision aids in practice in primary care. *BMC Health Services Research*, **8**, 5.

Charles, C., Whelan, T., and Gafni, A. (1999). What do we mean by partnership in making decisions about treatment? *British Medical Journal*, **319**, 780.

Chew-Graham, C.A., May, C.R., and Roland, M.O. (2004). *The Harmful Consequences of Elevating the Doctor-Patient Relationship to be a Primary Goal of the General Practice Consultation*. Oxford University Press.

Collective, B.W.S.H. (1973). *Our Bodies, Ourselves*. New York: Simon and Schuster.

Darzi, (2008). *High Quality Care for All*: NHS Next Stage Review final report', Crown.

Dean, M. (2007). *Governing Societies*: Open University Press.

Dent, M. (2006). Patient choice and medicine in health care. *Public Management Review*, **8**, 449–462.

Ehrenreich, B. and English, D. (1973). *Witches, Midwives, and Nurses: A History of Women Healers*, Feminist Press.

Ehrenreich, B. and English, D. (2005). *For Her Own Good: Two Centuries of the Experts' Advice to Women*. New York: Anchor Books.

Florin, D. and Dixon, J. (2004). Public involvement in health care. *British Medical Journal*, **328**, 159.

Foucault, M., Martin, L.H., Gutman, H. *et al.* (1988). *Technologies of the Self: A Seminar with Michel Foucault*. University of Massachusetts Press.

Friedson, E. (1970). *The Profession of Medicine*. New York: Dodd Mead.

Gothill, M. and Armstrong, D. (1999). Dr. No-body: The construction of the doctor as an embodied subject in British General Practice 195597'. *Sociology of Health & Illness*, **21**, 1–12.

Greco, M. (1993). Psychosomatic subjects and the 'duty to be well'. Personal agency within. *Economy Society*, **22**, 357–372.

Heath, C. (1984). Participation in the medical consultation: The co-ordination of verbal and nonverbal behavior between the doctor and patient. *Sociology of Health & Illness*, **6**, 311–338.

Illich, I. (1976). *Limits to Medicine: Medical Nemesis: The Expropriation of Health*, London: Boyars.

Jewson, N.D. (1974). Medical knowledge and the patronage system in 18th century england. *Sociology*, **8**, 369.

Lemke, T. (2001). The birth of bio-politics: Michel Foucault's lecture at the Collège de France on neo-liberal governmentality. *Economy Society*, **30**, 190–207.

Litva, A., Coast, J., Donovan, J. *et al.* (2002). The public is too subjective: Public involvement at different levels of health-care decision making. *Social Science & Medicine*, **54**, 1825–1837.

May, C., Allison, G., Chapple, A. *et al.* (2004). Framing the doctor-patient relationship in chronic illness: A comparative study of general practitioners' accounts'. *Sociology of Health & Illness*, **26**, 135–158.

Murtagh, M.J. (2008). A funny thing happened on the way to the journal: A commentary on Foucault's ethics and Stuart Murray's Care of the self. *Philosophy, Ethics, and Humanities in Medicine*, **3**, 2.

Murtagh, M.J. and Hepworth, J. (2003). Feminist ethics and menopause: Autonomy and decision-making in primary medical care. *Social Science & Medicine*, **56**, 1643–1652.

Nettleton, S. (2006). *The sociology of health and illness* (2nd Edition). Cambridge, MA: Polity Press.

Parsons, T. (1991). *The Social System*, Routledge.

Rapley, T. (2008). Distributed decision making: The anatomy of decisions-in-action. *Sociology of Health & Illnes*, **30**, 3.

Rose, N.S. (1999). *Powers of Freedom: Reframing Political Thought*. Cambridge University Press.

Ruzek, S. (2007). Transforming doctor–patient relationships. *Journal of Health Services Research and Policy*, **12**, 181–182.

Say, R., Murtagh, M., and Thomson, R. (2006). 'Patients' preference for involvement in medical decision making: A narrative review. *Patient Education and Counseling*, **60**(2), 102–114.

Stimson, G.V. and Webb, B. (1975). *Going to See the Doctor: The Consultation Process in General Practice*. Routledge & Kegan Paul Books.

Strong, P.M. (1979). *The Ceremonial Order of the Clinic: Parents, Doctors, and Medical Bureaucracies*. Routledge & Kegan Paul Books.

Waitzkin, H. (1984). Doctor–patient communication. Clinical implications of social scientific research. *JAMA*, **252** (17), 2441–2446.

Zola, I.K. (1972). Medicine as an institution of social control *Sociol. Rev.*, **20** (4), 487–504.

Section 3

Conceptual developments

Chapter 13

Informed Choice: A construct in search of a name

Theresa M. Marteau

Introduction

'Informed choice' is a relatively recent addition to the lexicon of health care providers and policy makers. This reflects broader social trends in the changing status and roles of consumers and professionals and a revolution in the accessibility of information.

This chapter sets out to define informed choice and describe how it relates to similar other terms of informed consent, autonomy, and shared decision-making. Ways of measuring informed choice are outlined prior to considering the extent to which health-related choices are, can, and indeed, should be informed. The chapter ends by acknowledging the failure of the term *informed choice* to capture its central concept of people acting in line with deeply held values.

Informed choice

Many different terms are used, often interchangeably, to encompass informed choice, including informed or effective decisions and evidence-based choices. Two core characteristics emerge: first, the decision maker understands the relevant evidence, and second, the choice reflects the values of the decision-maker (Bekker *et al.*, 1999, Entwistle and Watt, 2006). Based on O'Connor and colleagues' definition of an effective decision (1989), the first operational definition of an informed choice comprises a third characteristic, namely the enactment of the choice, resulting in the following definition:

> An informed choice is one that is based on relevant knowledge, consistent with the decision-maker's values and behaviourally implemented
>
> Marteau, Dormandy and Michie, 2001

These three key elements of an informed choice are also echoed in definitions of *informed decision-making* (Rimer *et al.*, 2004; Bekker *et al.*, 2004; Irwig *et al.*, 2006; Jepson *et al.*, 2005; Dowie, 2002). This definition does, however, beg a number of questions – principally concerning the definition of relevant knowledge and salient values. The former has been the focus of discussion elsewhere (e.g. Marteau *et al.*, 2001; Michie *et al.*, 2003; Irwig *et al.*, 2006). The latter is considered below.

Measuring informed choice

Based on O'Connor's definition of a good decision as one that is informed, consistent with the decision-maker's values, and behaviourally implemented, choices can be classified as informed or not; depending upon the extent to which the individual making the choice has the information

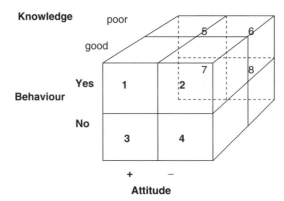

Figure 13.1 Classifying choices and informed, based on the three dimensions of knowledge, attitudes, and behaviour. Eight cells denote informed (cells 1 and 4) and uninformed (2, 3, 5, 6, 7, 8) choices, depending upon knowledge and attitude-behaviour consistency.

judged relevant, the choice reflects their values, and they act upon it (Marteau *et al.*, 2001; Michie *et al.*, 2003; Figure 13.1).

Using this operationalization, services can be classified in terms of the proportions of their populations making informed choices, as has been done in the context of screening in pregnancy (Dormandy *et al.*, 2002; van den Berg *et al.*, 2005; Rowe *et al.*, 2006; Kellar *et al.*, 2008). The nature of uninformed choices (i.e. whether reflecting lack of knowledge or value-behaviour inconsistency) can also be described, and the characteristics of those least likely to make informed choices can be characterized (e.g. Dormandy *et al.*, 2005). Our measure, based around this analysis, is the first measure to attempt to capture three components of informed choices (Marteau et al., 2001). While a useful beginning, further conceptual and psychometric work is needed, particularly in the measurement of values and value-choice consistency.

While the measurement of knowledge is not a trivial matter (requiring an agreed domain of knowledge as well as valid measurement) there are many examples of good measures (O'Connor *et al.*, 2003). Measurements of values and value-consistent choices have received less attention. Thus, despite a consensus that decision aids should facilitate treatment choices that reflect patients' values, Kennedy (2003) found no study that attempted to measure value-choice consistency. In O'Connor's review of 35 trials of decision aids, just four attempted to assess value-choice consistency (O'Connor *et al.*, 2003). Not only are values central to the concept of informed choice and decision-making, but also they are better predictors of enacted choices than are knowledge (Dormandy *et al.*, 2002; Kellar 2008). In the context of screening, for example, increasing knowledge does not affect either attitudes towards screening, intentions to attend, or actual attendance (Fox, 2006; Kellar *et al.*, 2008; Mathieu *et al.*, 2007; Trevena *et al.*, 2008).

Values can be considered as principles that reflect broad goals that apply across contexts and time (Rokeach, 1973; Schwartz 1992; Bardi and Schwartz, 2003). Each person holds numerous values with varying degrees of importance, and the potential to be in conflict with each other. Two related approaches are discernible to measuring values that inform decisions. The first involves the assessment of individual's attitudes towards themselves selecting different options (Marteau *et al.*, 2001). The other involves the use of expected utilities (EU) *i.e.* the incorporation into assessments of both the utility of an outcome and its perceived likelihood (Holmes-Rovner *et al.*, 1999). The strength of association between attitudes or expected utilities of a choice with the enacted choice is then used to assess the extent to which a choice is consistent with the values of the decision-maker. The extent to which these measures are tapping core values, as traditionally conceptualized and measured (Rokeach, 1973; Schwartz, 1992) is unknown. These simple measures also provide little insight into the potentially competing values individuals may hold when contemplating health-related decisions including the extent to which ambivalence (the holding of both positive and negative attitudes) undermines the enactment of informed choices (Dormandy *et al.*, 2005). Conceptual development, drawing upon a wider range of philosophical and psychological theories than currently inform research in this area, should lead to measures that better capture the values that underlie human health-related decisions.

Informed choice, shared decision-making, informed consent, and autonomy

These terms differ in the extent to which they focus upon the processes by which a decision is made (shared decision-making) or the components of the decision *per se* (informed choice, informed consent, and autonomy).

Shared decision-making

Shared decision-making characterizes the process by which a decision is made, not the characteristics of the actual decision (Entwistle and Watt, 2006). It is, therefore, possible for the process by which a decision is made to be shared between doctor and patient but for the decision to be characterized as uninformed either because the patient lacked relevant knowledge or because they acted inconsistently with their values. While this delineation between process and outcome of decision-making is blurred in some descriptions of informed choice or decision-making (e.g., Davey *et al.*, 2005; Irwig *et al.*, 2006; Bekker *et al.*, 2004), it seems vital to maintain the distinction between process and outcome to achieve much needed conceptual clarity in this area.

Informed consent

Informed consent is primarily a legal construct referring to consent based on an understanding of the implications of an action before proceeding. The operationalization of informed consent varies in different jurisdictions. In English law, the information an individual needs to have understood is that which a majority of practitioners would usually provide although recent judgments suggest that patients need to be informed of all 'material' risks. In the United States, Canada, and Australia significant risks require disclosure (what a reasonable patient might want to know) as well as risks which may be of importance to the particular individual. This simplistic account of the concept belies its contested nature (O'Neill, 2003). For a fuller account, see Chapter 23 by Mazur. Informed consent, however defined, differs from informed choice in two important ways. First, informed consent is not explicitly concerned with the understanding of those not consenting. Second, it is not explicitly concerned with the consenting individual's values.

Autonomy

The concept of autonomy has long roots into a number of philosophies (for review, see Ryan and Deci, 2006). Building on these and related psychological theories, autonomy can be defined as regulation by the self, a construct closely related to choice and freedom, the opposite being heteronomy or controlled regulation (Ryan and Deci, 2006). Autonomy is thus defined not by an absence of external influences but by the individual's assent to any such influences or inputs. By defining autonomous acts as those that are endorsed by the whole self, Ryan and Deci (2006) note that individuals can be autonomously dependent, or forced into independence.

This definition allows one to see the false opposition in such statements as '. . . the reaction of sick doctors can ironically be to prefer paternalism to personal autonomy' (from Stirrat and Gill, 2005). By conceptualizing autonomy as distinct from acting independently, a preference for paternalism can arguably be seen as compatible with autonomy. The extent to which scholars and practitioners see it this way will depend upon their concepts of autonomy and the extent to which these reflect the moral principles as envisaged, for example, by Kant (O'Neill, 2002) as opposed to an individual rights perspective invoked by the worst excesses of 'American Bioethics' (Wolpe, 1998).

Realizing informed choices

One reason for developing measures of informed choice is to be able to describe the extent to which choices are informed as a basis for evaluating and improving services that set out to facilitate such choices. There is good evidence that written information and more elaborate decisions aids are effective in improving short-term knowledge, with more intensive interventions being most effective (Fox, 2006; Rimer et al., 2004; O'Connor et al., 2003).

By contrast, there is little evidence regarding the most effective ways of increasing value–behaviour consistency (Rimer, 2004; Kellar et al., 2008). In a review of decision aids, there is little evidence that their use increases the value consistency of decisions (Feldman-Stewart et al., 2006). Value-choice inconsistency can occur when individuals act upon desires that – after reflection – they prefer not to have acted upon, reflecting a concept of autonomy as 'acting in ways that upon reflection are those that are preferred' (Frankfurt, 1971; Sen, 1977). Environmental interventions such as bans on smoking in public places or the use of incentives to motivate behaviour that meets valued or so-called second-order desires (i.e. those that we have reflected on and which might override our basic desires (Dworkin, 1988) can enhance value-choice consistency. While some consider such approaches coercive, others suggest that they can be seen as forms of *paternalistic liberalism* which allow individuals to act in ways they prefer, *i.e.* consistent with their values (Thaler and Sulstein, 2008).

Another approach to increasing the likelihood that individuals enact the choices that reflect their values is *action planning*. This involves individuals stating when, where, and how they propose to implement their intended actions (Gollwitzer and Sheeran, 2006). Recent research on unconscious processing of information suggests that distraction rather than deliberation upon the pros and cons of different options may also increase value-consistency (Dijksterhuis et al., 2006).

To what extent should choices be informed?

The value of informed choices in different health care contexts is debated. For some health-related interventions individual choice is neither possible nor desirable. Choice may not be possible given the nature of the intervention, such as water fluoridation (O'Neill, 2003), or may be constrained by an individual's cognitive capacity (Applebaum, 2007). Its use may also be deemed undesirable when an intervention seems to pose no substantive individual risk but substantive population benefit, such as the use of medical records in anonymized form for research (Metcalfe et al., 2008). This raises the question of who decides on which options the resources should be spent in facilitating informed choices. Salmon and Hall (2004) argue that many patients do not value the various offers of choice that characterize contemporary health care in many economically developed countries. They argue that its imposition can be seen, ironically, as health care professionals are imposing their choices (*i.e.* to offer choices) on patients. O'Connor et al. (2003) suggest that the effort expended in facilitating informed choices should vary depending upon whether the decision concerns an 'effective' or a 'preference-sensitive' intervention. Others have argued that it should depend upon the level of risk involved in a decision (O'Neill, 2003).

Beyond these considerations, the desire to be engaged in decision-making varies with health status, personality, and education, as well as between cultures (Auerbach, 2001; Degner and Sloan 1992; Flynn and Smith, 2007; Chirkov *et al.*, 2003). Evaluation of the benefits (including the value) and cost of facilitating informed choices for different individuals in different health care contexts might usefully inform the question of the extent to which choices should be informed.

Concluding comment

The core concept characterizing an 'informed choice' is that of an individual acting in line with deeply held values, a concept that this and similar other terms, fail to communicate. Such a failing is also reflected in the paucity of research on value-consistent choices under the various terms of informed choice and informed decision-making. Grounding future work on informed choice and its related constructs in the richer theoretical terrains of philosophical and psychological work on autonomy has the potential to address this failing. A term is now needed that captures the multiple concepts of 'informed, enacted, value-consistent choices' that comprise an informed choice.

Acknowledgements

I am extremely grateful to my colleagues for discussions on the ideas in this chapter, in particular Elizabeth Dormandy, Ian Kellar, Eleanor Mann, Rachel Crockett, Ann Louise Kinmonth, Richard Ashcroft, and Ainsley Newson.

References

Applebaum, P. (2007). Assessment of patient's competence to consent to treatment. *N. Engl. J. Med.*, **357**, 1834–1840.

Auerbach, S. (2001). Do patients want control over their own health care? A review of measures, findings and research issues. *Journal of Health Psychology*, **6**, 191–203.

Bardi, A. and Schwartz, S.H. (2003). Values and behavior: Strength and structure of relations. *Personality and Social Psychology Bulletin*, **29**, 1207–1220.

Bekker, H., Thornton, J., Airey, M., *et al.* (1999). *Informed Decision-Making: An Annotate Bibliography and Systematic Review.* Health Technology Assessment. **3**(1).

Bekker, H.L., Hewison, J., and Thorton, J.G. (2004). Applying decision analysis to facilitate informed decision making about prenatal diagnosis for Down's syndrome: A randomised controlled trial. *Prenatal Diagnosis*, **24**, 265–275.

Chirkov, V., Ryan, R., Kim, Y., *et al.* (2003). Differentiating autonomy from individualism and independence: A self-determination theory perspective on internalization of cultural orientations and well-being. *J. Pers. Soc. Psychol.*, **84**, 97–110.

Davey, C., White, V., Gattellari, M., *et al.* (2005). Reconciling population benefits and women's individual autonomy in mammographic screening: In-depth interviews to explore women's views about 'informed choice'. *Australian and New Zealand Journal of Public Health*, **29**, 69–77.

Degner, L.F., Sloan, J.F. (1992). Decision making during serious illness: What role do patients really want to play? *J Clinical Epidemiology*, **45**, 944–950.

Dijksterhuis, A., Bos, M.W., Nordgren, L.F., *et al.* (2006).On making the right choice: The deliberation-without-attention effect. *Science*, **311**, 1005–1007.

Dormandy, E., Hooper, R., Michie, S., *et al.* (2002). Informed choice to undergo prenatal screening: A comparison of two hospitals conducting testing either as part of a routine visit or requiring a separate visit. *Journal of Medical Screening*, **9**, 109–114.

Dormandy, E., Michie, S., Hooper, R., *et al.* (2005). Low uptake of prenatal screening for Down syndrome in minority ethnic groups and socially deprived groups: A reflection of women's attitudes or a failure to facilitate informed choices? *International Journal of Epidemiology*, **34**, 346–352.

Dowie, J. (2002). The role of patients' meta-preferences in the design and evaluation of decision support systems. *Health Expert*, **5**, 16–27.

Dworkin, G. (1988). *The Theory and Practice of Autonomy*. Cambridge: Cambridge University Press.

Entwistle, V.A. and Watt, I.S. (2006). Patient involved in treatment decision-making: The case for a broader conceptual framework. *Patient Education and Counseling*, **63**, 268–278.

Feldman-Stewart, D., Brennenstuhl, S., Brundage, M.D., *et al.* (2006). An explicit values clarification task: Development and validation. *Patient Education and Counseling*, **63**, 350–356.

Flynn, K.E. and Smith, M.A. (2007). Personality and health care decision-making style. *Journal of Gerontology*, **62b**, 261–267.

Fox, R.(2006). Informed choice in screening programmes: Do leaflets help? A critical literature review. *J. Public Health*, **28**, 309–317.

Frankfurt, H.(1971). Freedom of the will and the concept of a person. *The Journal of Philosophy*, **68**, 5–20.

Gollwitzer, P. and Sheeran, P. (2006). Implementation intentions and goal achievement: A meta-analysis of effects and processes. *Advances in Experimental Social Psychology*, **38**, 69–87.

Holmes-Rovner, M., Kroll, J., Rovner, D., *et al.* (1999). Patient decision support intervention: Increased consistency with decision analytic models. *Medical Care*, **37**, 270–284.

Irwig, L., McCaffery, K., Salkeld, G., *et al.* (2006). Informed choice for screening: Implications for evaluation. *Br. Med. J.*, **332**, 1148–1150.

Jepson, R., Hewison, J., Thompson, A., *et al.* (2005).How should we measure informed choice? The case of cancer screening. *J. Med. Ethics*, **31**, 192–196.

Kellar, I., Sutton, S., Griffin, S., *et al.* (2008). Evaluation of an informed choice invitation for type 2 diabetes screening. *Patient Education & Counseling*, **72**, 232–238.

Kennedy, A.D.M. (2003). On what basis should the effectiveness of decision aids be judged? *Health Expectations*, **6**, 255–268.

Marteau, T.M., Dormandy, E., and Michie, S. (2001). A measure of informed choice. *Health Expectations*, **4**, 99–108.

Mathieu, E., Barratt, A., Davey, H.M., *et al.* (2007). Informed choice in mammography screening: A randomized trial of a decision aid for 70-Year-Old Women. *Arch. Intern. Med.*, **167**, 2039–2046

Metcalfe, C., Martin, R.M., Noble, S., *et al.* (2008). Low risk research using routinely collected identifiable health information without informed consent: Encounters with the Patient Information Advisory Group. *J. Med. Ethics*, **34**, 37–40.

Michie, S., Dormandy, E., and Marteau, T.M. (2003). Informed choice: Understanding knowledge in the context of screening uptake. *Patient Education and Counseling. Couns.*, **50**, 247–253.

O'Connor, A., Stacey, D., Entwistle, V., *et al.* (2003). Decision aids for people facing health treatment or screening decisions. Cochrane Database of Systematic Reviews, 1. CD001431. DOI: 10.1002/14651858. CD001431.

O'Connor, A. and O'Brien-Pallas, L. (1989). Decisional conflict. In G.K. Mcfarlane and E.A. Mcfarlane (eds) Nursing Diagnosis and Intervention. Toronto: Mosby. pp 486–496.

O'Connor, A.M., Legare, F., and Stacey, L.D. (2003). Risk Communication in practice: The contribution of decision aids. *Br. Med. J.*, **327**, 736–740.

O'Neill O. (2002). *Autonomy and Trust in Bioethics*. Cambridge: Cambridge University Press.

O'Neill O. (2003). Some limits of informed consent. *J. Med. Ethics*, **29**, 1–5.

Rimer, B., Briss, P., Zeller, P., *et al.* (2004). Informed decision making: What is its role in cancer screening. *American Cancer Society*, **101**, 1214–1228.

Rokeach, M. (1973). *The Nature of Human Values*. New York: Free Press.

Rowe, H., Fisher, J., and Quinlivan, J. (2006). Are pregnant Australian women well informed about prenatal genetic screening? A systematic investigation using the multidimensional measure of informed choice. *Australian and New Zealand Journal of Obstetrics & Gynaecology*, **46**, 433–439.

Ryan, R.M. and Deci, E.L. (2006). Self-regulation and the problem of human autonomy: Does psychology need choice, self-determination, and will? *J. Pers.*, **74**, 1557–1586.

Salmon, P. and Hall, G. (2004). Patient empowerment or the emperor's new clothe. *Journal of the Royal Society of Medicine*, **97**, 53–56.

Schwartz, S.H. (1992). Universals in the context and structure of values: Theoretical advances and empirical tests in 20 countries. In M.P. Zanna (ed). *Advances in Experimental Social Psychology* New York: Academic Press. Vol. **25**. pp. 1–65.

Sen, A. (1977). Rational fools: A critique of the behavioural foundations of economic theory. *Philosophy and Public Affairs*, **6**, 317–344.

Stirrat, G.M. and Gill, R. (2005). Autonomy in medical ethics after O'Neill. *J. Med. Ethics*, **31**, 127–130.

Thaler, R.H. and Sulstein, C.R. (2008). Nudge: Improving decisions about health, wealth and happiness. New Haven, CT: Yale University Press.

Trevena, L.J., Irwig, L., and Barratt, A. (2008). randomised trial of a self-administered decision aid for colorectal cancer screening. *J. Med. Genet.*

van den Berg, M., Timmermans, D., Ten Kate, L., *et al.* (2005). Are pregnant women making informed choices about prenatal screening? *Genetic Medicine*, **7**, 332–338.

Wolpe, P.R. (1998). The triumph of autonomy in American bioethics: A sociological view. In R. Devries and J. Subedi (eds) *Bioethics and Society: Sociological Investigations of the Enterprise of Bioethics*. Englewood Cliff, NJ: Prentice Hall. pp. 38–59.

Chapter 14

Developing expert patients

Anne Rogers

Introduction

In the recent past, the concept of an 'Expert Patient' has been associated with patient-centred consultations within health care, and primary care in particular. In the ground breaking publication 'A Meeting Between Experts' by David Tuckett and colleagues, patients were viewed as experts by virtue of the experience of living with an illness which placed them on an equal, if different, footing with health professionals in the consultation (Tuckett, 1985). The notion has recently been re-surfaced in the UK policy context of the *Expert Patients' Programme* which is associated with a particular vision of a future ideal-type patient (see http://www.expertpatients. co.uk/). A patient perspective in health care policy and practice is not new and a philosophy of 'consumerism' has been evident in many health policies over the last 20 years (Calnan, 2001). However, the fulfilment of the contemporary policy vision of chronic disease management goes further, requiring a certain type of patient – the 'empowered' or 'expert' self-caring individual, and includes the need for individuals to have the capacity to be more confident and internalize control. This is in order to promote the monitoring and management of chronic conditions whilst allowing a person to be influenced by external supply constraints such as the need to limit demands on services (Chapple, 1999).

The context in which Expert Patients are expected to operate was laid out in the UK's 'Wanless review'. This explored three different scenarios, including a 'fully engaged' scenario in which the level of public engagement in relation to health is high, life expectancy goes beyond current forecasts, health status improves dramatically, use of resources is more efficient, and the health service is responsive with high rates of technology uptake. The fully engaged scenario was *both* the least expensive scenario modelled and delivered better health outcomes (Wanless, 2003). Wanless viewed the benefits of becoming Expert Patients:

'My inquiry showed that encouraging and supporting self-care was one of a number of actions which could potentially save the economy billions of pounds ... patients remain far from fully engaged in their own care; opportunities are being lost and inequalities reinforced.'

(www.healthfoundation.co.uk)

Subsequently, policy makers have presented different desirable facets of what it is to be an Expert Patient in the context of preventing poor health, managing health, and illness in the health service. Additionally, there has been a proliferation of associated terms ('empowered', 'autonomous', 'future', 'expert', 'activated', 'wireless', 'co-producer', or 'flat pack patient') representing an idealized individual with the abilities to bring about a desirable relationship between the self-managing patient and health services. The notion of an activated patient is of particular salience as it involves the formulation of a number of desirable outcomes for assessing 'activation' in self- management, involving four 'developmental' stages: (1) coming to believe the patient role is important, (2) learning enough and developing enough confidence and knowledge necessary to take action, (3) actually taking action to maintain and improve one's health, and

(4) staying as healthy as possible (Hibbard, 2007). A key mechanism for achieving this vision of a re-engineered patienthood is self-care skills training.

Making expert patients through the use of self-care skills training for long-term conditions

The UK Department of Health envisages service delivery for long-term conditions designed around three tiers:

+ *case management* for people with complex conditions
+ *disease management* for patients at some risk, through programmes in primary care
+ *self-care support* for low-risk patients (70–80% of those with long-term conditions).

In relation to the last of these, the Expert Patients Programme (EPP) in England aimed to improve the quality-of-life of a person with long-term conditions, by developing generic self-care skills, confidence, and motivation to take more effective control over one's life and illness. The 6 week course based on the Chronic Disease Self Management Programme (CDSMP) developed at the University of Stanford California operates on an open referral basis available to anyone with a long-term condition and is designed to be delivered by trained volunteers or paid trainers licensed to deliver the course (see http://patienteducation.stanford.edu/programs/cdsmp.html). Kate Lorig views the CDSMPCDMSP as being able to deliver 'confident, knowledgeable patients practicing self-management who will experience improved health status and will utilise fewer health care resources' (Lorig, 2003). The course is orientated to Expert Patients learning relaxation, better breathing, healthy eating and nutrition, exercise and how to build levels of fitness, flexibility and strength, how to communicate more effectively, making informed choices, dealing with anger, fear, frustration, isolation, fatigue and depression, using problem solving skills, how to make plans that work for individuals, and working with health care professionals.

The evidence base includes randomized controlled trials of the CDSMP from the United States and elsewhere, using an evaluative framework as shown in Figure 14.1. These have suggested that chronic disease self-management could improve health status while reducing hospitalization (Lorig, 1999, 2003; Fu, 2003). However, when considering the roll-out of a similar programme in England, the results of these studies were not viewed as directly transferable to the NHS. The application scope was limited by the lack of an economic analysis. Additionally, whereas previous trials centred on specific conditions, the UK programme centred around a generic course for long-term conditions. An evaluation produced results showing a medium effect on self-efficacy and little effect on routine utilization of services. There were small improvements in secondary outcomes which included improvements to social role, emotions, health distress, exercise, relaxation, and partnership working between patients and professionals (Kennedy, 2007). The programme is, however, likely to be cost-effective with the intervention group showing better EQ5D scores (0.020 QALY gain) and is found to have reduced costs, estimated to be about £27 per patient (Richardson, 2008). Other UK trials have shown similar results (Griffiths, 2007).

Patient experience of the EPP

Self-efficacy is considered to be a central construct of how the EPP programme is designed to work (Rogers, 2006). Self-efficacy as an outcome was valued amongst the participants of the EPP trial during its pilot phase (Richardson, 2008). However, the importance of self-efficacy as an outcome measure more generally may have been overplayed compared to other expected outcomes and experiences of patients. For example, in a study using mixed qualitative methods

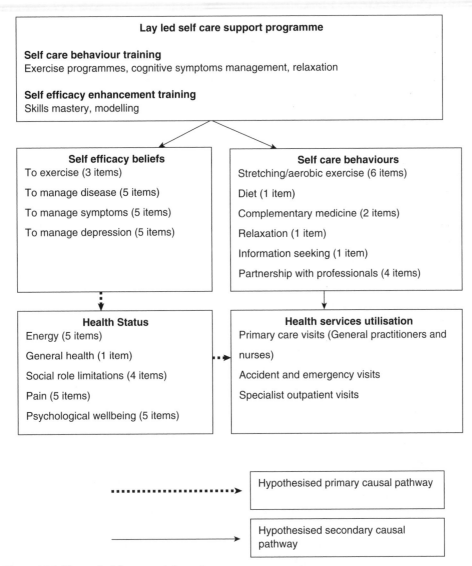

Figure 14.1 Theoretical framework for outcomes measurement.

some peoples' expectations and problems were not adequately dealt with because the self-care skills training programme prioritized improvements in self-efficacy and did not engage with patients' material and social needs (Kennedy, 2007). Thus, an approach which emphasizes improvements in self-efficacy may inadvertently sideline the relevance of the existence of social inequalities in chronic illness and the personal experience of chronic illness. For instance, a social comparison, which group-based programs rely on for mediating self-efficacy, can have a negative effect if positive comparisons by individuals cannot be made. Being poor and ill brings with it the possibility of shame and insecurity (Wilkinson, 2005) that may be reinforced in group situations, and the relatively poor uptake and attendance indicate the failure of the course to appeal to a wide range of patients (Griffiths, 2005).

The use of the term Expert Patient has itself caused controversy because of its lack of resonance and appeal to those it is aimed to win over - exemplified by this comment from a respondent from the process evaluation of the EPP (Kennedy, 2005):

> Everybody says they hate it. Even the patients ... have said they don't like it because they say just because they've got some sort of disability or disease doesn't mean they're a patient ... And of course the GPs and the consultants don't like the 'expert' part of it because ... they see it in a threatening, 'I know what's best, you know kind of way.
>
> (PCT ID 61)

The EPP also seems to attract people with values and behaviour already congruent with policy rather than to address those who do not hold such values. Those people who prefer to normalize chronic illness and its management rather than to participate in active engagement and constant self-surveillance and reflexivity are not embraced by the EPP (Gately, 2007).

There is some evidence which suggests that even if patients were to adopt the values of Expert Patients, this would not necessarily lead to improvements. Recent research suggests that patients with or at risk of developing a chronic condition who say they prefer to take an active role in their health care could be unhealthier in some respects than patients who prefer doctors to act in a more traditional way. Baldwin et al. showed that respondents who said that patients and doctors should be on a more equal footing when it came to treatment decisions had higher blood pressure and cholesterol scores than their peers (Baldwin, 2008). This raised the question whether being a more active participant actually translates into better biomedical health outcomes (Hibbard, 2007).

Finally, the absence of a link between participating in self-management interventions for chronic illness and activation is also evident. A controlled trial of a self-management intervention for people with chronic illness found there were no significant differences in activation between the intervention and control groups, begging the question also as to what type of intervention would improve activation (Kennedy, 2007).

So what is the future for the competencies associated with the ideal of the Expert Patient? It is clear from the existing evidence that the challenge for both self-skills training and the notion of an Expert Patient requires location in a wider context of professional behaviour change and community engagement. Effective self-care support requires two key changes in thinking. Firstly, a whole systems perspective that engages patient, practitioner, and service organization levels in the delivery of self-care support and secondly, widening the evidence base, to acknowledge recent research on the way in which patients and professionals respond to long-term conditions (Richardson, 2006). Such a whole systems perspective has been utilized in a model developed at the University of Manchester (the WISE model) which envisages the interaction between three levels: informed patients who receive support and guidance from trained practitioners working within a health care system geared up to be responsive to the needs of self-caring patients (Wilkinson, 2005). Whether or not such an approach can be adopted to complement the current financial incentivised Chronic Disease Management approach in general practice (the 'Quality Outcomes Framework') is a moot point.

Conclusion

The idea of an Expert Patient is associated with an agenda of patient empowerment in which the use of information and attitudinal attributes are seen as a means of democratization. Self-skills training programmes have been the key mechanism to achieve a policy vision of widespread expert patienthood compatible with an effective and cost-efficient patient-centred health service. The challenge for this vision includes the need to capture a broad appeal to those most likely to benefit from adopting the values of being an expert patient. A further challenge is the equivocal evidence that these values will lead to the desired outcomes envisaged by policy makers. The desire for normalization in conducting everyday life and suspicions about the advantages of self-care activities are reminiscent of the prevention paradox which has been identified as a key barrier to adoption of healthy lifestyles in primary prevention (Davison, 1992). Therefore, some people may be cautious about engaging with interventions such as the EPP. Currently, the evidence points to the need for a negotiated individually tailored approach and a key issue for success will be the extent to which variegated patient expertise and experience can be embedded into the routine activities of the health service.

References

Baldwin, A., Cvengros, J., Christensen, A., *et al.* (2008). Preferences for a patient-centered role orientation: Association with patient-information-seeking behavior and clinical markers of health. *Ann. Behav. Med.*, 35, 80–86.

Calnan, M. and Gabe, J. (2001). From consumerism to partnership? Britain's National Health Service at the turn of the century. *Int. J. Health. Serv.*, 31, 119–131.

Chapple, A. and Rogers, A. (1999). 'Self-care' and its relevance to developing demand management strategies: A review of qualitative research. *Health. Soc. Care. Community*, 7, 445–454.

Davison, C., Franke, S. and Smith, G. (1992). The limits of lifestyle: Re-assessing 'fatalism' in the popular culture of illness prevention. *Soc. Sci. Med.*, 34, 675–685.

Fu, D., Fu, H., McGowan, P., *et al.* (2003). Implementation and quantitative evaluation of chronic disease self-management programme in Shanghai, China: Randomized controlled trial. *Bull. World. Health. Organ.*, 81, 174–182.

Gately, C., Rogers, A. and Sanders, C. (2007). Re-thinking the relationship between long-term condition self-management education and the utilisation of health services. *Soc. Sci. Med.*, 65, 934–945.

Griffiths, C., Foster, G., Ramsay, J., *et al.* (2007). How effective are expert patient (lay led) education programmes for chronic disease? *Br. Med. J.*, 334, 1254–1256.

Griffiths, C., Motlib, J., Azad, A., *et al.* (2005). Randomised controlled trial of a lay-led self-management programme for Bangladeshi patients with chronic disease. *Br. J. Gen. Pract.*, 55, 831–837.

Hibbard, J., Mahoney, E., Stock, R., *et al.* (2007). Do increases in patient activation result in improved self-management behaviors? *Health. Serv. Res.*, 42, 1443–1463.

Kennedy, A., Gately, C., Rogers, A., *et al.* (2005), *Process Evaluation of the EPP Report II: Examination of the implementation of the Expert Patients Programme within the structures and locality contexts of the NHS in England (PREPP study).* Manchester: NPCRDC.

Kennedy, A., Reeves, D., Bower, P., *et al.* (2007). The effectiveness and cost effectiveness of a national lay-led self care support programme for patients with long-term conditions: A pragmatic randomised controlled trial. *J. Epidemiol. Community Health*, 61, 254–261.

Kennedy, A., Rogers, A., and Bower, P. (2007). Support for self care for patients with chronic disease. *Br. Med. J.*, 335, 9689–9670.

Kennedy, A., Rogers, A., and Crossley, M. (2007). Participation, roles, and the dynamics of change in a group-delivered self-management course for people living with HIV. *Qual. Health. Res.*, 17, 744–758.

Lorig, K., Sobel, D., Stewart, A., *et al.* (1999). Evidence suggesting that a chronic disease self-management program can improve health status while reducing hospitalization: A randomized trial. *Med. Care*, 37, 5–14.

Lorig, K., Ritter, P., and Gonzalez, V. (2003). Hispanic chronic disease self-management: A randomized community-based outcome trial. *Nurs. Res.*, 52, 361–369.

Richardson, G., Kennedy, A., Reeves, D., *et al.* (2008). Cost effectiveness of the Expert Patients Programme (EPP) for patients with chronic conditions. *J. Epidemiol. Community. Health*, 62, 361–367.

Richardson, G., Lee, V., Rogers, A., *et al.* (2008). What outcomes are important to patients with long term conditions? A discrete choice experiment. *Value Health.*

Richardson, G., Sculpher, M., Kennedy, A., *et al.* (2006). Is self-care a cost-effective use of resources? Evidence from a randomized trial in inflammatory bowel disease. *J. Health. Serv. Res. Policy,* **11**, 225–230.

Rogers, A., Bower, P., Gardner, C., *et al.* (2006). *Final Report National Evaluation of the Expert Patients Programme*, NPCRDC.

Tuckett, D., Olsen, C., and Williams, A. (1985). *A Meeting Between Experts: An Approach to Sharing Ideas in Medical Consultations.* London: Tavistock.

Wanless Review on Population Health (2003). Available at http://www.hm-treasury.gov.uk/consultations_and_legislation/wanless/consult_wanless03_index.cfm#document

Wilkinson, R. (2005), The impact of inequality Social Research, Department of Health. *Public Attitudes to Self Care: Baseline Survey*, London, **73**, 2.

Chapter 15

Health literacy – achieving consumer 'empowerment' in health care decisions

Michelle Edwards, Sophie Hill, and Adrian Edwards

Introduction

The term 'health literacy' was first used in a monograph describing the impact of health information on the educational system, the health system, and mass communication (Simonds, 1974). Since the United States' National Adult Literacy Survey (Kirsch *et al.*, 1993) identified 90 million adults as having inadequate literacy skills to meet the needs of the 21st century, there has been a concern about people's abilities to function in health contexts. The Organization for Economic Cooperation and Development (OECD) (Darcovich *et al.*, 2000) reports results from the International Adult Literacy survey showing that in 14 out of 20 industrialized countries more than 15 per cent of adults have only rudimentary literacy skills, making it difficult for them to cope with the demands of the information age. The implications of these results for health have instigated a refocus on health literacy and its meaning.

There are many definitions that reflect a wide range of skills that determine individuals' understanding of health and health care and their effectiveness in using health care services. The USA's Institute of Medicine (IOM) report *Health literacy: a prescription to end confusion* (2004) uses the most cited definition of health literacy:

> The degree to which individuals have the capacity to obtain, process, and understand basic health information and services needed to make appropriate health decisions.
>
> (Ratzan and Parker, 2000)

The IOM suggests several health literacy abilities and skills that are needed to participate in health care. These include the ability to

- promote and protect health and prevent disease;
- understand, interpret, and analyse health information;
- apply health information to a variety of life events and situations;
- navigate the health care system;
- actively participate in encounters with health care providers;
- understand and give consent; and
- understand and advocate for rights.

The World Health Organization (WHO) uses a definition (Nutbeam, 1998), which elegantly describes health literacy and information use, but which includes a goal of good health:

> Health literacy represents the cognitive and social skills which determine the motivation and ability of individuals to gain access to, understand, and use information in ways which promote and maintain good health.

Health literacy means more than transmitting information, developing skills to be able to read pamphlets and successfully make appointments. By improving people's access to health information and their capacity to use it effectively, health literacy is critical to empowerment.

From his WHO definition, Nutbeam (2000) has proposed three levels of health literacy that can be achieved through health education:

- *Functional health literacy* is an outcome of health education and involves basic reading and writing skills that facilitate knowledge of health risks and use of health care services.

- *Interactive literacy* represents the development of personal skills in a supportive environment and involves the social and personal skills and capacity that enables individuals to derive meaning from different forms of communication and to apply new information to changing circumstances.

- *Critical health literacy* represents the cognitive and social skills that enable individuals to critically analyse information and also use it to support effective social and political action, in addition to individual action.

A large systematic review of US studies (Paasche-Orlow *et al.*, 2005) revealed that over a quarter of US citizens have 'inadequate' health literacy and another fifth have 'marginal' health literacy as measured by either of the two most widely used health literacy assessment tools. These are the Rapid Estimate of Adult Literacy in Medicine (REALM) (Davis *et al.*, 1993) and the Test of Functional Health literacy in Adults (TOFHLA) (Parker *et al.*, 1995). Although these tests arguably assess literacy more than health literacy, inadequate health literacy assessed by these tests has been independently associated with several negative outcomes for both patients and the health care service. These include higher health care costs, higher utilization of health care services (Baker *et al.*, 1997), poorer understanding of chronic disease management techniques, under use of preventative health services (Scott *et al.*, 2002), and poorer knowledge and management of chronic disease (Powell *et al.*, 2007).

Information provision

Much research shows that patients desire a wide range of information related to their own health (Sihota and Lennard, 2004). In order to support these information needs and contribute to health literacy, appropriate and high-quality health information materials need to be accessible, readable, and comprehensible for the general public. However, there are a number of challenges that need to be addressed.

Despite a proliferation of health information sources and information tools on the internet, a digital divide is ever-present where the internet is not accessible to various groups (such as low income, low literacy, ethnic minority, disabled, or elderly people) (Eng *et al.*, 1998). An 'inverse information law' has been suggested whereby those in the greatest need of information about preventable or treatable conditions are least likely to have access to the necessary technologies (Ziebland, 2004). However, even if people have access to information, poor quality information diminishes the value of access.

Concerns over the quality of internet health information include fringe, nonscientific theories (Cline and Haynes, 2001); dangerous (McKinley *et al.*, 1999), misleading or fraudulent (McLeod, 1998), or incomplete content or it can be contradictory or based on insufficient evidence. Written information has also been found to be sometimes inadequate, inaccurate, misleading, and insufficient to support treatment decision-making (Coulter *et al.*, 1998). The average patient has to select, evaluate, and differentiate between various sources of information and various solutions to health problems. A substantial body of research has shown that many health information materials are written above the average reading ability and are difficult for many to comprehend (Berland *et al.*, 2001; Pasche-Orlow *et al.*, 2003; Rudd *et al.*, 2000). Efforts by UK health care organizations and providers of health care information to produce clear and understandable health information are also supported by the Plain English Campaign (www.plainenglish.co.uk) that provides a quality certification (Crystal Mark) for ensuring the readability of their health information materials.

However, the appraisal of health information and application of it to one's own circumstances is an 'interactive health literacy' skill (Nutbeam, 2000). This requires sufficient cognitive ability on the part of a patient and exceeds the functional level of health literacy that is currently underachieved by so many. Some commentators suggest it unreasonable to expect patients to critically evaluate information they retrieve from the internet, especially since few health professionals have the necessary critical appraisal skills (Ziebland, 2004). Therefore, it is important that high-quality health information is available and research evidence is presented in a balanced and accessible way. A number of initiatives have been developed and implemented in order facilitate consumer access to quality health information. These include accreditation and certification for providers (Health on the Net Foundation Code of Conduct: http://www.hon.ch/) and training in critical appraisal skills for those providing consumer information (e.g. Critical Appraisal Skills Programme: http://www.phru.nhs.uk/Pages/PHD/CASP.htm).

Interventions

A range of interventions are currently available that address challenges associated with the provision of health information and health literacy of the public. Coulter and Ellins (2006) categorize interventions into four types:

Written health information

Written information (e.g. health information leaflets) is a useful form of intervention for improving functional health literacy (Nutbeam, 2000). The English Department of Health has produced a Toolkit for producing patient information in collaboration with the Patient Information Forum, Royal National Institute for the Blind and Plain English campaign (www.nhsidentity.nhs.uk/patientinformationtoolkit). The toolkit offers advice, checklists, and leaflet templates to those who produce written information for patients.

Alternative format sources

Alternative format resources (e.g. internet health information services) have the potential to facilitate improvements in both functional and interactive health literacy. One example is CHESS (Comprehensive Health Enhancement Support System http://chess.chsra.wisc.edu/Chess/projects/about_chess.aspx), an internet-based patient information and support system providing personalized information, social support, decision-making, and problem-solving tools, that is accessible from home, community centres, health centres, colleges, and the workplace.

Low literacy initiatives

Low literacy initiatives have the potential to facilitate improvements in functional, interactive and to some extent critical health literacy. There are a number of initiatives focusing on this in different countries. For example, the California Health Literacy Initiative (CHLI, http://cahealthliteracy.org) in the United States and the Skilled for Health Program (Sfh, http://www.dfes.gov.uk/readwriteplus/bank/ACFEE55.pdf) in the UK both aim to combat low literacy and basic skills with regards to health. The CHLI is the largest state-wide health literacy project in the United States. Its goal is to provide information and partnership with individuals and organizations to develop solutions to low literacy that have a positive influence on the health and well-being of individuals with low literacy skills, their families, and their communities. The CHLI participates in advocacy and awareness raising campaigns in addition to providing a resource centre for health professionals and patients. In the United Kingdom, the Skills for Health programme is a joint partnership between the Department of Health (DH), the Department for Education and Skills (DfES), and the adult learning charity Continyou (www.continyou.org.uk). The programme produces learning materials for specific community groups with common health issues (young parents, older people, black and minority ethnic groups, mental health, etc). Its aim is to facilitate the improvement of basic skills and health literacy simultaneously.

There are also specific resources to assist decision-making by consumers with low literacy. For example, researchers at the University of Sydney, Australia, developed and are testing a decision aid to help people (aged 55–64) decide whether to self-test for bowel cancer (http://www.health. usyd.edu.au/shdg/current/low_literacy_fobt.php). This is in the context of a national bowel cancer screening programme, but may also be made available in primary care. The screening procedure is the faecal occult blood test ('FOBT'; see Chapter 46 for more detail on the test itself). Readability has been the focus for most products for low literacy user groups, but this resource was developed and based on a linguistic framework to support users in deciding about whether to use the test and participate in the screening programme (Smith et al., 2007, 2008). It is being tested now in a randomized controlled trial, measuring the primary outcomes of understanding and involvement in decision-making about bowel cancer screening with FOBT.

Targeted mass media campaigns

Targeted health communication through the mass media has the potential to facilitate improvements in functional, interactive, and critical health literacy levels. 'Developing Patient Partnerships' (DPP) is a UK charity, part funded by the Department of Health, that specializes in providing health information through mass media. The DPP produces health education campaigns for schools, primary care trusts, GP practices, pharmacies, work places, and local authorities. Its aims are to improve access to health services, tackle inequalities in public health, support health providers meet local targets, promote self-care, prevent ill health, and improve health literacy.

Interventions for consumer groups

Consumer groups have a key role in supporting consumer participation, and undertake many initiatives that promote health literacy. In terms of influencing policy and service delivery this particularly requires critical health literacy. For example the International Alliance of Patients' Organizations (IAPO: http://www.patientsorganizations.org/index.pl) provides training and resources for consumer groups to be more active in the quality and safety area. Similarly, the Patient Information Forum (PIF: www.pifonline.org.uk) is an independent organization aimed at helping both organizations and individuals to provide high-quality health information. They are involved in sourcing and sharing good practice and the training of health information professionals. In addition to raising awareness of health literacy and the importance of clear health communication, the PIF also provide workshops, advice, resources, tools and to help organizations and individuals design, produce, disseminate and evaluate health information, operate information services and involve patient and public involvement in the development of health information.

How effective are health literacy initiatives?

Coulter and Ellins (2006, 2007) summarize the research evidence of effectiveness of these types of interventions, by studying the existing systematic reviews in the field:

- Written information was found to improve health knowledge but not screening rates or health status.
- Alternative format resources mostly improved health knowledge and improved some clinical outcomes.
- Low literacy initiatives provided mixed results for knowledge and comprehension, no change in health care utilization, and no improvement on
- health status.
- Targeted mass media campaigns were effective in raising awareness and had some effect on health care utilization and health behaviour.

Overall, there were mostly positive effects on knowledge (10 out of 13 reviews), patients' experiences (10 out of 16 reviews), use of health services (9 from 14 reviews), and to a lesser extent on health behaviour and status (4 from 14 reviews). The interventions reviewed by Coulter and Ellins (2006) address challenges that represent a number of indicators of health literacy. For example, improvements in health knowledge and comprehension reflect 'functional health literacy', and improvements in health care utilization, health behaviours, and preventative health behaviours reflect 'interactive health literacy'. However, there are arguments that current measures of health literacy do not reflect current definitions (Neilsen-Bohlam *et al.*, 2004). None of the studies reviewed used specific health literacy measures, and the outcome variables used did not fully encapsulate the concept of health literacy. Hence, the effectiveness of the interventions reviewed by Coulter and Ellins (2006) may only partly reflect actual impacts on health literacy. Their review shows that there are gaps in what is known about the effectiveness of these interventions for aspects of health literacy and that improvements in health literacy are still only partly achieved.

Conclusion

More than 30 years after the term was first used, 'health literacy' has gained fresh currency, reflecting the rise in interest in informed health consumers. It is a paradox that so many populations in the world are better educated than at any time in history, yet the need for people to become even more highly educated about how to manage their health has grown commensurately, a process highlighting the complex dynamics of empowerment and inequality. Health literacy involves skills that enable a person to access and understand health information (functional health literacy), successfully apply it to their own circumstances (interactive health literacy), and critically appraise health care issues in order to vote on health policy or advocate for patient rights (critical health literacy). In order to facilitate improvements in health literacy, information providers must produce accessible, high quality, balanced, and comprehensive information that is presented in a clear and readable format. Various interventions are currently available to support health information providers in their efforts to achieve this. Other consumer-focused interventions also help patients make sense of health information and use that information to make better health choices. At present, these interventions may only partly address health literacy and mostly focus on skills associated with functional health literacy and interactive health literacy. Critical health literacy has been mostly addressed through the mass media and provider–patient partnerships. Future initiatives should develop these areas, and also enhance governmental support and training for consumer groups to enable them to be involved in health policy formulation and delivery. Future research efforts should focus on testing and evaluating health literacy interventions using measures based on a fully comprehensive definition of health literacy. This would provide a strong evidence base which could be used to refine existing health literacy interventions and develop more effective interventions that facilitate the improvement of health communication, health and preventive health behaviours, the use of health care services, self-care, and health status.

References

Baker, D.W., Parker, R.M., Williams, *et al.* (1997). The relationship of patient reading ability to self-reported health and use of health services. *American Journal of Public Health*, **87**, 1027–1030.

Berland, G.K., Elliott, N.M., Morales, L.S., *et al.* (2001). Health information on the internet: Accessibility, quality and readability in English and Spanish. *Journal of the American Medical Association*, **285**, 2612–2621.

Cline, R.J. and Haynes, K.M. (2001). Consumer health information seeking on the internet: The state of the art. *Health Education Research*, **16**, 671–692.

Coulter, A. and Ellins, J. (2006). Patient-focused interventions: A review of the evidence. London: The Health Foundation.

Coulter, A., Entwistle, V., and Gilbert, D. (1998). *Informing Patients: An Assessment of the Quality of Patient Information Materials.* London: King's Fund.

Darcovich, N., Hasan, A., Jones, S., *et al.* (2000). Literacy in the Information Age: Final report of the *International Adult Literacy Survey.* Organisation for Economic Co-operation and Development.

Davis, T.L., Long, S.W., and Jackson, R.H. (1993). Rapid estimate of adult literacy in medicine: A shortened screening instrument. *Family Medicine*, **25**, 391–395.

Eng, T.R., Maxfield, A., Patrick, K., *et al.* (1998). Access to health information and support: A public highway or private road. *Journal of American Medical Association*, **280**, 1371–1375.

Kirsch, I., Jungeblut, A., Jenkins, L., *et al.* (1993). Adult Literacy in America. Washington, DC: US. Department of Education.

McKinley, J., Cattermole, H., and Oliver, C.W. (1999). The quality of surgical information on the Internet. *Journal of the Royal College of Surgeons of Edinburgh*, **44**, 265–268.

McLeod, S.D. (1998). The Quality of medical information on the internet: A new public health concern. *Arch. Ophthalmol.*, **116**, 1663–1665.

Nutbeam, D. (1998). Health promotion glossary. *Heallth Promotion International*, **13**, 349–364.

Nutbeam, D. (2000). Health literacy as a public health goal: A challenge for contemporary health education and communication strategies into the 21st century. *Heallth Promotion International*, **15**, 259–267.

Paasche-Orlow, M.K., Parker, R.M., Gazmararian, J., *et al.* (2005). The prevalence of limited health literacy. *Journal of General Internal Medicine*, **20**, 175–184.

Pasche-Orlow, M., Taylor, H., and Brancati, F. (2003). Readability standards for informed-consent forms as compared with actual readability. *New England Journal of Medicine*, **348**, 721–726.

Powell, C.K., Hill, E.G., and Clancy, D.E. (2007). The relationship between health literacy and diabetes knowledge and readiness to take health actions. *Diabetes Educato.*, **33**, 144–151.

Rudd, R.E., Moeykens, B.A., and Colton, T.C. (2000). Health and literacy: A review of medical and public health literature. In J. Comings and B. Garner (eds) *The Annual Review of Adult Learning and Literacy.* San Francisco: Jossey-Bass.

Scott, T.L., Gazmararian, J.A., Williams, M.V., *et al.* (2002). Health literacy and preventative healthcare among Medicare enrollees in a managed care organization. *Med. Care*, **40**, 475–482.

Sihota, S. and Lennard, L. (2004). Health literacy: Being able to make the most of health. National Consumer Council.

Simonds, S. (1974). Health education as social policy. *Health Education Monograph*, **2**, 1–25.

Smith, S., McCaffery, K., and Trevena, L. (2007). Using decision aids to facilitate informed health care decision making among adults with low literacy: The case of bowel cancer screening. *Health Issues*, **92**, 28–32.

Smith, S., Trevena, L., Nutbeam, D., *et al.* (2008). Information needs and preferences of low and high literacy consumers for decisions about colorectal cancer screening: Utilising a linguistic model. *Health Expectations*, in press.

Ziebland, S. (2004). The importance of being expert: The quest for cancer information on the internet. *Social Science and Medicine*, **59**, 1783–1793.

Chapter 16

Conceptual variation and iteration in shared decision-making: The need for clarity

Marla L. Clayman and Gregory Makoul

What is shared decision-making?

The medical encounter is filled with potential decision points. How best to make decisions about tests, medications, procedures, referrals, or behaviours and whom to involve in these decisions are questions that have received increasing attention over the last several decades. Shared decision-making (SDM) is frequently advocated in teaching and research about the provider – patient interaction. Interest in SDM, in particular, has grown over the last several years (Makoul and Clayman, 2006), and recent articles have highlighted the conceptual variation that has become evident as educators and researchers grapple with the topic (Makoul and Clayman, 2006; Moumjid et al., 2007b).

Several journals have devoted issues to the topic (e.g., Health Expectations; German Journal for Quality in Health care; Medical Decision Making; Patient Education and Counseling). The range of journals in which SDM research is published shows its scope, in terms of both clinical area and geography. Shared decision-making (SDM) is often positioned as a 'middle ground' between paternalism (i.e., physicians make the decisions) and informed choice (i.e., patients make the decisions) (Charles et al., 1997, 1999a, 1999b; Elwyn et al., 1999). In that context, there is considerable overlap between SDM and constructs with similar connotations, such as informed decision-making (Braddock et al., 1999; Mullen et al., 2006), concordance (Jordan et al., 2002; Taylor et al., 1989), evidence-based patient choice (Ford et al., 2003; Ruland and Bakken, 2002), enhanced autonomy (Stubblefield and Mutha, 2002), and mutual participation (Stubblefield and Mutha, 2002).

However, the concept of SDM has been variably, and often loosely, defined. Some have acknowledged confusion surrounding the term (Charles et al., 1997, 2003; Jansen, 2001; Makoul and Clayman, 2006; Thornton et al., 2003), but variation in definition and measurement still exists. The lack of synthesis is problematic for several reasons. First, inconsistent conceptual definitions lead to inconsistent measurement of SDM (Charles et al., 1997, 2003; Elwyn et al., 2001a). Second, the lack of a core definition of SDM complicates efforts to identify the relationships between SDM and outcome measures. Third, variable coding schemes and measurements of SDM definitions make comparisons across studies difficult, if not impossible.

Similarly, as has been noted previously (Charles et al., 2003), models of SDM vary in the way they position the roles and responsibilities of each party. For example, competencies have been suggested for both physicians and patients as relatively equal partners (Towle and Godolphin, 1999), whereas other models place more responsibility on the physician to elicit or respond to patients' views (Elwyn et al., 2000a). There has also been increasing attention to patients' preferred role in decision-making, with some asserting that for SDM to occur, patients must share equally

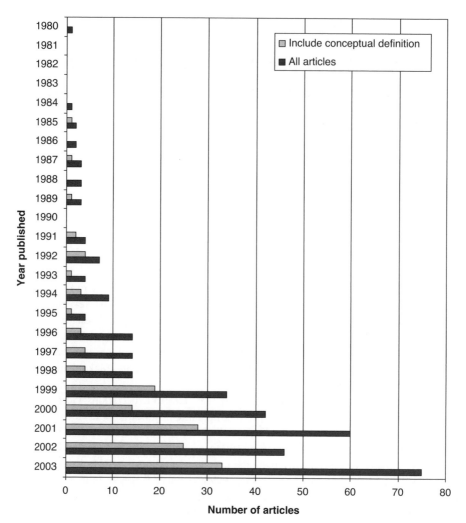

* *All articles* = results of the primary search strategy from Makoul and Clayman 2006, which captured articles that were indexed in Pubmed (Medline) through 31 December 2003, included the words *shared decision making* in the title or abstract, and met the following two inclusion criteria: (1) in the context of patient-provider encounters; (2) published in English. *N* = 342.

Figure 16.1 Growth in Pubmed-indexed articles on SDM (Reprinted from Makoul and Clayman 2006).

in the decision-making process (Charles *et al.*, 1997, Charles *et al.*, 1999a), while others contend that patients' role preferences should be discussed and accepted (Elwyn *et al.*, 2000a).

Most models of SDM recognize it as a process, rather than a single point in time (Charles *et al.*, 1997; Elwyn *et al.*, 1999; Makoul and Clayman, 2006). However, there is still debate about whether the term 'shared decision-making' implies that the resulting (or 'final') decision be equally shared (Charles *et al.*, 1997; Shepherd *et al.*, 2007; Weiss and Peters, 2008) or if sharing the process itself is the goal (Edwards and Elwyn, 2006; Makoul and Clayman, 2006). There has also been discussion about the appropriate contexts for SDM – is it only appropriate in cases of true medical equipoise (in which there is no clearly preferable medical option; Elwyn *et al.*, 2000a)?

Or is the process of SDM itself, particularly its focus on the incorporation of patients' preferences and values, applicable to almost any decision (Makoul and Clayman, 2006)?

Reviewing the literature

We previously conducted a systematic review of the literature (Makoul and Clayman, 2006), with four goals: (1) to determine the range of conceptual definitions of articles that specifically address SDM; (2) to identify the most frequently invoked elements of SDM; (3) to determine the most frequently cited models of SDM; and (4) to offer a model of SDM that integrates the extant literature base. We found that only about one-third of the articles that met our search criteria had a conceptual definition of SDM. Of the characteristics named in articles with a conceptual definition, we found that only patient values/preferences (67.1%) and options (50.9%) appeared in more than half of the conceptual definitions. We also found that the term 'shared decision-making' gained prominence in the 1990s, with the most commonly cited models being those of Towle and Goldolphin (1999), Elwyn and colleagues (Elwyn *et al.*, 1999, 2000a, 2000b, 2001a, 2001b,), Coulter and colleagues (Coulter, 1997), and Charles and colleagues (Charles *et al.*, 1997). These models afford different emphasis to different elements of the process of SDM, as summarized in Table 16.1.

This lack of coherence about what SDM is, or is not, results primarily from its atheoretical genesis. The group that first defined the term (President's Commission for the Study of Ethical Problems in Medicine and Biomedical and Behavioral Research, 1982) focused primarily on informed consent and framed the inclusion of patients as coming from the bioethical principle of autonomy, or respect for persons. Later incarnations of SDM focused on principles to be upheld (e.g., consideration of patient preferences) or tasks to be completed (e.g., discussion of risks).

Observing and measuring shared decision-making

Whereas models of SDM generally focus on what should ideally occur, measurement of what does occur in provider-patient encounters is still in its early stages. Perhaps most problematic is that, given that some elements of SDM rarely occur (e.g., discussion of risks for each option, checking for patient understanding; Braddock *et al.*, 1999), researchers who code encounters may find themselves trying to document what is lacking instead of what is present. In addition, coding systems that use a binary approach (i.e., either the element is present or it is not) do not capture the quality of discussion for a particular item. A recent article (Weiss and Peters, 2008) compared two decision-making coding systems: informed decision-making (Braddock *et al.*, 1999) and the OPTION scale (Elwyn *et al.*, 2003). The authors found that the two systems had very little overall agreement. However, some specific items within each system were conceptually similar and significantly related to one another (e.g. discussion of pros and cons). The authors conclude that coding for SDM may not be attainable, as current coding systems do not adequately capture the qualitative essence of sharing decisions.

Another option is to try and measure changes in decision-making, and more specifically, shared decision-making, through the testing of decision aids. The implicit goal of decision aids is often to assist patients in making decisions that are informed by the best evidence and in line with patient preferences (O'Connor *et al.*, 2007). However, decision aids also often lack a theoretical foundation. A recent review of decision aids found that only 17 of 50 decision aids tested in randomized controlled trials and included in a Cochrane systematic review had any theoretical underpinnings as part of their development (Durand *et al.*, 2008) – see also Chapter 29. Similar to the proliferation of research into what makes for a 'good' decision, there is also a great deal of discussion into

Table 16.1 Essential elements, ideal elements, and general qualities of SDM: emphasis in prominently cited models (modified from Makoul and Clayman 2006)

	President's commission (1982)	Charles, Gafni and Whelan (1997)	Coulter et al. (1997)	Towle and Godolphin (1999)	Elwyn et al. (2000)
Essential elements					
Define/explain problem	X		X		X
Present options	X	X	X	X	X
Discuss pros/cons (benefits/risks/costs)		X	X	X	X
Patient values/preferences	X	X	X	X	X
Discuss patient ability/self-efficacy[a]					
Doctor knowledge/recommendations	X	X			
Check/clarify understanding		X			X
Make or explicitly defer decision		X	X	X	X
Arrange follow-up				X	X
Ideal elements					
Unbiased information	X	X			X
Define roles (desire for involvement)		X	X	X	X
Present evidence		X	X	X	
Mutual agreement	X	X	X	X	X
General qualities					
Deliberation/negotiation	X	X		X	
Flexibility/individualized approach	X	X	X		X
Information exchange		X			
Involves at least two people		X		X	
Middle ground		X			
Mutual respect	X			X	
Partnership	X	X	X	X	
Patient education		X			X
Patient participation	X	X			X
Process/stages	X	X	X	X	X

[a] This category was added by the authors.

what makes a 'good' decision aid. The International Patient Decision Aids Collaboration (IPDAS) has developed standards by which decision aids can be judged (discussed further in Chapter 33). Several of the quality criteria recommended by IPDAS are similar to features in the models of SDM, including description of the clinical problem, description of options, and explicit values clarification (O'Connor *et al.*, 2007). Although decision aids standardize information, they may vary in their capacity to facilitate SDM between health care provider and patient. In addition to differences inherent in the decision aids themselves, the process through which they are implemented is also important. Many decision aids are intended for the patient to use without the physician present. The impact these decision aids have on the physician – patient interaction itself is also unclear.

International comparisons of shared decision-making in practice

Several articles devoted to the current state of SDM appeared, in English, in a German journal last year (Evans *et al.*, 2007; Goss & Renzi, 2007; Holmes-Rovner *et al.*, 2007; Legare *et al.*, 2007; Loh *et al.*, 2007; McCaffery *et al.*, 2007; Moumjid *et al.*, 2007a; van der Weijden *et al.*, 2007). Although several countries are represented, it is clear that there is a Western bent to the research and implementation of SDM. Whether based on the principle of respect for persons or the inherent equality between actors, the egalitarian approach that supporters of SDM espouse is a cultural ideal only in some societies. Having a cultural ideal in common is not enough to ensure that SDM is implemented. As Holmes-Rovner and colleagues point out, the myriad of providers, payers, and organizations involved in the delivery of health care in the United States means that consistent implementation of even proven interventions is difficult, if not impossible (Holmes-Rovner *et al.*, 2007). In countries with a national health care system, whether single payer or not, policies that embrace SDM have the potential to be implemented more consistently, with the government imprimatur (Evans *et al.*, 2007; Goss and Renzi, 2007; Legare *et al.*, 2007; Loh *et al.*, 2007; van der Weijden *et al.*, 2007). Each country has its own challenges, but those without a clear policy towards improving patient participation and SDM seem to focus primarily on patient activation and education (Holmes-Rovner *et al.*, 2007; McCaffery *et al.*, 2007), taking advantage of only one component of what others tackle in a multilevel approach. For a fuller discussion of international variations, we refer readers to Chapter 22 by Coulter.

How shared decision-making may evolve in further practice

There are currently several shortcomings to SDM as a concept and as a goal of measurement. Further research is needed to determine if an integrated model of SDM has a practical value in addition to conceptual appeal (Makoul and Clayman, 2006). Certainly, there is a need to modify coding schemes for different contexts, as the options, risks, and clinical uncertainties vary. However, there may be fundamental differences among types of decisions: models may differ according to, among other things, the timeframe in which the decision needs to be made (immediate versus delayed), disease context (prevention versus treatment), and participants (patient and doctor; patient and team of doctors or other health professionals; or patient, family, and doctor) (Legare *et al.*, 2008). One could think of these additional factors to consider as part of a single expansive model of SDM, or several, more narrowly constrained versions. As stated previously, existing models account for SDM as a process. However, the practice of measuring decision-making still focuses on the cross-sectional nature of a single clinician–patient encounter.

The current state of measuring SDM does not incorporate a realistic timeline for certain decisions, nor does it include the possibility of revisiting decisions. For example, a man with prostate cancer could choose among different treatment options or watchful waiting. He might take several days or weeks to make his decision. If he chooses watchful waiting, he might reconsider his position and choose a different option several months down the line, even if his clinical condition and test results are similar. Similarly, the current concepts of SDM do not represent the reality of integrating the contributions of family members and multiple health care providers.

For many of the decisions that have been most closely studied, such as those for cancer treatment, this is a glaring omission. Again, we refer readers to Chapter 8 (Rapley) for a fuller discussion of these issues, but we note that all these areas require attention in future research and practice.

Why focus on shared decision-making, anyway?

If we cannot agree on what SDM is and how it should be measured, why should we care about it at all? The research cited as evidence of positive outcomes of SDM usually refers to studies on improving 'patient participation' (Greenfield *et al.*, 1985, Greenfield *et al.*, 1988) or tests of decision aids (O'Connor *et al.*, 2007). While these studies are relevant, they do not directly test the benefits of SDM. We need to clearly define the entirety of SDM, and then elucidate the contribution of its individual parts to achieving a good decision. In addition to sharpening the focus on SDM in research, this approach can illuminate the ultimate goals of SDM in practice: namely that patients' choices are informed, in line with their values, and respected.

Acknowledgements

Some sections and Figures in this chapter have been published previously in *Patient Education and Counseling* (Makoul and Clayman 2006), reproduced with kind permission from Elsevier.

References

Braddock, C.H., 3rd, Edwards, K.A., Hasenberg, N.M., *et al.* (1999). Informed decision making in outpatient practice: Time to get back to basics. *JAMA*, **282**, 2313–2320.

Charles, C., Gafni, A. and Whelan, T. (1997). Shared decision-making in the medical encounter: What does it mean? (or it takes at least two to tango). *Soc. Sci. Med.*, **44**, 681–692.

Charles, C., Gafni, A., and Whelan, T. (1999a). Decision-making in the physician-patient encounter: Revisiting the shared treatment decision-making model. *Soc. Sci. Med.*, **49**, 651–661.

Charles, C., Whelan, T., and Gafni, A. (1999b). What do we mean by partnership in making decisions about treatment? *BMJ*, **319**, 780–782.

Charles, C.A., Whelan, T., and Gafni, A., *et al.* (2003). Shared treatment decision making: What does it mean to physicians? *J. Clin. Oncol.*, **21**, 932–936.

Coulter, A. (1997). Partnerships with patients: The pros and cons of shared clinical decision making. *J. Health. Serv. Res. Policy.*, **2**, 112–121.

Durand, M.A., Stiel, M., and Boivin, J., *et al.* (2008). Where is the theory? Evaluating the theoretical frameworks described in decision support technologies. *Patient. Educ. Couns.*, **71**, 125–135.

Edwards, A. and Elwyn, G. (2006). Inside the black box of shared decision making: Distinguishing between the process of involvement and who makes the decision. *Health Expect*, **9**, 307–320.

Elwyn, G., Edwards, A., and Gwyn, R., *et al.* (1999). Towards a feasible model for shared decision making: Focus group study with general practice registrars. *British Medical Journal*, **319**, 753–756.

Elwyn, G., Edwards, A., and Kinnersley, P., *et al.* (2000a). Shared decision making and the concept of equipoise: The competences of involving patients in healthcare choices. *Br. J. Gen. Pract.*, **50**, 892–899.

Elwyn, G., Edwards, A., and Mowle, S., *et al.* (2001a). Measuring the involvement of patients in shared decision-making: A systematic review of instruments. *Patient. Educ. Couns.*, **43**, 5–22.

Elwyn, G., Edwards, A., and Wensing, M., *et al.* (2001b). Shared decision making observed in clinical practice: Visual displays of communication sequence and patterns. *J. Eval. Clin. Pract.*, **7**, 211–221.

Elwyn, G., Edwards, A., and Wensing, M., *et al.* (2003). Shared decision making: Developing the OPTION scale for measuring patient involvement. *Qual. Saf. Health. Care.*, **12**, 93–99.

Elwyn, G., Gray, J., and Clarke, A. (2000b). Shared decision making and non-directiveness in genetic counselling. *J. Med.Genet.*, **37**, 135–138.

Evans, R., Edwards, A., and Coulter, A. (2007). Prominent strategy but rare in practice: Shared decision-making and patient decision support technologies in the UK. *Z. Arztl. Fortbild. Qualitatssich*, **101**, 247–253.

Ford, S., Schofield, T., and Hope, T. (2003). What are the ingredients for a successful evidence-based patient choice consultation? A qualitative study. *Soc. Sci. Med*, **56**, 589–602.

Goss, C. and Renzi, C. (2007). Patient and citizen participation in health care decisions in Italy. *Z. Arztl. Fortbild. Qualitatssich.*, **101**, 236–240.

Greenfield, S., Kaplan, S., and Ware, J.E., Jr. (1985). Expanding patient involvement in care. Effects on patient outcomes. *Ann. Intern. Med.*, **102**, 520–528.

Greenfield, S., Kaplan, S.H., and Ware, J.E., *et al.* (1988). Patients participation in medical care: Effects on blood sugar control and quality of life in diabetes., *J. Gen. Intern. Med.*, **3**, 448–457.

Holmes-Rovner, M., Gruman, J., and Rovner, D.R. (2007). Shared decision-making in the US–research & development outpaces delivery. *Z. Arztl. Fortbild. Qualitatssich.*, **101**, 254–258.

Jansen, L.A. (2001). Deliberative decision making and the treatment of pain. *J. Palliat.Med.*, **4**, 23–30.

Jordan, J.L., Ellis, S.J., and Chambers, R. (2002). Defining shared decision making and concordance: Are they one and the same? *Postgrad. Med. J.*, **78**, 383–384.

Legare, F., Stacey, D., and Forest, P.G. (2007). Shared decision-making in Canada: Update, challenges and where next! *Z. Arztl. Fortbild. Qualitatssich.*, **101**, 213–221.

Legare, F., Stacey, D., and Graham, I.D., *et al.* (2008). Advancing theories, models and measurement for an interprofessional approach to shared decision making in primary care: a study protocol. *BMC. Health. Serv. Res.*, **8**, 2.

Loh, A., Simon, D., and Bieber, C., *et al.* (2007). Patient and citizen participation in German health care–current state and future perspectives. *Z. Arztl. Fortbild. Qualitatssich.*, **101**, 229–235.

Makoul, G. and Clayman, M.L. (2006). An integrative model of shared decision making in medical encounters. *Patient Educ. Couns.*, **60**, 301–312.

McCaffery, K.J., Shepherd, H.L., and Trevena, L., *et al.* (2007). Shared decision-making in Australia. *Z. Arztl. Fortbild. Qualitatssich.*, **101**, 205–211.

Moumjid, N., Bremond, A., and Mignotte, H., *et al.* (2007a). Shared decision-making in the physician-patient encounter in France: A general overview. *Z. Arztl. Fortbild. Qualitatssich.*, **101**, 223–228.

Moumjid, N., Gafni, A., and Bremond, A., *et al.* (2007b). Shared decision making in the medical encounter: Are we all talking about the same thing? *Med. Decis. Making.*, **27**, 539–546.

Mullen, P.D., Allen, J.D., and Glanz, K., *et al.* (2006). Measures used in studies of informed decision making about cancer screening: A systematic review. *Ann. Behav. Med.*, **32**, 188–201.

O'Connor, A.M., Bennett, C., and Stacey, D., *et al.* (2007). Do patient decision aids meet effectiveness criteria of the international patient decision aid standards collaboration? A systematic review and meta-analysis. *Med. Decis. Making.*, **27**, 554–574.

President's Commission for the Study of Ethical Problems in Medicine and Biomedical and Behavioral Research (1982). *Making Health Care Decisions. The Ethical and Legal Implications of Informed Consent in the Patient-Practitioner Relationship'*. Washington, DC.

Ruland, C.M. and Bakken, S. (2002). Developing, implementing, and evaluating decision support systems for shared decision making in patient care: A conceptual model and case illustration. *J. Biomed. Inform.*, **35**, 313–321.

Shepherd, H.L., Tattersall, M.H., and Butow, P.N. (2007). 'The context influences doctors' support of shared decision-making in cancer care. *Br. J. Cancer.*, **97**, 6–13.

Stubblefield, C. and Mutha, S. (2002). Provider-patient roles in chronic disease management. *J. Allied. Health.*, **31**(2), 87–92.

Taylor, S.G., Pickens, J.M., and Geden, E.A. (1989). Interactional styles of nurse practitioners and physicians regarding patient decision making. *Nurs. Res.*, **38**, 50–55.

Thornton, H., Edwards, A., and Elwyn, G. (2003). Evolving the multiple roles of 'patients' in healthcare research: Reflections after involvement in a trial of shared decision-making, *Health Expect.*, **6**, 189–197.

Towle, A. and Godolphin, W. (1999). Framework for teaching and learning informed shared decision making. *Br. Med. J.*, **319**, 766–771.

van der Weijden, T., van Veenendaal, H., and Timmermans, D. (2007). Shared decision-making in the Netherlands–current state and future perspectives. *Z. Arztl. Fortbild. Qualitatssich.*, **101**, 241–246.

Weiss, M.C. and Peters, T.J. (2008). Measuring shared decision making in the consultation: A comparison of the OPTION and Informed Decision Making instruments. *Patient. Educ. Couns.*, **70**, 79–86.

Chapter 17

Shared decision-making: From conceptual models to implementation in clinical practice

Glyn Elwyn and Cathy Charles

Introduction

Shared decision-making (SDM) has been a topic of growing interest among health care providers, medical ethicists, social scientists, and others. A number of SDM models have been developed. Makoul and Clayman's (2006) review concluded that whilst full agreement had not been achieved, the model developed by Charles *et al.* (1997) was the one most commonly cited in the relevant literature. It was this model that was the starting point for the competencies described by Elwyn *et al.* (2000), and it is the one we use in this chapter.

The essential elements of the model include health professional and patient participation in all stages of the decision-making process including the exchange of information, deliberation about options, and arriving at an agreement on a decision to implement. In the information exchange process, the physician informs the patient about the relevant treatment options and describes their benefits and risks. The patient is assisted to identify their beliefs, values, and preferences (including cultural factors) that may influence their views of the choice of management options. In the deliberation stage, the pros and cons of the available treatment options are discussed in light of the evidence, patient preferences, and other factors. In the final stage, both patient and health professional work together, with the aim of achieving consensus, and the professional offers a specific recommendation that contributes to the decision-making. Arriving at agreement is sometimes problematic and often requires negotiation and perhaps additional consultations and compromises. The shared decision-making approach accommodates these processes. If the eventual outcome remains a disagreement then having a shared decision is not possible, even though the process was shared. In this situation, either the patient will decide to accept the professional's view (a reluctant agreement of sorts we imagine) or will need to seek alternative advice. Implementing each of these stages of SDM is clearly a complex set of tasks. In this paper, we review these stages and suggest ways in which health care professionals can facilitate patient involvement in the decision-making process.

The implementation of SDM involves a set of reciprocal role expectations for both the health professional and patient. In this chapter, we focus solely on the professional role and set out the core tasks that need to be mastered. We recognize that this approach has limitations, given that these interactions are interdependent, and rely on dyadic processes between actors who are recursively influencing each other. Nevertheless, we cannot escape from the fact that the power relationships in the majority of health care consultations are asymmetric, as is the possession of relevant technical knowledge. A professional's approach typically dominates and guides the interactional processes. Some patients will ask to be involved in decision-making, and the professional will (hopefully) respond accordingly. In the main however, professionals will need to facilitate the process. We, therefore, describe how this can be done in a sensitive way, without a threat to patient well-being.

Information exchange stage of shared decision-making

At the heart of shared decision-making is the concept of choice and that a deliberative process is either required or would be advantageous in order to arrive at a decision that integrates professional opinion, scientific data, and the personal preferences of patients. However, it is clear from an examination of both empirical practice (Edwards and Elwyn, 2006) and from interviews with professionals (Elwyn, 1999) that many factors play a part in making the idea of choice both visible and relevant for the patient. We do not have space to go into more detail but it is apparent that choice comes into focus more vividly when the problem being addressed is one in which a range of options exist, and there is *recognition* of two ever-present conditions, namely uncertainty about the best course of action at the individual patient level and the importance of personal preferences for relevant potential outcomes. The phrase, 'portrayal of equipoise' has been used to convey situations in which the professional (or the patient) feels that it is important and legitimate to highlight choices and emphasize that a deliberation process should be initiated. A debate exists as to whether equipoise exists in all clinical situations (whether a choice of one kind or another always exists) but the concept of making the choice visible is one that is pivotal in changing the power balance in clinical interactions. A key task then for health professionals is to define the nature of the decision task and to outline the relevant option set. This is important because seemingly similar decisions (e.g. to use hormone therapy) may actually derive from different clinical concerns. For instance, the decisions to take hormone replacement for short-term menopausal symptom control rather than to prevent long-term bone mass loss are different decisions and depend on different outcome datasets. Being able to describe the decision task is therefore of key importance. Failure easily results in crossed purposes – where the health professional and patient are unclear about the decision being considered, and so the next step – presenting data about options – may result in confusion for one or both parties.

While presenting data about options is a critical task for the professional, patients will also have information that needs to be integrated. It is known that the range of options provided by the clinician will influence how choices are considered by the patient (Redelmeier, 1995). Decisions vary in their urgency, salience, and stakes. A decision whether to switch medication because of a gradual deterioration of chronic disease control is one that can be considered over many weeks whereas a decision to undertake an amniocentesis, with its inherent risk of spontaneous abortion, has to be completed in a few days. Urgency and a high stakes decision will influence the emotional climate, making it more difficult for patients to both consider information and manage emotions.

Where two concrete options exist, i.e. a choice between A and B, professionals should list both options prior to giving more detail, perhaps highlighting areas of contrast. This task can be undertaken with the use of some form of decision support technology. If the option set is more complex, e.g., A or B or C, perhaps with permutations, it becomes more difficult to present options in a balanced way and decision support technologies (decision aids) will often be helpful to make options more visible. Sometimes, it is wise in health care to consider taking no action but the presentation of no action presents problems. Patients may find the idea of 'doing nothing' difficult, preferring to take the view that action is better than inaction (Charles, 1998). One solution, where interventions can be deferred, is to use a positive term such as 'watchful waiting'. It is also important to explore what options patients feel may be available and *relevant*.

Too often it seems that biomedical options are provided and little time is spent exploring what other strategies patients may consider relevant.

Providing information on the pros and cons of options (benefits and harms) is an essential but difficult information exchange. Unless an effort has been made to gather high-quality research information about the various options in different populations, it is impossible to provide relevant outcome probabilities for different pathways. Moreover, research information on the probabilities of different risks and outcomes refers to populations in the aggregate, not to individual patients. Tailoring this type of information to reflect outcomes for more homogeneous subgroups, similar in key characteristics to the patient, can help, but comparisons across studies are often difficult to make. The limitations of population level data for individual level patient decisions need to be carefully discussed with the patient (Charles, 2005).

Descriptive accounts of options are essential. These may include providing information about the processes involved in either agreeing to procedures or starting and maintaining treatment regimens. Providing numerical probability estimates is also important. However, the presentation of this type of information is problematic because research data are seldom designed so that they can be used to compare event rates in accessible absolute and relative risk formats (Edwards *et al.*, 2002). Physicians also need to check patient understanding. This task is about safety-netting, ensuring that the information exchange has been conducted successfully, that comprehension of knowledge and preferences is satisfactory on both sides, and that a good platform exists on which to proceed to the deliberation stage.

Elicitation of patient preferences is another complex task facing the health professional during information exchange. This area is problematic because, firstly, the concept of patient preferences has never been defined in terms of either the types or levels of preferences that are relevant to consider; secondly, the terminology is confusing. The terms values, beliefs, and preferences are often used interchangeably and there is a need for conceptual clarification in this area. Moreover, it is difficult for professionals to elicit patient preferences (Gafni, 1998). Although 'clarification exercises' have been developed as components of decision support technologies, there remains a possibility that these deliberative exercises may actually transform rather than reflect patient preferences. Cultural values, which are likely to be very important in shaping individuals' preferences about what to do and what might count as a legitimate options, have also rarely been researched (Charles, 2006). In short, how exactly to elicit and share preferences in SDM interactions is an under-researched area. Yet, it is the step that actively provides patients with decision-making agency, as they consider the relevance of option and attribute information against their own experience, circumstances, and attitudes.

Deliberation stage of shared decision-making

Patients are often uncertain when asked to integrate their own preferences, typically because the requirement is novel and because they *may* feel unfamiliar with biomedical information. Skilled professionals will be aware of the difficulty that can arise that patients will doubt their ability and self-efficacy. The skilled professional will help patients express their views and guide them to explore their feelings and reactions to the relevant choices. Some patients *may* prefer not *to make* decisions and decline decisional responsibility. Professionals at this point will need to decide whether or not they support the patient's preference in this or whether they advocate 'mandatory autonomy' (Schneider, 1998) and risk making the patient feel 'abandoned' (Quill and Cassel, 1995). We view the patient's choice do delegate decision-making to the physician as an expression of preference, and unless the physician has a compelling reason not to, ought to be respected.

One of the central tenets of shared decision-making is that there should be an exchange not only of information about options but also a sharing of both viewpoints. Both patients and professionals need to be aware of each others' perspectives with the aim, if possible, of arriving at an agreed decision. Hence, in this model of decision-making, it is appropriate for the professional to provide both information and, during deliberation, his or her preferred option and the background reasoning.

Implementation stage of shared decision-making

Interactions in clinical practice will always and inevitably be time-limited. Yet, presenting a set of options will invariably take more time than presenting a cut and dried solution. Where decisions are urgent, it is necessary to be able to arrive at a decision efficiently. However, few decisions are so urgent as to need immediate answers. Where it is feasible, agreeing to defer the decision, to facilitate the arrival of further data or other views, and to allow time for further deliberation would be helpful. If decisions seem clear to both patient and professional, it may nevertheless be wise to suggest review. Patients may wish to reconsider their choice after searching for more information or after discussing the issues with family, friends, or with other patients in similar predicaments.

These then are the competences involved in a SDM process (Elwyn *et al.*, 2000). Note that the model implicitly assumes that shared decision-making occurs in the context of a dyadic interaction between a professional and a patient. However, several important contextual factors also influence this process and are discussed briefly below.

Contextual factors influencing shared decision-making implementation

It seems likely that the information exchange contribution to SDM interactions may increasingly be mediated in the future by decision support technologies. These are artefacts (leaflets, videos, DVDs, or websites) which help patients make decisions. Some are intended for independent use prior to encounters but others are designed to be used also in the consultation, by a professional who discusses the components with the patient. These technologies have been considered 'adjuncts' to help professional interactions with patients but there is some evidence that their comprehensiveness may give the implicit message that they are to help patients act autonomously (Frosch in press). While evidence exists on the effectiveness of decision aids, particularly on patient knowledge acquisition (O'Connor, 2004), there is still debate over which outcomes are most appropriate (Charles, 2005; Nelson, 2007). There remains a significant lack of evidence of how health professionals might integrate these tools into routine practice: firstly, the few research studies that have investigated this report some resistance to their use (Silvia, 2008) and it is likely that a range of barriers exist, many of which are as yet not fully investigated. Secondly, as newer and expensive drugs and procedures become available, how to deal with options that may not be covered by public insurers is a concern: this area needs further research (Jefford, 2005; Thomson, 2006). Thirdly, there is a realization that decision-making seldom occurs in isolation of other actors and agents; the influence of family members, friends, and peers is constant (Rapley, 2008). In addition, health professionals and supporting staff are increasingly working in the complex milieu of inter-professional teams whose members may have different perspectives on prevailing or emerging decisions for a given patient (Legare, 2008), and research studies have yet to consider how SDM occurs across and between different professionals along the patient's journey.

References

Charles, C., Gafni, A., *et al.* (1997). Shared decision making in the medical encounter: What does it mean? (Or it takes at least two to tango). *Social Science & Medicine*, **44**, 681–692.

Charles, C., Gafni, A., *et al.* (2005). Treatment decision aids: Conceptual issues and future directions. *Health Expectations*, **8**, 114–125.

Charles, C., Gafni, A., *et al.* (2006). Cultural influences on the physician-patient encounter: The case of shared treatment decision-making. *Patient Education & Counseling*, **63**, 262–267.

Charles, C., Redko, C., *et al.* (1998). Doing nothing is no choice: Lay constructions of treatment decision-making among women with early-stage breast cancer. *Sociology of Health and Illness*, **20**, 71–95.

Edwards, A. and Elwyn, G. (2006). Inside the black box of shared decision making: Distinguishing between the process of involvement and who makes the decision. *Health Expectations*, **9**, 307–320.

Edwards, A., Elwyn, G., *et al.* (2002). Explaining risks: Turning numerical data into meaningful pictures. *British Medical Journal*, **324**, 827–830.

Elwyn, G., Edwards, A., *et al.* (1999). Towards a feasible model for shared decision making: A focus group study with general practice registrars. *British Medical Journal*, **319**, 753–757.

Elwyn, G., Edwards, A., *et al.* (2000). Shared decision making and the concept of equipoise: Defining the competences of involving patients in healthcare choices. *Br. J. Gen. Pract.*, **50**, 892–899.

Frosch, D.L., Legare, F., *et al.* (2008). Using decision aids in community-based primary care: A theory-driven evaluation with ethnically diverse patients. *Patient Education & Counseling*, **73**(3), 490–496.

Gafni, A., Charles, C., *et al.* (1998). The physician-patient encounter: The physician as a perfect agent for the patient *versus* the informed decision-making model. *Social Science & Medicine*, **47**, 347–354.

Jefford, M., Savulescu, J., *et al.* (2005). Medical paternalism and expensive unsubsidised drugs. *British Medical Journal*, **331**, 1075–1077.

Legare, F., Stacey, D., *et al.* (2008). Advancing theories, models and measurement for an interprofessional approach to shared decision making in primary care: A study protocol." *BMC Health Serv. Res.*, **8**, 2.

Makoul, G. and Clayman, M.L. (2006). An integrative model of shared decision making in medical encounters. *Patient Education & Counseling*, **60**, 301–312.

Nelson, W.L., Han, P.K., *et al.* (2007). Rethinking the objectives of decision aids: A call for conceptual clarity. *Medical Decision Making*, **27**, 609–618.

O'Connor, A.M., Stacey, D., *et al.* (2004). Decision aids for people facing health treatment or screening decisions (Cochrane Review) Issue 1. Chichester, UK, John Wiley & Sons, Ltd.

Quill, T.E. and Cassel, C.K. (1995). Non-abandonment: a central obligation for physicians. *Annals of Internal Medicine*, **122**, 368–374.

Rapley, T. (2008). Distributed decision making: The anatomy of decisions-in-action. *Sociology of Health and Illness*, **30**, 429–444.

Redelmeier, D.A., Koehler, D.J., *et al.* (1995). Probability Judgment in Medicine: Discounting unspecified possibilities. *Medical Decision Making*, **15**, 227–230.

Schneider, C.E. (1998). *The Practice of Autonomy: Patients, Doctors, and Medical Decisions*. New York: Oxford University Press.

Silvia, K.A., Ozanne, E.M., *et al.* (2008). Implementing breast cancer decision aids in community sites: Barriers and resources. *Health Expectations*, **11**, 46–53.

Thomson, J., Schofield, P., *et al.* (2006). Do oncologists discuss expensive anti-cancer drugs with their patients? *Annals of Oncology*, **17**, 702–708.

Chapter 18

Values clarification

Hilary A. Llewellyn-Thomas

Introduction

The background argument to this chapter relates to the context of preference-sensitive health care situations, where there is no single therapeutic action appropriate for all patients (Wennberg, 2002). Decision support is a systematic, theory-based clinical strategy for helping an individual in such a situation to arrive at an evidence-based patient choice among the relevant options – including the status quo (O'Connor *et al.*, 1998a, 1998b).

What is an evidence-based patient choice?

One condition for an evidence-based patient choice is that the patient accurately comprehends a clear synthesis of high-quality, balanced empirical reports about the clinical diagnosis, the available therapeutic options, and their inherent advantages and disadvantages – that is, the 'objective evidence'. While this is a necessary condition, it may be insufficient. We could argue that the patient's personal appraisal of the decision dilemma is an equally important form of evidence. Therefore, decision support should help the patient not only to comprehend the objective evidence but also to gain insight into his or her personally relevant 'subjective evidence', in order to make a choice that is more fully evidence-based.

There are at least three types of subjective evidence. One consists of information about whether the patient is experiencing either inadequate social support to engage with decision-making, or inappropriate social pressure to choose or reject a particular option. The second consists of awareness about the potential barriers to acting on the patient's preferred option, and the resources that he or she could draw upon to overcome those barriers.

The third type of subjective evidence can be coarse-grained or fine-grained. Coarse-grained subjective evidence consists of an overview of the patient's attitudes about the relative desirability of each therapeutic option. Fine-grained subjective evidence consists of detailed insight into the patient's attitudes about the relative desirability of each of the possible benefits and harms – or attributes – inherent in each option (O'Connor *et al.*, 2004). In the context of decision support, these evaluative attitudes are referred to as the patient's decision-focused 'values'. Thus, in this context, the term is limited; it is not intended to also refer to the patient's existential values.

The process of values clarification

'Values clarification' refers to the phase of decision support during which the third type of subjective evidence – in particular, the patient's evaluative attitudes at the fine-grained level – is revealed and brought to the mutual awareness of the patient and the clinician. However, it is very important to note four caveats.

First, values clarification may be helpful for patients who have not already formulated a strong prior preference, who wish to participate in shared decision-making but are in decisional conflict due to uncertainty about their own evaluative attitudes towards the relevant options and their attributes and who believe that assistance in sorting out those attitudes may be helpful (O'Connor, 1995). By corollary, it would not be imposed on patients who do not wish to engage in shared decision-making or who believe that attempts to sort out their evaluative attitudes would be distressing rather than helpful.

Second, it would be motivated by a genuine interest in helping the patient to identify and weigh the attributes that are personally important to him or her, to communicate those unique evaluative attitudes to their health care provider, to select a therapeutic option that is consistent with those decision-focused values, and to negotiate the system so that their informed choice is acknowledged and acted upon.

Third, the process ideally would be carried out in a manner that (a) avoids imposing providers' assumptions about what are the most relevant attributes of the options under consideration and (b) is free of deliberate or inadvertent framing and sequencing effects that could covertly influence the patient to favour or dismiss particular options.

Fourth, the process ideally would be carried out in a manner that leaves room for iteration because the formulation and reporting of values and the subsequent selection of a preferred therapeutic option are often dynamic, unfolding phenomena. Some individuals' attitudes about the attributes and their overall favoured option may remain constant, while others may report shifts as they gain deeper insights and experience with their decision situation (Fischhoff *et al.*, 1980; Llewellyn-Thomas, 1993, 2000; Sprangers and Schwartz, 2000; Wilson and Gilbert, 2003).

Values clarification methods

Various methods can be used to serve this complex process (see Figure 18.1). These can be loosely categorized as 'implicit/non-interactive' and 'explicit/interactive' approaches (O'Connor *et al.*, 2005). Here, for the ease of discussion, they are described as they would appear in formal patient decision aids (PtDAs).

Non-interactive methods

Some PtDAs – such as decision boards, videotapes, and DVDs (see Table 18.1) – are linear in format, in that their content is presented in a pre-determined sequence (Levine *et al.*, 1992; Detsky *et al.*, 2000). The sequence tends first to focus on providing objective information about two or more therapeutic options, and then to encourage the patient to consider their evaluative attitudes about those options. There are various non-interactive ways to provide this encouragement.

In the first example, the objective evidence about each option could be supplemented with detailed or vivid descriptions of the physical, social, and emotional effects of experiencing each option's potential benefits and harms (Nisbett and Ross, 1980). The assumption here is that, by making a hypothetical situation easier to imagine, patients are better able to clarify their evaluative attitudes, and then formulate their overall therapeutic preference.

In the second example, the objective evidence about each option could be supplemented with information about how different groups of patients might make different choices because they value the attributes of each option differently. The assumption here is that these illustrative examples help patients to sort through their personal values by considering which illustrative examples most closely match their own situation and which do not.

In the third example, the objective evidence about each option could be supplemented with presentations of 'patient testimonials'; these are often seen in video- or DVD-based decision aids.

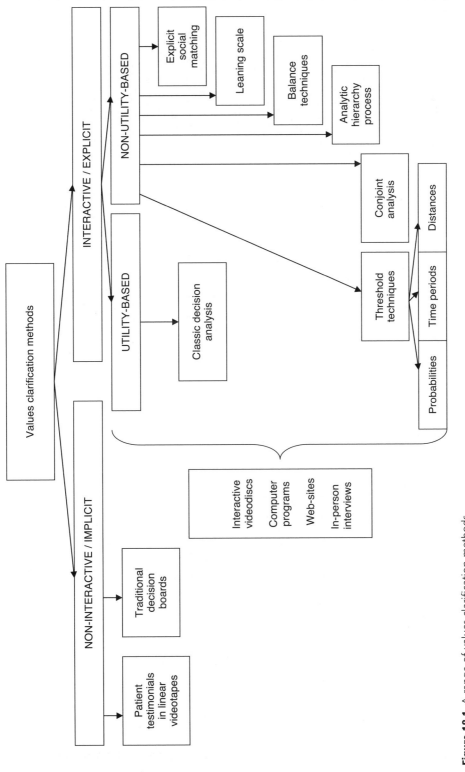

Figure 18.1 A range of values clarification methods.

Table 18.1 Examples of decision aids

	Sources	Procedure	End result	Advantages	Disadvantages
LINEAR VIDEOTAPES	Detsky, A. et al. (2000). A randomized trial of the ischemic heart disease shared decision making program: An evaluation of a decision aid. J. Gen. Intern. Med., 15, 685–693.	Linear videotape portrayal of diagnostic situation, treatment options and their associated risks/side effects; potential outcomes of each treatment option; and illustrations of other individuals' various treatment selections and their rationales. Underlying assumption is that patient engages in 'social matching' to formulate preferences.	Identify and select treatment option most preferred by patient, or defer selection until later.	Deliberately designed as formal patients' decision aid. Video suites could be prepared in an attempt to tailor to particular risk profiles. Icons, graphic illustrations of probabilities, and clinical sequences can increase comprehension. Portrayals of other individuals' rationales and selections can be interesting. Flexible to use in clinical setting. Patient also can work through on own, and then follow-up with clinician.	Cannot carry out process tracing to identify decision patterns. Difficult to build in explicit values-clarification exercises to assess which process/outcome attributes are affecting choice, unless accompanied by workbook. Expensive to produce, and for updating with new clinical information and preparing individualized components. Require technical equipment to display. Some patients may avoid technology.
TRADITIONAL DECISION BOARDS	Levine, M.N. et al. (1992). A bedside decision instrument to elicit a patient's preference concerning adjuvant chemotherapy for breast cancer. Ann. Intern. Med., 117, 53–58.	Velcro-backed cards on large boards systematically build up key information re. Diagnostic situation, treatment options, and their associated risks/side effects; potential beneficial outcomes of each treatment option; illustrations of individuals' various treatment selections, and their rationales.	Identify and select treatment option most preferred by patient, or defer selection until later.	Deliberately designed as formal patients' decision aid. Less expensive to produce, and for updating with new clinical information and preparing individualized components. Can be individualized and tailored to particular risk profiles. Icons, graphic illustrations of probabilities and clinical sequences can increase comprehension. Portrayals and interactive components can be engaging. Process tracing can be done to identify decision patterns. Flexible to use in clinical setting.	Require the presence of professional to provide background script, build up board systematically. Versions currently in the literature usually do not have explicit values clarification component, therefore can be difficult to assess which process/outcome attributes are affecting choice.

	Reference	Description	Purpose	Advantages	Disadvantages
INTERACTIVE VIDEODISCS / COMPUTER PROGRAMS / WEB-BASED PROGRAMS	Barry, M.J. et al. (1997). A randomized trial of a multimedia shared decision making program for men facing a treatment decision for benign prostatic hyperplasia. Disease Management and Clinical Outcomes, **1**, 5–14. Also: Spunt, B.S. et al. (1996). Health Educ. Res., **11**, 535–541.	Interactive videodisc or computer portrayal of diagnostic situation, treatment options, and their associated risks/side effects; potential beneficial outcomes of each treatment option; and illustrations of other individuals' various treatment selections and their rationales.	Identify and select treatment option most preferred by the patient, or defer selection until later.	Deliberately designed as formal patients' decision aid. Can be individualized and tailored to particular risk profiles. Icons, graphic illustrations of probabilities, and clinical sequences can increase comprehension. Portrayals and interactive components can be engaging. In PC versions can build in explicit value-clarification exercises to assess which process/outcome attributes are affecting choice. Process tracing can be done to identify decision patterns. Flexible to use in clinical setting. Patient also can work through on own, and then follow-up with clinician.	Expensive to produce and for updating with new clinical information and preparing individualized components. Require technical equipment to display. Some patients may be avoidant of technology.
AUDIOTAPES, WORKBOOKS & BALANCE SCALES	O'Connor A.M. et al. (1998). Randomized trial of a portable, self-administered decision aid for postmenopausal women considering long-term preventive hormone therapy. Med. Decis. Making, **18**, 295–303.	'Books-on-tape' format: audiotape and accompanying workbook systematically build up key information about diagnostic situation, treatment options, and their associated risks/side effects; potential beneficial outcomes of each treatment option; illustrations of individuals' various treatment selections and their rationales.	Identify and select treatment option most preferred by patient, or defer selection until later.	Deliberately designed as formal patients' decision aid. Less expensive to produce, and for updating. Suites of tapes/workbooks can be individualized and tailored to particular risk profiles. Icons, graphic illustrations of probabilities, and clinical sequences can increase comprehension. Portrayals and interactive components can be engaging. Balance scale explicitly assesses which process/outcome attributes affect choice. Flexible to use in clinical setting. Patient can work through on own, and then follow-up with clinician.	Process tracing to identify decision patterns cannot be done when patient works on own.

(continued)

Table 18.1 (continued) Examples of decision aids

Sources	Procedure	End result	Advantages	Disadvantages
ANALYTIC HIERARCHY PROCESS *Dolan, J.G. et al. (1989).* The analytic hierarchy process in medical decision making: A tutorial. *Med. Decis. Making,* **9**, 40–50. Also: Dolan JG. (1995). *Med. Decis. Making,* **15**, 76–80.	Problem structured re: goal of treatment; criteria to be satisfied; treatment actions to achieve the goal. Pairwise choices used to rank the criteria in terms of importance for goal achievement; then pairwise choices used to rank the actions relative to the achievement of each criterion.	Pairwise comparison matrix transformed, via algebraic vector analysis, into relative weights for different treatments. Identify and select treatment option most preferred by patient, or defer selection until later.	Could serve as both practitioners' and patients' decision aid. Less expensive to produce and for updating with new clinical information and preparing individualized components. Can be individualized and tailored to particular risk profiles. Icons, graphic illustrations of actions, criteria, and goal can increase comprehension. Interactive pairwise comparisons can be engaging and explicit values clarification exercise. Flexible to use in clinical setting.	Computation of final result complex, not intuitively obvious to patient. Not yet widely used to assess patient preferences at individual or group level– unexplored potential as patients' decision aid? Requires the presence of professional to provide background script, build up hierarchy, take patient through pairwise comparisons, do analysis.
CONJOINT ANALYSIS *Singh J et al. (1998).* Medical decision making and the patient: understanding preference patterns for growth hormone therapy using conjoint analysis. *Med. Care,* **36**(8), AS31–AS45. Also: *Wigton RS et al.* (1986). *Med. Decis. Making,* **6**, 2–11.	Set of treatment scenarios. Each scenario has several attributes (i.e. 4); each attribute at one of several levels (i.e 3). Fractional factorial designs often used so the full set of combinations is not necessary. Patients rank order scenarios from most to least preferred.	Resultant ordinal data subjected to conjoint analysis to estimate main effects of each attribute on patients' reports of overall treatment preferences. Cluster analysis can be used to identify aggregate preference structures.	Less expensive to produce, and for updating attributes/levels with new information. Flexible problem structure. Aggregate perspective can reveal attribute effects on across-therapy attitudes at social policy level – so, can be used to assess distributions of preferences in populations, and may be potentially a useful tool for policy negotiation?	Not really designed for use at an individual level as explicit values clarification exercise re. across-therapy attitudes. Icons, graphic illustrations of attributes/ levels not used; may be comprehension and fatigue problems. Computation of final result complex, not intuitively obvious to patient groups. Requires the presence of professional to provide background script, present scenario set, take patient through rank-ordering, do analysis.

THRESHOLD TECHNIQUES

Llewellyn-Thomas, H.A. (1997). Investigating patients' preferences for different treatment options. *Canadian J. Nursing Res.*, **29**, 45–64. Also: *Llewellyn-Thomas, H.A. et al. (1996) Med. Decis. Making*, **16**, 162–172.	Patient considers 2 (or more) alternative processes of care linked to different outcomes. Each process/outcome path contextually plausible. Asked to choose preferred path, and then attribute (probability or time) varied until patient switches to process/outcome path originally rejected. Selection of attribute that is varied and direction of systematic variation, are dependent on research purpose.	Elicits attitudes towards different process/outcome care paths, under conditions of risk or uncertainty. Can identify relative strength of preference (RSP), minimal clinically important difference (MCID), demanded risk reduction (DRR), maximally acceptable risk increment (MARI).	Very adaptable to a wide variety of clinical and health policy decision situations. Less expensive to produce and for updating with new clinical information and preparing individualized components. Can be individualized and tailored to particular risk profiles. Can be incorporated into videodiscs, decision boards. Icons, graphic illustrations of probabilities, and clinical sequences can increase comprehension. Requirement to make trade-off explicit is engaging. Less suitable for formal patients' decision aid. Requires the presence of professional to provide background script, build up trade-off systematically. Selection of process/outcome attribute to use in trade-off is tricky. Does not reveal if other process/outcome attributes are affecting choice; however, can collect qualitative data to identify such decision patterns.

Testimonials are recorded interviews with patients who talk about how they based their choices on their evaluative attitudes towards the options' different attributes (also see Chapter 30 by Winterbottom). The assumption here is that these personal stories help patients to appreciate the important role to be played by their own values in the decision situation.

Therefore, non-interactive approaches to values clarification rest on the general assumption that, as patients view the content of a decision aid, they will implicitly weigh out their subjective attitudes towards the relative desirability of the options and their attributes, and then derive an overall preference for one option compared to the others.

Interactive methods

Interactive approaches rely on hands-on exercises (see Table 18.1). These directly involve the patient in (a) considering an overview of each therapeutic option's positive and negative attributes, (b) adding other personally salient options and attributes, and then (c) explicitly revealing their evaluative attitudes towards this full roster of options and attributes. The exercises may take the form of rating or ranking the degree of personal importance the patient ascribes to each attribute and/or revealing the kinds of trade-offs across those attributes that the patient considers to be preferentially acceptable or unacceptable.

Interactive methods can, in turn, be *utility based* or *non-utility based*. Utility-based methods employ the standard gamble technique to elicit a patient's overall utility scores for the possible outcomes of each of the different options, and then fold those utilities into a formal decision analysis, and thereby indirectly identify the option with the highest expected utility for that patient (Llewellyn-Thomas, 1994, 1997; Holmes-Rovner, 1999).

The hands-on exercises used in non-utility-based methods do not involve the standard gamble. Instead, they use a wide range of either 'coarse-grained' or 'fine-grained' exercises that directly reveal the patient's evaluative attitudes. Coarse-grained exercises – such as O'Connor's leaning scale (O'Connor, 1998a) – directly reveal the patient's overall attitude towards each therapeutic option. Fine-grained exercises – such as O'Connor's balance technique (O'Connor, 1998a), Dolan's analytic hierarchy process (Dolan, 1995), and the threshold technique (Llewellyn-Thomas, 2002; Kopec, 2007) – directly reveal the patient's attitudes about the specific attributes of each option (see Table 18.1).

Interactive approaches rest on the general assumption that, by engaging with these hands-on tasks, the patient gains a deeper insight into his or her own constellation of decision-relevant values than that would be gained by passively viewing a decision aid. A further assumption is that these kinds of tasks help to reveal and communicate that unique set of values to others – such as the family and the clinician – which may, in turn, help to ensure that the patient receives the preferred therapeutic option (Guimond *et al.*, 2004).

Values clarification research

The systematic study of the values clarification process is very important; patients' decision aids are, by definition, used for decision support in *preference-sensitive* care contexts, and we need to know what we are doing at the interface between our provision of information and the patient's formulation of their preferences (Blank *et al.*, 2006).

Implicit approaches: Testing the assumptions underlying the use of patient stories

In high-quality video- or DVD-based decision aids, a considerable effort is devoted to ensuring that patient stories – whether they are in the form of hypothetical illustrative examples or actual recorded testimonials – are balanced, in that equal attention is devoted to patients' experiences with the pros and cons of various therapeutic options. However, there are a number of issues associated with using patients' stories in this way. For example, little is known about whether the attempt to present vivid stories may inadvertently push a patient's choice one way or the other, depending on whether he or she personally identifies with the socio-demographic characteristics of the people who are illustrated in or narrating their stories.

Furthermore, the attempt to present a fully 'balanced' set of patient stories in a decision aid may affect viewers' choices in invalid ways. For a fully balanced set, the decision aid should present a story for each possible combination of (a) experiencing either a positive or a negative treatment process while undergoing a particular option and (b) experiencing either a positive or a negative treatment outcome after undergoing a particular option. Therefore, for a two-option decision situation, a decision aid should present eight patients' stories, which could not only over-whelm the patient but also introduce order and sequencing effects that could bias their choices in unanticipated ways. Furthermore, in the attempt to present a 'balanced' roster of stories, a decision aid may over-represent relatively rare negative outcomes or under-represent common positive outcomes, which, in turn, could inadvertently push patients' choices one way or the other (Ubel *et al.*, 2001; Barnato *et al.*, 2007).

Explicit approaches: Which are most acceptable, feasible, and helpful?

Given the burgeoning complexity of preference-sensitive health care situations, it is increasingly important to launch comprehensive research programs to address the research questions inherent in using explicit values clarification exercises (O'Connor *et al.*, 1999; Feldman-Stewart *et al.*, 2006).

For example, within a particular patient population, are there different sub-groups of individuals who would prefer to be 'triaged' to different kinds of utility-based and non-utility-based methods? How well do different utility-based and non-utility-based methods work with different kinds of media, such as audiotapes, linear or interactive videos, personal computer programs, or in web-based format?

Are the results of a particular direct non-utility-based method for revealing a therapeutic preference consistent with the preference implied by indirect utility-based decision analysis, and under what conditions would consistency or inconsistency matter? Within the arena of direct non-utility-based approaches, are the results of different methods such as the balance technique/leaning scales and the analytic hierarchy process consistent with each other, and under what conditions does that matter?

As they work through explicit values-clarification exercises that are deliberately built into computer- or web-based interactive decision aids, can patients' values-formation pathways be tracked, as they sort out their attitudes towards the desirability or undesirability of different options and their potential benefits and harms? Are particular pathway patterns associated with different patient socio-demographic or clinical characteristics, or with different levels of information comprehension or anxiety?

How stable or labile are the results generated by coarse-grained and fine-grained explicit approaches to values clarification? Are the preferences revealed by subsequent actual behavior consistent with the preferences implied by earlier values clarification? Are the classic measure-ment concerns with stability and consistency of primary importance here, or are there decision support outcomes of greater clinical significance – such as reductions in decisional distress, increased information comprehension, self-reported readiness for decision-making, higher levels of self-reported decision self-efficacy, and down-stream adherence with therapy?

Conclusion

This chapter outlined how values clarification can play a role in the process of decision support, outlined a taxonomy of values clarification methods, and highlighted some of the research issues inherent in using these different implicit and explicit methods.

References

Barnato, A.E., Llewellyn-Thomas, H.A., Peters, E. *et al.* (2007). Communication and decision making in cancer care: Setting research priorities for decision support/patients decision aids. *Medical Decision Making*, **27**, 626–634.

Blank, T., Graves, K., Sepucha, K., and Llewellyn-Thomas, H. (2006). Understanding treatment decision making: Contexts, commonalities, complexities, and challenges. *Annals of Behavioral Medicine*, **32**, 211–217.

Detsky, A., Morgan, M., Deber, R., *et al.* (2000). A randomized trial of the ischemic heart disease shared decision making program: an evaluation of a decision aid. *Journal of General Internal Medicine*, **15**, 685–693.

Dolan, J.G. (1995). Are patients capable of using the analytic hierarchy process and willing to use it to help make clinical decisions? *Medical Decision Making*, **15**, 76–80.

Feldman-Stewart, D., Brennenstuhl, S., Brundage, M.D. (2006). An explicit values clarification task: Development and validation. *Patient Education and Counseling.*, **63**, 350–356.

Fischhoff, B., Slovic P., and Lichtenstein S. (1980). Knowing what you want: Measuring labile values. In T.S. Wallsten (ed) *Cognitive Processes In Choice And Decision Behavior*. Hillsdale, NJ: Lawrence Erlbaum Associates.

Guimond, P., Bunn, H., O'Connor, A., *et al.* (2004). Validation of a tool to assess health practitioners' decision support and communication skills. *Patient Education and Counseling.*, **50**, 235–245.

Holmes-Rovner, M., Kroll, J., Rovner, D., *et al.* (1999). Patient decision support intervention: Increased consistency with decision analytic models. *Medical Care*, **37**, 270–284.

Kopec, J.A., Richardson, C.G., Llewellyn-Thomas, H. *et al.* (2007). A probabilistic threshold technique showed that patients' preferences for specific tradeoffs between pain relief and each side effect of treatment in osteoarthritis varied. *Journal of Clinical Epidemiology.*, **60**, 929–938.

Levine, M.N., Gafni, A., Markham, B. *et al.* (1992). A bedside decision instrument to elicit a patient's preference concerning adjuvant chemotherapy for breast cancer. *Annals of Internal Medicine.*, **117**, 53–58.

Llewellyn-Thomas, H.A., Sutherland, H.J., and Thiel, E.C. (1993). Do patients evaluations of a future health state change when they actually enter that state? *Medical Care*, **31**, 1002–1012.

Llewellyn-Thomas, H.A. (1994). Turning decision analysis around. *Annals Royal College Physicians Surgeons of Canada*, **27**, 175–178.

Llewellyn-Thomas, H.A. (1997). Investigating patients' preferences for different treatment options. *Canadian Journal of Nursing Research,* **29**, 45–64.

Llewellyn-Thomas, H.A., and Schwartz, C.E. (2000). Response shift effects in patients' evaluations of health states: sources of artefact. In C.E. Schwartz and M.A.G. Sprangers (eds). *Adaptation to Changing Health: Response Shift in Quality-of-Life Research*. Washington, DC: American Psychological Association Press. pp. 109–122.

Llewellyn-Thomas, H.A., Paterson, J.M., Carter, J.A., *et al.* (2002). Primary prevention drug therapy: Can it meet patients' requirements for reduced risk? *Medical Decision Making*, **22**, 326–339.

Nisbett, R, and Ross, L. (1980). Assigning weights to data: The vividness criterion. *Human Inference: Strategies and Shortcomings of Social Judgment*. Englewood Cliffs, NJ: Prentice-Hall Inc., 43–62.

O'Connor, A.M. (1995). Validation of a decisional conflict scale. *Medical Decision Making*, **15**, 25–30.

O'Connor, A.M., Llewellyn-Thomas, H.A., and Stacey, D. (ed) (2005). *International Decision Aids Standards (IPDAS) Collaboration: Background Document*. Ottawa, Canada: Ottawa Health Research Institute. http://ipdas.ohri.ca/IPDAS_Background.pdf

O'Connor, A.M., Stacey, D., Entwistle, V., *et al.* (2004) Decision aids for people facing health treatment or screening decisions (Cochrane review). *The Cochrane Library*, 2. Chichester, UK: John Wiley & Sons, Ltd.

O'Connor, A.M., Tugwell, P., Wells, G.A., *et al.* (1998a). Randomized trial of a portable, self-administered decision aid for postmenopausal women considering long-term preventive hormone therapy. *Medical Decision Making*, **185**, 295–303.

O'Connor, A.M., Tugwell, P., Wells, G., *et al.* (1998b). A decision aid for women considering hormone therapy after menopause: Decision support framework and evaluation. *Patient Education and Counseling*, **33**, 267–279.

O'Connor, A.M., Wells, G., Tugwell, P., *et al.* (1999). The value of an explicit values clarification exercise in a women's decision aid regarding postmenopausal hormone therapy. *Health Expectations*, **2**, 21–32.

Sprangers, M.A.G and Schwartz, C.E. (2000). Integrating response shift into health-related quality-of-life research: A theoretical model, In C.E. Schwartz and M.A.G. Sprangers (eds.) *Adaptation to Changing Health: Response Shift in Quality-of-Life Research*. Washington, DC: American Psychological Association Press. pp. 11–23.

Ubel P.A., Jepson, C., and Baron, J. (2001). The inclusion of patient testimonials in decision aids: Effects on treatment choices. *Medical Decision Making*, **21**, 60–68.

Wennberg, J.E. (2002). Unwarranted variations in healthcare delivery: Implications for academic medical centers. *British Medical Journal*, **325**, 961–964.

Wilson, T.D., and Gilbert, D.T. (2003). Affective forecasting, in M.P. Zanna (ed) *Adv. Exp. Soc. Psychol.*, *Vol. 35*. San Diego, CA: Academic Press, Elsevier Science, 345–411.

Chapter 19

Risk communication – making evidence part of patient choices

Adrian Edwards

The challenge

Risk communication is an essential part of shared decision-making and evidence-based patient choice. It also needs to meet some complex needs for consumers, and is difficult to achieve well. The following quotations from Prior's study of risk discussions in genetics clinics illustrate the challenging 'pragmatic' setting in which any proposals need to be implemented (Wood *et al.*, 2003).

> 'I wasn't particularly worried about the genetic aspect of it, because as far as I am concerned I am more at risk anyway. I don't need a gene to tell me that. You know the fact that two sisters have had it, even if statistically I am not, in my mind I am more at risk. ... But I wasn't looking for a gene test to say I had the gene or anything. It was just really I wanted increased supervision ...'
>
> (Consumer assessed as 'moderate risk', breast cancer)

> 'I mean ... you know you read magazines and on the TV and they talk about 1 in 3 or 1 in 5 people in the population. And then you do a quick calculation in your head and there is my mum, my uncle and my auntie. And so that really puts me higher than 1 in 3. So I reckon I have got about 50:50 chance.'
>
> (Consumer assessed as 'moderate risk', colorectal cancer)

Addressing risk perceptions and communicating about the harms and benefits of health care options are difficult, but the initiatives undertaken are also often poorly thought through. For example, in the United Kingdom in 1995, information about the risk of venous thrombo-embolism among 'second generation' oral contraceptive pill users was primarily based on the relative risk – approximately doubling the risk. This raised alarm, and many users stopped taking their pills. Termination rates rose by almost 15,000 in the following year in the United Kingdom. Whilst this was over 10 years ago, other similar 'stories' indicate that the lessons have not been fully learned. For example, Hippisley-Cox and Coupland published data about the cardiac effects of non-steroidal anti-inflammatory drugs (Hippisley-Cox and Coupland, 2005). International media reported that 'Anti-inflammatory medications including COX-2 inhibitors and drugs like ibuprofen may be linked to an increased risk of heart attack, new research suggests' (Canadian media). But 'the authors of the study say no one should stop taking the drugs based on their results, which need to be confirmed by further research.' The absolute risk was hard to find reported, but, for example, for ibuprofen, one patient for every 1005 patients was at risk.

At a more general level, it is also clear that risk communication interventions have only modest effects on consumers. Across a range of settings and interventions, the mean effect size in an early systematic review of 100 intervention studies was only 0.15 (Edwards *et al.*, 2000). Risk communication interventions were, however, more effective in the context of making choices

---

Box 19.1: Uncertainty in the clinical encounter

- collective professional uncertainty
  which we address with more and better research

- individual professional uncertainty
  which we address with professional education and decision support

- stochastic uncertainty (irreducible chance element)
  which we address with effective 'risk communication' about the harms and benefits
  of different treatment or care options

(Edwards *et al.*, 2002)

---

about treatments (mean effect size 0.26) and if they used individual risk calculations (mean effect size 0.27), but these effects are still modest (Cohen and Manion, 1994).

Definition and context

The issue arises about how to improve risk communication. First, it is important to define it and see where this element fits in a context of clinician–consumer communication and the important influences on this interaction.

Ahl defined risk communication as 'the open two-way exchange of information and opinion about risk, leading to better understanding and better (clinical) decisions' (Ahl *et al.*, 1993). This is still a useful definition and basis for identifying improvements. However, it is also important to see the context for this element of communication. In our previous article about risk communication, Mulley identified three levels of uncertainty in the consultation (see Box 19.1) (Edwards *et al.*, 2002). Elwyn and colleagues have also identified the competences of shared decision-making (see Box 19.2). The two stages in the middle (italicized) represent the main contributions of risk communication, located within a process of shared decision-making. This process is described in more detail elsewhere in this volume (see Chapter 17) but here it is worth noting also that the process is often novel for both consumer and clinician, and both parties have to learn how to achieve it successfully. We should also be aware that the 'need' for risk communication isarguable driven more by professional and service agendas, perhaps more than consumers – in studies in clinical genetics, where risk communication is a particularly prominent element of the counselling, it is more often the supportive or emotional elements of counselling that provide benefits to users, rather than the informational or educational elements – (Edwards *et al.*, 2008).

Theory and practice of risk communication

There are several principles that can apply to either communication to populations or to individuals. Poortinga and Pidgeon identified the importance of ensuring the credibility of the source, being explicit about agendas, competing interests, and previous experience, understanding people's or public values and concerns, building trust, and maximizing the clarity of the message (Poortinga and Pidgeon, 2004).

When coming to put this into practice with individual consumers, many types of interventions have been tried and evaluated, but with limited effectiveness (Edwards *et al.*, 2000). Part of the reason for this may stem from inadequate attention to the notions of risk that individual consumers

Box 19.2: Competences of involving patients in decision-making

- Implicit or explicit involvement in decision-making process
- Identification of problem(s)
- Option portrayal
- Equipoise statements
- *Provide information in preferred format*
- *Checking:*
  understanding & reactions;
  acceptance of process & D-M role preference
- make, discuss or defer decision
- follow-up arrangements

(Elwyn *et al.*, 2000)

have, and often an atheoretical basis for the design of interventions. There is a need to base the interventions more on consumers' ideas about risk, perhaps modwwwwifying them where indicated and to use a stronger theoretical base than is evident in the literature to date.

Sivell and colleagues reviewed the way risk is 'constructed' – perceived, interpreted, and understood – in clinical genetics studies (Sivell *et al.*, 2008). The construction of risk is multi-factorial, but many common strands were evident. It is often influenced by past experiences, and a range of perceived causal factors was identified, including

- environmental factors,
- occupation,
- diet,
- stress and worry,
- physical resemblance to an affected relative, and
- genetic or family history factors.

Individuals experience difficulties in understanding numerical risk individuals, but they use their framework for understanding risk to aid *coping* with the risk. They live with it and experience it, as opposed to it being a detached, stand-alone concept (Sivell *et al.*, 2008). These perceptions and beliefs arguably need to be addressed more in design of risk communication interventions. A number of theories also offer potentially valuable frameworks to design interventions. Some mainly address the cognitive aspects of risk perception and communication. Others – and perhaps increasingly so recently – address the affective elements of risk as these are at least as if not more important in managing risk perceptions and behaviours (Slovic *et al.*, 2005).

Fuzzy-trace theory principally addresses cognitive aspects. This theory postulates that people have 'gist-based' representations of risk. These are often biased or have errors. The errors in risk estimation stem from distinct sources, each of which can then be targeted to minimize those errors (Reyna and Adam, 2003). It predicts 'unpacking' and memory effects. Interventions can be designed to improve risk perception by addressing in stepwise sequence: knowledge deficits, mental representations of risk (correcting where required), enabling the user to retrieve known information in the context and overcome 'processing interference' for overlapping risk categories. The aim is to design a theory-based intervention consistent with users' experiences, knowledge, and cognitive strategies (Reyna and Adam, 2003).

Protection motivation theory (Rogers and Prentice-Dunn, 1997) suggests that the impact of health risk information, and motivation for risk-reducing behaviour, is predicted by perceptions of the health threat and perceptions of strategies for reducing the threat. Interventions could be structured around these elements, addressing individuals' perceived severity of the threat, their vulnerability to the threat, the perceived effectiveness of a behaviour to reduce the threat and perceived confidence in one's ability to perform the behaviour (e.g. quitting smoking). Meta-analytic evidence indicates small-to-medium effects of each component on behaviour (Milne et al., 2000) so risk communication interventions might reasonably address each in turn.

There has been increasing attention to different 'modes' of information processing. These include 'dual-process theories of information processing' such as the Elaboration Likelihood Model (Petty and Cacioppo, 1986). Two fundamental ways in which people comprehend risk have been identified. The first is the *'analytic'* or deliberative system, which uses rules, logic, and risk assessment, and in which behaviour is viewed as being mediated by conscious appraisal of events. The second is the *'experiential'* or affective system – intuitive, fast, mostly automatic, and not very accessible to conscious awareness. Behaviour is often based on more holistic and affective appraisals. Slovic and colleagues describe these two ways of comprehending risk, respectively, as 'risk as analysis' and 'risk as feeling' (Slovic et al., 2004). (They also note drily that where the two differ it becomes 'risk as politics'.)

The common sense model of illness perceptions suggests that cognitive and emotional representations determine coping and emotional responses to risk. It is based on five key constructs – the identity, cause, and timeline of an illness, what its consequences are and whether it is curable or controllable (Leventhal et al., 1980). These elements can be used to structure the design for instance of decision aids, perhaps complementing other theories such as the Theory of Planned Behaviour (Ajzen, 1985, 1991) (e.g. see www.bresdex.com). According to the TPB, whether someone intends to behave in a certain way depends on the extent to which they perceive themselves to be in control over a given behaviour, as well as their attitudes and the 'perceived social norms'. Additional constructs to the TPB have been suggested, including anticipated affective reactions, which may be key determinants of both attitudes and intentions (Triandis, 1977; van der Pligt and de Vries, 1998). One such construct is anticipated regret – an emotion experienced when an individual believes feelings of regret will occur following inaction, or opting for one course of action over another (Abraham and Sheeran, 2003).

Rothman and Kiviniemi have separated the 'antecedents' and the 'consequences' of a risk or behaviour – again potentially as a basis for designing risk communication interventions (Rothman and MT, 1999). The antecedent information is about whether the risk is voluntary or controllable. Such information helps people think how a problem could develop, and how to alter their chances of developing a condition. Consequence information is about whether the illness can be detected or whether it would be 'catastrophic' and what it would be like to have the health problem. These elements are influential in people's perceptions of risk – it remains for evaluation as to how influential they may be in the design of risk communication and decision aids.

The 'Mental models' approach also adds another dimension, this time by explicitly juxtaposing expert and users' views. Users' concerns, experiences of health, knowledge of protective measures, and concerns about information are identified. Interventions can be based on these, reinforcing appropriate knowledge, filling in gaps in knowledge, and restructuring misinterpretations where indicated (Cox et al., 2003).

Where does this lead?

The above theoretical models represent a sample only of the range of models that may help to improve the design and application of risk communication interventions, both for face-to-face

Box 19.3: Competences of risk communication

Remind patients that virtually all treatment options are associated with some possibility of risks

Avoid explaining risks in purely descriptive terms (e.g. 'low risk').

♦ descriptive terms may convey a totally different order of magnitude to the patient than you intend

Have a clear reference class – who or what does the risk refer to?

Avoid percentages – use natural frequency format

♦ e.g. '1 in 5 people', or '12 in 100 people' is much less open to misinterpretation

Use consistent denominator

♦ e.g. 40 out of a thousand, 5 out of a thousand instead of 1 in 25 and 1 in 200

Balanced framing

♦ i.e. chances of survival and chances of death; etc.

Use absolute numbers wherever possible, not relative risks.

♦ e.g. 1995 Contraceptive Pill scare or 2005 NSAIDs

Seek appropriate visual aids

♦ can help a range of consumers see the risk numbers in context, providing information and not just data

Discussing these visual aids makes the doctor and patient come together

♦ non-verbal communication in consultations provides positive opportunities

Explore the significance of the risk to the individual

♦ a 'stroke' means different things to different people

♦ sharing understanding may be at least as important as sharing the numerical information

Share uncertainty if it is genuinely unclear what the best course of action might be.

♦ honesty may lead to greater professional respect in the long run

(Paling, 2003)

counselling contexts and for example for use in decision aids. The latter offer scope particularly to make information (and decision support) available to consumers, and this can achieve shorter consultations but which are able to focus more on the supportive elements of counselling (Edwards *et al.*, 2008). As above also, the effects of more theoretically based interventions remain to be evaluated, but this also reminds us about the question of what risk communication is for? What is 'effectiveness'? Thomson and colleagues have debated this, particularly when it influences public health challenges (Thomson *et al.*, 2005). There are ways of persuading people to make behavioural changes and other risk reductions, to achieve public health gain (Edwards *et al.*, 2006). However, it is more justifiable to see risk communication as building into a model of informed decision-making for the individual, based on ethical principles of autonomy, fairness, and veracity (Eriksson *et al.*, 2007; Thomson *et al.*, 2005).

Clinicians also need to know where their contribution to the process of informed decision-making is appropriate from an ethical perspective, and where it is not. Jensen and colleagues note how clinicians have professional authority to 'present the facts' but they should avoid the temptation to exercise professional authority in making value judgments. The individual consumer has legitimate interests in the discussion, and their value judgments are valid. We react with resistance when someone tries to change our value judgments by appealing to their authority in the matter (Jensen *et al.*, 2005).

Is there a 'new medical conversation'?

Nonetheless 'experts' probably do understand the lay perspective quite well, and lay people are also not necessarily insensitive to frequencies (Jensen *et al.*, 2005). Humans have 'evolved into reasonable intuitive statisticians and should have the chance to use these attributes' (Cosmides and Tooby, 1996). A 'new medical conversation' is taking shape (Mazur, 2002). Paling identified a number of competences and principles that clinicians and designers of risk communication should adhere to. These are summarized in Box 19.3 and enlarged on elsewhere (Paling, 2006). Gigerenzer tells of a surgeon who said 'I went into surgery because I knew I didn't want anything to do with psychology or statistics . . . but now I know I must deal with all of them' (Gigerenzer, 2002). The challenge is to continue trying to improve risk communication in health care, turning data into something more meaningful, relevant, and useful for individual consumers. By adopting simple and practical strategies (Box 19.3) and with a stronger theoretical base from other disciplines, the prospects would now seem more promising.

References

Abraham, C. and Sheeran, P. (2003). Acting on intentions: The role of anticipated regret. *British Journal of Social Psychology*, **42**, 495–511.

Ahl, A.S., Acree, J.A., Gipson, P.S., *et al.* (1993). Standardisation of nomenclature for animal health risk analysis. *Reviews of Scientific & Technical Office, UK Government*, **12**, 1045–1053.

Ajzen, I. (1985). From intention to actions: A theory of planned behaviour. *In* J. Kuhl and J. Beckmann (eds) *Action-control: From Cognition to Behavior*. Heidelberg: Spring.

Ajzen, I. (1991). The theory of planned behaviour. *Organizational Behavior and Human Decision Processes*, **50**, 179–211.

Cohen, L. and Manion, L. (1994). *Research Methods in Education*. London: Routledge.

Cosmides, L. and Tooby, J. (1996). Are humans good intuitive statisticians after all? Rethinking some conclusions from the literature on judgment under uncertainty. *Cogn.*, **58**, 1–73.

Cox, P., Niewohmer, J., Pidgeon, N., *et al.* (2003).The use of mental models in chemical risk protection: Developing a generic workplace methodology. *Risk Analysis*, **23**, 311–324.

Edwards, A., Elwyn, G., and Mulley, A.G. (2002). Explaining risks: Turning numerical data into meaningful pictures. *British Medical Journal*, **324**, 827–830.

Edwards, A., Evans, R., Dundon, J., *et al.* (2006). Personalised risk communication for informed decision making about taking screening tests. *Cochrane Database of Systematic Reviews*, **4**.

Edwards, A., Gray, J., Clarke, A., *et al.* (2008). Interventions to improve risk communication in clinical genetics: Systematic review. *Patient Education & Counselling*, **71**, 4–25.

Edwards, A., Hood, K., Matthews, E., *et al.* (2000). The effectiveness of one-to-one risk communication interventions in health care: systematic review. *Medical Decision Making*, **20**, 290–297.

Elwyn, G., Edwards, A., Kinnersley, P., *et al.* (2000) Shared decision-making and the concept of equipoise: Defining the 'competences' of involving patients in health care choices. *British Journal of General Practice*, **50**, 892–899.

Eriksson, T., Nilstun, T., and Edwards, A. (2007). The ethics of risk communication in lifestyle interventions - towards a new view on medical ethical principles. *Health, Risk & Society*, **9**, 19–36.

Gigerenzer, G. (2002). Ch 12: How Innumeracy can be exploited. *Reckoning with risk – learning to live with uncertainty* (1st Edition). London: Penguin Press.

Hippisley-Cox, J. and Coupland, C. (2005). Risk of myocardial infarction in patients taking cyclo-oxygenase-2 inhibitors or conventional non-steroidal anti-inflammatory drugs: Population based nested case-control analysis. *British Medical Journal*, **330**, 1366.

Jensen, K., Lassen, J., Robinson, P., *et al.* (2005). Lay and expert perceptions of zoonotic risks: Understanding conflicting perspectives in the light of moral theory. *International Journal of Food Microbiology.*, **99**, 245–255.

Leventhal, H., Meyer, D., and Nerenz, D. (1980). The common-sense representation of illness danger. *In* S. Rachman, (ed) *Medical Psychology*, New York: Pergamon Press.

Mazur, D. (2002). *The New Medical Conversation.* Boulder, CT: Rowman and Littlefield Inc.

Milne, S., Sheeran, P., and Orbell, S. (2000). Prediction and intervention in health-related behavior: A meta-analytic review of protection motivation theory. *Journal of Applied Social Psychology*, **30**, 106–143.

Paling, J. (2003). Strategies to help patients understand risks. *British Medical Journal*, **327**, 745–748.

Paling, J. (2006). *Helping Patients Understand Risks.* Gainesville, FL: The Risk Communication Institute.

Petty, R. and Cacioppo, J. (1986). *Communication and Persuasion: Central and PeripheralRroutes to Attitude Change.* New York: Springer-Verlag.

Poortinga, W. and Pidgeon, N. (2004). Trust, the asymmetry principle, and the role of prior beliefs. *Risk Anal.*, **24**, 1475–1486.

Reyna, V.F. and Adam, M.B. (2003). Fuzzy-trace theory, risk communication, and product labeling in sexually transmitted diseases. *Risk Anal.*, **23**, 325–342.

Rogers, R. and Prentice-Dunn, S. (1997). Protection motivation theory. *In* D. Gochman, (ed) *Handbook of Health Behavior Research 1: Personal and Social Determinants.* Springer, New York.

Rothman, A.J. and MT, K. (1999). Treating people with information: An analysis and review of approaches to communicating health risk information. *Journal of the National Cancer Institiute Monographs*, **25**, 44–52.

Sivell, S., Elwyn, G., Gaff, C., *et al.* (2008). How risk is perceived, constructed and interpreted by clients in clinical genetics, and the effects on decision making: Systematic review. *J. Genet. Couns.*, **17**, 30–63.

Slovic, P., Finucane, M., Peters, E., *et al.* (2004). Risk as analysis and risk as feelings: Some thoughts about affect, reason, risk and rationality. *Risk Anal.*, **24**, 311–322.

Slovic, P., Peters, E., Finucane, M., *et al.* (2005). Affect, risk and decision making. *Health Psychology*, **24**, S35–S40.

Thomson, R., Murtagh, M. and Khaw, F. (2005). Tensions in public health policy: Patient engagement, evidence-based public health and health inequalities. *Qual. Saf. Health Care*, **14**, 398–400.

Triandis, H. (1977). *Interpersonal Behavior.* CA: Brookes-Cole.

van der Pligt, J. and de Vries, N. (1998). Expectancy-value models of health and behaviour: The role of salience and anticipated affect. *Psychol. Health*, **13**, 289–305.

Wood, F., Prior, L., and Gray, J. (2003). Making decisions in a cancer genetics clinic. *Health Risk Soc.*, **5**, 185–198.

Chapter 20

Measuring 'decision quality': Irresolvable difficulties and an alternative proposal

Glyn Elwyn, Benjamin Elwyn, and Talya Miron-Shatz

Introduction

Although the task of involving patients in decision-making tasks has become the focus of increasing attention over the last decade, there is also a realization that we struggle to measure what would constitute success in this area. Important questions remain, such as what constitutes a good decision or a high-quality decision and how to measure decision quality. We recognize that definitions of decision quality and other similar terms have been put forward. In this paper, it is our intention to examine these definitions, to highlight the ways in which they converge, and to explain why we have some concerns about their emphasis on post hoc evaluations. We proceed to offer an alternative, which parses 'decisions' into a pre-decisional *process* and a post-decisional *outcome*.

The emphasis on involvement in decisions comes about partly because of the realization that in many medical scenarios evidence for the effectiveness of interventions is scarce and partly because the patients' contribution – their views and preferences – is being given a central place in clinical encounters (Schneider, 1998). This marks a definite shift away from paternalism to a process where patients are offered support to become actively engaged in decision-making tasks (Elwyn *et al.*, 1999). Efforts are therefore being made to involve patients in decision-making steps and research into this topic has expanded significantly over the last decade, with terms such as 'shared decision-making' (Charles *et al.*, 1997), 'evidence-based patient choice' (Hope, 1996), and 'informed choice' (Raffle, 2001) becoming common parlance.

The main approaches made to improve the quality of decision-making in health care to date have been as follows. Firstly, there has been an interest in developing the skills of practitioners to involve patients in decisions – a process often known as shared decision-making – with the aim of increasing the role patients play and ultimately – although arguably implicitly – to improve decision quality. Secondly, decision support technologies (decision aids) (O'Connor *et al.*, 2007) – information resources that are also designed to help patients take part in health care decisions – are being introduced as additional tools to assist this process of enhancing engagement in decision-making and enhance decision quality. Both approaches suggest that the patient becomes actively engaged in deciding a course of rather than the professional acting alone. We start by examining different approaches to the assessment of decisions and continue to pose the question of whether decisions can be attributed as having high or low quality and how this can be measured. Finally, we offer an alternative, perhaps the more modest approach, focusing on the quality of the decision process, rather on the end result.

We feel that this examination is necessary because in addition to the move away from paternalism to a patient-centred choice model (Coulter, 1999; Elwyn *et al.*, 2003), evidence-based medicine has emphasized the need to integrate empirical research data into clinical practice. However, paradoxically, this emphasis has drawn attention to the considerable uncertainty that surrounds most medical interventions and to the fact that a single correct course of action can seldom be advocated. Therefore, there is recognition that patient preferences should be given central voice in decision-making processes. Given the prominence and importance of this trend to involve patients in decision-making and the lack of consensus over metrics, we are motivated to add to the debate on what would constitute a high-quality decision. A better answer would help make progress in designing and evaluating decision support and doctor–patient communication strategies, as well as improve decisions and decision-making processes (Ratliff *et al.*, 1999). We start by considering a range of definitions. Below we offer our perspective on some converging aspects of these definitions and propose a modest alternative which leaves the decision outcome outside the evaluation picture and which places emphasis on the quality of deliberative processes, which *de facto* have to be founded on the acquisition of knowledge and the construction of preferences.

Existing definitions of *decision quality*

The conceptual question 'what is a good decision' was considered by a number of experts in a series of short essays (Ratliff *et al.*, 1999), although they did not offer formal definitions and did not offer suggestions as to how to measure 'good decisions'. A notable consistency in most essays was the view that although assessing decision quality was complex, it was important to avoid dependence on the outcomes of decisions. Good (or bad) decisions have good or bad outcomes by virtue of chance, at the individual level. For instance, Fisher and Fisher (Ratliff *et al.*, 1999) place emphasis on both how the decision is achieved and how satisfied the relevant parties are with the decision. Interestingly, they conclude by stating that 'because a good or bad outcome may powerfully influence perceptions (of decision quality) . . . such a judgement is best made before the outcome is known' (page 190). As the relevant parties cannot possess *a priori* certain knowledge of the outcome, we embrace the need for pre-outcome judgement of a decision. However, we note that recent definitions, as will be shown below, do not fully attend to the difficulty of post hoc judgements.

Ratliff (Ratliff *et al.*, 1999) argues a definite need for *knowledge* – that the person is informed – and that decisions reflect an individual's *preferences*. Her views are picked up by more recent work, which reflects, almost a decade later, increasing interest in definitions and the design of measurement tools for decision quality, although these remain contentious. For instance, Sepucha *et al.* (2007) proposed that '. . . the quality of a preference-sensitive clinical decision can be defined as the extent to which the implemented decision reflects the considered preferences of a well-informed patient.' p. 262. In a similar vein, O'Connor proposed that 'decision quality can be measured by. . . knowledge about the options and outcomes, realistic perceptions of outcome probabilities, and agreement between patients' values and choices.' p. 3 (O'Connor *et al.*, 2003). Marteau, adding to O'Connor, proposes a slight variant with the construct of 'informed choice': 'an informed choice is one that is based on relevant knowledge, consistent with a decision-maker's values and behaviourally implemented' (Marteau *et al.*, 2001). Inherent in her definition, however, is that the enacted choice (the decision effectively) is one based on adequate knowledge and is consistent with the individual's views, values, or preferences.

Critique of existing definitions of decision quality

In this section, we offer a criticism of prevailing definitions of decision quality regarding three elements: the knowledge they propose to measure, the preferences they propose to use as a yardstick of 'true' will, and the timing in which they propose to evaluate the decision. Almost all attempts at defining good decisions propose that knowledge about the options and consequences is necessary. Putting aside for the moment those who propose that intuition trumps knowledge-based deliberative work (Dijksterhuis *et al.*, 2006), we need to acknowledge that the assessment of this construct is problematic – knowledge about *what* for instance? About the nature of outcomes plus the probabilities of those outcomes? About the *features* (attributes) of short-, medium-, and long-term future states, given likely pathways? About the experiences of others who have chosen different options? Can we specify the optimal degree of search for information (as a proxy for knowledge) or when to stop the search? Can we specify the degree of knowledge that is necessary and sufficient (as well as different for every clinical scenario), or is this a quantity that we allow the decision maker to determine? Do we assume that knowledge (informedness) equates to understanding or does this not worry us? Efforts so far to operationalize the knowledge component of 'decision quality' scales have proposed key 'facts', typically about the nature and outcomes of options (Sepucha *et al.*, 2007). In addition, given what we know about the tendency for knowledge retention to decay over time, when is the correct time to assess this (Edwards, 2006) knowledge? To sum, although seemingly attractive to measure, knowledge as a necessary component of decision quality is difficult to operationalize and, at a deeper level, may be an untested feature of our theoretical stance – a belief that standardized and pre-specified levels of knowledge are necessary for good decisions. Furthermore, as we claim throughout this chapter, 'good decisions' are yet to be defined.

The second area of consensus is based on declaring the importance of what are most commonly called values or preferences – that these entities are fundamental in allowing individuals to express their own control over decisions. Nevertheless, difficulties abound in this area as well. First, there is confusion over terms. The use of the term 'values' in decision-making is commonly linked to the concept of utility assessment as required by expected utility theory. Utility assessment, in the classical sense, requires a numerical estimation (typically between zero and one) using a person's global assessment of the value of different options, often characterized as likely outcomes. Sometimes, however, the term is also used to describe broader approaches or attitudes – such as risk aversion for example or a general stance on, say, the avoidance of medication. The term 'preferences' is often used interchangeably with values but seems to refer most often to *attributes* of options that some options have a more significant or more worrying range of disadvantages, e.g. drug side-effects that a patient *prefers* to avoid, and hence avoids the associated option. As Marteau notes in an accompanying chapter (Marteau, 2009), measurement of 'value-consistent choices have received less attention' and suggests that this area requires more attention.

Another term used in the decision-making literature is 'the construction of preferences'. This implies that preferences do not exist in advance, waiting to be revealed. There is indeed evidence that preferences are constructed as individuals gain information, obtain representations of the options, and weigh alternatives against each other (Lichtenstein, 2006). Furthermore, people are often inconsistent in what they state as their 'values' and what they actually choose (Lichtenstein, 2006). For instance, work on transitivity, one of the axioms of the rationalistic expected utility theory, has demonstrated that people who prefer A to B and B to C often do not follow the mathematical logic of preferring A to C because the alternatives do not share the same features. The fluidity and malleability of preferences make it hard to suggest preferences as a yardstick against which decisions are made. It seems, therefore, problematic to operationalize a measure of decision quality when there is drift both in the understanding of the terms, values, and preferences and as to how these entities are integrated during deliberation processes.

The final critique is about the notion of when a decision can be evaluated. Our major concern is that decisions cannot be evaluated *after* they have been performed. Sepucha uses the term 'implemented decision' (Sepucha *et al.*, 2007), which we think implies that the decision's quality will be judged after the event, when the decision has been taken and – importantly – the outcome is known. Similarly, Marteau used the term 'behaviourally implemented' (Marteau *et al.*, 2001), suggesting that the decision or some action has been performed prior to the assessment of (in her case) informed choice. O'Connor's definition contains the phrase 'agreement between patients' values and choices made' (O'Connor *et al.*, 2003), again implying that an assessment of decision quality would be made after the decision had been made. To date, O'Connor's measurement of decision quality and, specifically, of congruence between values and actions is done post hoc. The issue of *when* the decision quality is to be measured is not spelled out in these definitions, so we may be interpreting these definitions incorrectly. Yet the way in which Sepucha *et al.* have operationalized 'decision quality' measures – i.e. as instruments to be used *after* decision-making interventions have been implemented and decisions achieved – indicates that they propose to assess decision quality, i.e. consistency between knowledge and declared preferences *after* decisions have been made, when preferences may have accordingly shifted. Marteau, in fact, explicitly proposes measurement after decisions have taken place. Our concern is that measuring decision quality after the outcome is known inevitably leads to bias in the appraisal of that decision.

Irresolvable problems with current definitions?

We cannot argue with the view that knowledge and preferences seem fundamental to the measurement of a capacity to take a decision but have concerns about the specificity of such measurement aims and about yardsticks, given the indeterminate nature of these constructs and that sufficient knowledge might vary from one person to another. The timing of measurement is also critical. As we have shown above, there are important reasons to avoid post hoc measurement of *decision quality*. The first problem with this post hoc measurement is that of time. The period of time after any decision is infinite and it is unclear at which point in time a judgement should be made about the quality of a decision. Given this indeterminate duration, appraisals are inevitably fleeting: judgements about decisions can be negative at first, and then positive (or vice versa), and then keep switching depending on the point of assessment. The second problem is that of the role of chance. Decisions are in effect wagers: 'A good decision cannot guarantee a good outcome. All real decisions are made under uncertainty. A decision is therefore a bet, and evaluating it as good or not must depend on the stakes and the odds, not on the outcome.' (p. 7, (Edwards, 1984)). While a good decision maker might assess the outcome probabilities for each option, gambles by definition cannot be predicted ahead of time. The impossibility of ever knowing *outcomes in advance* leads to the conclusion that assessments of decision 'quality' seem time-bound, and that from one moment to the next, views about their quality can shift, if judgements are based on outcomes as Fischoff, Baron, and Hershey have demonstrated (Fischhoff, 1975; Baron and Hershey, 1988). The difficulty posed by this realization is challenging and seemingly irresolvable. Whilst we can and do appraise our decisions, as good or bad decisions, based on how well we fared when we followed the path we chose, we cannot really equate this to being the same as a high-quality decision: time works against us and colours our judgement. This problem is augmented when *decision outcome* quality serves as the ultimate measure against which knowledge and preferences are evaluated.

If not outcomes, should we measure process?

Having dismissed the possibility of using of post hoc assessment of decision quality on the grounds that they are dominated by outcomes we need to *consider what other alternatives are possible?* We face the argument that decisions, once they have been made, are always viewed retrospectively.

This difficulty cannot be resolved if we accept that there is a border between the *processes of deliberating* about decisions and the *making and enactment* of decisions (Edwards, 2006). Although this may appear equivalent to dancing on the head of a pin – the distinction between decision process and decision enactment – between the deliberation process and the act of either taking route A or route B is key to the debate about the measurement of decision quality. Whoever wishes to define a good decision and to facilitate such decisions needs to differentiate clearly between the *quality* of the deliberative process and an *appraisal* of the decision – the choice made and any associated short-, medium-, or long-term outcomes. If we accept that outcomes are not a sound basis for assessing the quality of a decision, and that they taint any post-decisional evaluation, we are left with the contention that we would better focus on the quality of the deliberation and shift our measurement focus to the quality of a decision process.

Moving to a measure of deliberation – a decision process measure

An underpinning theoretical construct to measurement would be based on the following premises. First, accept that humans have to act on limited information availability when making decisions but contend that decisions made without any information are mere guesses. It follows, therefore, that data about the nature of the decision, the relevant option set, the positive and negative attributes of options, the probabilities that they occur over relevant time horizons should be both available and formatted in high-quality representations. Ample work (Gigerenzer, 1996; Miron-Shatz *et al.*, 2008) has demonstrated that certain formats (namely natural frequencies) are conducive to the comprehension of numeric risk information. Setting aside for a moment the sensitive issue of various farming effects, and the notion that information is invariably represented in one way or another, and that representation will influence understanding, a good decision process would ensure the availability of relevant, well-presented information and that a process of assimilation and, if necessary, clarification was undertaken, to gain maximum understanding. Second, accept that preference construction is a temporal and inter-subjective process that involves both cognitive and emotional contributions and is a fundamental step in decision-making, as it is ultimately the integration and the weighting of preferences, based on new information about attributes of options that leads to the ability to make a choice. For a theory of deliberation, wherein deliberation process quality is fulcrum, we make the premise that it is helpful to elicit preferences, to examine them, by discussion with other if necessary, and to either rank or weigh the negative and positive attributes of options, irrespective of the evidence that humans may not have the ability to achieve complete transitive accuracy. Given mental processing limitations and the fact that most reasoning is based on scarce input (Gigerenzer and Todd, 1999), it might suffice to allow the person to articulate what does she seek in an alternative and what she wishes to avoid. We propose that a good decision process would, therefore, provide opportunities to undertake these tasks, prior to a decision-making steps. It seems obvious but nevertheless important to state that these two processes of providing information and constructing preference assessments are co-dependent: one cannot form a view about preferences unless one has data about their attributes and probabilities. We suggest that, while it is the patient who makes the decisions, it is the professional's responsibility to present the information properly and to encourage an open preference elicitation process. Both these are prerequisites for a good quality deliberation process.

It also follows that measurement could be based on a number of data collection methods. The deliberation process could be observed and analysed; although as most deliberative processes occur over time and involve numerous interactions, the research burden is considerable.

Another method is to assess the patient's perspective on the deliberation steps. Have they received information and was it sufficient for them to be able to visualize the choice, the options and their respective attributes? Have they been able to elicit, examine, and assess their preferences, to the degree that it was sufficient for them to be in a position to make judgements? Ours is not a prescriptive tool in the sense that we do not decree how much information or how much deliberation is sufficient *for the particular patient*. Such a proposed measure suffers from being a subjective tool with no pre-set benchmarks or gold standards, but represents a method of gauging an individual's journey from a position of not understanding that choices exists, each with option attributes that need assessment, to a position of having deliberated to a level where they feel able to decide.

Conclusion

A focus on measure of deliberation provides potential benefits: it would help to distinguish and illuminate those parts of the global decision endeavour that are in the realm of one's control and responsibility. It focuses on pre-decision and ties in with the advances in patient–professional communication, as well as in the proliferation of decision support. By disentangling the process from the outcome, we allow for the evaluation not to hinge on whether a procedure succeeded, which can colour judgements on how well prepared, how ready one is to take decisions. In the final analysis, this is as much as we can do: the rest we have to leave to chance.

Acknowledgements

We thank Dominick Frosch, Adrian Edwards, Paul White, and Natalie Joseph for comments on drafts of this chapter.

References

Baron, J. and Hershey, J.C. (1988). Outcome bias in decision evaluation. *Journal of Personality and Social Psychology*, **54**, 569–579.

Charles, C., Gafni, A., *et al.* (1997). Shared decision-making in the medical encounter: What does it mean? (Or it takes at least two to tango). *Soc. Sci. Med.*, **44**, 681–692.

Coulter, A. (1999). Paternalism or partnership? *British Medical Journal*, **319**, 719–794.

Dijksterhuis, A., Bos, M.W., *et al.* (2006). On making the right choice: The deliberation-without-attention effect. *Science*, **311**, 1005–1007.

Edwards, A. and Elwyn, G. (2006). Inside the black box of shared decision making: Distinguishing between the process of involvement and who makes the decision. *Health Expect.*, 307–320.

Edwards, W. (1984). How to make good decisions. (Selected proceedings *9th research conference on subjective probability, utility and decision making*). *Acta Psychologica*, **56**, 5–27.

Elwyn, G., Edwards, A., *et al.* (1999). Shared decision making: The neglected second half of the consultation. *BJGP*, **49**, 477–482.

Elwyn, G., Rhydderch, M., *et al.* (2003). Shared decision making. In C. Silagy and N. Britten (eds) Oxford Textbook of Primary Medical Care. Oxford: Oxford University Press.

Fischhoff, B. (1975). Hindsight ≠ Foresight: The effect of outcome knowledge on judgement under uncertainty. *J. Exp. Psychol.*: Hum. Percept. Perform., **1**, 288–299.

Gigerenzer, G. (1996). The Psychology of good judgement: Frequency formats and simple algorithms. *Medical Decision Making*, **16**, 273–280.

Gigerenzer, G. and Todd, P.M. (1999). Simple Heuristics that Make us Smart. New York: Oxford University Press.

Hope, T. (1996). Evidence-Based Patient Choice. London: King's Fund Publishing.

Lichtenstein, S. and Slovic, P. (2006). The Construction of Preference. Cambridge: Cambridge University Press.

Marteau, T. (2009). Informed choice: A construct in search of a name. In A. Edwards and G. Elwyn (eds) Evidence-Based Patient Choice. Oxford: Oxford University Press.

Marteau, T.M., Dormandy, E., et al. (2001). A measure of informed choice. Health Expectations, **4**, 98–108.

Miron-Shatz, T., Hanoch, Y., et al. (2008). Presentation format, numeracy, and emotional reactions: The case of prenatal screening. Journal of Health Communication (**in submission**).

O'Connor, A.M., Wennberg, J., et al. (2007). Towards the 'tipping point': Decision aids and informed patient choice. Health Aff., **26**, 716–725.

O'Connor, A. M., Stacey, D., et al. (2003). Decision aids for people facing health treatment or screening decisions. Cochrane Database of Systematic Reviews, 2, CD001431.

Raffle, A.E. (2001). Information about screening: Is it to achieve high uptake or to ensure informed choice? Health Expectations., **4**, 92–98.

Ratliff, A., Angel, M., et al. (1999). What is a good decision? Eff. Clin. Pract., **2**, 185–197.

Schneider, C.E. (1998). The Practice of Autonomy: Patients, Doctors, and Medical decisions. New York: Oxford University Press.

Sepucha, K., Ozanne, E., et al. (2007). An approach to measuring the quality of breast cancer decisions. Patient Education and Counselling, **65**, 261–269.

Chapter 21

A practical approach to measuring the quality of preference-sensitive decisions

Karen R. Sepucha and Albert G. Mulley

Introduction

A patient with knee osteoarthritis and her doctor schedule surgery to replace her knee. A decision has been made but not yet enacted, and one might ask whether this is a good decision. This decision and many like it have certain features worth highlighting. First, there is a decision to be made because more than one reasonable alternatives are available to the patient and her doctor. Second, clinical evidence and clinical information, such as results of x-rays or even patient-reported symptoms scores though necessary, are not sufficient to determine the best alternative. Third, patients feel differently about the impact of the illness in their lives and the importance of the potential good and bad outcomes of the options. In these situations, the best treatment is the one that reflects what is most important to patients who are well informed about the options and potential outcomes.

The International Patient Decision Aids Standards collaboration found strong support for a definition of *decision quality* (DQ) as 'the match between the features that matter most to the informed patient and the option chosen' (Elwyn *et al.*, 2006). We have proposed a slight variation in this definition, as 'the extent to which a decision reflects the considered preferences of a well-informed patient, and is implemented' (Sepucha *et al.*, 2007, 2004). These and other definitions of good decisions consistently focus on two dimensions: one is that patients are informed and another that treatments reflect what is most important to patients. However, the minor wording changes may have significant implications, such as whether the chosen option needs to be implemented or not (see also Chapters 13, by Theresa M Marteau, and 20, by Elwyn *et al.*). This chapter presents the approach we have taken to define decision quality and describes the development process for decision quality instruments (DQIs) used to assess the quality of preference-sensitive medical decisions.

Defining decision quality

For decades, Jack Wennberg and others have documented a wide variation in treatment rates for many common medical conditions. This research calls into question the quality of clinical decision-making, and as a result, the validity of the pervasive medical decision-making heuristic, 'follow the doctor's recommendation'. Widespread variations in treatments, driven largely by geography and local practice patterns, lead to the troubling conclusion that where people live and the doctor they see has more to do with what treatment they receive than who they are and what they care about (Wennberg *et al.*, 2002).

In fact, treatment rates alone do not provide much information about the quality of the decisions as they cannot distinguish whether the right person is being matched with the right treatment.

The shared decision-making model takes a prescriptive approach to clinical decision-making that recognizes the importance of the doctor – patient relationship in decision-making, as well as the importance of engaging the patient in order to determine which treatment is best (Mulley, 1989, 1990; Sepucha and Mulley, 2003, 2008). The DQIs based on this framework are designed to provide an assessment of the quality of medical decisions across groups, or populations of patients. The instruments gather data to assess (a) the extent to which patients are informed, (b) the extent to which treatments or tests, on average (and controlling for other factors), are consistent with patients' goals and concerns, and (c) the extent to which the interactions between patients and providers support shared decision-making. The rest of the chapter expands on the work done to assess the first two of these areas.

What does it mean to be informed? Assessing decision-specific knowledge

There are different approaches that can assess the extent to which patients are informed. It is possible to ask them generically, for example on a scale of 1–10 where 1 is not at all informed and 10 is extremely well informed, how informed they felt. However, patient reports of their knowledge have been shown to have little if any correlation to scores on specific knowledge tests (Sepucha *et al.*, 2007). These types of assessments are not a good proxy for knowledge because people cannot reliably report on what they do not know.

The DQIs use decision-specific knowledge questions to assess whether patients are well informed. This approach requires identifying a minimally required body of knowledge—determining those pieces of information that are essential for all patients to understand before making a decision. This core set of facts can be generated through a rigorous process that begins with a review of the clinical evidence, supplemented with provider and patient focus groups and interviews. Then, a multidisciplinary group of providers and a group of patients rate and rank the importance, accuracy, and completeness of the set of facts. After revisions, the set of facts are then translated into multiple choice questions and responses by experts in survey research methods. The multiple choice items are then subject to three additional reviews: they are cognitively tested with patients, reviewed by medical experts for accuracy, and reviewed by an expert in health literacy. Table 21.1 provides examples of the multiple choice items used to assess common concepts for different conditions. After these reviews, the draft instrument is field tested with the target population and items are revised again as needed.

Being able to answer a set of multiple choice knowledge items correctly does not necessarily indicate that patients have made a good decision. In other words, the DQI recognizes that being informed is a necessary, but not sufficient, condition for achieving decision quality. The second core part of the DQIs is a set of items that assess what is most important to patients. A minimal set of goals and concerns salient to the decision are identified using the same rigorous process as for the knowledge items.

What are patients' values and preferences?

There is a great deal of confusion in the literature around what exactly constitute patients' preferences or values. The term 'patients' preferences' has been used interchangeably in the literature to refer to patient's preference for participation in the decision-making process, their preferred treatment, their utilities, risk attitudes and time preferences, and their attitudes and opinions about different features or attributes. Focus groups and cognitive testing have also suggested that the term 'values' is problematic as well. Several patients reacted negatively to the

Table 21.1 Sample decision quality instrument items covering common facts and goals for different conditions

Condition	Type of fact	Sample DQI item
Treatment of hip osteoarthritis	Natural history of symptoms:	Without surgery, what usually happens to hip pain from osteoarthritis? ❑ Get better ❑ Stays same ❑ Gets worse ❑ I don't know
Treatment of herniated disc	Symptom relief:	Which treatment is most likely to provide faster relief from pain caused by a herniated disc? ❑ Surgery ❑ Non-surgical treatment ❑ Both are about the same ❑ I don't know
Early stage breast cancer	Likelihood of serious complication:	How often do serious side effects, such as getting another kind of cancer or having heart problems, happen as a result of chemotherapy? ❑ Usually ❑ Sometimes ❑ Rarely ❑ Never ❑ I don't know
Condition	**Type of goal or concern**	**Sample DQI item**
Benign prostate disease	Symptom relief	On a scale of 0 to 10, where 0 is not at all important and 10 is extremely important, how important is it to you to relieve your symptoms?
Prostate cancer	Avoid complications	On a scale of 0 to 10, where 0 is not at all important and 10 is extremely important, how important is it to you to avoid problems with dripping or leaking urine?

notion that providers needed to know their values. When pressed for a reason, one consumer remarked, 'Well, I don't care if my doctor knows whether I'm a Republican or a Democrat or what I think about guns' (Seidman and Sepucha, 2008). The lack of clarity around these terms makes it difficult to determine what should be elicited and measured.

The shared decision-making model recognizes that the same illness and treatment may have very different meaning in different peoples' lives. Benign prostatic hyperplasia (BPH) causes urinary problems in men. The impact of these problems differs as one man may feel that getting up twice a night to go to the bathroom is a small inconvenience, whereas another may find that it is a huge problem adversely affecting his life. Surgery is effective at relieving symptoms, but causes problems with sexual function. For the DQIs, we examine the condition and the treatments to identify a set of goals and concerns that are most salient to each decision. For BPH, it includes items such as the importance of symptom relief and avoiding sexual problems. Then, we use the same process described earlier for the knowledge items, with multiple reviews by provider and patients, to validate the items. Table 1 provides examples of the scaling task to assess what is most important to patients. This is an area in need of more research and we are actively studying and experimenting with the items and scaling tasks as well as the models to determine concordance.

Do treatments meet patients' goals?

Once patients' goals and concerns are assessed, it is necessary to determine the extent to which treatments reflect patients' goals and concerns. In prior work, we used the term 'value concordance' to refer to this concept, although that terminology is problematic for the reasons raised earlier. The main approach follows that used by Barry et al. in which patients' subjective assessment of health outcomes are included in a multivariate regression model to determine the amount of variance in the treatments implemented that could be predicted by what was most important to patients, as opposed to other factors such as age, disease stage, or provider. Men, who were well-informed about BPH and who were very concerned about potential sexual side-effects of surgery, were one fifth as likely to have surgery compared to those who were not as bothered (Barry et al., 1995). The study did not have a control group, but one could imagine that men who were not informed or involved in decision-making would not demonstrate such a significant association.

One problem with this approach is that odds ratios or regression coefficients as measures of 'value concordance' are fairly inaccessible to consumers and most clinicians. If decision quality is meant to be widely used, it needs to be understandable and transparent. As a result, we have pursued some other approaches that translate this into a more accessible metric. Kearing and colleagues have adapted and extended this method to create a summary statistic that indicates the percentage of patients in a given population whose decisions 'matched' their goals (Kearing et al., 2007).

Multivariate regression models provide an assessment at the level of a population or group of patients. Although Kearing's approach does calculate a 'match' for an individual decision, the interpretation is most valid on the population level, and any assessment of concordance needs to control for other factors that may also influence treatments, including patient and clinical characteristics. These models are still evolving and will require more validation to evaluate whether and how generalizable they are across different populations.

Preliminary evaluations of decision quality instruments

We have implemented this process of assessing decision quality across 19 different preference-sensitive decisions that generally fall into three main categories: decisions about symptom relief, decisions about risk reduction, and decisions about screening. Overall, the process has worked very well across these varied decision situations. Several hundred patients and providers have participated in identifying a minimal body of knowledge and set of goals and concerns. One challenge to date is that the diversity of views between and among patients and providers has made it difficult to narrow down the items. As a result, we have included many more items in the draft DQIs than we had originally planned.

As we move forward with field testing draft DQIs, we are also learning about the impact of the timing of the administration on the results. Ideally, the DQIs would be administered after a decision has been made, but before the treatment has started. In practice, the timing of the administration depends largely on the most practical and reliable point to integrate the instruments into the clinical care path. Early results in some conditions do show that administering the DQIs after a decision results in some expected changes (e.g. knowledge declining over time and goals and concerns getting more concordant over time); however, many of the changes are fairly modest. Further research will demonstrate whether and how much flexibility there is in the timing, or whether it needs to be tightly controlled.

Probably, the most interesting finding throughout this process has been the interest expressed by many clinicians for a short version of the DQI to use *before* the consultation. For example, the Comprehensive Breast Program at Dartmouth Hitchcock Medical Center has developed a worksheet version of the DQIs that patients fill out before their visit, and a summary of the data is fed to the surgeons and used by surgeons to guide conversation (Collins *et al.*, 2008). This approach, using the DQIs to screen for problems, helps build in decision quality support from the beginning of the process and is important means to promote learning and improvement.

Conclusion

The core concepts in the DQIs are based on Mulley's shared decision-making framework and focus on how informed patients are about the key aspects of the decision, how well treatments reflect what is most important to these informed patients, and the nature of the interaction between patients and providers. The structured development process for the DQIs has resulted in a large item bank that covers the issues critical to decisions about symptom relief, decisions about reducing risk, and decisions about testing and screening. Further work is needed to understand the performance of these items in diverse populations and to validate models of assessing concordance for common conditions.

References

Barry, M., Fowler, F.J., Mulley, A., *et al.* (1995). Patient reactions to a program designed to facilitate patient participation in treatment decisions for benign prostatic hyperplasia. *Medical Care*, **33**, 771–782.

Collins, E., Moore, C., Clay, K., *et al.* (2008). Can women make an informed decision for mastectomy? *Journal of Clinical Oncology,* in press.

Elwyn, G., O'Connor, A., Stacey, D., *et al.* (2006). Developing a quality criteria framework for patient decision aids: Online international Delphi consensus process. *British Medical Journal*, **333**, 417.

Kearing, S., Sepucha, K., O'Connor, *et al.* (2007). Can video decision aids improve the match between patients.' Preferences and Choices? *Society for Medical Decision Making* Pittsburgh, PA.

Mulley, A. (1989). Assessing patients' utilities: Can the ends justify the means? *Medical Care,* **27**, S269–S281.

Mulley, A. (1990). Methodological issues in the application of effectiveness and outcomes research to clinical practice. *Effectiveness and Outcomes in Health Care.* Washington, DC: National Academy Press.

Seidman, J. and Sepucha, K. (2008). Navigating a changing healthcare system: How consumers, clinicians and policymakers can make sense of shared decision making and information therapy. Available at http://www.ixcenter.org/publications/documents/whitepaper319.pdf. Accessed 20 May 2008.

Sepucha, K. and Mulley, A. (2003). Extending decision support: Preparation and implementation. *Patient Education and Counseling,* **50**, 269–271.

Sepucha, K. and Mulley, A. (2008). A perspective on the patient's role in treatment decisions. *Medical Care Research and Review,* in press.

Sepucha, K., Ozanne, E., Silvia, K., *et al.* (2007). An approach to measuring the quality of breast cancer decisions. *Patient education and counseling,* **65**, 261–269.

Sepucha, K., Fowler, F., and Mulley, A. (2004). Policy support for patient-centered care: The need for measurable improvements in decision quality. *Health Affairs (Project Hope)*, Suppl Web Exclusive, VAR54–VAR62.

Wennberg, J., Fisher, E., and Skinner, J. (2002). Geography and the debate over medicare reform. *Health Affairs,* Suppl Web Exclusive, W94–W114.

Section 4

Shared decision-making in health care practice

Chapter 22

What's happening around the world?

Angela Coulter

Introduction

In democracies, those responsible for health care must ensure that they retain public support for the way health care is organized and delivered. For many governments and health authorities, this means searching for ways to ensure that health services are sufficiently responsive to patients' needs and preferences. Often there is a perceived need to respond to 'consumer pressure' and make health care more like other consumer experiences. But the need for 'patient engagement', where the patient is encouraged to take an active role as a key player in choosing appropriate treatments for episodes of ill-health and managing chronic disease, has often been ignored in the past. As other chapters in this volume show, substantial evidence now exists that this not only improves patients' experience and satisfaction, but can also be clinically and economically effective. As a result, the issue is creeping up the health policy agenda. This chapter looks at approaches adopted in a number of countries to promote and support shared decision-making.

International variations in patients' preferences for involvement

Not being properly informed about their condition and the options for treating is a very common source of patient dissatisfaction worldwide. Many patients want more information and a greater share in the process of making decisions about how they will be treated, but the proportion of people wanting a high level of active involvement varies within and between countries (Grol *et al.*, 2000; Schoen *et al.*, 2007).

For example, a population survey in Germany, Italy, Poland, Slovenia, Spain, Sweden, Switzerland, and the United Kingdom found generally high levels of desire for involvement in these eight European countries (Coulter and Jenkinson, 2005; Coulter and Magee, 2003). Telephone interviewers asked 1000 randomly selected people in each of the countries for their views on who should take the lead in making treatment decisions. Respondents were asked to select one of five responses taken from the Control Preferences Scale (Degner *et al.*, 1997): the patient alone, the patient after consultation with the doctor, the doctor and patient together, the doctor after discussion with the patient, or the doctor alone. Overall, 5% saw themselves (the patient) as the sole decision-maker and a further 18% said the patient should make the decision after consulting the doctor, giving a total of 23% who said the patient should have the primary role. In contrast, 10% said the doctor alone should decide and 16% said the doctor should make the decision after discussion with the patient, a total of 26% who preferred to assign the role of main decision-maker to the doctor. The shared decision-making model, in which doctor and patient are jointly responsible for making treatment decisions, was the most popular, with 51% of the total sample opting for it. Older people in this survey were significantly more likely than those in the younger age group to view the doctor as the primary decision-maker: 31% of those aged 55 and over said the doctor should decide, compared to 24% of those aged under 35.

Patients' expectations of involvement in decisions about their care differed significantly between the eight countries, with people in Spain and Poland exhibiting a much greater preference for a paternalistic style than those in Switzerland and Germany, while those in Sweden, Slovenia, Italy, and the United Kingdom formed a middle group. While 91% of Swiss respondents and 87% of those in Germany felt the patient should have a role in treatment decisions, either sharing responsibility for decision-making with the doctor or being the primary decision-maker, the proportion of Polish patients who felt the same way was only 59% and in Spain it was only 44%. However, the trend for younger people to want a more patient-centred approach than older people was consistent in all the countries, suggesting that demand for involvement is likely to increase everywhere, albeit at a different pace in different countries.

Patients' expectations of involvement are shaped by their previous experiences. The extent to which they expect to be actively involved in treatment decisions varies according to the prevailing medical culture, which in turn is subject to wider cultural influences. If the prevailing culture is paternalistic, both doctors and patients are likely to assume that decisions should be the responsibility of the doctor only, whereas in a more egalitarian culture a partnership or shared decision-making approach is more likely to be preferred. Policy-makers who want to promote shared decision-making must, therefore, persuade clinicians to change established practices, and they must also find ways to encourage patients to express their preferences more effectively.

Approaches to shared decision-making in different countries

In 2007, a special issue of the *German Journal for Evidence and Quality in Health Care* included a number of articles about progress with implementing shared decision-making in various countries. Highlights from these articles are summarized below.

Australia: Patient involvement in health care is fairly high up; the policy agenda in Australia at both federal and state levels and the consumer movement are active and relatively powerful. A commitment to shared decision-making is evident in many policy documents, for example those produced by the National Health and Medical Research Council and various professional associations. However, despite this commitment and an apparently favourable clinical culture, diffusion into mainstream clinical practice has been slow (McCaffery *et al.*, 2007). The results of various observational studies suggest that there is a considerable gap between the decision-making styles that doctors and nurses profess to practice and what actually happens, with only a small proportion of consultations exhibiting the essential attributes of shared decision-making. Clinical guidelines reinforce the need for shared decision-making, and clinicians are expected to ensure that patients give fully informed consent to medical interventions, but understanding of what is required to implement this effectively appears limited. In their review of the situation, McCaffery and colleagues concluded that greater emphasis should now be placed on educating patients to ask questions and insist on a more active role in decisions.

Canada: A tradition of community governance is well established in the hospital sector in Canada, which has also seen some highly ambitious attempts to encourage democratic involvement and even citizen control of health services (Legare *et al.*, 2007). There is extensive experience of research into shared decision-making in Canada, with several groups playing leading roles in the international research effort, notably those at the universities of Ottawa and McMaster. Several medical schools run 'Mini Med' schools for the general public to educate them in various aspects of health information, and decision aids are incorporated into 24-hour nurse-led call centres in some provinces. Yet, a 2002 survey of general practitioners indicated that they perceived their main role as relieving patients' anxiety rather than engaging them in informed decision-making. This is despite the fact that the Canadian code of good medical practice, CanMEDS, includes shared decision-making as one of the key competencies expected of all doctors (available at http://rcpsc.medical.org/canmeds/index.php). A number of training courses for clinicians have been introduced to tackle this problem, and the Canadian government has made funds available for research and education, including two research professorships in shared decision-making.

France: Various legal judgements since the early 1990s have clarified and strengthened patients' rights to information in France (Moumjid *et al.*, 2007). These culminated in the law of March 4th 2002 which stipulated that all patients are entitled to information on their health and to take their own decisions with the help of, and in agreement with, their physician. This stimulated a number of agencies, including the French National Authority for Health and the French Federation of Cancer Centres, to invest in the production of high-quality information for patients. Decision aids have been developed and evaluated by a team working with cancer patients at Centre Leon Berard in Lyon, but shared decision-making research has not yet attracted significant interest or investment in France. There is evidence of public demand for more information and greater participation in decision-making, but health professionals appear reluctant to adopt this approach, citing lack of time and lack of willingness on the part of patients to play an active role.

Germany: Patient participation in policy-making bodies is well established in Germany, and several national agencies are supporting the development of good-quality evidence-based patient information (Loh *et al.*, 2007). In 1999, the Conference of German Health Ministers adopted a document 'Patient rights in Germany today' which stated that patients have the right to clear, expert, and satisfactory education and counselling to explain the use, risks, and benefits of diagnostic and treatment options and their likely outcomes. For their part, doctors have a duty to ensure that patients have understood this information. Until recently the topic of shared decision-making has attracted sparse interest from academics, but in 2001, the German Ministry of Health provided 3.3 million Euros to establish a national research consortium 'Patient as partner in medical decision-making'. This has led to a dramatic increase in research activity and outputs. The products are being disseminated to clinicians in the normal way via publications and through the establishment of several new training programmes. Patient decision aids are being developed and evaluated, and the first ever patient university has been established in Hanover. Patient participation in decision-making is increasingly seen as a quality indicator for medical care to be included in quality reports required for licensing procedures.

Italy: The importance of patient and citizen participation is acknowledged in Italy's National Health Plan, but much work is needed to translate this commitment into practical action (Goss and Renzi, 2007). There are large numbers of patients' associations but they tend to be marginalized by health professionals and managers. Research into shared decision-making is at a very early stage in Italy and to date there have been no national funding initiatives similar to the one in Germany to kick-start the process.

The Netherlands: In contrast to Italy, there has been a concerted effort in the Netherlands to empower patients to play an active role in decision-making (van der Weijden *et al.*, 2007). The Dutch government is keen to make the health care system much more patient-oriented and responsive than it currently is. Among a number of initiatives, they have funded a national programme to develop and implement decision aids, publishing them on a governmental health care internet portal. Other bodies, such as the Dutch Cancer Society, have also invested in web-based patient information, and the Netherlands Organization for Health Research and Development has launched a special programme on patient information and empowerment. At least five of the eight academic medical centres in the Netherlands have active research programmes in shared decision-making. In a recent survey of general practice patients, nearly two-thirds said they were involved in decisions about their care, but there is still a need to strengthen medical education on this topic.

The United Kingdom: The British government is also concerned to make health care more patient-centred, and the Department of Health in England has published a number of policy documents stressing the need to involve patients in decisions about their care (Evans *et al.*, 2007). There is a long history of research into shared decision-making in the United Kingdom, carried out in many academic departments around the country, and a number of randomized controlled trials have evaluated the use of patient decision aids. The General Medical Council, the doctors' regulatory body, has emphasized the need for doctors to engage patients actively in decision-making and described the required standard for this in some detail. A large number of active patient organizations have called for more and better quality information for patients and some of them have become major information providers. The government-funded NHS Choices website is developing into a major portal for all types of health information, but it does not include any decision aids as yet (available at http://www.nhs.uk/Pages/homepage.aspx). Despite all these activities, surveys show that many patients are still not given a say in important health care decisions, and professional education programmes have been slow to recognize the need to give shared decision-making a central place in undergraduate and postgraduate curricula.

The United States: Shared decision-making was invented in the United States, and the vast majority of the research effort is located there. The US-based Society for Medical Decision-Making attracts many participants to its conferences which regularly include sessions on shared decision-making. A large number of organizations, both for profit and not for profit, market decision aids to employers, insurers, and providers, and these are also provided on websites and through telephone counselling centres (Holmes-Rovner *et al.*, 2007). There are many powerful patient organizations in the United States, including the American Association of Retired People (AARP) which has 35,000,000 members and disease-related groups such as the American Heart Association and the American Cancer Society, yet none of these has taken up the cause of shared decision-making as a priority. Unlike European countries, progress in the United States is unlikely to be driven by regulatory approaches. In the market-based American system, the various players need to be convinced that shared decision-making is in their self-interest. Holmes-Rovner and colleagues have argued for a new synthesis between shared decision-making and other aspects of patient participation in order to move forward. This should include an emphasis on patient involvement in decisions about plan selection, service use, self-management and health behaviours, as well as screening and treatment decisions.

Conclusions

The desire to promote greater patient engagement in health care decision-making is on the policy agenda in many western developed countries. The United States, with its strong tradition of health services research and commitment to consumerism, led the way. These developments attracted attention in other countries, and in some countries, for example Canada, Germany, the Netherlands, and the United Kingdom, governmental initiatives and funding have stimulated considerable research and development activity in recent years. While it is very encouraging to see professional and regulatory bodies picking up the baton, for example the Royal College of Physicians and Surgeons of Canada, the College of General Practitioners in the Netherlands, and the General Medical Council in the United Kingdom, the generally slow pace of diffusion into mainstream practice is disappointing.

If shared decision-making is to permeate the medical culture, a more concerted effort will be required to get it onto the curricula for medical and nursing education programs. Efforts will have to be made to tackle the various barriers to implementation, in particular, time pressures and lack of appropriate skills and techniques to convey complex information about treatment risks and outcome probabilities. There is no comprehensive source of information on the total level of activity in this field across the world, including the less developed countries; but even from this brief review of efforts in a small number of countries, it is clear that the collective research endeavour is now quite substantial. As it grows and spreads more widely, it will offer a great opportunity to learn how to shift the balance of power in favour of the patient, with potentially important benefits to health systems worldwide.

References

Coulter, A. and Jenkinson, C. (2005). European patients views on the responsiveness of health systems and healthcare providers, *Eur. J. Public. Health.*, **15**, 355–360.

Coulter, A. and Magee, H. (2003). *The European Patient of the Future.* Maidenhead: Open University Press.

Degner, L. F., Sloan, J. A., and Venkatesh, P. (1997). The Control Preferences Scale. *Canadian Journal of Nursing Research.*, **29**, 21–43.

Evans, R., Edwards, A., Coulter, A., and Elwyn, G. (2007). "Prominent strategy but rare in practice: shared decision-making and patient decision support technologies in the UK", *Zeitschrift fur arztliche Fortbildung und Qualitat im Gesundheitswesen*, **101**, 247–253.

Goss, C. and Renzi, C. (2007). "Patient and citizen participation in health care decisions in Italy", *Zeitschrift fur arztliche Fortbildung und Qualitat im Gesundheitswesen*, **101**, 236–240.

Grol, R., Wensing, M., Mainz, J., Jung, H. P., Ferreira, P., Hearnshaw, H., Hjortdahl, P., Olesen, F., Reis, S., Ribacke, M., and Szecsenyi, J. (2000). "Patients in Europe evaluate general practice care: an international comparison", *British Journal of General Practice*, **50**, 882–887.

Holmes-Rovner, M., Gruman, J., and Rovner, D. R. (2007). "Shared decision-making in the US – research and development outpaces delivery", *Zeitschrift fur arztliche Fortbildung und Qualitat im Gesundheitswesen*, **101**, 254–258.

Legare, F., Stacey, D., and Forest, P.-G. (2007). "Shared decision-making in Canada: update, challenges and where next!", *Zeitschrift fur arztliche Fortbildung und Qualitat im Gesundheitswesen*, **101**, 213–221.

Loh, A., Simon, d., Bieber, C., Eich, W., and Harter, M. (2007). "Patient and citizen participation in German health care-current state and future perspectives", *Zeitschrift fur arztliche Fortbildung und Qualitat im Gesundheitswesen*, **101**, 229–235.

McCaffery, K. J., Shepherd, H. L., Trevena, L., Juraskova, I., Barratt, A., Butow, P. N., Hazell, K. C., and Tattersall, M. H. N. (2007). "Shared decision-making in Australia", *Zeitschrift fur arztliche Fortbildung und Qualitat im Gesundheitswesen*, **101**, 205–211.

Moumjid, N., Bremond, A., Mignotte, H., Faure, C., Meunier, A., and Carrere, M.-O. (2007). "Shared decision-making in the physician-patient encounter in France: a general overview", *Zeitschrift fur arztliche Fortbildung und Qualitat im Gesundheitswesen*, **101**, 223–228.

Schoen, C., Osborn, R., Doty, M. M., Bishop, M., Peugh, J., and Murukutia, N. (2007). "Toward higher performance health systems: adults' health care experiences in seven countries 2007", *Health Affairs*, **26**, w717–w734.

van der Weijden, T., van Veenendaal, H., and Timmermans, D. (2007). "Shared decision-making in the Netherlands – current state and future perspectives", *Zeitschrift fur arztliche Fortbildung und Qualitat im Gesundheitswesen*, **101**, 241–246.

Chapter 23

Medical-legal aspects of evidence-based choice and shared decision-making

Dennis J. Mazur

Introduction

Evidence-based patient choice and shared decision-making may begin to have medical – legal consequences as they enter into the patient care arena. These two emerging contemporary approaches to information in patient care will have to face the long history of the judge-made law of consent and informed consent that has evolved in the high courts around the world. In this chapter, I will describe the different ways shared decision-making may be viewed medico – legally, using particular examples available from the courts of Great Britain, the United States, Canada, and Australia in relation to the patient – physician relationship and the duties of care and disclosure owed by physicians to their patients.

Standard of care

'Standard of care' of physicians is the degree of prudence and caution required of a physician who is under a duty of care for a patient. A practitioner's duty of care can be extended to include the provision of advice and information to a patient concerning proposed screening, diagnosis, and therapy. Evidence in the landmark Australian High Court case, *Rogers versus Whitaker*, was viewed as being based on whether there was 'a body of opinion in the medical profession at the time' (*Rogers v. Whitaker* 1992, p. 491).

Standards of disclosure

From 1767 to the present, there have been three standards of disclosure considered in the judge-made law of consent and informed consent:

- Under the *professional standard* (a physician-based standard), a physician is to provide that information that a physician in good standing in the physician's community-of-peers would provide to his or her patient.

- Under a *reasonable person standard*, a physician is to provide that information that a reasonable person in the position of the patient would want to know.

- Under a *subjective patient* standard, a physician is to provide that information that the individual patient would want to know.

Judge Spottswood Robinson in the landmark US federal decision in informed consent in the District of Columbia argued against a subjective patient standard because of 'hindsight bias' (*Canterbury v. Spence*, 1972, pp. 790–791). A patient after the fact of injury occurrence could not reasonably be expected to state without bias what his or her position would have been at a time before the intervention in which the injury occurred, whether he or she would have rejected the intervention had the possibility of that injury which in fact occurred in his or her case had been disclosed by the physician. Hence, Judge Robinson argued in support of the reasonable person standard of disclosure in the patient–physician relationship. However, this is not the same in all countries, as will be described below.

What is consent and informed consent in the courts?

The higher courts have not at all considered the notion of consent and informed consent similarly in terms of the required standards of disclosure. Examples of this variation from selected countries are shown in Box 23.1.

Higher court emphasis on 'PARQ'

Higher courts have emphasized four types of information in consent and informed consent. Shared decision-making adds at least two additional types of information not considered by the courts, unless it is brought up by the questioning patient (see Box 23.2).

Both consent and informed consent in the high courts are considered as part of a two-party relationship between a patient and his or her physician. In the ideal model considered by the courts, there is one recommended intervention by the physician and a set of alternatives and risks that will need to be disclosed, and then the patient can ask as many questions as he or she wishes regarding the physician's opinion for the one intervention out of the set of alternatives judged in terms of benefits and risks.

What is shared decision-making?

It is not clear what concepts are included and what concepts are excluded from the notion of shared decision-making. At the present time, there are many uses of the term shared decision-making, and it is difficult to see when use of the term is based on a clear concept of the term

---

Box 23.1: Consent and informed consent in courts and higher courts, from selected countries

Consent
- ◆ **Professional Standard**
  - Great Britain
- ◆ **Reasonable Person Standard**
  - Australia

Informed consent
- ◆ **Professional Standard**
  - About 50% of states in the United States
- ◆ **Reasonable Person Standard**
  - About 50% of states in the United States
  - Canada

Box 23.2: Four types of information: "PARQ"

- **P (Procedure)**
  - Nature of the physician-recommended medical intervention recommended in the patient's care
- **A (Alternatives)**
  - Alternatives to that physician-recommended intervention
- **R (Risks)**
  - Risks of intervention and its alternatives
- **Q (Questions)**
  - Doctor providing honest answers to the patient's questions

Two Additional Types of Information in Shared Decision Making
- **SE (Scientific Evidence)**
  - Whether there is any scientific evidence
  - If scientific evidence is present, its quality
- **U (Uncertainty)**
  - Related to the scientific evidence available
  - Related to the decision

starting with a clear definition (Moumjid *et al.*, 2007). In particular, in some forms of shared decision-making, there is an exclusion of physician's opinion on what is the best course of action for the patient from a medical perspective. It is on this point—exclusion of physicians from shared decision-making—one finds the most fundamental difference between the courts and higher courts' views of consent and informed consent and the different forms of shared decision-making.

Fundamental difference

The fundamental difference between the court approaches in consent and informed consent and key shared decision makers is whether the doctor's opinion on what should be done in the patient's care medically is to count or not in the information provided to the patient.

Some would argue that the core of the concepts of consent and informed consent found in courts and higher courts is based on the physician's medical opinion that in turn is based on his or her training and experience as a physician. Here, for the courts and the higher courts, the basis of consent and informed consent is the two-party relationship between a patient and a doctor where the doctor provides the patient with the doctor's opinion on what should be done in the patient's care (presuming the doctor has a reasonable opinion based on the doctor's training and experience). In essence, the doctor argues for the benefits and risks of the recommended intervention in relationship with the reasonable alternatives available, including not doing anything at all and allowing nature to take its course or postponing the decision to a later time when new information may be available. Here, the patient must also recognize that delaying the decision may well mean that the disease is allowed to progress while the decision is delayed. Such is the case of aggressive cancers and leukaemia or accelerating heart disease, where the disease process will not wait for the decision.

Some would argue that shared decision-making's emphasis on scientific evidence as opposed to court emphasis on physician's opinion based on training and clinical experience is the biggest challenge shared decision-making faces in the years to come as a recognized concept in the court room.

In a widely known but (legally) largely unreported court verdict in the state of Virginia, the attorney of a patient's wife whose husband had died due to advanced prostate cancer argued as follows:

> Due to the minimal risks associated with performing a PSA (a simple blood test), the plaintiff's attorney argued that the standard of care in Virginia was to order the test without discussing it with the patient. With four physician witnesses from the state of Virginia to support his claim, the plaintiff's attorney won his case against Merenstein's residency program, and seemingly against the use of evidence-based medicine and shared medical decision-making.
>
> (King and Moulton, 2006, p. 434)

Jaime Staples King and Benjamin Moulton argued the shared decision-making side of the case as follows:

> To his surprise, Dr. Merenstein listened to the plaintiff's attorney argue that despite the fact that practice guidelines established by the American Academy of Family Physicians, the American Urological Association, and the American Cancer Society all recommended that physicians discuss the risks and benefits of PSA screening with patients, this behavior constituted malpractice in Virginia. In all states, to win a medical malpractice case, the plaintiff must prove that the physician violated the standard of care, which in turn resulted in the patient's injury.
>
> (King and Moulton, 2006, p. 434)

King and Moulton are correct that in a medical malpractice case in the United States, the plaintiff must prove that the physician violated the standard of care. But particular state laws determine how that standard of care is to be determined in a court trial. Standard of care is not necessarily determined by what national experts say or recommend, but rather depends heavily on what the law is in a particular state. If the law says that the standard of care is defined by how local physicians practice medicine, then this is the law. If there was such a uniform practice of local physicians to order a PSA test, and then discuss the result with the patient, and local physicians are brought into court to testify regarding what the local practice is, this testimony may well then be considered the local standard of care.

Indeed, the fact that the cost of the PSA test was small, one alternative that exists is first checking the PSA test, and then discussing the result of the PSA test with the patient as at least an alternative way of screening for prostate cancer. Here, for example, an extremely elevated PSA may well lead to further discussions with the individual patient for both further diagnostic pursuit of the disease and biopsy and pathologic diagnosis and consideration of a vast array of therapeutic modalities open to patients before the spread of cancer beyond the prostate capsule. One of the alternative screening approaches that exist for any patient is to first check the PSA test, blood test, and then discuss the patient's chances of having or not having prostate cancer after the PSA test result is back.

At this point, one must ask what is the most important question to ask: is it 'how many patients will want to proceed with further diagnostic workup after hearing the interpretation of their own PSA obtained as a screening test?' or is it 'how many patients would rather proceed with a full discussion of risks and benefits of alternative approaches of diagnosis and treatment without knowing what their own PSA result is at the time?' These two questions also raise a third question: 'how much detail in discussion of screening, diagnosis, range of screening, and diagnostic test results, plus discussion of the range of treatment options for non-metastatic versus metastatic prostate cancer is gone into the screening discussion with the patient?'

Box 23.3: How was the shared decision making session carried out by the physician?

- ◆ What explicitly was said and what was not said in the shared decision making session about:
  - Benefits
  - Risks
  - Alternatives
  - And how elaborate was the presentation in terms of information?
    - How would the decision change with the following PSA results?
      - ○ Non-elevated PSA
      - ○ Mildly elevated PSA
      - ○ Moderately elevated PSA
      - ○ Extremely elevated PSA
- ◆ How was the shared decision making session about PSA screening carried out:
  - As "a stand-alone session" about prostate cancer screening as an informed consent session in its own right?
  - As just one of brief mention along a long list of other items discussed in a global screening session along with preventive point like wearing sunscreen, wearing a seatbelt, among others?
- ◆ How specific were the definition of shared decision making and how shared decision making sessions were to be carried out as recommended by the guidelines of the various societies and task forces that had recommendations on shared decision making sessions for PSA screening?

Also missing from the report of the court trial are answers to the following questions (see Box 23.3):

Here, we see the complexity of shared decision-making involving PSA screening in contrast to our higher court opinions in consent and informed consent where the classic cases involve a surgeon's disclosure of risk from the surgeon-recommended intervention to secure the patient's consent or informed consent to the intervention in question.

Challenges facing shared decision-making in the courts and higher courts

At the present time, there are a number of challenges facing the proponents of shared decision-making in the courts and higher courts of our countries of interest.

First, today, there are increasing efforts to conduct screening for prostate cancer in younger men aged 45–49, based on evidence in the United States that men younger than 50 had elevated PSA levels when in their 40s, and that this was associated with prostate cancer (Hamdy 2007).

Second, there is the challenge of specifically defining what share decision-making is as a framework in relationship with the current standard of care that is physician-based (physician-based standard) or based on a reasonable person (reasonable person standard). Can it be held as one session about a set of screening topics or is it to be considered as a session devoted to the elaboration of one topic area? In the specific case of PSA screening, is it a session that is introduced by a nurse in a screening session, and then elaborated upon by the physician in a shared decision-making session focused solely on the issues of PSA screening for prostate cancer?

Research here needs to discover if preferences change when PSA screening is discussed in a long list of screening points of a varying nature or as discussed as a separate topic in a specialized PSA screening discussion section.

Third, it needs to be recognized that there would be no problem if shared decision-making was accepted by the body of physicians in a locality, across a state, or across a nation. The courts rely on what the body of physicians would do, so it follows that if the body of physicians were to accept a form of shared decision-making, the courts would agree with what the profession has developed as a new approach within the profession. The problem is that at the present time the body of physicians in the countries we have considered does not recognize shared decision-making as its standard of disclosure or its primary method of decision-making in the patient – physician relationship. And the body of physicians recognizes that physician's opinion has important weight in the patient – physician relationship. In addition, patients recognize the important weight of physician's opinion in their own decision-making related to their individual care (Mazur *et al.*, 2005).

Fourth, shared decision-making could be accepted (legally) as a procedure offered by an alternative non-physician group within patient care within a clinic system or hospital system. For example, this might comprise nursing or social work colleagues, who could constitute a consultancy service to which physicians could refer their patients or for which patients could ask themselves.

Fifth, how is a case argued by a physician's attorney? Clearly, state courts in the United States may well be more interested in the practice of local physicians related to a screening topic than to experts imported from other states or countries to give testimony on a screening topic. In addition, we do not know the number of physicians within the institutions of interest and what their own views are regarding shared decision-making.

The conceptual development of shared decision-making is itself still at an early stage. Continued careful consideration of the definition as to what shared decision-making is about is the first step needed to develop the concept among physicians and other professionals. Then, the courts will be able to judge and influence how it operates in routine practice across a variety of settings.

References

Canterbury v. Spence (1972) 464 F.2d 772.

Hamdy, F. (2008). Should the UK lower the age for prostate cancer detection? (Prostate cancer detection in an unselected young population: Experience of the Protect study). *British Medical Journal*. Available at http://www.bmj.com/content/vol335/issue7628/press_release.dtl#2. Accessed on 7 March 2008.

King, J.S. and Moulton, B.W. (2006). Rethinking informed consent: The case for shared medical decision-making. *American Journal of Law and Medicine*, **32**, 429–501.

Mazur, D.J., Hickam, D.H., Mazur, M.D., *et al.* (2005). The role of doctor's opinion in shared decision making: What does shared decision making really mean when considering invasive medical procedures? *Health Expectations*, **8**, 97–102.

Moumjid, N., Gafni, A., Brémond, A., *et al.* (2007). Shared decision making in the medical encounter: Are we all talking about the same thing? *Medical Decision Making*, **27**, 539–546.

Reibl v. Hughes. (1980). 2 SCR 885.

Rogers v. Whitaker. (1992). 175 CLR 479.

Sidaway v. Board of the Governors of the Bethlem Royal Hospital and the Maudsley Hospital and Others. (1985). 1 AC 871.

Chapter 24

Helping consumers with their information needs

Paul Kinnersley and Adrian Edwards

Introduction

When people are ill or feel unwell, they want good information from their doctors and nurses about what is wrong and what needs to be done to help them feel better. However, as health care becomes more complex, providing patients with the information they want at the time they want remains a challenge. Clinicians may underestimate patients' needs for information or may overestimate the amount they provide. Alternatively, they may use jargon and not allow sufficient opportunity for patients' questions. In addition, patients themselves may be reluctant or otherwise feel unable to ask questions, particularly if they are suffering from serious or life threatening diseases.

Improving information giving and the answering of patients' questions presents challenges. Training clinicians is time-consuming and there is very limited evidence of effectiveness. As an apparently straightforward alternative, encouraging patients directly to ask questions in consultations has been proposed. Methods such as coaching the patient or showing them a video in the waiting room have been tested along with question prompt sheets which encourage the patient to list in advance the questions they want to ask. There are now websites such as 'Ask Me 3' which help patients identify questions to ask in consultations (see http://www.npsf.org/askme3/). However, despite there being a number of reviews with positive conclusions, these methods of helping patients are not widely used which suggests their effectiveness is questionable or not fully understood. To clarify this, we undertook a Cochrane systematic review (Kinnersley et al., 2007, 2008).

Summary of Cochrane review methods

We conducted a search of electronic databases (Cochrane Central Register of Controlled Trials, Medline, Embase, PsycINFO, ERIC, CINAHL from their start dates) using the following inclusion criteria:

(i) Randomized controlled trials;

(ii) Interventions directed at patients of all ages consulting with doctors or nurses in health care settings;

(iii) Interventions targeted at patients delivered before specific consultations and intended to help patients address their information needs by encouraging, identifying, or otherwise facilitating question asking.

We studied five main outcomes (question asking, satisfaction, anxiety, knowledge, consultation length) that enabled assessment of the effects on both the consultation process and outcomes for patients and service providers. During the review, we found that anxiety was measured both before and after consultations. When measured before consultations, in some cases, it was a baseline measure taken at the same time the intervention was delivered; in other trials, it was measured after the intervention (but still before the consultation) and was thus used as an outcome.

Study characteristics

We identified 35 papers describing 33 trials involving a total of 8244 patients. Seventeen trials were conducted in the United States, 7 in the United Kingdom, 4 in Australia, and 5 in other countries. Fourteen were conducted in family (general) practice, 9 in Oncology and the remaining 10 in other settings. For a full list of included studies, please see Kinnersley *et al.* (2007).

Study quality

All of the studies were described as randomized controlled trials although we considered their quality to be variable. Methods of randomization were generally described only briefly, and for the three studies where it was appropriate, there was no attempt to account for clustering. Only six studies provided sample size calculations and only four trials provided sufficient evidence of adequate concealment of allocation. In the 17 studies that used audio or videotapes to gather data about the consultation, 7 studies reported that those who assessed the tape were blind to the patients' group allocation. Eight studies reported reliability checks on the gathering of these data, with double rating of a sample or of all tapes. Most studies did not report about the blinding of assessors for other outcomes. However, as most studies used patient-reported measures (questionnaires), there may be low risk of ascertainment bias. Only two studies stated they used intention-to-treat analyses.

The interventions

A range of interventions was used. Twenty-five trials used written materials (question prompt sheets). In six of these, additional patient coaching was provided. Five trials used patient coaching alone. In two trials, patients were briefly instructed in the waiting room to think of the questions, they might want to ask. One trial combined coaching with the use of a computer programme and another combined coaching with video and written materials. In one trial, access to the medical record of the patient's previous consultation was provided as a question prompt and similarly another trial provided patients with audiotapes of their previous consultations. In five trials, in addition to the patient interventions, clinicians received brief training to help them answer patients' questions.

Effectiveness of the interventions

With regard to our outcomes of interest, 6 of 17 studies found statistically significant increases in patient question asking and the remainder no effects. Two studies found a reduction in anxiety before consultations, one an increase, and one no effect. Two of nine studies reported a reduction in patient anxiety after the consultation, one an increase, and six studies no effect. Two of five studies found reductions in knowledge and the remainder no effects. However, in both the studies showing a decrease in knowledge, we considered that the intervention for the control group could increase patient knowledge and that this may have affected the results. In 5 of 23 studies, there was

Table 24.1 The results of the meta-analyses undertaken (Kinnersley et al., 2008)

Outcome	Number of studies with extractable data	Number of patients	Effect size	95% Confidence Interval	Outcome
All studies					
Question asking	14	2020	SMD 0.27	0.19 to 0.36	Increased, statistically significant
Patient satisfaction	17	3316	SMD 0.09	0.03 to 0.16	Increased, statistically significant
Anxiety before consultations	3	372	WMD −1.56	−7.10 to 3.97	Reduced, not statistically significant
Anxiety after consultations	6	809	SMD −0.08	−0.22 to 0.06	Reduced, not statistically significant
Knowledge	5	378	SMD −0.34	−0.94 to 0.25	Reduced, not statistically significant
Consultation length	13	3406	SMD 0.10	−0.05 to 0.25	Possible increase, not statistically significant
Written materials versus coaching					
Question asking					
Written materials	6	563	SMD 0.42	0.26 to 0.59	Increased, statistically significant
Coaching	5	414	SMD 0.36	0.16 to 0.56	Increased, statistically significant
Patient satisfaction					
Written materials	10	2354	SMD 0.08	0.00 to 0.16	Possible increase, not statistically significant
Coaching	6	722	SMD 0.23	0.08 to 0.38	Increased, statistically significant
Consultation length					
Written materials	10	2534	SMD 0.13	0.05 to 0.21	Increased, statistically significant
Coaching	3	872	SMD 0.07	−0.07 to 0.20	Possible increase, not statistically significant
Clinician training					
Patient satisfaction					
Clinician training	3	821	SMD −0.01	−0.15 to 0.12	No change
No clinician training	15	2569	SMD 0.13	0.05 to 0.21	Increased, statistically significant
Consultation length					
Clinician training	2	682	SMD 0.17	0.01 to 0.32	Increased, statistically significant
No clinician training	12	2798	SMD 0.17	0.10 to 0.24	Increased, statistically significant

SMD = standardized mean difference; WMD = weight mean difference.

increased patient satisfaction; in two additional studies, there were increases for particular aspects of satisfaction (depth of relationship, interpersonal satisfaction); in one study, child satisfaction was increased but parental satisfaction was unchanged; and in another, there was no immediate effect but satisfaction was increased at three months. For the remaining 14 studies, there were no changes in patient satisfaction. Three of 17 studies reported increases in consultation length, and one other study found a reduction in length of the first consultation after the intervention and an increase for the third consultation. The remaining studies found no change to consultation length. Meta-analyses of the extractable data for each of these outcomes are presented in Table 24.1

We compared the effects of the two main types of intervention (written materials versus coaching) and separately the effects of clinician training (in addition to the patient intervention) for those studies with appropriate data (Table 24.1). Overall we found similar effects for both written materials and coaching for the outcomes of question asking, consultation length, and patient satisfaction. Similarly, we found that additional clinician training provided little tadditional benefit.

Discussion

This review identified 33 randomized trials of interventions to help patients ask questions and gather information in consultations in a range of settings and countries. While some individual papers reported positively on their results, our meta-analyses demonstrate little consistent benefit from these interventions. The most direct effect of the interventions is an increase in question asking, and this appears to lead on to a small increase in patient satisfaction which is consistent with the findings of the application of other patient-centred consulting styles (Lewin *et al.*, 2003). However, there was little information about the types of question asked, although Brown (1999, 2001) and Butow (1994) reported increases in questions asked by cancer patients about their prognosis.

A possible explanation for the limited effects of the interventions is that most of them were delivered immediately before consultations to patients who were waiting to see their clinician and were not expecting to be encouraged to ask questions. Most patients naturally feel slightly anxious before their consultations (and this would be increased if that consultation were with an oncologist as it was in nine of these studies). They are likely to find it difficult to change their approach to the consultation at short notice. Furthermore, only a small number of studies provided training to the clinician and in those that did it was quite brief. Without adequate training, there is the possibility of an empowered patient consulting with a clinician who adopts their usual style of consulting and struggles to respond appropriately to the patients' questions. It is notable that Bolman (2005), for example, found that fewer patients used the intervention at successive consultations despite providing brief clinician training and that anxiety before the consultations increased with over the three consultations.

The finding that the interventions had little effect on consultation length is important since many clinicians might regard the interventions with suspicion, anticipating that encouraging patients to ask questions will increase consultation length. It is also notable that more complex interventions such as coaching had no clear additional benefits over the written interventions which require little additional clinic time to administer.

Further research

Some patients may find the interventions more helpful than others and they may be more appropriate for some consultations than others. No study explored the use of the same intervention in different settings but only one studied the effect of repeatedly using the intervention through a series of consultations. Further research is needed but it is also dependent on a clear culture change. This must be to one of greater patient empowerment, in which patients expect to and are encouraged to ask questions and clinicians are trained to respond helpfully supported by appropriate written materials or other aids.

Conclusions

The benefits of the interventions reviewed here are limited. While question prompt sheets are attractive as an inexpensive (compared to coaching patients or training clinicians) method of encouraging question asking, they can only be viewed as part of the solution to improving communication between patients and clinicians. Focusing on the patient alone may not produce long-term patient benefits because of the complexity of the dialogue between patient and clinician (Roter, 2000).

References

Brown, R., Butow, P.N., Boyer, M.J., *et al.* (1999). Promoting patient participation in the cancer consultation: Evaluation of a prompt sheet and coaching in question asking. *British Journal of Cancer*, **80**, 242–248.

Brown, R.F., Butow, P.N., Dunn, S.M., *et al.* (2001). Promoting patient participation and shortening cancer consultations: A randomised trial. *British Journal of Cancer*, **85**, 1273–1279.

Bolman, C., Brug, J., Bar, J., *et al.* (2005). Long-term efficacy of a checklist to improve patient education in cardiology. *Patient Education and Counseling*, **56**, 240–248.

Butow, P.N., Dunn, S.M., Tattersall, M.H.N., *et al.* (1994). Patient participation in the cancer consultation: Evaluation of a question prompt sheet. *Annals of Oncology* **5**, 199–204.

Kinnersley, P., Edwards, A., Hood, K. *et al.* (2007). Interventions before consultations for helping patients address their information needs. *Cochrane Database of Systematic Reviews*, 3. CD004565. DOI: 10.1002/14651858.CD004565.pub2

Kinnersley, P., Edwards, A., Hood, K., *et al.* (2008). Interventions before consultations to help patients address their information needs by encouraging question asking: A systematic review. *British Medical Journal*, **337**, 335–339.

Lewin, S., Skea, Z., Entwistle, V., *et al.* (2003). Effects of interventions to promote a patient centred approach in clinical consultations [review]. *Cochrane Database of Systematic Reviews*, 2.

Roter, D. (2000). The enduring and evolving nature of the patient–physician relationship. *Patient Education and Counseling*, **39**, 5–15.

Chapter 25

Helping consumers to know their chances

Lisa M. Schwartz, Steven Woloshin, and H. Gilbert Welch

Introduction

People face a bewildering array of medical decisions: for example, should I have the genetic test for BRCA1 breast cancer gene? Should I be screened for prostate cancer? Should I take a medication to lower my cholesterol? Should I have chemotherapy to treat my breast cancer? If people are to make informed decisions, they need to understand their chances: What is my chance of a health outcome if I undergo this intervention and what is my chance of a health outcome if I forgo it?

There are many ways to describe the 'chance of a health outcome'. We believe (Schwartz, 1997) – as do many other experts (Elwyn, 2006) – that the best way is to use 'absolute risks'. But using absolute risks means lots of numbers: twice as many numbers as using the corresponding relative risk. And the numbers quickly multiply as the number of outcomes grows. The result is often unreadable: long blocks of text containing number after number. The solution is to use tables – structured displays of data, typically organized into columns for the intervention and controls and rows for the outcome.

Tables are the most efficient and practical way to look at and compare a series of numbers. Try to imagine a journal article with no tables. Nevertheless, there seems to be a hesitancy to use tables in communications with the general public. Although medical journals routinely use tables, none of the major medical journals' 'patient summary' pages include them, nor are tables a regular element in most news stories reporting on medical research. In part, this may reflect an assumption by writers and editors – and even by some in the risk communication research community – that numeric data – in any format – may be too difficult for even highly educated members of the general public.

But our research suggests that it is not. In this chapter, we review our work demonstrating that people – even those with limited formal education – can understand absolute risks in tables and desire them. We go on to some actual applications of tables and end with a way to prepare people to be better able to understand the risk information presented in tables.

People can understand tables – using the 'drugs facts box'

Background

US consumers rarely get accurate and understandable information about prescription drugs. Instead, they are exposed to billions of dollars of marketing designed to generate enthusiasm for new products using advertisements that highlight benefit and minimize harm (Woloshin, 2001). It is not surprising that consumers tend to overestimate how well drugs work – particularly heavily advertised drugs which typically offer little marginal benefit over existing drugs and have a much weaker track record for safety.

To get accurate information to the public, we created the 'drug facts box'. A drug facts box is a standardized 1-page table presenting prescription drug benefit and side-effect data. The top of the box provides descriptive information about the drug: its indication, who might consider taking it, who should not take it, recommended testing or monitoring, and other things to consider doing to achieve the same goals as the drug. Figure 25.1 is a drug facts box for Lunesta, a drug for chronic insomnia.

Prescription Drug Facts: Lunesta (Eszopiclone)

What is this drug for?	To make it easier to fall or to stay asleep
Who might consider taking it?	Adults age 18 and older with insomnia for at least 1 month
Who should NOT take it?	People under age 18
Recommended testing	No blood tests, watch out for abnormal behavior
Other things to consider doing	Reducing caffeine (especially at night), exercise, regular bedtime, avoid daytime naps

LUNESTA STUDY FINDINGS

788 healthy adults with insomnia for al least 1 month – sleeping less than 6.5 hours per night and/or taking more than 30 minutes to fall asleep – were given LUNESTA or a sugar pill nightly for 6 months. Here's what happened:

What difference did LUNESTA make?	People given a suge pill	People given LUNESTA (3 mg each night)
Did LUNESTA help?		
LUNESTA users feel asleep faster (15 minutes faster)	45 minutes to fall asleep	30 minutes to fall asleep
LUNESTA users slept longer (37 minutes longer)	5 hours 45 minutes	6 hours 22 minutes
Did LUNESTA have side effects?		
Life threatening side effects		
No difference between LUNESTA and a suger pill	None observed	
Symptom side effects		
More had unpleasant taste in their mouth (additional 20% due to drug)	6% 6 in 100	26% 26 in 100
More had dizziness (additional 7% due to drug)	3% 3 in 100	10% 10 in 100
More had drowsiness (additional 6% due to drug)	3% 3 in 100	9% 9 in 100
More had dry mouth (additional 5% due to drug)	2% 2 in 100	7% 7 in 100
More had nausea (additional 5% due to drug)	6% 6 in 100	11% 11 in 100

How long has the drug been in use?

Lunesta was approved by FDA in 2005. As with all new drugs we simply don't know how its safety record will hold up over time. In general, if there are unforeseen, serious drug side effects, they emerge after the drug is on the market (when a large enough number of people have used the drug).

Figure 25.1 Drug facts box for Lunesta.

Benefit of AVASTAT (Avaprastatin)			
In a study, people with high cholesterol either took AVASTAT or a sugar pill. Here are the percents of people who experienced the following over 5 years.			
	Given Sugar pill	Given AVASTAT	Effect of AVASTAT
Have a heart attack	8%	6%	Fewer
Die from heart attack	2%	1%	Fewer
Die (from anything)	4%	3%	Fewer

Figure 25.2 Simple table used to present benefit for AVASTAT (which is actually pravastatin). Reproduced with permission from Woloshin, S., Schwartz, L., and Welch, H. The value of benefit data in direct-to-consumer drug ads. Health Affairs 2004 : W234–245.

The heart of the drug facts box is a table summarizing data drawn from randomized trials used in the FDA's drug approval process. The table includes 2 columns of numbers providing the chance of various outcomes for people who do or do not take the drug. The first half of the table summarizes the benefit of the drug; the second half summarizes side effects. The last element of the box reports how long the drug has been in use (i.e. when it was approved by FDA) and reminds consumers that unanticipated safety issues sometimes emerge after approval - generally in the first 5 years that a drug is on the market.

Evidence that consumers understand simple tables

We conducted a study to test how well consumers understood simple tables (i.e. 3 rows and 2 columns of data) each summarizing the benefit of a drug (Woloshin, 2004). Trained interviewers showed 203 individuals in the greater Boston area actual direct to consumer advertisements (with only the name of the drug and the drug company changed) – and then showed them the same ads with the drug facts tables. Figure 25.2 shows one of the simple tables – also called 'benefit boxes' – used in the study.

Most (91%) participants rated the information in the benefit box as 'very important' or 'important'. Almost all said that the data were easy to understand (median rank of 9 on a scale from 0 [extremely hard] to 10 [extremely easy]). Most were able to navigate the table above: 97% correctly identified the percentage of people given AVASTAT who had a heart attack. In a similar example, as shown in Figure 25.3, consumer perception of the drug's effectiveness was diminished – appropriately, given the data – after seeing the benefit data.

Evidence that consumers can understand complex tables

We conducted another study to test how well consumers understood a complex table (i.e. 9 rows and 2 columns of data) summarizing the benefit and side-effects of a drug – included in a complete drug facts box (Schwartz, 2007). This study included a convenience sample of 274 people with a wide range of socioeconomic status who were mailed a drug facts box (without any training on how to read it) and asked to complete a survey. In this way, we could test how people used the table in a realistic setting. Figure 25.4 shows the complex table which summarized the data on tamoxifen for the primary prevention of breast cancer.

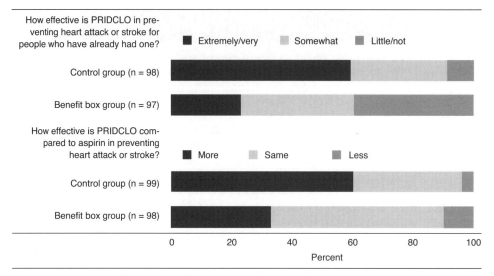

Figure 25.3 Perceived effectiveness of PRIDCLO (which is actually clopidogrel,) by people randomized to see an advertisement with ('benefit box group') or without ('control group') a benefit box. Reproduced with permission from Woloshin, S., Schwartz, L., and Welch, H. The value of benefit data in direct-to-consumer drug ads. Health Affairs 2004 : W234–245.

TAMOXIFEN STUDY FINDINGS TABLE		
13,000 women at high risk of getting breast cancer were given TAMOXIFEN or a sugar pill for 6 years. Here's what happened:		
What difference did TAMOXIFEN make?	Women given a sugar pill	Women given TAMOXIFEN (20 mg a day)
Did TAMOXIFEN help?		
Fewer women got invasive breast cancer	2.7%	1.4%
Fewer women died from breast cancer	0.09%	0.05%
Did TAMOXIFEN have side effects?		
Life threatening side effects		
More women had a blood clot in their leg or lungs	0.4%	0.8%
More women had a stroke	0.4%	0.6%
More women got invasive uterine cancer	0.2%	0.5%
Symptom side effects		
More women had hot flashes	69%	81%
More women had vaginal discharge	35%	55%
More women had cataracts needing surgery	1.1%	1.7%
Other things to know		
Dying for any reason	1.1%	0.9%

Figure 25.4 The benefits and harms of taking tamoxifen to prevent breast cancer. Reproduced with permission from Schwartz, L., Woloshin, S., and Welch, H. The drug facts box: providing consumers simple tabular data on drug benefit and harm. Med Decis Making 2007; 27: 655–662.

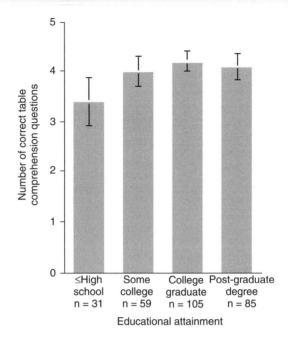

Figure 25.5 The effect of educational attainment on comprehension of a complex table. Reproduced with permission from Schwartz, L., Woloshin, S., and Welch,H. The drug facts box: providing consumers simple tabular data on drug benefit and harm. Med Decis Making 2007; 27: 655–662.

Participants were asked five comprehension questions which tested the ability to find specific data in the table, use data to calculate an absolute risk difference (i.e. subtractions), and compare the effect of tamoxifen to hypothetical drugs with different benefits. Comprehension was high. For example, 89% of participants correctly wrote in '0.8%' as the answer to what percentage of people given tamoxifen got a blood clot in their leg or lung, and 71% correctly answered that tamoxifen 'lowers the chance of getting breast cancer by 1.3%'. On average, participants correctly answered four of the five table comprehension questions. As shown in Figure 25.5, comprehension was good even at the lowest level of educational attainment.

Applications of tables

Newspaper tables

We have used a table to communicate the findings of the Women's Health Initiative study about the value of hormone replacement therapy in preventing chronic disease to the public in a newspaper. The original findings, as published in the medical journal article, presented relative changes (e.g. '41% increase in strokes, 29% increase in heart attacks') and the 1-year absolute risk differences but did not provide the absolute risks themselves (e.g. 'the data indicate that if 10,000 women take the drugs for a year, eight more will develop invasive breast cancer compared with 10,000 not taking HRT . . .'). These are challenging formats. In an earlier study of numeracy – we found that only about 10% of respondents were able to accurately interpret information in the relative format if it were given without the underling absolute risks. Only about 5% could interpret the information: it was given in an absolutely different format without the absolute risks themselves. In contrast, about 35% could interpret the same information when given both absolute risks (with and without treatment) (Schwartz, 1997).

Many people found the presentation of Women's Health Initiative data confusing. In fact, our own local health news reporter contacted us for help in understanding, and then communicating

**Results of Study
of Prempro Hormone Replacement Therapy**

Number of women who will experience:＊

	FOR THE NEXT YEAR		FOR THE NEXT 5 YEARS	
	Do not take HRT	Take HRT	Do not take HRT	Take HRT
Benefits				
Hip fracture	2 in 1,000	1 in 1,000	8 in 1,000	5 in 1,000
Colon cancer	2 in 1,000	1 in 1,000	8 in 1,000	5 in 1,000
Harms				
Heart disease	3 in 1,000	4 in 1,000	15 in 1,000	19 in 1,000
Stroke	2 in 1,000	3 in 1,000	11 in 1,000	15 in 1,000
Blood clots	2 in 1,000	3 in 1,000	8 in 1,000	18 in 1,000
Breast cancer	3 in 1,000	4 in 1,000	15 in 1,000	20 in 1,000

＊Number are rounded to the newest whole number

Source: Analysis by Steve Woloshin and Lisa Schwartz of the local VA Outcomes Group

Figure 25.6 Presenting data from the Women's Health Initiative study on the effects of hormone replacement therapy. Originally published in the Valley News, reproduced with permission.

the study results to her readers. Figure 25.6 shows the table we helped her draft for the newspaper. Note that to allow women to appreciate the difference between short- and long-term HRT use, the table includes the absolute risks at 1 year and at 5 years (the latter reflecting the average duration of the Women's Health Initiative trial).

Putting risk into context

We have also used tables to help people put a variety of health risks into context. We felt that these tables were needed because, typically, risk messages describe a single disease in isolation. For example, one message may state 'there are 3700 deaths attributed to cervical cancer in the United States each year', while another might say '1 in 6 men get prostate cancer in their lifetime'. The differing formats, outcomes, and time frames make it difficult to understand how big each risk really is, or how it compares to others.

To create useful messages about health risks – messages which tell people how big each individual risk is and how each compares to the others – we created tables called 'risk charts'. Risk charts help in two ways: they standardize the presentation of information by providing the absolute risk of the same outcome – death in the next 10 years – from the various causes, facilitating comparisons across diseases. They also help put each disease risk into a larger context by also providing the 10-year chance of dying from all causes combined. Since the chance of dying is strongly influenced by gender and smoking history, we created separate charts for men and women who currently smoke, used to smoke, or have never smoked, using data from the national center for health statistics and the US Census Bureau. We first published the charts in 2002 (Woloshin, 2002), and in response to methodological concerns, we recently updated the charts, using a revised algorithm and the most recent mortality data (Woloshin, 2008). Figure 25.7 shows the newest chart for men who currently smoke and never smoked. Of note, here the columns are the outcomes (causes of death) and the rows are the exposure (age groups).

Helping consumers better understand tables with risk information

While we are optimistic that most people can understand and use tabular data, getting the numbers is only one piece of understanding the risk. People need a set of skills to give the numbers real meaning, for example, how to put the numbers in context, and how to recognize exaggerated

Risk Chart for Men (current and never smokers)*

Find the line closest to your age and smoking status. The numbers tell you **how many of 1000 men will die in the next 10 years from...**

		Vasular Disease		Cancer			Infection			Lung Disease	Accidents	All Causes Combined
Age	Smoking status	Heart Disease	Stroke	Lung	Colon	Prostate	Pneumonia	Flu	AIDS	COPD		
35	Never smoker	1	1			Less than 1 death			2		5	15
	Smoker	7	1	1		Less than 1 death			2		5	42
40	Never smoker	3	1	1	1				2		6	24
	Smoker	14	2	4	1				2	1	6	62
45	Never smoker	6	1	1	1				2		6	35
	Smoker	21	3	8	1		1		2	1	6	91
50	Never smoker	11	1	1	2	1	1		1		5	49
	Smoker	29	5	18	2	1	1		1	3	5	128
55	Never smoker	19	3	1	3	3	1		1	1	5	71
	Smoker	41	7	34	3	1	2		1	7	4	178
60	Never smoker	32	5	2	5	3	2		1	1	5	115
	Smoker	56	11	59	5	3	3		1	16	4	256
65	Never smoker	52	9	4	8	6	3			3	6	176
	Smoker	74	16	89	7	6	5			26	5	365
70	Never smoker	87	18	6	10	12	6			5	7	291
	Smoker	100	26	113	9	10	9			45	6	511
75	Never smoker	137	32	8	13	19	11			6	11	449
	Smoker	140	39	109	11	15	16			60	9	667

* A never smoker has smoked fewer than 100 cigarettes in his life and a current smoker has smoked at least 100 cigarettes or more in his life and smokes (any amount) now. The numbers in each row do not add up the chance of dying from all causes combined because there are many other causes of death besides the ones listed here.

Figure 25.7 Risk chart for men who currently smoke or who have never smoked. Reproduced with permission from Woloshin, S., Schwartz, L., and Welch, H. The risk of death by age, sex, and smoking status in the United States: putting health risks in context. *J Natl Cancer Inst* 2008; 100: 845–853.

or incomplete representations of risk data. To help people develop these basic skills, we developed an instruction booklet (called 'Know your chances'). The first part of the booklet teaches people how to understand their risk of disease by working through an example based on a public service advertisement about colon cancer. The second part focuses on how to understand the benefits and harms of interventions; we use a direct-to-consumer advertisement (for Zocor, a statin) for secondary heart disease prevention as the example.

We tested the booklet in two, parallel, randomized controlled trials done in populations with high and low socioeconomic status (SES) comparing the booklet with a general health information pamphlet (which does not provide any guidance on interpreting risk information) (Woloshin, 2007). In both trials, the booklet improved skills, demonstrated by a higher proportion achieving a 'passing grade' (a score of 75 points or higher on a 100-point scale) on the medical data interpretation test than the control group: 74% versus 56% in the high SES trial and 44% versus 26% in the low SES trial (Figure 25.8). The medical data interpretation test is an outcome measure we developed and validated in a separate study (Schwartz, 2005).

An expanded version of 'Know your chances' is being published by the University of California press (Schwartz, 2008).

Conclusion

Consumers need information in order to make wise medical decisions. Unfortunately, many consumers are ill-prepared to receive messages about risk and risk reduction. Despite this, we have found that they can use tables and it is not that difficult to improve their skills.

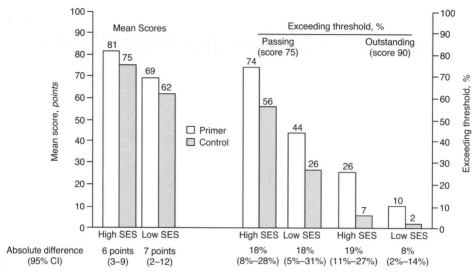

Figure 25.8 Effectiveness of booklet ('primer') on medical data interpretation skills. Reproduced with permission from Woloshin, S., Schwartz, L., and Welch, H. The effectiveness of a primer to help people understand risk: Two randomized trials in distinct populations. *Ann. Intern Med* 2007; 146: 256–265.

Communicators can do much to improve the quality of their messages by using simple tables with absolute risks helping consumers understand what is likely to happen if they do or do not take some action. Good decision-making requires more than data, and we are not suggesting that simply providing consumers with the numbers would solve all problems. But without numbers, consumers are left flying blind.

References

Elwyn, G., O'Connor, A., Stacey, D., *et al.* (2006). Developing a quality criteria framework for patient decision aids: Oonline international Delphi consensus process. *British Medical Journal*, **333**, 417–419.

Schwartz, L.M., Woloshin, S., Black, W.C., *et al.* (1997). The role of numeracy in understanding the benefit of screening mammography. *Ann. Intern. Med.*, **127**, 966–972.

Schwartz, L.M., Woloshin, S., and Welch, H.G. (2005). Can patients interpret health information? An assessment of the medical data interpretation test. *Med. Decis. Making*, **25**, 290–300.

Schwartz, L., Woloshin, S., and Welch, H. (2007). The drug facts box: Providing consumers simple tabular data on drug benefit and harm. *Med. Decis. Making*, **27**, 655–662.

Schwartz, L., Woloshin, S., and Welch, H. (2008). Know your chances: Understanding health statistics. University of California Press; (in press).

Woloshin, S., Schwartz, L., Tremmel, J., *et al.* (2001). Direct to consumer drug advertisements: What are Americans being sold? *Lancet*, **358**, 1141–1146.

Woloshin, S., Schwartz, L., and Welch, H. (2002). Risk charts: Putting cancer in context. *J. Natl. Cancer Inst.*, **94**, 799–804.

Woloshin, S., Schwartz, L., and Welch, H. (2004). The value of benefit data in direct-to-consumer drug ads. *Health Aff.*, W234–W245.

Woloshin, S., Schwartz, L., and Welch, H. (2007). The effectiveness of a primer to help people understand risk: Two randomized trials in distinct populations. *Ann. Intern. Med.*, **146**, 256–265.

Woloshin, S., Schwartz, L., and Welch, H. (2008). The risk of death by age, sex, and smoking status in the United States: Putting health risks in context. *J. Natl. Cancer Inst.*, **100**, 845–853.

Chapter 26

Making information available to patients and the general public: The example of *'Informed Health Online'* from Germany

Hilda Bastian, Marco Knelangen, and Beate Zschorlich

Introduction

Informing the public about the latest evidence and strengthening patients' autonomy in decision-making, these goals were set by legislators for Germany's national evidence assessment agency, the Institute of Quality and Efficiency in Health Care (IQWiG) (German Parliament, 2003). This remit for patients and the general public encompasses both an evidence monitoring role and a communication one (Bastian, 2008). It raises several central questions. What research evidence do patients and the public want to know about? How can high-quality evidence-based information be produced on a large scale? And how can evidence-based patient information on the internet – which is the primary communication medium available to the Institute – strengthen patient autonomy?

The Institute began operating in October 2004. The first two years were primarily developmental, concentrating on conceptual, methodological, and system requirements as well as staff development. We were a small department within the Institute, both in size (from one person in 2004 to five full-time staff by the end of 2006) and information output. Our website for the general public went online early in 2006, in both German (www.gesundheitsinformation.de) and English (www.informedhealthonline.org) (Figure 26.1).

A year later, in early 2007, the legislation governing IQWiG had been amended to strengthen and broaden the Institute's role in informing the public. An accompanying increased resource commitment saw us grow to a full-time staff of 14 by the end of 2007, publishing an average of four small to large information products every week in two languages. We scan all systematic reviews of evidence and health technology assessments published in English and German to identify new evidence that could be a basis for patient information (up to 10 reviews a day in 2008). The goal is to achieve an evidence-based encyclopaedia with over 2000 information items by the end of 2012 and to keep it reasonably up-to-date. The aim of this chapter is to describe how we got to this point, some of the key choices that were made along the way, and how users and others are reacting to this relative newcomer on the internet.

The genesis of health information at IQWiG

Central to the structure and formation of IQWiG as a national evidence assessment agency are its scientific independence and its advisory role. The Institute does not take decisions on behalf of others, but rather provides scientific assessments and analysis. This is also true for our role in

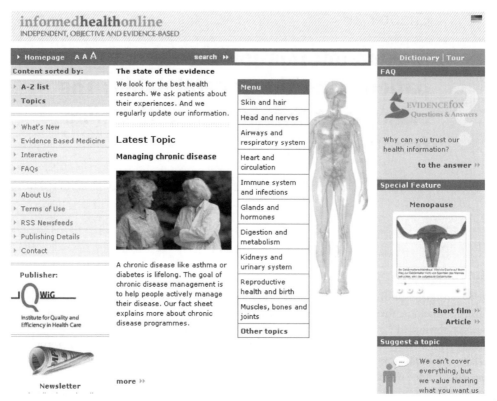

Figure 26.1 Screenshot – www.gesundheitsinformation.de / www.informedhealthonline.org

information provision to patients and the general public. We are expressly excluded from offering advice to individuals.

Our independence is protected legislatively and structurally. The Institute is governed by a non-government, non-profit foundation where major stakeholders in health have an oversight and advisory role. However, final scientific, content and editorial responsibility lies within the Institute. Funding is via a small levy on the public statutory health insurance, although the Federal Ministry of Health can also provide funding for commissioned activities.

Creating an independent and trusted national information provider was not the central motivation in the establishment of IQWiG, but it was a key function for the Institute from its legislative inception (German Parliament, 2003). Health information providers in Germany have been described as falling into four key groupings (Dierks *et al.*, 2006) as follows:

◆ Dependent institutions: actors within the health services who have other functions within health, such as providers and payers of services, and who cannot be regarded as independent by virtue of their other interests in the field;

◆ Independent institutions: organizations which are structurally and financially independent, and ideally not associated with provider functions in health;

◆ Government institutions: public agencies such as the Federal Centre for Health Education, which are directly governed and accountable to ministries; and

◆ Private and commercial information providers, including the manufacturers of health products.

A combination of community demand and political support for expanding independent health information options led to the inclusion of health information as part of IQWiG's remit, as well as other national initiatives such as an independent national network of patient counseling centres and a research program to support the development of patient information materials and projects to support patient autonomy (Dierks *et al.*, 2006; Loh *et al.*, 2007). Further, in the same year that IQWiG was grounded, a new parliamentary post of Federal Commissioner for Patients' Issues was established (Dierks *et al.*, 2006).

Two key factors were combined to ensure that health information for the public would be a major focus for the Institute: ongoing political commitment to an independent, national evidence-based health website and the appointment of a leading medical figure in the area of evidence-based patient education and autonomous self-management in Germany as the Director of IQWiG (Professor Peter Sawicki). This was critical in ensuring that patient information was not lost as a minority stream within the larger primary core business of the Institute (evidence assessment).

The challenges of large-scale production of evidence-based health information

Evidence-based health information is not simply health information that quotes evidence: Table 26.1 outlines IQWiG's definition of evidence-based health information. This incorporates aspects relevant not only to the content of the information, but also to its form being effective and to keeping the contents up-to-date as the evidence itself changes over time (Bastian, 2008; IQWiG, 2008). This is a labour-intensive endeavour, requiring a broad range of skills to achieve. Cost-effectiveness has not been a key feature of research on health information products to date, although there has been evaluation of some 'model' health information products (e.g. interactive decision aids – see also Chapter 54), and some development practices, which have been developed but are hard to realize on a large scale with public resources (such as randomized trials to investigate the impact of a particular product).

The contents of national websites generally draw together large amounts of information from a wide variety of sources and providers, produced according to highly varying standards, often with limited resources. Unsurprisingly, their contents do not then consistently meet either the criteria for evidence-based information or other criteria such as readability scores below the university level (Petch, 2004; Glenton *et al.*, 2005).

Table 26.1 IQWiG definition of evidence-based health information

The Institute defines evidence-based health information as information, where

- the content is based on evidence, particularly systematic reviews;
- the information is developed following systematic methods which aim to minimize bias and maintain neutrality;
- evidence-based communication techniques are used to meet the goals of informing, supporting, and empowering consumers and patients;
- uncertainties as well as the potential for benefit and harm are discussed;
- language and framing are neutral and non-directive, so that decisions are made in accordance with the patients' own values; and
- the information is updated so that it remains evidence-based.

The Institute also assesses the results of qualitative research and produces all elements of the information (including commissioning original visual artwork and audio-visual materials). Producing evidence-based health information in accordance with IQWiG's methods, therefore, requires a multi-disciplinary team as well as external support. That range of skills and experience is essential to being able to work at a high level of productivity on topics ranging across the health care spectrum in a reasonably short period of time. However, we need to achieve results in a cost-effective framework. Little has been published about the costs of developing information and national websites, although we were able to find one such descriptive analysis conducted for the European Union on NHS Direct (eHealth IMPACT, 2005). The expenditure on the development of *Informed Health Online* and its contents through to the end of its first year of operation was about 10% of those reported in that study. However, these two websites are far from identical, and the data are not directly comparable for this and other reasons.

The department within the Institute includes members with backgrounds in health care (including medicine, nursing, and dentistry), medical journalism and editing, health promotion, health consumer advocacy, public relations, qualitative research and undertaking systematic reviews of the effects of health care, and communication interventions. The work of department members is also supported by others in the Institute, including the Medical Statistics Department, as well as external contractors and experts. As information is produced in English as well as German, we are able to draw on the authors of research internationally to verify the accuracy of our explanation of the evidence.

IQWiG's information is being produced as somewhat 'official' information for Germany, so it also needs to go through a number of steps that are not required from other information providers. For example, there is a month-long consultation period incorporating a wide variety of stakeholders in health. This includes the Institute's Board of Governors, its Scientific Advisory Board, and its Board of Trustees. The Board of Governors includes representatives of the Ministry of Health and the statutory insurance funds. The Board of Trustees includes representatives of services providers (doctors, dentists, hospitals, and others), national patient and disability representatives, the Federal Commissioner for Patients' Issues, representatives of community stakeholder organizations such as employers and churches, and the pharmaceutical industry.

Within this consultation process, some stakeholders take the opportunity to push their interests quite aggressively. This can widen into post-publication pressure to change information seen to be unfavourable, such as to industry. A fact sheet similar to that produced by the Food and Drugs Administration in the USA on using dietary supplements and complementary medicine products, for example, resulted in a press release from the pharmaceutical industry association entitled 'IQWiG disseminates false patient information', and accusing the Institute of aiming to discredit medicinal products (National Federation of the Pharmaceutical Industry, 2008). Our experience with these processes underscores the need for independent national provision of evidence-based health information, but it also illustrates some of the operational and political challenges of this role.

Content, form, and style: choices along the path to an evidence-based encyclopaedia

We publish our information free of charge on the internet, although reproduction (with permission) is encouraged. About two-thirds of the population in Germany over the age of 14 years uses the internet now, and the importance of the internet in health information is increasing (van Eimeren *et al.*, 2008; Andreassen *et al.*, 2007). The internet might be the first port of call before a consultation for perhaps half of patients in Germany, at least for some conditions (Pennekamp *et al.*, 2006; Richter *et al.*, 2004).

This group of internet information seekers is a relatively literate group of people, and they offer a means of reaching into families and social circles with health information. We have a range of products, with varying degrees of detail and ease of reading, from detailed lengthy articles through to simpler audio-visual animations and patients' stories to interest and reach different audiences. We have developed only one decision aid to date. That has received a mixed reception in an independently conducted qualitative evaluation of users (Schmacke *et al.*, 2008). Although the decision aid does attract some visitors, users are mostly choosing the more traditional information options in our information modules. This suggests that decision aids are not a cost-effective option for us at this stage. It may be that the format of decision aids is still unfamiliar to average internet users (Schmacke *et al.*, 2008).

In developing major information modules, our starting point is patient's interest and perspectives. This involves a rapid review of qualitative studies in the topic area as well as studies on information needs, interviews with patient representatives, and often an online survey of reader interests and needs (Bastian, 2008). Individual patients are often interviewed to develop short patient stories, which are a critical element of our modules. These patients also contribute to the quality assurance of our products. In 2008, we also added a stage of user-testing to all our draft products, conducted externally from IQWiG either in focus groups or by an individual interview (IQWiG, 2008). These users may or may not be personally affected by the topic of the information, and the information is assessed using a guided interview or focus group structure addressing comprehension, comprehensiveness, readability, credibility, and relevance.

Along with readability testing, monitoring of website use, and external qualitative evaluation of our products, this routine use of externally conducted focus groups and interviews forms the backbone of our evaluation strategy. Evidence-based information is challenging for users who are used to less critical patient information. Nevertheless, our initial experience suggests we may be able to build a significant readership for evidence-based health information in Germany. Our information has also been endorsed for use within the NHS (UK), and translation and adoption into the French health care system is also on the horizon. In 2008, a major statutory health insurance fund in Germany printed the first booklet edition of one of our disease modules, sending hundreds of thousands of copies into circulation.

Conclusion

We have established that it is possible to produce evidence-based health information on a scale that can enable a multi-lingual, free, and up-to-date encyclopaedia to become a reality. Whether or not this makes an important contribution to patient autonomy, and better-informed use of health care in Germany will depend on reaching a wide audience, and continually improving in response to what we learn from our own experience and the research now accruing on enhancing evidence-based patient choice.

References

Andreassen, H.K., Bujnowska-Fedak, M.M., Chronaki, C.E., *et al.* (2007). European citizens use of E-health service: A study of seven countries. *BMC Public Health*, **7**, 53.

Bastian, H. (2008). Health literacy and patient information: Developing the methodology for a national evidence-based health website. *Patient Educ. Couns.* (in press).

Dierks, M.L., Seidel, G., Schwartz, F.W., *et al.* (2006). Citizen and patient orientation in the healthcare services. Bürger- und Patientenorientierung im Gesundheitswesen.] National Health Reports – Number 32. [Gesundheitsberichterstattung des Bundes - Heft 32.] Berlin: Robert Koch Institute.

eHealth IMPACT. (2005). Descriptive report on site study results. NHS Direct, UK – NHS Direct Online (NHSDO) information serve. Project: Study on economic impact of eHealth. Bonn: eHealth Impact. Accessed on 13 August 2008. Available at http://www.ehealth-impact.org/case_studies/index_en.htm

German Institute for Quality and Efficiency in Health Care (IQWiG). (2008). General Methods. Version 3.0. Cologne: German Institute for Quality and Efficiency in Health Care (IQWiG). Accessed on 31st August 2008. Available at: (*will add when the English version goes online – due late August 08*)

German Parliament [Deutscher Bundestag]. (2003). Draft of legislation to modernise social health insurance (the social health insurance modernisation act). [Entwurf eines Gesetzes zur Modernisierung der gesetzlichen Krankenversicherung (GKV-Modernisierungsgesetz – GMG)]. Drucksache 15/1525. Berlin: Deutscher Bundestag.

Glenton, C., Paulsen, E.J., and Oxman, A.D. (2005). Portals to wonderland: Health portals lead to confusing information about the effects of health care. *BMC. Med. Inform. Decis. Mak.*, **5**, 7.

Loh, A., Simon, D., Bieber, C., *et al.* (2007). Patient and citizen participation in German health care – current state and future perspectives. *Z. Arztl. Fortbild. Qualitatssich.*, **101**, 229–235.

National Federation of the Pharmaceutical Industry [Bundesverband der pharmazeutischen Industrie]. (2008). IQWiG disseminates false patient information. Press Release. Berlin: National Federation of the Pharmaceutical Industry (BPI). Accessed on 23 June 2008.

Pennekamp, P.H., Diedrich, O., Schmitt, O., *et al.* (2006). Frequency and utility of internet use by orthopaedic patients [Prävalenz und Stellenwert der Internetnutzung orthopädischer Patienten]. *Z. Orthop.*, **144**, 459–463.

Petch, T. (2004). Content analysis of selection health information websites: Final report. Vancouver. ACTION for Health, Centre for Clinical Epidemiology and Evaluation, Simon Fraser University. Accessed on 30 July 2008. Available at http://www.sfu.ca/~act4hlth/pub/working/Content%20Analysis.pdf

Richter, J.G., Becker, A., Specker, C., *et al.* (2004). Disease-oriented internet use in outpatients with inflammatory rheumatic diseases. *Z. Rheumatol.*, **63**, 216–222.

Schmacke, N., Kolip, P., Müller, V., *et al.* Evaluation of the health information feature "Menopause": Interviews with users on the Institute for Quality and Efficiency in Health Care's information module "menopause". Final report. Bremen: Health Services Research Working and Coordination Group, Bremen University. Accessed on 14 August 2008. Available at http://www.akg.uni-bremen.de/pages/projektBeschreibung.php?ID=4

van Eimeren, B. and Frees, B. (2008). Internet use: biggest increase by "silver-haired surfers". Results of the ARD/ZDF online study 2008 [Internetverbreitung: Größter Zuwachs bei Silver-Surfern. Ergebnisse der ARD/ZDF-Onlinestudie 2008]. *Media Perspektiven*, **7**, 330–344.

Chapter 27

The role of decision aids in promoting evidence-based patient choice

Annette M. O'Connor and Adrian Edwards

Introduction

Health care decisions are often difficult to make. This may be because there is insufficient scientific evidence about benefits and harms or because the options have known benefits and harms that patients value differently. Among the 2500 health care interventions evaluated by the *Clinical Evidence* group (*Clinical Evidence*, 2005), 13% were classified as 'beneficial', 23% as 'probably beneficial', 8% as 'need to weigh benefits versus risks', 6% as 'probably non-beneficial', 4% as 'probably useless or dangerous', and 46%, the largest number, as having insufficient evidence of usefulness. Patient decision aids have been developed to supplement existing communication between professionals and patients (O'Connor *et al.*, 2003b). In general their aim is to prepare patients for decision-making so that they can

1 understand the range of options available;

2 understand the probable consequences of options;

3 consider the value they place on the consequences; and

4 participate in decision-making with their practitioner to the extent that they wish (Edwards and Elwyn, 2006).

In this chapter, we provide a brief overview of patient decision aids and their role in promoting 'evidence-based patient choice'. We begin by defining decision aids and describe their methods and efficacy. We also introduce a number of key areas which are explored in more detail in the following chapters, particularly regarding design (Chapters 29 by Durand, 30 by Winterbottom), development (Chapter 33, IPDAS), evaluation (Chapter 28 by Stacey), and implementation (Chapters 34, 51 and 52 by Llewellyn-Thomas, Legare and May).

What is a patient decision aid?

Decision aids prepare patients to participate with their health care professionals in making deliberated, personalized choices about health care options. They supplement counselling by providing information on options. The aim is that patients are better able to judge the value of the benefits versus the harms. The Cochrane review of decision aids (O'Connor *et al.*, 2003a) has defined what decisions aids include and do not include:

1 Inclusion criteria: Interventions were designed to help people make specific and deliberative choices among options by providing (at the minimum) information on the options and outcomes relevant to the person's health status. Additional strategies may include providing information on the disease/condition; the probabilities of outcomes tailored to a person's health risk factors; an explicit values clarification exercise; information on others' opinions; and guidance or coaching in the steps of decision-making and communicating

with others. Decision aids are delivered using media such as decision boards, interactive videodiscs, personal computers, audiotapes, audio-guided workbooks, pamphlets, and group presentations.

2 Exclusion criteria: Passive informed consent materials, educational interventions that are not geared to a specific decision, or interventions designed to promote compliance with a recommended option rather than an informed choice based on personal values.

Despite the common elements of information provision to help patients judge the value of options, there is considerable variability in the level of detail, additional elements, and delivery. Sources and examples are listed in Figure 27.1. Decision aids have been developed for a range of situations such as

1 medical therapies for atrial fibrillation; benign prostatic hypertrophy; low back pain; cancers of the breast, lung and prostate, leukaemia, lymphoma; male newborn circumcision; and ischaemic heart disease;

2 diagnostic tests such as amniocentesis and screening for colon and prostate cancers;

Center	Type	Example	url
ACADEMIC RESEARCH CENTERS			
McMaster University	Decision board	Breast cancer	http://www.fhs.mcmaster.ca/slru/ sccru/decisionboard.html
Ottawa Health Decision Center	Booklets; audio-booklets; worksheets	Tube feeding Generic	http://decisionaid.ohri.ca/ AZsumm.php?ID=1174 http://decisionaid.ohri.ca/ decguide.html
Oregon Health Sciences Eisenberg Center, Portland Oregon USA Funded by AHRQ to develop template for AHRQ evidence reviews centers	Booklets for patients and clinicians	Osteoarthritis Other topics	http://effectivehealthcare.ahrq.gov/ reports/ topic.cfm?topic=4&sid=31&rType=1 http://effectivehealthcare.ahrq.gov/ reports/ index.cfm?sType=5#subList101
Cardiff University, Wales	Interactive decision support technology	PSA test Other topics	http://www.prosdex.org.uk/ index_content.htm http://www.informedhealthchoice.com/ prosdex.htm
Center for Disease Control	Online	PSA test	http://www.cdc.gov/cancer/prostate/ publications/decisionguide/
Toronto	Adapted Ottawa template	Breast cancer	http://www.cancer.ca/ccs/internet/ miniapp/0,2939,3543_16897665_ 19702640_langId-en,00.html
U. Sydney, Australia	Online	Mammogram other	http://www.mammogram.med. usyd.edu.au/ http://www.health.usyd.edu.au/ shdg/resources/decision_aids.php

Figure 27.1 Examples of patient decision aids.

Center	Type	Example	url
LARGE SCALE NOT FOR PROFIT/ COMMERCIAL PRODUCERS			
Health Dialog, Boston USA [content produced by Foundation for Informed Medical Decision-Making	DVD, videos, booklets	Several	Ottawa Hospital Consumer Library has suite of DVDS URL below is to website profiling their web-based product for breast cancer http://www.collaborativecare.net/
Healthwise, Boise Idaho; sells content to several health plans in US and Canada [BC, Sask] and internet providers [Preferred care, WEbMD, etc.]	Decision points. Format is under revision	Breast cancer	http://www.healthwise.net/ preferredcare/Content/ StdDocument.aspx?DOCHWID= tv6530&SECHWID=tv6530-Intro
		Others	Browse A to Z website at OHRI http://decisionaid.ohri.ca/ AZinvent.php
Mayo Clinic	Decision guides	Breast cancer	http://www.mayoclinic.com/health/ mastectomy-lumpectomy/BC99999
		Other Mayo	http://www.mayoclinic.com/health/ TreatmentDecsionIndex/Treatment DecisionIndex
National Cancer Institute, U.S.A	Online	Breast cancer	http://www.nci.nih.gov/cancertopics/ breast-cancer-surgery-choices
		Prostate cancer	http://www.cancer.gov/ cancertopics/ prostate-cancer-treatment-choices
		Others	http://www.cancer.gov/ cancertopics/Genetic-Testing-for- Breast-and-Ovarian-Cancer-Risk http://www.cancer.gov/ cancertopics/i131/makingchoices http://www.cancer.gov/ cancertopics/factsheet/Risk/BRCA

Note: Browse through other examples of patient decision aids at http://decisionaid.ohri.ca/AZinvent.php

Figure 27.1 (continued)

3 preventive therapies such as Hepatitis B vaccine;

4 clinical trial entry decisions; and

5 end-of-life decisions such as resuscitation in seniors.

We refer readers to the Chapters 35–49 for illustrations of the decision aids available in a number of medical, surgical, and screening scenarios. Arguably, it may have been envisaged in the early days of decision aid development that they might reduce the need for consultation time (and be cheaper) but they are now clearly seen as complementary to the health care consultation. Such consultations with practitioners are likely to be similar in duration, but able to focus more on the patient's individual needs, exploring emotional issues and reactions, and providing support (Edwards *et al.*, 2008).

The media used to present decision aids are varied, and it is important to note that each of these (paper-based, decision board, video, online) is likely to have its place according to the nature of the setting and the clinical problem being addressed. A further variation occurs in terms of whether the decision aids are thought most helpful if used as support before, during, or after a consultation. Some decision aids are provided for consumers to work through on their own (outside the consultation or at home) as a platform for discussions in a further consultation. These aids vary in their use of explicit links to the health care encounter, such as guiding patients to communicate values, preferences for participation, and questions with their practitioner. Others are offered within consultations. Each is likely to have its place according to the situation; but where decision aids are discussed *outside* consultations, it is important to ensure that both patient and professional contribute to the process of making a decision about treatment and that the patient feels adequately supported in decisions about their treatment or care (see also Chapter 17, Elwyn and Charles). Moreover, structured counselling approaches for the professional (Lerman *et al.*, 1997) may also be important to ensure that linkage with the decision aid. As more research accumulates, it will become clearer which types of interventions are likely to be most effective for which types of patients and clinical circumstances. All of the decision aids, however, seek to enhance consumer involvement, on the basis of evidence, and thus facilitate 'evidence-informed patient choice'.

When do you need a decision aid?

The development of decision aids across North America, Australasia, and Europe is motivated by several trends as follows:

1 the rise of consumerism with an emphasis on informed choice rather than informed consent;

2 the evidence-based practice and knowledge translation initiatives in which evidence to support decision-making is provided to patients as well as to professionals and policy makers;

3 the use of patient-mediated strategies to reduce regional practice variations;

4 the identification of treatment decisions that are 'utility' or 'value' sensitive and consequent implications in practice guidelines and health policy;

5 the quality improvement reforms that include patient-oriented care.

Kassirer (1994) lists some indications for explicitly eliciting patients' preferences in clinical practice: firstly, when options have major differences in outcomes or complications; secondly, when decisions require trade-offs between short-term and long-term outcomes; thirdly, when one choice can result in a small chance of a grave outcome; and finally, when there are marginal differences in outcomes between options. When these situations are evident, a decision aid may be particularly helpful. Patient characteristics may also determine the need for a decision aid, for example, if patients are very risk-averse, or attach unusual importance to certain possible outcomes.

Do decision aids work?

Evaluation studies from a review out of 10 concluded that decision aids improved patients' participation, increased knowledge of their treatment options and probable outcomes, and improved agreement between patients' values and subsequent treatment decisions (Coulter and Ellins, 2007). The use of discretionary surgery decreased without apparent adverse effects on health outcomes. The readers are referred to a recent update of the Cochrane systematic review described in Chapter 28 (Stacey).

How do you develop and evaluate a decision aid?

There are several issues that need to be considered during the process of development and evaluation. The reader is referred to Chapter 33 (IPDAS) in which standards for development and evaluation are discussed in more detail (Elwyn *et al.*, 2006). Researchers will strive to improve on current versions of decision aids, based on their desired objectives. Moreover, mass producers of patient decision aids will need to grapple with 'essential' elements, delivery, and evaluation. Future trends will challenge both groups. For example, the number of options and potential effects are proliferating. How do we help patients sort through these issues? Another related issue is the integration of decision support tools into chronic condition management. How will decision aids be adapted for patients whose main issue is priority setting according to clinical and personal needs?

Are decision aids being implemented in practice?

In 2006, patient decision aids from four large-scale producers were accessed over 8 million times, primarily through the internet (O'Connor *et al.*, 2007). The integration into clinical care processes is more of a challenge. Delivery of decision support may require some combination of clinical consultation, counselling, provision of patient decision aids, and coaching, an exemplar of which is the Dartmouth Hitchcock Medical Center 'decision lab' (see Chapter 34, Llewellyn-Thomas). The sequence, combination, and professionals involved need to be adapted to the type of decision, the population, and service context in which care is provided. These should be spelled out in clinical and care pathways.

Other examples of implementation in clinical care including a network of US practice centers supported by the Foundation for Informed Medical Decision Making include the Massachusetts General Hospital; the White River Junction Veterans Administration; University of California at San Francisco and Los Angeles; University of North Carolina; and Allegheny General Hospital.

This shift in the way care is delivered, promoting decision aids to facilitate patients' active participation in decisions about their treatment or care, is beginning to be taken up in other countries too. For example, in the United Kingdom, several Urology centres in the National Health Service have care pathways for benign prostatic hyperplasia and early stage prostate cancer treatments. In Canada, the Ottawa Hospital is beginning to embed decision support into its care pathways. For example, patients on the waiting list to see a surgeon are screened for surgical eligibility, and then use patient decision aids and complete a personal decision form. Summarized data on clinical and decisional needs are forwarded to the surgeon, if patients prefer surgery and to the referring physician, if patients decline surgery.

However, it has to be said that such developments are as yet quite limited in prominence and impact on everyday health care. This has raised a significant concern to identify, understand, and develop effective strategies to overcome 'implementation barriers'. These may include the traditional hindrances of time and money, but may also include professional attitudes and cultural adaptation and implementation issues. They may also include patient resistance. These issues are examined in more detail by Legare and May, and colleagues (Chapters 51 and 52). It is also possible that decision aids are not as widely valued as developers might wish, and that they are not a vehicle through which shared decision-making is most effectively promoted. We refer readers to Chapters 11 (Gafni and Charles) and 50 (Price) which ask whether we are really clear that we 'know where we are going', to explore this aspect further.

1. Is there a need for a decision aid?

What are the decision-making needs of patients and practitioners? Conduct key informant interviews, focus groups, or surveys to elicit patients' and practitioners' perceptions of decisions perceived as important and difficult; usual roles and decision-making practices; barriers & facilitators in providing/accessing decision support, potential strategies for overcoming barriers. Conduct marketing surveys regarding demand for an aid and preferred method of delivery.

What makes the decision difficult? Review systematic overviews, decision analyses, and preference studies to determine whether benefits marginal or uncertain; risks material/uncertain; value tradeoffs between benefits and risks; variation in preferences for outcomes.

Are sufficient numbers affected and how are they affected? Review databases, demographic, morbidity statistics; population surveys.

Is there sufficient variation in utilisation? Review practice atlases, utilization data, practice variation studies.

Are there decision aids available to meet these needs? Review published overviews, reports. Contact centres that produce aids.

2. Is it feasible to develop a decision aid?

Are there adequate resources?
Assess finances, availability of experts with credibility, networks, and commitment to ongoing update. Link to established overview & dissemination networks.

Is there enough evidence of benefits and risks to incorporate into a decision aid?
Review systematic overviews with appraisals of the quality of evidence.

How quickly is the evidence expected to change? Review ongoing trials.

Can delivery be accessible/ acceptable to users? Conduct focus groups, market surveys.

3. What are the objectives of the decision aid?

Objectives will depend on one's frame of reference.
e.g. Improve decision quality (Sepucha *et al.*, 2004).
Improve knowledge of the clinical problem, options, outcomes, variation in patient or practitioner opinions and practices.
Create realistic expectations of outcomes, consistent with available evidence.
Promote congruence between patients' values and choice.

4. Which framework will drive its development?

Charles, Gafni & Whelan distinguish shared decision-making from other decision-making approaches (Charles *et al.*, 1999)
Entwistle defines evidence-informed choice; outlines different criteria for evaluations depending on objective (Entwistle *et al.*,1998)
Hersey & Lohr Framework for AHCPR with a health services and informatics perspective (Hersey *et al.*, 1997).
Llewellyn-Thomas Framework has a special focus on types of preferences; placement in socio-political context (Llewellyn-Thomas, 1995)
Makoul and Clayman has an integrative model of shared decision-making in medical encounters (Makoul & Clayman, 2005)
Mulley places shared decision-making in the context of outcomes research (Mulley, 1995).
O'Connor *et al.* Ottawa Decision Support Framework focuses on decision support as a clinical skill by preparing both the practitioner and patient for decision-making (O'Connor *et al.*, 1998a)
Rothert *et al* describe mutual roles of patients and practitioners in decision-making; focus on information and values (Rothert & Talarczyk, 1987).
Ruland and Bakken describe decision support systems for shared decision-making.
Stacey *et al.* describes the role of coaches in supporting decision-making.
Whitney examines the limits of applying shared decision-making (Whitney, 2003).
Durand *et al.* describe the need for strong theoretical basis for design of decision aid (Durand *et al.*, 2008)

5. Which methods will be included in the decision aid?

Patient/Client Decision Support

1. **Information Re Options and Outcomes** content: clinical problem, options, outcomes
2. **Probabilities:** (a). none; numerical frequencies/ percents (Barratt *et al.*, 2004; Barry *et al.*, 1997; Man-Son-Hing *et al.*, 2002); graphic pie charts (Schapira *et al.*, 2001; Whelan *et al.*, 1995), 100 people qualitative (low, moderate, high) (Gigerenzer & Edwards, 2003); (b). tailored probabilities: not tailored; stratified by personal risk factors; (c). evidence for statements: references included/not
3. **Values clarification:** (a). Implicit describing processes outcomes in sufficient detail [physical, emotional, social effects] to judge their value (Barry *et al.*, 1997; Whelan *et al.*, 1995) (b). explicit methods such as weigh scale exercise (O'Connor *et al.*, 1998a); treatment tradeoff task (Dowding *et al.*, 2004); balance scales (O'Connor *et al.*, 1998b); formal utility assessments (Pauker S.P. and Pauker S.G., 1987); (c). relevance chart (Rothert *et al.*, 1997)
4. **Information on others:** none; cases of different choices (Barry *et al.*, 1997; O'Connor *et al.*, 1998a; Rothert *et al.*, 1997); statistics on variation in patients' decisions or professionals' opinions
5. **Coaching or guidance** in deliberation, communication, and implementation: not included; steps in weighing the benefits, risks (O'Connor *et al.*, 1998a; Rothert *et al.*, 1997); steps in discussing decision with a professional (O'Connor *et al.*, 1998a; Rothert *et al.*, 1997); tips on managing consequences of choices.
6. **Delivery:** personal counselling supplemented by: generic tools; decision board (Carrere *et al.*, 2000; Whelan *et al.*, 1995); take home audio-guided workbook (O'Connor *et al.*, 1998a); interactive videodisc or linear video (Barry *et al.*, 1997); computer-based tool elwyn (Evans *et al.*, 2007); group lecture, workshop (Rothert *et al.*, 1997).

Professional Decision Support

1. **Content:** scientific evidence re decision; rationale for decision aid; efficacy of decision aid; timing and use in practice; scientific references.
2. **Delivery:** manual; video; lecture; workshop; hot-line; academic detailing

Figure 27.2 Developing and evaluating decision aids: questions and methods.

6. Which designs and measures will be used to develop and evaluate decision aid?

Development Panel	Participants:	researchers, clinicians, educators, patients, opinion leaders;
	Methods:	iterations of drafts, feedback, revisions, feedback etc.
Review Panels	Participants:	potential users (practitioners, patients who have already made decisions)
	Methods:	focus groups, personal interviews, questionnaires to elicit acceptability, etc.
Pilot Studies	Participants:	patients at the point of decision making
	Designs:	**before/after study** – e.g. baseline questionnaire, decision aid, post-test questionnaire or **post-test only**, with pre-established criteria for success (e.g. 70% knowledge test)
Trials__	Participants:	patients at point of decision-making; practitioners
	Designs:	**quasi experiment** or **randomized trial** with unit of randomization patient or practitioner

Criteria For Evaluation	Measurement Tools
Knowledge	Knowledge/Comprehension test specific to decision
Expectations of outcomes	Probability scales (Palda *et al.*, 1997; Schwartz *et al.*, 1999; Woloshin and Schwartz, 1999) Likelihood scales (Azjen & Fishbein, 1980; O'Connor, 1995)
Clarity of values	Values subscale of Decisional Conflict Scale (O'Connor, 1995)
Agreement between choice & values	Statistical relationship between values and choices (Barry *et al.*, 1995; Dodin *et al.*, 2001; Holmes-Rovner *et al.*, 1999; O'Connor *et al.*, 1998a; Sepucha *et al.*, 2004)
Realistic perceptions of others'	Perceptions of % of practitioners/patients choosing options; subjective norms (Azjen & Fishbein, 1980)
Decision	Choice Question (option *x*, option *y*, unsure); choice predisposition (O'Connor *et al.*, 1998a)
Decisional conflict	Decisional conflict scales for patients and providers (Dolan *et al.*, 1996; O'Connor, 1995)
Skill in decision-making	Self-efficacy scale (Rothert *et al.*, 1997)
Satisfaction with decision-making	Decision Satisfaction Inventory (Barry *et al.*, 1997); Satisfaction with Decision; (Holmes-Rovner *et al.*, 1996; Sainfort and Booske, 2000) Satisfaction with Preparation for Decision Making (Rothert *et al.*, 1997)
Acceptability	Acceptability Questionnaires (Liao *et al.*, 1996)
Use of decision aid	Utilisation data
Participation according to needs	Congruence between preferred and actual role in decision making (Degner *et al.*, 1997; Strull *et al.*, 1984)
Persistence with decisions	Survey of decision over time; implementation data
Reduced distress from outcomes	Condition-specific symptom and side effects distress scales; distress from risk (Lerman *et al.*, 1996)
Health-related quality of life	Generic, condition-specific, preference-based
Use of resources	Analysis of utilisation data (Cohen *et al.*, 2004)
Costs	Cost-effectiveness model (Nease and Owens, 1994)

See also IPDAS documents at http://www.ipdas.ohri.ca/IPDAS_Background.pdf for further resources

---

7. How should the decision aid be implemented? {Logan & Graham 1998 ID: 58}

What are potential adopters': attitudes toward innovation/change; knowledge, attitudes and skills to use aid; preference for shared decision making?
Conduct focus groups, key informant interviews, environmental scans, surveys of potential users.

What are the environmental barriers & supporters? Conduct focus groups, surveys to identify the following factors
Social: likely supporters and opposers; presence of opinion leaders as supporters; predominant belief system regarding shared decision-making.
Structural: operational tools and processes, regulations, quality assurance criteria, to encourage/hinder use of aid; resources to support dissemination of aid.
Other incentives and disincentives

Will the evidence-based innovation meet expectations of target audience?
Conduct focus groups, surveys.

Which implementation strategies should be used?
Tailor strategies according to needs.
Diffusion strategies: advertisements, publications, internet;
Dissemination strategies: targeted mailings;
Implementation strategies: education programs, feedback, administrative changes

Is the aid being adopted and is it having the expected effect on outcomes?
Analyse data bases, conduct quality assurance studies, surveys and implementation studies to determine whether the aid is being used by the expected audience in the expected manner and whether it is having the expected effect on expected outcomes and evidence-based decision making among patients/clinicians.

Figure 27.2 (continued)

Conclusion

In this chapter, we have defined patient decision aids, their rationale, their efficacy and signalled issues in their development, evaluation, and dissemination. From the wider literature on decision aids, there is a large body of evidence about their benefits in the research setting where study populations may be highly selected. Implementation of decision aids is more commonly practiced via the internet than in routine practice. Whilst some of the reasons for this are generic to the transfer of any research into practice, some more specific issues are also relevant. Developers of decision aids must continue to refine their methods and content. Meeting the needs of the individual patient with a package developed for many remains a challenge. However, if these needs continue to be addressed in developing future aids then there is great potential for the benefits currently shown in research to be available to patients across a wide range of settings and for a variety of health care choices. Decision aids build on the conceptual frameworks of shared decision-making and seek to implement effective risk communication and values clarification. As such they offer a very practical way in which evidence-based patient choice can be facilitated.

References

Azjen, I. and Fishbein, M. (1980). *Understanding Attitudes and Predicting Behaviour*. Englewood Cliffs, New Jersey: Prentice-Hall.

Barratt, A., Trevena, L., Davey, H., *et al.* (2004). Use of decision aids to support informed choices about screening. *British Medical Journal*, **329**, 507–510.

Barry, M.J., Cherkin, D., Chang, Y., *et al.* (1997). A randomized trial of a multimedia shared decision-making program for men facing a treatment decision for benign prostatic hyperplasia. *Disease Management and Clinical Outcomes*, **1**, 5–14.

Barry, M.J., Fowler, F.J., Jr., Mulley, A.G., *et al.* (1995). Patient reactions to a program designed to facilitate patient participation in treatment decisions for benign prostatic hyperplasia. *Medical Care*, **33**(8), 771–782.

Carrere, M.O., Moumjid-Ferdjaoui, N., Charavel, M., *et al.* (2000). 'Eliciting patients' preferences for adjuvant chemotherapy in breast cancer: Development and validation of a bedside decision-making instrument in a French Regional Cancer Centre. *Health Expectations.*, **3**, 97–113.

Charles, C., Gafni, A., and Whelan, T. (1999). Decision-making in the physician-patient encounter: Revisiting the shared treatment decision-making model. *Social Science & Medicine*, **49**, 651–661.

Clinical Evidence. (2005). A guide to the text: Summary page. British Medical Journal, http://clinicalevidence. bmj.com/ceweb/about/knowledge.jsp.

Cohen, D., Longo, M., Hood, K., *et al.* (2004). Resource effects of training general practitioners in risk communication skills and shared decision making competencies. *Journal of Evaluation in Clinical Practice*, **10**, 439–445.

Coulter, A. and Ellins, J. (2007). Effectiveness of strategies for informing, educating and involving patients. *British Medical Journal*, **335**, 24–27.

Degner, L., Kristjanson, L.J., Bowman, D., *et al.* (1997). Information needs and decisional preferences in women with breast cancer. *Journal of the American Medical Association*, **277**, 1485–1492.

Dodin, S., Legare, F., Daudelin, G., *et al.* (2001). Prise de decision en matière d'homonothérapie de remplacement *Canadian Family Physician*, **47**, 1586–1593.

Dolan, J.G., Markakis, K., Beckman, H., *et al.* (1996). Further evaluation of the provider decision process assessment instrument (PDPAI): A process-based method for assessing the quality of health providers' decisions [abstract]. *Medical Decision Making*, **16**, 465.

Dowding, J., Swanson, V., Bland, R., *et al.* (2004). The development and preliminary evaluation of a decision aid based on decision analysis for two treatment conditions: Benign prostatic hyperplasia and hypertension. *Patient Education & Counseling*, **52**, 209–215.

Durand, M., Stiel, M., Boivin, J., *et al.* (2008). Where is the theory? Evaluating the theoretical frameworks described in decision support technologies. *Patient Education & Counseling*, **71**, 125–135.

Edwards, A. and Elwyn, G. (2006). Inside the black box of shared decision making – distinguishing between the process of involvement and who makes the decision. *Health Expectations*, **9**, 307–320.

Edwards, A., Gray, J., Clarke, A., *et al.* (2008). Interventions to improve risk communication in clinical genetics: Systematic review. *Patient Education & Counseling*, **71**, 4–25.

Elwyn, G., O'Connor, A., Stacey, D., *et al.* (2006). Developing quality indicators for patient decision aids: An online international Delphi consensus process. *British Medical Journal*, **333**, 417–419.

Entwistle, V., Sheldon, T., Sowden, A., *et al.* (1998). Evidence-informed patient choice. Practical issues of involving patients in decisions about health care technologies. *Int. J. Technol. Assess. Health Care*, **14**, 212–225.

Evans, R., G., E., Edwards, A., Watson, E., *et al.* (2007). Toward a model for field-testing patient decision-support technologies: A qualitative field-testing study. *Journal of Medical Internet Research*, **9**(3), e21.

Gigerenzer, G. and Edwards, A. (2003). Simple tools for understanding risks: From innumeracy to insight. *British Medical Journal*, **327**, 741–744.

Hersey, J., Matheson, J., and Lohr, K. (1997). Consumer health informatics and patient decision-making. (AHCPR Pub. No. 98-N001)'. Research Triangle Institute, Agency for Health Care Policy and Research.

Holmes-Rovner, M., Kroll, J., Rovner, D., *et al.* (1999). Patient decision support intervention: Increased consistency with decision analytic models. *Medical Care*, **37**, 270–284.

Holmes-Rovner, M., Kroll, J., Schmitt, N., *et al.* (1996). Patient satisfaction with health care decisions: The satisfaction with decision scale. *Medical Decision Making*, **16**, 58–64.

Kassirer, J. (1994). Incorporating patients preferences into medical decisions. *New England Journal of Medicine*, **330**, 1895–1896.

Lerman, C., Biesecker, B., Benkendorf, J.L., *et al.* (1997). Controlled trial of pretest education approaches to enhance informed decision-making for BRCA1 gene testing. *Journal of the National Cancer Institute*, **89**, 148–157.

Lerman, C., Schwartz, M.D., Miller, S.M., *et al.* (1996). A randomized trial of breast cancer risk counseling: Interacting effects of counseling, educational level, and coping style. *Health Psychology*, **15**, 75–83.

Liao, L., Jollis, J.G., DeLong, E.R., *et al.* (1996). Impact of an interactive video on decision making of patients with ischaemic heart disease. *Journal of General Internal Medicine*, **11**, 373–376.

Llewellyn-Thomas, H.A. (1995). Patients' health care decision-making: A framework for descriptive and experimental investigations. *Medical Decision Making*, **15**, 101–106.

Makoul, G. and Clayman, M. (2005). An integrative model of shared decision making in medical encounters. *Patient Education & Counseling*, **60**, 301–312.

Man-Son-Hing, M., O'Connor, A., Drake, E., *et al.* (2002). The effect of qualitative and quantitative presentation of probability estimates on patient decision making: A randomised trial. *Health Expectations*, **5**, 246–255.

Mulley, A. (1995). Outcomes research: Implications for policy and practice In R. Smith, and D. T. (eds), *Outcomes in Clinical Practice*. London: BMJ Publishing Group.

Nease, R. and Owens, D. (1994) A method for estimating the cost-effectiveness of incorporating patient preferences *Medical Decision Making*, **14**, 382–392.

O'Connor, A., Stacey, D., Entwistle, V., *et al.* (2003a). Decision aids for people facing health treatment or screening decisions [Cochrane Review]', *Update Software: Cochrane Library*, 2.

O'Connor, A., Stacey, D., and Legare, F. (2003b). Risk communication in practice: The contribution of decision aids. *British Medical Journal*, **327**, 736–740.

O'Connor, A., Tugwell, P., Wells, G., *et al.* (1998a). A decision aid for women considering hormone therapy after menopause: Decision support framework and evaluation. *Patient Education and Counselling*, **33**, 267–279.

O'Connor, A., Wennberg, J., Legare, F., *et al.* (2007). Toward the 'tipping point': Decision aids and informed patient choice. *Health Affairs,* **26**, 716–725.

O'Connor, A.M. (1995). Validation of a decisional conflict scale. *Medical Decision Making,* **15**, 25–30.

O'Connor, A.M., Tugwell, P., Wells, G.A., *et al.* (1998b). Randomized trial of a portable, self-administered decision aid for postmenopausal women considering long-term hormone therapy. *Medical Decision Making,* **18**, 295–303.

Palda, V., Llewellyn-Thomas, H., Mackenzie, R., *et al.* (1997). 'Breast cancer patients' attitudes about rationing post-lumpectomy radiation therapy: Applicability of the probability trade-off method to policy-making. *Journal of Clinical Oncology,* **15**, 3192–3200.

Pauker, S.P. and Pauker, S.G. (1987). The amniocentesis decision: Ten years of decision analytic experience. *Birth Defects: Original Article Series,* **23**(2), 151–169.

Rothert, M. and Talarczyk, G. (1987). Patient compliance and the decision making process of clinicians and patients. *Journal Compliance Health Care,* **2**, 55–71.

Rothert, M.L., Holmes-Rovner, M., Rovner, D., *et al.* (1997). An educational intervention as decision support for menopausal women. *Research in Nursing and Health,* **20**, 377–387.

Ruland, C. and Bakken, S. (2002). Developing, implementing, and evaluating decision support systems for shared decision making in patient care: A conceptual model and case illustration. *Journal of Biomedical Informatics,* **35**, 313–321.

Sainfort, F. and Booske, B.C. (2000). Measuring post-decision satisfaction. *Medical Decision Making,* **20**, 51–61.

Schapira, M., Nattinger, A., and McHorney, C. (2001). Frequency or probability? A qualitative study of risk communication formats used in health care. *Medical Decision Making,* **21**, 459–467.

Schwartz, L., Woloshin, S., and Welch, G. (1999). Risk communication in clinical practice: Putting cancer in context. *Journal of the National Cancer Institute Monographs,* **25**, 124–133.

Sepucha, K., Fowler, F., and Mulley, A. (2004). Policy support for patient-centered care: The need for measurable improvements in decision quality. *Health Affairs* Suppl Web Exclusive, VAR54–VAR62.

Stacey, D., Murray, M., Legare, F., *et al.* (2007). 'Decision coaching to support shared decision making: A framework, evidence, and implications for nursing practice, education, and policy. *Worldviews on Evidence-Based Nursing,* **5**, 25–35.

Strull, W., Lo, B. and Charles, G. (1984). Do patients want to participate in medical decision making? *Journal of the American Medical Association,* **252**, 2990–2994.

Whelan, T.J., Levine, M., Gafni, A., *et al.* (1995). Breast irradiation postlumpectomy: Development and evaluation of a decision instrument. *Journal of Clinical Oncology,* **13**, 847–853.

Whitney, S. (2003). A new model of medical decisions: Exploring the limits of shared decision making. *Medical Decision Making,* **23**, 275–280.

Woloshin, S. and Schwartz, L. (1999). How can we help people make sense of medical data? *Effective Clinical Practice,* **2**, 176–183.

Chapter 28

How effective are patient decision aids?

Dawn Stacey, Carol Bennett, Anton Saarimaki,
Sara Khangura, Karen Eden, and Nananda Col

Introduction

The first randomized controlled trials of patient decision aids, published in 1983, were focused on the decision to circumcise a newborn boy (Maisels *et al.*, 1983; Herrera *et al.*, 1983). Findings revealed that compared to usual care, couples exposed to patient decision aids were more likely to make a decision and were more knowledgeable, but there was no significant difference between groups on whether they chose to have their baby circumcised. Subsequently, there have been over 10 systematic reviews of patient decision aids, most recently with the updated Cochrane review of patient decision aids including 55 randomized controlled trials (Coulter and Ellins, 2007; O'Connor *et al.*, 2007a). This chapter summarizes the evidence on the effectiveness of patient decision aids, highlights evidence changes over time, and reports quality rating of publicly available patient decision aids.

Summary of Cochrane review methods

The purpose of the Cochrane Review of Patient Decision Aids is to describe the effectiveness of patient decision aids for improving the quality of decisions and the decision-making process for people facing difficult treatment or screening decisions (O'Connor *et al.*, 2003). The review was conducted based on a search of electronic databases (MEDLINE, PsycINFO, CINAHL, EMBASE, Cochrane Controlled Trials Register) until July 2006. Additionally, known patient decision aid developers and evaluators were contacted directly in December 2006 for reports of newly completed trials. Two reviewers independently screened each study for inclusion criteria (see Table 28.1), extracted data, and assessed study quality using standardized forms. Interventions focused solely on lifestyle changes, hypothetical situations, clinical trial entry, or advanced directives; education programs were not geared to a specific decision, and interventions designed to promote adherence or to elicit passive informed consent regarding a recommended option were excluded. Inconsistencies were resolved by consensus. Meta-analysis was used only for outcomes with similar measures and only if the effects were expected to be independent of the type of decision (e.g. knowledge tests, realistic perceptions of the chances of benefits/harms, decisional conflict, proportion undecided). Review Manager 4.2 (2003) was used to estimate a weighted treatment effect, defined as weighted mean differences (WMD) for continuous measures and pooled relative risks (RR) for dichotomous outcomes. All data were analysed with a random effects model due to the diverse nature of the trials.

Types of decisions

Of 22,778 citations reviewed, 55 randomized controlled trials of patient decision aids were identified. Table 28.2 shows that the 22 unique decisions were addressed in the patient

Table 28.1 Inclusion criteria

Participants	Individuals deciding about screening or treatment options for themselves, for a child, or for an incapacitated significant other.
Intervention	Patient decision aids defined as interventions designed to help patients make specific, deliberate choices among options (including the status quo), by providing information about the options and outcomes (e.g. benefits, harms) in sufficient detail that an individual could personally judge their value.
Comparison	Randomized controlled trials comparing patient decision aids to usual care controls or comparing detailed to simple patient decision aids.
Outcomes	Determined *a priori* based on theoretical frameworks and included knowledge, realistic expectations, agreement between patients' values and choice, decision-making process criteria, decisional conflict, patient – practitioner communication, participation in decision-making, satisfaction, decisions, adherence to chosen option, health status and quality of life, anxiety, depression, emotional distress, regret, confidence, cost, cost-effectiveness, consultation length, litigation rates.

decision aids. The most common decisions are hormone replacement therapy for menopause, prostate-specific antigen screening, breast cancer genetic testing, and cancer surgery (mastectomy, prostatectomy). Formats for these tools include video-cassettes, DVDs, decision boards, audio-guided booklets, internet-based materials, and, most often, paper-based booklets.

Effectiveness of patient decision aids on key outcomes

Decision quality: When patient decision aids are used as adjuncts to practitioner counselling, they have consistently demonstrated superior effects relative to usual practices on the following indicators of decision quality (see also Chapter 21 by Sepucha and Mulley for more detailed discussion of 'decision quality'): increased knowledge scores and improvement in the proportion of patients with realistic perception of the chances of benefits and harms (see Table 28.3). Complex patient decision aids have been shown to have advantages over simpler patient decision aids in ensuring patient values match the option chosen. These improvements in decision quality have generally occurred without deleterious effects on patient satisfaction, patient anxiety, or practitioner consultation time.

Decision-making process: Compared to standard care, patient decision aids have been shown to significantly reduce decisional conflict, a measure of uncertainty about choosing a course

Table 28.2 Typology of decisions in patient decision aids

Surgery	Medications	Obstetrics	Screening	Other
4 mastectomy	9 hormone therapy	1 vaginal birth after cesarean	8 prostate specific antigen	1 infant vaccine
4 prostatectomy	2 atrial fibrillation anti-coagulation	1 termination	5 BRCA1/2 gene	1 Hepatitis B vaccine
2 hysterectomy	1 hypertension		3 colon cancer	1 pre-op autologous blood donation
2 dental	1 hyperlipidaemia		3 prenatal	
1 circumcision	1 osteoporosis			
1 back	1 chemotherapy for breast cancer			
2 coronary revascularization				

Table 28.3 Effects on decision quality, decision-making process, decisions

Outcome	Comparator	1999		2007	
		Number of trials (N = 17)	Pooled weighted differences (95% CI)	Number of trials (N = 55)	Pooled wighted differences (95% CI)
Decision quality outcomes (informed, values-based)					
Knowledge of options and outcomes (0–100 scale)	Standard care only	4	WMD 20.6 (16.5, 24.8)*	18	WMD 15.2 (11.7, 18.7)*
	Simple patient decision aid	4	WMD 3.1 (0.6, 5.5)*	9	WMD 4.6 (3.0, 6.2)*
Realistic expectations of outcomes with and without treatment	No outcome probability information	2	RR 1.3 (0.9, 1.8)	11	RR 1.6 (1.4, 1.9)*
Match between choice and patients' values (benefits/ harms that matter most)	Simple patient decision aid	0	—	3	Improved match in 2* of 3 studies
Decision-making process outcomes					
Decisional Conflict: perceived uncertainty and related deficits in knowl-edge, values clarity, support (0–100 scale)	Standard care only	2	WMD −6.1, (−15.7, 3. 5)	10	WMD −6.1 (−8.6, −3.6)*
	Simple patient decision aid	1	WMD −5.0, (−9.6, −0.4)*	7	WMD −1.3 (−3.3, 0.6)
Proportion remaining undecided	Standard care only	1	RR 0.4 (0.2, 0.8)	4	RR 0.5 (0.3, 0.8)*
Participation in decision-making	Standard care only	3	More active RR 2.27 (1.3–4)	8	Less passive RR 0.6 (0.5, 0.8)*
Decisions					
Major Elective Surgery (breast cancer, back, prostatectomy, hysterectomy, cardiac revascularization)	Standard care only	3	RR 0.8 (0.6, 0.9)	8	RR 0.8 (0.6. 0.9)*
	Simple patient decision aid	1	RR 0.6 (0.3, 1.3)	2	RR 0.8 (0.6, 1.0)
Medication: hormone replacement therapy	Simple patient decision aid	1	RR 0.9 (0.4, 1.8)	3	RR 0.7 (0.5, 0.9)
Prostate specific antigen screening	Standard care only	2	RR 1.0 (0.6, 1.5)	5	RR 0.8 (0.7, 1.0)

Abbreviations: WMD = weighted mean difference; CI = confidence interval; RR = relative risk.
*$p < 0.05$.

of action. Patient decision aids have also been shown to decrease the proportion of patients who are passive in decision-making, the proportion of patients remaining undecided, and practitioner controlled decision-making.

Patient health outcomes: There is no consistent evidence to indicate that patient decision aids are superior to standard care with respect to patient health outcomes. However, patient decision aids are typically used for decisions with multiple viable options and one in which there are competing benefits and harms that patients may value differently. In these 'toss-up' decisions the 'best decision' is one in which the expected outcomes of the decision are consistent with the patient's values and preferences. One patient may prefer a treatment option with a lower risk of side-effects and not necessarily one that will result in a better health outcome. For example, an older man with slow progressing prostate cancer may prioritize avoiding incontinence that often follows treatment over a somewhat increased risk of the cancer advancing.

Uptake rates for different options: Exposure to patient decision aids has been shown to reduce, overall by 24%, the uptake of more invasive surgical options in favour of more conservative surgical or medical options, without adverse effects on health outcomes (O'Connor *et al.*, 2003; O'Connor and Stacey, 2005). Patient decision aids have also been shown to reduce uptake of medications such as hormones for menopause and warfarin for atrial fibrillation. Patient decision aids have had more variable effect on the uptake of other treatment options (hepatitis B vaccination, chemotherapy for breast cancer, circumcision of male newborns, high blood pressure treatment, and minor dental surgery). There is insufficient evidence on the effect that patient decision aids have on adherence to chosen options.

Economic evaluation: Four trials evaluated the impact of patient decision aids compared to usual care on cost and resource use (Kennedy *et al.*, 2002; Murray *et al.*, 2001a, 2001b; Vuorma *et al.*, 2004). One trial evaluated the cost-effectiveness of patient decision aids for women experiencing heavy uterine bleeding (Kennedy *et al.*, 2002). These women who had a patient decision aid plus coaching to help them express their preferences had greater satisfaction and reduced the hysterectomy rate, resulting in lower health system costs. Two different trials of video-based patient decision aids (hormone replacement therapy; benign prostatic hypertrophy) in a primary care setting revealed that the patient decision aid intervention had no effect on the use of health care resources but increased the overall cost of care when the expense of the multi-media patient decision aid intervention was included (Murray *et al.*, 2001a, 2001b). At the time when these trials were conducted, interactive video discs were very expensive to produce and disseminate. The authors then estimated the cost to conduct a similar intervention via the internet and found no increased cost. Finally, a trial that included a booklet patient decision aid for Finnish women considering hysterectomy found no significant difference in costs between the patient decision aid and usual care groups (Vuorma *et al.*, 2004).

Changes from first to latest systematic review

Table 28.3 compares the findings from the first Cochrane Review of Patient Decision Aids which included 17 trials (O'Connor *et al.*, 1999) to the most recent update with 55 trials (O'Connor *et al.*, 2007a). Over this 8-year period, results have remained consistent across the knowledge of options, expectations of outcomes, decision processes, and decisions. More recently, trials have been reporting economic evaluation results. As well, with the publication of the International Patient Decision Aid Standards (IPDAS) (Elwyn *et al.*, 2006), the recent update is more focused on the key effectiveness criteria that researchers, clinicians, and patients think are important.

Inventory of quality rated patient decision aids

An essential strategy proposed for successful implementation of patient decision aids as part of the process of care (O'Connor *et al.*, 2007b) is improving access to a comprehensive library of patient decision aids. Of concern is the quality of those patient decision aids that are easily available on the internet, particularly given that such patient decision aids were accessed over

8 million times in 2006. The development of IPDAS was a major first step in specifying quality criteria for patient decision aids. This is described in more detail in Chapter 33 by Elwyn and O'Connor. Here, we report initial operationalization of these standards on the Ottawa A to Z Inventory of Patient Decision Aids (Inventory). This was established in 2007 as a clearinghouse for available patient decision aids (http://decisionaid.ohri.ca/AZinvent.php).

Each patient decision aid in the Inventory was described and rated using 24 IPDAS items (30 items for patient decision aids addressing screening decisions) (see Table 28.4). Results were verified by the patient decision aid producer. Currently, the Inventory focuses on patient decision aids developed

Table 28.4 Quality ratings of patient decision aids in the A to Z Inventory ($N = 215$)

	Producer 1 N = 26	Producer 2 N = 137	Producer 3 N = 16	Producer 4 N = 13	Other N = 23
Content	(%)	(%)	(%)	(%)	(%)
Condition related to the decision.	100	100	100	100	78
The decision*	88	100	19	100	96
Options*	96	99	100	100	70
Natural course of the condition	69	69	75	92	65
Procedures involved	92	55	100	62	70
Positive features of options*	100	100	100	100	100
Negative features of options*	100	99	100	100	100
Probabilities of option outcomes	92	34	19	77	61
event rates for probabilities	77	10	6	77	30
same denominator for probabilities	81	11	6	77	39
probabilities over the same time period	62	7	6	77	35
diagrams use the same scales	77	1	6	69	35
Asks what features of options matter most	96	100	100	100	83
Makes it easy to compare features of options	65	99	94	100	61
Shows features of options with equal detail	100	99	100	100	91
Development process	(%)	(%)	(%)	(%)	(%)
Users were asked what they need to prepare them to discuss a specific decision	85	0	0	69	0
Reviewed by people who previously faced the decision (not involved in its development)	85	0	0	100	9
Field tested with people who were facing the decision	85	0	0	54	13
Patient decison aid was acceptable to users	85	0	0	92	9

(continued)

Table 28.4 (continued) Quality ratings of patient decision aids in the A to Z Inventory (N = 215)

	Producer 1 N = 26	**Producer 2** N = 137	**Producer 3** N = 16	**Producer 4** N = 13	**Other** N = 23
Undecided people felt information was presented in a balanced way	85	0	0	23	9
The patient decision aid provides references to scientific evidence used	100	100	0	100	52
Reports date when it was last updated	85	100	100	77	83
Reports if authors or affiliations stand to gain or lose by choices people make	100	99	100	46	4
Reports readability level	0	99	94	69	9
Effectiveness	(%)	(%)	(%)	(%)	(%)
Helps people know the available options	100	0	0	54	9
Improves match between patients' informed values for outcomes and option chosen.	0	0	0	23	4

*Grey shading indicates more than two-thirds of patient decision aids meeting that criteria.

by higher volume producers. Developers are invited to enter their patient decision aid(s) into the Inventory with the help of a user-friendly, web interface. Developer-entered data will be verified by the research staff.

The 2007 Inventory contained 215 decision aids of variable quality produced by 10 developers. The IPDAS criteria are used to assess the quality of patient decision aids in three areas: content, development process, and evaluation of effectiveness. Most developers produced patient decision aids that met all the content related criteria. A notable exception is that few included the probabilities of outcomes associated with options (e.g. the chance of incontinence with prostate cancer surgery). Concerning the development process, most developers provided references to scientific evidence, provided the date when it was last updated, disclosed potential conflicts of interest, and reported readability levels. Although, the inclusion of patients within the development process has been identified as important (Feldman-Stewart et al., 2004) and included within the IPDAS criteria, few developers reported assessing the needs of users or field testing to determine its acceptability. Other gaps were also evident: most developers also did not report whether they evaluated users' perceptions about whether the patient decision aid had a balanced presentation of options. Only one developer, without fail, evaluated the effect of patient decision aids on improving knowledge and no developers consistently evaluated the effect of patient decision aids on decision quality.

Conclusions

In view of findings from systematic reviews of patient decision aids, there is consistent evidence indicating that patient decision aids facilitate patient involvement in decision-making and improve decision quality. Patient decision aids show promise in decreasing practice variations and preventing over- or underuse of health care options. However, the Inventory shows that the quality of publicly available patient decision aids is generally variable and relatively few have been formally evaluated with patients.

References

Coulter, A. and Ellins, J. (2007). Effectiveness of strategies for informing, educating, and involving patients. *British Medical Journal*, **335**, 24–27.

Elwyn, G., O'Connor, A., Stacey, D., *et al.* (2006). For International Patient Decision Aids Standards (IPDAS) Collaboration. Developing a quality criteria framework for patient decision aids: Online international Delphi consensus process. *British Medical Journal*, **333**, 417.

Feldman-Stewart, D., Brundage, M., Van Manen, L., *et al.* (2004). Patient-focussed decision-making in early-stage prostate cancer: Insights from a cognitively based decision aid. *Health Expectations*, **7**, 126–141.

Herrera, A.J., Cochran, B., Herrera, A., *et al.* (1983). Parental information and circumcision in highly motivated couples with higher education. *Pediatrics*, **71**, 233–234.

Kennedy, A.D., Sculpher, M.J., Coulter, A., *et al.* (2002). Effects of decision aids for menorrhagia on treatment choices, health outcomes, and costs: A randomized controlled trial. *JAMA*, **288**, 2701–2708.

Maisels, M.J., Hayes, B., Conrad, S., *et al.* (1983). Circumcision: The effect of information on parental decision making. *Pediatrics*, **71**, 453–455.

Murray, E., Davis, H., Tai, S., *et al.* (2001a). Randomised controlled trial of an interactive multimedia decision aid on benign prostatic hypertrophy in primary care. *British Medical Journal*, **323**, 493–496.

Murray, E., Davis, H., Tai, S., *et al.* (2001b). Randomised controlled trial of an interactive multimedia decision aid on hormone replacement therapy in primary care. *British Medical Journal*, **323**, 490–493.

O'Connor, A.M., Bennett, C., Stacey, D., *et al.* (2007a). Do patient decision aids meet effectiveness criteria of the International Patient Decision Aid Standards Collaboration? A systematic review and meta-analysis. *Medical Decision Making*, **27**, 554–574.

O'Connor, A.M., Rostom, A., Fiset, V., *et al.* (1999). Decision aids for patients facing health treatment or screening decisions: Systematic review. *British Medical Journal*, **319**, 731–734.

O'Connor, A.M. and Stacey, D., (2005). Should patient decision aids (PtDAs) be introduced in the health care system? WHO Regional Office for Europe, World Health Organization. Health Evidence Network.

O'Connor, A.M., Stacey, D., Entwistle, V., *et al.* (2003). Decision aids for people facing health treatment or screening decisions. *Cochrane Database of Systematic Reviews*, CD001431.

O'Connor, A.M., Wennberg, J., Legare, F., *et al.* (2007b). Toward the 'tipping point': Decision aids and informed patient choice. *Health Affairs*, **26**, 716–725.

Vuorma, S., Teperi, J., Aalto, A., *et al.* (2004). A randomized trial among women with heavy menstruation – impact of a decision aid on treatment outcomes and costs. *Health Expectations*, **7**, 327–337.

Chapter 29

Examining the theoretical foundation of decision support technologies

Marie-Anne Durand and Glyn Elwyn

Introduction

Many decision-making theories exist and their applications have improved our understanding of how individuals make decisions, but the association between decision-making theories and decision support tools is relatively rare in practice. This chapter is based on a theoretical review of existing decision support technologies (DSTs) for patients facing treatment or screening decisions (Durand *et al.*, 2008) and examines the current use of theory in designing and evaluating DSTs.

Theories of decision-making are divided into normative, descriptive, or prescriptive theories (Bekker *et al.*, 1999). Normative theories examine how individuals should process information and make a decision under what are presumed ideal conditions. Descriptive theories describe how individuals make decisions in real life situations and prescriptive theories recognize that decision makers have limited reasoning and computational abilities and examine ways of overcoming those difficulties.

The conceptual and theoretical basis of DSTs has remained largely unexplored. While the number of published DSTs has tripled since 1999 (O'Connor *et al.*, 2008), it is noteworthy that their development has been largely independent of theoretical frameworks. A literature review of 547 studies of health technologies revealed that 82 % of the studies did not make use of any theory or model of decision-making (Bekker *et al.*, 1999). Similarly, Bowen *et al.*, (2006) investigated the theoretical basis of interventions promoting patient's informed decision-making in the clinical context of cancer screening. The findings showed that 5 out of 14 interventions referred to a theoretical framework but did not specify how each theory had shaped the design of the intervention. In brief, there is no clear description of a deliberate avoidance of theory nor is there detailed attention to how some DSTs, albeit a minority, used theory to guide their conception, prototype development, and evaluation. Furthermore, the impact of theory on the DSTs' efficacy has not been formally evaluated. DSTs that are based on theory may be more efficient and reliable than interventions which are atheoretical. However, for the time being, we are unable to assess this area.

The first section of this chapter examines the method used in describing and analysing the theoretical foundation of rigorously developed DSTs. In the second part, the results of the theoretical review will provide a reflection on the relationship between existing DSTs and theory. Finally, we will identify major implications for the development, efficacy, and implementation of future DSTs.

Section 1: Theoretical review of decision support technologies

The theoretical review was based on 55 trials of 'patient decision aids for people facing health treatment or screening decisions', included in the Cochrane systematic review (O'Connor *et al.*, 2008).

The DST selection was based on the assumption that DSTs evaluated by randomized controlled trials included in a Cochrane review would have been amongst those most rigorously developed. The DSTs focused on 23 different screening and treatment decisions and were independently evaluated by two raters.

Full text articles were reviewed to examine references to a theoretical framework in the text. If present, the use of each theoretical framework was discussed. Where a theoretical framework was identified, DST developers were contacted and asked how theory had informed the design and evaluation. They were informed that the theoretical review would be based on their published work if they did not provide a reply within two months.

The extent to which decision-making theories guided the conception of the DST, the prototype development, field testing (if applicable), and evaluation was examined. Field testing was defined as the process whereby the DST's prototype is shown to patients faced with the relevant decision and asked to comment on its content, usability and utility (Evans *et al.*, 2007).

Section 2: DST development and theories of decision-making: An unlikely association

Prevalence of atheoretical DSTs

Fifty DSTs and their associated publications (78 full text articles) were analysed. The analysis revealed that 17 out of 50 DSTs referred to a theory or model of decision-making: the majority of analysed DSTs (33 out of 50) did not rely on any theory or conceptual framework.

All 17 authors of theory-based DSTs were contacted and asked to provide additional information regarding the use of theory in conceiving, developing, and evaluating the intervention. Seven authors answered, providing additional literature or describing and elaborating on the use of a specific theoretical framework. The DSTs' characteristics and use of theory at some or all of the four essential phases of development (conception, prototype development, field testing, and evaluation) are described in Table 29.1.

The theoretical analysis revealed significant variations in the extent to which theory guided the development, field testing, and evaluation of the 17 interventions. Half of the theory-based DSTs made poor or partial use of their cited theoretical framework. More importantly, none of the theory-based DSTs reported field testing prior to evaluation.

Heterogeneity of theoretical foundations used

Ten theories or models of decision-making were used in developing DSTs (see Figure 29.1). The field of shared decision-making (and DST development) has emerged and developed without solid theoretical anchor. As a consequence, the issues surrounding the integration of theory to the design of DSTs have remained largely unexplored. We are currently unable to assess whether some theoretical foundations might be more appropriate than others.

The results of the theoretical review described above reflect the emerging nature of this field. The theories or models chosen to guide the DSTs'development are diverse (cognitive, behavioural, normative, descriptive, and prescriptive theories of decision-making) and do not always fit the purposes of the interventions. The following theories or models were used:

- ◆ Decision analysis (five DSTs): Based on the expected utility theory, decision analysis (Bernoulli 1954; Von Neumann and Morgenstern, 1944) is based on a normative theory of decision-making which has been widely adopted in designing DSTs. Patients are asked to assign a cost or utility to each possible health outcome (on a numerical scale from 0 to 100)

Table 29.1 Characteristics of theory-based DSTs included in the review (Durand et al., 2008)

Theoretical foundation	DST components informed by theory	First author, year	Health decision addressed in the DST	Format
Decision analytic method based on the expected utility theory	◆ Conception ◆ Prototype development ◆ Evaluation	Bekker, 2004	Prenatal diagnostic screening for Down syndrome	Decision analysis plus consultation
Decision analytic method based on the expected utility theory	◆ Conception ◆ Prototype development ◆ Evaluation	Clancy, 1988	Hepatitis B vaccine	Leaflet + decision analysis
Decision analytic method based on the expected utility theory	◆ Conception ◆ Prototype development ◆ Evaluation	Montgomery, 2003	Hypertension treatment	Decision analysis
Decision analytic method based on the expected utility theory	◆ Conception ◆ Prototype development ◆ Evaluation	Rothert, 1997 Holmes Rovner, 1999	Hormone replacement therapy	Discussion or personalized decision exercise
Decision analytic method based on the expected utility theory	◆ Conception ◆ Prototype development ◆ Evaluation	Van Roosmalen, 2004	Treatment options for BRCA1/2 mutations carriers	Video + leaflet with decision analytic method
Multiple attribute and multiple criteria decision-making theories	◆ Conception ◆ Prototype development ◆ Evaluation	Dolan, 2002	Colon cancer screening	Standardized interview (using the analytic hierarchy process) + Leaflet
Ottawa decision support framework	◆ Conception ◆ Evaluation (partial use of the theories)	Hunter, 2005	Prenatal diagnostic testing	Audiotape and booklet
Ottawa decision support framework	◆ Conception ◆ Prototype development ◆ Evaluation (partial use)	Lalonde, 2006	Cardiovascular health treatment	Video + booklet

(continued)

Table 29.1 (continued) Characteristics of theory-based DSTs included in the review (Durand et al., 2008)

Theoretical foundation	DST components informed by theory	First author, year	Health decision addressed in the DST	Format
Ottawa decision support framework	◆ Conception ◆ Prototype development ◆ Evaluation (partial use)	O'Connor, 1998	Hormone replacement therapy	Audiotape + booklet
Ottawa decision support framework	◆ Conception ◆ Prototype development ◆ Evaluation (partial use)	Shorten, 2005	Birthing options after previous caesarean	Booklet
Combination of behavioural models of decision-making	◆ Unclear	Lerman, 1997	Breast cancer genetic testing	Discussion and counselling
Cognitive-social health information processing model (C-SHIP)	◆ Conception ◆ Prototype development ◆ Evaluation	Miller, 2005	Breast cancer genetic testing	Discussion + leaflet
The preventive health Model	◆ Conception ◆ Prototype development	Myers, 2005	PSA testing	Discussion + leaflet
Social cognitive theory	◆ Conception (partial use) ◆ Prototype development (partial use) ◆ Evaluation	Partin, 2004	PSA testing	Video
Health belief model	◆ Early conception ◆ Evaluation	Schapira, 2000	Prostate cancer screening	Booklet
The transtheoretical model	◆ Unclear	Pignone, 2000	Colon cancer screening	Video
Empowerment model	◆ Early conception	Davison, 1997	Prostate cancer treatment	Written information package + audiotape + discussion

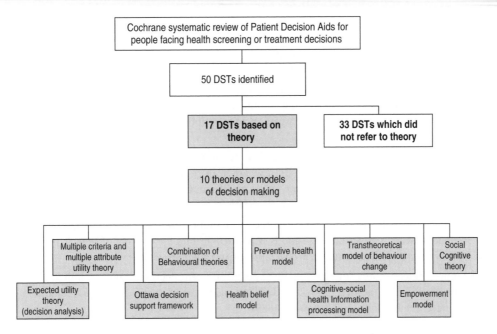

Figure 29.1 17 DSTs based on 10 different theories or models of decision-making.

and to multiply this number by the outcome probability in order to identify the option with the highest subjective utility.

- Multiple criteria decision-making and multiple attribute utility theory (one DST): derived from normative and mathematical theories of problem solving (Dyer *et al.*, 1992).

- Ottawa decision support framework (four DSTs): This framework combines the expectancy value model, decision analysis (described earlier), prospect theory, the conflict theory model of decision-making, and the theory of reasoned action. The 'expectancy value model' (Fishbein, 1975) postulates that decision makers are more likely to opt for the option with the highest expected values and success. The 'prospect theory' (Kahneman and Tversky, 1979) recognizes limited computational capacities and postulates that decision-making is biased by the way the options are described or framed. The 'conflict theory model of decision-making' (Janis and Mann, 1977) assumes that making adecision generates stress, uncertainty, and conflict that constrain decision makers to search for and evaluate information and alternatives. Finally, the 'theory of reasoned action' (Ajzen and Fishbein, 1980) considers that the intention to engage in a behaviour is determined by the decision maker's attitudes and associated subjective norms.

- Behavioural models of decision-making (four DSTS)

Combination of theory of reasoned action, consumer behaviour model, and conflict theory model of decision-making (one DST): The theory of reasoned action and conflict theory model of decision-making are described above. The consumer behaviour model (Engel *et al.*, 1978) identifies a set of variables that shape decision-making (i.e. individual differences, environmental influences, or psychological processes).

The health belief model (one DST): The way individuals perceive the susceptibility, seriousness, benefits, and barriers associated with each health option is assumed to determine the final decision (Rosenstock, 1974).

The preventive health model (one DST): Created by the DST's developers (Myers, *et al.*, 2005; Myers and Wolf, 1990), the model assumes a series of internal and external factors (e.g. socio-cultural background, cognitive and affective representations associated with the disease or condition) that influence people's intention to act on their health.

The transtheoretical model of behaviour change (one DST): The model describes how people acquire or modify a behaviour (using emotional, cognitive, and behavioural components) in five stages: precontemplation, contemplation, preparation, action, and maintenance (Prochaska and Velicer, 1997).

◆ Cognitive-social health information processing model (one DST): Decision makers favour a systematic processing of information where both cognitive and emotional components (individual perception of risk, knowledge, beliefs, and expectancies) are integrated in the decision-making process (Miller, *et al.*, 2005, 1996).

◆ Social cognitive theory (one DST): The theory (Bandura 1989) describes the developmental changes that individuals undergo and is structured around the concept of agency, defined as an intentional involvement in self-development and adaptation.

◆ Empowerment model (one DST): When given sufficient decisional power, individuals are more likely to assume an active role in decision-making and to achieve their desired outcomes (Conger, 1989; Conger and Kanungo, 1988).

Section 3: Implications

This chapter draws attention to the difficulty of integrating theories or models of decision-making into the development and evaluation of DSTs. This reflects the emergent nature of the field of shared decision-making, where the design and evaluation of supportive technologies are still issues that have not been resolved. The lack of theoretical foundations may relate to the difficulty in applying abstract theoretical constructs to the practical design and evaluation of those applied interventions. There is a need to carefully consider how to transfer theoretical constructs into the conception, design, and evaluation of DSTs. Using theories to develop DSTs may prove beneficial to decision makers provided appropriate theories are used and correctly transferred into practice.

The lack of theoretical basis underpinning the development and evaluation of DSTs points to a paradox. Practical technologies intended to facilitate decision-making processes do not build on key concepts of how individuals make decisions. However, theories or models of decision-making do attempt to explain and predict how individuals make complex decisions. They also describe the factors or situations likely to impair the decision-making process and lead to poor decision outcomes and decisional regret. It would, therefore, seem appropriate to integrate theoretical constructs into the development and evaluation of DSTs, anticipating a significant impact on the decision quality and outcomes.

Attempts at creating standards for the development of DSTs are taking place. The IPDAS collaboration (Elwyn, *et al.*, 2006) is working on the validation of a quantitative instrument (IPDASi) to evaluate the quality of DSTs and provide guidelines for their development. It is noteworthy that the IPDAS criteria also do not mention a theory base as important. In spite of improvements being made to the overall development of DSTs, the evidence base for the contribution of theory to the design of DST components and their effectiveness is not yet available.

References

Ajzen, I. and Fishbein, M. (1980). *Understanding Attitudes and Predicting Human Behaviour*. Englewood Cliffs, NJ: Prentice-Hall.

Bandura, A. (1989). Social cognitive theory. *Annals of Child Development*. vol 6, Greenwich, CT: JAI Press.

Bekker, H., Thornton, J.G., Airey, C.M., *et al.* (1999). Informed decision making: An annotated bibliography and systematic review. *Health Technol. Assess.*, **3**, 1–156.

Bernoulli, D. (1954). Exposition of a new theory on the measurement of risk *Econometrica*, **22**, 23–36.

Bowen, D.J., Allen, J.D., Vu, T., *et al.* (2006). Theoretical foundations for interventions designed to promote informed decision making for cancer screening. *Annals of Behavioral Medicine*, **32**, 202–210.

Conger, J.A. (1989). Leadership: The art of empowering others. *Acad. Manag. Exec.*, **3**, 17–24.

Conger, J.A. and Kanungo, R.N. (1988). The empowerment process: Integrating theory and practice. *The Academy of Management Review*, **13**, 471–482.

Durand, M.A., Stiel, M., Boivin, J., *et al.* (2008). Where is the theory? Evaluating the theoretical frameworks described in decision support technologies. *Patient Education and Counseling*, **71**, 125–135.

Dyer, J.S., Fishburn, P.C., Steuer, R.E., *et al.* (1992). Multiple criteria decision making, multiple attribute utility theory: The next ten years. *Management Science*, **38**, 645–654.

Elwyn, G., O'Connor, A.M., Bennett, C., *et al.* (2009). Assessing the quality of decision support technologies using the International Patient Decision Aid Standards instrument (IPDASi). *Plos One*, In Press

Elwyn, G., O'Connor, A., Stacey, D., *et al.* (2006). Developing a quality criteria framework for patient decision aids: Online international Delphi consensus process. *British Medical Journal*, **333**, 417.

Engel, J., Kollatt, D. and Blackwell, R. (1978). *Consumer Behaviour*. Dryden Press.

Evans, R., Elwyn, G., Edwards, A., *et al.* (2007). Toward a model for field-testing patient decision-support technologies: A qualitative field-testing study. *J. Med. Internet Res.*, **9**, e21.

Fishbein, M. (1975). *Belief, Attitude, Intention, and Behavior: An Introduction to Theory and Research*. Reading, MA: Addison-Wesley.

Janis, I.L. and Mann, L. (1977). *Decision-Making: A Psychological Analysis of Conflict, Choice and Commitment*. New York: Free Press.

Kahneman, D. and Tversky, A. (1979). Prospect theory: An analysis of decision under risk. *Econometrica*, **47**, 263–292.

Miller, S.M., Fleisher, L., Roussi, P., *et al.* (2005). Facilitating informed decision making about breast cancer risk and genetic counseling among women calling the NCI's Cancer Information Service. *Journal of Health Communication*, **10**, 119–136.

Miller, S.M., Shoda, Y., and Hurley, K. (1996). Applying cognitive-social theory to health-protective behaviour: Breast self-examination in cancer screening. *Psychological Bulletin*, **119**, 70–94.

Myers, R.E., Daskalakis, C., Cocroft, J., *et al.* (2005). Preparing African-American men in community primary care practices to decide whether or not to have prostate cancer screening. *Journal of National Medical Association*, **97**, 1143–1154.

Myers, R.E. and Wolf, T. (1990). Instrument development for a colorectal cancer screening survey. *Fox Chase Cancer Center Scientific Report*. Philadelphia, PA: Fox chase cancer center.

O'Connor, A.M., Bennett, C., Stacey, D., *et al.* (2008). Patient decision aids for people facing health screening or treatment decisions: A systematic review and meta-analysis. *Cochrane Systematic Review*.

Prochaska, J.O. and Velicer, W.F. (1997). Behavior change: The transtheoretical model of health behavior change. *American Journal of Health Promotion*, **12**, 38–48.

Rosenstock, I.M. (1974). The health belief model and preventative health behavior *Health Educ. Monogr.*, **2**, 354–386.

Von Neumann, J. and Morgenstern, O. (1944). *Theory of Games and Economic Behavior*. Princeton, NJ: Princeton University Press.

Chapter 30

Should patient stories be used in decision aids?

Anna Winterbottom and Hilary Bekker

Purpose of the chapter

The use of patient stories in decision aids is popular yet the evidence base supporting their use is less clear. Many questions remain about the optimal way of presenting such stories in decision aids. This chapter explores how their inclusion might bias the decision-making process and how research in this area is hampered by a lack of a cohesive definition or guidelines on their usage. To date, four reviews of the literature exist providing mixed evidence of the persuasive effect of patient stories on decision-making. More research into the impact of using patient stories is needed and the use of real world settings to explore such ideas is discussed. We recommend that until there is a greater understanding of how patient stories might affect decision-making processes, decision aids that include patient stories should be implemented in practice with caution.

The use of patient stories in decision aids

Patient stories are frequently used in decision aids and estimates of their prevalence vary between 20 and 74% (Feldman-Stewart *et al.*, 2006; O'Connor *et al.*, 2003). Several reasons for their popularity have been proposed. It is thought that the description of one person's experience is more concrete and appealing than abstract statistical data, which are limited to expressing the patient experience solely through the use of numbers (Feldman-Stewart *et al.*, 2006). Patients' stories can illustrate a range of views about a health condition as well as provide guidance from the process that others have used to make a decision. They may also help people make sense and cope with their (ill) health, (Butow *et al.*, 2005; Herxheimer and Ziebland, 2004).

The value of using the patient experience has also been recognized in other health contexts. This is seen, for example, in the development of the Database of Personal Experiences of Health and Illness (www.dipex.org/; Herxheimer and Ziebland, 2004), which describes a range of patient narratives about a variety of illnesses to help guide individuals facing a similar dilemma through the decision-making process. Using patient stories to describe different health treatments or procedures is also recognized as a way of providing an authentic picture of the lived experience of illness and as such is an established part of medical training and clinical skills acquisition (Chisholm and Askham, 2006; Greenhalgh and Hurwitz, 1999; Ubel *et al.*, 2001).

How have patient stories been conceptualized?

The effect of using people's stories on decision-making in both health and non-health contexts has received considerable attention in the literature (for a review see Reinard, 1988).

Box 30.1: Patient stories presented in the first and third person

First person patient story	Third person patient story
A narrative account of an individual's experience described in the first person. For example, 'I was diagnosed with end-stage renal failure 3 years ago, and I was given three treatment options to choose ...'	A narrative account of an individual's experience described in the third person. For example, 'Michael suffered from a stroke; he must make a decision about which type of treatment to choose ...'

Patient stories have appeared under several guises, such as, narratives (Green & Brock, 2000), exemplars (Brosius, 1999), anecdotal evidence (Slater & Rouner, 1996), testimonial evidence (Ubel *et al.*, 2001) and case histories (Dickson, 1982). Not surprisingly then there lacks a cohesive definition for what constitutes narrative evidence, although many have been proposed (Green and Brock, 2000; McLauglin, 1984; Reinard, 1988; Slater, 2002). Typically, narratives are story-like prose '[which] focus on elaborating one example of an event, and they provide appealing detail, characters, and some plot' (Greene and Brinn, 2003) and are presented in either the first or third person (Lee and Leets, 2002). Box 30.1 provides an example of a first and third person patient story.

What are the issues surrounding the use of narratives?

There is little information about how researchers develop patient stories for inclusion in decision aids (Clarke *et al.*, 2005; O'Connor *et al.*, 2003) and there is considerable variation in the content of those presented. Often patient stories contain multiple messages such as describing the causes and consequences of illness and/or treatment seeking behaviour (Greene and Brinn, 2003; Wilson *et al.*, 2005). The optimal way of presenting 'balanced' health information as narrative is unknown. At present, there are no guidelines for the length, breadth, and/or content of patient stories, and stories normally conclude with the patient being satisfied with the outcome of their decision (Khangura *et al.*, *in press*). Not surprisingly then, the inclusion of patient stories as part of quality criteria for the development of decision aids is contentious due to the lack of an evidence base (Elwyn *et al.*, 2006).

With a dearth of guidance on the use of patient stories, there remain many empirical questions about how they may impact on individuals' decision-making. Decision aids work, in part, by providing information about the advantages and disadvantages of all the treatment options. This is presented in a balanced way that enables individuals to process this information with minimal bias. They also encourage patients to evaluate systematically more of the decision-relevant information, in accord with their own beliefs and emotions, than those making the same decision unaided (Bekker *et al.*, 2003). However, patient stories are likely to be biased (see Redelmeier, 1993). They are unlikely to mention all the possible consequences of a decision problem, and the experience of a few can never be truly representative of the population as a whole (Butow *et al.*, 2005). They may also encourage information to be processed 'heuristically', whereby individuals generally assimilate the information swiftly and based on rules-of-thumb, their observations, and past experiences. In such circumstances, the context of the message, such as who is delivering the informtion, may be more influential in decision-making than the message content, such as infomation about the risks and benefits of treatment options (Chaiken, 1980).

What does wider research show about the use of narratives in decision-making?

To date, four reviews exist that examine the influence of narrative evidence on decision-making. Three reviews found support for the greater persuasiveness of narrative information (Reinard, 1988; Taylor and Thompson, 1982; Winterbottom *et al.*, *under review*), and one found support for the persuasiveness of statistical information (Allen and Preiss, 1997). They provide equivocal findings, which are in part explained by their different inclusion criteria, aims, and methods used to synthesize the data.

Our recent review of the literature (Winterbottom *et al.*, *2008*) identified 17 studies completed in a health context. Of these, approximately a third of the studies (5/17) found evidence of the persuasiveness of narrative evidence (Fagerlin *et al.*, 2005a,b; Rook, 1987a,b; Ubel *et al.*, 2001a,b). Ten of the studies included in the review assessed variables to explain the effect of narrative information on decision-making (Cox & Cox, 2001a,b; Greene and Brinn, 2003; Kopfman *et al.*, 1998; Morman, 2000; Rook, 1986, 1987a,b,c; Slater and Rouner, 1996) including vividness, credibility of information, causal relevance, number of thoughts and feelings, prior thought and intent, and affect. However, identifying mechanisms that might explain the persuasiveness of narrative is hampered by discrepancies in the operationalization of mediating or moderating variables. For example, one of the most common explanations for the appeal of narrative information is the idea that narrative is more 'vivid' than statistical information (Rook 1986, 1987a,b,c; Sherer and Rogers, 1984; Wilson *et al.*, 2005). Three mechanisms have been proposed that underlie the vividness construct, increasing the emotional interest, proximity, and/or concreteness of the information (Nisbett and Ross, 1980); yet only one study in the review operationalized each of these components (Sherer and Rogers, 1984). Findings were mixed as to whether or not the vividness might mediate the persuasiveness of narrative. Similarly, 'credibility' was measured by several of the studies and operationalized in a variety of different ways, such as using a believability index (Sherer and Rogers, 1984), measuring realism (Greene and Brinn, 2003), measuring the credibility and expertise (Kopfman *et al.*, 1998), or the informational value of the message (Cox D. and Cox A.D. 2001a; Rook, 1986, 1987a,b,c). Not surprisingly, there was only mixed support for credibility mediating the persuasiveness of the narrative evidence.

Assessing the impact of narrative information on decision-making is difficult. Studies define and operationalize patient stories in different ways. Many (6/17) of the studies were carried out using hypothetical decision scenarios and almost half (8/17) used a student population. The length of narratives and their content varied considerably between studies; none of the studies included narratives that guided patients through steps on how to make a 'good' decision. Hypothetical scenarios are unlikely to be reflective of real world settings. Non-clinical populations do not experience the same emotions or potential consequences of illness as those facing real life health decisions. This may lower motivation for participants to respond or provide truthful answers (Wiseman and Levin, 1996). Findings from studies set in non-health contexts are equally ambiguous. Whilst some studies have found support for the biasing effect of narrative evidence (Dickson, 1982; Koballa, 1986), others have failed to produce such findings (Baesler, 1997; Morman, 2000).

Recommendations and future research

The literature that underpins the practical application of narratives in decision aids is confused and at present it is not possible to say why narratives affect the decision-making process. Nor can we be certain whether narratives might facilitate or bias decision-making or whether narratives affect the quality or outcome of the decision being made. The research is also limited by the use of hypothetical decision scenarios. Manipulating the content of patient stories in real world settings could, however, have serious consequences for the patient. However, the use of non-student or patient populations or scenarios informed by current health practice will strengthen study validity in future research. Studies would also be greatly improved by the use of validated measures in the measurement of constructs such as vividness and credibility to allow a comparison of the findings between studies.

Further research is required to examine the impact of including different narrative types in hypothetical decision scenarios. For example, narratives may impact on decision-making differently when they are presented in the first or third person, and the optimal method for presenting 'balanced' narrative information may be dependent on the medical context. If these processes were better understood, they would allow the application of narrative evidence to be appropriately integrated into decision aid interventions or omitted if unhelpful. We suggest that decision aid designers should use patient stories only with great caution until there is evidence to explain what type of narrative encourages or minimizes bias in information processing and decision-making and which mechanisms are mediating the effects.

References

Allen, M. and Preiss, R.W. (1997). Comparing the persuasiveness of narrative and statistical evidence using meta-analysis. *Communication Research Reports,* **14**, 125–131.

Baesler, J.E. (1997). Persuasive effects of story and statistical evidence. *Argumentation and Advocacy,* **33**(4), 170–175.

Bekker, H.L., Hewison, J., and Thornton, J.G. (2003). Understanding why decision aids work: Linking process and outcome. *Patient Education & Counselling,* **50**, 323–329.

Brosius, H. (1999). Research note: The influence of exemplars on recipients judgements. The part played by similarity between exemplar and recipient. *European Journal of Communication,* **14**(2), 213–224.

Butow, P., Fowler, J., and Ziebland, S. (2005). Using personal stories. In A. O'Connor, H. Llewelyn-Thomas, and D. Stacey (eds) *IPDAS International Collaboration Document, International Patient Decision Aids Standards (IPDAS) Collaboration,* pp. 24–27.

Chaiken, S. (1980). Heuristic versus systematic information processing and the use of source versus message cues in persuasion. *Journal of Personality and Social Psychology,* **38**, 752–766.

Chisholm, A. and Askham, J. (2006). *What do you think of your doctor? A review of questionnaires for gathering patients' feedback on their doctors.* Europe: Picker Institute.

Clarke, A., Jacobsen, M.J., O'Connor, *et al.* (2005). Using a systematic development process. In A. O'Connor, H., Llewellyn-Thomas, D. Stacey (eds) IPDAS Collaboration Background Document Available from: http://ipdas.ohri.ca/. (2005). Accessed at 04/06/2008.

Cox, D. and Cox, A.D. (2001a,b). Communicating the consequences of early detection: The role of evidence and framing. *Journal of Marketing,* **65**, 91–103.

Dickson, P.R. (1982). The impact of enriching case and statistical information on consumer judgments. *Journal of Consumer Research,* **10**, 398–406.

Elwyn, G., O'Connor, A., Stacey, D., *et al.* (2006). The International Patient Decision Aids Standards (IPDAS) Collaboration. Developing a quality criteria framework for patient decision aids: Online international Delphi consensus process. *British Medical Journal,* **333**(7565), 417–413.

Fagerlin, A., Wang, C., and Ubel, P.A. (2005a,b). Reducing the influence of anecdotal reasoning on people's health care decisions: Is a picture worth a thousand statistics? *Medical Decision Making,* **25**, 398–405.

Feldman-Stewart, D., Brennenstuhl, S., McIssac, K., *et al.* (2006). A systematic review of information in decision aids. *Health Expectations,* **10**, 46–61.

Greene, K. and Brinn, L.S. (2003). Messages influencing college women's tanning bed use: Statistical versus narrative evidence format and a self-assessment to increase perceived susceptibility. *Journal of Health Communication,* **8**, 443–461.

Green, M.C. and Brock, T.C. (2000). The role of transportation in the persuasiveness of public narratives. *Journal of Personality and Social Psychology*, **79**, 701–721.

Greenhalgh, T. and Hurwitz, B. (1999). Narrative based medicine: Why study narrative? *British Medical Journal*, **318**, 48–50.

Herxheimer, A. and Ziebland, S. (2004). The DIPEx project: Collecting personal experiences of illness and health care. In B. Hurwitz, T. Greenhalgh, and V. Skultans, (eds) *Narrative Research in Health and Illness*. Blackwell; pp. 115–131.

Khangura, S., Bennett, C., Stacey, D., *et al.* (2008). Personal stories in publicly available patient decision aids. *Patient Education and Counseling*, **73**, 456–464.

Koballa, T.R. (1986). Persuading teachers to re-examine the innovative elementary science programs of yesterday: The effect of anecdotal versus data-summary communications. *Journal of Research in Science Teaching*, **23**(5), 437–449.

Kopfman, J.E., Smith, S.W., Ah Yun, J.K. and Hodges, A. (1998). Affective and cognitive reactions to narrative versus statistical evidence organ donation messages. *Journal of Applied Communication Research*, **26**, 279–300.

Lee, E. and Leets, L. (2002). Persuasive storytelling by Hate Groups Online. American Behavioral Scientist, **45**(6), 927–957.

Morman, M.T. (2000). The influence of fear appeals, message design and masculinity on men's motivation to perform the testicular self-examination. *Journal of Applied Communication Research*, **28**, 91–116.

Nisbett, R.E. and Ross, L. (1980). Human Inference: *Strategies and Shortcomings of Social Judgment*. Englewood-Cliffs: Prentice-Hall.

O'Connor, A.M., Stacey, D., Entwistle, V., *et al.* (2003). Decision aids for people facing health treatment or screening decisions. *The Cochrane Database of Systematic Reviews*, 1.

Redelmeier, D.A., Rosen, R. and Kahneman, D. (1993). Understand patients decisions. Cognitive and emotional perspectives. *Journal of the Amercian Medical Association*, **270**, 72–76.

Reinard, J.C. (1988). The empirical study of the persuasive effects of evidence: The status after fifty years of research. *Human Communication Reports*, **15**, 3–59.

Rook, K.S. (1986). Encouraging preventative behaviour for distant and proximal health threats: Effects of vivid versus abstract information. *Journal of Gerontology*, **41**, 526–534.

Rook, K.S. (1987a,b,c). Effects of case history versus abstract information on health attitudes and behaviours. *Journal of Applied Social Psychology*, **17**, 533–553.

Sherer, M. and Rogers, R.W. (1984). The role of vivid information in fear appeals and attitude change. *Journal of Research in Personality*, **18**, 321–334.

Slater, M.D. (2002). Entertainment education and the persuasive impact of narratives. In M.C. Green, J.J. Strange, and T.C. Brock, (eds). Narrative Impact: *Social and Cognitive Foundations*. Mahwah, NJ: Erlbaum.

Slater, M.D. and Rouner, D. (1996). Value-affirmative and value-protective processing of alcohol education messages that include statistical evidence or anecdotes. *Commun. Res.*, **23**, 210–235.

Taylor, S.E. and Thompson, S.C. (1982). Stalking the elusive "vividness" effect. *Psychol. Rev.*, **89**, 155–181.

Ubel, P.A., Jepson, C., and Baron, J. (2001a,b). The inclusion of patient testimonials in decision aids: Effects on treatment choices. *Medical Decision Making*, **21**, 60–68.

Wilson, K., Mills, E.J., Norman, G., *et al.* (2005). Changing attitudes towards polio vaccination: A randomized trial of an evidence-based presentation versus a presentation from a polio survivor. *Vaccine*, **23**, 3010–3015.

Winterbottom, A., Bekker, H.L., Conner, M., and Mooney, A. (2008). Does narrative information bias individual's decision making? A systematic review. *Social Science Medicine*, **67**(12), 2079-2088.

Wiseman, D.B. and Levin, P.I. (1996). Comparing risky decision making under conditions of real and hypothetical consequences. *Organizational Behaviour and Human Processes*, **66**, 241–250.

Chapter 31

The role of internet-delivered interventions in self-care

Elizabeth Murray

Introduction

People with long-term conditions need a great deal of support, including access to high quality, timely information, emotional support, social support, help with making and implementing decisions, and help with adopting healthier behaviours. Self-care is an essential part of good management of long-term conditions, but poses considerable challenges for patients. In this chapter, I discuss how Internet-delivered Interventions can meet user needs and hence promote self-care.

Why are Internet-delivered Interventions important?

The challenge of long-term conditions and the need for self-care

In the United Kingdom, some 17.5 million people or 1 in 3 of the population are living with a long-term condition (Department of Health, 2005). There is an urgent need to determine ways of reducing the costs associated with long-term conditions, both by health promotion (to reduce the incidence of diabetes, heart disease, and cancer) and by improving the quality and efficiency of care for people with these conditions. One of the clearest expositions of the financial imperative underpinning these efforts is a recent report written by Derek Wanless for the British Treasury in 2002 (Wanless, 2002).

The Wanless report considered three hypothetical scenarios for British health and health care in 2022, which were named 'slow uptake', 'solid progress' and 'fully engaged' (Wanless, 2002). Slow uptake reflected little change in the population's health behaviours, with little engagement by the public in health promotion. The solid progress scenario assumed that people become more engaged in relation to their health, while the fully engaged scenario considered a population fully engaged in health and health care. The difference in these three scenarios, in terms of life expectancy, healthy life expectancy, and costs to the NHS is stark with the difference between the slow uptake and the fully engaged scenario being about half the total NHS expenditure in 2002 (Box 31.1).

Wanless (2002) considered that there were two major drivers which would determine which of these three hypothetical scenarios came to pass: use of information technology (IT) and self-care. In particular, the use of IT would promote progress from slow uptake to solid progress, while self-care was necessary for the fully engaged scenario, which provides a strong rationale for exploring the role of the Internet in self-care.

What is needed for self-care?

Corbin and Strauss (1988) defined three tasks faced by those living with a long-term condition: medical management, emotional management, and role management. Medical management is

Box 31.1: Wanless projections for 2022–2023 (Wanless, 2002)

Scenarios	Life expectancy in years[1] (male/female)	Healthy life expectancy[2]	Costs to the NHS in £ billion, 2002–03 prices
2002–03	75.8/80.6		68
Slow uptake	78.7/83.0	Worse	184
Solid progress	80.0/83.8	About the same	161
Fully engaged	81.6/85.5	Better	154

[1] Life expectancy at birth in a given year is the average number of years of life that a new-born baby would be expected to live assuming the death rates of that year.

[2] Number of years of life a person can expect to live before being affected by an illness which makes them unable to perform at least one domestic task (such as shopping or cooking a main meal) and/or at least one personal care task (e.g. bathing or going to the toilet).

what most health professionals focus on, which includes monitoring symptoms; changing health behaviours (such as eating a healthier diet, taking more exercise, taking medications regularly); and working with health professionals. For the patient, emotional management, i.e. dealing with the emotional consequences of having a long-term condition, which include anger, guilt, despair, and frustration, can be equally challenging and equally important for quality of life. Role management, i.e. coming to terms with a change in life role (e.g. from 'healthy' to 'sick', or from 'provider' to 'cared for', with its connotation of 'burden') is also a significant challenge (Corbin and Strauss, 1988).

Achieving these three tasks requires a considerable degree of informational, behavioural, emotional, and social support (Box 31.2). People need access to information, including information about their condition (likely prognosis, potential complications); treatments available (indications, effects, adverse effects); and what they can do to help themselves (Lorig and Holman, 2003). Information is necessary, but not sufficient, for people to engage in self-care (Stephenson et al., 2003). Changing health behaviours, such as diet, exercise, alcohol consumption, or smoking is hard – and people need considerable help and support to achieve a sustained change. This can take the form of assistance with identifying small achievable goals, identifying barriers and facilitators to change, making definite action plans, and providing monitoring and feedback over time (Lorig and Holman, 2003; Noar et al., 2008). Emotional support is much needed as people try to come to terms with the strong negative emotions that commonly occur during long-term conditions (Corbin and Strauss, 1988), as is social support. Social support can be a practical, informational, affectionate, or positive social interaction (Sherbourne and Stewart, 1991).

People with long-term conditions have to make a great number of decisions. Some of these occur daily – for example, modifying the dose of asthma inhaler according to weather conditions, whereas others occur infrequently – e.g. to start or stop a treatment, undertake surgery, or change jobs to one better suited to current capacities. Decision support, aimed at helping people make better quality decisions, (defined as decisions more in line with their underlying personal goals – see also Chapters 20 (Elwyn) and 21 (Sepucha)) is helpful (Dowie, 2002).

Box 31.2: What people need for selfcare

- Information – what to do, why do it, when to do it
- Emotional support – depression, guilt, role change
- Social support
- Behaviour change support – how to do it?
- Decision support – which treatment or behaviour?
- Monitoring and feedback – how am I doing?

What can internet interventions provide?

The internet can convey a great deal of information, and because there are no space limitations, one site can combine the sort of basic information needed by a novice or newly diagnosed patient, with advanced scientific information suitable for use by a health professional or a patient who has become expert in self-care. Complex information can be made accessible and comprehensible through the use of video, graphics, and audio. Information can easily be updated as new research evidence becomes available. People use the internet for emotional and social support – both by reading about other people who are in a similar position and by joining on-line support groups or posting on bulletin boards. There are a number of formal behaviour change support tools delivered via the internet, which contain self-assessment tools, action plans with opportunities for goal setting, identification of barriers and facilitators to change, and on-going monitoring. An example is shown in Box 31.3. Long-term monitoring and feedback can also be provided through the internet, either by self-completed questionnaires (e.g. on mood or diet), or through objective measurements such as weight, blood pressure, or blood glucose, which can be done by portable telemedicine devices. In either case, the feedback can be presented visually, with easily comprehensible graphs showing progress over time. Feedback can be coupled with tailored information, as tailoring is known to improve the impact of information in promoting behaviour change (Noar *et al.*, 2007). Decision aids (dealt with elsewhere in this book (Chapters 27–49)) can be incorporated into internet interventions, and the internet is a particularly suitable medium for complex aids which use underpinning software to calculate individual risks and benefits according to data provided by the user (O'Connor *et al.*, 2003).

There are also some specific advantages to internet-delivered interventions from a user perspective. For those with internet access at home – 67% of the UK population in 2007 (Dutton and Helsper 2007) – it is convenient and accessible. It can be used at any time of day or night; hence, can be fitted round busy schedules. The user can control the amount of use – more when they need more, less when they are feeling well or stable. It can be anonymous, so receiving treatment via the internet may help users avoid stigma. Internet interventions have the potential to be highly cost-effective. For interventions which are designed to be accessed directly by the user, and do not require any health professional facilitation or support, the main costs are associated with the development of the intervention. Finally, the internet provides a virtual meeting space for people with rare conditions, who might otherwise never encounter each other.

It is worth noting that, to a great extent, the internet is simply an efficient and convenient means of delivery. Interventions which contain high-quality information with additional interactive services can also be delivered using static systems such as CD-ROM, or, with the rapid convergence of digital technology, other mobile systems such as mobile phones or digital technology Although I use the term internet interventions throughout this chapter, much of the information also applies to other interactive computer-based interventions (ICBI) (Bailey *et al.*, 2007).

What do users think about internet interventions?

There are relatively few data on user perceptions of the benefits and potential of internet interventions. A qualitative study of people who either had, or cared for someone with, a long-term condition found that participants were overwhelmingly positive about the potential

Box 31.3: DownYourDrink as an example of internet intervention. (http://www.downyourdrink.org.uk/)

DownYourDrink (DYD) is an internet intervention aimed at heavy drinkers, currently (2006–2010) being evaluated through an on-line randomized controlled trial at UCL. The site contains three phases: Phase 1 uses motivational interviewing techniques to help users decide whether they want to tackle their drinking; Phase 2 is based on behavioural self-control and cognitive behavioural therapy and focuses on helping people reduce their drinking; while Phase 3 focuses on relapse prevention (Linke *et al.*, 2008).

Figure 31.1 DYD front page. © Copyright Alcohol Concern 2007.

Box 31.3: DownYourDrink as an example of internet intervention. (http://www.downyourdrink.org.uk/) *(continued)*

There are multiple 'e-tools' in Phase 2. The most powerful is probably the drinking diary, which allows users to record what they drank, the conditions that they drank under, and their thoughts and feelings before and after drinking.

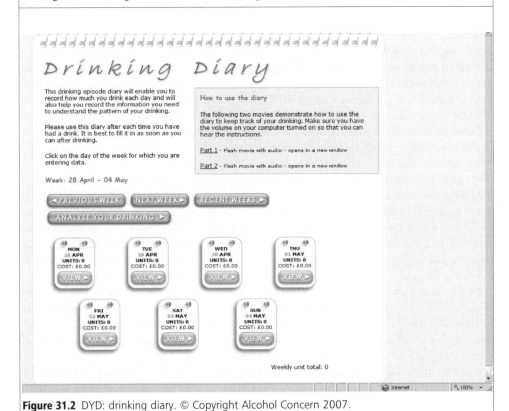

Figure 31.2 DYD: drinking diary. © Copyright Alcohol Concern 2007.

of such interventions, wishing that they had been available when they were first diagnosed, and keenly aware of their potential for future use. One participant described them as having *'Totally unbounded potential, the potential to step in and alleviate lots of conditions'* (Kerr *et al.*, 2005). Participants stated that they would use such interventions to help them understand their condition, manage their condition better and prevent complications, augment information and advice from health professionals, meet emotional needs, and improve access to services (Kerr *et al.*, 2005). Although this was a relatively small study, the findings are similar to those of other studies exploring patients requirements of internet treatments (Rozmovits and Ziebland, 2004).

Plenty of potential: What about the evidence?

There is a very large body of literature on the effectiveness of internet interventions, both for self-care and for health promotion. A recent 'review of reviews' identified 17 systematic reviews, defined as reviews of the literature which had used an explicit, rigorous and transparent methodology, examining the effectiveness of internet interventions (Murray, 2008). The main findings are summarized here.

It appears that well-designed internet interventions can have a number of beneficial effects on users. They can improve user knowledge about their condition and available treatment options (Eysenbach et al., 2004; Kirsch and Lewis, 2004; Murray et al., 2005; Wantland et al., 2004; Ybarra and Eaton 2005). They appear to be able to improve users' 'self-efficacy'. Self-efficacy is a psychological construct, referring to an individual's belief in their capacity to undertake a specific action (Bandura, 1977). People with high self-efficacy for a behaviour are more likely to attempt that behaviour, and more likely to succeed in that behaviour. Internet interventions can provide social support in various ways – either by providing 'personal stories' (or illness narratives) from other people who have experienced similar health problems (see e.g. DIPEX (Database of Individual Patient Experiences) http://www.dipex.org/DesktopDefault.aspx) (Herxheimer and Ziebland, 2003) or by providing on-line discussion groups (Eysenbach et al., 2004).

Increases in knowledge, self-efficacy, and social support appear to be related to changes in health behaviours. Health behaviours as diverse as diet (Norman et al., 2007; Saperstein et al., 2007; Weinstein, 2006), exercise (Norman et al., 2007; van den Berg et al., 2007; Vandelanotte et al., 2007), smoking (Walters et al., 2006), alcohol consumption (Linke et al., 2007), sexual behaviour (Bailey et al., 2007), medicines management, and engagement in health care have all been targeted by different internet interventions, with varying degrees of success (Murray et al., 2005). It seems as if some internet interventions can improve health behaviours for some people, under some conditions, but a great deal of research is still needed to determine the essential components (active ingredients) that make an internet intervention effective in achieving behaviour change, and which people, with which problems, are most likely to benefit.

Finally, health care providers and policy makers are interested in clinical outcomes – Can using an internet intervention improve the health of the user? Again, it seems as if well-designed internet interventions can indeed improve the health of the user, particularly in conditions which are amenable to self-care. The evidence is particularly strong for mental health and computerised cognitive behavioural therapy (CCBT). Cognitive behavioural therapy (CBT) aims to identify and modify maladaptive cognitions (thoughts) and behaviours. Traditional, therapist-led CBT has been shown to be effective for a wide range of mental health problems, including anxiety, depression, and phobias. Reviews of both CCBT and internet-delivered CBT (ICBT) have concluded that delivering CBT by computer can be at least as effective as therapist-led CBT (Kaltenthaler et al., 2002; Spek et al., 2007). One freely available programme that has been extensively evaluated is the Australian MoodGym, suitable for people with mild to moderate depression (http://www.moodgym.anu.edu.au). CCBT has also been shown to improve quality of life and clinical outcomes in people with physical health problems, such as tinnitus and chronic headache (Cuijpers et al., 2008).

Internet interventions that do not use CBT approaches have also been shown to be effective in improving clinical outcomes in people with a wide range of long-term conditions, such as diabetes, asthma, encopresis (faecal soiling in children), and obesity (Murray et al., 2005). It is not clear from the available data how these Interventions achieved their beneficial effect, but one possibility is that the combination of improved knowledge with enhanced self-efficacy leads to improved health behaviours and hence improved clinical outcomes.

There is a presumption that if internet interventions are effective, they are likely to be cost-effective, as the majority of the costs are associated with the initial development and design of the Intervention. There is often little or no marginal cost per additional user, and indeed, one of the great attractions of internet interventions is their scalability – i.e. the relative ease with which an internet intervention can be made available to millions of people simultaneously with very little additional cost. Unfortunately, there are very few empirical data on the cost-effectiveness of internet interventions, and this is an area that needs further research. One noted feature of internet interventions is the high attrition rate amongst users (Eysenbach, 2005; Linke et al., 2007). This may explain why one systematic review found greater effectiveness in those interventions which had more facilitation (Spek et al., 2007). This would have implications both for cost-effectiveness and scalability, although as the main role of the health care worker appears to be simple encouragement and monitoring of the use of the Intervention by the patient, relatively unskilled staff could be used for this.

Conclusions

Internet interventions have considerable potential as a means of enhancing self-care in people with long-term conditions. Initial research evidence supports this potential, in terms of enhancing user knowledge, self-efficacy, perceived social support, health behaviours, and clinical outcomes. However, the costs associated with internet interventions and their subsequent cost-effectiveness have not been well described. Further research is urgently needed on this, and also on determining how internet interventions achieve their desired effects. We need to determine the essential components (active ingredients) of internet interventions, and also what features of users are associated with effectiveness, in terms of health problems experienced, psychological or demographic profile, and other key features.

References

Bailey, J.V., Murray, E., Rait, G., et al. (2007). Interactive computer-based interventions for sexual health promtion (protocol). The Cochrane Database of Systematic Reviews, 2.

Bandura, A. (1977). Self-efficacy: Toward a unifying theory of behavioral change. Psychological Review, **84**, 191–215.

Corbin, J.M. and Strauss, A. (1988). Unending Work and Care (1st edition). San Francisco: Jossey-Bass Inc. Cuijpers, P., van Straten, A., and Andersson, G. (2008). Internet-administered cognitive behavior therapy for health problems: A systematic review. Journal of Behavioral Medicine.

Department of Health (2005). Supporting People with Long Term Conditions, Leeds: Department of Health.

Dowie, J. (2002). The role of patients' meta-preferences in the design and evaluation of decision support systems. Health Expect., **5**, 16–27.

Dutton, W.H. and Helsper, E. (2007). The Internet in Britain: 2007. Oxford: Oxford Internet Institute, University of Oxford.

Eysenbach, G. (2005). The law of attrition. J. Med. Internet. Res., **7**, e11.

Eysenbach, G., Powell, J., Englesakis, M., et al. (2004) Health related virtual communities and electronic support groups: Systematic review of the effects of online peer to peer interactions. British Medical Journal, **328**, 1166.

Herxheimer, A. and Ziebland, S. (2003). DIPEx: Fresh insights for medical practice. J. R. Soc. Med., **96**, 209–210.

Kaltenthaler, E., Shackley, P., Stevens, K., et al. (2002). A systematic review and economic evaluation of computerised cognitive behaviour therapy for depression and anxiety. Health Technol. Assess., **6**, 1–89.

Kerr, C., Murray, E., Stevenson, F., et al. (2005). Interactive health communication applications for chronic disease: Patient and carer perspectives. J. Telemed. Telecare., **11**(1), 32–34.

Kirsch, S.E. and Lewis, F.M. (2004). Using the World Wide Web in health-related intervention research. A review of controlled trials. Comput. Inform. Nurs., **22**, 8–18.

Linke, S., McCambridge, J., Khadjesari, Z., *et al.* (2008) Development of a psychologically enhanced interactive on-line intervention for hazardous drinking. *Alcohol & Alcoholism,* **43**, 669–674.

Linke, S., Murray, E., Butler, C., *et al.,* (2007). Internet-based interactive health intervention for the promotion of sensible drinking: Patterns of use and potential impact on members of the general public. *J. Med. Internet. Res.,* **9**, e10.

Lorig, K.R. and Holman, H. (2003). Self-management education: History, definition, outcomes, and mechanisms. *Ann. Behav. Med.,* **26**, 1–7.

Murray, E. (2008). Internet-delivered treatments for long-trem conditions: Strategies, efficiency and cost-effectiveness. *Expert Review of Pharmacoeconomics Outcomes Research,* **8**, 3.

Murray, E., Burns, J., See Tai, S., *et al.* (2005). *Interactive Health Communication Applications for people with chronic disease,* The Cochrane Library.

Noar, S.M., Benac, C. N., and Harris, M.S. (2007). Does tailoring matter? Meta-analytic review of tailored print health behavior change interventions. *Psychol. Bull.,* **133**, 673–693.

Noar, S.M., Chabot, M., and Zimmerman, R.S. (2008). Applying health behavior theory to multiple behavior change: Considerations and approaches. *Prev. Med.,* **46**, 275–280.

Norman, G. J., Zabinski, M. F., Adams, M.A., *et al.* (2007). A review of eHealth interventions for physical activity and dietary behavior change. *Am. J. Prev. Med.,* **33**, 336–345.

O'Connor, A.M., Stacey, D., Entwistle, V., *et al.* (2003). Decision aids for people facing health treatment or screening decisions (*Cochrane Review*). *The Cochrane Library,* 2.

Rozmovits, L. and Ziebland, S. (2004). What do patients with prostate or breast cancer want from an Internet site? A qualitative study of information needs. *Patient. Educ. Couns.,* **53**, 57–64.

Saperstein, S.L., Atkinson, N.L., and Gold, R.S. (2007). The impact of Internet use for weight loss, *Obes. Rev.,* **8**, 459–465.

Sherbourne, C.D. and Stewart, A.L. (1991). The MOS social support survey. *Soc. Sci. Med,* **32**, 705–714.

Spek, V., Cuijpers, P., Nyklicek, I., *et al.* (2007). Internet-based cognitive behaviour therapy for symptoms of depression and anxiety: A meta-analysis. *Psychol. Med.,* **37**, 319–328.

Stephenson, J.M., Imrie, J., and Bonell, C. (2003). *Effective Sexual Health Interventions. Issues in experimental evaluation.* Oxford, New York: Oxford University Press.

van den Berg, M.H., Schoones, J.W., and Vliet Vlieland, T.P. (2007). Internet-based physical activity interventions: A systematic review of the literature. *J. Med. Internet. Res.,* **9**, e26.

Vandelanotte, C., Spathonis, K.M., Eakin, E.G., *et al.* (2007). Website-delivered physical activity interventions a review of the literature. *Am. J. Prev. Med.,* **33**, 54–64.

Walters, S.T., Wright, J.A., and Shegog, R. (2006). A review of computer and Internet-based interventions for smoking behavior. *Addict. Behav.,* **31**, 264–277.

Wanless, D. (2002). *Securing our Future Health: Taking a Long-Term View.* London: HM Treasury.

Wantland, D.J., Portillo, C.J., Holzemer, W.L., *et al.* (2004). The effectiveness of Web-based vs. non-Web-based interventions: A meta-analysis of behavioral change outcomes. *J. Med. Internet Res.,* **6**, e40.

Weinstein, P.K. (2006). A review of weight loss programs delivered via the Internet. *J. Cardiovasc. Nurs.,* **21**, 251–258.

Ybarra, M.L. and Eaton, W.W. (2005). Internet-based mental health interventions. *Ment. Health Serv. Res.,* **7**, 75–87.

Chapter 32

Decision analysis – utility for everyday use?

Richard Thomson

Introduction

The challenge in health care choices, from system-wide decisions on new treatments through to individual decisions on treatment options, is to find ways of supporting good – or better – decisions. Decision-analytic (DA) techniques can address questions about the use of treatment for groups of patients, for example to underpin health policy decisions, or might be used to guide the management of individual patients (Ginsberg and Lev, 1997; Lilford and Royston, 1998). Their use to support individual treatment choices, though, is far less developed. This chapter will describe the potential value of decision analysis in shared decision-making, critique the method with reference to both practical and theoretical concerns, and consider the implications for practice and research.

What are the challenges of shared decision-making?

Treatment choices are difficult. They often involve the integration of complex information from multiple sources; imperfect or incomplete information; the presence of uncertainty; and a complex interaction between the clinician and the patient, each bringing different personal values to the decision. Many clinical decisions are not supported by clear evidence; nonetheless decisions have to be made even in the absence of robust information (Detsky *et al.*, 1997). Even if, all the necessary information is available, it is argued that the human mind lacks the ability to easily integrate it.

Even when the problem structure is clearly articulated, uncertainty remains, based both on particularizing evidence from population-based studies to an individual patient and the nature of evidence itself. The relationships between treatments and outcomes are generally probabilistic, rather than deterministic, and a good decision can still lead to a poor outcome (or *vice versa*). Hence, the attitude of the clinician and patient towards risk will also have a bearing on what constitutes a 'good decision'. One way of dealing with these difficulties is formal problem structuring and analysis using decision analysis.

What is decision analysis?

Decision analysis is based on expected utility theory, first described by von Neumann in the 1920s (Von Neumann and Morgenstern, 1947). The potential application of decision analysis to medical problems was first described as early as 1959 (Ledley and Lusted 1959) and in 1967, a published application of decision analysis considered whether radical neck dissection was beneficial in patients with oral cancer but no tangible neck tumour (Henschke and Flehinger, 1967). Decision analysis is firmly rooted in rational choice and expected utility theory.

Figure 32.1 is a simplified structure of a decision analysis for the choice of warfarin, or not, to prevent stroke in atrial fibrillation. Analysis requires intgration of data from different sources to determine (or advise upon) the optimal choice.

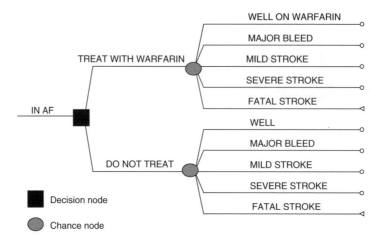

Figure 32.1 Basic decision model.

The data required include

♦ the risk of stroke and the range of outcomes in the absence of treatment – in this case in terms of severity – preferably derived from cohort studies;

♦ the effectiveness of treatments, preferably derived from randomized trials;

♦ the risk of adverse treatment effects, preferably derived from inception cohort studies; and

♦ the values placed on outcomes (adverse events and relevant health states), potentially derived from the individual patient or patients like the one making the decision.

Expected utility theory is usually described as a normative theory, and in a decision analysis framework the optimal choice is that which produces the greatest expected utility (usually measured in quality adjusted life years). This is calculated by multiplying the values of the outcomes for each limb of the decision tree by the probability of the outcomes in that limb and rolling this back to give a calculated summary measure for each choice; the choice that gives the greater value is preferred.

What are the limitations of decision analysis in shared decision-making?

So far so good, but there are a number of problems and limitations to decision analysis. These include problems with the data needed to populate any model, but also theoretical and practical problems with decision analysis itself. There may be a dearth of epidemiological data, especially that enable risks to be personalized to the individual patient. In cardiovascular disease, predictive equations (Wolf *et al.*, 1991) are widely used and can be used in decision analysis. However, in many clinical settings, such high-quality data do no exist. Even with the Framingham equations, questions have been raised about applicability outside the source population (Haq *et al.*, 1999; Quirke *et al.*, 2003; Ramachandran *et al.*, 2000). And a study showed that the choice of the predictive equation for stroke in atrial fibrillation might have a significant impact upon risk communication and decision-making (Thomson *et al.*, 2007).

There are problems with the availability of robust treatment effectiveness data from randomized trials and the capacity to personalize this to the individual. Equally, data on adverse treatment effects may be in short supply; a systematic review on the risk of bleeding on warfarin found 274 papers but only one was a robust inception cohort study (Thomson *et al.*, 2000).

Finally, there are challenges to deriving utility data. There is considerable evidence that the method used has an impact on the size of the derived utility. Scores derived using the standard gamble method are generally higher than those using time trade-off, which are in turn higher than those derived from visual analogue scales (Post *et al.*, 2001; Torrance *et al.*, 1996). This is due to methodological differences in the three approaches. People who have experienced a health state, e.g. those who have had a stroke, value that health state higher than the general public or those at risk of stroke (Post *et al.*, 2001), generally thought to be due to accommodation to a new health state. So which should best be used in modelling decisions?

Concerns go beyond data adequacy and reliability. Thus, should decision analysis use values derived from the patient involved in the decision, or use representative population data? If the former this is not only time-consuming, but may also be difficult for an individual to understand and complete the exercise. A randomized trial of a patient decision aid incorporating explicit utility elici-tation employed an embedded observational study (Murtagh *et al.*, 2007). The arm with the explicit tool was abandoned when six of eight patients had significant problems with the standard gamble component, despite extensive testing and iterative development (Thomson *et al.*, 2002), largely reflecting problems with the hypothetical nature of the exercise. On the other hand, if population data are used, then any decision advised will be true to an aggregate average population level, but may not be to the individual patient, thus rather undermining the value in individualizing choice.

There is also concern about the 'black box approach' – the model can be very complex in itself, and patients (and doctors) may have difficulty dealing with outputs from a model that they do not fully comprehend. Furthermore, there may be features that are important to decision-making that cannot be incorporated within a decision analysis. For example, choosing a drug therapy is a decision which can be kept under review and changed if a patient's experience differs from their expectations. However, surgery, once undertaken, is irrevocable. There may be process utility in keeping options open. Decision analyses that focus on net expected values ignore the utility gained from options retained.

There are also concerns about a mechanical approach replacing judgement and clinical interac-tion; this is probably more to do with how any such approach is incorporated within a decision aid or process. Some have used the output of a model as an adjunct to the shared decision, rather than a prescriptive guide, which is more in keeping with the philosophy of SDM (see for example Chapter 39 by Protheroe).

Finally, there is the fundamental issue as to whether expected utility theory and the rational choice approach is the right model to underpin decision-making. There is increasing evidence that people who are asked to make choices using explicit criteria make decisions with which they are less satisfied, that are less likely to match expert opinion, and are less reliable (Nelson *et al.*, 2007). One explanation of this is that the human mind uses heuristics (rules of thumb) to make decisions in preference to a more rational integrated approach. Gigerenzer has argued, therefore, that the question to pursue is how we can support better use of 'fast and frugal heuristics to sup-port good decisions rather than pursue rational choice methods' (Gigerenzer 2007; Gigerenzer and Todd, 1999). Elwyn *et al.* (2001) have argued that *bounded rationality models* are more akin to the reality of decision-making in practice than unbounded rationality models such as expected utility theory and that we need to understand the trade-offs between accuracy and frugality; they describe fast and frugal heuristics as 'the next frontier'.

Examples of decision analysis in use and evaluation

The number of evaluated patient decision aids incorporating decision analysis is still small. A recent systematic review of patient decision aids (Durand *et al.*, 2008), limited to those assessed by randomized trials, sought to look at the theoretical basis for their design, field testing, and evaluation (see also Chapter 29). Only 17 out of 50 decision aids were based on a theoretical framework, of which 5 were based on expected utility theory.

Looking at published examples reveals several ways of using decision analysis within patient decision aids. Whilst expected utility theory has been described as a normative theory, this is not always the mode of use. For example, one patient decision aid for patients with atrial fibrillation incorporated a standard gamble to derive patient utilities, and then incorporated these into a Markov model running behind the decision aid (Brown *et al.*, 2008; Thomson *et al.*, 2002). The output of the model was presented to patients after expressing their preference following both the standard gamble and personalized risk and benefit data being presented; that is, it was an adjunct to decision-making, with the underlying concept that values elicitation and individualized risk communication would in themselves support preference expression. In contrast, another patient decision aid for the same condition used individual utilities derived using time trade-off in an observational study and equated preference for treatment with the output of the model, i.e. assuming that the patient would accept treatment if the expected utility of 'treatment' exceeded that of 'no treatment' (Protheroe *et al.*, 2000).

More recent decision analysis-based decision aids, for example to support choice between a trial of labour and repeat caesarean section after previous section, have used the visual analogue scale to derive utilities (Emmett *et al.*, 2007; Montgomery *et al.*, 2007). Women ran through the computerized decision aid, facilitated by a researcher, and were then given a print out with the results of a hidden decision analysis model (suggested optimal mode of delivery). They were then encouraged to use this as a basis for discussion of their choice with their obstetrician. The decision analysis-based model was both feasible and acceptable to patients when delivered and supported in this way, although in the development work a simpler information model was found easier to use and understand (Emmett *et al.*, 2007).

Another example was developed for a woman's decision on whether or not to have a prophylactic oophorectomy (removal of ovaries) when having a hysterectomy, in order to prevent subsequent ovarian cancer (Pell *et al.*, 2002). This was a more complex tool that used time trade-off methods for deriving utilities in its pilot version, and then presented the output in terms of quality adjusted life expectancy, stating that 'the program, given what it has been told about you and your preferences, favours the [. . .] option' before decision-making.

The way forward – applications and research

Whilst there is an undoubted value in the use of decision analysis methods in helping to structure and understand decisions, and to model the impact of decisions to support health policy decisions, their utility within patient decision aids for shared decision-making remains unproven. There are theoretical and practical arguments both for and against decision analysis, but evaluation in practice has been limited and there are examples where use has failed, due to problems with patient understanding, or of tools that have been designed and evaluated but not crossed the divide between research and wider practical use (not limited by any means to decision analysis-based tools). Patient decision aids that have become more widely implemented tend to eschew decision analysis and prefer to use implicit value elicitation processes.

Nonetheless, there may be a place for decision analysis-based decision aids for some patients and in some settings. For example, it may be that the use of decision trees populated with risk and outcome data would help communicate and explore decision-making even without going on to full decision analysis. This is testable.

Dowie (2001) has pointed out that as well as preferences for treatments, patients have preferences for being engaged in decisions (he has called this meta-preference). It is also likely to be the case that different patients (and clinicians) have different preferences for the type of patient decision aids. This might, for example, reflect their preferences for numerical or graphical presentation of risk; in our study of a patient decision aid using an individual standard gamble, two patients found it very helpful and both had a knowledge and experience of gambling. Thus, evaluative research might usefully concentrate on identifying which patients and which settings might be better matched to decision analysis-based tools and on comparing the value of different patient decision aids (decision analysis and non- decision analysis) in the same condition or choice.

Conclusions

In conclusion, there are reasons to imagine that decision analysis within the context of patient decision aids and shared decision-making may have value, but the evidence base and practical experience is to date limited. Decision analysis can help characterize a decision and may help people understand the factors that might affect decision-making. It may be that the complexity of decision analysis, or the disjunction between the rational choice model and the cognitive workings of the human mind in decision-making, will limit its use and usefulness in shared decision-making, but in the absence of more robust and applied research, the jury must remain out.

References

Brown, C., Hofer, T., Johal, A. *et al.* (2008). An epistemology of patient safety research: A framework for study design and interpretation: Part 1. Conceptualising and developing interventions. *Quality & Safety in Health Care*, **17**, 158–162.

Detsky, A.S., Naglie, G., Krahn, M.D. *et al.* (1997). Primer on medical decision analysis: Part 1. Getting started. *Medical Decision Making*, **10**, 181–194.

Dowie, J. (2001). Decision analysis and the evaluation of decision technologies. *Quality & Safety in Health Care*, **10**, 1–2.

Durand, M-A., Stiel, M., Boivin, J. *et al.* (2008). Where is the theory? Evaluating the theoretical frameworks described in decision support technologies. *Patient Education and Counseling*, **71**, 125–135.

Elwyn, G., Edwards, A., Eccles, M. *et al.* (2001). Decision analysis in patient care. *Lancet*, **358**, 571–574.

Emmett, C.L., Murphy, D.J, Patel, R.R. *et al.* (2007). Decision making about mode of delivery after previous caesarean section: Development and piloting of two computer-based decision aids. *Health Expectations*, **10**, 161–172.

Gigerenzer, G. (2007). Gut feelings. London: Penguin.

Gigerenzer, G. and Todd, P. (1999). Simple heuristics that make us smart. New York: Oxford University Press.

Ginsberg, G.M. and Lev, B. (1997). Cost-benefit analysis of riluzole for the treatment of amyotrophic lateral sclerosis. *Pharmacoeconomics*, **12**, 578–584.

Haq, I.U., Ramsay, L.E., Yeo, W.W. *et al.* (1999). Is the Framingham risk function valid for northern European populations? A comparison of methods for estimating absolute coronary risk in high risk men. *Heart*, **81**, 40–46.

Henschke, U.K. and Flehinger, B.J. (1967). Decision theory in cancer therapy. *Cancer*, **20**, 1819–1826.

Ledley, R.S. and Lusted, L.B. (1959). Reasoning foundations of medical diagnosis: Symbolic logic, probability and value theory aid our understanding of how physicians reason. *Science*, **130**, 9–21.

Lilford, R. and Royston, G. (1998). Decision analysis in the selection, design and application of clinical and health services research. *J. Health Serv. Res. Policy*, **3**, 159–166.

Montgomery, A.A., Emmett, C.L., Fahey, T. *et al.* (2007). Two decision aids for mode of delivery among women with previous caesarean section: Randomised controlled trial. *British Medical Journal,* **334**, 1305–1312.

Murtagh, M.J., Thomson, R.J., May, C.R. *et al.* (2007). Qualitative methods in a randomised controlled trial: The role of an integrated qualitative process evaluation in providing evidence to discontinue the intervention in one arm of a trial of a decision support tool. *Quality & Safety in Health Care,* **16**, 224–229.

Nelson, W.L., Han, P., Fagerlin, A. *et al.* (2007). Rethinking the objectives of decsison aids: A call for conceptual clarity. *Medical Decision Making,* **27**, 609–618.

Pell, I., Dowie, J., Clarke, A. *et al.* (2002). Development and preliminary evaluation of a clinical guidance programme for the decision about prophylactic oophorectomy in women undergoing a hysterectomy. *Quality & Safety in Health care,* **11**, 32–39.

Post, P.N., Stigglebout, A., and Wakker, P.P. (2001). The utility of health states after stroke: A systematic review of the literature. *Stroke,* **32**, 1425–1429.

Protheroe, J., Fahey, T., Montgomery, A.A. *et al.* (2000). The impact of patients' preferences on the treatment of atrial fibrillation: Observational study of patient-based decision analysis. *British Medical Journal,* **320**, 1380–1384.

Quirke, T.P., Gill, P.S., Mant, J.W. *et al.* (2003). The applicability of the Framingham coronary heart disease prediction function to black and minority ethnic groups in the UK. *Heart,* **89**, 785–786.

Ramachandran, S., French, J.M., Vanderpump, M.P.J. *et al.* (2000). Using the Framinhgam model to predict heart disease in the United Kingdom: Retrospective study. *British Medical Journa,* **320**, 676–677.

Thomson, R., Eccles, M., Wood, R. (2007). A cautionary note on data sources for evidenced-based clinical decisions: Warfarin and stroke prevention. *Medical Decision Making,* **27**, 438–447.

Thomson, R.G., Parkin, D., Eccles, M. *et al.* (2000). Decision analysis and guidelines for anticoagulant therapy to prevent stroke in patients with atrial fibrillation. *Lancet,* **355**, 956–962.

Thomson, R.G., Robinson, A., Greenaway, J. *et al.* (2002). Development and description of a decision analysis based decision support tool for stroke prevention in atrial fibrillation. *Qual. Saf. Health Care,* **11**, 25–31.

Torrance, G.W., Feeny, D.H., Furlong, W.J. *et al.* (1996). Multiattribute utility function for a comprehensive health status classification system: Health utilities index mark 2. *Medical Care,* **34**, 702–722.

Von Neumann, J. and Morgenstern, O. (1947). Theory of games and economic theory. New York: Wiley.

Wolf, P.A., D'Agostino, R.B., Belanger, A.J. *et al.* (1991). Probability of stroke: A risk profile from the Framingham Study. *Stroke,* **22**(3), 312–318.

Chapter 33

The International patient decision aids standards (IPDAS) collaboration: The checklist, the instrument, and next steps

Glyn Elwyn and Annette O'Connor

Section 1: The origin and aims of the collaboration

The growth in the development of decision aids for patients and others who need support to make wise health care decisions has been one of the most important health communication innovations over the last decade, given that they make a difference to the way patients are treated (O'Connor et al., 2007b). We will not rehearse here the evidence base for their effectiveness, merely point to the relevant literature (Coulter and Ellins, 2007; O'Connor et al., 2004b) and summarize by saying that these decision support technologies have important effects on decisions (Godlee F, 2007; Holmes-Rovner M et al., 2007; O'Connor AM et al., 2004a; O'Connor AM et al., 2007b). For example, they reduce the use of some procedures (such as fewer mastectomies in favour of breast conservation surgery or a reduction in hysterectomy rates (Kennedy ADM et al., 2002; Whelan T et al., 2004), and increasing the use of others (such as the uptake of colon cancer screening (O'Connor et al., 2004b). These effects are desirable when decision aids are unbiased and the motivation is to rectify variations in practice due to poor comprehension or disregarding of patients' preferences. However, concerns will emerge if decision aids affect uptake rates because of bias or inaccuracy.

Over the last decade, the interest in developing decision aids has moved beyond research groups and entered the commercial world. Many are easily available on the internet. However, their quality varies; some do not cite their evidence sources, and others have presentational biases. Furthermore, debate exists about underlying concepts (Charles et al., 2005) and about the lack of agreed quality criteria for these tools. Because patient decision aids can have an important influence on choices made, developers need to have followed recognized methods, avoided bias, and cited valid evidence sources. A global interest in developing and using decision aids has emerged, by both for-profit and not-for-profit organizations creating potential for conflicts of interest. One could argue that enthusiasm for developing these tools has overtaken the science that needs to underpin their design, development, and methods to ensure their quality and safety. It is, therefore, essential to have a set of internationally accepted standards to assess their quality and to assess whether interests are declared and whether they are unduly biased (Holmes-Rovner et al., 2007; O'Connor et al., 2004a).

Acting on this need, the International Patient Decision Aids Standards (IPDAS) Collaboration was established at the 2nd International Shared Decision-Making conference at Swansea in 2003 (see in chapter 2). The proposal to generate a quality framework was also supported at the Society for

Medical Decision-Making (Chicago, 2003) and Society for Information Therapy (Utah, 2003). We reviewed existing checklists for assessing the quality of randomized trials (CONSORT), meta-analyses (QUOROM), practice guidelines (AGREE), and general patient information. However, these technologies differ from scientific studies and practice guidelines and aim to do more than provide general information for patients. They are interventions that recognize the need for both patients and professionals to consider, at the individual level, the impact of uncertainties surrounding many health care decisions; they communicate risk probabilities and use methods to clarify values and guide deliberation. Moreover, they use powerful and potentially misleading strategies that have not been used in other quality checklists. Aware of best practice regarding the development of quality criteria, IPDAS adapted an approach used for appraising clinical guidelines (AGREE collaboration) (Cluzeau *et al.*, 2003) and established an international collaboration of different stakeholder groups. The aim was to achieve an international consensus-based framework of quality criteria for patient decision aids that would act as a guide for developers and users.

Section 2: Arriving at the IPDAS checklist

Full details of the modified Delphi consensus methods used are available in an online publication (Elwyn *et al.*, 2006), and so we only summarize here the key issues of relevance and provide the published IPDAS checklist – see Table 33.1. The first step was to create background evidence documents, reviewing the literature in key areas of relevance for decision support. From these documents, a set of 80 quality criteria were written and formatted so that it was possible to rate their importance. Second, multiple stakeholders groups were formed of patients, professionals, policy makers, and developers or researchers. These stakeholders were asked to vote on the quality criteria and did so in two rounds, after they had reviewed a synopsis that defined the criteria, provided a theoretical rationale, and summarized the empirical data supporting or refuting inclusion. The results of the first round, and qualitative comments, were provided at the second round, so as to guide the second vote. We included the following quality domains in the final quality framework: (1) systematic development process; (2) providing information about options; (3) presenting probabilities; (4) clarifying and expressing values; (5) using patient stories; (6) guiding or coaching in deliberation and communication; (7) disclosing conflicts of interest; (8) delivering patient decision aids on the internet; (9) balancing the presentation of options; (10) using plain language; (11) basing information on up-to-date scientific evidence; and (12) establishing effectiveness. A total of 41 criteria were given the maximum score of 9 out of 9 (for full details see published article (Elwyn *et al.*, 2006)). The Delphi process provided substantial consensus about a framework of quality criteria for patient decision aids. The criteria that were most strongly endorsed also had the greatest empirical support. Where stakeholder groups' ratings differed, the researcher group tended to give lower ratings, presumably because these participants were more conservative about the feasibility of simultaneously achieving a large number of quality criteria and perhaps more aware of the difficulty in obtaining supportive empirical evidence. The checklist has been made widely available and has been used to assess the extent to which existing tools have met the criteria (Evans *et al.*, 2007; O'Connor *et al.*, 2007a).

Section 3: From IPDAS checklist to instrument: IPDASi

Although it has been influential in changing development practice, the IPDAS checklist was not designed to provide precise, quantitative assessments, such that judgements could be made about the quality of decision aids, either at the item, domain, or global levels. In addition, because

Table 33.1 IPDAS Patient decision aid user checklist

Area 1. Information and value clarification

Does the patient decision aid provide information about options in sufficient detail for decision-making?

- describe the health condition
- list the options
- list the option of doing nothing
- describe the natural course without options
- describe procedures
- describe positive features [benefits]
- describe negative features of options [harms/side-effects/disadvantages]
- include chances of positive/negative outcomes

Additional items for tests

- describe what test is designed to measure
- include chances of true positive, true negative, false positive, false negative test results
- describe possible next steps based on test result
- include chances the disease is found with/without screening
- describe detection/treatment that would never have caused problems if one was not screened

Present probabilities of outcomes in an unbiased and understandable way?

- use event rates specifying the population and time period
- compare outcome probabilities using the same denominator, time period, scale
- describe uncertainty around probabilities
- use visual diagrams
- use multiple methods to view probabilities [words, numbers, diagrams]
- allows the patient to select a way of viewing probabilities [words, numbers, diagrams]
- allow patient to view probabilities based on their own situation [e.g. age]
- place probabilities in context of other events
- use both positive and negative frames [e.g. showing both survival and death rates]

Include methods for clarifying and expressing patients' values?

- describe the procedures and outcomes to help patients imagine what it is like to experience their physical, emotional, social effects
- ask patients to consider which positive and negative features matter most
- suggest ways for patients to share what matters most with others

Include structured guidance in deliberation and communication?

- provide steps to make a decision
- suggest ways to talk about the decision with a health professional
- include tools [worksheet, question list] to discuss options with others

Area 2. Development process

Does the patient decision aid present information in a balanced manner?

- able to compare positive/negative features of options
- shows negative/positive features with equal detail [fonts, order, display of statistics]

Have a systematic development process?

- have developers' credentials/qualifications
- find out what users [patients, practitioners] need to discuss options
- have peer review by patient/professional experts not involved in development and field testing

(continued)

Table 33.1 (continued) IPDAS Patient decision aid user checklist

- is field tested with users [patients facing the decision; practitioners presenting options]
- the field tests with users [patients, practitioners] show the patient decision aid is acceptable
- the field tests with users show that the patient decision aid is balanced for undecided patients
- understood by those with limited reading skills

Use up-to-date scientific evidence that is cited in a reference section or technical document?

- provides references to evidence used
- report steps to find, appraise, summarize evidence
- report date of last update
- report how often patient decision aid is updated
- describe quality of scientific evidence [including lack of evidence]
- uses evidence from studies of patients similar to those of target audience

Disclose conflicts of interest?

- report source of funding to develop and distribute the patient decision aid
- report whether authors or their affiliations stand to gain or lose by choices patients make after using the patient decision aid

Use plain language?

- is written at a level that can be understood by the majority of patients in the target group
- is written at a grade 8 equivalent level or less according to readability score [SMOG or FRY]
- provides ways to help patients understand information other than reading [audio, video, in-person discussion]

Meet additional criteria if the patient decision aid is internet based

- provide a step-by-step way to move through the web pages
- allow patients to search for key words
- provide feedback on personal health information that is entered into the patient decision aid
- provides security for personal health information entered into the decision aid
- make it easy for patients to return to the decision aid after linking to other web pages
- permit printing as a single document

Meet additional criteria if stories are used in the patient decision aid

- use stories that represent a range of positive and negative experiences
- reports if there was a financial or other reason why patients decided to share their story
- state in an accessible document that the patient gave informed consent to use their stories

Area 3. Effectiveness

Does the patient decision aid ensure decision-making is informed and values based?

- recognize a decision needs to be made
- help patients to know about options and their features
- understand that values affect decision
- be clear about option features that matter most
- discuss values with their practitioner
- become involved in preferred ways

Decision quality. The patient decision aid

- improves the match between the chosen option and the features that matter most to the informed patient not all checklist items were applicable to every decision aid, comparability, even at the checklist level, was not possible. Given interest in being able to assess these interventions at a more precise level of detail - in terms of how they were developed, field tested, whether their content was valid, and whether or not they had been evaluated – the IPDAS Collaboration agreed that achieving this objective would require an instrument capable of quantitatively assessing the quality of decision aids. The development of the IPDAS instrument (IPDASi) took place in four stages. The detail is described elsewhere (Elwyn et al., 2008), so a summary is provided here. In stage 1, the checklist was used to assess three decision aids by six raters. Based on these initial assessments where interpretation difficulties were encountered, a new set of items was generated that had more precise statements. This was called IPDASi v2 and in stage 2, five independent raters were again asked to assess the same three tools and a website created for data collection (http://www.ipdasi.org/). Their scores were analysed (intra-class correlations) and problems discussed. A new version, IPDASi v3 was created. In stage 3, 30 randomly selected decision aids were assessed by eight raters, four in North America (Ottawa and Providence) and four in the United Kingdom (Cardiff) and the scores analysed for inter-rater agreement. In stage four, a core set of items (a short form version of IPDASi) was selected and also analysed.

Full details of the results are available elsewhere (Elwyn et al., 2008). In summary, adjusted IPDASi scores ranged widely from 33 to 82. The intra-class correlation for the weighted overall score was 0.80. Correlations of domain scores with the weighted overall score were all positive (0.31–0.68). Cronbach's alpha values for the eight raters ranged from 0.72 to 0.93. We, therefore, conclude that IPDASi has the potential to assess the quality of decision aids. The four stage process revealed the need to make significant changes in the IPDAS checklist and modifications to the set of assumptions so that a measurement tool could be applied across the range of all possible decisions. Having undertaken this work, we also suggest that IPDASi could provide formative feedback about domains in which developers could make improvements in subsequent versions. A short form may also be developed to support the development of quality standards and enhance patient safety. In addition, the study demonstrated the high correlation between IPDASi and IPDASi-Short Form (SF) – high quality scores at detailed domain assessment correspond with high scores on a version which focuses on fewer items. Further work is now in progress to refine the IPDASi items, to improve the inter-rater calibration of raters and to offer IPDASi as a method to assess existing tools and also as a formative check against tools that are in development (http://www.ipdasi.org/).

Section 4: Future developments

This field is a fast moving area of research and the IPDAS Collaboration needs to be able to be confident that it is working with the latest evidence base and reflecting expertise at an international level. A decision was taken in mid 2008 to expand the steering group and to prepare an agenda for the ISDM conference in Boston, 2009. At that meeting, proposals were planned to update background documents and to ensure that both the checklist and the instrument are updated. There is no doubt that technologies that have the power to influence preference-sensitive decisions in health care need to be based on the highest quality evidence, as free from bias as possible and developed in accordance with best practice. These are not easy tasks to accomplish and it is our hope that the IPDAS Collaboration – both the checklist and the instrument – provides helpful guidance.

References

Charles, C., Gafni, A., Whelan, T. *et al.* (2005). Treatment decision aids: Conceptual issues and future directions. *Health Expect*, **8**, 114–125.

Cluzeau, F.A., Burgers, J.S., Brouwers, M. *et al.* (2003). Development and validation of an international appraisal instrument for assessing the quality of clinical practice guidelines: The AGREE project. *Quality and Safety in Health Care*, **12**, 18–23.

Coulter, A. and Ellins, J. (2007). Effectiveness of strategies for informing, educating, and involving patients. *British Medical Journal*, **335**, 24–27.

Elwyn, G., O'Connor, A., Stacey, D. *et al.* (2006). The International Patient Decision Aids Standards Collaboration. Developing a quality criteria framework for patient decision aids: Online international delphi consensus process. *British Medical Journal*, **333**, 417–421.

Elwyn, G., O'Connor, A.M., Bennett, C. *et al.* (2008), Assessing the quality of decision support technologies using the International Patient Decision Aid Standards instrument (IPDASi). *PLoS One,* Submitted.

Evans, R., Elwyn, G., Edwards, A. *et al.* (2007) Toward a model for field-testing patient decision-support technologies: A qualitative field-testing study. *J. Med. Internet Res.*, **9**, e21.

Godlee, F. (2007). Evidence to inform, *British Medical Journal*, **334** doi:10.1136/bmj.39252.523519.47 1

Holmes-Rovner, M., Nelson, W.L., Pignone, M. *et al.* (2007). Are patient decision aids the best way to improve clinical decision making? Report of the IPDAS Symposium. *Med. Decis. Making*, **27**, 599–608.

Kennedy, A.D.M., Sculpher, M.J., Coulter, A. *et al.* (2002). Effects of decision aids for menorrhagia on treatment choices, health outcomes, and costs. *Journal of the America Medical Association*, **288**, 2701–2708.

O'Connor, A.M., Bennett, C., Stacey, D. *et al.* (2007a). Do patient decision aids meet effectiveness criteria of the international patient decision aid standards collaboration? A systematic review and meta-analysis. *Med. Decis. Making*, **27**, 554–574.

O'Connor, A.M., Llewellyn-Thomas, H.A. and Flood, A.B. (2004a). Modifying unwarranted variations in health care: Shared decision making using patient decision aids. *Health Aff. (Millwood)*, Suppl Web Exclusive:VAR, 63–72.

O'Connor, A.M., Stacey, D., Entwistle, V. *et al.* (2004b), *Decision Aids for People Facing Health Treatment or Screening Decisions: (Cochrane Review) Issue 1*, Chichester, UK: John Wiley & Sons, Ltd.

O'Connor, A.M., Wennberg, J., Legare, F. *et al.* (2007b). Towards the 'tipping point': Decision aids and informed patient choice. *Health Affairs*, **26**, 716–725.

Whelan, T., Levine, M., Willan, A. *et al.* (2004). Effect of a decision aid on knowledge and treatment decision making for breast cancer surgery: A randomized trial. *Journal of the America Medical Association*, **292**, 435–441.

Chapter 34

The decision research 'lab'

Hilary Llewellyn-Thomas

Introduction

Considerable progress has been made in the science and infra-structure needed to incorporate high-quality decision support (DS) and patients' decision aids (PtDAs) into regular clinical practice in preference-sensitive situations. On the basis of these achievements, investigators can now justifiably focus future efforts entirely on the development and testing of pragmatic, sustainable strategies for the widespread introduction of DS and PtDAs into the mainstream of care.

However, one could argue that there still remain notable gaps in our knowledge about what is fundamentally going on inside the 'black box' of decision-making (Llewellyn-Thomas 1995). If our efforts exclusively address pragmatic issues, we would miss opportunities to gain deeper insights into those fundamental decision-making processes. Without these insights, we could, at best, fall short of the goal of fostering informed patient choice, or, at worst, inadvertently undermine the achievement of that goal.

If we agree that it is important to fill the gaps in our fundamental knowledge, we would, ideally, investigate these basic processes in actual decision-making situations. However, there are questions about the appropriateness of superimposing research projects onto mainstream care, about confirming patient eligibility, and about controlling for covariate and confounding effects. Therefore, an argument could be made for establishing research 'laboratories' in informed patient choice.

The structure of such a research laboratory would depend on a wide range of factors, including the research team's scientific philosophy, funding sources, high-priority research questions, target populations and sampling capabilities, and available research tools. For example, the lab may need to be housed in an actual physical space in order to accommodate volunteer participants, but require only minimal equipment because the team's research program involves comparisons of simple DS tools and requires simple paper-and-pencil data-capturing strategies. In another example, the lab may need not only to take the form of an actual physical space, but also to house highly technical equipment in order to present simulated decision dilemmas, to video-tape full-length DS transactions, to use complex multi-media DS tools, and to use multi-method approaches for interactively capturing both quantitative and qualitative data. In a third example, the lab could take the form of a 'virtual laboratory', in which investigators rely wholly on interactive websites to recruit volunteer participants from geographically dispersed populations, to present decision situations, to provide interactive DS tools, and to collect online response data.

For the purposes of this chapter, I shall set aside considerations about the structure of a laboratory in patients' decision-making and explore some speculative ideas about the kinds of studies in informed patient choice that such a lab might undertake (Llewellyn-Thomas, 2005).

The decision lab's research program

The overall aim would be to contribute new knowledge about the underlying processes whereby patients make informed choices among options in preference-sensitive decision situations. The strategy would involve creating laboratory conditions for collecting responses from different groups of patient–volunteers towards different elements of DS and PtDAs specifically designed to test particular research hypotheses. Thus, there would be two major cross-cutting research themes. The first focuses on the constituent elements of DS and PtDAs, and the second on the different groups of patients engaged with those elements.

Researching the constituent elements of decision support/decision aids

Information studies

A major design element is the information provided to the patient about his or her condition and the relevant therapeutic options. Current evidence indicates that, overall, patients understand this information better after working with paper-, audiotape-, and video-based decision aids, compared with usual care alone. However, it will be worthwhile to use interactive electronic media to probe deeper, given (a) the heuristics and biases that can affect how patients and practitioners use information to draw inferences, make judgments, and arrive at choices; (b) the comprehension errors and inconsistency in decision-making demonstrated by particular sub-groups of patients who may need particular kinds of help; and (c) the increasing interest in web-based PtDAs available via the internet, which could quickly become a primary dissemination route for new generations of patients.

There are many fundamental research questions about how patients engage with the information in decision aids. Do some patients come into the decision situation with exaggerated subjective assumptions about the chances of risks and benefits? If so, and if those erroneous baseline assumptions interfere with accurately understanding subsequently provided objective information, could different ways of portraying probabilities (for example, icons, graphic displays, numeric displays, nested scales), or different probability formats (for example, absolute risk, relative risk, numbers-needed-to-treat) be used to help moderate those assumptions? Can we foster greater comprehension of the objective risk/benefit information presented in PtDAs by providing learning templates about probabilities (for example, illustrations and application exercises) before the patient actually begins to work with a decision aid? What would be the effects of providing decision aids with tailored interactive components (for example, probability sliding scales) that allow the patient to visualize the meaning of changes in probabilities?

There are also rich opportunities to learn about the processes whereby other types of information are attended to, learned, and used by patients. When patients are choosing among options, do they tend to consider only the information about the therapeutic protocols and their pros and cons, or would they also consider information about geographic variations in reported preferences, in uptake rates, and in outcomes? As they work through the array of information presented in interactive computer- or web-based decision aids, can patients' information-processing pathways be tracked? If so, can sub-groups of patients who use characteristic information-processing pathways be identified? Are these path patterns differentially affected by using different systems for navigating around the content of different decision aids? Are these patterns affected by using different presentation sequences (like risks before benefits, or vice versa)? Do particular patterns relate to differences in decisional conflict, in comprehension, in self-reported readiness for decision-making, in actual treatment choice, and in adherence with therapy?

Research about values clarification

Another major DS and Patient Decision Aid design element involves the approaches used to help patients formulate and reveal their evaluative attitudes towards the therapeutic options and their attendant attributes. See the 'Values Clarification' chapter for overviews of the implicit and explicit methods that can be used to support this process, of the assumptions underlying those methods, and of the kinds of values-clarification research questions that we could test in the decision lab.

Studies in guidance and coaching

A third DS and PtDAs design element consists of different strategies for fostering shared patient–practitioner deliberation about the decision at hand. One example involves using a worksheet that summarizes the information that the patient understands as well as the areas in which he or she is having comprehension difficulties. This can summarize the key preference-sensitive issues in which the patient has formulated clear preferential attitudes, as well as those in which he or she is unclear about what is personally more or less important. This individualized worksheet could guide subsequent decision-related discussions between the patient and their clinician. In another example, a decision aid intervention could be designed to coach the patient in the communication and negotiation skills needed for active involvement in all the steps of decision-making.

Research questions about guidance and coaching are wide-ranging, and offer a rich, relatively untapped area of research in the field of DS and PtDAs. To begin with, what are the determinants of patients' 'informed' (as opposed to 'naive') preferences for participating (or not) in decision-making about preference-sensitive care, in the first place (Llewellyn-Thomas, 2006a; Llewellyn-Thomas, 2006b)? What are the processes whereby participatory preferences are revealed (or not) to practitioners? What happens when participatory preferences are acted upon (or not) by practitioners?

Are there 'core' guidance or coaching elements that are common to all effective DS and PtDAs? Are there 'modular' elements that are specific to particular kinds of preventive, screening or treatment decision situations, or to particular disease conditions? Are the principles of good decision aid-driven guidance common to all health care disciplines, or are some guidance or coaching principles discipline-specific? Can we characterize 'best practices' for decision aid-driven guidance or coaching with patients? What outcome measures should be used – the patients' level of confidence, deliberative skills, and communication skills after they work with a decision aid? Does guidance or coaching affect the communication patterns between patients and clinicians, and, if so, what are the effects of altered communication patterns on patients' decision quality? What study designs and measures can be used to investigate the effects of decision aid-driven guidance and coaching on how patients engage with new decision situations in the future?

Media questions

Early decision aid media included videos, decision boards, interactive computer programs, audio-guided workbooks, and pamphlets. Many decision aids involve more than one medium, and there is a recent shift towards internet-based delivery systems. There are several pragmatic issues about media selection, including the cost of updating decision aids as new clinical evidence emerges; feasibility and acceptability; patients' readiness; clinicians' usual practice patterns; whether a decision aid is to be self-administered or practitioner-administered; whether it is to be used in one-to-one or group situations; and the timing and manner in which it is to be integrated into the pathway of care. Besides these pragmatic issues, there are also several research questions of methodological interest.

For example, are various kinds of media differentially effective for different types of decision situations (e.g. acute versus chronic illness; screening situations versus life-threatening illnesses), or at different points in the decision trajectory (e.g. screening, diagnostic testing, initial treatment selection, treatment for recurrent disease, during palliative care)? Regardless of the decision situation or the decision point, do these media vary in their abilities to help patients understand objective information or reveal their evaluative attitudes towards relevant therapeutic options? How well do these media handle different formats for presenting probabilistic information, or different kinds of values clarification exercises? Do these media differ in terms of the ease and effectiveness of incorporating guidance and coaching design elements?

Research about different patient populations

The decision lab's second major cross-cutting research theme refers to the different groups of patients engaging with the constituent elements of DS and PtDAs.

Socio-demographic sub-groups

There are several different motivations for studying the role of DS and PtDAs in any particular clinical context. Health services researchers are interested in whether DS and PtDAs could modify unwarranted variations in preference-sensitive health care. Researchers in quality improvement argue that DS and PtDAs might rectify shortfalls in the 'centeredness' of patient-centered care. Clinical investigators study the role of DS and PtDAs in helping patients who want to be involved in choosing among therapeutic options, but are experiencing decisional conflict. Basic decision scientists work with DS and PtDAs to gain insights into the cognitive processes underlying patients' decision-making in close-call situations.

Across all of these research motivations, there is an increasing emphasis on the need to investigate differences in the causes and consequences of effective decision-making among the various ethnic, racial, gender, age, and educational sub-groups of patients engaging with a particular clinical choice. Laboratory studies about information provision, values clarification, guidance and coaching, and media that proceed without identifying and characterizing these potential differences could lead to invalid generalizations about the preferences of different patient sub-populations. These invalid interpretations could, in turn, lead to inappropriate practice policies that unwittingly reinforce problems such as unwarranted variations and gaps in patient-centered care (Wennberg and Peters 2004; King and Moulton 2006).

Multiple chronic conditions and multiple options

Two challenges to our current approaches for designing DS and PtDAs are rapidly emerging and carry important implications for a decision lab's research program.

First, as more new 'high-tech' interventions, devices, and materials appear, we anticipate the need to design novel decision aids that help patients comprehend this complex information and sort through multiple options' conflicting pros and cons. For example, patients with osteoarthritis who consider knee replacement surgery may not only be involved in opting for or against surgery, but also, if they opt for surgery, in choosing among different surgical approaches and prosthetic materials. However, to date, the tendency has been to design decision aids for deliberating about single-event 'cross-roads' in care, rather than for choosing among nested, contingent options.

Second, as the proportion of older patients with multiple chronic conditions increases – with some aspects of their care clearly indicated by high-quality clinical evidence and other aspects resting squarely in the preference-sensitive arena – we anticipate the need for multiple-conditions and multiple-objectives DS systems. These complex, novel systems would be required (a) to integrate patient education materials (which are designed to help patients to understand their practitioners' clearly-indicated recommendations for care) with DS and PtDAs (which are designed to help patients make values-based informed choices among relevant preference-sensitive care options); (b) to clarify, communicate, and establish patients' priorities for both recommended and optional care; and (c) subsequently, to help with the coordinated implementation of these individualized health care management plans. Decision laboratories could not only carry out the early developmental work required to design and pilot-test such innovations, but also play a notable role in their subsequent patient-based health technology assessment.

In both of these challenging areas, the research program would require collaborative links between experts in multi-attribute and multi-objective decision-making, experts in patients' decision support, and experts in health technology assessment (Bridges 2003, 2005; Bridges and Jones 2007).

Conclusion

When carried out in conjunction with the development and testing of pragmatic, sustainable strategies for the widespread introduction of DS and PtDAs into the mainstream of care, these laboratory-focused efforts would be entirely consistent with the current emphasis on the importance of translational research (Woolf 2008). This conjoint strategic approach to the science of Decision Support and Patient Decision Aids could increase our chances of fostering informed patient choice in an evidence-based, cost-effective, and sustainable way.

References

Bridges, J. (2003). Stated preference methods in health care evaluation: An emerging methodological paradigm in health economics. *Applied Health Economics and Health Policy*, **2**, 224.

Bridges, J. (2005). Future challenges for the economic evaluation of healthcare: Patient preferences, risk attitudes and beyond. *Pharmacoeconomics*, **23**, 317–321.

Bridges, J.F.P. and Jones, C. (2007). Patient-based health technology assessment: A vision for the future. *International Journal of Technology Assessment in Health Care*, **23**, 30–35.

King, J.S. and Moulton, B. (2006). Rethinking informed consent: The case for shared medical decision making. *American Journal of Law and Medicine*, **32**, 429–501.

Llewellyn-Thomas, H.A. (1995). Society for Medical Decision Making Presidential Address – Patients' health care decision making: A framework for descriptive and experimental investigations. *Medical Decision Making*, **15**, 101–106.

Llewellyn-Thomas, H.A. (2005). Decision making needs of older people: The role of patients' decision aids. *National Academies Center for Studies of Behavior & Development: Workshop on Decision Making Needs of Older People*. Washington DC: November 2005. Commissioned by the National Research Council under U.S. Department of Health and Human Services Contract N01-OD-4-2139, TO147. Available at http://www7.nationalacademies.org/csbd/presentations_archive.html. Accessed on 31 May 2008.

Llewellyn-Thomas, H.A. (2006a). Comment: Why it's tricky to measure patients' preferences for participating in decisions about elective spine surgery. *Spine*, **31**, 2861–2862.

Llewellyn-Thomas, H.A. (2006b). Measuring patients' preferences for participating in health care decisions: Avoiding invalid observations. *Health Expectations*, **9**, 305–306.

Wennberg, J.E. and Peters, P.G. (2004). Unwarranted variations in the quality of health care: Can the law help medicine provide a remedy/remedies? Specialty Law Digest. *Health Care Law*, **305**, 9–25.

Woolf, S.H. (2008). The meaning of translational research and why it matters. *Journal of the American Medical Association*, **299**, 211–213.

Chapter 35

Decision aids for preventing cardiovascular disease

Alan Montgomery

The health care problem and choices available

Cardiovascular disease accounts for around 40% of all deaths in Europe and the USA, is a major cause of disability, and impacts economically through health care costs, productivity losses, and informal care of people with cardiovascular disease (Allender *et al.*, 2008; American Heart Association 2008). Individuals at increased risk of suffering a cardiovascular event (mainly myocardial infarction or stroke) can be identified using one of several risk scoring equations derived from large cohort studies (Anderson *et al.*, 1990; Hippisley-Cox *et al.*, 2007). Once identified, these individuals may be offered one or more treatments known to be effective in reducing their risk of a cardiovascular event (Blood Pressure Lowering Treatment Trialists' Collaboration 2003; Law *et al.*, 2003). Guidelines for assessment of cardiovascular risk and treatment strategies are available to physicians (British Cardiac Society *et al.*, 2005; National High Blood Pressure Education Program, 2003), but such guidelines contain no explicit instructions for how individual patient preferences might be included in decisions about treatment. For asymptomatic patients in particular, for example with raised blood pressure or cholesterol, individualized estimation of the risk and availability of effective treatments can generate a difficult choice. Do they begin lifelong treatment, reducing the chances of an event that may or may not happen but with the possibility of side-effects? Or do they opt for no treatment or only lifestyle changes with more modest effects, knowing that their risk of a cardiovascular event remains higher than could otherwise be the case? And for patients with known cardiovascular disease such as atrial fibrillation, a further choice exists between treatment types, with differing effects on risks of stroke and major side-effects such as bleeding complications.

Atrial fibrillation

Decision aids for choice of antithrombotic therapy among patients with atrial fibrillation have been developed and evaluated in Canada (Man-Son-Hing *et al.*, 1999; McAlister *et al.*, 2005; Holbrook *et al.*, 2007) and the United Kingdom (Thomson *et al.*, 2007). A summary of each is shown in Table 35.1.

   When compared with usual care, Man-Son-Hing *et al.* (1999) found that the audio booklet resulted in a higher proportion of patients able to make a definite choice of preferred treatment (99% versus 94%) and fewer chose warfarin (8% versus 11%). McAlister *et al.* (2005) reported a greater proportion of patients receiving therapy appropriate to their stroke risk at 3 months in the decision aid group compared with usual care (adjusted difference = 12%).

Table 35.1 Studies of decision aids for choice of antithrombotic therapy among patients with atrial fibrillation

Study	Country	Study sample	Description of decision aid
Man-Son-Hing et al., 1999	Canada/ USA	Patients with atrial fibrillation, all on aspirin, otherwise at relatively low risk of stroke.	29-page information booklet, 20 min audiotape, and 1-page personal worksheet. Population estimates of stroke risk. Designed to be used by patients at home in advance of a physician consultation.
McAlister et al., 2005	Canada	Patients in primary care, mean duration with atrial fibrillation = 5 years, at varying stroke risk, 80% on warfarin.	Same as Man-Son-Hing et al., except with patient-specific estimates of stroke risk.
Thomson et al., 2007	UK	Treated or newly diagnosed atrial fibrillation identified in primary care.	Two computer-based decision aids for use in consultation with doctor.* Individualized presentation of treatment risks and benefits, section to support shared decision-making.
Holbrook et al., 2007	Canada	Aged over 65 years, ≥1 stroke risk factor, no known atrial fibrilla tion diagnosis or treatment with warfarin.	Outcome descriptions, probabilities, and treatment choices, as decision board, audio booklet, computer program, and probabilities as either pie chart or pictogram. Population estimates of probabilities.

*One of the interventions, employing explicit utility assessment and formal decision analysis, had to be discontinued in the study due to confusion among users (Murtagh et al., 2007).

This outcome is interesting in that it suggests concordance with treatment guidelines as a goal; however, it is possible that a patient at the sufficiently high risk of stroke to warrant treatment with warfarin, after full consideration of all the information available, legitimately opts for aspirin because of its lower associated risk of bleeding side-effects. This illustrates the potential conflict between individual preferences and evidence-based treatment guidelines aimed at reducing mortality and morbidity in populations. Both studies found increased knowledge and more realistic expectations of treatment, and although there was a little effect on overall decisional conflict, there were reductions in both studies on the 'uninformed' subscale consistent with improved knowledge scores. McAlister et al. did not measure resource use, but Man-Son-Hing et al. reported no difference in length of visit.

Thomson et al.'s (2007) computer-based decision aid resulted in reduced overall decisional conflict compared with a doctor consultation using evidence-based guidelines, but no effect on knowledge or anxiety. Patients not already on warfarin in the decision aid group were much less likely to start than those in the guideline group (25% versus 94%). Assuming that patients not on warfarin in each group had similar risk profiles, this again demonstrates the potential for a decision aid to result in treatment choices that may contradict evidence-based recommendations. Clinic visits in the decision aid group were 10 min longer on average but with much overlap between the groups, and there were no differences in the number of health care consultations in the subsequent 3 months.

Holbrook and colleagues reported before to after benefits but no between-group differences for any outcome, suggesting that the type of media used to deliver material and the type of picture to represent probability information may not matter (Holbrook *et al.*, 2007). Their most interesting finding was that 36% of participants changed their preference when the treatment names were revealed – mainly those who had initially chose warfarin switching to aspirin.

Blood pressure, cholesterol, multifactorial risk reduction

Decision aids have been developed and evaluated for treatment choices for individual cardiovascular risk factors (Montgomery *et al.*, 2003; Dowding *et al.*, 2004; Weymiller *et al.*, 2007), and for multifactorial risk reduction (Sheridan *et al.*, 2006). These are summarizsed in Table 35.2.

Individualized decision analysis for hypertension involves presenting information about hypertension and its treatment patients, eliciting individual values regarding outcomes, and finally combining these with individual cardiovascular risk estimates in a decision tree to produce a recommended 'best' treatment option for each patient. This appears to be an acceptable method of assisting patient decision-making (Dowding *et al.*, 2004; Montgomery *et al.*, 2003). Further, it appears effective in reducing decisional conflict and anxiety and increasing knowledge among patients with a new diagnosis of hypertension (Montgomery *et al.*, 2003). It did not though have any effect on either the proportion of patients at 3 months who have started medication, or treatment adherence or blood pressure control at 3 years (Emmett *et al.*, 2005).

The *Statin Choice* decision aid was also reported as highly acceptable to patients (Weymiller *et al.*, 2007). Additionally, they reported reduced decisional conflict, improved knowledge, and

Table 35.2 Studies of decision aids for choice of therapy among patients with raised blood pressure, cholesterol, and cardiovascular risk

Study	Country	Study sample	Description of decision aid
Montgomery *et al.*, 2003	UK	Newly diagnosed hypertensive patients in primary care.	1. Individualized cardiovascular risk calculation, utility assessment, and decision analysis. 2. Information video and leaflet.
Dowding *et al.*, 2004	UK	Hypertensive patients in primary care.	Individualized cardiovascular risk calculation, utility assessment, and decision analysis.
Weymiller *et al.*, 2007	USA	Patients with Type II diabetes.	*Statin Choice*: Detailed information booklet, plus individualized cardiovascular risk estimate, potential advantages and disadvantages of taking statins, question asking patient what action they want to take now.
Sheridan *et al.*, 2006	USA	Patients aged 35–75 with no known cardiovascular disease, attending internal medicine clinic.	*Heart to Heart*: internet-based decision aid, calculates individualized coronary heart disease risk, presents pros and cons of treatment options for modifiable risk factors, re-calculates risk based on one or more treatments, print-out for discussion with doctor.

improved estimation of cardiovascular risk and risk reduction with treatment, and these effects were generally greater when the consultation was with a doctor rather than a researcher. There was some evidence of increased uptake of statin therapy but no evidence of adherence to treatment choice at 3 months.

Subject only to pilot evaluation so far, the *Heart-to-Heart* decision aid explores treatment of various risk factors for coronary heart disease, rather than focusing on treatment of single cardiovascular risk factors (see Figure 35.1). It appears promising in that it resulted in a greater proportion of patients discussing CHD risk reduction with their doctor, and making a specific plan to reduce CHD risk (Sheridan *et al.*, 2006). There was no change in the proportion of patients who viewed this as a shared decision, but there was a 10% reduction in patients who considered it as their own decision, and a concomitant increase who viewed it as the doctor's decision. It is possible this may not be replicated in a study with larger numbers, but it may signify recognition by some patients that individual preference plays a secondary role when there is compelling evidence of effective treatments for CHD risk reduction.

Future developments

Cardiovascular disease risk reduction, particularly as a preventive strategy for individuals with raised levels of one or more modifiable risk factors, is an important area for the development of patient decision aids. That there have been relatively few subjected to evaluation thus far is

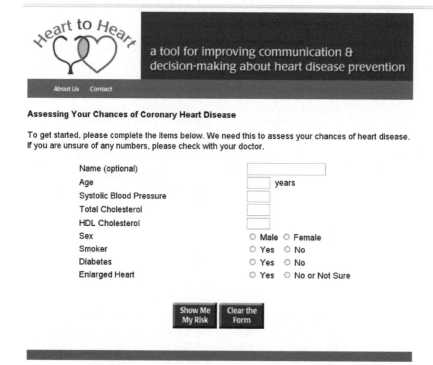

Figure 35.1 The Heart to Heart decision aid for heart disease prevention (courtesy, Stacey Sheridan, and Mike Pignone, Duke University, USA).

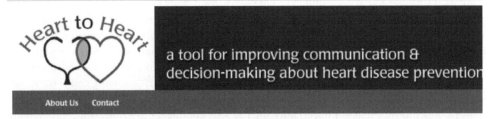

How Much Strategies Can Reduce Your Chances of Heart Disease
This is the maximal amount you can lower your chances of heart disease using proven options. You may receive additional benefits if you eat right and exercise, but doctors can't say exactly how much. Talk with your doctor about reducing your chances of heart disease by eating right and being active.

Your original risk is **37%**,

By choosing the following actions:

Take Aspirin
Stop Smoking
Take Blood Pressure Medication
Take Cholesterol Medication

You can lower your risk to **7%**

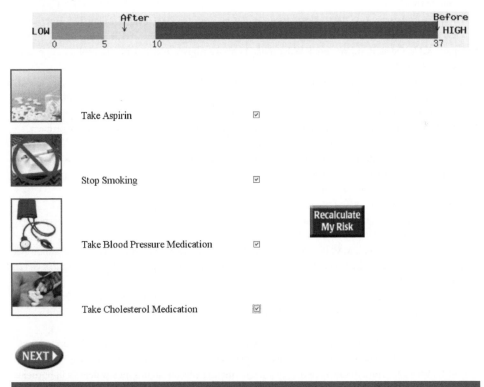

Figure 35.1 (continued)

somewhat surprising. Given the shift in recent years toward overall risk estimation and treatment, rather than identification and treatment of single risk factors, it seems sensible that decision aids adopt the same approach. Tools that offer individual risk estimation must keep pace with other developments in this area – for example, the Framingham risk equations are known to under- or overestimate risk in certain groups and do not take into account factors such as social deprivation, BMI or family history (Brindle *et al.*, 2006). Improvements in risk scoring calibration and discrimination must be reflected in interventions to assist patient and clinician decision-making. This may include estimates of uncertainty such as 95% confidence intervals, which are notably absent in most presentations of either individual cardiovascular risk or treatment effects.

Given that we now know from RCTs that cardiovascular disease decision aids are generally effective in improving the decision-making process for patients who want to be involved, the next major challenge is implementation. Tools that are flexible enough in mode of presentation and amount and format of content to satisfy all patients with a desire to know more about their condition and be involved in treatment decision-making are likely to be most successful. Studies that move away from addressing the question 'does this work?' to 'how can we get patients and clinicians to use this in normal practice?' are now required.

References

Allender, S., Scarborough, P., Peto, V., *et al.* (2008), *European Cardiovascular Disease Statistics*. European Heart Network.

American Heart Association (2008). *Heart disease and stroke statistics 2008 update*. Dallas, TX: American Heart Association.

Anderson, K.M., Odell, P.M., Wilson, P.W.F., *et al.* (1990). Cardiovascular disease risk profiles. *American Heart Journal*, **121**, 293–298.

Blood Pressure Lowering Treatment Trialists' Collaboration. (2003). Effects of different blood-pressure-lowering regimens on major cardiovascular events: Results of prospectively-designed overviews of randomised trials. *Lancet*, **362**, 1527–1535.

Brindle, P., Beswick, A., Fahey, T., *et al.* (2006). Accuracy and impact of risk assessment in the primary prevention of cardiovascular disease: A systematic review. *Heart*, **92**, 1752–1759.

British Cardiac Society, British Hypertension Society, Diabetes UK, HEART UK, Primary Care Cardiovascular Society, and The Stroke Association (2005). JBS2: Joint British Societies' guidelines on prevention of cardiovascular disease in clinical practice. *Heart*, **91**, 1–52.

Dowding, D., Swanson, V., Bland, R., *et al.* (2004). The development and preliminary evaluation of a decision aid based on decision analysis for two treatment conditions: Benign Prostatic Hyperplasia and Hypertension. *Patient Education and Counseling*, **52**, 209–215.

Emmett, C.L., Montgomery, A.A., Peters, T.J., *et al.* (2005). Three-year follow-up of a factorial randomised controlled trial of two decision aids for newly diagnosed hypertensive patients. *British Journal of General Practice*, **55**, 551–553.

Hippisley-Cox, J., Coupland, C., Vinogradova, Y., *et al.* (2007). Derivation and validation of QRISK, a new cardiovascular disease risk score for the United Kingdom: Prospective open cohort study. *British Medical Journal*, **335**, 136.

Holbrook, A., Labiris, R., Goldsmith, C.H., *et al.* (2007). Influence of decision aids on patient preferences for anticoagulant therapy: A randomized trial. *Canadian Medical Association Journal*, **176**, 1583–1587.

Law, M.R., Wald, N.J., and Rudnicka, A.R. (2003). Quantifying effect of statins on low density lipoprotein cholesterol, ischaemic heart disease, and stroke: Systematic review and meta-analysis. *British Medical Journal*, **326**, 1423–1429.

Man-Son-Hing, M., Laupacis, A., O'Connor, A.M., *et al.* (1999). A patient decision aid regarding antithrombotic therapy for stroke prevention in atrial fibrillation. *Journal of the American Medical Association*, **282**, 737–743.

McAlister, F.A., Man-Son-Hing, M., Straus, S.E., *et al.* (2005). Impact of a patient decision aid on care among patient with nonvalvular atrial fibrillation: A cluster randomized trial. *Canadian Medical Association Journal*, **173**, 496–501.

Montgomery, A.A., Fahey, T., and Peters, T.J. (2003). A factorial randomised controlled trial of decision analysis and an information video plus leaflet for newly diagnosed hypertensive patients. *British Journal of General Practice*, **53**, 446–453.

Murtagh, M.J., Thomson, R.G., May, C.R., *et al.* (2007). Qualitative methods in a randomised controlled trial: The role of an integrated qualitative process evaluation in providing evidence to discontinue the intervention in one arm of a trial of a decision support tool. *Quality and Safety in Health Care*, **16**, 224–229.

National High Blood Pressure Education Program. (2003). *The seventh report of the Joint National Committee on prevention, detection, evaluation, and treatment of high blood pressure.* NIH, 03-5233.

Sheridan, S.L., Shadle, J., Simpson Jr, R. J., *et al.* (2006). The impact of a decision aid about heart disease prevention on patients' discussions with their doctor and their plans for prevention: A pilot randomized trial. *BioMed Central Health Services Research*, **6**, p. 121.

Thomson, R.G., Eccles, M.P., Steen, I.N., *et al.* (2007). A patient decision aid to support shared decision-making on anti-thrombotic treatment of patients with atrial fibrillation: Randomised controlled trial. *Quality and Safety in Health Care*, **16**, 216–223.

Weymiller, A.J., Montori, V.M., Jones, L.A., *et al.* (2007). Helping patients with type 2 diabetes mellitus make treatment decisions. *Archives of Internal Medicine*, **167**, 1076–1082.

Chapter 36

Decision aids in multiple sclerosis

Sascha Köpke and Ingrid Mühlhauser

Multiple sclerosis

Multiple sclerosis (MS) is a recurrent inflammatory disorder of the central nervous system usually starting in early adult life. The cause and mechanisms of the disease remain mostly unexplained. All features of MS are characterized by uncertainty – in fact, it has been claimed that the most constant feature of the disease is uncertainty (NCC-CC, 2004). Diagnostic criteria are based mostly on experts' consensus rather than evidence as an individual patient's course and prognosis is variable and hard to predict. The disease is commonly characterized by periodic relapses with a large variety of possible presentations from mild sensory dysfunctions to severe and highly disabling symptoms like complete loss of vision or paraplegia. However, at least one-third of people with a diagnosis of MS seem to remain relatively unaffected by the disease (Ramsaransing and De Keyser, 2006).

There is still no cure available, but a number of so-called disease-modifying (immuno-modulatory and immuno-suppressive) drugs have been licensed with Interferons, Glatiramer Acetat, and Natalizumab the most prominent. They reduce relapses and slow down disease progression, but long-term effects remain unclear. Relapses are commonly treated with high-dose intravenous steroids despite weak and ambiguous evidence (Köpke et al., 2004). Also, there are a number of symptomatic therapeutic options available such as for bladder dysfunction or spasticity. However, disease modifying drugs have regular and pronounced adverse effects (Filippini et al., 2003) and are very expensive. Furthermore, limited specificity of diagnostic tests and a 'hit hard and early' treatment approach increasingly promoted by experts and pharmaceutical stakeholders is likely to result in over-diagnosis and over-treatment (Whiting et al., 2006).

Recently, the European Union has published a 'Code of Good Practice' on the rights of people with MS (European Multiple Sclerosis Platform (EMSP), 2007), demanding the provision of clear and concise high-quality information from diagnosis onwards, to empower patients to manage their disease. In practice, most people with MS claim autonomous roles in decision-making although there may be cultural differences (Solari et al., 2007). This contrasts with poor disease related knowledge (Heesen et al., 2004). We have previously shown that provision of honest, evidence-based information about risks, treatment options, and possible outcomes does not disturb or upset people with MS (Heesen et al., 2004; Kasper et al., 2006).

Shared decision-making, decision aids, and evidence-based patient information

In the light of the multitude of uncertainties related to MS, informed shared decision-making appears prototypic for decisions in MS (Heesen et al., 2007). Probably, decision aids are the most appropriate tools to support informed choice in the care of people with MS. These require high-quality evidence-based patient information, including the strength of available evidence, patient-relevant outcomes, presentation of risks in absolute numbers, displaying gains and losses together, and using a reassuring but non-patronizing style (Steckelberg *et al.*, 2005).

Available decision aids for persons with multiple sclerosis

A systematic database and internet search in May 2008 identified only five decision aids for persons with MS (Prunty *et al.*, 2008; UCLH *et al.*, 2006; Healthwise, 2008; Kasper *et al.*, 2008; Köpke *et al.*, 2008a). Three of these aim to support decision about disease modifying drugs (UCLH *et al.*, 2006; Healthwise, 2008; Kasper *et al.*, 2008). Two of these (UCLH *et al.*, 2006; Healthwise, 2008) only partially fulfil the criteria for evidence-based patient information and high-quality decision aids. For example, in both decision aids information about chances of both favourable and unwanted outcomes is lacking or inconsistent. The American decision aid (Healthwise, 2008) relies on recommendations by experts strongly supporting disease modifying drugs which diverges from the above principles of balanced information.

Prunty *et al.* (2008) published the results of a randomized controlled trial evaluating a decision aid on family planning for women with MS. The tool aims to support women with MS to make decisions on different issues of family planning. Although the decision aid meets several of the IPDAS criteria, a number of relevant inconsistencies remain. For example, probabilities of possible outcomes are not given consistently which makes an unbiased comparison of different options difficult. Other important criteria are met, e.g. patients have been involved throughout the development process and the effectiveness of the decision aid has been evaluated (Prunty *et al.*, 2008).

The remaining two decision aids have been developed by our group based on a number of pre-studies. Two randomized controlled trials evaluating the effectiveness of the decision aids have been completed. The first decision aid is delivered as an educational program on relapse management (Köpke *et al.*, 2008a). People with MS are provided with a preparatory 40-page brochure, which is available for download (Köpke *et al.*, 2006). People then attend a 4-hour educational programproviding information, working with decision trees, and group discussion. Participants are offered a prescription for oral steroids for self-treatment as a further treatment option to enhance self-management. Although a somewhat unusual approach for a decision aid, it meets the aforementioned criteria. Evidence-based patient information is provided on relapses and management options including to refrain or delay steroid therapy or to use oral steroids for self-medication. The group format allows people to listen to and to discuss other participants' 'stories' on relapse management and to reflect on their own preferences.

The second decision aid targets disease-modifying drugs and consists of a comprehensive 100-page brochure and a decision support chart (Kasper *et al.*, 2008). The brochure starts with the description of the different natural courses of MS without treatment. The brochure is structured according to disease courses, so that readers can easily assess personally relevant passages, and at levels of detail of their choosing. Each chapter discusses the range of disease-modifying drugs available. Benefits and risks are communicated as absolute risks using pictograms of 100 human stick figures (Figure 36.1). Also, numbers needed to treat (NNTs), 95% confidence intervals, strengths of evidence and references are displayed. The brochure is available for download (Heesen *et al.*, 2005). An English version is in preparation.

Evidence of implementation, effectiveness, and cost-effectiveness

There is little evidence about the implementation of these decision aids in clinical practice. As there is an abundance of 'patient information' materials provided by the pharmaceutical industry,

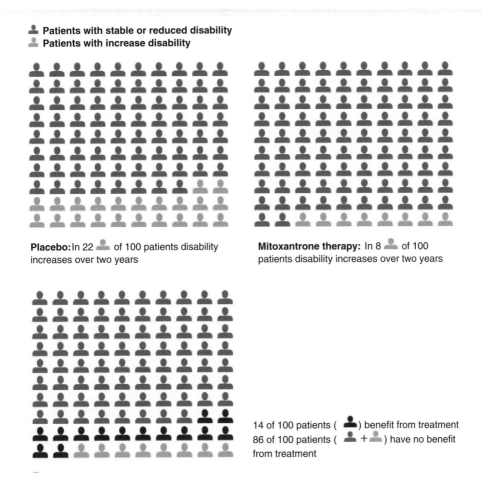

Figure 36.1 Mitoxantrone: Effects on disability over two years of therapy.

high-quality decision aids might not easily squeeze in. There is no information about the implementation and effectiveness of the decision aids that are available on the internet (UCLH *et al.*, 2006; Healthwise, 2008). The decision aid on family planning has been implemented in Australia and shown to increase knowledge, decision certainty and to decrease decisional conflict (Prunty *et al.*, 2008). Cost-effectiveness data are not yet available.

Both decision aids of our own group have been evaluated in randomized controlled trials with people with MS throughout Germany. The decision aid on relapse management increased knowledge and decision autonomy. Importantly, it also altered relapse management as a further indicator of increased autonomy. Over 2 years of follow-up, participants reported a better disease course compared to controls and had fewer physician contacts, suggesting cost-effectiveness (Köpke *et al.*, 2008a). Presently, a formal cost-effectiveness analysis is in progress. An implementation study in rehabilitation clinics indicated that the decision aid is transferable into practice (Köpke *et al.*, 2008b).

In contrast, the decision aid on immunotherapy hardly yielded any meaningful differences between groups. Although participants rated the decision aid as particularly helpful and knowledge was increased, there were no differences in role preferences and the proportion of participants who were able to realize their preferred decision role in consultations. Also, there were no differences in decisions absut treatment with disease-modifying drugs (Kasper *et al.*, 2008).

Keeping decision aids up-to-date with evidence advances in multiple sclerosis

There is an accumulating evidence base about disease-modifying drugs and we expect various new drugs to arrive in the near future. Also, interest in diagnostic criteria and their implications for treatment decisions is increasing. In theory, this should provide fertile ground for development and use of high-quality evidence-based information about treatment options for people with MS, engaging them in decisions about their care. However, there are currently only a few research groups involved in the development of decision aids for people with MS. The many uncertainties related to MS urge collaboration and networking in the field of decision support for people with MS. There are no powerful networks of researchers in the field, and influential institutions like neurological societies or health insurance companies currently show little engagement in activities that support people with MS and enable informed decision-making.

Conclusion for future development and maintenance of decision aids

There is an appalling and surprising paucity of decision aids for MS. Paradoxically, this may be a consequence of the many uncertainties inherent to MS. Many physicians and other stakeholders like self-help group officials seem convinced that doctors should have a strong role in decisions and, despite contrary research results, suspect that informing patients about uncertainties might lead to anxiety and depression. This is also in stark contrast to recent recommendations to involve patients in decision-making and empower them to make informed decisions based on their needs and the best-available evidence (NCC-CC, 2004; EMSP, 2007). Most importantly of all, however, most people with MS want to share decisions with their physicians and a considerable proportion prefers more autonomous roles (Heesen *et al.*, 2004). More high-quality decision aids for people with MS, rigorously developed and evaluated, are needed. Based on our own study results, we are currently developing an educational program to complement the brochure-based decision aid on disease-modifying drugs. Also, supported by the National MS Society, USA, we are presently working on further decision aids and evidence-based patient information for symptomatic treatments as well as diagnosis and prognosis in MS.

References

European Multiple Sclerosis Platform. (2007). European Code of Good practice on the rights and quality of life of people affected by multiple sclerosis. Available at. http://www.ms-in-europe.org/enews/2006-12-28/EMSP_CODE_in_its_current_draft_version.pdf. Accessed on 23 May 2008.

Filippini, G., Munari, L., Incorvaia, B., *et al.* (2003). Interferons in relapsing remitting multiple sclerosis: A systematic review. *Lancet*, **361**, 545–552.

Healthwise. (2008). Should I have disease-modifying therapy for multiple sclerosis? Available at http://www.healthwise.net/preferredcare/Content/StdDocument.aspx?DOCHWID=tf2571&SECHWID=tf2571-Intro. Accessed on 23 May 2008.

Heesen, C., Köpke, S., Richter, T., *et al.* (2007). Shared decision making and self-management in multiple sclerosis-a consequence of evidence. *J. Neurol.*, **254**, II116–121.

Heesen, C., Schwickert, Y., Kasper, J., *et al.* (2005). Immuntherapien der MS [MS immunotherapies]. Available at http://www.download.ms-netz-hamburg.de/download.php?downloadfile=immuntherapien_der_ms_2005.pdf. Accessed on 23 May 2008.

Heesen, C., Kasper, J., Segal, J., *et al.* (2004). Decisional role preferences, risk knowledge and information interests in patients with multiple sclerosis. *Multiple Sclerosis*, **10**, 643–650.

Kasper, J., Köpke, S., Mühlhauser, M., *et al.* (2008). Informed shared decision making about immunotherapy for patients with multiple sclerosis (ISDIMS): A randomised controlled trial (submitted for publication).

Kasper, J., Köpke, S., Mühlhauser, I., *et al.* (2006). Evidence-based patient information about treatment of multiple sclerosis—a phase one study on comprehension and emotional responses. *Patient Education & Counseling*, **62**, 56–63.

Köpke, S., Kasper, J., Nübling, M., *et al.* (2008a). Patient education programme to enhance decision autonomy in multiple sclerosis relapse management: A randomised controlled trial. (submitted for publication).

Köpke, S., Richter, T., Kasper, J., *et al.* (2008b). *Shared Decision Making in Multiple Sclerosis: The Need and Effects of Evidence-Based Patient Education*. Poster. *13th Annual Conference of RIMS*, Leuven, May 2008.

Köpke, S., Richter, T., Kasper, J., *et al.* (2006). Schubtherapie der MS [MS relapse therapy]. Available at http://www.download.ms-netz-hamburg.de/download.php?downloadfile=Schubtherapie_der_MultiplenSklerose.pdf. Accessed on 23 May 2008.

Köpke, S., Heesen, C., Kasper, J., *et al.* (2004). Steroid treatment for relapses in multiple sclerosis – the evidence urges shared decision-making. *Acta. Neurol. Scand.*, **110**, 1–5.

Prunty, M., Sharpe, L., Butow, P., *et al.* (2008). The motherhood choice: A decision aid for women with multiple sclerosis. *Patient Education & Counseling*, **71**, 108–115.

Ramsaransing, G., and De Keyser, J. (2006). Benign course in multiple sclerosis: A review. *Acta Neurologica Scandinavica*, **113**, 359–369.

Solari, A., Giordano, A., Mattarozzi, K., *et al.* (2007). Do people with multiple sclerosis want to participate in medical decisions? *Multiple Sclerosis*, **13**, S88.

Steckelberg, A., Berger, B., Köpke, S., *et al.* (2005). Kriterien für evidenzbasierte Patienteninformationen [Criteria for evidence-based patient information]. *Z. Arztl. Fortbild. Qualitatssich.*, **99**, 343–351.

The National Collaborating Centre for Chronic Conditions (NCC-CC) (2004). Multiple Sclerosis. National clinical guideline for diagnosis and management in primary and secondary care. Royal College of Physicians. Available at http://www.rcplondon.ac.uk/pubs/books/MS/MSfulldocument.pdf. Accessed on 23 May 2008.

University College (UCLH) NHS Trust *et al.* (2006).Available at. http://www.msdecisions.org.uk Accessed on 23 May 2008.

Whiting, P., Harbord, R., Main, C., *et al.* (2006). Accuracy of magnetic resonance imaging for the diagnosis of multiple sclerosis: Systematic review. *British Medical Journal*, **332**, 875–884.

Chapter 37

Decision aids and shared decision-making in inflammatory bowel disease

Anne Kennedy

Inflammatory bowel disease and consumer involvement in decision-making

Crohn's disease and ulcerative colitis are inflammatory bowel diseases (IBD) that affect about 240,000 people in the United Kingdom (Carter *et al.*, 2004). The cause is unknown and current medical treatment is to ameliorate rather than cure. Many patients take long-term drug treatment to control their condition, but surgery is sometimes an option when such treatment becomes ineffective. Symptoms include bloody diarrhoea, abdominal pain, and weight loss, and often follow a relapsing course with periods of remission. Management guidelines (Carter *et al.*, 2004; Wexner *et al.*, 1997) state that patients should be provided with information on treatment options and choice, with recognition of the patient's perspective, experience, and expectations. In this chapter, I will look at how this can be achieved.

Whilst there is currently limited empirical evidence of improved clinical outcomes, better shared decision-making in IBD consultations should result in patients and clinicians:

- Having a better understanding of the risks and benefits of the various treatment options.
- Feeling able to voice concerns and come to terms with uncertainties.
- Reaching concordance about drug regimes, resulting in better adherence to treatment.
- Clarifying when to initiate self-treatment for relapses.
- Making more timely and considered decisions on the need for surgery.
- Moving beyond a focus on medical treatment to incorporate lifestyle issues in management plans.

IBD is a condition where there are many treatment options and where even the most effective drugs only work for a minority of patients (Travis 2006; Westwood and Travis 2008). Most treatment decisions are reached through a process of trial and error as it does not seem possible to predict which patients will respond well to a particular drug treatment. However, research has shown that 'guided self-management' of ulcerative colitis accelerates treatment provision and reduces doctor visits, and does not increase morbidity (Robinson et al., 2001). There is growing evidence that involving patients in making informed decisions about management has positive, beneficial outcomes for the individual and the health service (Kennedy et al., 2004; Richardson et al., 2006).

Another factor driving the need to involve patients in decisions about treatments is the low adherence to medication regimens in IBD; it is possible that more than 40% of patients do not follow the treatment recommendations of their doctor (Robinson, 2008; Kane *et al.*, 2008). Low adherence may result in increased risks of flare ups and hospital admissions. Research on medication beliefs and non-adherence has shown that patients' attitudes may be medication specific (e.g. often relating to concerns about steroids) and may change over time as people gain more experience in managing their IBD (Hall *et al.*, 2007). Patients seek permission from practitioners to self-treat – but often do this from a low information base.

Table 37.1 outlines the domains where involvement in decision-making is relevant for patients with IBD.

Available decision aids

A search through the literature provides few examples of decision aids being used with IBD patients. There are no examples of computerized decision aids but there are reports which indicate that preliminary work is being undertaken in the USA, Australia, and France on patient preferences linked to risks and benefits of treatment which could lead to their development (Byrne *et al.*, 2007; Jaisson-Hot *et al.*, 2004; Johnson *et al.*, 2007; Siegel, 2008). There is a growing body of work from the USA and UK looking at how decision-making in IBD is linked to patients' health beliefs and which aims to find the best way to frame messages to increase adherence to medication (Goldring *et al.*, 2002; Hall *et al.*, 2007).

Work has been done in the United Kingdom on how preferences and choice can be incorporated into written information (Kennedy *et al.*, 2004; Kennedy and Robinson, 2000, 2006; Kennedy and Rogers, 2002; Rogers *et al.*, 2005). The approach taken by the Manchester team,

Table 37.1 Areas of relevance for shared decision-making in IBD

Decision-making domain	Examples of choices for patients
1. Choice of drug treatment	
a. '5-ASA' drugs for maintenance therapy	Range of drugs available with different properties and methods of delivery. Feedback from patient required to determine what works best.
b. Use of steroids for flare ups	Balance benefits and risks of short-term gain in symptom relief versus long-term side-effects.
c. Use of immuno-suppressants and biologics	Treatment decision requires knowledge of likely benefits of treatment in achieving remission versus serious adverse risks.
d. Treatment with topical drugs (suppositories, liquid enemas or foam enemas)	1. Treatment decision regarding preferred mode of delivery (topical versus oral medication) 2. Decision about which preparation is easiest to tolerate and retain
2. When to initiate self-treatment for a relapse	Decision based on patient's experience and recognition of symptoms which indicate a flare up.
3. When to have surgery	Decision based on severity of symptoms and response to medical treatment and on the surgical options available.
4. Medication during pregnancy	Decision based on risk to foetus of uncontrolled IBD versus risk to foetus of toxic effects of medication.
5. Regular surveillance for colon cancer by biopsy and colonoscopy	Balance of risks and benefits of early detection of cancer versus risks and discomfort of colonoscopy.
6. Nutritional therapy in Crohn's disease	Balance the risks and benefits of using nutritional therapy versus steroids or surgery.

of which I am a member, is to integrate the decision-making with a whole systems approach (Kennedy *et al.*, 2007) termed 'WISE' (Whole systems informing self-management engagement; http://www.npcrdc.ac.uk/WISEApproachSelf-management.cfm). In this approach, patients and clinicians are engaged in a shared approach to self-management within a supportive health service context (see Figure 37.1). Clinicians were successfully trained in the WISE intervention to adopt patient-centred approaches to supporting self-management of IBD (Kennedy *et al.*, 2005), and patients were provided with information designed to promote patient choice (for example Figure 37.2).

Evidence of implementation, effectiveness, and cost-effectiveness

So far, the evidence for including patient preferences in decisions about treatment comes mainly from a series of three randomized controlled trials of the WISE approach in IBD. The first trial focused on the guided self-management plan and patient directed follow-up (Robinson *et al.*, 2001). The second trial focused on the use and effect of the patient guidebook (Kennedy *et al.*, 2003). The third trial was a pragmatic evaluation of the complete WISE approach (clinician training plus patient guidebooks plus open access to clinics) (Kennedy *et al.*, 2004). The latter – pragmatic – trial was designed to assess whether the WISE approach could alter clinical outcome and affect health service use. Results showed that 1 year after the intervention, self-managing patients had made fewer hospital visits (difference 21.04 (95% confidence interval (CI) 21.43–20.65); $p < 0.001$) without an increase in the number of primary care visits; quality of life was maintained without evidence of anxiety about the program. The two groups were similar with respect to satisfaction with consultations. Immediately after the initial consultation, those in the intervention group reported greater confidence in being able to cope with their condition (difference 0.90 (95% CI 0.12–1.68); $p = 0.03$).

A cost-effectiveness analysis showed the WISE method was likely to reduce health care costs without adversely affecting patient outcomes (Richardson *et al.*, 2006). Qualitative research (Rogers *et al.*, 2005) demonstrated limitations to the approach since even in the context of an intervention designed to promote shared decision-making in a patient-centred way, patients found it hard to bring their voice into decisions about treatment. Medical treatment decisions were generally made by the consultants – who had core beliefs that patients need guidance on medical treatment. This meant that rather than mutual shared decision-making, doctors

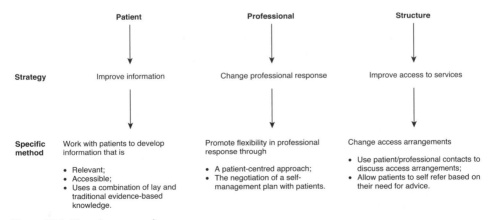

Figure 37.1 The wise approach.

Surgery for ulcerative colitis

The symptoms of ulcerative colitis can totally ruin your life. You can become dominated by frequent and urgent trips to the toilet.

You may be worried about the long-term effects of steroids.

You may be fed up with having to go to hospital or to see your doctor so often.

At this point it will be worth thinking about surgery. Removing your colon will cure your ulcerative colitis and you may be able to reduce or stop your medication.

Your choice

You may decide that surgery is best for you because:

● it will cure your ulcerative colitis;

● you have symptoms which have gone on for a long time and ruin your life;

● you have severe extra-intestinal manifestations; or

● you have a risk of cancer of the colon.

You can always refuse to have surgery even when your doctor strongly advises it, but it is worth talking to someone who has had surgery. Many people say they wish they had had surgery much earlier because they now feel so much better.

Surgery means removing you colon, so the surgeon has to make a way for your faeces to leave your body. He or she can do this by:

● joining the end of your small intestine to your anus as a pouch; or

● bringing the end of the small intestine out through your abdomen to form a stoma.

52

Most people now have pouch surgery. This is where a part of your small intestine is made into a pouch which acts like a rectum to store your faeces until it is convenient for you to go to the toilet.

You will need to find out as much as you can about the different operations you could have. You might not be able to have operations to make a pouch if you have problems with anal disease, or if the muscles around your anus do not work very well.

Ask your surgeon as many questions as you can about the operation.

If you are going to have an ileostomy, you will see a stoma therapist. The stoma therapist will teach you how to look after your stoma. Before your operation, he or she will help you choose the best place for your stoma, and will give you advice on how to look after you stoma.

You may decide not to have surgery because:

● all operations carry a small risk of complications; and

● there is a small risk of nerves to the bladder or sexual organs being damaged during the operation.

A quote from a patient involved in developing this guidebook:

" Taking into consideration the choice options (in this guidebook), I requested surgery, not as a last resort, but as a positive choice as the action I wished to take. That was the turning point of my life. Almost six years after the first symptoms I underwent a pan-protocolectomy and ileostomy, from which I made a rapid recovery and regained control of my life "

53

Surgery for ulcerative colitis

Figure 37.2 Example of information from WISE programm for patients considering surgery.

concentrated on using guided self-management to increase compliance and adherence. Treatment plans clarified patients' responsibilities for self-treatment and maintenance therapy, but were problematic for complex cases. Patients tended not to disclose concerns about decisions they made about day-to-day self-care activities that might allow them to lead as normal life as possible at home and work. These limitations are being addressed as the WISE approach that evolves in response to research findings (Kennedy *et al.*, 2007).

Implementation of decision support in IBD

The growing recognition amongst gastroenterologists that patient preferences should guide treatment decisions is hampered by the lack of resources available to help physicians include patients in decision-making. Currently, clinicians rely largely on their own knowledge and experience when making decisions (Carter *et al.*, 2004; Marshall and Irvine, 2000). However, there is evidence that patients' preferences between surgical and medical treatments differ from those of clinicians (Byrne *et al.*, 2007). Furthermore, patients with IBD have well-defined treatment preferences and appear willing to accept higher risks of serious adverse events in exchange for improved control of their condition (Johnson *et al.*, 2007). Further studies, though, suggest that patients may often overestimate the benefits of treatments for IBD and underestimate risks (Siegel, 2008). Computerized decision tools have the potential to help in this situation – meeting requirements to portray the options, identify the risks and benefits for each of these, and engage users in exploring their preferences, in the context also of clinician opinions about how to manage their condition. Currently however, such decision support remains only rudimentary and with limited availability to patients and clinicians, so investment and further development are urgently required.

Will decision aids keep up to date with therapeutic or evidence advances in this field?

Once such decision support tools are available, they will need continued attention to maintain their currency and relevance to clinical practice. Therapeutic advances in IBD tend to be in the development and refinement of drugs and surgical techniques. The shared-decision domains as outlined in Table 37.1 are unlikely to change much in the future, but information sources developed to aid shared decision-making will need to be regularly updated to include new drugs licensed for treatment and the most up-to-date evidence about the risks and benefits of different options for treatment or care. Clearly, both development and maintenance of decision support for IBD require investment of time, resources, and evaluation to realize the full potential of involving patients in the management of IBD.

The WISE program showed that patients can successfully be involved in decision-making and encouraged to self-manage their conditions with appropriate health care support when required. This requires service re-arrangement and re-design, along with training of clinicians to facilitate patient involvement and autonomy in dealing with their condition with confidence. There remains scope and opportunity, however, to develop and enhance the information and decision support materials that patients require to do this effectively. Computerized decision support, with the interactive opportunities this affords, may be particularly appropriate in this setting, and a valuable area to focus further efforts to improve care and quality-of-life for the many patients affected by IBD.

References

Byrne, C.M., Solomon, M.J., Young, J.M., *et al.* (2007). Patient preferences between surgical and medical treatment in Crohn's disease. *Diseases of the Colon & Rectum*, **50**, 586–597.

Carter, M.J., Lobo, A.J., and Travis, S.P.L. (2004). Guidelines for the management of inflammatory bowel disease in adults. *Gut*, **53**, v1–v16.

Goldring, A.B., Taylor, S.E., Kemeny, M.E., *et al.* (2002). Impact of health beliefs, quality of life, and the physician–patient relationship on the treatment intentions of inflammatory bowel disease patients. *Health Psychology*, **21**, 219–228.

Hall, N.J., Rubin, G.P., Hungin, A.P., *et al.* (2007). Medication beliefs among patients with inflammatory bowel disease who report low quality of life: A qualitative study. *BMC Gastroenterol.*, **7**, 20.

Jaisson-Hot, I., Flourie, B., Descos, L., *et al.* (2004). Management for severe Crohn's disease: A lifetime cost-utility analysis. *International Journal of Technology Assessment in Health Care*, **20**, 274–279.

Johnson, F.R., Ozdemir, S., Mansfield, C., *et al.* (2007). Crohn's disease patients' risk-benefit preferences: Serious adverse event risks versus treatment efficacy. *Gastroenterology*, **133**, 769–779.

Kane, S.V., Brixner, D., Rubin, D.T., *et al.* (2008). The challenge of compliance and persistence: Focus on ulcerative colitis. *Journal of Managed Care Pharmacy*, **14**, S2–S12.

Kennedy, A., Gask, L., and Rogers, A. (2005). Training professionals to engage with and promote self-management. *Health Education Research.*, **20**, 567–578.

Kennedy, A.P., Nelson, E., Reeves, D., *et al.* (2004). A randomised controlled trial to assess effectiveness and cost of a patient orientated self-management approach to chronic inflammatory bowel disease. *Gut*, **53**, 1639–1645.

Kennedy, A. P. and Robinson, A. (2000). *A Handy Guide to Managing Crohn's Disease.* Southampton: RTFB Publishing Ltd.

Kennedy, A. P. and Robinson, A. (2006). *A Handy Guide to Managing Ulcerative Colitis.* (3rd edition), Southampton: RTFB Publishing Ltd.

Kennedy, A.P., Robinson, A., Hann, M., *et al.* (2003). A cluster-randomised controlled trial of a patient-centred guidebook for patients with ulcerative colitis: Effect on knowledge, anxiety and quality of life. *Health and Social Care in the Community,* **11**, 64–72.

Kennedy, A.P. and Rogers, A. (2002). Improving patient involvement in chronic disease management: The views of patients, GPs and specialists on a guidebook for ulcerative colitis. *Patient Education and Counseling,* **47**, 257–263.

Kennedy, A., Rogers, A., and Bower, P. (2007). Support for self care for patients with chronic disease. *British Medical Journal,* **335**, 968–970.

Marshall, J.K. and Irvine, E.J. (2000). Putting rectal 5-aminosalicylic acid in its place: The role in distal ulcerative colitis. *The American Journal of Gastroenterology,* **95**, 1628–1636.

Richardson, G., Sculpher, M., Kennedy, A., *et al.* (2006). Is self-care a cost-effective use of resources? Evidence from a randomised trial in inflammatory bowel disease. *Journal of Health Service Research Policy,* **11**, 225–230.

Robinson, A., Wilkin, D., Thompson, D.G., *et al.* (2001). Guided self-management and patient-directed follow-up of ulcerative colitis: A randomised trial. *Lancet,* **358**, 976–981.

Robinson, A. (2008). Review article: Improving adherence to medication in patients with inflammatory bowel disease. *Alimentary Pharmacology & Therapeutics,* **27**, 9–14.

Rogers, A., Kennedy, A., Nelson, E., *et al.* (2005). Uncovering the limits of patient centredness: A qualitative investigation of implementing a self-management trial for chronic illness. *Qualitative Health Research,* **15**, 224–239.

Siegel, C.A.M. (2008). Patient perceptions of the risks and benefits of infliximab for the treatment of inflammatory bowel disease.(Article). *Inflammatory Bowel Diseases,* **14**, 1–6.

Travis, S.P.L. (2006). New thinking: Theory vs. practice. A case study illustrating evidence-based therapeutic decision making. *Colorectal Disease,* **8**, 25–29.

Westwood, N. and Travis, S.P.L. (2008). Review article: What do patients with inflammatory bowel disease want for their clinical management? *Alimentary Pharmacology & Therapeutics,* **27**, 1–8.

Wexner, S.D., Rosen, L., Lowry, A., *et al.* (1997). Practice parameters for the treatment of mucosal ulcerative colitis – supporting documentation. The standards practice task force. The American Society of Colon and Rectal Surgeons. *Diseases of the Colon and Rectum,* **40**, 1277–1285.

Chapter 38

Shared decision-making in mental health

Daniela Simon, Celia E. Wills, and Martin Härter

The importance of shared decision-making in mental health

Shared decision-making (SDM) was originally described as an approach for physician-patient communication in the context of health decisions for which several treatment options exist (Charles *et al.*, 1997). Positive outcomes of SDM including increased patient knowledge, satisfaction, and treatment adherence have been reported for various "physical" health conditions, but less research has been done on SDM for mental health conditions. Research on SDM in mental health care is a high priority for quality-of-life, autonomy, and health outcomes reasons (Wills and Holmes-Rovner 2006b), and results of early studies are favourable regarding the potential of SDM to improve mental health care (Loh *et al.*, 2007; Swanson *et al.*, 2007). SDM is highly relevant in mental health care due to the presence of multiple treatment decision options and the preferences of many consumers to participate in decision-making (Hamann *et al.*, 2005). With its focus on mutual information sharing and respect for individual preferences, SDM can be an empowerng experience, assisting mental health recovery for people who have encountered stigmatization and discrimination due to mental illness (Pinninti and Bokkala-Pinninti, 2007). In the US, the incorporation of mental health consumer preferences into person-centered treatment focused on recovery is supported by the President's New Freedom Commission Report (Hogan, 2003). Consumer participation in decision-making is also advocated by international clinical practice guidelines for mental disorders, e.g. in the UK and Germany, as well as training manuals (Härter *et al.*, 2007, Härter *et al.*, 2008, NICE 2002; Lehman *et al.*, 2004). Individual values, explicit negotiation, empowerment, and self-determination are essential values for the treatment of people with mental illness and have been in the focus of psychiatric rehabilitation for decades (Anthony, Cohen and Pierce 1980; Anthony, Cohen and Farkas 1999; Deegan and Drake 2006; Lazare, Eisenthal and Wasserman 1975). SDM is also consistent with a fundamental assumption that rehabilitation is done *with* the person and not *to* the person (Schauer, Everett and del Vecchio, 2007).

Despite the apparent opportunity for SDM in mental health, there is controversy about capacity for consumer participation in decision-making (Forrest, 2004). Practitioners have expressed scepticism about ability to participate due to cognitive deficits (Angel, 1984; Auerbach 2000). Involuntary mental health treatment is contrary to an autonomy assumption in SDM (Vollmann *et al.*, 2003; Swartz *et al.*, 2003). However, the stereotype of impaired decision-making capacity is inconsistent with evidence, as consumers have been reported to be interested in and capable of participating in decision-making in most situations (Carpenter *et al.*, 2000; Grisso and Appelbaum, 1995; Hamann *et al.*, 2007a; Loh *et al.*, 2004). Advance crisis planning and psychiatric advance directives can be helpful in situations where decision-making capacity is truly impaired (Deegan and Drake, 2006). Nevertheless the practice of SDM in these situations could still be useful o build a therapeutic alliance with individuals who do not acknowledge their condition or refuse treatment (Adams and Drake, 2006), and is consistent with person-centeredness and recovery goals. Although some aspects of SDM are incorporated in usual mental health care, explicit research on SDM for patients with mental illness is just beginning (Adams *et al.*, 2007), and little is known about SDM in mental health compared to the current state of research in other medical fields (Adams and Drake, 2006).

Approaches to shared decision-making in mental health

Studies on SDM in mental health have focused primarily on schizophrenia and depression, and have examined consumers' preferences, experiences with decision-making, and effects of specific SDM interventions (Table 38.1). Overall these studies show that there is generally strong interest in information and involvement among mental health consumers, while at the same time there are unmet information, decision support, and involvement needs. Hamann *et al.*, (2007) reported that mental health patients' preferences for participation do not differ considerably from patients' preferences in somatic conditions. A study in a community mental health centre showed that 39% of the consumers preferred a more active role than they experieinced and were less likely to prefer a passive role in psychiatric medication decisions than in general medical decisions (23% vs. 76%; Adams *et al.*, 2007). In a study of primary care patients with depression, Loh *et al.*, (2004) found a high preference for information, regardless of depression symptom severity. Bunn *et al.*, (1997) reported that people with schizophrenia who were uncertain about continuing medication treatment had higher decisional conflict and lower decision self-efficacy and indicated lower expectations of benefits and higher expectations of side effects if treatment continued. A survey of over 2,000 mental health patients in the UK reported that 75% of health care providers discuss medication with patients, but almost two thirds of the patients indicated no involvement in decision-making (Corry, 2001). Simon *et al.*, (2007a) investigated depressed patients' perceptions of past treatment decision-making and found that a lack of acknowledgement of depression severity substantially delayed patient engagement in treatment seeking and decision-making. Patients also expressed serious concerns about certain aspects of depression treatment such as stigmatization. Stacey *et al.*, (2008) explored the decision-making needs of depressed patients considering treatment options and found that 2/3 of the patients were uncertain about their decision. These patients also felt less informed, less supported and less clear about how they valued the benefits and risks of options. Patients who did feel more certain were more likely to have made a decision.

Hamann *et al.*, (2008) reported that the most frequently cited decisions by patients with schizophrenia and physicians were about medication and leave from hospital. Patients reported involvement for 70% of these decisions, whereas psychiatrists indicated involvement in 83% of the situations. Patients who did not feel involved reported significantly more often that they would have decided differently. Clever and colleagues (2006) found an association between involvement of primary care patients with depression and a greater likelihood of guideline-concordant care and clinically significant improvement in depression over time. Loh *et al.*, (2007a) studied the impact of patient participation on adherence and clinical outcome in primary care of depression and found that participation predicted adherence but did not directly affect clinical outcome. Furthermore, Loh *et al.*, (2006) conducted more specific analyses of patient involvement in primary care of depression with an observational instrument (OPTION-Scale), and found very low scores of involvement. A recent study by Young *et al.*, (2008) investigated interactions between physicians and standardized patients in depression care, also finding low levels of involvement on the OPTION Scale. Longer visit duration was associated with greater involvement and older physicians performed fewer SDM behaviours. In addition physicians showed more SDM behaviour with standardized patients who made medication requests (Young *et al.*, 2008).

Table 38.1 Studies on shared decision-making in mental health

Authors	Sample	Condition	Intervention	Outcomes	Results
Adams et al. (2007)	N=30	Severe mental illness	—	Preference for participation in decision-making	39% preferred a more active role than they experienced and were less likely to prefer a passive role in psychiatric medication decisions than in general medical decisions (23% vs. 76%)
Bunn et al. (1997)	N = 94	Schizophrenia	—	Uncertainty with regard to treatment options Decisional conflict Decision self-efficacy	Uncertain clients had higher decisional conflict and less decision self-efficacy as well as lower expectations of benefits and higher expectations of side-effects if treatment continued
Clever et al. (2006)	N = 1706	Depression (primary care)	Training in guideline concordant care	Guideline concordant care Patient involvement	Association between patient involvement and greater likelihood of guideline-concordant care and clinically significant improvement in depression over time
Corry et al. (2001)	N = 2222	Schizophrenia, Depression	—	Information about medicine, involvement in decision about medicine	◆ 75% of health care providers discuss medication with patients ◆ 2/3 of the patients report no involvement in decisions about medication
Hamann et al. (2007)	N = 1393	Depression, schizophrenia, hypertension, breast cancer, multiple sclerosis, minor traumas	—	Preference for participation in decision-making	No differences between mental health and somatic patients were found.
Hamann et al. (2006)[1]	N = 107	Schizophrenia (inpatient)	Decision aid, planning talk	Knowledge Patient involvement	◆ Increased knowledge and higher perceived involvement for most patients ◆ SDM feasible for most patients ◆ No increase in consultation time

(continued)

Table 38.1 (continued) Studies on shared decision-making in mental health

Authors	Sample	Condition	Intervention	Outcomes	Results
Hamann et al. (2007)[1]	N = 107	Schizophrenia (inpatient)	Decision aid, planning talk	Rehospitalization Medication Compliance	◆ No clear beneficial effect on long-term-outcomes ◆ Positive trend towards fewew hospitalizations in intervention group
Hamann et al. (2008)[1]	N = 60 N = 30	Schizophrenia (inpatient) psychiatrists	—	Clinical decisions	Most frequent decisions: medication and leave from hospital (70% of patients report involvement vs. 83% of psychiatrists) Patients, who did not feel involved reported significantly more often that they would have decided differently
Katon et al. (1999)	N = 228	Depression (primary care)	Enhanced education Increased frequency of physician visits to improve pharmacologic treatment	Medication adherence Satisfaction with care Depression severity	Significant improvements in medication adherence, satisfaction with care and depression outcome for patients in the intervention group
Loh et al. (2004)[2]	N = 405	Depression (primary care)	—	Preferences for information and participation	Patients indicate a high information preference regardless of symptom severity and a lower participation preference
Loh et al. (2006)[2]	N = 405	Depression (primary care)	—	Observed patient involvement	Very low levels of patient involvement
Loh et al. (2007a)[2]	N = 405	Depression (primary care)	—	Involvement, treatment adherence, clinical outcome	◆ Participation predicted adherence ◆ Effect of adherence on clinical outcome
Loh et al. (2007b)[2]	N = 405	Depression (primary care)	SDM training for physicians Decision board	Patient involvement Patient satisfaction Depression severity	◆ Higher level of patient involvement ◆ Higher patient satisfaction with treatment ◆ No effect depression severity ◆ No difference in consultation time

Simon et al. (2007a)	N=40	Depression	—	Perceptions of previous treatment decision-making	◆ Lack of perception of depression severity delayed patient engagement in treatment seeking and decision-making. ◆ Patients mentioned serious concerns about certain aspects of depression treatment such as stigmatization.
Simon et al. (2007b)	n.a. yet	Depression	Web-based interactive decision aid	Decisional conflict, knowledge, preparation for decision-making	Results of RCT not yet available
Stacey et al. (2008)	N = 94	Depression	—	Needs for treatment decision-making	◆ 2/3 of the patients uncertain about decision ◆ Uncertain patients felt less informed, less supported and less clear about how they valued benefits and risks of options ◆ Patients feeling certain were more likely to have made a decision.
Young et al. (2008)	N = 287	Depression	—	Observed patient involvement	◆ Very low level of patient involvement ◆ Older physicians performed less patient involvement ◆ Physicians enacted more patient involvement when standardized patients made medication requests

1 These publications by Hamann et al. are based on the same study
2 These publications by Loh et al. are based on the same study

Intervention studies have incorporated SDM on different levels. The results of these early studies support the positive impact of SDM, including increased knowledge, satisfaction, decision-making involvement, social functioning, and reduced psychological distress. A randomized controlled trial comparing a SDM program (decision aid, training of physicians and nurses) with routine care of schizophrenic in-patients showed increased knowledge and higher perceived involvement. SDM did not increase physician time workload (Hamann et al., 2006). Effects on long-term-outcomes could not be found, but higher participation preferences and better knowledge significantly predicted hospitalization and the intervention showed a positive trend towards fewer hospitalizations (Hamann et al., 2007). In a randomized controlled trial comparing physician training and a decision aid to usual care in primary care of depression, physicians' facilitation of patient participation improved significantly, but no intervention effect could be found for depression severity reduction. Patient satisfaction at post-intervention was higher in the intervention group. The consultation time did not differ between groups (Loh et al., 2007). The studies of Loh et al., (2007) and Hamann et al., (2006, 2007) were both embedded in a larger research consortium on SDM in ten different conditions funded by the German Ministry of Health. Katon et al., (1999) have included SDM to enhance patient involvement in stepped collaborative care interventions for depression. Because of the use of a multi-faceted intervention, the positive outcomes cannot be attributed solely to SDM.

Recently the authors of this chapter have been involved in two projects on decision support in depression. Wills et al., (2006a) have developed a patient-centered decision support intervention for depression in people with diabetes. Results of short-term pilot-testing ($N = 32$; 4–6 week follow-up period) showed increases in knowledge, decision stage, and activation of decision-making. In addition, among those making a depression-related decision at any point in the study, there was a significant reduction in numbers of depressive symptoms and stress severity, with a trend for reduced depressive symptom severity. Those who made decisions were on average satisfied with their decisions. Simon et al., (2007b) developed a web-based individually-tailored patient information system on depression to support patient involvement in the consultation. It has been evaluated in comparison to a static web-based patient information system within a randomized controlled trial on a sample of 273 patients. First results show a high acceptability and general satisfaction with the interactive system.

Conclusions and future agendas

Compared to other fields in health care, less is known about SDM in mental health. There has been an increasing number of studies in recent years that focus on people with depression and schizophrenia. These studies show that mental health consumers are generally interested in information and participation in decision-making, and often desire more participation compared to what has been experienced. Positive impact of SDM has been shown for improved treatment adherence, satisfaction, knowledge, involvement in decision-making, activation of decision-making, reduced numbers of depressive symptoms and stress, social functioning, and a trend for reduced hospitalization.

Based on these positive outcomes, more research is needed to identify decision-making variables which play a central role in mental health. In addition, specific adaptations of SDM for mental health decision-making situations need to be further investigated. The need for more mental health specific research on SDM also requires attention to valid and reliable assessment instruments that are sensitive to the special requirements of the mental health context (Wills and Holmes-Rovner 2006; Hamann et al., 2007). As many instruments for the measurement of SDM have not yet been validated in mental health (Wills and Holmes-Rovner 2003; Simon et al., 2007c), validation studies and potential adaptations are required in order to precisely investigate effects of SDM in mental health.

In order to enhance SDM in routine mental health care, specific decision aids suitable for use by mental health consumers, feasible curricula for training health care professionals in SDM, and SDM training programs for consumers need to be developed and broadly implemented (Adams *et al.*, 2006; Hamann *et al.*, 2007). These interventions should focus on the elicitation of consumers' preferences and on achieving optimum matches between preferences and decisions, as this has been shown to be an essential factor for concordance with decisions and longer-term treatment adherence (Hamann *et al.*, 2007b). If results of future studies further support the need and importance of SDM in mental health, this could not only contribute to the improvement of mental health care, but could also support the destigmatization of mental health issues.

References

Adams, J.R. and Drake, R.E., (2006). Shared Decision-Making and Evidence-Based Practice. *Community Mental Health Journal*, **42**, 87–105.

Adams, J.R., Drake, R.E., and Wolford, G.L. (2007). Shared Decision-Making Preferences of People With Severe Mental Illness. *Psychiatric Services*, **58**, 1219–1221.

Angel, M. (1984). Respecting the autonomy of competent patients. *New England Journal of Medicine*, **310**, 1115–1116.

Anthony, W.A., Cohen, M.R., and Pierce, R.M., (1980). Instructors' guide to the psychiatric rehabilitation practice series. Baltimore: University Park Press.

Anthony, W.A., Cohen, M., and Farkas, M., (1999). The future of psychiatric rehabilitation. *International Journal of Mental Health*, **28**, 48–68.

Auerbach, S.M. (2000). Should patients have control over their own health care?: Empirical evidence and research issues. *Annals of Behavioral Medicine*, **22**, 246–259.

Bunn, M.H., O'Connor, A.M., Tansey, M.S., Jones, B.D., and Stinson, L.E. (1997). Characteristics of clients with schizophrenia who express certainty or uncertainty about continuing treatment with depot neuroleptic medication. *Archives of Psychiatric Nursing*, **11**, 238–248.

Carpenter, W.T. Jr., Gold, J.M., Lahti, A.C., *et al.* (2000). Decisional capacity for informed consent in schizophrenia research. *Archives of General Psychiatry*, **57**, 533–538.

Clever, S.L., Ford, D.E., Rubenstein, L.V., *et al.* (2006). Primary care patients' involvement in decision-making is associated with improvement in depression. *Medical Care*, **44**, 398–405.

Corry, P., Hogman, G., and Sandamas, G. (2001). That's just typical. (National Schizophrenia Fellowship, London)

Deegan, P.E. and Drake, R.E. (2006). Shared decision making and medication management in the recovery process. *Psychiatric Services*, **57**, 1636–1639.

Forrest, E. (2004). Mental health. The right to choose. *Health Services Journal*, **114**, 24–26.

Grisso, T. and Appelbaum, P.S. (1995). The MacArthur treatment competence study. III: Abilities of patients to consent to psychiatric and medical treatments. *Law and Human Behavior*, **19**, 149–174.

Härter, M., Bermejo, I., and Niebling, W. (2007). Praxismanual Depression – Diagnostik und Therapie erfolgreich umsetzen. (Köln: Deutscher Ärzte-Verlag)

Härter, M., Klesse, C., *Bermejo, I., et al. (2008)*. Development of national guidelines for depression. *Bundesgesundheitsbl - Gesundheitsforsch – Gesundheitsschutz*, **51**, 451–457.

Hamann, J., Cohen, R., Leucht, S., Busch, R., and Kissling, W. (2005). Do patients with schizophrenia wish to be involved in decisions about their medical treatment? *American Journal of Psychiatry*, **162**, 2382–2384.

Hamann, J., Langer, B., Winkler, V., *et al.* (2006). Shared decision making for in-patients with schizophrenia. *Acta Psychiatrica Scandinavica*, **114**, 265–273.

Hamann, J., Neuner, B., Kasper, J., *et al.* (2007a). Participation preferences of patients with acute and chronic conditions. *Health Expectations*, **10**, 358–363.

Hamann, J., Cohen, R., Leucht, S., Busch, R., and Kissling, W. (2007b). Shared decision making and long-term outcome in schizophrenia treatment. *Journal of Clinical Psychiatry*, **68**, 992–997.

Hamann, J., Mendel, R.T., Fink, B., Pfeiffer, H., Cohen, R., and Kissling, W. (2008). Patients' and psychiatrists' perceptions of clinical decisions during schizophrenia treatment. *Journal of Nervous and Mental Disease*, **196**, 329–332.

Hogan, M.F. (2003). The President's New Freedom Commission: recommendations to transform mental health care in America. *Psychiatric Services*, **54**, 1467–1474.

Katon, W.J., von Korff, M., Lin, E., *et al.* (1999). Stepped collaborative care for primary care patients with persistent symptoms of depression: A randomized trial. *Archives of General Psychiatry*, **56**, 1109–15.

Lazare, A., Eisenthal, S., and Wasserman, L. (1975). The customer approach to patienthood. Attending to patient requests in a walk-in clinic. *Archives of General Psychiatry*, **32**, 553–558.

Loh, A., Kremer, N., Giersdorf, N., *et al.* (2004). Information and participation interests of patients with depression in clinical decision making in primary care. *Zeitschrift für ärztliche Fortbildung und Qualitatssicherung*, **98**, 101–107.

Loh, A., Simon, D., Hennig, K., Hennig, B., Härter, M., and Elwyn, G. (2006). The assessment of depressive patients' involvement in decision making in audio-taped primary care consultations. *Patient Education and Counseling*, **63**, 314–18.

Loh, A., Leonhart, R., Wills, C.E., Simon, D., and Härter, M. (2007a). The impact of patient participation on adherence and clinical outcome in primary care of depression. *Patient Education and Counseling*, **65**, 69–78.

Loh, A., Simon, D., Wills, C.E., Kriston, L., Niebling, W., and Härter, M. (2007b).The effects of a shared decision-making intervention in primary care of depression: a cluster-randomized controlled trial. *Patient Education and Counseling*, **67**, 324–32.

Pinninti, N.R. and Bokkala-Pinninti, S. (2007). Shared decision making and humanistic care. *Psychiatric Services*, **58**, 414–415.

Schauer, C., Everett, A., del Vecchio, P., and Anderson, L. (2007). Promoting the value and practice of shared decision-making in mental health care. *Psychiatric Rehabilitation Journal*, **31**, 54–61.

Simon, D., Loh, A., Wills, C.E., and Härter, M. (2007a). Depressed patients' perceptions of depression treatment decision-making. *Health Expectations*, **10**, 62–74.

Simon, D., Vietor, C. Loh, A., Hecke, T., and Härter, M. (2007b). Development and evaluation of a web-based interactive information system for low back pain and depression. In: Härter, Simon, Loh: *International Shared Decision Making Conference 2007.* Pabst Science Publishers, Lengerich: Germany.

Simon, D. Loh, A., and Härter, M. (2007c). Measuring (shared) decision-making – a review of psychometric instruments. *Z Arztl Fortbild Qualitatssich*, **10**, 259–267.

Stacey, D., Menard, P., Gaboury, I., *et al.* (2008). Decision-making needs of patients with depression: a descriptive study. *Journal of Psychiatric and Mental Health Nursing*, **15**, 287–295.

Swanson, K.A., Bastani, R., Rubenstein, L.V., Meredith, L.S., and Ford, D.E. (2007). Effect of mental health care and shared decision making on patient satisfaction in a community sample of patients with depression. *Medical Care Research and Review*, **64**, 416–430.

Swartz, M.S., Swanson, J.W., Wagner, H.R., Hannon, M.J., Burns, B.J., and Vollmann, J., Bauer, A., Danker-Hopfe, H. and Helmchen, H. (2003). Competence of mentally ill patients: A comparative empirical study. *Psychological Medicine*, **33**, 1463–1471.

Wills, C.E. and Holmes-Rovner, M. (2003). Preliminary validation of the Satisfaction With Decision scale with depressed primary care patients. *Health Expectations*, **6**, 149–159.

Wills, C.E. (2006a). *Feasibility and outcomes testing of a patient-centered decision support intervention for depression in people with diabetes.* (Lansing, MI: Michigan Department of Community Health, Division of Chronic Diseases. MDCH contract #20063027.)

Wills, C.E. and Holmes-Rovner, M. (2006b). Integrating Decision Making and Mental Health Interventions Research: Research Directions. *Clinical Psychology*, **13**, 9–25.

Young, H.N., Bell, R.A., Epstein, R.M., Feldman, M.D., and Kravitz, R.L. (2008). Physicians' shared decision-making behaviors in depression care. *Archives of Internal Medicine*, **168**, 1404–1408.

Chapter 39

Decision aids and shared decision-making in menorrhagia

Joanne Protheroe

Clinical condition

Menorrhagia or heavy menstrual bleeding is a common problem for women. In the United Kingdom, over 5% of women aged 30–49 consult their general practitioner each year with this complaint and 12% of all referrals to gynaecology outpatient departments are to investigate and treat menorrhagia (Prentice, 1999; Royal College of Obstetricians and Gynaecologists, 1998).

Historically, menorrhagia has been defined as menstrual blood loss of greater than 80 ml per period, but reality the presentation is a woman complaining that her periods are heavier than usual. The definition of menorrhagia as menstrual blood loss of over 80 ml per cycle was taken from Scandinavian population studies of menstrual blood loss, and guidelines for treatment have previously been based on this (Hallberg *et al.*, 1966). However, it is widely accepted that as well as it being impractical to measure menstrual blood loss outside research studies, there is no correlation between women's subjective assessment of their blood loss as heavy, and their actual blood loss, which is often less than 80 ml (Higham, 1999; O'Flynn and Britten, 2000). Recent UK guidance published by the National Institute for Health and Clinical Excellence (NICE: http://www.nice.org.uk/) has included a useful new definition of heavy menstrual bleeding based on the impact on quality of life rather than measured blood loss:

> 'Heavy menstrual bleeding should be defined as excessive menstrual blood loss which interferes with the woman's physical, emotional, social and material quality of life, and which can occur alone or in combination with other symptoms. Any interventions should aim to improve quality of life measures.'
> (National Collaborating Centre for Women's and Children's Health 2007)

Once history and examination have excluded other pathologies, the treatment options for menorrhagia can be broadly described as 'watchful waiting', non-hormonal and hormonal medical treatments (including the hormonal intrauterine system, 'Mirena' coil), and surgical management (including endometrial resections and hysterectomies) (Protheroe, 2004; Royal College of Obstetricians and Gynaecologists, 1998). Treatment decision-making is challenging because not even one treatment option is superior overall, all the options vary according to a trade-off between risks and benefit. Accordingly, evidence-based guidelines, including the recent NICE guidelines, for menorrhagia recommend that patient preferences must be taken into account (Royal College of Obstetricians and Gynaecologists, 1998).

It has been argued that decision support is of most value in 'preference sensitive' decisions, such as those faced by women with menorrhagia (O'Connor *et al.*, 2002). A further compelling reason for the use of decision aids in menorrhagia is that, despite the existence of best-practice guidelines, health professionals have been criticized for being dismissive of menstrual problems and not taking account of patient concerns (O'Flynn and Britten, 2000). In addition, previous research by this author has shown that women diagnosed by their general practitioner as having menorrhagia and referred to secondary care had limited and often inaccurate knowledge of treatment options available (Protheroe and Chew-Graham, 2005).

Decision aids

Despite the evident need for decision aids about menorrhagia, a review of the literature identified only three randomized trials evaluating the effectiveness of these interventions, including one by Protheroe *et al.*. The decision aids differed in complexity and included (see Table 39.1)

- information booklets;
- a video with accompanying booklet and nurse coaching; and
- interactive computerized decision aid based on decision analysis.

Evidence for implementation, effectiveness, and cost-effectiveness

Kennedy et al., 2002

This was a large trial (involving 625 women) conducted in gynaecology outpatient departments of six hospitals in the United Kingdom. The decision aid consisted of a specially designed booklet and accompanying video was sent six weeks before the patient's consultation in outpatients. These emphasized the importance of patient preference in choosing the appropriate treatment and discussed menorrhagia, its causes, and the risks and benefits of treatment options, both medical and surgical. This was compared with a group who received the same materials and also underwent an interview with a research nurse immediately before their consultation. The purpose of this interview was to help patients clarify and articulate their preferences. A third group received usual care.

Self-reported health status was the main outcome; secondary outcomes included treatments received and costs. The results of the study showed that neither intervention had a consistent effect on health status. However the 'decision aid plus interview' group had lower hysterectomy rates than the other two groups, and as a consequence lower costs of treatment (assessed at 2 years) than both the usual care group and the 'decision aid alone' group. There was no difference in hysterectomy rates between the 'decision aid alone' group and the usual care group. This reduction in rates of surgery has been shown in other studies of decision aids, particularly with the more complex decision aids (O'Connor *et al.*, 2003). An advantage of this study is that it compares both a relatively simple decision aid, the information group, with a relatively complex decision aid, the interview group in the same study.

Vuorma et al., 2004

This was a trial of a simple decision aid, an information booklet, in women with menorrhagia, in 2003. The trial was again conducted in the gynaecology outpatients, this time in 14 hospitals in Finland. The decision aid was a 25-page information booklet about heavy menstruation and its treatment options. This was posted to the intervention group at least 7 days before their outpatient appointment. The booklet contained information about menorrhagia and the treatment options including their benefits and risks. The booklet is described as encouraging women to consider different aspects of each treatment and the outcomes that they would prefer, but did not include a formal values clarification exercise, nor any guidance on making decisions. The comparison was with usual care.

Table 39.1 Trials of decision aids in menorrhagia

Study	Methods	Participants	Intervention	Outcomes	Results
Kennedy et al., 2002	Video + booklet + nurse coaching vs. video + booklet vs. usual care	215 + 206 + 204 UK women with menorrhagia at hospital outpatients	DECISION AID: video + booklet on options, outcomes, probabilities, and values clarification COACHING: 20-min coaching with nurse prior appointment with physician COMPARISON: usual care	Uptake of option; satisfaction; quality of life; menorrhagia severity; and cost-effectiveness.	No effect on health status Decision aid + coaching – lower surgery rates – increased cost-effectiveness
Vuorma et al., 2003	Information booklet vs. usual care	184 + 179 Finnish women with menorrhagia at hospital outpatients	DECISION AID: Information booklet about clinical problem and treatment options COMPARISON: usual care	Treatment option; knowledge; satisfaction; anxiety; menstrual symptoms; and cost.	Decision aid group more likely to make a treatment choice, including newer treatments: endometrial ablation or the hormonal intrauterine system - LNG-IUS (21% and 29% more than control group, respectively). No effect on knowledge, satisfaction, anxiety, health outcome, or cost
Protheroe et al., 2007	Computerized decision aid + booklet vs. booklet alone	74 + 74 UK women with menorrhagia in primary care	DECISION AID: interactive, individualized computer programme: provides options, outcomes, probabilities and values clarification using decision analysis + Information booklet about clinical problem and treatment options COMPARISON: Information booklet about clinical problem and treatment options	Decisional conflict scale; anxiety; menorrhagia-specific utility scale; knowledge; treatment preference and treatment chosen	Decision aid group had decreased decisional conflict, increased knowledge and menorrhagia-specific quality of life and more likely to make a treatment choice. No effect on anxiety or treatment option chosen.

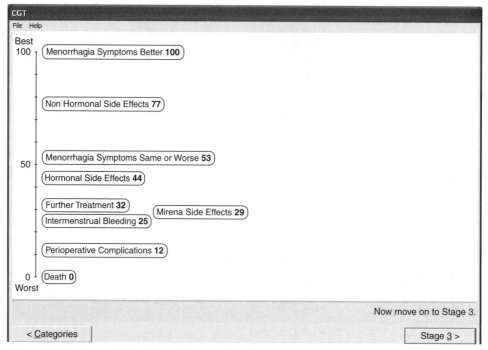

Figure 39.1 Patients ranked their preferences for different outcomes.

The effects of the decision aid were measured in terms of their effects on health-related quality of life, psychological well-being, menstrual symptoms, satisfaction with treatment outcome, and use and cost of health care services. The results showed no marked differences in health outcomes between the study groups at 1-year follow-up. The decision aid did not significantly affect health costs, despite some differences in treatments; however, the intervention group tended towards a lower rate of treatment and investigation episodes during the follow-up time period. The authors commented that providing an additional information booklet to women did influence treatment choices: they were more likely to have made a treatment decision within 3 months (96% in the intervention group and 89% in the control group) (Vuorma *et al.*, 2003). The intervention group was also more likely to choose oral medication and they less frequently chose what the study described as 'newly introduced treatments' (that is, endometrial ablation or the hormonal intrauterine system – LNG-IUS) than the control group.

The authors found that use of the decision aid did not increase the number of surgical procedures used, improve knowledge, or influence satisfaction or anxiety. An extensive systematic review of decision aids conducted by O'Connor *et al.* for the Cochrane Library found, amongst its conclusions, that complex decision aids are more effective than simpler ones. The fact that simple information in this study had no measurable impact on knowledge is consistent with those conclusions from the Cochrane review (O'Connor *et al.* 2003). Other studies contained within the Cochrane review have also reported sometimes no effects on satisfaction or anxiety.

Both the Kennedy and Vuorma decision aid trials were recruited from patients already referred to gynaecology outpatients. These will represent a different population to those women presenting to primary care.

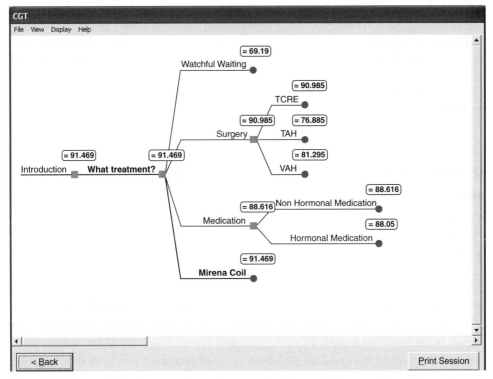

Figure 39.2 Suggested treatment pathway for one patient from decision analysis.

Protheroe et al., 2007

This was a trial to evaluate whether adding a computerized decision aid to existing written information would reduce decisional conflict (uncertainty over which course of action to take) in women presenting to their general practitioner with menorrhagia. The decision aid was a self-directed, interactive computerized decision aid based on decision analysis, the 'Clinical Guidance Tree' (CGT). The CGT program elicited information from the patient, which allowed the tree to be tailored to her as an individual, ensuring that the treatment information she received was appropriate (see Figure 39.1). Next, information was provided about menorrhagia and the risks and benefits of the treatment options; patient preferences were incorporated into a decision analysis (Figure 39.2), and the programme produced a printout detailing a suggested preferred treatment option. The decision aid was presented to the women on a laptop computer in their own homes by a researcher, prior to a follow-up appointment to discuss treatment options with their GP. The information leaflet that all women in the trial received was a freely available information leaflet which provided information on menorrhagia and its treatment options, both medical and surgical.

The effects of the decision aid were measured in terms of its effects on decisional conflict, anxiety, a menorrhagia-specific quality-of-life scale and knowledge – all collected using postal questionnaires. The results showed that there was significantly less decisional conflict in the group who had received the decision aid. This group also showed significantly better knowledge about menorrhagia and higher quality of life in terms of their menorrhagia. There was no difference in anxiety between the two groups. This study did not assess cost-effectiveness.

Although attempts had been made to minimize the effect of the presence of the researcher (meant only to facilitate the use of the decision aid, not to answer patient enquiries), the fact still remains that the researcher must be considered part of the intervention in this study. The authors concluded that a computerized decision aid, used outside of the primary care consultation, is effective in increasing patient involvement in decision-making in primary care. This is important as one of the main barriers to the use of decision aids in primary care in the United Kingdom is restricted time during consultations.

Currently, in the United Kingdom at least, decisions aids for menorrhagia are not implemented in routine practice outside of clinical trials.

Maintaining the evidence base and relevance of decision aids in this field

A decision aid for use in menorrhagia developed to take advantage of the benefits of all the above research would need

- to be readily adaptable to take account of new guidelines (for example the recent NICE guidelines for menorrhagia referred to above, http://www.nice.org.uk/guidance/index.jsp?action=byID&o=11002);
- it should be available for self-directed completion, or with guidance by a facilitator;
- it should be available in different languages and in versions suitable for patients with low-health literacy skills; and
- it needs to contain more than simple information, and should include clarification of patient values and preferences.

The most practical way to achieve these requirements would be to develop decision aids available for use from the internet. However, not all patients have access to, or feel able to use web-based decision aids without some direction (Protheroe et al., 2007). In primary care settings, one way to provide access to decision aids for many different conditions, including menorrhagia, could be the provision of web-based versions available on computer terminals in a resource room in a health centre (similar to a patient library), staffed by a professional skilled in facilitating the use of decision aids. An example, at least in the secondary care domain, is the Center for Shared Decision Making at Dartmouth Hitchcock Medical Center, New Hampshire, USA (http://www.dhmc.org/shared_decision_making.cfm, see Chapter 34). Web-based versions of decision aids can be adapted to take account of new evidence and guidelines, and different versions could be made available as required. A commitment to continuing investment of resources to updating the content is crucial for any decision aid about menorrhagia where treatments and the range of options available to women are already increasing and are likely to continue to develop rapidly in the coming years.

References

Hallberg, L., Hogdahl, A.M., Nilsson, L., et al. (1966). Menstrual blood loss – A population study. *Actu. Obstet. Gynaecol. Scand.*, **45**, 320–351.

Higham, J.M. (1999). Clinical associations with objective menstrual blood loss. *Eur. J. Obstet. Gynaecol. Repro. Biol.*, **82**, 73–76.

National Collaborating Centre for Women's and Children's Health, N. (2007). *NICE Clinical Guideline 44: Heavy Menstrual Bleeding*. London: National Institute for Health and Clinical Excellence.

O'Connor, A.M., Jacobsen, M.J., and Stacey, D. (2002). An evidence-based approach to managing women's decisional conflict. *J. Obstet. Gynecol. Neonatal Nurs.*, **31**, 570–581.

O'Connor, A.M., Stacey, D., Entwistle, V., *et al.* (2003). Decision aids for people facing health treatment or screening decisions, A Cochrane review. *The Cochrane Library, 2*, Update Software, Oxford.

O'Flynn, N. and Britten, N. (2000). Menorrhagia in general practice – Disease or illness. *Social Science & Medicine* **50**, 651–661.

Prentice, A. (1999). Medical management of menorrhagia. *British Medical Journal*, **319**, 1343–1345.

Protheroe, J. and Chew-Graham, C.A. (2005). The role of primary care in the diagnosis and management of menorrhagia: A qualitative study of women with menorrhagia. *Primary Health Care Research and Development*, **6**, 217–223.

Protheroe, J. (2004) Modern management of menorrhagia. *J Fam Plann Reprod. Health Care*, **30**, 118–122.

Protheroe, J., Bower, P., and Chew-Graham, C. (2007). The use of mixed methodology in evaluating complex interventions: Identifying patient factors that moderate the effects of a decision aid. *Fam. Pract.*, **24**, 594–600.

Royal College of Obstetricians and Gynaecologists. (1998). *The initial management of menorrhagia*. London.

Vuorma, S., Rissanen, P., Aalto, A.M., *et al.* (2003). Impact of patient information booklet on treatment decision – A randomized trial among women with heavy menstruation. *Health Expect.*, **6**, 290–297.

Chapter 40

Decision aids in diabetes

Matthias Lenz and Ingrid Mühlhauser

Diabetes

Diabetes is usually not considered a typical disease for shared decision-making (SDM) even by protagonists of SDM (O'Connor et al., 2003). The belief is still widely held that control of blood glucose and other cardiovascular risk factors is beyond any doubt beneficial, and therefore, supporting patients in adherence increasing behaviour rather than SDM has been standard procedure in diabetes care (IDF, 2005; Nathan et al., 2006; ADA, 2008).

However, there has rarely been a disorder where recommendations have been driven to such a high extent by stakeholders and opinion leaders rather than evidence (Richter and Berger, 2000; Hauber and Gale, 2006). Targets for blood glucose and other risk factors have been continuously decreased, and normalization of glycosylated haemoglobin (HbA1c) values has been set as a primary treatment goal for most patients (IDF, 2005; Nathan et al., 2006; ADA, 2008). Even the newest guidelines of the American Diabetes Association define the overall (glycaemic) objective for persons with type 2 diabetes as 'to achieve and maintain glycemic levels as close to the non-diabetic range as possible and to change interventions at as rapid a pace as titration of medications allows' (ADA 2008).

However, the recent ACCORD study has shown that such an indiscriminate and poly-pragmatic approach may lead to almost doubling of mortality within a few years (ACCORD, 2008). Furthermore, and despite lack of evidence, blood glucose self-monitoring (BGSM) has been extensively propagated even for patients without insulin therapy (IDF, 2005; ADA, 2008) but emerging evidence proves harm rather than benefit of BGSM for patients with type 2 diabetes (Simon et al., 2008; O'Kane et al., 2008).

Based on randomized controlled trials (RCT) and using patient relevant outcomes (Berger and Mühlhauser, 1999), only a few glucose lowering drug therapies have been shown to do good as well as harm. This includes insulin and glibenclamide (UKPDS, 1998b). Metformin which is now the first line drug worldwide has been reported to reduce mortality, although this is based on a subgroup of only little more than 300 patients followed in the United Kingdom Prospective Diabetes Study (UKPDS, 1998a, 1998b). Results have never been replicated in another RCT. The most frequently used regimen in Germany and other countries is a combination of metformin and a sulfonylurea, which increased mortality in the UKPDS (1998b). No other RCT has ever cleared the concerns completely. In addition, an increasing plethora of novel diabetes drugs and combinations thereof are prescribed in routine care. Some of them have already been shown to be harmful, and others have not yet been properly evaluated (Gale, 2006; Hauber and Gale, 2006; Richter 2006, 2007, 2008; Holleman and Gale, 2007).

Improving HbA1c from high to moderate values, such as from 9% to 7% as part of intensive care may reduce diabetic complications in younger patients with type 1 diabetes. However, in middle-aged newly diagnosed patients with type 2 diabetes, intensive care resulting in HbA1c changes from about 8% to 7% is of limited benefit (UKPDS 1998a, 1998b). In the UKPDS, 10 years of intensified blood glucose therapy using diet, insulin, or glibenclamide resulted in benefit for 5 out of 100 patients as they could prevent or delay diabetes-related endpoints, whereas 95 out 100 patients did not benefit. Here, 41 experienced an endpoint despite intensive therapy, whereas 59 did not. In the control group (conventional therapy), 46 out of 100 patients experienced an endpoint, whereas 54 did not (Mühlhauser and Berger, 2000).

It is worrying that diabetes experts largely overestimate possible benefits of blood glucose lowering interventions in patients with type 2 diabetes. Also, they generally have a poor understanding of clinical study results and misinterpret possible benefits of interventions to prevent diabetes (Mühlhauser et al., 2006).

In contrast to blood glucose lowering therapies, control of blood pressure (UKPDS, 1998c) and use of statins (Costa, 2006) do have the potential to improve prognosis for people with diabetes. In addition, educating and empowering patients to engage in self-control and self-treatment, both of diabetes and hypertension, is an indispensable part of diabetes care. Self-management reduces acute complications and the need for drug interventions, improves metabolic and blood pressure control, and enhances quality of life as well as patients' independence from medical institutions (Lenz et al., 2007).

Traditional management of diabetes still relies on strong physician roles. Patients are not explicitly involved in defining treatment goals or in the selection of therapeutic regimens. Rather, an array of behavioural directives are imposed on patients such as quitting smoking, increasing exercise, normalizing weight, and adhering to monitoring, dietary, and medication schedules (IDF 2005; ADA 2008). Not surprisingly, long-term compliance is poor even with the most promising interventions such as blood pressure control and statin use (Yusuf et al., 2000; WOSCOPS, 1997).

Shared decision-making, decision aids, and evidence-based patient information

The doubtful benefit of normalizing HbA1c values on the one hand and the availability of other treatment options to improve prognosis but with low adherence on the other hand, urge shared decision-making. Patients have a right to know about the limited evidence of recommendations and about all options to improve prognosis. They have a right to make good decisions on their treatment goals and treatment regimens. Confronted with the large variety of options to improve prognosis, patients should be supported to define a hierarchy of individual goals and to triage interventions. This might facilitate long-term adherence to albeit a few but individually acceptable and possibly the most effective treatment interventions. From this point of view, diabetes might even be prototypic for evidence-based patient information and SDM.

Available decision aids for people with diabetes

The early 'Ottawa Inventory' (Stacey and O'Connor, 2001) listed one diabetes decision aid as publicly available (BMJ Publishing Group, 2003). We have browsed the internet perpetually and undertook systematic literature searches in June 2008 using PubMed, EMBASE, CINAHL, PsycINFO, and PSYNDEXplus. Sixteen publicly available diabetes-relevant decision aids were identified. Thirteen of these primarily target cardiovascular risk management and are therefore not further considered in this article. In addition, the material provided by the BMJ Publishing

Group (2003) is conventional patient information rather than a decision aid as it does not include probabilities about outcomes and does not support users to weigh positive and negative features of options. Therefore, this material is also not further considered. The remaining three decision aids were specifically designed for people with diabetes (Healthwise Inc., 2007, 2008; Montori et al., 2007; Weymiller et al., 2007). One additional decision aid was identified by personal contact (Health Dialog, 2007). One publication about a diabetes decision aid was identified, which is still under evaluation and currently not available (Corser et al., 2007). Our research group developed a decision aid for coronary prevention in type 2 diabetes, designed to support patients defining a hierarchy of individual goals and to triage interventions. This decision aid has been pilot-tested but is not yet available (Lenz et al., 2008).

Characteristics of the four currently available and diabetes-specific decision aids are summarized in the table. One of these refers to the use of an insulin pump in type 1 diabetes (Healthwise Inc., 2007). Patients are asked to deliberate about positive and negative features of options. Scientific references are cited. However, probabilities of benefits and harms are lacking. The second decision aid (Healthwise Inc., 2008) was designed for women with type 1 diabetes deliberating about getting pregnant. The contents rely on expert recommendations. Evidence-based risk information that could help to deliberate about options is not provided. Sources of information are not transparently reported.

The Health Dialog decision aid for patients with type 2 diabetes (Health Dialog, 2007) promotes modification of health behaviour in addressing smoking, diet, and physical activity. A hierarchy of targets is suggested with emphasis on control of blood pressure and cholesterol rather than on blood glucose. Risk information on benefits and harms of options is not provided. Rather, patients are referred to their physicians. References are not listed. The 'Statin Choice' decision aid targets treatment with statins in patients with type 2 diabetes (Montori et al., 2007). This decision aid meets nearly all IPDAS-criteria (Table 40.1). A limitation is that the external validity of the included risk calculator is unclear and problems with reliability of risk prognosis are not discussed.

Evidence of implementation, effectiveness, and cost-effectiveness

Evidence about the implementation of these decision aids in clinical practice is lacking. Background information on development and evaluation was identified for one decision aid only (Montori et al., 2007; Weymiller et al., 2007; Christianson et al., 2006). Weymiller et al. (2007) randomly assigned 98 patients to the decision aid or a standard educational pamphlet. The decision aid was rated more helpful and found effective concerning knowledge, improving estimated cardiovascular risk, potential risk reduction with statin drugs, and decisional conflict. Follow-up was 3 months so long-term effects are unknown.

Keeping decision aids up to date with evidence advances in type 2 diabetes

There is much clinical research about diabetes, and many topics are controversial. This appears to be fertile ground for developing diabetes-related decision aids, but currently, only a few research groups appear to be involved in this area. This is surprising since powerful networks of researchers in the field exist. Providing high-quality evidence-based information and keeping them up to date appear to be presenting a number of challenges which must be overcome.

Table 40.1 Decision aids for people with diabetes

Title	Should I get an insulin pump?	I have diabetes. Should I get pregnant now?	Living with diabetes. Making life style changes to last a life time	Statin choice
Publisher	Healthwise, USA	Healthwise, USA	Health Dialog, Foundation for Medical Informed Decision Making, US	Mayo Foundation, US
Scientific background publication(s)	Unknown	Unknown	Unknown	Montori 2007; Weymiller et al. 2008
Type of diabetes	Type 1 diabetes	Type 1 diabetes	Type 2 diabetes	Type 2 diabetes
Topics	Insulin pump	Getting pregnant	Losing weight, physical activity, healthy eating quitting smoking, controlling blood pressure, controlling cholesterol, controlling blood sugar	Statin use
Last update	2007	2008	2007	2008
Format	Web	Web	Video, booklet, diabetes management worksheet, and "Questions to Ask My Doctor About my Diabetes" form	Booklet, Coronary Heart Disease Calculator; decision sheets (average, elevated, and high coronary risk)
Language	English	English	English	English, Spanish
Availability	Publicly available for free from a number of Web sites.	Publicly available for free from a number of Web sites.	The DA can be requested from the Foundation for Medical Informed Decision Making	Publicly available for free from http://mayoresearch.mayo.edu
IPDAS-Criteria (IPDAS 2005)				
◆ The DA describes the condition related to the decision.	Yes	Yes	Yes	Yes

◆ The DA describes the decision that needs to be considered.	Yes	Yes	Yes	Yes
◆ The DA lists the options	Yes	Yes	Yes	Yes
◆ The DA describes what happens in the natural course of the condition if no action is taken.	No	NA	Yes	Yes
◆ The DA has information about the procedures involved	Yes	NA	Yes	Yes
◆ The DA has information about the positive features of the options	Yes	Yes	Yes	Yes
◆ The DA has information about negative features of the options	Yes	Yes	Yes	Yes
◆ The information about outcomes of options (positive and negative) includes the chances they may happen.	No	No	Only for quitting smoking	Yes
◆ The DA presents probabilities using event rates in a defined group of people for a specified time.	No	No	No	Yes
◆ The DA compares probabilities of options using the same denominator.	No	No	No	Yes
◆ The DA compares probabilities of options over the same period of time.	No	No	No	Yes
◆ The DA uses the same scales in diagrams comparing options.	No	No	No	Yes

(continued)

Table 40.1 (continued) Decision aids for people with diabetes

Title	Should I get an insulin pump?	I have diabetes. Should I get pregnant now?	Living with diabetes. Making life style changes to last a life time	Statin choice
◆ The DA asks people to think about which positive and negative features of the options matter most to them.	Yes	Yes	No	Yes
◆ The DA makes it possible to compare the positive and negative features of the available options.	Yes	Yes	Only for quitting smoking	Yes
◆ The DA shows the negative and positive features of the options with equal detail.	Yes	Yes	No	Yes
◆ Users (people who previously faced the decision) were asked what they need to prepare them to discuss a specific decision.	No	Unknown	General policy of Health Dialog	Yes
◆ The DA was reviewed by people who previously faced the decision who were not involved in its development and field testing.	No	Unknown	Unknown	Yes
◆ People who were facing the decision field tested the decision aid.	Unknown	Unknown	Unknown	Yes
◆ Field testing showed that the DA was acceptable to users.	Unknown	Unknown	Unknown	Yes
◆ Field testing showed that people who were undecided felt that the information was presented in a balanced way.	Unknown	Unknown	Unknown	Unknown

Criterion				
◆ The DA provides references to scientific evidence used.	Yes	No	Yes	Yes
◆ The DA reports the date when it was last updated.	Yes	Yes	Yes	Yes
◆ The DA reports whether authors of the DA or their affiliations stand to gain or lose by choices people make after using the decision aid.	No	No	Yes	Yes
◆ There is evidence that the DA helps people know about the available options and their features.	Unknown	Unknown	Unknown	Yes
◆ There is evidence that the DA improves the match between the features that matter most to the informed person and the option that is chosen.	Unknown	Unknown	Unknown	Unknown
Additional Criteria according to MATRIX (Lenz 2007)*				
◆ The objectives of the DA are reported.	No	No	No	Yes
◆ An explicit rationale for the selection of the objectives is reported.	No	No	No	Yes
◆ The contents of the DA are evidence-based	NA (references not cited)	NA (references not cited)	NA (references not cited)	Yes
◆ Structure, complexity, and used media are appropriate and support users to deliberate about options.	Yes	Yes	Yes	Yes

(continued)

Table 40.1 (continued) Decision aids for people with diabetes

Title	Should I get an insulin pump?	I have diabetes. Should I get pregnant now?	Living with diabetes. Making life style changes to last a life time	Statin choice
◆ Randomized controlled trial(s) is/are published assessing the efficacy of the decision aid	No	No	No	Yes
◆ Design and methods (randomization, allocation, blinding, etc.) of these trial(s) is/are transparently described	NA	NA	NA	Yes
◆ Used outcome measures are patient relevant and represent the particular objectives of the decision aid.	NA	NA	NA	Yes
◆ Implementation trials assessed the effectiveness under uncontrolled conditions (reproducibility).	No	No	No	No

NA = not applicable.
*selected criteria extracted from the MATRI X-instrument (Lenz and Kasper, 2007).

Conclusion for future development and maintenance of decision aids

Transparency is an important quality criterion for the development and evaluation of a decision aid. Authors should state whether and in which way a decision aid includes patient-relevant evidence-based information (including the strength of available evidence), and whether and in which way users are supported to deliberate about positive and negative features of options (Lenz and Kasper, 2007).

Decision aids usually consist of various elements related to different topics (glucose control, blood pressure treatment, etc.). Furthermore, a decision aid can be part of a decision-making program, which additionally comprises a strategy for patient counselling or an introductory educational module. Thus, decision aids are 'complex interventions', whose development and evaluation require qualitative and quantitative methods (Campbell *et al.*, 2007; Lenz *et al.*, 2007). It appears impossible to systematically extract all necessary background information about theoretical concept, development, and evaluation of decision aids using current database search strategies (Lenz *et al.*, 2006). Hence, an electronic database would be helpful to make informed decision-making programs accessible together with their relevant background information.

Evidence-based decision aids need to be kept inline with current scientific development. Therefore, a 'flexible' medium should be used that enables keeping the contents up to date. The internet seems to be appropriate as updating of information can easily be performed. However, some people with type 2 diabetes might still prefer a paper-based format so this must also be made available by developers. Finally, it is challenging for users to assess the reliability of internet contents so current quality criteria should be enhanced to also support users to easily evaluate the level of evidence of the content of a decision aid.

References

Action to Control Cardiovascular Risk in Diabetes (ACCORD) Study Group. (2008). Effects of intensive glucose lowering in type 2 diabetes. *N. Engl. J. Med.* **358**, 2545–2559.

American Diabetes Association (ADA 2008). Standards of Medical Care in Diabetes. *Diabetes Care*, **31**(1), 12–S54.

Berger, M. and Mühlhauser, I. (1999). Diabetes care and patient-oriented outcomes. *JAMA*, **281**, 1676–1678.

BMJ Publishing Group (2003). Diabetes. Available at http://www.besttreatments.co.uk. Accessed on 23 May 2008.

Campbell, N.C., Murray, E., Darbyshire, J., *et al.* (2007). Designing and evaluating complex interventions to improve health care. *British Medical Journal*, **334**, 455–459.

Christianson, T.J., Bryant, S.C., Weymiller, A.J., *et al.* (2006). A pen-and-paper coronary risk estimator for office use with patients with type 2 diabetes. *Mayo. Clin. Proc.*, **81**, 632–636.

Corser, W., Holmes-Rovner, M., Lein, C., *et al.* (2007). A shared decision-making primary care intervention for type 2 diabetes. *Diabetes Educ.*, **33**, 700–708.

Costa, J., Borges, M., David, C., *et al.* (2006). Efficacy of lipid lowering drug treatment for diabetic and non-diabetic patients: Meta-analysis of randomised controlled trials. *British Medical Journal*, **332**, 1115–1124.

Gale, E.A. (2006). Troglitazone: The lesson that nobody learned? *Diabetol.*, **49**, 1–6.

Hauber, A. and Gale, E.A. (2006). The market in diabetes. *Diabetol.*, **49**, 247–252.

Health Dialog (2007). Living with diabetes. Making lifestyle changes to last a lifetime. Boston: Foundation for Informed Medical Decision Making.

Healthwise Inc. (2007). Healthwise decision point: Should I get an insulin pump? http://www.healthwise. net/preferredcare/. Accessed on 23 May 2008.

Healthwise Inc. (2008). Healthwise decision point: I have diabetes. Should I get pregnant now? Available at http://www.healthwise.net/hillhealth/ http://www.healthwise.net/preferredcare/. Accessed on 23 May 2008.

Holleman, F., Gale, E.A. (2007). Nice insulins, pity about the evidence. *Diabetologia*, **50**, 1783–1790.

International Diabetes Federation (IDF). (2005). Clinical Guidelines Task Force. Global guideline for Type 2 diabetes. Brussels: International Diabetes Federation.

International Patient Decision Aid Standards (IPDAS) Collaboration. (2005). Criteria for Judging the Quality of Patient Decision Aids. Available at http://ipdas.ohri.ca/resources.html Accessed on 23 May 2008.

Lenz, M., Kasper, J., Mühlhauser, I. (2006). Searching for diabetes decision aids and related background information. *Diabet. Med.*, **23**, 912–916.

Lenz, M. and Kasper, J. (2007). MATRIX – Development and feasibility of a guide for quality assessment of patient decision aids. *GMS Psychosoc. Med.*, **4**, Doc10.

Lenz, M., Kasper, J., Mühlhauser, I. (2008). Development of an evidence based patient decision aid for coronary prevention in type 2 diabetes – Theoretical concept and preliminary testing. (unpublished manuscript).

Lenz, M., Steckelberg, A., Richter, B., *et al.* (2007). Meta-analysis does not allow appraisal of complex interventions in diabetes and hypertension self-management. A methodological review. *Diabetologia*, **50**, 1375–1383.

Montori, V.M., Breslin, M., Maleska, M., *et al.* (2007). Creating a conversation: Insights from the development of a decision aid. *PLoS Med.*, **4**, e233

Mühlhauser, I. and Berger, M. (2000). Evidence-based patient information in diabetes. *Diabet. Med.*, **17**, 823–829.

Mühlhauser, I., Kasper, J., Meyer, G., *et al.* (2006). Understanding of diabetes prevention studies: Questionnaire survey of professionals in diabetes care. *Diabetologia*, **49**, 1742–1746.

Nathan, D.M., Buse, J.B., Davidson, M.B., *et al.* (2006). Management of hyperglycemia in type 2 diabetes: A consensus algorithm for the initiation and adjustment of therapy: A consensus statement from the American Diabetes Association and the European Association for the Study of Diabetes. *Diabetes. Care*, **29**, 1963–1972.

O'Connor, A., Légaré, F., and Stacey, D. (2003). Risk communication in practice: The contribution of decision aids. *British Medical Journal*, **327**, 736–740.

O'Kane, M.J., Bunting, B., Copeland, M., *et al.* (2008). Efficacy of self monitoring of blood glucose in patients with newly diagnosed type 2 diabetes (ESMON study): Randomised controlled trial. *British Medical Journal*, **24**, 1174–1177.

Richter, B., Bandeira-Echtler, E., Bergerhoff, K., *et al.* (2007). Rosiglitazone for type 2 diabetes mellitus. *Cochrane Database Systematic Review*, 3:CD006063

Richter, B., Bandeira-Echtler, E., Bergerhoff, K., *et al.* (2006). Pioglitazone for type 2 diabetes mellitus. *Cochrane Database Systematic Review*, 4:CD006060

Richter, B., Bandeira-Echtler, E., Bergerhoff, K., *et al.* (2008). Dipeptidyl peptidase-4 (DPP-4) inhibitors for type 2 diabetes mellitus. *Cochrane Database Systematic Review*, 2:CD006739

Richter, B. and Berger, M. (2000). Randomized controlled trials remain fundamental to clinical decision making in Type 2 diabetes mellitus: A comment to the debate on randomized controlled trials. *Diabetologia*, **43**, 254–258.

Simon, J., Gray, A., Clarke, P., *et al.* (2008). Cost-effectiveness of self monitoring of blood glucose in patients with non-insulin treated type 2 diabetes: Economic evaluation of data from the DiGEM trial. *British Medical Journal*, **336**, 1177–1180.

Stacey, D. and O'Connor, A.M. (2001). Cochrane Inventory of Existing Patient Decision Aids. Ottawa Health Decision Centre, University of Ottawa. Available at http://decisionaid.ohri.ca/. Accessed on 23 May 2008.

The West of Scotland Coronary Prevention Study Group (WOSCOPS 1997). Compliance and adverse event withdrawal: Their impact on the West of Scotland Coronary Prevention Study. *Eur. Heart J.*, **18**, 1718–1724.

University Group Diabetes Program (UGDP 1982). Effects of hypoglycemic agents on vascular complications in patients with adult-onset diabetes: VIII. Evaluation of insulin therapy: Final report. *Diabetes*, **31**, (Suppl 5), 1–81.

UK Prospective Diabetes Study (UKPDS) Group (1998a). Effect of intensive blood-glucose control with metformin on complications in overweight patients with type 2 diabetes (UKPDS 34). *Lancet*, **12**, 854–865.

UK Prospective Diabetes Study (UKPDS) Group (1998b). Intensive blood glucose control with sulphonylureas or insulin compared with conventional treatment and risk of complications in patients with type 2 diabetes (UKPDS 33). *Lancet*, **352**, 837–853.

UK Prospective Diabetes Study (UKPDS) Group (1998c). Tight blood pressure control and risk of macrovascular and microvascular complications in type 2 diabetes: UKPDS 38. *British Medical Journal*, **317**, 703–713.

Yusuf, S., Sleight, P., Pogue, J., *et al.* (2000). Effects of an angiotensin-converting-enzyme inhibitor, ramipril, on cardiovascular events in high-risk patients. The heart outcomes prevention evaluation study investigators. *N. Engl. J. Med.*, **20**, 145–153.

Weymiller. A.J., Montori, V.M., Jones, L.A., *et al.* (2007). Helping patients with type 2 diabetes mellitus make treatment decisions: Statin choice randomized trial. *Arch. Intern. Med.*, **28**, 1076–1082.

Chapter 41

Promoting critical reflection in breast cancer decision-making

Jeff Belkora

The health care context

Breast cancer occurs when cells in the ducts or lobules of the breast begin to proliferate out of control and spread through the lymph system or bloodstream to other parts of the body, where they can interfere with vital functions, leading to death. No one knows for sure what causes breast cancer; and although survival is increasing overall and the 5-year survival rate exceeds 90% for localized disease, there is no definite cure (American Cancer Society, 2007). Breast cancer treatments are invasive and life altering. Treatment options include surgery, radiation, hormone therapy, chemotherapy, and biologic therapy. Patients and health care professionals face many other decisions about breast cancer.

The choices

Decisions about breast cancer treatment are characterized by

+ inadequate evidence about benefits and harms;
+ material individual variation in outcomes; and
+ material variation in how patients feel about the value, the timing, or the probabilities of known benefits and harms.

For example, there is inadequate evidence about new treatment approaches, such as total skin-sparing mastectomies or biologic therapies because only short-term follow-up is available to date.

Even where there is scientifically adequate evidence about outcomes for large samples of patients, such as for chemotherapy, the distribution of individual outcomes such as survival can be extremely broad, ranging from 0 to 20 years or more.

Also, patients may feel differently about whether the benefits are worth the risks. For example, chemotherapy has been shown, on average, to increase 10-year survival by 3–11% (Cole et al., 2001). However, it is historically associated with a treatment death rate of about 0.5%, many patients require hospitalization or other invasive treatments to deal with its side-effects, and it disrupts patients' lives for a year or more (Fisher et al., 2001; Smith et al., 2003). Therefore, different patients feel differently about taking chemotherapy, depending on how they feel about the value, the timing, and the probabilities of the benefits and harms.

To complicate the situation even further, 50% of newly diagnosed breast cancer patients experience clinically significant levels of anxiety, distress, or depression (Hegel et al., 2006). Some patients face other barriers to coping with a new diagnosis, including poverty, discrimination, illiteracy, or innumeracy. How are patients to cope, facing such barriers, with the issues of inadequate or conflicting evidence, variation in individual outcomes, and variation in how they feel about the value, timing, and probabilities of the outcomes?

The critical reflection cycle

One answer is that patients must rely on critical reflection to cope with breast cancer or indeed any life-threatening condition. Along with colleagues, I develop, evaluate, and implement approaches that guide patients to decisions based on critical reflection. I define critical reflection as the process of formulating issues, analyzing each part, synthesizing the parts into holistic insight, and translating the insight into action (Figure 41.1). The action can be to start a new cycle of critical reflection, or to allocate resources and create a change in the world, such as surgery. An individual can reflect critically in their head or using external symbols (e.g. writing and drawing), and can involve others in the process of critical reflection, by communicating (e.g. talking and writing).

The goals of critical reflection include reducing the individual's confusion about what to do, reducing anxiety about how to decide, and reducing conflict with other parties needed to carry out the decision. Stated positively, the goals of critical reflection include promoting clarity about what to do, serenity about having chosen wisely, and harmony with needed and valued collaborators.

I have mapped the patient journey through the breast care center where I work and identified critical times at which our institution can support critical reflection.

Figure 41.2 shows a model of how patients come into contact with health care systems, including our breast care center at the University of California, San Francisco. They monitor their health, detect a problem, schedule an appointment, and prepare for and attend the appointment. The next step after any given appointment, as patients debrief or make sense of what happened, is often to schedule another appointment and repeat steps 4, 5, and 6. Ideally, patients then develop a strategy to respond to their condition, a strategy being a coherent set of linked decisions, such as taking chemotherapy before surgery to shrink a tumour, and then surgery, radiation, and hormone therapy. Then, patients take action and return to step 1, monitoring their health.

Health professionals can engage patients in critical reflection at any of the stages mentioned above, to address some of the potential lapses that patients might wish to revisit.

- Patients may not monitor their health adequately, and for example miss a breast lump or other symptom, which they might feel upon critical reflection, was unwise and did not lead to clarity, serenity, and harmony.

- If patients do find a problem, such as a lump, they may ignore it, in some cases out of fear and denial. They might become aware of their denial upon further review.

- Patients who do take note of, say, a breast lump, may not engage with the medical system and schedule appointments or tests, in some cases due to poverty, insurance barriers, lack of faith in medical science, or lack of conviction about the importance of an issue. Health disparities

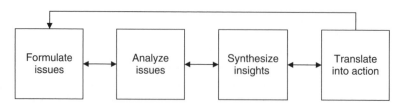

Figure 41.1 Critical reflection cycle.

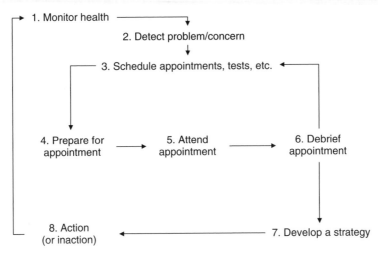

Figure 41.2 The patient journey.

are, by definition, difficult to overcome. However, after critical reflection, patients might be able to move towards their goals.

- If patients do schedule appointments, they may not show up or may show up unprepared. Patients might revise these behaviors after critical reflection.

- Patients who do attend appointments may be unable to absorb the information and advice offered by physicians or other professionals. Some strategies, such as note-taking and audio-recording, allow patients to shift the time and place of critical reflection to allow repetition in a more comfortable setting. Having a meeting facilitator can generally improve critical reflection as well (Doyle, 1982).

- In debriefing appointments, patients may be unable to make sense of what was said. Again, notes and recordings can facilitate critical reflection after the appointment.

- Patients may never develop a coherent strategy with their medical providers. For example, a patient may be treated by many specialists working, unknowingly, at cross-purposes. A patient may see an oncologist only after having had surgery, when neo-adjuvant (pre-surgery) chemotherapy might have been an option. More critical reflection could surface interdependences among specialists and prevent this kind of conflict.

- Even if a coherent strategy does emerge for medical care, the patient may not implement it. Again, critical reflection at this stage could lead patients to confirm whether a strategy is in their long-term interests and follow through if appropriate.

Using this map of the patient journey, I identified the points of intersection where the breast care center where I work, at the University of California, San Francisco, can provide decision support to patients. Our starting point has been what we call the visit cycle, steps 4, 5, and 6. We intervene with patients before, during, and after their consultations with surgeons and medical oncologists. We implement and evaluate proven decision support interventions.

Before consultations, we send patients the decision aids produced by the Foundation for Informed Medical Decision Making (FIMDM, www.fimdm.org) in collaboration with Health Dialog (www.healthdialog.com). We send the decision aids by mail in the form of digital videodiscs (DVDs) or video home system (VHS) tapes, along with printed information booklets.

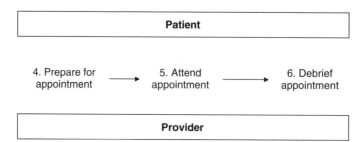

Figure 41.3 The visit cycle.

Each of the five titles represents what FIMDM calls a *decision crossroad*. The crossroads represent decisions about ductal carcinoma *in situ* (a pre-cancerous condition); surgery for early-stage breast cancer; reconstruction after mastectomy; adjuvant therapy for early stage breast cancer; and living with metastatic breast cancer. These and similar decision aids have proven associations with improved educational and psychological outcomes, such as patient knowledge and reduced decisional conflict (O'Connor *et al.*, 2003).

We identify eligible patients through our scheduling system and send them whichever title fits their situation. We are now reaching most if not all of the 600 or so eligible patients every year – around 90% in our most recent quarter. We invite patients to use the decision aids to prepare for their consultations rather than make definitive decisions. In particular, we invite patients to make a list of questions and concerns based on the information, perspectives, and prompts provided in the videos. Thus, we initiate the process of critical reflection with patients before their consultations, supporting them in formulating informed views of their condition, and questions about it. FIMDM funds the distribution of the videos, and evaluation of survey responses, as part of a demonstration project.

Our website and the new patient binder available to all newly diagnosed patients also provide a set of links to useful resources online. Among others, we refer patients to specific online offerings from the Mayo Clinic (http://www.mayoclinic.com/health/breast-cancer-treatment/AT99999/PAGE=AT00004) from Healthwise (http://www.healthwise.net/preferredcare/Content/StdDocument.aspx?DOCHWID=tv6530&SECHWID=tv6530-Intro) and from the National Cancer Institute (http://www.cancer.gov/cancertopics/breast-cancer-surgery-choices).

Supporting patients

We also offer patients the opportunity to be accompanied to their consultations. We do this on a first-come, first-served basis, subject to our capacity of about 250 patients a year (approximately 1 per clinic day). This program is made possible through a premedical internship program. We use the term internship to refer to the fact that we recruit young people interested in gaining 1–2 years of experience before they apply to medical school. The interns work primarily as research assistants or study coordinators, but one day per week they accompany patients. We train the interns to further facilitate critical reflection by patients by means of consultation planning, recording, and summarizing.

Consultation planning, recording, and summarizing begins before the patient – physician visit. Interns meet with patients, either by telephone or in person, to facilitate the development of a word-processed list of questions and concerns known as a consultation plan. Other researchers have established associations between this type of visit preparation and increased patient asking,

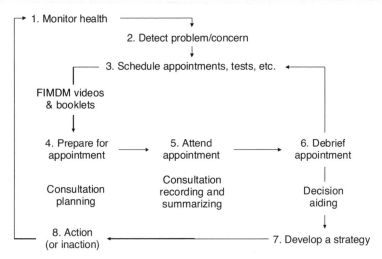

Figure 41.4 Integrating critical reflection into the patient journey.

reduced anxiety, and increased self-efficacy (Brown *et al.*, 1999, 2001; Butow *et al.*, 1994; Greenfield *et al.*, 1985, 1988; Griffin *et al.*, 2004; Harrington *et al.*, 2004; Kinnersley *et al.*, 2007; Roter, 1977) as also discussed by Kinnersley and Edwards in Chapter 24.

Consultation recording consists of the intern creating a digital audio-recording of the patient's visit with a surgeon or medical oncologist. Other researchers have established associations between audio-recordings or summaries and increased patient retention of information and satisfaction (Hack *et al.*, 2003; Ong *et al.*, 2000; Scott *et al.*, 2003). Consultation summarizing consists of the intern creating a word-processed written summary of the advice and information presented by the attending physician during the visit.

The consultation planning, recording, and summarizing (CPRS) program is mostly funded by the Breast Care Center faculty, who pay 100% of the intern salaries while donating 20% of the intern time to the program. In return, the faculty benefit from highly qualified, motivated, and productive research assistants and study coordinators, who view the CPRS program as a job enhancement that offers the opportunity for meaningful interactions with patients and their families. The United States Agency for Healthcare Research and Quality has recognized this program as one of the top 100 innovations in its Innovation Exchange (AHRQ Health Care Innovations Exchange).

Supporting clinicians

Since we began evaluating the distribution of FIMDM decision aids and the CPRS program, we have documented increases in patient knowledge and decision self-efficacy, and reductions in decisional conflict, as patients proceed through the visit cycle (Belkora *et al.*, 2008a). We hope to expand our program by routinely implementing software-based decision aids, towards the end of physician–patient consultations, after appropriate formulation and analysis of issues. Many of our medical oncologists already use a software-based prognostic model called Adjuvant! Online (www.adjuvantonline.com). This model was created and is maintained by an oncologist based on registry data combined with clinical trial results (Ravdin, 1995, 1996; Ravdin *et al.*, 2001). It has been shown to predict patient 10-year survival and recurrence-free survival within 2–5% on average, as a function of six inputs (Olivotto *et al.*, 2005). These inputs are age, tumor size, tumor grade, and node, hormone receptor, and comorbidity status. The Adjuvant! model is probably the most widely used physician decision aid in medicine, with 40–70% of oncologists using it as a reference tool (Love, 2005).

Some of our oncologists consult the model prior to meeting with patients and report the risk estimates during the consultation; others print screenshots to use as visual aids; and still others access the model online in the exam room side by side with the patient. Our preliminary studies suggest that the model's interface, which was designed for use as a reference tool by oncologists, communicates risk clearly to some patients, but leaves a majority of patients confused about their prognosis (Belkora *et al.*, 2008b). We have designed a common interface for use by any physician presenting information to any patient and are now testing it for various decision crossroads in breast cancer.

Conclusion

The content of decision aids will always lag behind scientific advances. At the UCSF Breast Care Center, we rely on our physicians, who specialize in breast cancer, to synthesize recent research and incorporate it into the consultations. We promote and support the fact that patients continue to see their physicians as their preferred source of information (Hesse *et al.*, 2005). We see our commitment to critical reflection as leveraging physician expertise, alleviating some of the time pressures during visits and allowing specialists to focus their conversations on areas where they add the most value. We send videos and booklets to patients in advance in order to provide them with background information. We prompt patients to write down questions in advance so that specialists can tailor their presentations, which will increasingly use software teaching tools, to patient biology and preferences. We provide notes and audio-recordings after the visit to allow patients to absorb, retain, and act upon physician insights.

We are still in the early days of identifying what is good and true about interventions that support critical reflection, and in what ways such interventions do not deliver on their promise. Having developed supportive interventions directed mostly at patients, we are now turning our attention to supporting our physicians and helping them to better leverage our videos, software-based decision aids, and consultation plans, summaries, and recordings.

Acknowledgments

Thanks to the patients who have participated in decision support programs and provided feedback over the years at Stanford University; University of California, San Francisco (UCSF); Breast Cancer Connections; Cancer Resource Center of Mendocino County; Humboldt Community Breast Health Project, and the several funding bodies. Thanks to colleagues who have collaborated on elements of the decision support programs, including (among others) Laura Esserman, Karen Sepucha, Shelley Volz, and Meredith Loth.

Competing interests

Part of the author's salary is covered by a grant from the Foundation for Informed Medical Decision Making, which produces decision aids discussed in this chapter.

References

AHRQ Health Care Innovations Exchange 'Innovation Profile: Personalized support improves patient-physician communication and enhances decision making for breast cancer patients.' AHRQ Health Care Innovations Exchange (Web site).

American Cancer Society (2007). *Breast Cancer Facts and Figures 2007–2008*. Atlanta: American Cancer Society, Inc.

Belkora, J.K., Loth, M.K., Chen, D.F., *et al.* (2008a). Monitoring the Implementation of Consultation Planning, Recording, and Summarizing in a Breast Care Center. *Patient Educ. Couns.*.

Belkora, J.K., Rugo, H.S., Moore, D.H. *et al.* (2008b), Risk communication with breast cancer patients: A cautionary note about printing Adjuvant! screenshots. *Lancet Oncol.*

Brown, R., Butow, P.N., Boyer, M.J., *et al.* (1999). Promoting patient participation in the cancer consultation: Evaluation of a prompt sheet and coaching in question-asking. *Br. J. Cancer*, **80**, 242–248.

Brown, R.F., Butow, P.N., Dunn, S.M., *et al.* (2001). 'Promoting patient participation and shortening cancer consultations: A randomised trial. *Br. J. Cancer*, **85**, 1273–1279.

Butow, P.N., Dunn, S.M., Tattersall, M.H., *et al.* (1994). Patient participation in the cancer consultation: Evaluation of a question prompt sheet. *Ann. Oncol.*, **5**, 199–204.

Cole, B.F., Gelber, R.D., Gelber, S., *et al.* (2001). Polychemotherapy for early breast cancer: An overview of the randomised clinical trials with quality-adjusted survival analysis. *Lancet*, **358**, 277–286.

Doyle, M. and Straus D. (1982), *How to Make Meetings Work*. New York: Jove Books.

Fisher, B., Anderson, S., Tan-Chiu, E., *et al.* (2001). Tamoxifen and chemotherapy for axillary node-negative, estrogen receptor-negative breast cancer: Findings from National Surgical Adjuvant Breast and Bowel Project B-23. *J. Clin. Oncol.*, **19**, 931–942.

Greenfield, S., Kaplan, S., and Ware, J. (1985). Expanding Patient Involvement in Care: Effects on patient outcomes. *Annals of Internal Medicine*, **102**, 520–528.

Greenfield, S., Kaplan, S., Ware, J. (1988). 'Patients' participation in medical care: Effects on blood sugar control and quality of Life in diabetes. *J. Gen. Intern. Med.*, **3**, 448–457.

Griffin, S.J., Kinmonth, A.L., Veltman, M.W., *et al.* (2004). Effect on health-related outcomes of interventions to alter the interaction between patients and practitioners: A systematic review of trials. *Ann. Fam. Med.*, **2**, 595–608.

Hack, T.F., Pickles, T., Bultz, B.D., *et al.* (2003). Impact of providing audiotapes of primary adjuvant treatment consultations to women with breast cancer: A multisite, randomized, controlled trial. *J. Clin. Oncol.*, **21**, 4138–4144.

Harrington, J., Noble, L.M., and Newman, S.P. (2004). Improving patients communication with doctors: A systematic review of intervention studies. *Patient Educ. Couns.*, **52**, 7–16.

Hegel, M.T., Moore, C.P., Collins, E.D., *et al.* (2006). Distress, psychiatric syndromes, and impairment of function in women with newly diagnosed breast cancer. *Cancer*, **107**, 2924–2931.

Hesse, B.W., Nelson, D.E., Kreps, G.L., *et al.* (2005). Trust and sources of health information: The impact of the internet and its implications for health care providers: Findings from the first health information national trends survey. *Arch. Intern. Med.*, **165**, 2618–2624.

Kinnersley, P., Edwards, A., Hood, K., *et al.* (2007). Interventions before consultations for helping patients address their information needs. *Cochrane Database Systematic Review*, **3**, CD004565.

Love, N. (2005). Management of breast cancer in the adjuvant and metastatic settings. *Patterns Care*, **2**, 3.

O'Connor, A.M., Stacey, D., Entwistle, V., *et al.* (2003). Decision aids for people facing health treatment or screening decisions. *Cochrane Database Systematic Review*, **2**, CD001431.

Olivotto, I.A., Bajdik, C.D., Ravdin, P.M., *et al.* (2005). Population-based validation of the prognostic model ADJUVANT! for early breast cancer. *J. Clin. Oncol.*, **23**, 2716–2725.

Ong, L.M., Visser, M.R., Lammes, F.B., *et al.* (2000). Effect of providing cancer patients with the audio-taped initial consultation on satisfaction, recall, and quality of life: A randomized, double-blind study. *J. Clin. Oncol.*, **18**, 3052–3060.

Ravdin, P.M. (1995). A computer based program to assist in adjuvant therapy decisions for individual breast cancer patients. *Bull. Cancer*, **82**(5), 561s–564s.

Ravdin, P.M. (1996). A computer program to assist in making breast cancer adjuvant therapy decisions. *Semin. Oncol.*, **23**(2), 43–50.

Ravdin, P.M., Siminoff, L.A., Davis, G.J., *et al.* (2001). Computer program to assist in making decisions about adjuvant therapy for women with early breast cancer. *J. Clin. Oncol.*, **19**, 980–991.

Roter, D.L. (1977). Patient participation in the patient – provider interaction: The effects of patient question asking on the quality of interaction, satisfaction and compliance. *Health Educ. Monogr.*, **5**, 281–315.

Scott, J.T., Harmsen, M., Prictor, M.J., *et al.* (2003). Recordings or summaries of consultations for people with cancer. *Cochrane Database Systematic Review*, **2**, CD001539.

Smith, R.E., Bryant, J., DeCillis, A., *et al.* (2003). Acute myeloid leukemia and myelodysplastic syndrome after doxorubicin-cyclophosphamide adjuvant therapy for operable breast cancer: The n ational surgical adjuvant breast and bowel project experience. *J. Clin. Oncol.*, **21**, 1195–1204.

Chapter 42

Decision support in the treatment of aneurysms of the abdominal aorta

Anne M. Stiggelbout and J. Kievit

The nature of abdominal aortic aneurysm–a high-stakes decision

An aortic aneurysm is local dilatation of the aorta–the main artery supplying blood from the heart to all the major organs of the body–usually representing an underlying weakness in the wall of the aorta at that location. While the stretched vessel may occasionally cause discomfort, a greater concern is the risk of rupture, which causes severe pain, massive internal bleeding, and, without prompt treatment, quickly results in death. Abdominal aortic aneurysms, hereafter referred to as AAAs, are the most common type of aortic aneurysm. They are mostly detected as an incidental finding by ultrasound in the course of physical examination or imaging, e.g. for urological or bowel symptoms, although some screening programs are being initiated both in the United States and the United Kingdom and are being discussed in other Western countries. A Cochrane systematic review has shown evidence of a significant reduction in mortality from AAA (but not in all-cause mortality) in men aged 65–79 years who undergo ultrasound screening (Cosford and Leng, 2007).

The natural course of the condition

The prevalence of AAAs increases with age, and 5–10% of men aged between 65 and 79 years have an abdominal aneurysm in the area of the aorta, of which 10% are suitable for surgery (Cosford and Leng, 2008). An AAA may remain asymptomatic indefinitely. Mortality risk with an observation policy is mainly caused by non-AAA-related cardiovascular mortality. Risk of rupture increases with the size of the AAA, and there is a high risk of rupture at a diameter of 5 cm or more. Aneurysms of 5–6 cm diameter carry an annual risk of rupture of 5–10%, which increases to around 20% for 8 cm, and even higher for larger diameters. In contrast, small aneurysms, of 4 cm and below, carry a low risk of rupture (around 1–2% annually).

Surgery and other treatments

Unfortunately, rupture is usually the first hint of AAA. Only 10–25% of patients survive rupture, due to high pre- and post-operative mortality. Elective surgical replacement of the aneurysm by a vascular graft eliminates this risk, but carries the inherent risk of operative death. Mortality for open surgery is around 5%, but is highly dependent upon age and the patient's prior state of health. For this reason, 'endovascular' treatment of AAAs has emerged as an alternative to open surgery. It involves the placement of an endovascular stent (usually accessed through the femoral arteries in the groin) into the diseased portion of the aorta. Endovascular repair of AAAs is associated with lower short-term rates of death (around 1–2%) and fewer complications. On the other hand, it is less effective in eliminating rupture risk, as this risk may persist if the prosthesis does not totally exclude the aneurysm from the circulation and the associated blood pressure (the so-called endo-leak). Later re-interventions related to AAAs are more common after endovascular repair, but the survival advantage is more durable among older patients. (Schermerhorn *et al.*, 2008).

Not only diameter, but also expansion rate is predictive of impending rupture, so a rapidly expanding aneurysm should be operated on as soon as feasible. Stable or slowly expanding aneurysms may be followed by routine diagnostic testing (i.e. CT scan or ultrasound imaging). In men, if the aortic aneurysm is 5.5 cm or larger in diameter, grows at a rate of more than 1 cm/ year, or causes symptoms, surgical treatment should be electively performed. In women, surgery may be recommended for smaller aneurysms.

A preference-sensitive decision

The decision of when surgery should be performed is complex and specific to the individual. The overriding consideration seems to be when the risk of rupture exceeds the risk of surgery. The diameter of the aneurysm, its rate of growth, and co-existing medical conditions are all important factors in the decision. However, a decision about having surgery involves a trade-off between short-term and long-term risks and complications. In addition to mortality, complication rates are not negligible. Medical complications, such as heart attack and renal failure, may exceed 10%, and surgical complications, though less frequent, may involve amputation and paraplegia. Rehabilitation may take as long as 6 months. The decision can, therefore, be seen as a so-called preference-sensitive decision (O'Connor *et al.*, 2003), a decision for which the ratio of benefit to harm is affected by patients' values. For each patient with an AAA, there is the therapeutic dilemma of weighing the risks of rupture (and possibly of late elective surgery) against those of early elective surgery. These dilemmas can be expected to increase in the near future, since population screening is being discussed in many Western countries.

Decision aids for AAA decision-making

Surprisingly little research has been done on patient involvement in surgical decision-making for AAAs, and no research is available regarding screening decisions. At the Leiden University Medical Center, in the Netherlands, a randomized trial was carried out in the late 90s assessing the effect of an individualized evidence-based information brochure on decision-making behaviour (e.g. patient choice), quality of life, and autonomy ideals of abdominal aneurysm patients (Molewijk, 2006, Stiggelbout *et al.*, 2008). The individualized brochure presented survival information and a ranking of the treatment strategies (elective surgery, regular follow-up until a threshold, and no surgery/no follow-up), based on a decision-model (see Figure 42.1). The model estimated risks and benefits on the basis of 10 risk factors. The brochure was given to both patients and surgeons to be discussed at a subsequent additional consultation. The decision support was an information aid, and not a true decision aid according to IPDAS standards, since it did not help patients clarify and communicate the personal value they associate with different features of the options.

At the Academic Medical Center in Amsterdam, the Netherlands, an interactive CD-Rom is currently being developed as a decision aid for AAA surgery decisions (Ubbink *et al.*, 2008).

To our knowledge, no other decision aids are available for AAA. Many websites, such as WebMD (http://www.webmd.com/heart-disease/tc/aortic-aneurysm-overview) offer extensive information, but not as formal decision aids. With the advent of screening, the call for decision aids, therefore, becomes more urgent. This is not only for the decision to perform surgery or not, but also for the decision to participate in screening or not. Given the low mortality of small aneurysms, the fact that many aneurysms detected by screening are yet too small to justify

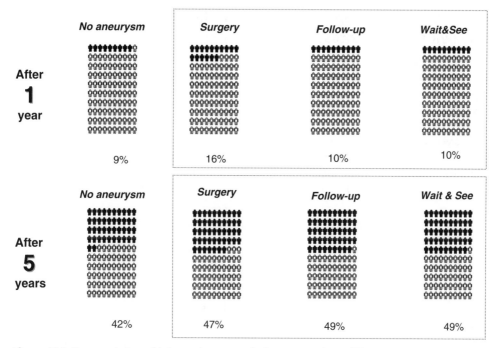

Figure 42.1 Representation of information on survival outcomes from different surveillance or intervention strategies for AAA (Molewijk, 2006).

surgery, and the absence of a reduction in all-cause mortality with screening, the decision to undergo screening may be a strongly preference-sensitive decision. Screening will detect small aneurysms that otherwise may have gone undetected, for which the benefit of surgery is surrounded by uncertainty.

Evidence of effectiveness and implementation

As stated above, the study of Molewijk (2006) has been the only one so far reporting some form of decision support in AAA. In that study, patients, who had received the individualized brochure had a better understanding of important issues in the treatment decision, had prepared more questions and were less satisfied with the duration of the consultation than patients who had received a more general brochure. However, they felt more strongly that the surgeon perceived them more as a 'medical problem' than a patient with a problem. They agreed less with the surgeon's advice and lost some of their belief in 'the doctor knows best'. Before receiving the brochure, this group had a stronger preference for patient-based decisions than the control group who received a general brochure. After the brochure, however, the resulting decision-making was more surgeon based. Apparently, some patients who realized the complexity of the decision preferred the burden of choice to rest upon the surgeon. No effects were seen on patients' quality of life. The authors concluded that individualized evidence-based information stimulated patients' active involvement, but led to less patient-based decisions in the context of this study (Stiggelbout et al., 2008). No update of their model has been carried out, however, and the individualized brochure is not implemented in practice.

Will information keep up to date with therapeutic and evidence advances?

With no true decision aids being available, it is difficult to speculate about the feasibility of keeping the aids up to date with advances in this field. The Molewijk information aid was developed in a period when the endovascular procedure was still experimental, and their model would clearly need updating. Endovascular repair is common practice now, which would seem to make any new surgery decision aid or information aid easy to keep updated. However, the start of population screening can be expected to lead to new information on large screening populations. In such populations, where many small aneurysms will be detected, it may be expected that patients and surgeons will resort to earlier surgery. More data on the harms and benefits of surgery in small aneurysms will accrue, which need to be incorporated into decision aids.

Can we maintain relevance and applicability in this field?

Patient decision aids take considerable effort to develop and can have an important effect on decision quality and the use of health services. Therefore, it is important that they are developed using a systematic and replicable process (O'Connor et al., 2005). The specific developmental steps that are to be taken for AAA decision aids are those common to many patient decision aids and are described in the background document of the IPDAS Collaboration (O'Connor et al., 2005). They include assessing decisional needs of patients; the formation of groups to develop and review patient decision aids (experts and potential users, both patients and practitioners); the iterative process of drafting, reviewing, and revising the aid (providing information about the condition, options, and outcomes; values clarification; and guidance in decision-making and communication); field testing; and, finally, external peer review. For the moment, we assume that these are important steps, but also note that little evidence is available yet on the impact of these steps on the quality of the decisions made in this particularly high-stakes preference-sensitive decision.

References

Cosford, P.A. and Leng, G.C. (2008). Screening for abdominal aortic aneurysm. *Cochrane Database Systematic Reviews*, Issue 2.

Molewijk, A.C. (2006). Risky business: Individualised evidence-based decision support and the ideal of patient autonomy (*PhD thesis*). Leiden University.

O'Connor, A., Llewellyn-Thomas, H., and Stacey, D. (2005). IPDAS Collaboration Background Document. International Patient Decision AidStandards (IPDAS) Collaboration. Available at.http://ipdas.ohri.ca/ IPDAS_Background.pdf. Accessed on 13 June 2008.

O'Connor, A.M., Légaré, F., and Stacey, D. (2003). Risk communication in practice: The contribution of decision aids. *British Medical Journal*, **327**, 736–740.

Schermerhorn, M.L., O'Malley, A.J., Jhaveri, A., et al. (2008). Endovascular versus open repair of abdominal aortic aneurysms in the medicare population. *New England Journal of Medicine*, **358**, 464–474.

Stiggelbout, A.M., Molewijk, A.C., Otten, W., et al. (2008). The impact of individualized evidence-based decision support on aneurysm patients' decision-making, ideals of autonomy, and quality of life. *Medical Decision Making*. **28**(5), 751–762.

Ubbink, D., Knops, A., Molenaar, S., et al. Design and development of a decision aid to enhance shared decision making by patients with an asymptomatic abdominal aortic aneurysm. *Patient Preference and Adherence 2008*; http://www. dovepress.com/articles.php?article_id=2536.

Chapter 43

From leaflets to edutainment: The evolution of PSA decision support tools

Rhodri Evans

Introduction

Decision support technologies (DSTs) have changed radically over the last 10 years. Coinciding with the web and multimedia revolution, developers have, over this period, employed the latest methods to produce DSTs of increasing sophistication. On the one hand this has allowed more information to be presented in different ways, with increasingly complex decision-making functionalities. On the other hand, however, developers have aimed to increase the usability and utility of these interventions. The extent to which these two, not necessarily opposing, aims have been achieved will be explored in this chapter. Specifically, I will consider a field of clinical medicine, prostate specific antigen (PSA) testing, where the uncertainty and controversy surrounding the test is a fertile ground for the evolution of DSTs.

Prostate cancer and PSA testing

PSA testing for prostate cancer is a significant health care issue worldwide. Prostate cancer is increasing in its prevalence in the developed world, partly due to an increase in the population of older men. The PSA test remains the only widely available investigation, and, as a blood test, it is both simple and cheap to undertake. However, it is not a diagnostic test, unlike the prostate biopsy for which men are frequently referred following a high PSA test result. Moreover, the value of the PSA test is limited due to poor sensitivity – around 2/3 of men with a raised PSA test will not have prostate cancer (Selley *et al.*, 1997) – and poor specificity – 20% of men with a 'normal' PSA test will eventually be found to have prostate cancer (Catalona, 1994). Nonetheless, demand for the PSA test is fairly high, and likely to rise. In the United Kingdom, Melia in 2004 reported the annual rate of testing in men with no previous diagnosis of prostate cancer to be 6%, and the annual rates of asymptomatic, symptomatic, and re-testing were 2.0%, 2.8%, and 1.2%, respectively(Melia, 2004). Moreover, there was a significant increase in the rate of PSA testing: a six-monthly testing rate of 2.7% in 1999 and 3.6% in late 2001(Melia, 2004). Higher rates of PSA testing result in a greater utilization of urological services, specifically ultrasound-guided prostate biopsies, and, if prostate cancer is diagnosed, costs related to further investigations and treatment are incurred. Balanced against the costs, nevertheless, is the potential benefit of reduced mortality from prostate cancer. The evidence base for such a reduction in mortality following large-scale PSA testing is, however, unclear. Because of these limitations, there is currently no systematic PSA screening for prostate cancer in most developed countries, although it is to be found in some regions, notably states in the USA.

Paper-based DSTs

One of the earliest paper-based PSA DSTs was a leaflet published in 1997 by the UK National Health Service Centre for Reviews and Dissemination: 'Screening for prostate cancer – information for men considering or asking for PSA tests'(NHS, 1997). In common with many other PSA DSTs, the content ranged from background information about prostate cancer to treatment options, under the following headings:

- ◆ Screening for prostate cancer – the issues.
- ◆ What is prostate cancer.
- ◆ Is screening for prostate cancer useful?
- ◆ The PSA test
- ◆ What if the test is normal?
- ◆ What if the test result is high?
- ◆ Treatment options for prostate cancer
- ◆ Surgery
- ◆ Radiation therapy
- ◆ Watchful waiting

The leaflet was published in a reputable publication, *Effectiveness Matters*, but was not the subject of wide professional consultation nor of an evaluation. In contrast, a paper-based DST from 1999, developed by the American Institute for Cancer Research, *'Reducing your risk of prostate cancer'* (1999), was reviewed by the American Academy of Family Physicians (American Institute for Cancer Research, 1999). Other notable features of that particular DST was that it discussed the influence of race and diet and had the following headings:

- ◆ Are particular races or nationalities more at risk than others?
- ◆ A diet to lower cancer risk?

By the turn of the century, there was an emerging consensus that certain quality criteria – in particular the involvement of professionals – had to be applied to the development of DSTs. A PSA DST from the Minneapolis Veterans Affairs Medical Centre, 2001, *Early prostate cancer: information you should know about testing and treatment'*, was said to be *developed from validated material determined to be important in shared decision-making about prostate cancer screening*. Moreover, the DST was reviewed by a *patient education specialist* and *pre-tested for readability* (VA Medical Centre Minneapolis, 2001). Finally, this DST demonstrated another emerging quality criterion: the need for evaluation. The results of the randomized controlled trial of the DST were published by Wilt and colleagues in 2001, and they found that in the 375 subjects, there was improved knowledge in the intervention group but no difference in PSA testing between the two groups (Wilt, 2001).

The principle of peer-review in the development process was taken to greater lengths by the developers of the UK Prostate Cancer Risk Management paper-based DST, 'PSA testing for prostate cancer: an information sheet for men considering a PSA test,' launched in 2002 (Brett, 2002). Over 100 GPs and primary care leads were consulted in addition to an expert review panel; also, 50 men over the age of 40 were interviewed as part of the development process. The resultant DST was distributed to all GPs in the United Kingdom and was the subject of a randomized controlled trial in 2006 which demonstrated improvements in knowledge about the benefits and risks of PSA testing; in addition, men who received the DST were significantly less positive about the PSA test, although there was no difference in the intention to undertake the test (Watson *et al.*, 2006).

Some of these quality criteria that we have seen developing in the evolution of paper-based PSA DSTs – peer review and evaluation, for instance – became, in 2005, key quality criteria in the IPDAS consensus statement for DSTs (Elwyn *et al.*, 2006). Another criterion which, in contrast, garnered some controversy was the use of testimonials, patient and professional, that resulted from the emergence of video DSTs at the turn of the century.

Video DSTs

The video-based PSA DST developed by The Foundation for Informed Decision Making, USA, (versions from 1994 to the present; Foundation for Informed Medical Decision-Making, 1994) was notable in many respects. First, it was groundbreaking in its presentation of testimonials in bite-sized video clips. Second, these testimonials were treated by the developers as information in their own right, not as diversions from the main textual information base; accordingly, the program scripts were reviewed for clinical accuracy and completeness. Third, was the utilization of field testing: patients viewed and commented on the DST prior to final production. Finally, this DST has probably been the subject of more evaluations than most extant DST (Foundation for Informed Medical Decision-Making, 1994). Frosch, for example, in a 2 × 2 factorial comparison, found that there was improved knowledge and reduced PSA testing in the intervention group that was shown the video (Frosch, 2001).

The controversy relating to the testimonials comes in two parts: first, the high impact of these video clips in comparison with the less engaging textual information; second is the difficulty in striking a balance in the testimonials presented, particularly in relation to a highly controversial issue such as PSA testing. Both of these problems can, to a certain extent, be addressed by placing the video-based testimonials in a web-based DST.

The advent of the web

When discussing web-based PSA DSTs, it is important to differentiate between web-based DSTs and documents that can be downloaded from the web. Indeed, many of the documents discussed earlier, 'paper-based DSTs', can, or could, be downloaded from various websites. Web-based DSTs, in contrast, can be defined in terms of two of the properties of the web: user interactivity and multimedia utilization. Both of these features were present in the web-based PSA DST, *Prosdex* (2005), launched in 2005. *Prosdex* was a development of the UK Prostate Cancer Risk Management paper-based DST, 'PSA testing for prostate cancer: an information sheet for men considering a PSA test,' mentioned earlier (Brett, 2002). Indeed, the textual content of the two DSTs was very similar, based as it was on the same evidence base. In *Prosdex*, however, the users were able to navigate freely through a contents menu, and many of the pages contained not only textual information but also video-clips and other illustrations (see Figure 43.1). The video-clips were of actors enacting the experiences of men who had undergone PSA testing, and also included the experiences of men who had subsequently been diagnosed with prostate cancer and had received various treatments. These experiences were verbatim quotations from a series of qualitative interviews with men who had undergone, or contemplated undergoing, PSA testing (Evans *et al.*, 2007). In contrast to traditional video, where viewers have to watch the whole program, these video-clips had to be selected to be viewed, giving users the freedom of choice and, possibly, addressing the concerns raised earlier of the power of these testimonials. Certainly, when the DST was field-tested, these testimonials proved to be very popular with viewers (Evans, 2007).

At a basic level, user interactivity was employed in *Prosdex* through the ability of users to navigate freely through the site. At a more complex level, however, user interactivity was utilized to develop a decision-making functionality known as the *decision stacker*. Users were able to weigh

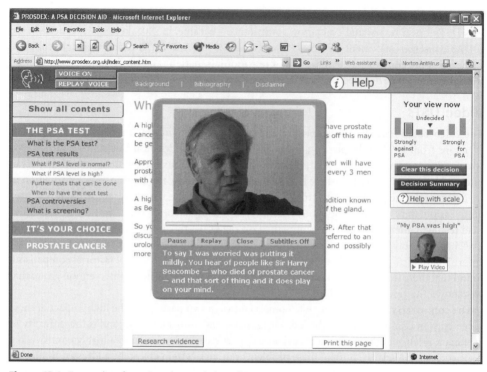

Figure 43.1 Screenshot from *Prosdex,* web-based PSA DST.

the impact of the information/video-clips in each web-page on their decision-making processes by indicating for that piece of information whether they were for, against, or undecided about PSA testing. Each decision was then added, or *stacked*, in the decision summary to produce a cumulative result for the pages viewed. This was a novel functionality, and the initial evidence from the field-testing of the DST suggested that it was under-utilized (Evans, 2007). There are a number of possible reasons for this: first, it may have been too complex for many users; second, it may have been poorly positioned in the site; third, it may not have added value to the users' decision-making process; finally, users may have simply found that there were too many features in the DST.

Edutainment

Multimedia technologies, as we have seen, allow for the presentation of information in a variety of formats. They also, however, provide a fertile ground for creative solutions in the development of DSTs. Arguably such creativity is now a requirement for DSTs, as they have to compete against a multiplex of sophisticated, captivating media such as digital television and commercial websites, for users' attention. And after capturing users' attention, it needs to be maintained – a challenging task considering the subject matter and the fact that many of the users have a low level of education and are unexperienced in viewing what are highly factual websites. One possible solution is to apply to these DSTs viewing formats with which the users would be familiar. Volk and colleagues have recently done this in a PSA DST, targeted to patients with a 'limited health literacy', which used short soap opera video clips to present information about PSA testing and prostate cancer screening (Volk, 2008). They described the technique as 'educational entertainment', and, in

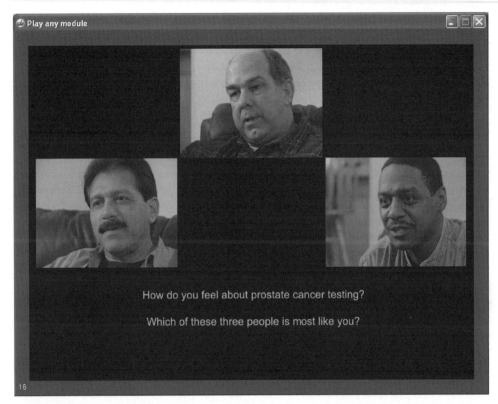

Figure 43.2 Screenshot from *Making informed decisions about testing for prostate cancer,* an entertainment education PSA DST.

a subsequent study, the DST was used by patients from a high-literacy and a low-literacy group. The patients were then asked to complete a 16 item user engagement measure, and user engagement was found to be greater among those from the low-literacy group compared to those from the high-literacy group. Significantly, the patients from the low-literacy group seemed to relate to both the characters and the storylines in the soap opera clips (Volk, 2008). Creative multimedia solutions such as soap opera clips, therefore, offer opportunities to capture and maintain the attention of certain patient groups. They are unlikely, however, to replace patient/professional testimonials, enacted or otherwise. Significantly, Volk and colleagues used entertainment education, dubbed edutainment, and testimonials in their DST (see Figure 43.2).

Edutainment does not currently feature as a quality criterion in IPDAS. Indeed, at the time of its instigation, patient testimonials were seen by the IPDAS collaboration as radical and untested. Of course, it has always been the fate of quality assurers in any field to lag behind the innovators, and the web brings this dilemma into sharp focus, particularly the set of technologies known as web 2.0.

Web 2.0

At the time of writing there are no Web 2.0 PSA DSTs in existence. Notwithstanding the dangers of futurology, it is this author's firm belief, however, that their development is only a matter of time, for the simple reason that web 2.0 is already a part of many patients' lives. The social web, to give web 2.0 its more popular name, includes web functionalities such as blogs, social networking sites, and web fora. The common theme is user interactivity: not only the ability to freely explore web-pages, but also the ability to contribute and, at its extremes, to create web-contexts which mirror users' 'real' social networks. The successful UK website of video patient experiences, *DIPEx*, already employs web 2.0 technology to good effect, through a number of specific health fora, including prostate cancer (DIPEx).

Conclusion

Creativity and innovation comes at a price. Although web-design costs have decreased, the time taken to develop sophisticated DSTs, particularly when features such as soap opera video-clips are involved, has increased significantly. Furthermore, it is expected now that new DSTs should be field-tested and evaluated: time-hungry and costly processes. Potential funders of new PSA DSTs may, therefore, justifiably question the economic rationale for what is, inevitably, a large investment. Presently, there exists no such economic assessment, though there is, in the United Kingdom, work beginning on mathematical modelling, the effect of PSA DSTs on large populations, specifically the urological health care costs. Therefore, it would be reasonable for these funders to argue that the current, publicly available, web-based DSTs are sufficient. The strongest argument against this is what has been demonstrated in this chapter: the relentless pace of change in the delivery of information to patients. Not only will patients expect attractive formats, but they will expect to find formats that are personalized to their background and needs. In a recent study, Frosch and colleagues found that public websites about prostate cancer provided less effective decision support than specifically designed DSTs (Frosch, 2008). PSA DSTs of the future will be bespoke, creative, and dynamic.

References

American Institute for Cancer Research. (1999). Reducing your risk of prostate cancer. Washington: American Institute for Cancer Research.

Brett, J., W.E., Bukach, C., *et al.* (2002). PSA testing for prostate cancer: An information sheet for men considering a PSA test. Oxford: Cancer Research UK Primary Care Education Research Group, University of Oxford.

Catalona, W.J. (1994). Management of cancer of the prostate. *New England Journal of Medicine,* **331**, 996–1004.

DIPEx. Available at http://www.dipex.org/Home.aspx

Elwyn, G., O'Connor, A., Stacey, D., *et al.* for the International Patient Decision Aids Standards Collaboration. (2006). Developing a quality criteria framework for patient decision aids: Online international Delphi consensus process. *British Medical Journal,* **333**, 417–421.

Evans, R., Edwards, A., Elwyn, G., *et al.* (2007a). 'It's a maybe test': Men's experiences of prostate specific antigen testing in primary care. *British Journal of General Practice,* **57**, 303–310.

Evans, R., E.G., Edwards, A., *et al.* (2007b). Toward a model for field-testing patient decision-support technologies: A qualitative field-testing study. *Journal of Medical Internet Research,* Available at http://www.jmir.org/2007/3/e21/.

Foundation for Informed Medical Decision-Making. (1994). The PSA decision: What you should know. Hanover, USA: Foundation for Informed Medical Decision Making.

Frosch, D.L., B.V., Tally, S., *et al.* (2008). Internet patient ecision support. A randomized controlled trial comparing alternative approaches for men considering prostate cancer screening. *Arch. Intern. Med.,* **168**, 363–369.

Frosch, D.L., K.R., and Felitti, V. (2001). Evaluation of two methods to facilitate shared decision making for men considering the prostate specific antigen test. *J. Gen. Intern. Med.,* **16**, 391–398.

Melia J, M.S., and Johns L. (2004). Rates of prostate-specific antigen testing in general practice in England and Wales in asymptomatic and symptomatic patients: A cross-sectional study. *British Journal of Urology International*, **94**, 51–56.

NHS Centre for Reviews and Dissemination. (1997). Screening for prostate cancer — Information for men considering or asking for PSA tests.

Effectiveness matters NHS Centre for Reviews and Dissemination'.

PROSDEX. (2005). PSA Decision explorer. Available at http://www.prosdex.com. Cardiff: Cardiff University.

Selley, S., Donovan, J., Faulkner, A., *et al.* (1997). Diagnosis, management and screening of early localised prostate cancer: A systematic review. *Health Technol. Assess.*, **1**, 2.

VA Medical Centre Minneapolis. (2001). Early prostate cancer information leaflet. Minneapolis.

Volk, R.J., J.-W.M., Hawley, S.T., *et al.* (2008). Entertainment education for prostate cancer screening among primary care patients with low health literacy. *Patient Education and Counseling*.

Watson, E., Hewitson, P., Brett, J., *et al.* (2006). Informed decision making and prostate specific antigen (PSA) testing for prostate cancer: A randomised controlled trial exploring the impact of a brief patient decision aid on men's knowledge, attitudes and intention to be tested. *Patient Patient Education and Counseling*, **63**, 367–379.

Wilt, T.J., P.J., Murdoch, M., *et al.* (2001). Educating men about prostate cancer screening. A randomized trial of a mailed pamphlet. *Effective Clinical Practice*, **4**, 112–120.

Chapter 44

Decision support in the treatment of prostate conditions

Michael J. Barry

Benign prostatic hyperplasia (BPH)

The health care problem

BPH is common among older men worldwide. For unclear reasons, as men age, the tissues of the prostate gland expand and coalesce, eventually causing prostate enlargement, bladder outlet obstruction, and secondary detrusor (bladder muscle) instability. The morbidity of BPH is largely due to its associated lower urinary tract symptoms (LUTS), including urgency, frequency, nocturia, incomplete emptying, straining, intermittency, and a weak stream. Men with BPH may also develop acute urinary retention, the inability to urinate at all; urinary tract infections; and rarely, renal insufficiency (Barry, 2006). Not all LUTS are attributable to BPH; and conversely, many men with BPH never develop bothersome symptoms.

Men with LUTS attributed to BPH who *are* 'bothered' by symptoms have a variety of treatment options, including two classes of drug therapy – alpha blockers and 5-alpha reductase inhibitors; minimally invasive treatments involving applying heat to the prostate via a transurethral approach; or surgery to remove or vaporize obstructing tissue with an electrified cutting loop or, more recently, lasers. In general, as treatment invasiveness increases, effectiveness increases, along with the risks, severity, and duration of potential side effects. If a man's symptoms are not bothersome enough, he may initially pursue "watchful waiting," unless and until symptoms become bothersome enough to merit risking the side-effects of treatment (Barry, 2006; AUA, 2003).

Because the optimal management decision for a man with LUTS attributed to BPH depends heavily on the bother of his symptoms and his feelings about the prospects of possible side effects, therapy for BPH is a classic "preference sensitive" decision. A shared decision making approach should allow for improvement in decision quality by ensuring those decisions are informed and consistent with the patient's values and preferences (Wennberg *et al.*, 2007). Current BPH treatment guidelines emphasize the importance of shared decision making (AUA, 2003).

Decision aids available and their effectiveness

Patient decisions aids are tools to facilitate the shared decision-making process, and a number of decision aids have been developed to help men and their clinicians optimize the quality of therapeutic decisions for LUTS attributed to BPH. The Ottawa Health Research Institute (OHRI) "A–Z Inventory" of decision aids lists four decision aids for BPH treatment (Table 44.1). One is video/DVD-based, with a supplemental booklet, while the other three are web or paper-based. Details about these decision aids, including their availability and the degree to which they meet quality criteria developed by the International Patient Decision Aids Standards (IPDAS) Collaboration, can be found at (http://decisionaid.ohri.ca/AZinvent.php).

Table 44.1 Summary of available benign prostatic hyperplasia (BPH) treatment decision aids, (from Ottawa Health Research Institute, http://decisionaid.ohri.ca, accessed on 7 June 2008)

Title	Options included				Format	Developer, Year of last update/review
	WW*	Medications	Surgery	Other		
Benign prostatic hyperplasia: choosing your treatment.	WW	Alpha blockers, Reductase inhibitors	TURP*, Prostatectomy, TUIP*, TUNA*, TUMT*	–	DVD, Video, Paper	Health Dialog, 2007
Enlarged prostate (BHP) guide.	WW	Medications	TURP, TUIP, Laser surgery, Open prostatectomy	TUMT, TUNA, Interstitial laser, Stents, Alternative therapies, Emerging therapies	Web, Paper	Mayo Clinic, 2006
Should I use medication or watchful waiting to treat benign prostatic hyperplasia (BPH)?	WW	Alpha blockers, Reductase inhibitors	–	–	Web, Paper	Healthwise, 2006
Should I have surgery or take medication to treat benign prostatic hyperplasia (BPH)?	–	Medications	Surgery	–	Web, Paper	Healthwise, 2006

*WW = watchful waiting; TURP = transurethral resection of the prostate; TUIP = transurethral incision of the prostate; TUNA = transurethral needle ablation; TUMT = transurethral microwave thermotherapy.

The Cochrane systematic review of patient decision aids (O'Connor *et al.*, 2003 and 2007) identified two randomized trials of decision aids among men with symptoms attributed to BPH, both using an early version of the Health Dialog decision aid (Table 44.1). In the first trial, conducted in a prepaid health plan in the U.S., 227 patients were randomized to use of the decision aid as part of the decision making process, or "usual care". Over the subsequent year, patients randomized to the decision aid had significantly higher scores on measures of BPH knowledge, satisfaction with the decision-making process, general health perceptions, and physical functioning. Scores on measures of BPH symptom severity and bother, social functioning, and autonomy preference were similar. About 8% of patients randomized to the decision aid versus 13% of control patients chose surgery, a non-significant difference (Barry *et al.*, 1997). The second trial was conducted in general practices in the U.K., where 112 men with symptomatic BPH were randomized to the same decision aid or usual care. In that trial, a significantly higher proportion of patients and their general practitioners felt that treatment decisions had been made mainly or only by patients randomized to the decision aid, and scores on a measure of decisional conflict were significantly lower three and nine months after the decision. No differences were found for measures of anxiety, general health status, symptoms, utility, or costs (Murray *et al.*, 2001).No additional trials were identified in an update of this search conducted in June, 2008, in preparing this chapter.

In addition to these randomized trials, a number of non-experimental studies provide complementary information on the impact of this same BPH decision aid. In one study in six U.S. urology practices, 373 men viewed the decision aid and provided ratings of the experience. Ratings of the amount and clarity of the information provided were generally high, with subjects with lower educational attainment more likely to indicate the amount of information was more than they wanted and that most things (not everything) were clear. Summary ratings of the value of the program were high and not dependent on educational level. A negative rating of their current symptom level was a strong and significant predictor of choosing surgery, while a negative rating of the prospect of post-operative sexual dysfunction was a strong and significant negative predictor (Barry *et al.*, 1995). When the BPH decision aid was implemented in selected regions of two health maintenance organizations in the U.S., surgical rates declined more than in control regions, though the effect could not be definitively attributed to the decision aid (Wagner *et al.*, 1995). In a multi-center Canadian study, 678 men viewed the BPH decision aid and provided high ratings of satisfaction and improvements in self-rated knowledge. In this study, about two thirds of patients undecided about treatment were able to express a treatment preference after viewing (Piercy *et al.*, 1999). Finally, in another U.S. study, subjects viewed the BPH decision aid in a study assessing also the impact of ethnicity and education. Knowledge increased in all groups, and the effect was independent of ethnicity and education (Rovner *et al.*, 2004). In that same study, however, some men still confused BPH and prostate cancer after viewing the decision aid (Holmes-Rovner *et al.*, 2006).

In summary, the literature addressing decision aids for BPH suggests their use in varied clinical settings can improve knowledge, reduce decisional conflict, strengthen the patient's role in decision making, and help undecided patients choose an appropriate therapy. Though decision aids may reduce the use of surgical treatment, the data are not definitive.

Therapy for BPH has become more complicated over the last 10–20 years with many more medical and surgical therapies available to patients, and data about more outcomes allowing the tailoring of treatment to patient characteristics. Despite these advances, the fundamental tenet that an informed patient should share in the decision making process remains unchanged.

Prostate cancer

The health care problem

Prostate cancer is a major cause of morbidity and mortality in developed countries worldwide. Among U.S. men, prostate cancer is the most common solid tumor, and the second most common cause of cancer death (Jemal *et al.*, 2007). With the advent of screening for prostate cancer with the prostate-specific antigen (PSA) test, prostate cancer incidence has increased dramatically, in part because of the over-diagnosis of indolent prostate cancers not destined to present clinically in the absence of screening (Ries *et al.*, 2008; Barry, 2008).

Treatment options for prostate cancer depend on the stage of disease. For prostate cancers that are judged likely to be confined to the prostate gland, many treatments are available including radical prostatectomy (open or laparoscopic surgery, including robotic-assisted), radiation therapy (external beam radiotherapy, intensity-modulated radiotherapy, brachy-therapy, and proton beam therapy), and watchful waiting (including delayed attempted curative treatment for cancer progression, also called "active surveillance"). For prostate cancers with a higher risk of extra-capsular disease, androgen deprivation therapy (reducing male hormone levels) may be added, particularly to radiation therapy (Thompson *et al.*, 2007). Androgen (male hormone) deprivation therapy is the mainstay of treatment for metastatic prostate cancer. Another common situation is a man presenting with a rising PSA after attempted curative treatment, with evidence of residual or recurrent disease. The timing of additional treatment for such men is particularly controversial (Loblaw *et al.*, 2007).

In the "PSA era" – that is, the context of regular PSA testing, virtually as a screening program, such as found particularly in the U.S. – the great majority of men present with clinically localized disease. Up to 25% of men who receive attempted curative therapy will have a rising PSA at some point after treatment (Freedland *et al.*, 2003). For such men, few ran-domized trials are available to guide decision making (Loblaw *et al.*, 2007; Wilt *et al.*, 2008). However, with several treatment choices and few data to guide decision-making, shared decision making for men diagnosed with prostate cancer has been endorsed (Thompson *et al.*, 2007; Loblaw *et al.*, 2007; O'Connor *et al.*, 2003b). The OHRI Inventory lists five decision aids for prostate cancer treatment (Table 44.2). Four focus on attempted curative treatment for clinically localized prostate cancer, three in web or paper format and one video/DVD-based with a supplemental booklet; another in video/DVD format with a booklet addresses the timing of androgen deprivation for a rising PSA after surgery or radiation therapy.

Decision aids available and their effectiveness

The Cochrane review identified two trials of decision aids for prostate cancer treatment (O'Connor 2003a and 2007); interestingly, neither used decision aids meeting the inclusion criteria for the OHRI Inventory (Table 44.2). The first trial randomized 60 men with prostate cancer to an "empowerment intervention" including a written information package, help in developing a list of questions for their physician, and the means to audiotape conversations with their physician; this was compared with receiving the information package alone. Men in the intervention group demonstrated a significantly more active role in decision-making, as well as lower anxiety six weeks later (Davison & Degner, 1997). The second trial, conducted in Finland, randomized 210 men with newly diagnosed prostate cancer of all stages to an "enhanced participation" arm including prostate cancer treatment information tailored to the subject's cancer stage (supplied orally and in writing), a discussion with the physician about the options, and an invitation to

Table 44.2 Summary of available prostate cancer treatment decision aids, (from Ottawa Health Research Institute, http://decisionaid.ohri.ca, accessed June 7, 2008)

Title	Options included				Format	Developer, Year of last update/review
	WW*	Surgery	Radiation	Other		
Treatment choices for prostate cancer	WW	Radical prostatectomy	External beam Seed implants	–	DVD, Video, Paper,	Health Dialog, 2006
Treatment choices for men with early-stage prostate cancer	WW	Surgery	Radiation therapy	–	Web, Paper, PDF	National (US) Cancer Institute, 2005
Prostate cancer guide	WW	Surgery	External beam Seed implants	Combination therapy Hormone therapies Emerging treatments	Web, Paper	Mayo Clinic, 2005
Should I have radiation therapy or a prostatectomy for localized prostate cancer?	WW	Radical prostatectomy	Radiation therapy	–	Web, Paper	Healthwise, 2006
Hormone therapy: When the PSA rises after prostate cancer treatment.	WW	–	–	Hormone therapy	DVD, Video, Paper,	Health Dialog, 2006

*WW = Watchful waiting

participate in the treatment decision; this was compared with the physician offering a single "treatment of choice" with brief mention of other options. Significantly fewer subjects in the enhanced participation arm chose the "treatment of choice" than in the control arm (Auvinen *et al.*, 2004).

In an update of this search through June 2008, an additional trial was identified. A total of 324 men with newly diagnosed prostate cancer were randomized to a "generic" decision aid versus receiving information in multiple formats tailored to the subject's disease stage and information preferences. Men randomized to the tailored information reported greater satisfaction with the decision-making process and their role played in decision making (Davison *et al.*, 2007).

Further non-experimental studies deserve mention. A study of the use of the Health Dialog decision aid for clinically localized prostate cancer (Table 44.2) showed improvements in self-rated knowledge after viewing (Onel *et al.*, 1998). A decision aid focused on the choice of radiation dose improved knowledge, aspects of decision satisfaction, and participation among men exposed to the decision aid versus men in a non-randomized control group (Stalmeier *et al.*, 2007; van Tol-Geerdink *et al.*, 2008). And finally, a "plain language" decision aid prototype showed promising results in early testing (Holmes-Rovner *et al.*, 2005).

Summary

In general, there appears to be less research on the role of decision aids for men with prostate cancer than for BPH, and no trials were identified using the currently available decision aids included in the OHRI inventory. Given the rapidly rising incidence of prostate cancer in many countries, this lack of data is both puzzling and problematic. On the one hand, the Cochrane review of 55 decision aid trials across many conditions suggests a "class effect" with beneficial effects on many domains of "decision quality" (O'Connor *et al.*, 2003a and 2007) (see also Chapters 20 and 21); on the other hand, specific evidence of the effectiveness of decision aids among prostate cancer patients would seem highly desirable but is currently lacking.

As with BPH, the range of therapies available for men with different stages of prostate cancer has broadened considerably, making decisions even more difficult for patients. A lack of comparative effectiveness data, especially from clinical trials, heightens this difficulty. Ongoing treatment trials will address some, but not all, of these questions. In this setting, patients often receive conflicting treatment advice, and make hurried decisions based on incomplete information (Fowler, *et al.*, 2000; Denberg *et al.*, 2006). The value of complete, unbiased information about treatment options in this situation seems obvious. On the other hand, the lack data also poses challenges for decision aid developers, who must assemble multi-disciplinary teams to create programs and materials that present the best available evidence, and update them frequently as new data become available.

Disclosure

Dr. Barry receives grant support from the Foundation for Informed Medical Decision-Making, which develops decision aids with Health Dialog, including some of the decision aids described in this chapter.

References

American Urological Association (AUA) Practice Guideline Committee. (2003). AUA guideline on management of benign prostatic hyperplasia. Diagnosis and treatment recommendations. *Journal of Urology*, **170**, 530–547.

Auvinen, A., Hakama, M., Ala-Opas, M., *et al.* (2004). A randomized trial of choice of treatment in prostate cancer: The effect of intervention on the treatment chosen. *British Journal of Urology International*, **93**, 52–66.

Barry, M., Fowler, F., Mulley, A., *et al.* (1995). Patient reactions to a program designed to facilitate patient participation in treatment decisions for benign prostatic hyperplasia. *Medical Care*, **33**, 771–782.

Barry, M., Cherkin, D., Chang, Y., *et al.* (1997). A randomized trial of a multimedia shared decision-making program for. *Disease Management & Clinical Outcomes*, **1**, 5–14.

Barry, M. (2006). Approach to benign prostatic hyperplasia. In A. Goroll and A.Mulley (eds). *Primary Care Medicine*. Philadelphia: Lippincott Williams and Wilkins; pp. 909–914.

Barry, M. (2008). Commentary: How serious is getting a diagnosis of prostate cancer? *Oncologist*, **13**, 306–308.

Davison, B.J. and Degner, L.F. (1997). Empowerment of men newly diagnosed with prostate cancer. *Cancer Nursing*, **20**, 187–196.

Davison, B.J., Goldenberg, S.L., Wiens, K.P., *et al.* (2007). Comparing a generic and individualized information decision support intervention for men newly diagnosed with localized prostate cancer. *Cancer Nursing*, **30**, E7–E15.

Denberg, T.D., Melhado, T.V., and Steiner, J.F. (2006). Patient treatment preferences in localized prostate carcinoma: The influence of emotion, misconception, and anecdote. *Cancer*, **107**, 620–630.

Fowler, F., McNaughton, Collins, M., *et al.* (2000). Comparison of recommendations by urologists and radiation oncologists for treatment of clinically localized prostate cancer. *Journal of the American Medical Association*, **283**, 3217–3222.

Freedland, S.J., Presti, J.C., Jr., Amling, C.L., *et al.* (2003). Time trends in biochemical recurrence after radical prostatectomy: Results of the SEARCH database. *Urology*, **61**, 736–741.

Holmes-Rovner, M., Stableford, S., Fagerlin, A., *et al.* (2005). Evidence-based patient choice: A prostate cancer decision aid in plain language. *BMC Med. Inform. Decis. Mak*, **5**, 16.

Holmes-Rovner, M., Price, C., Rovner, D.R., *et al.* (2006). Men's theories about benign prostatic hyperplasia and prostate cancer following a benign prostatic hyperplasia decision aid. *J. Gen. Intern. Med.* **21**, 56–60.

Jemal, A., Siegel, R., Ward, E., *et al.* (2007). Cancer Statistics, 2007. *CA-Cancer Journal for Clinicians*, **57**, 43–66.

Loblaw, D.A., Virgo, K.S., Nam, R., *et al.* (2007). Initial hormonal management of androgen-sensitive metastatic, recurrent, or progressive prostate cancer: 2007 update of an American Society of Clinical Oncology practice guideline. *Journal for Clinicial Oncology*, **25**, 1596–1605.

Murray, E., Davis, H., Tai, S.S., *et al.* (2001). Randomised controlled trial of an interactive multimedia decision aid on benign prostatic hypertrophy in primary care. *British Medical Journal*, **323**, 493–496.

O'Connor, A., Stacey, D., Entwhistle, V., *et al.* (2003a). Decision aids for people facing health treatment or screening decisions (Review). Cochrane Database of Systematic Reviews.

O'Connor, A., Mulley, A., and Wennberg, J. (2003b). Standard consultations are not enough to ensure decision quality regarding preference-sensitive options. *J. Natl. Cancer Inst.* **95**, 570–571.

O'Connor, A.M., Bennett, C., Stacey, D., *et al.* (2007). Do patient decision aids meet effectiveness criteria of the international patient decision aid standards collaboration? A systematic review and meta-analysis. *Medical Decision Making*, **27**, 554–574.

Onel, E., Hamond, C., Wasson, J.H., *et al.* (1998). Assessment of the feasibility and impact of shared decision making in prostate cancer. *Urology*, **51**, 63–66.

Piercy, G., Deber, R., Trachtenberg, J., *et al.* (1999). Impact of a shared decision making program on patients with benign prostatic hyperplasia. *Urology*, **53**, 913–920.

Ries, L., Melbert, D., Krapcho, M., *et al.* (2008). SEER Cancer Statistics Review, 1975–2005. Bethesda, MD: National Cancer Institute.

Rovner, D.R., Wills, C.E., Bonham, V., *et al.* (2004). Decision aids for benign prostatic hyperplasia: Applicability across race and education. *Medical Decision Making*, **24**, 359–366.

Stalmeier, P.F., van Tol-Geerdink, J.J., van Lin, E.N., *et al.* (2007). Doctors' and patients' preferences for participation and treatment in curative prostate cancer radiotherapy. *Journal of Clinical Oncology*, **25**, 3096–3100.

Thompson, I., Thrasher, J.B., Aus, G., *et al.* (2007). Guideline for the management of clinically localized prostate cancer: 2007 Update. *Journal of Urology*, **177**, 2106–2131.

van Tol-Geerdink, J.J., Leer, J.W., van Lin, E.N., *et al.* (2008). Offering a treatment choice in the irradiation of prostate cancer leads to better informed and more active patients, without harm to well-being. *Int. J. Radiat. Oncol. Biol. Phys.*, **70**, 442–448.

Wagner, E., Barrett, P., Barry, M., *et al.* (1995). The effect of a shared decision making program on rates of surgery for benign prostatic hyperplasia. *Medical Care*, **33**, 765–770.

Wennberg, J., O'Connor, A., Collins, E., *et al.* (2007). Extending the P4P agenda: Part I. How medicare can improve patient decision making and reduce unnecessary care. *Health Affairs*, **26**, 1564–1574.

Wilt, T.J., MacDonald, R., Rutks, I., *et al.* (2008). Systematic review: Comparative effectiveness and harms of treatments for clinically localized prostate cancer. Annals of International Medicine, **148**, 435–448.

Chapter 45

Decision aids and shared decision-making in mammography screening

Alexandra Barratt and Joan Austoker

The health care context

Mammography screening is offered in many developed countries to women aged approximately 50–69 years to reduce mortality from breast cancer. The main benefits and harms of mammography screening are outlined in Box 45.1 (Barratt *et al.*, 2005a) (for relative frequencies of these benefits and harms see Appendix 45.1). Information about screening generally emphasizes benefits and generally understates the harms (Jorgensen and Gotzsche, 2006), and there is a need for balanced, evidence-based patient decision aids on this topic, especially for younger women (Elmore and Choe, 2007; Qaseem *et al.*, 2007).

The choice

The main choice for women is at 50 years of age and is whether to participate in a 20-year course of mammography screening. Depending on the country, mammography might be offered 2 yearly or 3 yearly. Other choices are whether to start earlier (e.g. at age 40, such as might be offered for women with a strong family history of breast cancer, and if so whether to do annual screening) or whether to continue past age 70.

Benefits

The key benefit of mammography screening is reduced risk of dying from breast cancer (mammography screening does not *prevent* breast cancer). This has been well established by randomized trials for women aged 50–69 years (Gotzsche and Nielsen, 2008; IARC Expert Group, 2002). For example, among 1000 Australian women who participate in 2-yearly screening from 50–69 years of age, about five deaths from breast cancer will be prevented, reducing the number of breast cancer deaths from approximately 14 to 9 (Appendix 45.1).

The age trial recently reported a relative risk reduction for breast cancer death of 17% among women who begin annual screening from age 40 (Moss *et al.*, 2006). While this result was not statistically significant (relative risk 0.83 [95% CI 0.66–1.04]), it is in keeping with the results of the other trials of mammography screening and earlier estimates (Barratt *et al.*, 2005a). Many people are surprised to hear how few breast cancer deaths are prevented by screening (Larson *et al.*, 2005; Schwartz *et al.*, 2004; Webster, 2006), but this is because death from breast cancer is relatively rare in asymptomatic women of screening age.

Box 45.1: Balance sheet of the pros and cons of mammography screening

Benefits	Harms
Less likely to die of breast cancer	More likely to be diagnosed and treated for breast cancer. This includes increased diagnosis and treatment of pre-cancers (DICS), and increased diagnosis and treatment of invasive breast cancers.
Peace of mind	False positive results (abnormal mammograms) which lead to additional imaging and/or biopsies. False negative results (normal mammograms) but women later find they have breast cancer which was not detected by the previous screening mammogram. Anxiety and inconvenience of attending for the screening mammograms. Effects of repeated exposure to ionizing radiation.

Harms

On the other hand, harms from breast screening are relatively common. For example, among the same 1000 women, about 400 will receive a false positive result at some time during those 20 years of screening.

The two most important harms are over-detection and false positives. Over-detection refers to the diagnosis and treatment of pre-cancers (for example, ductal carcinoma *in situ*) and of invasive cancers which are not destined to become clinically important within a woman's lifetime (Biesheuvel *et al.*, 2007; Moss, 2005). This concept is familiar from prostate cancer screening, but is relevant in breast cancer screening too, and indeed applies generally to all cancer screening due to the lead time bias inherent in cancer screening (Barratt *et al.*, 1999). Unfortunately, it is not currently possible to distinguish which breast cancers will progress from those that will not. Thus, all screen detected breast cancers are treated, with treatment options including surgery, radiotherapy, and endocrine therapy. For those women who have these treatments for over-detected cancers, the psychological and physical morbidity must be substantial.

False positive screening has been shown to cause significant psychological morbidity in the short term (Brett *et al.*, 2005; Brewer *et al.*, 2007). There is conflicting evidence about whether the adverse psychological impact of mammographic screening persists long term. Some studies have shown that anxiety persists for months and even years in women receiving a false positive result (Brett and Austoker, 2001; Olsson *et al.*, 1999). This has been shown in some studies to result in significantly lower attendance for subsequent routine screening.

Other harms include the anxiety and inconvenience of attending for screening mammograms, pain and discomfort during screening, and the carcinogenic effect of radiation. Although each radiation dose is small, there is induction of breast cancer among screened women especially if screening begins early. For example, it is estimated that 10 years of annual screening of 1000 women from age 40 will cause 0.5 radiation-induced breast cancer deaths over these women's lifetimes. This was compared with 0.11 radiation-induced breast cancer deaths over the lifetimes

Appendix 45.1 Cumulative frequency of benefits and harms over 10 years of mammography screening for women aged between 50 and 60 years. (Barratt et al., 2005b)

Cumulative number out of 1000 women who, over 10 years:	Age 50 Begin screening at age 50 and have 5 biennial screens	Age 50 No Screening	Age 60 Have another 5 biennial screens	Age 60 No screening
Are recalled for more tests	242.0		184.6	
Are recalled for extra imaging (mammography and/or ultrasound) or clinical examination only	177.9		128.6	
Undergo biopsy (total having at least one biopsy)	64.1		56.0	
Fine needle aspiration biopsy	30.5		25.4	
Core Biopsy	27.2		25.3	
Open Biopsy	6.4		5.3	
Have screen detected invasive breast cancer	17.6		23.3	
Develop an interval cancer	10.4		9.2	
Total who receive a diagnosis of invasive breast cancer	28.1	19.8	32.5	23.9
Have DCIS*	4.9	0.4	5.5	0.5
Total who receive a breast cancer diagnosis of any kind	32.9	20.2	38.0	24.4
Die from breast cancer	4.0	5.9	5.1	8.1
Die from causes other than breast cancer	25.3	25.2	68.5	68.4
Total who die	29.3	31.1	73.6	76.5

*Ductal carcinoma in situ, detected by screening in the screening group, and presenting clinically with symptoms in the unscreened group.

of 1000 women who screen 3 yearly for a decade from age 50 (Berrington de Gonzalez and Reeves, 2005).

The setting

In some countries (for example the United Kingdom, Canada, Australia), access to screening may not need a referral from a doctor, and so women may be making this decision largely by themselves or with their friends and family, rather than jointly with their doctor. This means decision aids for mammography screening are developed for use in a different context from patient decision aids for most treatment choices. Given this context, full information about mammography screening should be available to women so they can, if they want to, make an informed choice about whether to participate in screening (Thornton et al., 2003).

Table 45.1 Mammography screening decision aids

Title	Target audience	Developer	Availability	Evaluation
Should I continue having mammograms to screen for breast cancer?	Women aged 70 who have been participating in screening	Sydney Health Decision Group, University of Sydney http://www.health.usyd.edu.au/shdg/	PDF can be downloaded from http://www.health.usyd.edu.au/shdg/resources/decision_aids.php	Yes, outcomes assessed in RCT (Mathieu et al., 2007).
Should I Start Having Mammograms to Screen for Breast Cancer?	Women aged 40	Sydney Health Decision Group, University of Sydney http://www.health.usyd.edu.au/shdg/	Accessible on line at www.mammogram.med.usyd.edu.au	Yes, outcomes assessed in RCT (being submitted for publication).
A Decision Aid for Breast Cancer Screening in Canada	Women aged 40–79 years	Canadian Breast Cancer Screening Initiative	Will be available in print and web from Public Health Agency of Canada from October 2008.	No, but development based on evaluated Australian decision aids
Mammography Decision Aid	Women 50–70 considering screening mammography, including women with low education levels.	Professor Valerie Lawrence and colleagues at University of Texas Health Science Centre San Antonio	Decision aid diagrams and script available in English and Spanish, on request from Professor Valerie Lawrence, University of Texas Health Science Centre San Antonio VLAWRENCE@uthscsa.edu	Yes, outcomes assessed in small sample of European American and Mexican American women including women with low educational status (Lawrence et al., 2000).
Personally relevant information about screening mammography (PRISM)	Women considering breast cancer screening	Professor Barbara Rimer, Cancer Control PLANET http://cancercontrolplanet.cancer.gov/	http://rtips.cancer.gov/rtips/index.do Click on "informed decision making", then click on Personally Relevant Information about Screening Mammography (PRISM), and agree to terms to access PRISM products including intervention and evaluation tools.	Yes, outcomes assessed in RCT (Rimer et al., 2002).
Becoming involved in the decision: Evidence-based information about early detection of breast cancer with mammography	Women considering breast cancer screening	Dr Birgitt Höldke University of Hamburg Germany	Interactive decision aid in German accessible on line at www.mammographie-screening-online.de (English translation in progress)	Yes, outcomes assessed in web based survey (Höldke, 2002).

The range of decision aids available

There are few decision aids about mammography screening although there are many information tools (e.g. leaflets, fact sheets, brochures, and consent forms) and many interventions designed to increase the uptake of mammography screening (e.g. reminder systems, personalized invitations, publicity campaigns). We searched the Ottawa Health Decision Centre and decision aid inventory and contacted colleagues working in the field to identify relevant decision aids (http://decisionaid.ohri.ca/AZinvent.php). Developers were contacted to confirm decision aid details and availability. Available (and soon to be available) decision aids are listed in Table 45.1.

Other resources

There are also some evidence-based information tools that set out the benefits and harms of screening. Guidance has been developed for the UK NHS Breast Screening Programme to provide women with written information to enable informed decision-making (Goldsmith *et al.*, 2007a, 2007b). Similarly, the European Breast Screening Communication Group, operating within the framework of the European Breast Cancer Network, has developed guidance on communicating information about breast screening to facilitate decision-making (Giordano *et al.*, 2006). In New Zealand, BreastScreen Aotearoa, the national screening program of New Zealand, has developed evidence-based information about the pros and cons of screening for women considering being screened (NZ Ministry of Health 2007 http://www.nsu.govt.nz/Current-NSU-Programmes/1313.asp, accessed on 19 May 2008).

These materials can play an important role in informing women because they are available to women when they participate in screening. However, in general, they are not sufficient for informed decision-making and have not been developed with the same rigour as patient decision aids which comply with IPDAS standards (Elwyn *et al.*, 2006).

Evidence of implementation, effectiveness, cost-effectiveness

As noted above, few decision aids have been developed and evaluated, and implementation of decision aids in screening programs has not yet occurred. While wanting to provide information to women, some screening services may be concerned about potentially negative impacts on participation targets. There is a perceived tension between maximizing participation and maximizing informed choice and consent (Raffle, 2001). This has been resolved in the United Kingdom in favour of ensuring informed participation (UK National Screening Committee), although as noted above the necessary materials to facilitate this have not been developed and implemented to date. In other countries, the issue remains unresolved and is probably one reason why decision aids are not available within screening services.

Will decision aids keep up to date with therapeutic/evidence advances in this field?

Emerging evidence on over-detection

The extent of over-detection in mammography screening remains unclear and estimates vary widely (Biesheuvel *et al.*, 2007; Moss, 2005). Furthermore, the physical and psychological impact of over-detection on women is unknown, although it is likely to be considerable (Schwartz *et al.*, 2000; Welch *et al.*, 2006, 2008). This is an important downside of screening, and it is important that updated information is included in decision aids as it becomes available. The complex and contested nature of this information will ensure that this continues to be challenging for decision aid developers.

New screening tests

New screening methods will continue to be developed. At present, there is evidence that screening with magnetic resonance imaging (MRI) is more sensitive than mammography alone among women with a high familial risk of breast cancer. Combined mammography and MRI is being used among young women (30–49 years) at a high risk of breast cancer who are likely to be carriers of genetic mutations that confer additional breast cancer risk (MARIBS study group, 2005; Saslow *et al.*, 2007). Screening with ultrasound as well as mammography may also be recommended for high-risk women based on clinical factors such as high breast density, previous abnormal biopsy or previous history of breast cancer (Berg *et al.*, 2008). The addition of these new methods not only increases the sensitivity of screening (correctly identifying cancer cases) but also increases the risk of false positive results, and potentially of over-detection (Irwig *et al.*, 2006). Such information should be included in decision aids for high-risk women.

The future

Evidence about the benefits and harms of screening is complex and susceptible to many biases. Future decision aid developers must recognize these issues, if the problems of the past (unbalanced information, focused on benefits) are not to be repeated.

Decisions about screening are extremely preference sensitive. This means there is a role for decision aids within screening programs. However, they do need to address additional challenges, compared to patient decision aids developed for treatment decisions. These challenges include being used by women to make decisions without input from doctors and being used in a context where there may be tension between maximizing participation and achieving informed choice.

Future decision aids should be tailored to women's individual risk of breast cancer, using online risk calculators (e.g. http://www.cancer.gov/bcrisktool/) in combination with decision aids in which benefits and harms are adjusted in accordance with breast cancer risk information for each woman.

References

Barratt, A., Howard, K., Irwig, L., *et al.* (2005a). Model of outcomes of screening mammography: Information to support informed choices. *British Medical Journal,* **330**, 936–938.

Barratt, A., Howard, K., Irwig, L., *et al.* (2005b). A model of the outcomes of screening mammography: Information to support informed choices. *British Medical Journal,* **330**, 936–938.

Barratt, A., Irwig, L., Glasziou, P., *et al.* (1999). Users Guides to the Medical Literature: XVII. How to use guidelines and recommendations about screening. *Journal of the American Medical Association,* **281**, 2029–2034.

Berg, W.A., Blume, J.D., Cormack, J.B., *et al.* (2008). Combined screening with ultrasound and mammography vs mammography alone in women at elevated risk of breast cancer. *Journal of the American Medical Association,* **299**, 2151–2163.

Berrington de Gonzalez, A. and Reeves, G. (2005). Mammographic screening before age 50 years in the UK: Comparison of the radiation risks with the mortality benefits. *British Journal of Cancer,* **93**, 590–596.

Biesheuvel, C., Barratt, A., Howard, K., *et al.* (2007). Effects of study methods and biases on estimates of invasive breast cancer overdetection with mammography screening: A systematic review. *The Lancet Oncology,* **8**(12), 1129–1138.

Brett, J. and Austoker, J. (2001). Women who are recalled for further investigation for breast screening: Psychological consequences 3 years after recall and factors affecting re-attendance. *Journal of Public Health Medicine*, **23**, 292–300.

Brett, J., Bankhead, C., Henderson, B., *et al.* (2005). The psychological impact of mammographic screening. A systematic review. *Psycho-Oncology*, **14**, 917–938.

Brewer, N.T., Salz, T., and Lillie, S.E. (2007). Systematic Review: The long-term effects of false-positive mammograms. *Annals of Internal Medicine*, **146**, 502–510.

Elmore, J. and Choe, J. (2007). Breast cancer screening for women in their 40s: Moving from controversy about data to helping individual women. *Annals of Internal Medicine*, **146**, 529–531.

Elwyn, G., O'Connor, A., Stacey, D., *et al.* (2006). Developing a quality criteria framework for patient decision aids: Online international Delphi consensus process. *British Medical Journal*, **333**, 417.

Giordano, L., Webster, P., Segnan, N., *et al.* European Breast Screening Group. (2006). *Guidance on Breast Screening Communication. European Guidelines for Quality Assurance in Breast Cancer Screening & Diagnosis*. Luxembourg: Office for Official Publications for the European Community.

Goldsmith, M., Bankhead, C., and J, A. (2007a). Improving the quality of the written information sent to women about breast screening. Evidence-based criteria for the content of letters and leaflets. NHS Cancer Screening Programmes.

Goldsmith, M., Bankhead, C., and J, A. (2007b). Improving the quality of the written information sent to women about breast screening. Guidelines on the content of letters and leaflets. NHS Cancer Screening Programmes.

Gotzsche, P.C. and Nielsen, M. (2008). *Screening for Breast Cancer with Mammography (Systematic review)*. *Cochrane Database of Systematic Reviews*, 1.

Höldke, B. (2002). Use of Evidence-based Patient Information about Mammography Screening as a Web-based decision aid. *World Conference on Breast Cancer*, Victoria, Canada.

IARC Expert Group. (2002). *IARC Handbooks of Cancer Prevention. Vol 7 Breast Cancer Screening*, IARC Press.

Irwig, L., Houssami, N., Armstrong, B., *et al.* (2006). Evaluating new screening tests for breast cancer. *British Medical Journal*, **332**, 678–679.

Jorgensen, K.J. and Gotzsche, P.C. (2006). Content of invitations for publicly funded screening mammography. *British Medical Journal*, **332**, 538–541.

Larson, R.J., Woloshin, S., Schwartz, L.M., *et al.* (2005). Celebrity endorsements of cancer screening. *J. Natl. Cancer Inst.*, **97**, 693–695.

Lawrence, V.A., Streiner, D., Hazuda, H.P., *et al.* (2000). A cross-cultural consumer-based decision aid for screening mammography. *Preventive Medicine*, **30**, 200–208.

MARIBS study group. (2005). Screening with magnetic resonance imaging and mammography of a UK population at high familial risk of breast cancer: A prospective multicentre cohort study (MARIBS). *Lancet*, **365**, 1769–1778.

Mathieu, E., Barratt, A., Davey, H.M., *et al.* (2007). Informed choice in mammography screening: A randomized trial of a decision aid for 70-year-old women (see comment). *Archives of Internal Medicine*, **167**, 20392046.

Moss, S. (2005). Overdiagnosis and overtreatment of breast cancer: Overdiagnosis in randomised controlled trials of breast cancer screening. *Breast Cancer Res.*, **7**, 230–234.

Moss, S.M., Cuckle, H., Evans, A., *et al.* (2006). Effect of mammographic screening from age 40 years on breast cancer mortality at 10 years' follow-up: A randomised controlled trial. *Lancet*, **368**, 2053–2060.

Olsson, P., Armelius, K., Nordahl, G., *et al.* (1999). Women with false positive screening mammograms: How do they cope? *J. Med. Screen.*, **6**, 89–93.

Qaseem, A., Snow, V., Sherif, K., *et al.* For the Clinical Efficacy Assessment Subcommittee of the American College of Physicians. (2007). Screening mammography for women 40 to 49 years of age: A clinical practice guideline from the American College of Physicians. *Ann. Intern. Med.*, **146**, 511–515.

Raffle, A.E. (2001). Information about screening – Is it to achieve high uptake or to ensure informed choice? *Health Expectations*, **4**, 92–98.

Rimer, B.K., Halabi, S., Sugg Skinner, C., *et al.* (2002). Effects of a mammography decision-making intervention at 12 and 24 months. *American Journal of Preventive Medicine,*, **22**, 247–257.

Saslow, D., Boetes, C., Burke, W., *et al.* For the American Cancer Society Breast Cancer Advisory Group. (2007). American Cancer Society Guidelines for Breast Screening with MRI as an Adjunct to Mammography. *CA - the Cancer Journal for Clinicians*, **57**, 75–89.

Schwartz, L.M., Woloshin, S., Fowler, F.J., Jr., *et al.* (2004). Enthusiasm for cancer screening in the United States. *Journal of the American Medical Association*, **291**, 71–78.

Schwartz, L.M., Woloshin, S., Sox, H.C., *et al.* (2000). US women's attitudes to false positive mammography results and detection of ductal carcinoma in situ: Cross sectional survey. *British Medical Journal*, **320**, 1635–1640.

Thornton, H., Edwards, A. and Baum, M. (2003). Women need better information about routine mammography. *British Medical Journal*, **327**, 101–103.

UK National Screening Committee. UK National Screening Committee's policy positions.

Webster, P.A., Joan. (2006). Women's knowledge about breast cancer risk and their views of the purpose and implications of breast screening – A questionnaire survey. *Journal of Public Health*, **28**, 197–202.

Welch, H.G., Schwartz, L.M., and Woloshin, S. (2006). Ramifications of screening for breast cancer: 1 in 4 cancers detected by mammography are pseudocancers. *British Medical Journal*, **332**, 727–729.

Welch, H.G., Woloshin, S., and Schwartz, L.M. (2008). The sea of uncertainty surrounding ductal carcinoma in situ – The price of screening mammography. *J. Natl. Cancer Inst.*, **100**, 228–229.

Chapter 46

Decision aids to promote shared decision-making for colorectal cancer screening

Carmen Lewis and Michael Pignone

Introduction

Colorectal cancer is a common and serious health issue. Worldwide, each year, it is estimated that almost 1 million new cases occur and almost 500,000 deaths result from colorectal cancer (Ferlay *et al.*, 2001).

Randomized trials have found that screening for colorectal cancer with fecal occult blood testing could reduce the incidence and mortality from colorectal cancer (Mandel *et al.*, 1993, 2000). These findings have been extrapolated to other CRC screening techniques, including newer occult blood tests, sigmoidoscopy, colonoscopy, and radiological imaging, that have been shown to have good accuracy for detecting cancers and pre-cancerous polyps. Although different techniques for screening have not been directly compared with one another, evidence from high-quality models suggest that several screening test options are both effective and cost-effective, but that no single method is clearly optimal for all patients (Pignone, 2005; Pignone *et al.*, 2002). This evidence has led US guidelines to recommend CRC screening for adults over 50; other countries are considering or now implementing screening programs as well (NHS, 2006; Sydney Health Decision Group).

Despite its potential effectiveness and recommendation for its routine use, only about half of age-eligible patients in the United States are up to date with current screening recommendations (MMWR, 2008). A consistent factor associated with screening (or lack thereof) is whether the individual patient has had an opportunity to discuss the issue of CRC screening and make an informed decision (Lafata *et al.*, 2006). Good decision-making in this context includes high awareness of the issue, review of the potential benefits and adverse effects of screening, discussion of options for how to be screened, and advice about how to communicate with one's provider to schedule and complete the preferred test. Decision aids offer one means of improving the decision-making process for CRC screening. In this chapter, we examine some of the key issues related to decision aids for CRC screening.

Consumer choices for colorectal screening

One important and basic issue is the intended effect of a CRC screening decision aid. Some would argue that because colorectal cancer screening has been shown to be effective and cost-effective, evaluations should focus on measuring whether the decision aid increases screening rates. Others would argue that, based on their values and preferences, the best decision for some patients would be to forego screening. From this point of view, the best measure of the effectiveness of a decision aid would be whether the aid can help patients become sufficiently informed and help them recognize their own values such that they can make a value-concordant decision. As such, measures of knowledge after viewing and measures to assess core values and preferences would be the best determinants of the effect of the decision aid. From either viewpoint, it may also be valuable to measure whether screening was discussed in the provider–patient encounter, and whether the agreed upon action (e.g. decision to have a colonoscopy) was actually performed.

Decision aids for colorectal cancer screening and evidence of effectiveness

We identified CRC screening decision aids from searching PubMed and the Web as well as from colleagues. Some CRC screening decision aids address the question about whether to obtain screening or not (Health Dialog and Foundation for Informed Medical Decision Making (FIMDM); Mayo Clinic Staff, 2008; Sydney Health Decision Group; Wolf and Schorling, 2000) and others address the issue of deciding which screening test is preferred (Dolan and Frisina, 2002; Health Dialog and Foundation for Informed Medical Decision Making (FIMDM); Healthwise, 2006; Pignone *et al.*, 2000) (see Table 46.1). The effects of these decision aids on various outcomes have been studied, including screening test interest and completion, intent to discuss screening with one's provider, screening test choice, knowledge about screening, and decisional conflict. The results of these studies will be reviewed below.

Pignone and colleagues developed a CRC screening decision aid and conducted a randomized trial of 249 patients in three primary care practices in North Carolina – see Figure 46.1 (Pignone *et al.*, 2000). The decision aid was effective in increasing interest in screening, intent to discuss screening with one's provider, the frequency of conversations between patients and providers about screening, test ordering and test completion by 14 percentage points.

In 2002, Pignone and colleagues developed a revised version of the decision aid in order to reflect the changes in CRC screening options (adding colonoscopy and barium enema) and advances in information technology and dissemination (making the decision aid modular and computer based). In an uncontrolled trial of 80 patients at the University of North Carolina in 2003–2004, patients found the aid useful and reported that it improved their knowledge about screening and increased their intent to ask providers for screening (from mean score 2.8 (1 = not at all likely to ask, 4 = very likely to ask) before to 3.2 after viewing the decision aid (difference, 0.4; $p < 0.0001$) (Kim *et al.*, 2005)). However, many (60%) patients who reported readiness for screening did not have a screening test ordered. Crucially, among the 45% who were screened, only 28% actually received the test they chose when using the decision aid. This finding highlights the barriers to implementing informed decision-making in practice.

Table 46.1 Colorectal cancer screening decision aids available for consumers

Whether to obtain screening or not	Screening test options
Colon Cancer Screening: Deciding What's Right For You, *Health Dialog* (Health Dialog and Foundation for Informed Medical Decision Making (FIMDM))	Colon Cancer Screening: Deciding What's Right For You, *Health Dialog* (Health Dialog and Foundation for Informed Medical Decision Making (FIMDM))
Making decisions: Should I have a screening test for bowel cancer? (Sydney Health Decision Group)	Which test should I have to screen for colorectal cancer? *Healthwise* (Healthwise, 2006)
About colon cancer: Do you need testing? *Mayo Clinic* (Mayo Clinic Staff, 2008)	

Figure 46.1 CHOICE communicating health options though interactive computer education for Screening for colon cancer (© 2007 University of North Carolina at Chapel Hill).

The Foundation of Informed Medical Decision Making recently created a patient decision aid for CRC screening, drawing on the work by Pignone and colleagues and new formative research. This decision aid was approximately 30 min in duration and added explicit information about the risk for CRC in the absence of screening. It also provided supplemental information about new modalities, such as CT scan 'colonography'. The FIMDM version was used to evaluate the effect of including or not including an explicit discussion of the option of not being screened in a decision aid. Those who viewed the version without the explicit discussion reported better subjective clarity about the benefits ($p < 0.01$) and disadvantages of screening ($p = 0.03$). We did not observe differences in knowledge or screening interest after viewing the decision aid (Griffith *et al.*, 2008).

The colorectal cancer screening decision becomes more complicated when considering whether elderly patients and patients with limited life expectancy due to co-morbid conditions should undergo screening. Wolf and Schorling performed a trial comparing brief information about CRC screening versus a decision aid administered verbally among 399 older patients in a US primary care setting. They found no difference in the intent to have (or not have) additional screening, with over 60% preferring additional screening in both groups. Intervention patients had more accurate perceptions of test accuracy and control patients rated the efficacy of screening higher (Wolf and Schorling, 2000).

Investigators have also begun to examine how the amount of detail in a decision aid affects its impact. Dolan and Frisina compared, in a randomized trial, the effect of a basic informational decision aid about colorectal cancer screening against a more intensive decision aid based on the analytic hierarchy process (Dolan, 2000). They found that the more intensive decision aid improved the decision-making process as measured by the Decision Conflict Scale, with improvements specifically noted in knowledge and clarity about values. Participants in the more intensive intervention were more likely than those receiving the basic intervention to choose an active screening strategy as opposed to a 'wait and see' (no testing) approach (82% vs. 63%). Despite these process differences, there was no difference in the proportion of patients completing a screening test 2–3 months after the index visit (49% for the intensive intervention group versus 52% for the basic information control group). These results suggest that for the outcome of screening test completion, a limited decision aid appears to be as effective as a more intensive decision aid.

The question of which tests to include in a CRC screening decision aid is another important dilemma. Griffith and colleagues examined the effect of including two (FOBT and colonoscopy) versus five options (FOBT, colonoscopy, sigmoidoscopy, barium enema, and the combination of FOBT and sigmoidoscopy). They found, in a small randomized trial that the number of options did not affect interest in screening, but did affect test choice when co-payments were assumed to be required for each test (Griffith *et al.*, 2008).

Implementing CRC screening decision aids

How best is to implement CRC screening decision aids and whether they will be adopted in clinical practices is currently unknown. One study, however, addressed this question in an academic setting in the United States. The FIMDM decision aid was distributed to all eligible patients by mail, unrelated to patient visits. To 'close the loop' and ensure decisions were carried out, standing orders for CRC screening tests were implemented so that patients could obtain the tests without having to rely on their personal physicians to order them, as this was a significant barrier identified in the previous work. The intervention was mailed to 137 patients of attending physicians and 100 served as wait list controls. Outcomes were assessed by written and phone surveys, and chart reviews to document screening.

Reported viewing of the decision aid was limited. Among the 57 patients who returned material, 11 reported viewing the decision aid. Among the 55 patients who were contacted by phone, 23 remembered getting the intervention materials, 14 looked at the materials, and 6 reported viewing the decision aid. However, using chart review to determine screening test completion, 15% of intervention group patients were screened versus 4% in the control group. The cost of the mailing the programs was estimated to be $94 per additional patient screened (Lewis *et al.*, In Press).

Challenges

As with all decision aids, one important challenge is to keep the information up to date, especially about different screening test options. Newer tests such as CT colonography, immunochemical stool cards, and stool DNA tests are becoming more available. The pros and cons for these newer tests must be weighed against the older tests, and decision aids focused on the choice of screening test option must be updated to reflect these comparisons.

Additionally, as newer tests become accepted, research is needed to determine the optimal number of screening tests that should be presented in CRC decision aids. On the one hand, choosing among equally effective options is a value-based decision; however, providing numerous options may overwhelm patients (Schwartz, 2004).

Future directions

In summary, several colorectal decision aids are available for decisions about whether to obtain screening and about the choice of screening test. They have been shown to facilitate decision-making using a variety of outcomes in research studies. However to date, there is a little evidence examining how best to implement decision aids for clinical use by people facing colorectal cancer screening decisions. Furthermore, it is not known, if implementing decision aids will be viable from a cost perspective. However, given the overall cost-effectiveness of CRC screening, modest costs associated with decision aid implementation may still be valuable. Future efforts are needed to gain a better understanding of how best to effectively and efficiently implement colorectal cancer screening decision aids in clinical arenas and beyond.

References

Dolan, J.G. (2000). Involving patients in decisions regarding preventive health interventions using the analytic hierarchy process. *Health Expectations*, **3**, 37–45.

Dolan, J.G. and Frisina, S. (2002). Randomized controlled trial of a patient decision aid for colorectal cancer screening. *Medical Decision Making*, **22**, 125–139.

Ferlay, J., Bray, F., Pisani, P., *et al.* (2001). *Globocan 2000. Cancer Incidence, Mortality and Prevalence Worldwide*. World Health Organization.

Griffith, J.M., Fichter, M., Fowler, F.J., *et al.* (2008). Should a colon cancer screening decision aid include the option of no testing? A comparative trial of two decision aids. *BMC Med. Inform. Decis. Mak.*, **8**, 10.

Health Dialog and Foundation for Informed Medical Decision Making (FIMDM). Colon Cancer Screening: Deciding What's Right For You. Health Dialog.

Healthwise. (2006). Which test should I have to screen for colorectal cancer? Healthwise.

Kim, J., Whitney, A., Hayter, S., *et al.* (2005). Development and initial testing of a computer-based patient decision aid to promote colorectal cancer screening for primary care practice. *BMC Med. Inform. Decis. Mak.*, **5**, 36.

Lafata, J.E., Divine, G., Moon, C., *et al.* (2006). Patient–physician colorectal cancer screening discussions and screening use. *American Journal of Preventive Medicine*, **31**, 202–209.

Lewis, C., Brenner, A., Griffith, J., *et al.* (2008). The uptake and effect of a mailed decision aid on colon cancer screening intervention A pilot controlled trial. *Implementation Science*, **3**, 32.

Mandel, J.S., Bond, J.H., Church, T.R., *et al.* (1993). Reducing mortality from colorectal cancer by screening for fecal occult blood. Minnesota Colon Cancer Control Study. *New England Journal of Medicine*, **328**, 1365–1371.

Mandel, J.S., Church, T.R., Bond, J.H., *et al.* (2000). The effect of fecal occult-blood screening on the incidence of colorectal cancer. *New England Journal of Medicine*, **343**, 1603–1607.

Mayo Clinic Staff. (2008). 'Do you need testing?' MayoClinic.com.

MMWR. (2008). Use of colorectal cancer tests – United States, 2002, 2004, and 2006. *Morbidity and Mortality Weekly Report*, **57**(10), 253–258.

NHS (2006). NHS Bowel Cancer Screening Programme. NHS.

Pignone, M. (2005). Is population screening for colorectal cancer cost-effective? *Nat. Clin. Pract. Gastroenterol. Hepatol.*, **2**, 288–289.

Pignone, M., Harris, R., and Kinsinger, L. (2000). Videotape-based decision aid for colon cancer screening. A randomized, controlled trial. *Annals of Internal Medicine*, **133**, 761–769.

Pignone, M., Rich, M., Teutsch, S.M., *et al.* (2002). Screening for colorectal cancer in adults at average risk: A summary of the evidence for the U.S. Preventive Services Task Force. *Annals of Internal Medicine*, **137**, 132–141.

Schwartz, B. (2004). *The Paradox of Choice: Why More Is Less*. HarperCollins.

Sydney Health Decision Group. (2008). Making decisions: Should I have a screening test for bowel cancer? University of Sydney.

Wolf, A.M. and Schorling, J.B. (2000). Does informed consent alter elderly patients' preferences for colorectal cancer screening? Results of a randomized trial. *Journal of General Internal Medicine*, **15**, 24–30.

Chapter 47

Shared decision-making in cardiovascular risk management: Experiences and challenges

Trudy van der Weijden, Ben van Steenkiste, and Marije S. Koelewijn-van Loon

Arguments for shared decision-making in primary prevention of cardiovascular disease

Primary prevention of cardiovascular disease (CVD) is focused on patients without CVD but at an elevated risk of CVD. Public knowledge about symptoms and signs of myocardial infarction and stroke, or its risk factors, is limited, even among more highly educated and experienced patients (Bachmann, 2007). CVD is perceived as an undetectable or 'sneaky' disease in its earlier stages (Angus, 2005).

Guidelines on CVD primary prevention have made a shift from separate risk factors, such as hypertension or hypercholesterolemia, to the overall risk profile as a guide for risk management. Identification of people at high risk is guided by so-called 'risk tables' – tools designed to assess an individual's absolute 5- or 10-year risk of a first (fatal) CVD event. Numerous CVD-risk tables are available (Sheridan, 2003). Risk tables differ in the risk factors included (usually gender, age, smoking, systolic blood pressure, and serum cholesterol/HDL-ratio) the way risks are framed and presented and the suggested options for risk reduction (Sheridan, 2003; Graham, 2006). Despite these considerations, risk tables can be looked upon as an established tool in primary prevention.

To date, however, there does not seem to have been a natural uptake of shared decision-making (SDM) in CVD risk management. Emancipation of patients as active and critical consumers was not reflected in a longitudinal analysis of hypertension consultations (Bensing, 2006). Following four reasons can be given to promote SDM in CVD risk management:

1 *Much high-quality evidence is available.* This can be used to estimate individuals' risk and different effective strategies for primary prevention of CVD and has been translated into guidelines including risk tables.

2 *Respecting patient autonomy.* CVD risk management is preventive health care, and the outcomes are uncertain (who benefits), but healthy people are being treated and lifestyle and effects on quality of life are important issues – decisions on CVD risk management are preference-sensitive decisions. Patients and their doctors are often faced with various options for risk reduction, either behaviour change (quit smoking, start physical exercise, change diet) or long-term medication (blood pressure or cholesterol lowering drugs), or both. It is

unrealistic to expect patients to agree on all available options, and therefore the target for risk reduction – after the patient has agreed that the risk should be reduced – should be based on a shared decision.

3 *Inappropriate risk perception and expectation of drug benefits.* Mismatches between a patient's risk perception and the actual CVD risk often occur in general practice among patients without CVD (van der Weijden, 2007). Patients have unrealistically high expectations from cholesterol-lowering drugs, and they also wish to be told the numerical benefit of preventive drugs (Trewby, 2002).

4 *Improve patient adherence.* Research suggests that patients vary widely in their preferences for risk reducing treatments (Montgomery, 2001) and may perceive greater control over their treatment when they are involved in decision-making (Bellg, 2003).

Experiences with shared decision-making support in cardiovascular risk management

There is much experience of feeding back patient-specific CVD risk profiles to clinicians to support their CVD risk management (van Steenkiste, 2008a). However, feeding back CVD risk profiles to patients to facilitate SDM on CVD risk management has only recently been studied. We describe some key randomized controlled experiments.

Montgomery evaluated the effect of simple (information video/leaflet) and complex (decision analyses including standard gamble method to elicit patient values) decision aids for treatment of hypertension in general practice. The patients in the intervention groups had lower decisional conflict and higher knowledge scores. Patients exposed to decision analysis were less likely to start drug treatment than patients exposed to the video information. Actual prescription of blood pressure lowering drugs did not differ between groups, suggesting that the decisions were more influenced by physicians than by patients (Montgomery, 2003).

Lalonde (2004) developed a decision aid booklet with a personal worksheet that in a pilot proved to be acceptable, increase knowledge, and decrease decisional conflict. Risk is framed by a population diagram and also presented as 'cardiovascular age', defined as patient's age + (average life expectancy of population of same age and sex – patient's life expectance according to the risk table). This decision aid was implemented in the community pharmacists' setting, given that actually starting or persistence with lipid-lowering and antihypertensive medications is very low even after they have been prescribed (LaLonde, 2006). The decision aid was mailed to patients before a consultation with the pharmacist. The control group received a personal CVD risk profile. No between-group differences in risk perception or decisional conflict were found. Retrieving the data on CVD risk profile from the treating physician appeared to be difficult.

Sheridan *et al.* invited patients with sustained raised blood pressure in the waiting room of an internal medicine clinic to use a computerized decision aid. A summary print out could be taken to the consultation. Patients were encouraged to choose treatment options that were acceptable and feasible to them. More patients in the intervention group compared to the control group discussed CVD prevention with the doctor (40% vs. 24%) and had a specific plan for CVD reduction (37% vs. 24%) (Pignone, 2004; Sheridan, 2006).

Weymiller *et al.* evaluated a one-page decision aid, to be used during the consultation, for patients with diabetes at endocrinology clinics who were considering cholesterol-lowering drugs. The patients in the intervention group, had lower decisional conflict and higher knowledge scores, were more likely to find the decision aid highly acceptable compared to the control pamphlet

(OR 2.8) and to recommend it to other patients. After 3 months, patients' self-reported adherence to statins was higher in the intervention group (Weymiller, 2007; Montori, 2007).

Van Steenkiste (2007) trained general practitioners to present a decision aid booklet at the first consultation and to invite the 'empowered' patients to return within 2 weeks for discussion about CVD risk management. After 6 months, there was an effect on just one aspect of self-reported lifestyle – physical activity. The physicians only invited 70% of the patients for a second consultation. All patients (returnees and non-returnees) had read the booklet (average time spent 22 min.), understanding was fair to good, but lower socio-economic status correlated with poorer understanding (van Steenkiste, 2008b).

Krones (2008) trained general practitioners in communication strategies to facilitate SDM and in applying a risk calculator during a consultation. Patients in the intervention arm were significantly more satisfied and participated more in the decision-making process. Decisional regret was lower in the intervention group after 6 months. CVD risk had dropped comparably for both arms.

Overcoming barriers

There is no simple overall interpretation due to differences in interventions and outcomes between studies. However, patients' acceptance of decision aids seems good, and the decision-making process seems to shift towards SDM (although this was only explicitly measured in one study (Krones, 2008)), but implementation of SDM seems awkward in primary care. We do not know yet if patients also benefit in terms of health outcomes. Interestingly, there was no greater desire for SDM in patients who had been exposed to decision aids compared to patients who were not exposed (Sheridan, 2006). It seems likely that skill building for both patient and doctor through coaching or training seems necessary, as well as decision aids, to facilitate patients' involvement in decisions about CVD risk. Doctors should adjust their risk communication to each patient's health literacy and numeracy (Hamm, 2007).

Most decision aids have been intended to be used (at home) before or during a consultation, together with a professional, or after the first consultation where risk assessment takes place, in preparation for a second consultation. Computerized self-completed decision analysis for measuring utilities took approximately 1 hour, with or without a researcher (Montgomery, 2001; Thomson, 2006). Weymiller et al. originally developed a computerized decision aid, to be used by patients without supervision in preparation for the visit. Because patients found themselves printing out the material to share its content with significant others, the decision aid was ultimately summarized into a one-page printed paper version to be used during the consultation (Montori, 2007).

Risk estimates were expressed as absolute 10-year risk of events in percentages, natural frequencies, or population diagrams. In some decision aids, comparisons were made to the risk of a peer without risk factors (Sheridan, 2006; van Steenkiste, 2007) or to the age- and sex-adjusted population risk (Krones, 2008), e.g. the so-called cardiovascular age (LaLonde, 2006). It is reassuring that communicating CVD risk did not induce anxiety (Montgomery, 2003; van Steenkiste, 2007). In the latest European risk table, risk is expressed as 10-year CVD mortality (de Backer, 2003). There is a dilemma in CVD risk tables; if we present the risk tables with mortality estimates only, we confront patients with the most precise data with small confidence intervals around the estimates. The downside of this high level of precision is that patients are not informed about the additional risk of non-fatal CVD events (van der Weijden, 2008).

Two studies explicitly described training for professionals. Krones trained general practitioners in two 2-hour group sessions to follow a 6-step script (agree on task, explore subjective risk, calculate objective risk, present preventive options, discuss pros and cons, agree on plan). This was successful regarding the higher rates on the SDM process reported by patients. Steenkiste trained general practitioners (4-hour duration) to follow a two-step model (present the booklet at the first consultation and involve the 'empowered' patients in decision-making in the second consultation), which was not easily implemented. In a new trial, nurses are trained in CVD risk management, including applying a risk communication tool that facilitates visualization of the risk and motivational interviewing as a method to elicit patients' values (Koelewijn, 2008). Probably more intensive strategies are needed to implement this on larger scale (Legare, 2008).

Reflections

Single risk factor decision aids should be abandoned. Following the latest guidelines, CVD risk management starts with assessing the complete risk profile to calculate the absolute overall risk score, and patients should then be given a choice about focusing on none, one, or more risk factors.

Applying CVD risk management is not easy for professionals, let alone adding SDM to CVD risk management. Good teamwork, nurse-led clinics, and smart software programs, integrated in the practice management system, seem to be promising strategies for patient selection and risk assessment (van Steenkiste, 2008a). Disseminating a decision aid to the patient, providing support in reading it (e.g. by a computerized, tailored decision aid available on the internet (Wright, 2004) or consulting a nurse (O'Connor, 2008), and planning a second consultation for SDM might be helpful. It seems most appropriate also to distribute a decision aid before the initial consultation where decisions on risk reducing strategies are introduced.

In conclusion, involving patients in cardiovascular risk management is important. Clinicians must be aware that the perceived risk is not necessarily associated with the actual risk. Effective and feasible (i.e. not too time-consuming) instruments for the explanation of risk and options for risk reduction should be available on the internet, although it seems advisable to support patients in using decision aids and to integrate SDM in cardiovascular risk management in general practice.

References

Angus, J., Evans, S., Lapum, J., et al. (2005). Sneaky disease: The body and health knowledge for people at risk for coronary heart disease in Ontario, Canada. *Social Science & Medicine*, **60**, 2117–2128.

Bachmann, L.M., Gutzwiller, F.S., Puhan, M.A., et al. (2007). Do citizens have minimum medical knowledge? A survey. *Medicine*, **5**, 14.

Bellg, A.J. Maintenance of health behavior change in preventive cardiology. (2003). *Behaviour Modification.*, **27**, 103–131.

Bensing, J.M., Tromp, F., van Dulmen, S., et al. (2006). Shifts in doctor–patient communication between 1986 and 2002: A study of videotaped general practice consultations with hypertension patients. *BMC Family Practice*, **7**, 62.

De Backer, G., Ambrosioni, E., Borch Johnsen, K., et al. (2003). European guidelines on cardiovascular disease and prevention in clinical practice. *Atherosclerosis*, **171**, 145–155.

Graham, I.M., Stewart, M., and Hertog, M.G. (2006). Factors impeding the implementation of cardiovascular prevention guidelines: Findings from a survey conducted by the European Society of Cardiology. *Eur. J. Cardiovasc. Prev. Rehabil.*, **13**, 839–845.

Hamm, R.M., Bard, D.E., Hsieh, E., et al. (2007). Contingent or universal approaches to patient deficiencies in health numeracy. *Medical Decision Making*, **27**, 635–637.

Koelewijn-van Loon, M.S., van Steenkiste, B., Ronda, G., *et al.* (2008). Improving patient adherence to lifestyle advice (IMPALA): A cluster-randomised controlled trial on the implementation of a nurse-led intervention for cardiovascular risk management in primary care (Protocol). *BMC Health Services Research,* **8,** 9.

Krones, T., Keller, H., Sönnichsen, A., *et al.* (2008). Absolute cardiovascular disease risk and shared decision making in primary care: A randomized controlled trial. *Annals of Family Medicine,* **6,** 218–227.

LaLonde, L., O'Connor, A.M., Drake, E., *et al.* (2004). Development and preliminary testing of a patient decision aid to assist pharmaceutical care in the prevention of cardiovascular diseases. *Pharmacotherapy,* **24,** 909–922.

Lalonde, L., *et al.* (2006). Evaluation of a decision aid and a personal risk profile in community pharmacy for patients considering options to improve cardiovascular health: The options pilot study. *Int. J. Pharm. Pract.* **14,** 51–62.

Legare, F., Elwyn, G., Fishbein, M., *et al.* (2008). Translating shared decision-making into health care clinical practices: Proof of concepts. *BMC Implementation Science,* **3,** 2.

Montgomery, A.A., Harding, J., and Fahey, T. (2001). Shared decision making in hypertension: The impact of patient preferences on treatment choice. *Family Practice,* **18,** 309–313.

Montgomery, A.A., Fahey, T., and Peters, T.J. (2003). A factorial randomised controlled trial of decision analysis and an information video plus leaflet for newly diagnosed hypertensive patients. *British Journal of General Practice,* **53,** 446–453.

Montori, V.M., Breslin, M., Maleska, M., *et al.* (2007). Creating a conversation: Insights from the development of a decision aid. *PLoS Medicine,* **4,** 1303–1307.

O'Çonnor, A.M., Stacey, D., and Légaré, F. (2008). Coaching to support patients in making decisions. *British Medical Journal,* **336,** 228–229.

Pignone, M., Sheridan, S.L., Lee, Y.Z., *et al.* (2004). Heart to heart: A computerized decision aid for assessment of coronary heart disease risk and the impact of risk reduction interventions for primary prevention. *Preventive Cardiology,* **7,** 26–33.

Sheridan, S., Pignone, M., and Mulrow, C. (2003). Framingham-based tools to calculate the global risk of coronary heart disease: A systematic review of tools for clinicians. *Journal of General Internal Medicine,* **18,** 1039–1052.

Sheridan, S.L., Shadle, J., Simpson, R., *et al.* (2006). The impact of a decision aid about heart disease prevention on patients' discussions with their doctor and their plans for prevention: A pilot randomized trial. *BMC Health Services Research,* **6,** 121.

Thomson, P., Dowding, D., Swanson, V., *et al.* (2006). A computerised guidance tree (decision aid) for hypertension, based on decision analysis. Development and preliminary evaluation. *European Journal of Cardiovascular Nursing,* **5,** 146–149.

Trewby, P.N., Reddy, A.V., Trewby, C.S., *et al.* (2002). Are preventive drugs preventive enough? A study of patients expectation of benefit from preventive drugs**.** *Clinical Medicine,* **2,** 527–533.

van der Weijden, T., van Steenkiste, B., Stoffers, H.E.J.H., *et al.* (2007). Primary prevention of cardiovascular diseases in general practice. Mismatch between cardiovascular risk and the patient's risk perception**.** *Medical Decision Making,* **27,** 754–761.

van der Weijden, T., Bos, L.B.J., and Koelewijn-van Loon, M.S., (2008). Primary care patients' recognition of their own risk for cardiovascular disease. Implications for risk communication in practice. *Current Opinion Lipid,* in press.

van Steenkiste, B., van der Weijden, T., Stoffers, H.E.J.H., *et al.* (2007). Improving cardiovascular risk management: A randomized controlled trial on the effect of a decision support tool for patients and physicians. *European Journal of Cardiovascular Prevention & Rehabilitation,* **14,** 44–50.

van Steenkiste, B., Grol, R., and van der Weijden, T. (2008a). Systematic review of implementation strategies for risk tables in the prevention of cardiovascular diseases. *Vascular Health Risk Management.* In press.

van Steenkiste, B.C., van der Weijden, T., Stoffers, J.H.E.H., *et al.* (2008b). Patients responsiveness to a decision support tool for primary prevention of cardiovascular diseases in primary care. *Patient Education & Counseling*, **72**,63–70.

Weymiller, A.J., Montori, V.M., Jones, L.A., *et al.* (2007). Helping patients with type 2 diabetes mellitus make treatment decisions. *Archives of Internal Medicine*, **167**, 1076–1082.

Wright, P., Belt, S., and John, C. (2004). Helping people assess the health risks from lifestyle choices: Comparing a computer decision aid with customized printed alternative. *Communication in Medicine*, **1**, 183–192.

Chapter 48

Decision aids for MMR vaccination

Lyndal Trevena and Julie Leask

Global strategies to prevent measles, mumps, and rubella through immunization

Measles is a highly contagious disease which is contracted by almost all exposed non-immune children and those affected bear considerable risk of serious illness or death (Table 48.1). Prior to the development of a vaccine for measles in the 1960s, there were approximately 135 million cases and over 6 million measles-related deaths around the world each year (Wolfson et al., 2007). By 1987, the World Health Organization estimated that this had fallen to 1.9 million and a new combined vaccine for measles, mumps, and rubella became available (MMR). Global health

Table 48.1 Common, less serious outcomes of MMR vaccination versus no vaccination in children

Outcomes of measles in unvaccinated children under 5 years	Outcomes of mumps in unvaccinated children and adolescents	Outcomes of rubella in unvaccinated children and adults	Outcomes of MMR vaccination in children
Most children with measles have the following symptoms ◆ Fever ◆ Loss of appetite ◆ Tiredness ◆ Cough ◆ Runny nose ◆ Red, painful eyes ◆ Rash which begins on face and then spreads to rest of body	Common symptoms of mumps include: ◆ Low grade fever ◆ Loss of appetite ◆ Tiredness ◆ Headache ◆ General aches and pains ◆ Runny nose and other common-cold symptoms ◆ About one third of children will have no symptoms	Common symptoms of rubella include ◆ Fever ◆ Tiredness ◆ Rash ◆ Swollen glands ◆ Aching joints ◆ Sore eyes Out of 100 children and adults who get rubella 50 will have some or all of the above common symptoms 70 will develop temporary arthritis/aching swollen joints (adults only)	Out of 100 children getting the MMR vaccine, the following will have problems: ◆ 4 will have a high fever ◆ 5 will develop a rash ◆ 1 will have swelling an/or less movement of a joint ◆ 4 will be irritable ◆ 1 will get swollen salivary glands ◆ 1 will have redness at the injection site Many of these will occur about 10 days after immunisation

strategies aim for greater than 90% immunization rates with MMR in the first year of life and a second opportunity for vaccination to boost immunity (WHO, 2001).

Most of the countries falling short of the global immunization targets for measles are in the developing world. However, according to WHO monitoring data, some developed nations also fell short of the >90% target in 2006. These include Austria (80%), Ireland (86%), Italy (87%), New Zealand (82%), Switzerland (86%), and the United Kingdom (85%) (WHO, 2008).

Debate about the safety of MMR vaccination

Low coverage in the UK, Ireland, and New Zealand is in part attributable to a major public controversy about the MMR vaccine. It began in 1998 when Andrew Wakefield, a gastroenterologist at the Royal Free Hospital in London, and colleagues, proposed that MMR vaccination may cause an increased risk of inflammatory bowel disease and autism (Wakefield *et al.*, 1998). Wakefield then suggested that single vaccine administration for each disease would reduce this risk and a flurry of negative publicity about MMR ensued. By 2003, MMR uptake had troughed at 80% and outbreaks began to occur (Savage *et al.*, 2005). Over the following years, Wakefield's research was refuted and he is currently under investigation by the General Medical Council in the UK but is still strongly supported by some parent organizations and lobby groups critical of vaccines.

Patterns of under-immunization in developed countries

Recent research in the UK has suggested that MMR under-immunization in developed countries comprises two major groups: those with indicators of disadvantage and social factors facing reduced access to immunization and those with higher education levels who delay or decline MMR vaccination for their children (Hilton *et al.*, 2007; McIntyre and Leask, 2008; Pearce *et al.*, 2008; Smith *et al.*, 2007). This latter group fall into two possible categories – 'reformists' who have concerns about some vaccine safety issues but are likely to support some aspects of immunization; and 'radicals' who actively oppose all forms of immunization and are not likely to be swayed in their attitudes (Hobson-West, 2007).

Evidence-based patient choice through tools such as decision aids may be an important intervention for 'reformist' parents and others who may experience high levels of decision conflict when their child is due for MMR vaccine. A recent report on a decade of parental attitudes to MMR vaccination in the UK supports the notion that parental attitudes can change over time. The proportion of parents believing that MMR was a greater risk than the diseases it protects against fell from 24% in 2002 to 14% in 2006 but the proportion of 'hard-core rejectors' remained stable at 6% (Smith *et al.*, 2007).

Ethical issues for evidence-based patient choice in immunization

If we consider how the four principles of modern medical ethics (beneficence, non-maleficence, justice, and autonomy) apply to the case of parents declining to immunize their child for measles, mumps, and rubella, there is a clear conflict between patient autonomy and justice (Salmon *et al.*, 1999). Whilst 'autonomy' requires a respect for the individual's capacity to make decisions, 'justice' requires fairness to all who might require protection against these potentially serious diseases. This includes the right of the child to be protected and the rights of other children who may not be able to be immunized for medical reasons (e.g. a young child or a child with immunodeficiency).

Similarly, 'non-maleficence' might add weight to the argument that refusing immunization avoids the risk of a serious adverse event. However, if one considers the balance of benefits and harms – 'beneficence' – then the benefits of avoiding the serious effects of measles, mumps, and rubella outweigh the rare chance of an adverse reaction to immunization.

The role of informed choice in autonomy

It might be one thing to respect the decision-making capacities of the autonomous patient (or parents in this case) but it is another thing if this autonomy is uninformed or even misinformed. Then perhaps the pendulum swings towards non-maleficence and health care providers have an ethical obligation to facilitate informed decision-making. Tools such as decision aids can help patients weigh up the benefits against the harms of options.

Beneficence, decision aids, and other evidence-based information: weighing up the benefits against the harms

An online decision aid has been developed by Australian researchers for parents with concerns about the safety of MMR vaccination. This tool summarizes the benefits and harms of MMR vaccination and helps parents weigh these up. It significantly increased the proportion of parents with a positive attitude to MMR, shifting this from 39% before using the DA to 55% after using it ($P < 0.0001$) (Wallace et al., 2006). The likelihood of key outcomes for their child are summarized in Tables 48.1 and 48.2, from sources listed in Box 48.1 and are shown graphically in Figure 48.1.

Justice and immunization decisions

Policy decisions such as providing free MMR vaccination to all children aim to benefit the whole community. This is particularly the case in the control of communicable diseases by immunization where a certain level of 'herd immunity' is required to prevent outbreaks. With a rise in the number of individuals who exercise their autonomous right to refuse immunization, the risk of outbreaks increases and those who are precluded from immunization for medical reasons will be at risk.

While this issue of 'justice' may not be something many health care workers feel adept at discussing with parents, one decision aid study showed that it was an important factor in swaying parents towards immunization. Not surprisingly, 'avoiding the serious but rare complications of measles, mumps, and rubella' was the most common factor in those leaning towards MMR (98%) but 'the fact that [their] child would be less likely to pass on diseases to the small number of children who could not be vaccinated for medical reasons' was the next most common reason in pro-vaccinators after the DA (68%). It seems that altruism and issues of

Box 48.1: Sources for evidence-based patient choice in MMR vaccination

MMR decision aid and fact sheet – http://www.ncirs.usyd.edu.au/

NHS Patient Website – MMR The Facts http://www.mmrthefacts.nhs.uk/

Centers for Disease Control www.cdc.gov

National Network for Immunization Information http://www.immunizationinfo.org/

Table 48.2 Rare but serious outcomes of MMR versus no MMR. NB: Some children may develop more than one of the above

Outcomes of measles in unvaccinated children under 5 years	Outcomes of mumps in unvaccinated children and adolescents	Outcomes of rubella in unvaccinated children and adults	Outcomes of MMR vaccination
◆ **3** in 1,000 may die ◆ **22** per 100,000 may get a fatal degenerative brain disease (SSPE or subacute sclerosing panencephalitis) ◆ **2** in 1,000 may experience inflammation of the brain (encephalopathy).	Out of 100 children & adolescents who get mumps: ◆ 66 get swollen cheeks ◆ 10 swelling under the jaw ◆ *25 swollen and painful testicles (if getting mumps after puberty) ◆ 5 swollen ovaries causing pelvic pain (if getting mumps after puberty) ◆ 4 inflamed pancreas causing pain and vomiting ◆ 8 mild and temporary inflammation of the lining of the brain (aseptic meningitis) ◆ 4 hearing loss that is usually temporary ◆ Less than three in one thousand may have serious brain inflammation with possible death (encephalitis) ◆ 1 in 20,000 may develop permanent deafness, usually on one side ◆ very rarely, a person may get serious anaemia, arthritis or inflammation of the heart	◆ 1 in 3000 get easy bruising and bleeding (thrombocytopenia) ◆ 1 in 6000 get brain inflammation (encephalitis) ◆ 90% of babies infected in the first 10 weeks after conception will have major congenital abnormality such as deafness, blindness, heart defects or intellectual disability ◆ very rarely, a person may get degenerative brain inflammation (progressive rubella pan-encephalitis (PRP)	◆ Between 25 and 34 per 100,000 may have a fever induced convulsion ◆ 4 per 100,000 may get temporary bruising due to low platelets (thrombocytopenia) ◆ Between 1 and 4 permillion may have a serious allergic reaction (anaphylaxis)

justice are important in those who are likely to adopt the vaccination recommendation. Indeed, previous research has pointed to the important role of altruism in vaccine decisions (Hershey et al., 1994).

On the other hand, those who remained against MMR vaccination were less likely to consider the risks to other children as important (25%) but were much more concerned about the rare chance of a serious vaccine side-effect (78%) and would feel 'guilty or responsible for getting him/her vaccinated' (77%).

Measles

Common symptoms of measles
Most children who have measles will have the common symptoms. These may include:

- Fever
- Loss of appetite
- Tiredness
- Cough
- Runny nose
- Red, painful eyes
- Rash which begins on face and spreads to the rest of the body

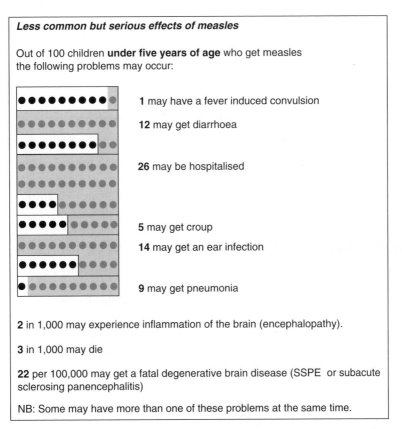

Figure 48.1 What are the potential risks of **measles** compared to the potential risks of MMR?

MMR vaccination

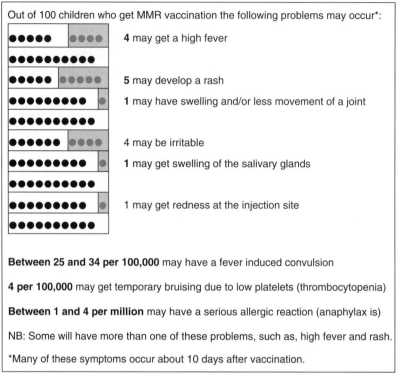

Out of 100 children who get MMR vaccination the following problems may occur*:

4 may get a high fever

5 may develop a rash

1 may have swelling and/or less movement of a joint

4 may be irritable

1 may get swelling of the salivary glands

1 may get redness at the injection site

Between 25 and 34 per 100,000 may have a fever induced convulsion

4 per 100,000 may get temporary bruising due to low platelets (thrombocytopenia)

Between 1 and 4 per million may have a serious allergic reaction (anaphylax is)

NB: Some will have more than one of these problems, such as, high fever and rash.

*Many of these symptoms occur about 10 days after vaccination.

Figure 48.1 (continued)

The role of legislation and regulation in promoting justice over autonomy

At some point, society needs to overrule autonomy for the sake of justice and impose regulation or even legislation. In the case of immunization, these measures might include compulsory vaccination, incentives provided to doctors or parents for children to be vaccinated, or exclusion of the unvaccinated during an outbreak of a vaccine preventable disease.

Implementation of MMR decision aids in practice

Despite evidence for its effectiveness in improving parental attitudes to MMR and being available free online, the tool into practice has not been systematically incorporated into immunization programmes. An unpublished pilot study in the UK has shown that the MMR decision aid was well received by parents (Jackson *et al.*). Decision aids hold promise for this and other vaccines where high levels of decision conflict occur and consumers seek balanced information to make an informed decision which takes into account the impact of their decision on themselves or their child and society in general.

References

Hershey, J., Asch, D., Thumasathit, T., *et al.* (1994). The roles of altruism, free riding, and bandwagoning in vaccination decisions. *Org. Behav. Hum. Dec. Process*, **59**, 177–187.

Hilton, S., Petticrew, M., and Hunt, K. (2007). 'Parents' champions vs vested interests: Who do parents believe about MMR? A qualitative study. *BMC Public Health*, 7, 42, doi:10.1186/1471-2458-7-42.

Hobson-West, P. (2007). Trusting blindly can be the biggest risk of all: Organised resistance to childhood vaccination in the UK. *Sociology of Health and Illness*, 29, 198–215.

McIntyre, P, Leask, J. (2008). Improving uptake of MMR vaccine. *British Medical Journal*, **336,** 729–730.

Pearce, A., Law, C., Elliman, D., *et al.* (2008). Factors associated with uptake of measles, mumps, and rubella vaccine (MMR) and use of single antigen vaccines in a contemporary UK cohort: Prospective cohort study. *British Medical Journal*, **336**, 754–757.

Salmon, D., Haber, M., Gangarosa, E., *et al.* (1999). Health consequences of religious and philosophical exemptions from immunization laws: Individual and societal risk of measles. *JAMA*, **282**, 47–53.

Savage, E., Ramsay, M., White, J., *et al.* (2005). Mumps outbreaks across England and Wales in 2004: Observational study. *British Medical Journal*, **330**, 1119–1120.

Smith, A., Yarwood, J., and Salisbury, D. (2007). Tracking mothers attitudes to MMR immunisation 1996–2006. *Vaccine*, **25**, 3996–4002.

Wakefield, A., Murch, S., Anthony, A., *et al.* (1998). Ileal-lymphoid nodular hyperplasia, non-specific colitis, and pervasive developmental disorder in children. *Lancet*, **351**, 637–641.

Wallace, C., Leask, J., and Trevena, L. (2006). A web-based decision aid pilot improves parental attitudes to MMR vaccination. *British Medical Journal*, **332**, 146–149.

WHO (2001). *Measles Technical Working Group: Strategies for Measles Control and Elimination*. Geneva.

WHO (2008). Immunisation, surveillance, assessment & monitoring: Vaccine preventable diseases. WHO.

Wolfson, L., Strebel, P., and Gacic-Dobo, M. (2007). Has the 2005 measles mortality reduction goal been achieved? A natural history modelling study. *Lancet*, **369**, 191–200.

Chapter 49

Supporting decisions in clinical genetics

Clara L. Gaff and Bettina Meiser

Introduction

Genetic conditions as a group have little in common beyond their familial nature – the fact that they can be passed through generations, potentially affecting multiple family members. This characteristic is a central aspect of decision-making in clinical genetics and one that adds complexity. A family member's decision impacts on the entire family and family considerations impact on the decision of that person.

The familial nature of genetic conditions is perhaps most immediately apparent in reproductive decision-making, where parents might choose to avoid the birth of a child known to be affected by a genetic condition. However, genetic testing to clarify personal health risks also has consequences for relatives. If a genetic test shows a mutation predisposing to an adult-onset condition such as breast cancer, then that person's children also have a 50% risk of inheriting the same predisposition. This knowledge inevitably leads to another area of decision-making in clinical genetics: to what extent to share information about genetics with family members. Although decision-making in clinical genetics is not limited to reproduction, genetic testing, and family communication[1], arguably they are the decisions most commonly faced by people attending genetic services.

Decision context

People at an increased risk of having a child with a genetic condition can have numerous reproductive options available to them (Table 49.1). Shiloh *et al.* (2006) reported that people find information about the consequences of options and about measures to defuse risk most helpful during reproductive decision-making, although no relationship exists between finding the information provided helpful and the difficulty of the decision. The difficulty experienced in making a decision appeared to relate more to the extent to which there is inherent uncertainty and moral dilemma (Shiloh *et al.*, 2006). Certainly reproductive decision-making is ultimately sensitive to personal values and psychosocial needs, rather than medical evidence for a particular course of action.

'Preference sensitivity' is also a characteristic, to an extent, of decision-making about genetic testing. Genetic tests have different health and psychosocial consequences that depend in part on the genetic condition and whether the person making the decision is affected or not (Sivell *et al.*, 2007;

....

[1] The process by which people make decsions about family communication and support provided for this has been reviewed elsewhere Gaff, C.L., Clarke, A.J., Atkinson, P., Sivell, S., Elwyn, G., Iredale, R., Thornton, H., Dundon, J., Shaw, C. and Edwards, A. (2007). Process and outcome in communication of genetic information within families: A systematic review. *Eur. J. Hum. Genet.*, **15**(10), 999–1011.

Table 49.1 Reproductive options

Prenatal screening for chromosome anomalies, e.g. Trisomy 21 (Down Syndrome)
Prenatal diagnosis for chromosome anomalies and/or specific genetic condition
Pre-implantation diagnosis for specific genetic condition
Donor egg or sperm
Adoption
No (further) children

Table 49.2).Commonly, people are motivated to undergo genetic testing to reduce uncertainty in relation to their own and their relative's risk (e.g. Esplen *et al.*, 2001; Meissen *et al.*, 1991). Unsurprisingly, people at the risk of conditions for which there are prevention or risk reduction strategies are more likely to decide to have testing than those at the risk of an untreatable (Meiser, 2005); the potential benefits are more likely to outweigh the potential for psychosocial harms such as adverse emotional reactions and discrimination. For 'treatable' conditions, testing can lead to further decision-making about participation in risk management and preventative care. Thus, decisions relating to genetic testing require consideration and integration of multiple layers of complex information including, the risk of having a mutation, risk of developing the condition, risk management options, residual risks if no mutation is found, and psychosocial consequences for both the person considering the test and their relatives.

Decision-making support

A key expectation of people attending genetic services is to obtain information (e.g. Michie *et al.*, 1997). Shiloh and colleagues suggests that people in risk situations are interested mainly in information about actions that are expected to control and decrease the risk (Shiloh *et al.*, 2006). Certainly, the value of information to consumers of genetic services appears to lie in the decisional control it imparts to themselves and also to their family members (MacLeod *et al.*, 2002; McAllister *et al.*, 2008).

Information to support decision-making is usually provided through the process of genetic counselling. In fact, genetic counselling is the main strategy for decisional support in

Table 49.2 Genetic testing

Type	Description
Mutation detection	Testing of a person with a genetic condition to identify the causative gene mutation(s), e.g. Creutzfeld-Jakob disease
Carrier testing	Testing of a healthy person for the presence of a single gene mutation which is unlikely to be detrimental to his or her health. There is a risk of having an affected child with a carrier of the same condition, e.g. cystic fibrosis
Predictive testing	Testing of an apparently unaffected person to determine if they have a genetic mutation(s) that predisposes to developing a health condition later in life, e.g. hereditary breast-ovarian cancer
Presymptomatic testing	Testing of an apparently unaffected person to determine if they will develop a health condition later in life, e.g. Huntington disease

clinical genetics. The US National Society of Genetic Counsellors defines genetic counselling as 'the process of helping people understand and adapt to the medical, psychological and familial implications of the genetic contribution to disease', elaborating that this includes counselling to promote informed choices (Resta *et al.*, 2006). Relatively little is known about how this is achieved in practice (Sivell *et al.*, 2007), but teaching and counselling models for clinical genetics have been described (Kessler, 1997). The teaching model 'tends to assume that human beings act and make decisions in a more or less rational manner and, when informed, clients should be able to make their own decisions' (Kessler, 1997, p. 287). In this model, expression of emotion is not encouraged. In contrast, the counselling model does not consider education an end in itself but aims to promote, among other things, the counselee's sense of control over the agenda of the genetic counselling session and of general competence and capacity to make decisions. The recently described 'reciprocal-engagement model' of genetic counselling considers the elements of counselling and information as complementary, integrating them by 'articulating a psychosocial basis to exploring genetic information' (Veach *et al.*, 2007). Attending to the supportive and emotional elements of genetic counselling during risk communication can provide greater benefit to consumers than the informational or educational elements alone (Edwards *et al.*, 2008).

Decision aids may serve to facilitate a shift in the focus of clinical consultations from information provision to psychosocial aspects (Braithwaite *et al.*, 2005; Green *et al.*, 2005). Edwards *et al.* (2008) provide an overview of the published literature on decision aids for use in the clinical genetics setting, and the Ottawa Health Research Institute's Inventory of Decision Aids (http://204.187.39.28/AZinvent.php) includes some decision aids which may not have been published in peer-reviewed journals. Together, these sources indicate that few tools have been developed specifically to facilitate decision-making in clinical genetics and almost without exception these have been for decisions relating to prenatal diagnosis of Down syndrome and to cancer genetics. Prenatal screening decision aids are discussed in Chapter 13, so we will focus on aids for those known to be at the increased risk of cancer on the basis of their family history or genetic testing.

Decision aids for people at increased risk for hereditary cancer

Many of the aids available for those at the increased risk of cancer provide support for decisions pertaining to risk assessment and management (Table 49.3). The primary focus is often on information provision; such resources typically lack the classic elements of decision aids (e.g. visual diagrams to describe probabilities, the ability to tailor content to the client, and values clarification exercises) or have not been developed specifically to facilitate decision-making in relation to a particular issue. Others, by contrast, incorporate several features of decision aids, such as values clarification exercises (O'Connor *et al.*, 2003) – that is structured step-by-step guidance, to encourage clients to imagine outcomes of different decision options and stories to describe clients making decisions in similar situations.

With few exceptions (Schwartz *et al.*, 2001; Warner *et al.*, 1999), almost all of the existing decision aids were designed to be used as an adjunct to genetic counselling rather than as stand-alone tools. Indeed, Green *et al.* (2004) found that a decision aid (a computer program) on its own was less effective than standard genetic counselling in reducing women's anxiety and facilitating more accurate risk perceptions; these authors concluded that the optimal use of the decision aid would be to supplement rather than substitute genetic counselling.

Table 49.3 Summary of decision aids in cancer genetics

Reference	Target group	Decision	Use	Format	Values clarification
(Cull et al., 1998)	High-risk hereditary breast-ovarian cancer: women	N/A (educational)	Prior to consultation	Videotape	No
(Green et al., 2001a, 2001b, 2005, 2004)	High-risk hereditary breast-ovarian cancer: women	Genetic testing	Prior to consultation	CD-ROM	Yes
(Kaufman et al., 2003)	BRCA1/2 carriers: women	Risk management options	Not reported	CD-ROM	Yes
(Lobb et al., 2006)	High-risk hereditary breast-ovarian cancer: women	N/A (educational)	During consultation	Booklet	No
(Mancini et al., 2006)	High-risk hereditary breast-ovarian cancer: women	Genetic testing	After consultation	Booklet	No
(Schwartz et al., 2001)	Moderate increased risk breast cancer: Ashkenazi Jewish women	N/A (educational)	Stand alone	Booklet	No
(Tiller et al., 2006, 2003)	Increased risk ovarian cancer	Risk management options	After consultation	Booklet	Yes
(van Roosmalen et al., 2004a)	High risk hereditary breast-ovarian cancer: women considering genetic testing	Risk management options	After consultation	Brochure & video	No
(van Roosmalen et al., 2004b)	BRCA1/2 carriers: women	Risk management options	After consultation	Time trade off interviews	Yes
(Wakefield et al., 2008a,b)	High-risk hereditary breast-ovarian cancer: women	Genetic testing	During consultation	Booklet	Yes
(Wakefield et al., 2008c.)	High-risk hereditary bowel cancer (Lynch Syndrome)	Genetic testing	After consultation	Booklet	Yes
(Wang et al., 2005)	High-risk hereditary breast-ovarian cancer: women	N/A (educational)	Prior to consultation	CD-ROM	No
(Warner et al., 1999)	Moderate increased risk breast cancer: women	N/A (educational)	Stand alone	Booklet & audiotape	No

N/A, Not applicable.

Impact of decision aids

Evidence suggests that decision aids are acceptable to clients at the increased risk for cancer and increase knowledge about the issue being considered (Cull *et al.*, 1998, Lobb *et al.*, 2006, Schwartz *et al.*, 2001, Wakefield *et al.*, 2008a, Warner *et al.*, 2003, Wakefield *et al.*, 2008c, Warner *et al.*, 1999). With few exceptions (Tiller *et al.*, 2006), studies generally show that decision aids generally have no adverse impact on levels of distress and/or anxiety (Tiller *et al.*, 2006; van Roosmalen *et al.*, 2004a; Wakefield *et al.*, 2008a, 2008b; Warner *et al.*, 1999).

By contrast, findings are inconsistent in terms of the impact of decision aids for clinical genetics on 'decisional conflict', that is the degree to which people feel uncertain about the decision under consideration (Green *et al.*, 2004, van Roosmalen *et al.*, 2004a, van Roosmalen *et al.*, 2004b, Wakefield *et al.*, 2008). The evidence on the effect of aids on the actual decision made and/or implemented is also inconsistent, with some studies showing no impact (Tiller *et al.*, 2006; Wakefield *et al.*, 2008a, 2008b, 2008c), while others show decreases in intention to undergo, or uptake of, genetic testing (Green *et al.*, 2001a, 2004; Schwartz *et al.*, 2001; Wang *et al.*, 2005).

To the best of our knowledge, no data are available on the cost-effectiveness of decision aids in this setting. Health economic evaluations of decision aids are clearly a priority area for future research, as is research on the value and impact of decision aids for clients at the risk of inherited conditions other than Hereditary Breast Ovarian Cancer.

Challenges

Genetic counselling and the use of decision aids appear to be complementary approaches: decision aids used prior to genetic counselling led to shorter consultations (Cull *et al.*, 1998; Wang *et al.*, 2005) and enable the counsellor to focus on supportive or emotional aspects that appear to provide benefit to consumers. However, a challenge, perhaps insurmountable, is decisional support for those declining genetic testing or deferring this decision. Decisions *not* to undergo genetic testing for adult onset disorders appear to be made frequently without any contact with clinical services (Taylor, 2004); current approaches provide little opportunity to reach this group and facilitate informed decision-making by addressing the misconceptions that can underlie this decision (McAllister, 2008, Taylor, 2004).

References

Braithwaite, D., Sutton, S., Mackay, J., *et al.* (2005). Development of a risk assessment tool for women with a family history of breast cancer. *Cancer Detect. Prev.*, **29**, 433–439.

Cull, A., Miller, H., Porterfield, T., *et al.* (1998). The use of videotaped information in cancer genetic counselling: A randomized evaluation study. *British Journal of Cancer*, **77**, 830–837.

Edwards, A., Gray, J., Clarke, A., *et al.* (2008). Interventions to improve risk communication in clinical genetics: Systematic review. *Patient Educ. Couns.*, **71**, 4–25.

Esplen, M., Madlensky, L., Butler, K., *et al.* (2001). Motivations and psychosocial impact of genetic testing for HNPCC. *American Journal of Medical Genetics*, **103**, 9–15.

Gaff, C.L., Clarke, A.J., Atkinson, P., *et al.* (2007). Process and outcome in communication of genetic information within families: A systematic review. *Eur. J. Hum. Genet.*, **15**, 999–1011.

Green, M., Biesecker, B., McInerney, A., *et al.* (2001a). An interactive computer program can effectively educate patients about genetic testing for breast cancer susceptibility. *American Journal of Medical Genetics*, **103**, 16–23.

Green, M., McInerney, A., Biesecker, B., *et al.* (2001b). Education about genetic testing for breast cancer susceptibility: Patient preferences for a computer program or genetic counselor. *American Journal of Medical Genetics*, **103**, 24–31.

Green, M.J., Peterson, S.K., Baker, M.W., *et al.* (2005). Use of an educational computer program before genetic counseling for breast cancer susceptibility: Effects on duration and content of counseling sessions. *Genet. Med.*, **7**, 221–229.

Green, M.J., Peterson, S.K., Baker, M.W., *et al.* (2004). Effect of a computer-based decision aid on knowledge, perceptions, and intentions about genetic testing for breast cancer susceptibility: A randomized controlled trial. *Journal of the American Medical Association*, **292**, 442–452.

Kaufman, E., Peshkin, B., Lawrence, W., *et al.* (2003). Development of an interactive decision aid for female BRCA1/BRCA2 carriers. *Journal of Genetic Counseling*, **12**, 109–129.

Kessler, S. (1997). Psychological aspects of genetic counseling: IX. Teaching and counseling. *Journal of Genetic Counseling*, **6**, 287–295.

Lobb, E.A., Butow, P.N., Moore, A., *et al.* (2006). Development of a communication aid to facilitate risk communication in consultations with unaffected women from high risk breast cancer families: A pilot study. *Journal of Genetic Counseling*, **15**, 393–405.

MacLeod, R., Craufurd, D., and Booth, K. (2002). Patient's perceptions of what makes genetic counseling effective: An interpretive phenomenological analysis. *Journal of Health Psychology*, **7**, 145–156.

McAllister, M., Payne, K., MacLeod, R., *et al.* (2008). Patient empowerment in clinical genetics. *Journal of Health Psychology*, **13**, 895–905.

Meiser, B. (2005). Psychological impact of genetic testing for cancer susceptibility: An update of the literature. *Psychooncology*, **14**, 1060–1074.

Meissen, G.J., Mastromauro, C.A., Kiely, D.K., *et al.* (1991). Understanding the decision to take the predictive test for Huntington disease. *Am. J. Med. Genet.*, **39**, 404–410.

Michie, S., Marteau, T.M., and Bobrow, M. (1997). Genetic counselling: The psychological impact of meeting patients' expectations'. *Journal of Medical Genetics*, **34**, 237–241.

O'Connor, A., Stacey, D., and Entwistle, V., *et.al.* (2003). Decision aids for peope facing health treatment or screening decsions. *Cochrane Database of Systematic Reviews*, **1**, 1.

Resta, R., Biesecker, B.B., Bennett, R.L., *et al.* (2006). A new definition of Genetic Counseling: National Society of Genetic Counselors' Task Force report'. *J. Genet. Couns.*, **15**, 77–83.

Schwartz, M., Benkendorf, J.L., Lerman, C., *et al.* (2001). Impact of educational print materials on knowledge, attitudes and interest in BRCA1/BRCA2 testing among Ashkenazi Jewish women. *Cancer*, **92**, 932–940.

Shiloh, S., Gerad, L., and Goldman, B. (2006). The facilitating role of information provided in genetic counseling for counselees decisions. *Genet. Med.*, **8**, 116–124.

Sivell, S., Elwyn, G., Gaff, C.L., *et al.* (2007). How risk is perceived, constructed and interpreted by clients in clinical genetics, and the effects on decision making: Systematic Review. *J. Genet. Couns*, **71**, 4–25.

Taylor, S.D. (2004). Predictive genetic test decisions for huntington's disease: Context, appraisal and new moral imperatives. *Soc. Sci. Med.*, **58**, 137–149.

Tiller, K., Meiser, B., Gaff, C., *et al.* (2006). A randomized controlled trial of a decision aid for women at increased risk of ovarian cancer. *Med. Decis. Making*, **26**(4), 360–372.

Tiller, K., Meiser, B., Reeson, E., *et al.* (2003). A decision aid for women at increased risk for ovarian cancer. *Int. J. Gynecol. Cancer*, **13**, 15–22.

van Roosmalen, M.S., Stalmeier, P.F., Verhoef, L.C., *et al.* (2004a). Randomized trial of a decision aid and its timing for women being tested for a BRCA1/2 mutation. *British Journal of Cancer*, **90**, 333–342.

van Roosmalen, M.S., Stalmeier, P.F., Verhoef, L.C., *et al.* (2004b). Randomized trial of a shared decision-making intervention consisting of trade-offs and individualized treatment information for BRCA1/2 mutation carriers. *Journal of Clinical Oncology*, **22**, 3293–3301.

Veach, P.M., Bartels, D.M., and Leroy, B.S. (2007). Coming full circle: A reciprocal-engagement model of genetic counseling practice. *J. Genet. Couns.*, **16**, 713–728.

Wakefield, C., Meiser, B., Homewood, J., *et al.* (2008a). A randomized controlled trial of a decision aid for women considering genetic testing for breast and ovarian cancer risk. *Breast Cancer Research and Treatment*, **107**, 289–301.

Wakefield, C., Meiser, B., Homewood, J., *et al.* (2008b). When and how should decision aids be used? A randomized trial of a breast/ovarian cancer genetic testing decision aid used as a communication aid during genetic counseling. *Psycho- Oncology.* In press.

Wakefield, C., Meiser, B., Homewood, J., *et al.* (2008c). A randomized trial of a decision aid for individuals considering genetic testing for hereditary non-polyposis colorectal cancer risk. *Cancer*, In press.

Wang, C., Gonzalez, R., Milliron, K., *et al.* (2005). Genetic counseling for BRCA1/2: A randomized controlled trial of two strategies to facilitate the education and counseling process. *American Journal of Medical Genetics*, **134A**, 66–73.

Warner, E., Goel, V., Ondrusek, N., *et al.* (1999). Pilot study of an information aid for women with a family history of breast cancer. *Health Expectations*, **2**, 118–128.

The next and possible future developments

Chapter 50

A devil's advocate: Do patients really want shared decision-making?

Christopher Price

Shared decision-making – recipe for disaster?

Monday morning 7:45

"Would you like seafood tagliatelle or chicken in basil for dinner?"

I inwardly groan, this is one of those Shared Decision-Making (SDM) sessions. I have five minutes before I leave for work and I have to negotiate dinner options with my wife. The other problem is that I have never had either before and I am expected to decide on something that will happen in the future with no guarantee of a successful outcome.

I suppose I need some more information: -

"Where did you get the recipes from?"

"It's that new book I had for my birthday; you can look at the pictures if you like"

Now I am stuck, I am aware that my wife knows a lot more about this than I and yet I am going to have to contribute to the decision, I examine the pictures, here goes:-

"I quite like the look of the seafood"

"O.K. I will need to see what they have at the market"

Now this is a disaster, what I have seen in the book does not necessarily directly relate to my dinner as it will affect me. Let's try another tack:-

"Would you like to try the chicken?"

"MMM I don't really mind, both recipes have their advantages and disadvantages, why don't you choose?"

Disadvantages? – I had not considered the disadvantages up to this point, this introduces another more worrying slant into the choice. I had better let the expert decide:-

"Which one would you prefer?"

"Aw, I wanted you to have the dinner you chose"

Now I am really stuck, so let's make a snap decision:-

"Seafood tagliatelle please"

Monday morning 8:00 I leave for work 10 minutes late and wonder if I have made the right decision.

The small vignette above illustrates many of the drawbacks of SDM.

The first and foremost principle is that there must be a choice to discuss, if there were fresh ingredients for a seafood dish in the refrigerator then seafood tagliatelle would have been this evening.

The lack of knowledge of these recipes (or worse the partial knowledge – I know what seafood, tagliatelle, chicken, and basil are – but as to the combination?) can be used as a metaphor for the patient contemplating the options for breast surgery (have heard of surgery, breast, mastectomy, and radiotherapy but have no concrete or personal experience of them).

The imbalance of knowledge on the one side with mixed emotions of worry over potential treatment options and a lack of knowledge about the outcomes (or the treatment for that matter) on the other.

The lack of time often present in an encounter between patient and physician, leading to either a rushed decision on the patients part or coaching or framing on the physicians side.

Edwards *et al.*, (2002) argue the case for pictorial representation of data to help the decision-making process. This relies on the ability of the patient to be able to interpret the pictorial data; however, more importantly the pictorial representation of the outcome of a recipe is related to many more variables as follows:

- Correct ingredients (does the patient fit exactly into the evidence base?)
- Correct proportions of ingredients (does the patient have the same age, sex, BMI, co-morbidity characteristics as the evidence base?)
- The chef (is the surgeon as skilful, the physician as well practiced?)
- The kitchen (are the same facilities available to the same standard)
- The serving bowl (do all physicians present the alternatives in a standard way?)
- The consumer (previous knowledge (right and wrong) personal preference)

To offer an à la carte menu the maitre d' has to be confident of all of the factors above and yet when the diner asks – 'what's good tonight?' he will pick out a few of the dishes that he prefers.

Practicing shared decision making

Monday morning 9:30

"Hello Doctor Price, Becky has an earache"

Still worrying if I have made the right choice for dinner I focus on my fourth patient of the morning, Becky Smith is 2 ½ and has an earache of 2 days duration, a mild fever and a red angry looking ear drum. Remembering the decision making ordeal my wife put me through less than an hour ago I decide that I will try out this SDM lark. I search for "explaining risks" and "otitis media" on Google and the first hit gives me a picture with nice smiley faces and proceed to explain to Mrs. Smith and the increasingly fractious Becky

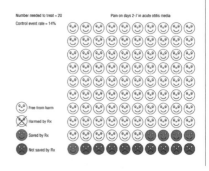

Courtesy Dr Chris Cates
http://www.nntonline.com/

"The yellow smiley faces show that most patients are free from harm"
"What does that mean doctor?"
I hastily read the accompanying text
"I think it means that if we don't treat patients all these yellow smileys are better within 2 days"
"And if we do treat?"
Becky starts crying and holding her ear.
"All the yellow smileys and the purple ones are better"
"Ah so what you are saying is that more children get better quicker with treatment than without"
"Yes but"
"And no one is harmed"
Becky chooses this moment to announce
"I feel sick"
Having furnished Mrs. Smith with a vomit bowl I sign the prescription for the amoxicillin and reflect on what could have gone better.

SDM cannot apply to all situations; there will be instances where the physician needs to move the fulcrum (see Figure 50.1) of the balance of the choice one way or another by framing or influencing the decision. There will equally be instances that the fulcrum is moved unconsciously by the physician and instances where the fulcrum is moved by the patient, either intentionally or unintentionally. The physician acting as an agent (see Chapter 11) may present the patients with options but suggest that one way is superior. How different is this to shared decision-making? It could be argued that in all consultations there is an agency approach but that the fulcrum of the balance just varies. Figure 50.1 shows the different roles and activities of physicians and patients in the shared, patient-led, and physician-led models usually described.

In the first example, there could be an argument that this represents true SDM; however, this is simply an agent/client relationship. At any stage, the physician can push the fulcrum and frame the situation to suit the physician's intended outcome.

Shared decision-making – the agent

Monday afternoon 2:00
"Well Doctor Price, have you decided yet – France Spain or Italy?"
The travel agent had decided that I had not made enough decisions for one day; however this was one choice I was going to make myself. I had promised myself a trip to Bordeaux for a few years – and this year ....
"France, Bordeaux region, hotel for 2 weeks please"
"You seem to have made up your mind, have you looked at the brochures?"
This flummoxed me; I thought this was what travel agents were for.
"No, I rather thought I would leave that up to you"
He fixed me with a withering look and resignedly pulled down three glossy magazines, worryingly one was headed "holidays in Italy" and another "the Spanish adventure"
"I would like to go to Bordeaux please"

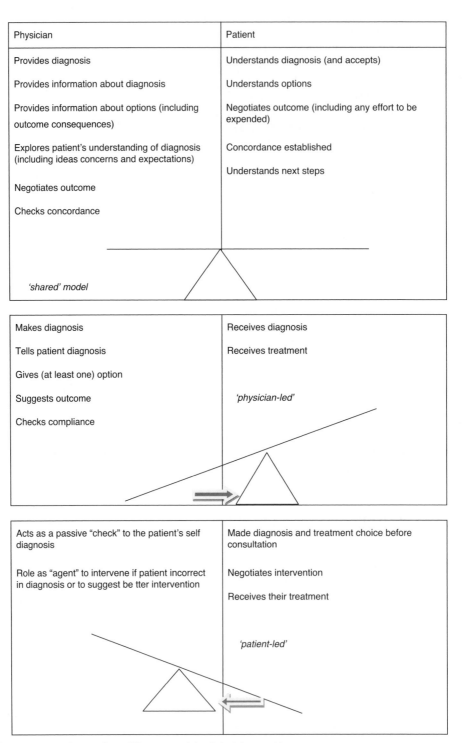

Physician	Patient
Provides diagnosis	Understands diagnosis (and accepts)
Provides information about diagnosis	Understands options
Provides information about options (including outcome consequences)	Negotiates outcome (including any effort to be expended)
Explores patient's understanding of diagnosis (including ideas concerns and expectations)	Concordance established
	Understands next steps
Negotiates outcome	
Checks concordance	
'shared' model	

Makes diagnosis	Receives diagnosis
Tells patient diagnosis	Receives treatment
Gives (at least one) option	
Suggests outcome	*'physician-led'*
Checks compliance	

Acts as a passive "check" to the patient's self diagnosis	Made diagnosis and treatment choice before consultation
Role as "agent" to intervene if patient incorrect in diagnosis or to suggest be tter intervention	Negotiates intervention
	Receives their treatment
	'patient-led'

Figure 50.1 Understanding different models of decision-making.

> *"We have some wonderful bargains in Tuscany and the Rio Oja areas, flights, hotels and a hire car all in the price"*
>
> I looked at the pictures, I looked at the restaurants, I looked at the wines and I looked at the price – and that's what got me, I could have two weeks in the Rioja region for the price of one in Bordeaux and a car thrown in. I felt the equipoise move.
>
> *"Let's go for Spain then"*
>
> I couldn't believe the words – but they were out. I was so pleased I had made a decision............... with the help of an agent.

The devil is out – the physician controls the consultation in the framing. Shared decision-making is not a level playing field and the skilled physician acts as the patient's agent. The skill is the art of convincing the patient they have (been given and) made the choice.

Gravel *et al.* (2006) highlight the three most often reported barriers to SDM as follows:

◆ Time constraints

◆ Patient characteristics

◆ Clinical situation

All three of these constraints are physician determined. Time is finite and is only constrained by a physician's practice. Patient characteristics are in, at least, part a subjective judgement on behalf of the physician, and the clinical situation again is determined by both physician and patient contact. The physician can make time – either by giving information to be taken away, digested, and a further encounter planned or extending the consultation time. The characteristics of the patient may influence their wish to be involved in decision making (McKinstry, 2000); however, this should only become apparent as the encounter progresses and the physician acting as an agent makes a judgement that the patient does not or cannot be involved in a SDM process. The clinical situation may impact in an emergency situation; however, this argument is surely one of the physicians deciding that it is inappropriate.

Shared decision-making – conclusion

> Monday evening 7.30
>
> *"Dinner's nearly ready, would you like some wine?"*
>
> I am getting the hang of this SDM by now and so I need to find out what's on offer
>
> *"What have we got there – white I think with the seafood?"*
>
> *"There's a nice Pinot Grigot or even a Chablis in the fridge"*
>
> Things are looking up, I have a choice to make, am familiar with both wines, both are chilled and either would be acceptable with dinner.
>
> *"Which would you prefer?"*
>
> My wife shrugs
>
> *"I like both – the Chablis is the better wine but the Pinot is more fruity"*
>
> I realise that I have at last found the answer to SDM – it works when the outcome stakes are low, there is no real loss in either choice and the person giving the choice has no view on the outcome. I close my eyes, open the fridge and grab the nearest bottle..................
>
> *"It looks like ketchup then"*
>
> The tagliatelle was delicious (eventually chose the Pinot) even if it didn't look quite like the picture in the book as there was no squid at the market. I suspect however the chicken in basil would have been as good.

SDM can work on low-stakes decisions where outcomes do not differ greatly (e.g. what is for dinner? antibiotics in otitis media), where there is no hidden agenda on either side (e.g. higher commission on Spanish holidays, prescribing projects to lower antibiotic prescribing), and both sides are in a position to negotiate (please Becky stop crying and do not be sick on my carpet, please Becky stop crying and do not be sick on Dr. Price). Once there are confounding factors introduced, the equipoise shifts, and there is an agency arrangement with (usually) the physician in the role of the agent.

Shared decision-making is another phrase for patient centeredness and describes good consultation skills; however, it does not mean shared (equal) decision (it is a choice of options provided by the physician) making (selecting from a pick list). The most well-informed patient still uses the doctor as an agent to some extent (checking decision, what would you do?) and as such SDM is a myth.

Competing interests

The author believes in shared decision-making (but disputes what it is), likes seafood tagliatelle, and prefers good claret to Rioja. He has worked in partnership in clinical practice with Adrian Edwards for the past 10 years, so may not feel free to say exactly what he thinks about these issues.

References

Edwards, A., Elwyn, G., and Mulley, A.G. (2002). Explaining risks: Turning numerical data into meaningful pictures. *British Medical Journal*, **324**, 827–830.

Gravel, K., Legare, F., and Graham, I. (2006). Barriers and facilitators to implementing shared decision-making in clinical practice: A systematic review of health professionals perceptions. *Implementation Science*, **1**, 16.

McKinstry, B. (2000). Do patients wish to be involved in decision making in the consultation? A cross sectional survey with video vignettes. *British Medical Journal*, **321**, 867–871.

Chapter 51

Barriers and facilitators to implementation of shared decision-making

France Légaré, Stéphane Ratté, Karine Gravel, and Ian D. Graham

Introduction

The expanded availability of health information, the consumer movement, the desire of patients to be actively involved in their health care, the need to manage public expectations, and the increased concern about patient safety are among the factors that support the idea of an extended role for patients in clinical decision-making. However, shared decision-making has not yet been adopted by health practitioners. Although there are very few data available on specific interventions found to be effective for implementing shared decision-making in clinical practice, a growing body of knowledge can inform us about those interventions most likely to be successful or worth considering in future initiatives. In this chapter, we highlight the specific challenges associated with the barriers and facilitators to the adoption of shared decision-making in clinical practice. The first section reports on a conceptual model for assessing the barriers and facilitators. It then addresses measurement issues and presents a few instruments that could be useful for assessing barriers and facilitators to the implementation of shared decision-making. The second section briefly reports on implementation studies of shared decision-making in clinical practice. The last section identifies strengths and limitations associated with a barriers and facilitators assessment approach as well as areas needing further research.

Assessment of barriers and facilitators to the implementation of shared decision-making, based on the clinical practice guidelines framework for improvement

One of the most often cited conceptual frameworks regarding barriers to knowledge use in health care is the Clinical Practice Guidelines Framework for Improvement (Cabana *et al.*, 1999). This framework was based on an extensive search of the literature of barriers to physician adherence to clinical practice guidelines and was organized according to knowledge, attitudes, and behaviour of physicians. Here, we define barriers as factors that limit or restrict implementation and facilitators as factors that promote or help implement shared decision-making in clinical practice. This is important because researchers tend to forget that the same factor may sometimes be identified both as a barrier and as a facilitator to knowledge use, demonstrating the importance of developing a more comprehensive and integrated understanding of both barriers and facilitators concurrently (Graham *et al.*, 2003).

Recently, this framework was used for systematically assessing published studies on barriers and/or facilitators to implementing shared decision-making in clinical practice (Gravel *et al.*, 2006). Briefly, 31 publications covering 28 unique studies were included. Eleven studies were from the United Kingdom, eight from the USA, four from Canada, two from the Netherlands, and one from each of the following countries: France, Mexico, and Australia. Overall, the vast majority of participants ($n = 2784$) were physicians (89%). Table 51.1 shows its main results. Overall, this systematic review showed that interventions to foster implementation of shared decision-making in clinical practice will need to address a broad range of factors. It also revealed that on this subject, there was very little known about health professionals other than physicians.

Table 51.1 Barriers and facilitators to implementing shared decision-making in clinical practices as perceived by health professionals

Factor as a barrier/facilitator	Barriers (number of studies in which this factor was identified as a barrier)	Facilitators (number of studies in which this factor was identified as a facilitator)
Knowledge		
Lack of awareness/awareness	0	0
Lack of familiarity/familiarity	5	0
Forgetting	1	Not applicable
Attitude		
Lack of agreement with specific components of shared decision making/ agreement with specific components of shared decision making	17*	11
Lack of agreement in general/agreement in general	7	6
Lack of expectancy/expectancy	2	15
Patient's outcome	1	10
Process expectancy	1	11
Feeling expectancy	0	1
Lack of self-efficacy/self-efficacy	6	0
Lack of motivation/motivation	4	15
Behaviour		
Factors associated with patient	9	9
Factors associated with shared decision making as an innovation	8	4
Factors associated with environmental factors	18**	7

*Includes lack of applicability due to patient characteristics and lack of applicability due to the clinical situation.
**Includes time constraints.

Measurement issues relating to the assessment of barriers and facilitators to implementation of shared decision-making

If researching barriers to knowledge use in health care practices, there is a need to assess such barriers validly and reliably. In this emerging field of research, valid and reliable instruments to assess barriers and facilitators to implementing shared decision-making in clinical practice are scarce. However, a number of instruments to assess barriers to knowledge use in health care practices exist and could be used. In turn, this would contribute to an enhanced knowledge base of implementation science by providing a means of comparing, in different settings and across different targets of implementation, in which factors are perceived to be the most likely to hamper the transfer of knowledge into clinical practice. A few examples are given below.

Based on the Clinical Practice Guidelines Framework for Improvement, a tool to assess barriers to adherence to hand hygiene guidelines was developed and tested on a group of 21 infectious disease clinicians (Larson, 2004). The tool has two sections: (a) attitudinal statements about practice guidelines in general and (b) specific statements regarding the Hand Hygiene Guideline. Also, Wensing and Grol (2005) reported on the development of another instrument designed to assess barriers and facilitators to knowledge use. This instrument was applied to 12 different implementation studies in the Netherlands. In a study on the prevention of cardiovascular diseases in general practice, the self-reported barriers that were identified explained 39% of the variation in self-reported performance. However, to the best of our knowledge, neither of these two instruments has been used in the context of implementation studies regarding shared decision-making in clinical practice.

In addition, instruments that assess barriers to perceived characteristics of innovations might be considered. For example, Moore and Benbasat (1991) proposed an instrument that measures the perceptions around adoption of an innovation in information technology based on the theory of diffusion of innovations. This instrument could be useful for assessing barriers and facilitators to the implementation of patient decision aids which aim to foster shared decision-making in clinical practice. Lastly, although quantitative approaches are useful for assessing barriers and facilitators to the implementation of shared decision-making in clinical practice, qualitative approaches based on content analysis of individual interviews or focus groups can also be very valuable.

Effective interventions to overcome barriers to implementation of shared decision-making

In one of the most extensive systematic reviews to date on interventions for implementing change in clinical practice, the authors concluded that overall, there was an imperfect evidence base to support decisions about which implementation strategies are likely to be efficient under different circumstances (Grimshaw *et al.*, 2004). Few studies had estimated the efficiency of dissemination and implementation strategies in the presence of different barriers and effect modifiers. The authors also concluded that interventions should be based on (a) the targeted clinical field; (b) an appreciation of the benefits and costs involved; and (c) an appreciation of the anticipated benefits and costs that will result. More importantly, they also emphasized the need for developing and validating a coherent theoretical framework of health professionals' and organizational behaviour change to better inform the choice of interventions in research and service settings. In other words, the authors concluded that one key gap in knowledge was the lack of theoretical foundations for implementation strategies and how to effectively tailor interventions to identified barriers.

Similar observations hold true concerning the implementation of shared decision-making in clinical practice. Nonetheless, a number of recently published studies point to interesting areas to pursue.

For example, in a randomized controlled trial conducted in Canada with a group of 41 nurses at a health call centre, participants were first interviewed about their perceived barriers to provide decision support to patients (Stacey *et al.*, 2006). Based on the Ottawa Model of Research Use, the researchers then developed a survey instrument to help identify barriers as well as facilitators to the implementation of decision support for patients and tailored their intervention accordingly. The implementation strategies that included a combination of a coaching protocol, online tutorial, skills building workshop, and performance feedback were shown to be effective. Indeed, compared with controls, nurses in the intervention group had better knowledge and better decision coaching skills.

More recently, in a trial of training primary care physicians in shared decision-making, patient decision aids for depression and mental health were shown to improve physician facilitation of patient participation and patient satisfaction (Loh *et al.*, 2007). However, there was no intervention effect for reducing depression severity. Interestingly, the consultation time did not differ between the two groups.

In short, although it remains important to continue research on the best strategies to improve the implementation of shared decision-making in clinical practice, the existing knowledge base informs us that there are a range of barriers and facilitators to implementing shared decision-making in clinical practice. In essence, a combination of interventions will likely be needed to overcome or neutralize the barriers and to use the facilitators.

Strengths and limitations of a barriers and facilitators assessment approach

The assessment of barriers and facilitators is still considered an important step in some of the most cited theories for implementation science. For example, in the theory of planned behaviour (Ajzen, 1988) as well as in the integrated model (Fishbein, 2000), one of the main constructs, perceived behavioural control, is defined as the amount of control the individual perceives he or she has over the behaviour in question. It reflects the individual's perception of barriers or facilitating factors likely to influence their adoption of the behaviour. In the case of non-volitional behaviour, perception of control may have a direct influence on the behaviour itself. These theories provide a theoretical account of the way in which attitude, social norms, and perceived behavioural control combine to predict a given behavioural *intention*. Successful behavioural change will occur only if the determinants of intention (i.e. attitude, social norm, and perceived behavioural control) change. In turn, the determinants will only be modifiable through their underlying salient *beliefs*. Applying this theoretical view to shared decision-making implementation, identifying and monitoring the barriers and facilitators to knowledge use over time has the potential to inform the nature, content, and impact of interventions targeting behavioural change and more specifically perceived behavioural control.

Notwithstanding the on-going interest in the assessment of barriers and facilitators approach to knowledge use (Kitson and Bisby, 2008), it may still be difficult to disentangle which factors at the individual, team or organization levels foster or hamper change and thus to elaborate effective implementation strategies. In recent years, new models have been proposed that take into account the inherent complexity associated with implementing change in health care contexts (Greenhalgh *et al.*, 2004; May *et al.*, 2007). In future years, we expect more implementation studies of shared decision-making to be performed based on these new models.

Gaps in knowledge and areas that require further research

As indicated in the previous sections of this chapter, although there are many current research initiatives that focus on assessing factors influencing the implementation of shared decision-making in clinical practice, many challenges remain that will need to be addressed by rigorous research. There is a need to standardize the identification and reporting of barriers and facilitators to implementing shared decision-making. Researchers in this field should consider using existing models that have been tested, such as the Clinical Practice Guidelines Framework for Improvement, to guide both qualitative and quantitative approaches for assessing and classifying identified factors. It will also be important to address both barriers and facilitators to implementing shared decision-making in clinical practice since one factor can be perceived as a barrier by some potential adopters at the same time as seen as a facilitator by others. Even if these questions are answered, there remains a need for more research on how to choose the right intervention to address a barrier or a facilitator.

Conclusion

Although the implementation of shared decision-making in clinical practice is a relatively recent phenomenon of interest, the results from previous and on-going systematic reviews suggest that this field is expanding very rapidly. However, many gaps in knowledge remain, some more crucial than others. There is a need for theory-driven implementation studies. There is also a need for measurement to be adapted and further developed for the assessment of barriers and facilitators to implementing shared decision-making. Lastly, there is a need for well-conducted research to identify the effective components of implementation strategies.

References

Ajzen, I. (1988). Attitudes, personality and behavior. M. Keynes (ed). Open University Press.

Cabana, M., Rand, C., Powe, N., et al. (1999). Why don't physicians follow clinical practice guidelines? A framework for improvement. *Journal of the American Medical Association, 282*, 1458–1465.

Fishbein, M. (2000). The role of theory in HIV prevention. AIDS Care, *12*, 273–278.

Graham, I. D., Logan, J., O'Connor, A., et al. (2003). A qualitative study of physicians perceptions of three decision aids. *Patient Education & Counseling, 2055*, 1–5.

Gravel, K., Légaré, F., and Graham, I. D. (2006). Barriers and facilitators to implementing shared decision-making in clinical practice: A systematic review of health professionals' perceptions. *Implement Science, 1*, 16.

Greenhalgh, T., Robert, G., Macfarlane, F., et al. (2004). Diffusion of innovations in service organizations: Systematic review and recommendations. *Milbank Quarterly, 82*, 581–629.

Grimshaw, J. M., Thomas, R. E., MacLennan, G., et al. (2004). Effectiveness and efficiency of guideline dissemination and implementation strategies. *Health Technology Assessment, 8*(6), iii–iv, 1–72.

Kitson, A. and Bisby, M. (2008). *Speeding up the Spread*. Putting KT research into practice and developing an integrated KT collaborative research agenda. Background paper. Edmonton: The Alberta Heritage Foundation for Medical Research. 43 p.

Larson, E. (2004). A tool to assess barriers to adherence to hand hygiene guideline. *Am American Journal of Infection Control, 32*, 48–51.

Loh, A., Simon, D., Wills, C. E., et al. (2007). The effects of a shared decision-making intervention in primary care of depression: A cluster-randomized controlled trial. *Patient Educ. Couns., 67*, 324–332.

May, C.R., Mair, F.S., Dowrick, C.F., et al. (2007). Process evaluation for complex interventions in primary care: Understanding trials using the normalization process model. *BMC. Family Practice., 8*, 42.

Moore, G. C., and Benbasat, I. (1991). Development of an instrument to measure the perceptions of adopting an information technology innovation. *Information Systems Research, 2*, 192–222.

Stacey, D., O'Connor, A. M., Graham, I. D., *et al.* (2006). Randomized controlled trial of the effectiveness of an intervention to implement evidence-based patient decision support in a nursing call centre. *Journal of Telemedicine & Telecare,* **12**, 410–415.

Wensing, M., and Grol, R. (2005). Methods to identify implementation problems. In R. Grol, M. Wensing, and M. Eccles (eds.), *Improving Patient Care. The Implementation of Change in Clinical Practice.* Oxford: Elsevier Butterworth Heinemann. pp. 109–121.

Chapter 52

Understanding factors that retard the normalization of decision-support technologies

Carl May, France Légaré, Trudy van der Wiejden, and Glyn Elwyn

Introduction

Shared decision-making over treatment and management of a wide range of conditions can be supported by decision-support technologies (DSTs) that help patients and doctors to work together to interpret high-quality clinical evidence and apply it to the specific circumstances of individuals. There are now a large number of DSTs, and although clinical trials and systematic reviews show that they can be useful and effective in practice (O'Connor *et al.*, 2004), it also clear that they are not being widely adopted by health care professionals (Edwards *et al.*, 2003; Blank *et al.*, 2006). Reviews suggest that a 'many barriers and facilitators' argument is used to explain this (Holmes-Rovner *et al.*, 2001; Gravel *et al.*, 2006), focusing on mainly structural features of the clinical encounter. Such factors draw attention to individualized problems of employing DSTs, and it is increasingly recognized that the successful adoption of interventions depends also on more complex interactions than one of overcoming barriers (Checkland *et al.*, 2007). We argue that an atheoretical 'many barriers' and facilitators' explanation is insufficient and that a different paradigm is necessary. If we wish to understand why DSTs seem not to be used by professionals, even when they are widely available, then it is how they fit in the work – and the workspaces – of clinical organizations that matters.

Why is implementing DSTs such a problem?

To understand why DSTs pose such significant implementation problems, we have used the Normalization Process Model (NPM) (May, 2006), an explanatory model of processes by which new techniques, technologies, or organizational interventions become routinely embedded in practice. The NPM is an explanatory model that seeks to balance group and individual contributions to routine embedding. It is empirically derived and limited in scope, focusing on the collective work that individuals and groups do with any new or modified way of thinking, acting, or organizing in health care practice.

   In a theory-refining review (Elwyn *et al.*, 2007) of shared decision-making and the related literature (e.g. Godolphin *et al.*, 2001; McKinstry, 2000; Gravel *et al.*, 2006; Charles *et al.*, 2004, 2005; Stacey *et al.*, 2005,2006; Wills and Holmes-Rovner, 2006; Holmes-Rovner *et al.*, 2001; Legare *et al.*, 2006; Gravel *et al.*, 2006), we mapped existing knowledge about factors that have retarded or fostered the employment of DSTs onto the NPM. The products of this process were organized as structured explanations of the collective work involved in shared decision-making processes and operationalizing DSTs. The model proposes four constructs that may be applied in the analysis of DSTs in practice, and in this chapter we make these explicit through a set of related hypotheses.

Interactional workability

In the clinical encounter, a DST must possess *interactional workability*. It will be disposed to normalize if it does not adversely affect congruence between participants about the structure and conduct of interactions that involve decision-making work or their beliefs about the proper disposal of problems. Both parties must agree that changes to their work and roles in consultations are legitimate and co-operate to achieve this. A DST will not normalize if its users, individually and collectively, do not accept the new work that it involves and embed this in their existing practice. This leads to our first hypothesis:

(H1) *The interactional workability of DSTs may be retarded because professional work aimed at disposal displaces patient work aimed at securing congruence.*

Here, we suggest that DSTs are a problem because professional and patient are not, in fact, doing coterminous work. The theory refining study showed that professional work is often procedural, focusing on operationalizing DSTs (making them available, enrolling patients, managing time) to dispose of clinical problems and decisions. Patient work, on the other hand, could be categorized as being about seeking congruence in adjusting identity (accepting the concept of shared decision-making, taking a new role as participant, engaging cognitively with DST, and accepting decisional responsibility). Disposal – understanding and assessing outcomes – meant that responsibility for the personal consequences of the decision was shifted towards the patient.

Relational integration

Across professional and lay networks, a DST must be supported by the *relational integration* of participants' knowledge and practice. It will be disposed to normalize if it does not adversely affect confidence in the knowledge that underpins shared decisions, or their accountability to others about ensuring its utility. Both parties must accept the credibility of the other's expertise. A DST will not normalize if its users do not accept the new ways of understanding the other that it requires, and if they do not embed these in the way that their work is organized. It leads to our second hypothesis:

(H2) *The relational integration of DSTs may be retarded because work aimed at sharing accountability displaces patient work aimed at securing confidence.*

Here, we can see that work about expertise is divided, with professionals being concerned with accountability across professional networks, whilst patients are concerned with localizing decisions in personal relationships. In our theory refining study, we found that the professional work was about the use of the DST as an intermediary to manage the link between abstract evidence and individual patients (it includes: matching clinical evidence with patient knowledge, deciding on patients' accountability for engaging with DSTs, dealing with safety and liability). Patient work was about engaging with a personal mediator (the professional) to make sense of clinical knowledge. But further, corporate entities (health care providers, managers, and regulators) also intruded into the relational integration work (assessing the value of evidence, appraising professional engagement, formally defining and evaluating 'best practice').

Skill-set workability

Within the formal and informal health care division of labour, a DST must possess *skill-set workability* that will allow patterns of shared decision-making to be distributed amongst different groups of users. It will be disposed to normalize if it is not adversely affected by participants' beliefs about the proper allocation of work stemming from shared decisions or about the ways that they are equipped to deliver its performance. A DST will not normalize if its users do not accept that their participation is founded on appropriate knowledge and practice. Managerial assumptions configure the environment in which DSTs are distributed to accomplish clinical tasks (specifying roles and competencies, defining standard operating procedures, and job descriptions). Our third hypothesis reflects this labour of division:

(H3)   *The skill-set workability of DSTs may be retarded because professional work aimed at allocating shared decision-making tasks displaces patient work aimed at securing performance.*

In this context, the allocation of work to the patient brings in its wake anxiety about their capacity to perform within the frame of the DST. The theory refining study showed professionals focusing on the allocation of tasks within shared decision processes (identifying appropriate patients and problems, delegating decision-making to other professionals and to autonomous patients). Once again, professional and organizational work seemed to have a procedural quality. Patient work, however, appeared to be focused on problems related to performance (gaining competencies and skills in participation, operationalizing delegated clinical decisions, and answering *their* questions).

Contextual integration

Within health care systems, a DST must be supported by the *contextual integration* of the shared decision-making work. It will be disposed to normalize if it is not adversely affected by the policies and procedure that link decisions to the execution of existing structures and procedures, and for the realization of personnel and fiscal resources. A DST will not normalize if its users do not embed it in the organizing structures of their work, or if they do not link it to patterns of resource allocation. Our fourth hypothesis tests differential resource allocation:

(H4)   *The contextual integration of DSTs may be retarded because work aimed at promoting realization displaces work aimed at securing execution.*

The progress of many clinical encounter-related innovations seemed to be retarded because they were poorly integrated with service delivery at a systems level. Patients were largely absent at this level, where the work of bringing DSTs into practice was characterized in terms of investment in new ways of working and of mobilizing resources for their realization (managing professionals *and* patients' choices and focusing their attention through new protocols and procedures). This displaced attention to the mundane problems of execution (governance and medico-legal boundaries, judgements about relative priorities, and the relative allocation of time and resources) on which integration is founded. Put simply, disproportionate effort is invested into showing that a DST works rather than in discovering how it can 'fit' properly with the health care service in which it is located.

Conclusion

Evaluations of DSTs focus on where the action seems to be – the clinical encounter between patient and professional – but tend to focus on technical properties of that interaction (May *et al.*, 2006), the delivery of information and patterns of communication between participants. The implication of the NPM is that to understand the factors that retard the embedding of DSTs – or any other technology – in clinical practice, we need to look at a lot more than the techniques of communication that they involve, or the mechanisms by which they are delivered. Instead, we need to look holistically at the *work* that participants do, and how it is done, understood, distributed, and resourced at a systems level. In this chapter, we have suggested four factors that have inhibited the routine employment of DSTs by using the NPM to identify problems of corporate or *collective action* rather than the *dyadic interaction* that extend the way beyond the boundaries of the consultation, and which suggest organizational rather than clinical dynamics of implementation and integration. Attention to these wider factors may identify methods to enhance the implementation of DSTs in usual health care practice.

Acknowledgements

We thank Adrian Edwards for his contribution to this chapter. We acknowledge support for CRM from the UK Economic and Social Research Council through a personal research fellowship (Grant RES 000270084)

References

Blank, T., Graves, K., Sepucha, K., *et al.* (2006). Understanding treatment decision making: Contexts, commonalities, complexities, and challenges. *Annals of Behavioral Medicine, 32*, 211–217.

Charles, C., Gafni, A., and Whelan, T. (2004). Self-reported use of shared decision-making among breast cancer specialists and perceived barriers and facilitators to implementing this approach. *Health Expectations, 7*, 338–348.

Charles, C., Gafni, A., Whelan, T., *et al.* (2005). Treatment decision aids: Conceptual issues and future directions. *Health Expectations, 8*, 114–125.

Checkland, K., Harrison, S., and Marshall, M. (2007). Is the metaphor of barriers to change useful in understanding implementation? Evidence from general medical practice. *J. Health Serv. Res. Policy, 12*, 95–100.

Elwyn, G., Legare, F., Edwards, A., *et al.* (2007). Arduous Implementation: Why is it so difficult to embed decision support technologies in clinical practice? *Proceedings: 4th International Shared Decision Making Conference.* Freiburg. May.

Edwards, A., Evans, R., and Elwyn, G. (2003). Manufactured but not imported: New directions for research in shared decision making support and skills. *Patient Education & Counseling, 50*, 33–38.

Godolphin, W., Towle, A., and McKendry, R. (2001). Challenges in family practice related to informed and shared decision-making: A survey of preceptors of medical students. *Canadian Medical Association Journal, 165*, 434–435.

Gravel, K., Legare, F., and Graham, I.D. (2006). Barriers and facilitators to implementing shared decision-making in clinical practice: A systematic review of health professionals perceptions. *Implement Science, 1*, 16.

Holmes-Rovner, M., Valade, D., Orlowski, C., *et al.* (2001). Implementing shared decision-making in routine practice: barriers and opportunities. *Health Expectations, 3*, 182–191.

Legare, F., O'Connor, A. M., Graham, I.D., *et al.* (2006). Primary health care professionals views on barriers and facilitators to the implementation of the Ottawa decision support framework in practice. *Patient Education and Counseling, 63*, 380–390.

May, C. (2006). A rational model for assessing and evaluating complex interventions in health care. *BMC. Health Services Research, 6*, 1–11.

May, C., Rapley, T., Moreira, T., *et al.* (2006). Technogovernance: Evidence, subjectivity, and the clinical encounter in primary care medicine. *Social Science & Medicine, 62*, 1022–1030.

McKinstry, B. (2000). Do patients wish to be involved in decision making in the consultation? A cross sectional survey with video vignettes. *British Medical Journal, 321*, 867–871.

O'Connor, A.M., Stacey, D., Entwistle, V., *et al.* (2004). *Decision Aids for People Facing Health Treatment or Screening Decisions (Cochrane Review), 1.* Chichester, UK: Wiley.

Stacey, D., Graham, I.D., O'Connor, A.M., *et al.* (2005). Barriers and facilitators influencing call center nurses decision support for callers facing values-sensitive decisions: A mixed methods study. *Worldviews Evid. Based Nurs.*, **2**, 184–195.

Stacey, D., Pomey, M.P., O'connor, A.M., *et al.* (2006). Adoption and sustainability of decision support for patients facing health decisions: An implementation case study in nursing. *Implement Science*, **1**, 17.

Wills, C.E. and Holmes-Rovner, M. (2006). Integrating decision making and mental health interventions research: Research directions. *Clin. Psychol.*, **13**, 9–25.

Chapter 53

Education and training of health care professionals

Angela Towle and William Godolphin

Introduction

The education of health professionals for shared decision-making (SDM) or Evidence Based Patient Choice (EBPC) has received increasing attention over the past decade. The knowledge, skills, and attitudes required for SDM, the gap between this ideal and current practice, and the types of training and education that are needed to bridge the gap were reviewed in the first edition (Towle and Godolphin 2001). We suggested approaches to teaching and assessment of SDM competencies, barriers to implementation, and strategies to overcome them. This chapter is an overview of how education and training of health professionals for SDM has developed since and how it has informed further understanding of the barriers and possible future directions.

The context of health professional education

In 2008 Lord Darzi introduced his vision for the UK National Health Service with the words 'An NHS that gives patients and the public more information and choice, works in partnership and has quality of care at its heart' (Darzi 2008). In North America, patient safety and quality of care are driving health care and educational reform. Reports from the US Institute of Medicine between 2000 and 2003 and the UK Department of Health response to the Bristol Inquiry in 2002 insist on patient involvement in decision-making and training of health professionals for 'new rules' for 21st-century health care that make the patient the 'source of control' and note that 'a key component of patient-centred care is shared and informed decision-making ...' (Institute of Medicine 2003). These trends ought to favour progress in training for shared decision-making – at least the words are frequently used.

Reports and guidelines from national medical training bodies in the UK, USA, Canada, and Australia now prescribe shared decision-making competencies such as 'explains options clearly and openly, encouraging patients ... to make informed decisions ...' (UK Foundation Programme Office 2007) or 'enable patient-centered therapeutic communication through shared decision-making ...' (Frank 2005) and regulatory bodies use language that promotes full involvement of patients in decisions about their care.

Although laws appear to require a high standard of informed consent that approaches the ethical standard for informed and shared decision-making, these are rarely invoked except when substantial harm has arisen. A change may be signaled by recent guidance to doctors in the UK (General Medical Council 2008) which prescribes:

'Whatever the context in which medical decisions are made, you must work in partnership with your patients to ensure good care. In so doing, you must:

(a) listen to patients and respect their views about their health;

(b) discuss with patients what their diagnosis, prognosis, treatment and care involve;

(c) share with patients the information they want or need in order to make decisions;

(d) maximise patients' opportunities, and their ability, to make decisions for themselves;

(e) respect patients' decisions.'

This is a remarkable statement. The words nearly fit descriptions of the elements of SDM; the GMC says this is an 'overriding duty or principle' and 'serious or persistent failure to follow this guidance will put your registration at risk'. Yet, there is substantial evidence that this rarely happens and reason to believe that most physicians do not have the communication skills to meet these criteria.

Another topical movement has been toward training for inter-professional collaborative practice, with some evidence and a great deal of interest in the potential for improved patient safety and patient-centred care (Hammick *et al.*, 2007; and see also Chapter 4 by Légaré). However, in this context, proposed competencies for SDM have so far only related to communications between professionals rather than between professionals and patients.

SDM competencies for health professionals

There is currently no definition or agreement on what we are trying to teach or a concept of a SDM curriculum. Makoul and Clayman (2005) examined 416 articles on SDM and found 31 separate concepts to explicate SDM, but only "patient values/preferences" (67%) and "options" (51%) appeared in more than half the 161 definitions (see also Chapter 16). They give a model of SDM that integrates the extant literature and identifies essential and ideal elements that could provide a common framework for teaching, learning and assessment of the ability of health professionals to engage in SDM.

Most competency statements that refer to SDM (e.g. Frank 2005) come under the broad domain of communication skills, although there are other relevant knowledge, skills, and attitudes, such as ethics, and evidence-based medicine. Thus, elements of SDM may be currently subsumed under a variety of curriculum topics and not explicitly labeled or identified to learners as SDM.

A further confusion occurs with the use of different terms for overlapping competencies (e.g. EBPC, SDM, Informed choice/consent, concordance). Our (non-systematic) search of the literature yielded several conclusions:

- SDM is a much more common term than EBPC.
- In health professional education literature, SDM appears primarily in Medicine.
- Papers on SDM in mainstream health professional *education* journals are rare.
- EBPC is not a term used in health professional education.
- Outside medicine, SDM is a term used in contexts other than decision-making between health professionals and patient.

In the models of practice for different health professionals, statements about patient-centred care are universal and provide a natural context for the teaching and learning of SDM. Bainbridge and Harris (2005) describe the application of competencies for informed shared decision-making (ISDM) as defined by Towle and Godolphin (1999) in a medical context to the client-centred practice models of physical therapy (PT) and occupational therapy (OT). In a pilot study at the University of British Columbia, PT, OT, and pharmacy students trained to use the ISDM framework during their clinical placements reported that this model was applicable to their disciplines – although the emphasis on specific competencies varied (e.g. pharmacy emphasizes evidence). Another approach, described by Stacey *et al.* 2008 is to enhance nurses' coaching skills for support of patients and families in decision-making. This has promise for other health professionals who have a counseling role. Actual educational interventions have not yet been described.

The confusion in terminology, lack of agreement about SDM competencies, and lack of a defined SDM curriculum hinder the uptake of SDM into the already crowded curricula of health professionals.

Educational interventions and their outcomes

A recent journal theme issue reviewed SDM in 8 countries and noted examples of programmes to educate health professionals in Canada (Légaré, *et al.*, 2007). Germany (Loh *et al.*, 2007). and The Netherlands (van der Weijden *et al.*, 2007).

We identified eight peer reviewed reports that describe interventions intended to train physicians in SDM (Table 53.1).

Seven studies report their outcomes. Six reported some improvement in ability to engage in SDM after the intervention but the practical importance of the improvement was not convincingly demonstrated and there is limited evidence that education changed practice. Edwards *et al.* (2005) found that, after training, doctors were selective about when they felt greater patient involvement was appropriate and feasible (based on their perceptions of patient characteristics such as age, educational level, and the clinical problem).

Towle and Godolphin (2001) identified a number of barriers to changing the communication behaviours of physicians. These include:

♦ Inadequate teaching about decision-making in communication skills courses.

♦ Lack of good role models, supervision, and feedback from preceptors.

♦ Culture of medical education and training.

♦ Tensions between patient autonomy and professional authority.

♦ Difficulty of providing effective continuing education and professional development.

♦ Organization of health care (including lack of time or incentives).

These barriers are still present. Even with intensive educational interventions (which may not be sustainable outside a research study) it is difficult to change established communication patterns. Physicians have difficulty integrating SDM into their script of the medical interview which is formed very early in the process of professionalisation (Towle *et al.*, 2006). There are also specific barriers in relation to individual SDM competencies. Studies of consultations consistently show that physicians rarely enquire about patient preferences for role in decision-making or preferences for information, even though this is the competency most frequently defined in SDM models (Makoul and Clayman 2005): educational interventions have not been effective in persuading doctors to ask questions that they find unnatural and they perceive will be puzzling for patients.

Recent studies in medical education highlight the important (often counter) influence of the learning environment (the informal or hidden curriculum) on physicians in training and on curriculum reform (Hafferty 1998). to such an extent that in North America a new accreditation standard addressing the learning environment was introduced by the Liaison Committee on Medical Education in 2008. Examples of the hidden curriculum of relevance to SDM are the lack of respected role models who practice SDM, and the rewarding of confidence, control and the 'right answer'. The American Medical Association's *Initiative to Transform Medical Education* (2007) includes among problems with the current preparation of physicians that 'physicians are trained to believe it is important to have the answer' and that 'physicians are socialized to be in charge and act as autonomous decision-makers in the care of patients'. They recommend a change to the student evaluation system to permit the acknowledgement of uncertainty.

Table 53.1 Educational interventions to train physicians to engage their patients in shared decision-making*

Taught	Sample	Audience (country)	Information	Feedback	Model	Practice
Competencies for SDM in general practice	20	Recently qualified GPs (UK)	Y	Y	Y	Y
Concordance for reducing non-adherence with prescribed medication - including core competencies for SDM.	8	GPs (UK)	Y	?	?	Y
Ten communication behaviours to facilitate SDM with patient and family (some palliative care specific)	> 100	Various (USA)	Y	Y	Y	Y
Competencies for ISDM in routine general practice	6	Family physicians (Canada)	Y	Y	Y	Y
"SDM" (specific learning objectives not described) about opioids for non-cancer pain.	22	Internal Medicine residents and attendants (USA)	Y	N	Y	N
Ottawa Decision Support Framework & Tools applied to difficult decisions e.g., management of hot flashes	60 & 15	Family physicians & residents (Canada)	Y	?	Y	
Informed consent to taking part in cancer clinical trials	10	Medical oncologists (Australia)	Y	Y	Y	Y
Improved communication skills for SDM in Fibromyalgia	4	Rheumatologists (Germany)	Y	?	?	Y

*Categories (columns) are according to Rao *et al* 2007.

Intensity	Comparison	Study design	Data collected	Outcomes	Report reference
High	No intervention	Randomized cross over; pre-post	OPTION scores on audiotaped consultations; patient-based outcomes (COMRADE)	Significant difference in post intervention compared to pre	Elwyn *et al.* 2004
High	No intervention	Pre-post	Knowledge questions & short essays; Skills with simulated patients on 13 item checklist. Attitudes on 20 item questionnaire	Increased knowledgeand skills from 14/26 to 16/26	Dowell *et al.* 2004
High	–	–	–	–	Weiner and Cole 2005
Moderate	No intervention	Pre-post	Transcribed audio taped office consultations of all-comers	No difference pre-post	Towle *et al.* 2006
Moderate	Written information	RCT	Self report of satisfaction, patient centeredness, prescribing changes and effectiveness of training	Significantly greater satisfaction, completion of patient treatment agreements, and methadone prescription rates.	Sullivan *et al.* 2006
Moderate	No intervention	Pre-post	Decisional conflict scores on 5 patients/ physician pre & post workshop; all comers	Difference between Decisional Conflict Scores of physicians and patients decreased	Légaré *et al.* 2006
Moderate	No intervention	Pre-post	Audiotaped consultation with oncology patients eligible for clinical trial, coded for 57 behaviours, of which 13 were SDM-specific	Increased check of understanding, offering of choice of no treatment and time given for discussion of patient concerns. Doctors increased some SDM aspects, used fewer coercive behaviours.	Brown *et al.* 2007
High	6 untrained	RCT	Patient assessment of quality of physician-patient interaction, Decisional Conflict Scale and Satisfaction With Decision scale	Patients reported higher quality of physician-patient interaction with trained physicians	Bieber *et al.* 2008 (training described in German publication)

Decision-making and sharing and professional–patient relationships are culturally defined. The growing international mobility of healthcare professionals, as a consequence of European Union directives and workforce shortages in developed countries, may counter efforts to decrease paternalism in health care. In the USA for example about 25% of current specialist training positions are held by international medical graduates. Many of these received their foundation training in societies where paternalism is strong and expected, and may find it difficult to adjust to different cultural norms for healthcare decision-making.

The future

Rhetoric and policy about involving patients in decision-making are getting stronger. Bodies responsible for the education of health professionals are including direct or indirect statements about SDM in their competency frameworks and practice models. At the same time, research into effective educational interventions and the development of sustainable programs are tentative. Direct educational interventions appear to have limited success in changing professional practice beyond the confines of the specific intervention. There are major barriers to the systematic implementation of SDM in practice.

While the search for effective focused educational interventions should not be abandoned, other strategies are required that seize opportunities afforded by those trends in health professional education that may be hooks for SDM. Recent experience has shown that accreditation bodies do develop new standards in relation to emerging 'hot topics' such as patient safety, community service learning, inter-professional teamwork and service user involvement in education. However, standards tend to follow after examples of good educational practice are in place. This calls for advocates of SDM to agree and define a core curriculum and a strategy to influence those responsible for delivering the education of health professionals.

One opportunity that may be invoked is the movement towards inter-professional education for collaborative patient-centred care that may force physicians to modify their assumptions of autonomy and shift the culture to SDM. However, there is also the danger of increasing decision-making among health professionals and diminishing the patient's voice. The use of simulation and virtual patients is an approach to the teaching and learning of SDM that is currently underdeveloped, although increasingly used in other areas of communication training. The Association of American Medical Colleges MedEd Portal repository only has one resource on SDM (a standardized patient case on asking consent for a procedure) but provides an opportunity to disseminate peer reviewed educational resources (www.aamc.org/mededportal, accessed July 2008). Movements toward the active involvement of patients as educators of health professionals also have the potential to change attitudes to SDM.

References

Functions and Structure of a Medical School. Standards for Accreditation of Medical Education Programs Leading to the M.D. Degree 2008 June, Liaison Committee on Medical Education, Association of American Medical Colleges, Washington, D.C.

Initiative to transform medical education. Recommendations for change in the system of medical education. 2007 June, American Medical Association.

Bainbridge, L.A. and Harris, S.R. (2006). "Informed shared decision-making: a model for physical therapy education and practice?", *Physiotherapy Canada*, **58**, 74–81.

Bieber, C., Müller, K.G., Blumenstiel, K., Hochlehnert, A., Wilke, S., Hartmann, M., and Eich, W. (2008). "A shared decision-making communication training program for physicians treating fibromyalgia patients: Effects of a randomized controlled trial", *Journal of Psychosomatic Research*, **64**, 13–20.

Brown, R.F., Butow, P.N., Boyle, F., and Tattersall, M.H. (2007). "Seeking informed consent to cancer clinical trials; evaluating the efficacy of doctor communication skills training", *Psycho-oncology*, **16**, 507–516.

Darzi, A. (2008). *High quality care for all. NHS next stage review final report.*, Dept of Health, London, UK.

Dowell, J., Pagliari, C., and McAleer, S. (2004). "Development and evaluation of a concordance training course for medical practitioners", *Medical Teacher* **26**, 384–386.

Edwards, A., Elwyn, G., Wood, F., Atwell, C., Prior, L., and Houston, H. (2005). "Shared decision-making and risk communication in practice: a qualitative study of GPs' experiences", *The British Journal of General Practice*, **55**, 6–13.

Elwyn, G., Edwards, A., Hood, K., Robling, M., Atwell, C., Russell, I., Wensing, M., Grol, R., and Study Steering Group (2004). "Achieving involvement: process outcomes from a cluster randomized trial of shared *decision-making* skill development and use of risk communication aids in general practice", *Family Practice*, **21**, 337–346.

Frank, J.R. (ed) (2005). *The CanMEDS 2005 physician competency framework. Better standards. Better physicians. Better care*, The Royal College of Physicians and Surgeons of Canada, Ottawa.

General Medical Council (Great Britain) (2008). *Consent: patients and doctors making decisions together*, General Medical Council, London.

General Medical Council Education Committee (2003). *Tomorrow's doctors*, General Medical Council, London, UK.

Great Britain. Dept. of Health. (2002). *Learning from Bristol: the Department of Health's response to the report of the public inquiry into children's heart surgery at the Bristol Royal Infirmary 1984–1995*, Stationery Office.

Hafferty, F.W. (1998). "Beyond curriculum reform: confronting medicine's hidden curriculum", *Academic Medicine*, **73**, 403–407.

Hammick, M., Freeth, D., Koppel, I., Reeves, S., and Barr, H. (2007). "A best evidence systematic review of inter-professional education: BEME Guide no. 9", *Medical Teacher*, **29**, 735–751.

Institute of Medicine (2003). *Health professions education: a bridge to quality*, National Academies Press, Washington, D.C.

Institute of Medicine (2000). *To err is human: building a safer health system*, National Academies Press, Washington, D.C.

Institute of Medicine. (2001). *Crossing the quality chasm: a new health system for the 21st century*, National Academies Press, Washington, D.C.

Légaré, F., O'Connor, A.M., Graham, I.D., Wells, G.A., and Tremblay, S. (2006). "Impact of the Ottawa Decision Support Framework on the agreement and the difference between patients' and physicians' decisional conflict", *Medical Decision-making*, **26**, 373–390.

Légaré, F., Stacey, D., and Forest, P. (2007). "Shared decision-making in Canada: update, challenges and where next!", *Zeitschrift für ärztliche Fortbildung und Qualität im Gesundheitswesen – German Journal for Quality in Health Care*, **101**, 213–221.

Loh, A., Simon, D., Bieber, C., Eich, W., and Härter, M. (2007). "Patient and citizen participation in German health care – current state and future perspectives", *Zeitschrift für ärztliche Fortbildung und Qualität im Gesundheitswesen – German Journal for Quality in Health Care*, **101**, 229–235.

Makoul, G., and Clayman, M.L. (2005). An integrative model of shared decision making in medical encounters. *Patient Education and Counselling*, **60**(3), 301–312.

Rao, J.K., Anderson, L.A., Inui, T.S., and Frankel, R.M. (2007). "Communication interventions make a difference in conversations between physicians and patients: a systematic review of the evidence", *Medical Care*, **45**, 340–349.

Sullivan, M.D., Leigh, J., and Gaster, B. (2006). "Brief report: Training internists in shared decision-making about chronic opioid treatment for noncancer pain", *Journal of General Internal Medicine*, **21**, 360–362.

Towle, A. and Godolphin, W. (2001). "Education and training of health care professionals" in *Evidence-based patient choice: inevitable or impossible?*, eds. A. Edwards & G. Elwyn, Oxford University Press, Oxford, pp. 245–269.

Towle, A. and Godolphin, W. (1999). "Framework for teaching and learning informed shared decision making", *British Medical Journal*, **319**, 766–771.

Towle, A., Godolphin, W., Grams, G., and LaMarre, A. (2006). "Putting informed and shared decision-making into practice", *Health Expectations*, **9**, 321–332.

UK Foundation Programme Office, *The Foundation Programme Curriculum. 2nd Edition. June 2007* [Homepage of The Academy of Medical Royal Colleges, Department of Health, NHS Scotland, DHSSPS, NHS Wales.], [Online]. Available: http://www.foundationprogramme.nhs.uk/pages/home/key-documents [2008, July/18].

van der Weijden, T., van Veenendaal, H. & Timmermans, D. (2007). "Shared decision-making in the Netherlands – current state and future perspectives", *Zeitschrift für ärztliche Fortbildung und Qualität im Gesundheitswesen - German Journal for Quality in Health Care*, **101**, 241–246.

Weiner, J.S. and Cole, S.A. (2005). "ACare: A communication training program for shared decision-making along a life-limiting illness", *Palliative & Supportive Care*, **2**, 231–241.

Chapter 54

Decision aids and beyond: The next decade of decision support technologies

Glyn Elwyn, Annette O'Connor, Dominick Frosch, Bob Volk, and Deb Feldman-Stewart

New challenges, new terminologies?

Decision aids – a term that has gained valuable currency in health care settings – are a form of decision support technology: they are tools which are designed to support individuals in making decisions about situations where deliberation is regarded as a useful process, i.e. where at least two reasonable options exist and where high-quality information needs to be presented, preferably in understandable formats. The label has been used for over a decade, in a wide range of settings and in research studies, including systematic reviews, and seems to differentiate tools that are designed specifically for patients (or users of health care services) from expert systems designed to support professional decision-making. Whereas the term is very well recognized and concise, some have worried that the term 'aid' does not do justice to the importance of what seems to be emerging as a key group of interventions in health care interactions, part of a family of health technologies that impact on patient outcomes.

Using a generic term such as 'decision support technology' or 'knowledge translation tools' might enable researchers to link their work to the internationally important fields of health technology assessments, implementation science, and knowledge translation. However, as a Google search will show, the term decision support technology is also used to cover a wide range of interventions, from chronic disease management decision support systems to artificial intelligence software systems and so 'decision support technology', although correct in its scope, seems too broad a category. Neither does it seem to be a term that can be used in day-to-day communication with consumers. Other terms exist, such as 'decision tools' and 'decision explorers', and as the field diversifies, commercial interests increase, and as Web 2 and Web 3 (the semantic web) influence this field, other terms may be introduced. The current suggestion that guidelines will need to address patient preferences is an indication of further impending development (Guyatt et al., 2008; Krahn and Naglie, 2008). 'Decision aid' remains an accessible user-friendly term but there may be a need to consider new terminology as innovations arrive. More important than the name is a definition and it is likely that the next decade will give this issue attention as well.

Further work on a definition and scope

The Cochrane Collaboration has led the way in defining decision aids. Their approach has enabled significant progress in building up an evidence base for these interventions. Nevertheless, there remain some areas where further consensus would be helpful. For instance, more could be done to be able to draw clear lines around what constitutes a 'decision aid'. The criteria used in the Cochrane systematic review were as follows (see also Chapter 28):

Did the intervention –

1 Describe a specific decision to be made? (Describe options).

2 Present positive and negative features of the options?

3 Provide outcomes that are relevant to health status?

4 Does the intervention avoid the promotion or compliance with a recommended option?

5 Does the intervention help patients to clarify values implicitly?

At a general level, it can be readily agreed that a 'decision' tool has to describe options in sufficient detail so as to enable the decision maker to recognize their positive and negative features. But after this cornerstone, there remain areas where questions have been raised.

There are calls for 'conceptual clarity' (Charles *et al.*, 2005; Holmes-Rovner *et al.*, 2007; Nelson *et al.*, 2007), which we will return to when we discuss 'value clarification'. Perhaps decision aids have multiple aims – yet we feel it would be helpful to scope the intended goals in more depth. For instance, is the decision aid to help patients become clearer about their preferred options, and know why, so they (a) know what they want, (b) can discuss it with their family and friends, should they want to, and/or (c) can participate in the decision to the extent that they want (which may be a shared decision but also may not), or is the decision aid intended explicitly to encourage shared decision-making.

The first criterion also needs further work: Is it enough to have two options or do all *possible* options need to be specified? How would option sets among competing or comparable options be determined? In terms of option features, What features are important – the process and procedural aspect of interventions (options) are just as important to many people as potential outcomes, and the definition is quiet on exactly what features are required, save that 'health outcomes' need to be described. Whilst no one will argue that it is important to describe health outcomes, it may be necessary to define a range of outcomes in more detail. There are large differences between immediate-, medium-, and long-term outcomes, and in making decisions, there is often a balance to be struck between potential evaluations at different time horizons. Long-term gain may be traded off against short-term discomfort for instance. It is not only health outcomes that determine decisions. More often than not, people put higher emphasis on social and psychological issues when making decisions or in sustaining behaviours, and future definitions may need to encompass a wider set of relevant outcomes.

What information should be incluped and how does that get decided? Shouldn't the issue of systematically consulting patients be raised in terms of a definition or is this an issue for standard setting? A review of information in decision aids made clear that patients are often not consulted and, when they are, the effort is generally limited in terms of quantity and quality (Feldman-Stewart *et al.*, 2007).

Moreover, there is debate about the concept of 'value clarification' as a necessary component of the decision aids and the distinction between the term implicit and explicit 'clarification'. We note that there is no compelling evidence that explicit values clarification methods such as utility assessments or importance ratings add value to the decision-making process. Therefore, the current Cochrane definition and IPDAS standards do not consider 'explicit' methods as a required feature of decisions aids (see also Chapter 33). Nevertheless, a considerable number of decision aids use explicit methods.

One possible position is that there is no need for preference clarification methods to be required parts of decision aids. Individuals by the very nature of their cognitive and emotional processes naturally and inevitably elicit, examine, and consider their preferences based on their under-standing of the attributes of the options described. Humans are preference determinants and so *explicit* methods may not be necessary. Moreover, psychologists have found that in some situations people are more accurate in making decisions intuitively rather than actively deliberating about attributes. People also tend to be poor at anticipating their feelings about future events, raising doubts regarding the stability of preferences.

An alternative position stems from the observation that people who support patients in decision-making (practitioners, families) are not very good at judging what matters most to patients. Patients need to communicate their views in a more systematic way. Just as practitioners now assess patients' pain by asking for ratings on a scale ranging from 0 (no pain) to 10 (the worst possible pain); they may find it helpful to know the personal importance that patients attach to the major attributes that distinguish the options. Patients may also gain insight into their personal views through such an exercise and be better at communicating their views. As discussed by Llewellyn-Thomas in Chapter 34, further research is needed to understand which types of decision processes work 'best' in different types of health care decisions.

Perhaps future research will also help resolve whether some methods – of deliberation or of preference elicitation and clarification – add value to decision processes. However, at the moment, preference clarification methods can be as simple as the provision of information about options in sufficient detail to judge their value.

Adjuncts or adversaries to shared decision-making?

It has always been proposed that decision aids should be seen as 'adjuncts' to health care interactions – as tools that should add value to the process where patients arrive at decisions in partnership with their health care providers. There is indeed some evidence that although decision aids help patients to become involved in informed decision-making, a reduction in personal uncertainty about the best course of action is not achieved until they interact with their provider in the health care encounter (Collins *et al.*, 2008). Some may debate the value of lowering patients' personal uncertainty about the best course of action. Although in the short term, raising uncertainty in someone who has arrived at a decision too precipitously may appear to have merit (McNutt, 2004) being in a persistent state of personal uncertainty and indecision can be agonizing. Practitioners aim to relieve suffering of those facing big decisions, not induce it; people feel relief when uncertainty about what is wrong with them and what will be done about it is resolved. The methods of supporting patients' decision-making need to be humane.

It is also true that the reactions of professionals and the difficulty encountered in the implementation of decision aids in real-world settings might provide some insight into the fact that these tools are not always welcomed as 'adjuncts' and not always perceived as useful technologies. Gravel's review about the barriers to shared decision-making, and the fact that the article is one of most often viewed reviews online, provides evidence that professionals face a number of problems. These include a lack of trust in the provenance of the tool, that it was 'not invented locally', that it lacks specific local data, and that it is not relevant or specific enough to the individual patients that the professional sees. In addition, it is very likely that professionals are sometimes blind-sided by the information contained in such tools. Having not had the time or the motivation to become familiar with the decision aid, professionals find it difficult to either agree or disagree with the information contained in the decisions tools. Faced with losing face in front of informed patients, professionals are likely to avoid using decision aids to their maximal impact.

In this context, Frosch has found that the Foundation for Informed Medical Decision Making videos about prostate and colon cancer screening decreased the patients' motivation to engage in a shared decision with professionals, especially when the patients were inclined not to receive cancer screening because the tool was perceived as promoting autonomous decision-making.

In addition, it is remarkable how little attention has been given to collecting detailed qualitative views of professionals about decision aids and how they could fit into routine practice (Frosch *et al.*, 2008). It may be that the decision tools of the future will have to pay more attention to the 'fit' for each individual context and that different versions will need to exist for different points along a patient's journey, as they prepare for encounters, interact in a number of interprofessional encounters, and deliberate with others over time. The 'one size fits all' type of decision aid, assumed to promote shared decision-making, will need, we conjecture, considerable re-design.

The focus of most decision aid research to date has arguably been on cognitive variables including patient knowledge, accurate risk perceptions, and preferences and so on. But shared decision-making is about much more than just cognition. It is also about behaviour, for physicians and patients, and the relationships that develop as a consequence. There is wide agreement that for many patients the process of engaging in shared decision-making requires behaviours that are often contextually novel and that many patients are not yet ready to play an active role in these type of clinical encounters (Makoul and Clayman, 2006). They may want to do so and many endorse the idea, but it may be questionable whether or not they have the skills and ability to do so. The time pressures in consultations raise further challenges, as patients ideally want to focus on the key issues and discuss these as a priority. Perhaps the focus of decision aids and related research needs to expand to also include help with the communication behaviors necessary for shared decision-making to occur.

Future developments

Two significant developments stand to happen in the next decade for this area of work. First, clinical guidelines will need to consider how to address scientific uncertainty and benefit/risks trade-offs, and in doing so, will need to encompass the need to address patient preferences (Guyatt *et al.*, 2008; Krahn and Naglie, 2008). Whether or not a hybrid evolves, where clinical guidelines and decision aids morph into a new set of tools is unknown – but seems likely (Krahn and Naglie, 2008). Second, shared decision-making will enter the language of the trend towards multidisciplinary care – towards what is often called interprofessional practice (see Legare, Chapter 4) – and will enter the fabric of micro systems and teams. Decision support technologies will have to develop new ways of being accessible and useful at different time points along the patients travel across health care systems (Legare *et al.*, 2008). There is evidence of increased uptake in some settings (O'Connor *et al.*, 2007b), but for the majority of health care systems at an international level, there remain significant, pragmatic barriers to the implementation of decision aids in clinical care (Gravel *et al.*, 2006).

In addition to these two major trends, it is worth noting that there will be increasing attention to the added value that informatics will deliver to this field. In the first edition, 2001, we speculated at length about the role of informatics. We now witness the development in platforms, web access in hand-held devices, interactive television merging with the web, and the as-yet-unrealized potential of mass collaboration in health information development – see Medpedia www.medpedia.com for a relevant example. The methods emerging on the web will have increased relevance for the design of decision aids. Web 2 technology has opened up the idea of social networking and collaboration among users to create new ways of communicating and sharing ideas. Some decision aids have begun to allow patient forums, adding comments, and sharing experiences, see for example www.amniodex.com, but the full potential of Web 2 and Web 3 methods are as yet unexplored. Interactive online games and 'virtual worlds' are also phenomena which could be adapted for decision support needs. Anonymity may be preserved in virtual online spaces and so difficult decisions can be explored in great detail whilst preserving privacy. Whether or not these methods are used for decision support purposes in health care contexts remains to be seen.

Delivering decision support to persons with low health literacy will remain a significant challenge. Patients who are poor readers and have limited skills to interpret quantitative information will have difficulty with many currently available decision aids. Alternative approaches such as entertainment education have recently been proposed to enhance the engagement and understanding of patients with low literacy (Jibaja-Weiss and Volk, 2007). The approach relies on interactive multimedia to present the patients with an engaging story (i.e., a soap opera) about a health care decision and integrates the story with interactive learning modules to provide key factual information and skill building through modeling behavior. Initial evaluations in breast cancer treatment and prostate cancer screening decision-making suggest patients are highly favorable to the approach, leading them to feel more assured about their choices, and becoming stronger advocates for themselves (Jibaja-Weiss and Volk, 2007; Volk RJ et al.). Clearly, there will be an ongoing need to consider literacy in development of patient decision aids. Similarly, aids in languages other than English and research on cultural factors in decision support will also be needed.

Another area ripe for development concerns the task of eliciting preferences, examining, and considering their contributions to final decisions – the area known as value clarification (see Chapter 34 by Llewellyn-Thomas). The role of compensatory versus non-compensatory decision strategies will need to be determined and whether decision aids can successfully incorporate deliberation tools from approaches that recognize that humans are bounded decision makers such as Svensons' differentiation approach (Svenson O, 1992) or Gigerenzer's fast and frugal heuristics (Gigerenzer and Todd, 1999). Could new deliberative tools be designed and introduced that integrate the wish to inform patients with the suggestion that decision-making is, inherently, adaptive and heuristic?

Conclusion

In summary then, the next decade promises to be as exciting as the one which has elapsed since the first edition of this book was published. The field has witnessed the consolidation of an evidence base in terms of the trials included in the Cochrane reviews (O'Connor et al., 2007a), there is an International Collaboration working to set quality standards (Elwyn et al., 2006), and we have seen a rapid growth in research outputs as well as the emergence of many commercial developers. We should, however, remain humble and challenge our assumptions as we go forward. We still struggle with many issues and, although we feel the imperative to support patients when they face tough decisions, we should openly debate the many unanswered questions.

References

Charles, C., Gafni, A., Whelan, T., et al. (2005). Treatment decision aids: Conceptual issues and future directions. *Health Expectations*, **8**, 114–25.

Collins, D., Moore, C., Clay, K., et al. (2008). Can Women with Early Stage Breast Cancer Make an Informed Decision for Mastectomy?' *Can Women with Early Stage Breast Cancer Make an Informed Decision for Mastectomy?*, In Press.

Elwyn, G., O'Connor, A., Stacey, D., et al. and The International Patient Decision Aids Standards Collaboration. (2006). Developing a quality criteria framework for patient decision aids: Online international Delphi consensus process. *British Medical Journal*, **333**, 417–421.

Feldman-Stewart, D., Brennenstuhl, S., McIssac, K., et al. (2007). A systematic review of information in decision aids. *Health Expectations*, **10**, 46–61.

Frosch, D.L., Legare, F., and Mangione, C.M. (2008). Using decision aids in community-based primary care: An evaluation with ethnically diverse patients. *Patient Educ. Couns.*

Gigerenzer, G. and Todd, P. (1999). *Simple Heuristics That Make Us Smart*, New York: Oxford University Press.

Gravel, K., Legare, F., and Graham, I.D. (2006). Barriers and facilitators to implementing shared decision-making in clinical practice: A systematic review of health professionals' perceptions. *Implement Sci.*, 1, 16.

Guyatt, G.H., Oxman, A.D., Kunz, R., *et al.* and GRADE Working Group (2008). Going from evidence to ecommendations. *British Medical Journal*, 336, 1049–1051.

Holmes-Rovner, M., Nelson, W.L., Pignone, M., *et al.* (2007). Are patient decision aids the best way to improve clinical decision making? Report of the IPDAS Symposium. *Med. Decis. Making*, 5, 599–608.

Jibaja-Weiss, M.L. and Volk, R.J. (2007). Utilizing computerized entertainment education in the development of decision aids for lower literate and naïve computer users. *Journal of Health Communication*, 12, 681–697.

Krahn, M. and Naglie, G. (2008). The next step in guideline development: Incorporating patient preferences. *JAMA*, 300, 436–438.

Legare, F., Stacey, D., Graham, I.D. *et al.* (2008). Advancing theories, models and measurement for an interprofessional approach to shared decision making in primary care: A study protocol. *BMC Health Serv. Res.*, 8, 2.

Makoul, G. and Clayman, M.L. (2006). An integrative model of shared decision making in medical encounters. *Patient Educ. Couns.*, 60, 301–312.

McNutt, R.A. (2004). Shared medical decision making: Problems, process, progress. *JAMA*, 292, 2516–2518.

Nelson, W.L., Han, P.K., Fagerlin, A., *et al.* (2007). Rethinking the objectives of decision aids: A call for conceptual clarity. *Med. Decis. Making*, 27, 609–618.

O'Connor, A.M., Bennett, C., Stacey, D., *et al.* (2007a). Do patient decision aids meet effectiveness criteria of the international patient decision aid standards collaboration? A systematic review and meta-analysis. *Med. Decis. Making*, 27, 554–574.

O'Connor, A.M., Wennberg, J., Legare, F., *et al.* (2007b). Towards the 'tipping point': Decision aids and informed patient choice. *Health Affairs*, 26, 716–725.

Svenson, O. (1992). Differentiation and consolidation theory of human decision making. *Acta Psychologica*, 80, 143–168.

Volk, R.J., Jibaja-Weiss, M.L., and Hawley, S.T. Entertainment education for prostate cancer screening: A randomized trial among primary care patients with low health literacy. *Patient Education and Counseling*, In Press.

Chapter 55

Information therapy: Tomorrow's promise is happening today – an example from the commercial sector

Donald W. Kemper

Introduction

Information is important. And it is always been available with health care. Until now, though, health education has generally meant giving patients information 'about' their care. Today's information therapy model changes the role of information in a subtle, yet defining, way. Instead of information being 'about' one's care, information can be a significant 'part' of one's care. Information *is* care. Information *is* therapy. Once the subtle shift is fully understood, the exceptional promise of information therapy is revealed.

It makes sense. Information can affect a person's health just as significantly as a lab test, a medication, or an operation. Information not only guides our treatment decisions, but it also motivates our self-management, prevention, and health behaviours.

Definition

Information therapy is the prescription of specific, evidence-based medical information to a specific patient, caregiver, or consumer at just the right time to help the person make a specific health decision or behaviour change (Kemper and Mettler, 2002).

The central point of information therapy is that the information is 'prescribed'. Whether it is prescribed by a physician, a nurse, a health insurer's computer system, or a family friend, this does not matter as long as the prescription is for evidence-based information and it is relevant to the individual's specific health concerns at that particular time (i.e. the right information to the right person at the right time).

What's an Ix®?

The meaning of 'Rx' is common knowledge – the prescription of a medication. An 'Ix' is a prescription of information within the context of information therapy. Information therapy advocates believe that the role of the information prescription is so key to solving current cost, quality, and workforce crises in health care that the prescription of an 'Ix' will become a standard of quality care within the next decade, worldwide.

The Ix solution: three rules (Kemper 2007)

Three simple rules define how Ix can be the solution for resolving the cost, quality, and workforce crises of health care today.

Rule 1. The self-care rule. Help people do as much for themselves as they can – give them self-care information

If people can be their own travel agents, stockbrokers, bankers, librarians, and grocery clerks, they can do more with their own health care.

With the right information and tools, people can

+ provide their own self-care in their own homes;

+ prepare for each visit so that the doctor can more quickly assess symptoms and concerns and give guidance on the right care plan;

+ gain mastery over the day-to-day management of their long-term illnesses.

Rule 2. Help people ask for the care they need – give them tools to understand the evidence-based guidelines

Every year, the resources of evidence-based guidelines for clinical conditions become richer and more in depth (Clancy and Cronin, 2005). Yet far too often these guidelines are ignored (McGlynn *et al.*, 2003). Rule 2 would give the guidelines to patients in plain language that they can understand. Over the past decade, the science of patient decision aids has advanced significantly (O'Connor *et al.*, 2004). Interactive tools now help each person apply the guidelines to his or her own situation. When patients know what the guidelines suggest, they become more involved in the treatment decision. And the clinician becomes more aware of the clinical guidelines. Both changes can lead to better care and, ultimately, lower cost.

Take note: Pay-for-performance (P4P) initiatives have begun to provide financial incentives for physicians who follow guidelines in their practices. Providing the guidelines to patients increases quality scores and can add to physician income. Everybody wins.

Rule 3. Help people say 'no' to care they do not need – give them a sense of their autonomy

A significant amount of unneeded health care spending could be avoided if people were given the confidence and opportunity to decline any tests, drugs, and procedures that add little or no value to their health.

Whether or not insurance pays for a medical service should depend on the scientific evidence base. Whether or not that treatment is provided at all should depend on whether the patient (with the doctor's advice) decides it is in his or her best interest. Patients have the ultimate authority to say 'no'.

Rule 3 promotes doctor – patient collaboration and can make a difference in three important areas:

1 Physicians and hospitals in the United States do a great deal of testing to reduce the risk of a malpractice claim. It is not always because good medicine requires it (Studdert et al., 2005). With good information, patients can decline unnecessary tests.

2 Supply-induced demand drives up the cost of care, sometimes with a negative impact on quality (Fisher et al., 2003). With good information, people can say 'no' to excessive care or unneeded surgeries when other options are viable.

3 Providers can give a great deal of care at the end of life more to defeat death than to improve life. With good information, patients and their advocates can regain control of those final weeks.

For testing, surgery, and end-of-life decision-making, value-based decision-support tools can help patients and their families assess the real value of their options.

Three levels of information therapy

Three different levels of information therapy are needed to implement these rules. Each level requires a different degree of information technology infrastructure to deliver it.

Level I: Self-serve Ix

Most people begin with a self-serve model of information therapy. They go directly to a book, health web site, or other information service to look for information that will help them better manage their health concerns. This is not truly 'prescribed information', except in the sense that it is self-prescribed. Still, in 2007 people turned to information produced by the non-profit organization, Healthwise, over 100 million times.

But, not every person is motivated and activated, and not every person knows how to find reliable information either on the web or at the bookstore. That is where Levels II and III can make a big difference.

Level II: Prescribed Ix

Level II Ix uses coded information in a medical record, medical claim, or some other source to predict the 'moment in care' that a person is entering. Information prescriptions are then selected automatically and delivered to the patient either as a printout in the clinic or through a link within a secure electronic message. Prescribed Ix is now available for most moments in care, including

- lab tests (pre-order, pre-test preparation, post-test explanation of results)
- medications (decision aid, adherence plan, side effects, etc.)
- new diagnoses (overview information, treatment overview, home treatment, etc.)
- prevention plans
- surgery (decision aid, informed consent, preparation, recovery, etc.)

Generally, Level II prescriptions are 1–2 page overviews that include links to decision aids or other relevant information.

Level III: Engagement Ix

The greatest payoff from the Ix solution will most certainly come from helping people better manage serious health conditions and major medical events. Level III engagements can help to turn around the crises of cost, quality, and staffing by guiding people over time through a comprehensive self-management plan for each of their long-term conditions.

Based on each person's medical condition, personal preferences, pace of learning, and specific medical events, a self-management communication and motivation plan is delivered through secure messaging and other means. The goal is to help people gain a sense of self-mastery over their conditions. Even if cure is not an option, the information can help people develop a sense of control over their symptoms and reduce some of the impact of the disease on their quality of life.

The quality of 'engagement' is aided by new interactive technology that allows virtual conversations between people and health education resources. (Access to conversation demonstrations from our nonprofit organization, Healthwise, can be requested at www.healthwise.org. Other organizations may also offer types of virtual coaching.)

Is Ix approaching a tipping point?

Change in health care happens slowly. On average, it takes 17 years for new research to move from proof in the lab to mainstream practice (Balas and Boran, 2000). Still, significant gains are evident in the spread of the concept:

◆ The Center for Information Therapy (www.ixcenter.org) now boasts a membership of 38 organizations in its Ix Action Alliance.

◆ The phrase 'information therapy' now turns up 47,000 hits on a Google search.

◆ The annual Ix Conference draws 200–300 participants each year.

◆ Information therapy presentations have been part of conferences in the Netherlands, the United Kingdom, Canada, Chile, Germany, the Czech Republic, India, and Luxembourg.

A number of US health organizations have begun using Ix strategies on a mainstream basis. For example

◆ Group Health Cooperative (Seattle) and Kaiser Permanente both have implemented information prescriptions in their after visit summaries that are given to patients at the end of each visit.

◆ Interactive Health Solutions, a provider of medical management services, is providing lab results in its personal health records with Ix links to relevant content.

◆ Saint Alphonsus Regional Medical Center provides patients with online access to their medical records, including Ix links to content about their conditions and lab test results.

◆ HealthPartners also provides patients with online access to their test results, medications, and health conditions and includes Ix links to relevant content.

Still, the information therapy movement is in its early launch phase.

Does Ix make a difference?

Despite its promise and the momentum behind its growth, the impact of information therapy on health care costs and outcomes is still unconfirmed. But a number of research universities have recently expressed interest in conducting studies to determine how much of the potential impact is achievable.

What do doctors think of Ix?

For doctors to embrace information therapy, they must first be convinced of three things.

1 That the information is evidence-based. When physicians are in the loop, it is absolutely essential that the information be 'prescription strength', up to date, referenced to the evidence base, and vetted by medical experts.

2 That patients appreciate their doctors prescribing the information. In most medical settings, the biggest patient complaint is, 'I was not informed well enough'. After Ix is implemented, doctors typically receive 'hero notes' from patients thanking them for the new service.

3 That the Ix process fits within their workflow. No matter how promising something new is, if it takes more time in the clinic visit, it would not get support. When Ix is embedded into the workflow of an electronic medical record, it actually saves time – and does a better job.

Many doctors lament the patient who walks into the appointment with an armful of computer downloads. But when doctors are introduced to information therapy systems that meet the three factors, they soon begin to see Ix as a tool to help them do a better job for their patients (Seidman, 2004).

Information therapy will be resisted when it is forced on physicians abruptly without training or support. But, when Ix is presented as a way to help each doctor do a better job with each patient – and in the same amount of time as before – acceptance levels will be very high.

The business model for information therapy

Four factors will drive Ix business models.

1 Ix that preempts phone or in-person service will significantly save money.

2 Ix that helps patients avoid medical errors will significantly reduce both remedial services and medical malpractice costs.

3 Ix that meets patient needs will reward sponsors with both lower costs and higher patient/ member loyalty.

4 Ix that helps clinicians and institutions score higher in pay-for-performance programs will increase same-service revenues and bring positive recognition to those involved.

Ix as innovation today – mainstream tomorrow

Information therapy is an innovation today. Some of the world's leading health care organizations have discovered its value and have implemented Ix programs. Physicians like it; employers like it; regulators like it; and consumers love it. Before long, this innovation will have become an expectation – and then, a mainstream reality.

Declaration of interests: Donald Kemper is Chairman and CEO, and Founding Chair of Healthwise's IxCenter Board of Directors. The Center for Information Therapy (IxCenter) is an independent, US tax-exempt, not-for-profit organization that aims to advance the practice and science of information therapy to improve health, consumer decision-making, and healthy behaviors.

References

Balas, E.A. and Boran, S.A. (2000). Managing clinical knowledge for healthcare improvement. *Yearbook of Medical Informatics*, National Library of Medicine, Bethesda, MD, 65–70.

Clancy, C.M. and Cronin, K. (2003). Evidence-based decision making: Global evidence, local decisions. *Health Affairs*. **24**, 151–162.

Fisher, E.S., Wennberg, D.E., Stukel, T.A., *et al.* (2003). The implications of regional variations in medicare spending: Part 1. The content, quality, and accessibility of care. *Annals of Internal Medicine* **138**, 273–287.

Kemper, D.W. (2007). The Healthwise Ix Solution. Available online at: https://www.healthwise.org/f_white_papers.aspx. Accessed on 4 June 2008.

Kemper, D.W. and Mettler, M. (2002). Information therapy defined. In *Information Therapy: Prescribed Information as a Reimbursable Medical Service*. Boise, ID: Healthwise. p. 3.

McGlynn, E.A., Asch, S.M., Adams, J., *et al.* (2003). The quality of health care delivered to adults in the United States. *The New England Journal of Medicine*. **348**, 2635–2645.

O'Connor, A.M., Stacey, D., Entwistle, V., *et al.* (2004). Decision aids for people facing health treatment or screening decisions (Cochrane Review) (Abstract). *The Cochrane Library*, 1. Chichester, UK: John Wiley & Sons Ltd.

Seidman, J. (2004). The Arrival of 21st-Century Health Care: Group Health Cooperative Reengineers Its Delivery System Around Information Therapy and Patient-Centered Informatics. Available online at http://www.ixcenter.org/publications/documents/e0067.pdf. Accessed on 4 June 2008.

Studdert, D.M., Mello, M.M., Sage, W.M., *et al.* (2005). Defensive medicine among high-risk specialist physicians in a volatile malpractice environment. *JAMA*. **293**, 2609–2617.

Chapter 56

'It's what we do around here': Shared decision-making as a future organizational competence

Glyn Elwyn and Adrian Edwards

You tend to know when someone takes you seriously. They listen and they indicate that they are doing so. They signal that they have understood. They might disagree but at least they have bothered to take your views seriously. It may not lead to better outcomes or to decisions which you would make yourself but it feels like a good process and is a clear mark of respect. Something similar may be said of involving patients in decisions and doing so with genuine intent (Edwards et al., 2001).

Many unanswered questions remain about the process of sharing decisions with patients but we now feel sufficiently confident to say that it is a concept that has found its time and place in the discourse of health care, and it is not going to go away. It is important to note, however, that this discourse is not supported by empirical evidence of significant long-term benefits in health outcomes (Joosten et al., 2008). Granted, there is evidence of positive trends, of increased adherence to chosen medication, of decreased decision conflict and increases in knowledge, and so forth, and there are indications that patients, when informed, are more cautious about discretionary, invasive, or risky procedures. But, alone, these trends would not sustain the level of interest in shared decision-making and decision support technologies. There is something else at the root of this trend.

We contend that these developments rest on a deeper foundation – that of respect for the person as a self-governing agent, capable of understanding, and deliberating about important choices. To respect the capability of the person is to respect the concept that has underpinned human development – and encapsulated in the idea that Horace called 'sapere aude', dare to know. Kant took up the idea in his seminal essay answering the question, *What is Enlightenment?* Kant argued for 'man's release from his self-incurred tutelage', advocating people to follow an ethos of individual liberty and knowledge. In addition, insights obtained from the field of evolutionary psychology is alerting us that altruism, co-operation, and collaboration are sustained by the benefits they provide at societal levels (Dennett, 1996). Given that our society places a high value on the ethical principles of veracity, self-determination and non-coercion, it is hardly surprising that the shared decision-making ethos has taken hold in health care and has been placed firmly at the heart of most health care policy documentation and professional guidance for consent and practice (Loh et al., 2007).

Yet, despite this lineage, we have to immediately acknowledge that this is a slow process, slower than the authors of the chapters in this book bear imagine perhaps. Shared decision-making has emerged from the idea of putting the patient at the centre of professional practice, of being careful to assess their needs in a holistic way, attending to social, psychological, as well as biomedical issues.

Patient-centredness has sometimes been difficult to define, implement, and measure (Lewin *et al.*, 2003), Whilst shared decision-making is perhaps slightly clearer in these respects, there is also considerable evidence that the concept is one that is more alive in journals and workshops than in the real world of patients and busy clinicians. Study after study demonstrates that professionals find it extremely difficult to really involve patients in decisions about their health care (Gravel *et al.*, 2006), even to educate and involve patients with life-long conditions such as diabetes, asthma, or epilepsy, where the pay-back, in theory, could be greatest (O'Connor *et al.*, 2003). Why is this the case, but also how and why do we think it will change?

System design and goals: The future drivers for shared decision-making

Health care practice has made spectacular advances in therapeutics and technological innovations to repair or replace diseased organs, resulting in improvements in both the quality and duration of life for millions of individuals every year, especially in the developed world. New advances in genetics may lead to even greater abilities to generate tailored therapeutic interventions or to predict and even prevent illness. However, even as such progress arrives in clinical practice, problems are visible and threaten the viability of the current supremacy of technical-led care systems. First, cost will be a barrier. We do not intend here to rehearse the many arguments that swirl around the rising cost of health care provision, merely to say that there is an inevitable point at which a society (our younger generations) will not be able to support the inexorable cost of health care inflation, where more is done to more people at ever decreasing marginal benefits. In this situation, choice will become a real issue – where one of the key attributes of the option set will be cost. Nothing focuses the mind as much as having to work out what the supposed extra benefit will deliver and for how much, and what will have to be foregone in order to achieve such benefits.

Secondly, as healthcare becomes more and more of a commodity, delivered by global multinational providers, it also risks becoming more anonymised and fragmented, delivered by organizations where clinicians become replaceable components, rather than professionals who engage in long-term relationships with a known cohort of individuals, either in specialist or generalist practice. These trends are not speculations, at least not in the developed world, and we think it safe to say that this future has already arrived, though not evenly distributed as yet.

We think two possible things may happen as a result of these trends. As described above, working out the extra benefit of additional interventions (a new joint, a new drug with new therapeutic profile) will increasingly drive shared decision-making as patients will have to become familiar with weighing up what is covered by their insurance (state or private). Secondly, patients will become inured to the anonymity of health care teams and will develop methods to ensure that they are getting the best care available to them. Data will be available about the performance of individual clinicians but, more to the point, data will also be available about a range of treatments, and patients will be much more aware of their need to review the pros and cons of alternatives.

Paradoxically, as the need for patients to engage in decision-making increases, so will the value placed on clinicians' skills and the tools that will enhance this facility. Ironically, the ethical goals of ensuring self-determination and self-management may not be the eventual driving forces. Paradoxically, the drivers of the market (creating long-term satisfaction among discerning consumers) and of defensive medicine (avoiding costly claims) will fuel the move to create environments for shared decision-making. As this occurs, organizations themselves will build incentives and performance measurements to ensure that professional align themselves with shared decision-making, securing the consistent and diligent use of decision support technologies that will also record the process of informing and involving patients.

Shared decision-making as an organizational competence

We, therefore, propose a future vision of how organizations will organize themselves to support shared decision-making – or, more in tune with the increasing emphasis on the 'patient choice' label, achieve an *informed (evidence-based) patient choice* environment. We draw on the model suggested by May, where it is conjectured that a set of exogenous and endogenous factors are important to the 'normalization' of a new practice (an intervention, a mode of working or a technology). Space precludes a detailed description of the model but Figure 56.1 illustrates how the four main factors (skill set workability, contextual integration, interactional workability, and relational integration) would influence how a new practice (such as shared decision-making or the use of a decision support technology) would interact with existing practice, and become assimilated or embedded into everyday clinical routines (May *et al.*, 2007).

Figure 56.2 illustrates how we can use the model to pre-suppose the determinants of an informed patient choice environment. At the highest and perhaps the most critical level of leadership and directorship, it is vital that the organizational culture places informed patient choice as a desired and prioritized organizational outcome, and that this is recognized throughout the institutional layers and working procedures. In other words, the organizational culture should directly mandate that organizational polices are aligned with patient involvement in treatment and management options as a key outcome, and that this aim would override the more recent managerial emphasis on efficiency (cost-effectiveness and productivity) as the most important performance target.

These two areas are necessary preconditions for the next set of determinants. Batalden notes the importance of translation of high-level policies into operating procedures that determine micro-system performance (clinical teams) (Nelson *et al.*, 2008). There are a multitude of such teams in all health provider organizations. It is at this level that professionals perform the routine delivery of patient care. Unless these teams have agreements about the situations where clinical equipoise exists and when and how to facilitate shared decision-making, the organization will be unable to generate an environment that supports patient choice. Similarly, data systems, especially the electronic medical record, need to be capable of supporting interprofessional collaboration,

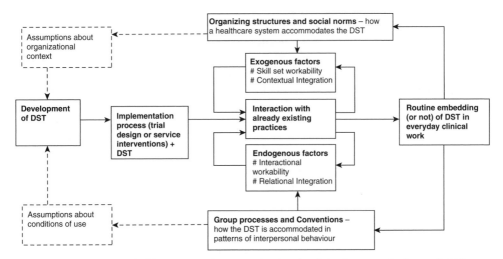

Figure 56.1 Integrating decision support into organizational policies (courtesy Professor Carl May, Newcastle University, UK).

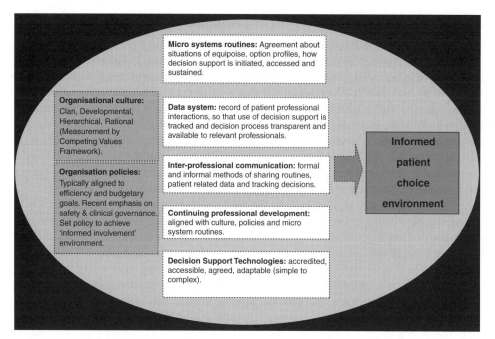

Figure 56.2 Organizational determinants for an informed patient choice environment.

either when patients interact with small groups of different professionals or, as is more often the case, patients interact with different professionals along a 'patient journey'. Tracking how options are offered, supported, and deliberated requires attention to a shared longitudinal record that is easily and permanently accessible to the relevant actors. These two areas of practice, operating procedures at the micro-system and the existence of shared clinical records are examples of what can be considered 'exogenous factors' in the normalization process model.

In addition to the exogenous factors, we propose other important determinants of an informed patient choice environment. Modern health care delivery is dependent on interprofessional collaboration, between different professionals in the same micro-system and between professional based in different micro-systems. For example, anaesthetists, theatre nursing staff, and surgeons need close co-operation when working in surgical teams. They also need excellent communication with other teams, with radiologists, or with intensive care staff, based in different teams. Excellent formal and informal communication routines are a recognized requirement of safe and effective delivery systems but this feature is also fundamental if professionals are to ensure that patients are carefully consulted and involved in making relevant decisions, and are they progress along their care journeys. Perhaps one of the most effective means of ensuring effective interprofessional communication is through high-quality professional development programs, especially if these are organized so that relevant professionals are engaged in collaborative work-based experiential learning.

Another pivotal determinant, familiar to the readers of this book, will be the need for decision support systems and technologies. The data required to inform and guide decision-making is hard won and the steps needed to help individuals deliberate about options and formulate clear, stable, confident preferences are not easily supported. Evidence to support the benefits of well-designed decision support technologies is slowly arriving (Elwyn *et al.*, 2006; O'Connor *et al.*, 2007) and these will be required tools in organizations that wish to create an informed patient choice environment.

In summary, surveying the contents of this book, and the development of a research field that has grown rapidly over the last decade and influenced the health care policies in many countries, we are confident that the concept of respecting the self-determination of patients is a component of the way in which human development is taking place, will therefore endure, although in ways which are difficult to predict. In addition to the ability to cooperate, humans seem alone in having the ability to imagine, and critically, to imagine futures states (Gilbert, 2006). We do indeed 'dare to know' and this in itself means that we are willing to confront uncertainties. As Dennett has argued, 'freedom evolves' (Dennett, 2003), and so, we think, does our willingness to tackle difficult decisions. Being willing to cooperate in order to make better decisions seems to us to be part of a wider set of developments. We believe that the interest in supporting people make 'good decisions' is an additional step along our evolutionary journey.

Acknowledgements

We gratefully acknowledge the contributions of all the authors of chapters in this volume. We are indebted to them, including many who have contributed to several chapters. There are also several others who have influenced our thinking and work in this area over many years, and whose work is reflected in the content of this volume, but not as named contributors. We are sorry that it has not been possible to include more. This pressure for space from several contributors reflects a vibrant field of research and health care practice of which we feel privileged to be a small part. We look forward to continuing exciting developments that improve health care and health, and also broaden our horizons and learning. We thank you.

References

Dennett, D.C. (1996). *Darwin's Dangerous Idea: Evolution and the Meanings of Life*. New York: Simon and Schuster.

Dennett, D.C. (2003). *Freedom Evolves*. New York: Viking Press.

Edwards, A., Elwyn, G., Smith, C., *et al.* (2001). Consumers views of quality in the consultation and their relevance to shared decision making approaches. *Health Expectations*, **4**, 151–162.

Elwyn, G., O'Connor, A., Stacey, D., *et al.* (2006). Developing quality indicators for patient decision aids: An online international Delphi consensus process. *British Medical Journal*, **333**, 417–419.

Gilbert, D. (2006). *Stumbling on Happiness*. New York: Alfred A Knopf.

Gravel, K., Legare, F., and Graham, I. (2006). Barriers and facilitators to implementing shared decision-making in clinical practice: A systematic review of health professionals perceptions. *Implementation Science*, **1**, 16.

Joosten, E., DeFuentes-Merillas, L., de Weert, G., *et al.* (2008). Systematic review of the effects of shared decision-making on patient satisfaction, treatment adherence and health status. *Psychother. Psychosom.*, **77**, 219226.

Lewin, S., Skea, Z., Entwistle, V., *et al.* (2003). Effects of interventions to promote a patient centred approach in clinical consultations: *Cochrane review*. 2.

Loh, A., Simon, D., Bieber, C., *et al.* (2007). Patient and citizen participation in German health care–current state and future perspectives. *Z. Arztl. Fortbild. Qualitatssich.*, **101**, 229–235.

May, C., Finch, T., Mair, F., *et al.* (2007). Understanding the implementation of complex interventions in health care: The normalization process model. *BMC Health Serv. Res.*, **7**, 148.

Nelson, E.C., Godfrey, M.M., Batalden, P.B., *et al.* (2008). Clinical microsystems: Part 1. The building blocks of health systems. *Jt. Comm. J. Qual. Patient Saf.*, **34**, 445–452.

O'Connor, A., Bennett, C., Stacey, D., *et al.* (2007). Do patient decision aids meet effectiveness criteria of the international patient decision aid standards collaboration? A systematic review and meta-analysis. *Med. Decis. Making*, **27**, 554–574.

O'Connor, A., Stacey, D., and Legare, F. (2003). Risk communication in practice: The contribution of decision aids. *British Medical Journal*, **327**, 736–740.

Index